PENGUIN BOOKS

UPON THE ALTAR OF THE NATION

Harry S. Stout is the Jonathan Edwards Professor of American Religious History at Yale University and the author of *The New England Soul*. He has received an N. E. H. Research Fellowship and a Guggenheim Foundation Fellowship, among other awards. Currently the editor of the twenty-seven volume series of *The Works of Jonathan Edwards*, Professor Stout has co-edited the seventeen-volume series *Religion and American Life* designed for public schools.

UPON THE ALTAR OF THE NATION

A MORAL HISTORY OF THE CIVIL WAR

HARRY S. STOUT

PENGUIN BOOKS

PENGUIN BOOKS

Published by the Penguin Group
Penguin Group (USA) Inc., 375 Hudson Street, New York, New York 10014, U.S.A.
Penguin Group (Canada), 90 Eglinton Avenue East, Suite 700, Toronto, Ontario, Canada M4P 2Y3
(a division of Pearson Penguin Canada Inc.)
Penguin Books Ltd, 80 Strand, London WC2R 0RL, England
Penguin Ireland, 25 St Stephen's Green, Dublin 2, Ireland (a division of Penguin Books Ltd)
Penguin Group (Australia), 250 Camberwell Road, Camberwell, Victoria 3124,
Australia (a division of Pearson Australia Group Pty Ltd)
Penguin Books India Pvt Ltd, 11 Community Centre, Panchsheel Park, New Delhi – 110 017, India
Penguin Group (NZ), 67 Apollo Drive, Mairangi Bay, Auckland 1311, New Zealand
(a division of Pearson New Zealand Ltd)
Penguin Books (South Africa) (Pty) Ltd, 24 Sturdee Avenue, Rosebank,
Johannesburg 2196, South Africa

Penguin Books Ltd, Registered Offices:
80 Strand, London WC2R 0RL, England

First published in the United States of America by Viking Penguin,
a member of Penguin Group (USA) Inc. 2006
Published in Penguin Books 2007

3 5 7 9 10 8 6 4

Map illustrations by Adrian Kitzinger

Illustration credits: American Antiquarian Society: pages 80, 96, 195, 268, and 399.
All others courtesy of the Library of Congress.

THE LIBRARY OF CONGRESS HAS CATALOGED THE HARDCOVER EDITION AS FOLLOWS:
Stout, Harry S.
Upon the altar of the nation : a moral history of the American Civil War / Harry S. Stout
p. cm.
Includes index.
ISBN 0-670-03470-3 (hc.)
ISBN 978-0-14-303876-4 (pbk.)
1. United States—History—Civil War, 1861–1865—Moral and ethical aspects.
2. Just war doctrine. I. Title.
E468.9.S94 2005
973.7'1—dc22   2005042420

Printed in the United States of America
Designed by Daniel Lagin

To the memory of my father, Harry Stober Stout (1923–2004), a warrior sailor in a just war. And to my grandchildren: James Benjamin Klapwijk, Helena Neeltje Klapwijk, and Wendell McCullough Stout. It is to the coming generation and the moral conclusions they reach that this book is ultimately dedicated.

CONTENTS

PART VI: PROPORTION
THE SOLDIERS' TOTAL WAR
MAY 1864 TO AUGUST 1864

PART VII: DISCRIMINATION
A CIVILIAN WAR
AUGUST 1864 TO FEBRUARY 1865

PART VIII: RECONCILIATION
MAKING AN END TO BUILD A FUTURE

INTRODUCTION

In the critical months of spring 1864, when Union and Confederate armies suffered horrendous and unprecedented casualties, Grant's Army of the Potomac faced Lee's Army of Northern Virginia in an area of open pines and deep ravines called Cold Harbor, Virginia. Both sides had already expended sixty-nine thousand casualties in four weeks of frontal assaults. Soldiers and their commanders were exhibiting unmistakable signs of shell shock. In the mistaken belief that Lee's lines were spread too thin, Grant ordered yet another frontal assault on June 3 intended to break through Lee's soft underbelly, roll up his army, and march on the gates of Richmond.

At 4:30 a.m. the assault began. In lockstep madness, each advancing Union corps was enfiladed by Lee's cannon and musket fire on the flanks while simultaneously receiving direct fire in front. Artillery batteries worked their Napoleons furiously with double charges of canister, turning the assault troops into a bloody mass of writhing humanity. Three assaulting Federal corps were repulsed in little over an hour, with staggering losses that totaled 7,000—a rate of roughly 116 men per minute. In surveying the carnage, Lee's horrified general Evander Law would write of the battle: "It was not war, but murder."

But *was* it murder? Talk about war or murder, right or wrong, is moral talk. And talk of past war or murder, right or wrong, is moral history—that is, professional history writing that raises moral issues of right and wrong as seen from the vantage points of both the participants and the historian, who, after painstaking study, applies normative judgments. Insofar as ordinary language is implicitly ethical, all history writing implies moral discernment; a moral history, however, calls more for a determination of right or wrong.

The historian writing a moral history does not presume to be a sort of Supreme Court justice adjudicating the past, trying actors for their crimes and then sentencing them. The dead no longer care, and they cannot be sentenced. Rather, it is for the living that the historian offers moral judgments in the hope that lessons for life today may ensue. Reflecting on a career of scholarship on Indian-white relations, the historian James Axtell observes that in writing moral history, "[t]he historian's justice is retrospective, not contemporary, and his goal is not to punish or rehabilitate historical malefactors—who are all mortally incorrigible—but to set the record straight for future appeals to precedent."[1] Moral history imbues the present with a heightened sensitivity to what actors *might* have done, what they *ought* to have done, and what, in fact, they *actually* did. It is in the distances between the oughts and the actualities that moral judgments emerge. One bears witness to the past with all possible integrity and disinterestedness for the sake of the present and the future.

Writing a serious history of war humbles the author and discourages self-righteous pretensions to a monopoly on the Truth. Does that mean that the historian has no interpretation or point of view? Of course not. But precisely because wars past and present exist in a gray zone of differing opinions among good people, the historian's primary task is to reveal the zone.

Current debates over American wars in the twenty-first century dramatically confirm the contested nature of war among good people. The reason is simple: At its most elemental, war is evil. War is killing. War is destroying. It may be a necessary evil, and in that sense "right," but it is nevertheless lethally destructive. So real-world questions about war will always strain any theory created to justify it and invite debate. In telling the story of the Civil War, I pay particular attention to those aspects of the war that raise moral issues. Such issues appear on the home front and in the trenches, among foot soldiers and civilians no less than generals and statesmen. I seek first to establish a narrative that frees the reader to make his or her judgments, while admittedly drawing conclusions of my own.

How then do I, as a historian, render moral judgments about a war? By holding up the actions against widely recognized, long-established principles of just war. The subject of war should not be consigned to some random zone of pure historical relativism or postmodern agnosticism. *Laws of war* and *rules of engagement* exist that civilized peoples agree to. Such laws and rules transcend personal opinion or individual caprice. War crimes tribunals of our modern era bear eloquent testimony to the ongoing relevance of laws of war. When particular battles and wars are laid alongside the laws of just war, judgments are called for that can be applied to all participants and to nations as a whole.

The ethical standards employed to judge the rightness or wrongness of war fall under the rubric of "just-war theory." Just-war theory refers to an intellectual tradition at least two millennia old designed to establish rules of war. These rules first govern whether a people are right to declare war. Once war is declared, they provide guidelines for how that war should be fought, with a view toward minimizing the violence and destruction of war and prompting a peaceful future of coexistence. Although just-war thinking is as old as warfare itself, a self-conscious body of literature on the subject in Western culture began with Saint Augustine of Hippo (354–430), who raised the question of when and how to wage war justly. Its first systematic expression dates from Saint Thomas Aquinas (ca. 1225–1274), whose *Summa theologica* presents the broad categories of what becomes just-war theory. Aquinas's thoughts became the foundation for later Catholic and Protestant jurists.[2]

In the twentieth and twenty-first centuries, just-war theory has undergone a rebirth in response both to the invention and deployment of nuclear weaponry and other weapons of mass destruction and to wars in Southeast Asia and the Middle East. Perhaps the single most important study has been Michael Walzer's *Just and Unjust Wars*, but other major scholarship appears in the work of Paul Ramsey, Jean Bethke Elshtain, Geoffrey Best, James Turner Johnson, and William V. O'Brien.[3]

In opposition to both pacifism on the one hand and amoral realism (Realpolitik) on the other, just-war theory offers a series of ethical principles that articulate a plausible moral framework.[4] Whether one is dealing with wars in the distant past or contemporary wars, two sets of principles are especially important. The first set of principles offers guidelines for when a war might justly be declared. The second set of principles offers guidelines for governing just and fair conduct in the actual fighting of the war.

With regard to the first set of principles governing just war (*jus ad bellum*), most theorists agree that initiating acts of aggression for selfish purposes is always wrong. The only rationale for a just declaration of war is self-defense, and this must be determined at the highest levels of state. In situations where imminent attack looms, a preventive or preemptive attack is justified—but real and present danger must be virtually beyond doubt. In other words, just wars are always *defensive* wars.

One corollary principle growing out of a just war for self-defense is that the war have a reasonable probability of success. The net balance of the war's costs and benefits, as well as its cause, must be calculated by a nation's leaders. Just-war theory argues against expending (that is, wasting) precious human and economic resources in an obviously uneven fight, though even here theorists concede that a nation must sometimes stand up to a bully in the hope that others will join the cause.

Jus ad bellum arguments are ideally suited to addressing wars of nation against nation, and, in particular, nations who share some common culture and expect at war's conclusion to live in some sort of measured peace. In civil wars, however, where significant numbers of belligerent citizens align themselves under warring banners, with substantial territories and competent leadership on both sides, it often becomes difficult to discern with finality who is the unjust aggressor and who the just defender.[5] Such was the case with the American Civil War, in which each of two considerable populations came to the conclusion that war was their last best option. With this conviction, each side joined the battle convinced that its cause was just and that God was on its side.[6]

As they moved relentlessly toward war, both sides focused on the issue of secession and discovered an ethical problem without a formula for a definitive moral response. There is no "just" or "unjust" behavior a priori. On the eve of civil war, Benjamin Russell Allen, the Congregational minister of Marblehead, Massachusetts, pointed to the ethical conundrum of secession. Recalling the American Revolution, he recognized that "[o]pposition to the Government, secession even, is a *revolutionary* right in certain circumstances, a right *above* all constitutions, the right of all people—everywhere; but not a right which any government provides for [emphasis added]."[7]

Did Norway have a right to secede from Sweden? Does modern-day Chechnya have a right to secede from Russia? It is a moral issue that recurs through the years, with no definitive answers. Did the South have a right to secede from the North? Yes. And no. Only a civil war would determine the answer.

The second category of just-war theory, and the one most central to this moral history, addresses the conduct of war (*jus in bello*). In asking how a just war should be fought, theorists isolate two primary principles: proportionality and discrimination. The former bridges the gap between declarations of war and methods of war by requiring that goals be proportional to the means employed. Even granting that all soldiers at some level give up their right to life by enlisting in armed forces, principles of proportionality still invoke limits to the carnage. This is precisely the issue that Evander Law raised when he said of Cold Harbor, "It was not war, but murder." In like manner, orders of "no quarter" (i.e., that all wounded and prisoners be killed) in the Seven Years' War violated the principle of proportionality—the battle had already been won when the orders were given.[8]

The principle of discrimination addresses the question of who should be considered legitimate targets in war. Noncombatants are deemed to stand outside the field of war proper; thus it is unjust to attack them. Just-war theory unanimously upholds the protection of civilians—no element of judgment or prudential weighing of costs and benefits is acceptable in deciding whether or not to target civilians or take them hostage; it is always wrong.

Of course, warfare sometimes unavoidably involves civilians who get caught up in the fighting. Today we use the term "collateral damage" to describe these tragic situations. Just-war theorists address the topic of collateral damage in terms of "double effect." The doctrine of double effect justifies killing civilians in war only if their deaths are not intended but accidental. So, for example, targeting an undefended city is not permissible but targeting a military establishment in the middle of a city is. The target is the military unit and not the civilians inadvertently caught up in the struggle.

Issues of proportionality of losses to strategic ends and discrimination of legitimate and illegitimate targets will recur in this book. While the theory remains clear in the abstract (i.e., without actual numbers in play), its application in the Civil War—the determination of right or wrong—is far from clear or unanimous, from the vantage point of both the participants and the later observers. This becomes especially true in the later years of the war, as it escalated from a limited war fought by armies in the field, far from cities and civilians, to a "total" war in which civilians and their property were deliberately targeted. As limited war transmogrified into a total war for unconditional surrender, the moral dimensions changed dramatically.

The phrase "total war," like "just war" or "immoral behavior," is vigorously contested but, I believe, necessary. The term "total war" did not exist during the Civil War, but I employ it anyway, taking into account its historical relativity. Why? Because I simply cannot come up with a better term. Words like "hard" or "destructive" are often used to distinguish the Civil War from the even greater tragedies of the twentieth century, but they do not penetrate the moral center of the Civil War, which I take to be a war waged deliberately on civilian populations with the full knowledge and compliance of commanders running all the way to the top. In this sense, the *spirit* of total war emerged quite clearly by 1864 and prepared Americans for the even more devastating total wars they would pursue in the twentieth century. In terms of the civilian victims, North and South, the Civil War differed so profoundly in scale from earlier American conflicts that participants could only understand and experience it as something *totally* new and unprecedented. Of course, total war in nineteenth-century America describes something very different—and less severe—than total wars in the twentieth or twenty-first century. There exists no equivalent of Dresden, or Coventry, or Tokyo, or Rwanda in the Civil War. But nineteenth-century participants *experienced* their war as total. If, God forbid, a total war in the twenty-first century were to claim hundreds of millions of casualties that dwarfed losses in World Wars I and II, it would not mean that the twentieth-century wars were no longer "total." The same is true of the Civil War, and attempts to minimize its destruction—military and civilian—reflect the historian's cardinal sin of anachronism, literally judging the past by the standards of the present rather than on its own terms.[9]

At the same time that the Civil War developed from a limited war into a total war, the moral justification changed in the North from a limited war for "Union" to a moral crusade for "freedom" and abolition. Unlike secession, slavery is not morally ambiguous. At first a background topic as the (initially unacknowledged) cause of the war, slavery would grow ever more powerful in its foreground role throughout the war. With emancipation, it would represent Lincoln's inner accelerator for mounting a total war on the Confederacy, soldier and civilian alike. And with abolition, it would provide an unambiguous moral triumph.

The justness of abolition and the freedom of four million dictates that any moral history of slavery unconditionally conclude that the right side won, no matter what the casualties and sacrifices. Lincoln was right when he said in his Second Inaugural Address that if God willed that the war "continue, until all the wealth piled by the bond-man's two hundred and fifty years of unrequited toil shall be sunk, and until every drop of blood drawn with the lash, shall be paid by another drawn with the sword . . . so still it must be said 'The judgments of the Lord, are true and righteous altogether.' "[10]

But this book is not a moral history of slavery. It is a moral history of a war, where questions of proportionality and discrimination continue to remain in play. In any moral history of slavery, Lincoln's Emancipation Proclamation would be unquestionably "right" and good. But in a moral history of the Civil War, the Emancipation Proclamation becomes more problematic if it was employed by Lincoln and Northern Republicans generally as a "lever" (Lincoln's term) for a total war on the Confederacy that deliberately targeted civilian farms, cities, and—in at least fifty thousand instances—civilian lives.[11] In a moral history of the Civil War, it is not enough merely to say that the end of human bondage in the United States was worth a million white lives, true as that may be. The separate question of war remains: was it just? Here it is possible, and, I believe, reasonable, to conclude that the right side won *in spite of itself*. Instead of declaring the Civil War a just war dictated by prudent considerations of proportionality and protection of noncombatants, I argue that in too many instances both sides descended into moral misconduct.

Any moral history of America's Civil War is as much a history of ideas and passions as of actions. The United States was first and foremost an idea built on a foundation of ideology and theology. So, when America was put to its ulti-

mate internal test, it would require not only a war of troops and armaments—
the stuff of geopolitics—but also a war of ideas. This war would require each
side, especially the South, to establish a legitimate identity as a moral "nation." It would also demand a moral campaign to establish the justness of a
resort to arms. Abstract political arguments would not suffice. They would
have to be augmented by moral and spiritual arguments that could steel millions of men to the bloody business of killing one another. Above all, it is crucial to understand how both sides needed to enlist God in their cause as both
justifier and absolute guarantor of their deliverance. Here the voices of clergymen in thousands of churches North and South would become especially
meaningful as critics or cheerleaders of the war's conduct.

Tragically, no less than everyone else, the clergy were virtually cheerleaders all. Throughout this book I have paid particular attention to the voices of
clergymen on both sides of the struggle, because they were the sources
where moral arguments *should* have prevailed. One more easily forgives generals, journalists, and soldiers for their moral silence. But clergy—especially
the majority Protestant clergy—had traditionally opposed reflexive patriotic
rhetoric from the pulpit. They supposedly answered to a higher authority.
True, the rare critical voices sounded among the clergy, as evidence that they
could have established a prophetic distance from their side. But these voices
are precious few, and for one simple reason—nationalism.

In exploring the Civil War through moral lenses, one sees just how unprepared Americans were for such a cataclysm in the moral sense no less
than the military or political. And unlike politics and military arsenals, which
geared up to meet the challenge, the ability to fix a moral stance never progressed. Rather, it regressed. On all sides—clerical, political, journalistic,
military, artistic, and intellectual—the historian searches in vain for moral
criticism directed at one's own cause. Talk of war certainly bristled from the
pages of the secular press and civic assemblies, and statesmen, clergy, and intellectuals raged against the unjust conduct of the enemy. Yet few directly addressed the question of what constitutes a just war, and what limitations
ought to be observed in the unpleasant event of war. In this avoidance and
unpreparedness appears an important clue to the savage ferocity of fighting
that would follow. As well, we discern important clues to the evolving meaning of America, and who (we) Americans are as a nation.

While few judged or questioned the recourse to total war, many saw in
the unprecedented destruction of lives and property something mystical taking place, what we today might call the birthing of a fully functioning, truly
national, *American* civil religion. It was a meaning difficult for anyone to articulate at the time; yet some—including soldiers, clergy and, most notably,

Abraham Lincoln—began to posit a moral high ground in the creation of a powerful national or "civil" religion. As the Civil War progressed onto increasingly eroded moral ground, something transformative simultaneously took place that would render the war *the* defining phenomenon in American history. Patriotism itself became sacralized to the point that it enjoyed coequal or even superior status to conventional denominational faiths.

Ever since Robert Bellah's seminal essay on civil religion, published in 1967, American scholars have awakened to a "religion" of American patriotism that exists alongside traditional religious faiths. American civil religion, Bellah observed, is "an understanding of the American experience in the light of ultimate and universal reality . . . at its best [it] is a genuine apprehension of universal and transcendent religious reality as seen in or, one could almost say, as revealed through the experience of the American people." The historian of religion Rowland Sherrill defined civil religion this way: "American civil religion is a form of devotion, outlook, and commitment that deeply and widely binds the citizens of the nation together with ideas they possess and express about the sacred nature, the sacred ideals, the sacred character, and sacred meanings of their country."[12] Though lacking transcendent revelations akin to the Abrahamic faiths, the religion of a sacralized patriotism enjoys a complete repository of sacred rituals and myths.

In fact, American civil religion borrows so heavily from the language and cadences of traditional faiths, many Americans see no conflict or distinction between the two. Many Americans equate dying for their country with dying for their faith. In America's civil religion, serving country can be coequal with serving God.

The evidences for an ongoing American civil religion are ubiquitous. The Bible prevails as America's most popular book, and often patriotism draws on familiar biblical themes to refer not to the church and its believers but to the nation and its citizens: "Exodus," "chosen people," "promised land," and "New Israel" all represent staple metaphors in American speech and letters that express America's messianic "mission" to be a "redeemer nation."

The rites and rituals of civil religion are discovered less in the laws of the nation than in more informal folkways and traditions. These include a myriad of sacred monuments, chief among them the Mall in Washington, D.C., with recent monuments to the Vietnam War and World War II, and, above all else, the majestic Lincoln Memorial, bracketed by the transforming phrases of the Gettysburg Address and the Second Inaugural Address. Key places evoke religious significance for many American tourists and patriots: Bunker Hill and Concord, Independence Hall, the Alamo, Gettysburg, and the Statue of Liberty all elicit reverential awe.

Though lacking a formal creed American civil religion does contain sacred texts, including most importantly the Declaration of Independence, the Constitution, and the two Lincoln orations. Patriotic songs identify America with the sacred. "God Bless America" was sung repeatedly after 9/11, not the "Star-Spangled Banner," generally viewed as lacking sacred gravitas. "My Country 'Tis of Thee" reminds Americans that the transcendent smiles on their cause in unique and self-empowering ways.

America's civil religion enjoys no weekly Sabbaths, but it does have its sacred days. For the first three centuries of America's existence, fast and thanksgiving days, called by civic authorities (rather than churches) and observed on weekdays to judge or celebrate the nation, predominated, especially in the North. They would later be joined by Memorial Day, Independence Day, Veterans Day, Presidents' Day, and Martin Luther King Day. Nonsectarian prayers sacralize political events, including inaugurals and opening sessions of Congress. Historically these have often been expressed in schools in conjunction with the Pledge of Allegiance.

The American flag stands as America's totem. Schoolchildren routinely pledge their allegiance *to the flag*—and the republic for which it stands, one nation under God. Until the late twentieth century, this pledge would be accompanied by prayers asking for God's blessing on "His" American people. Soldiers killed in battle are buried in flags. America at war is a nation festooned with flags in 2005 no less than in 1861. American patriots reflexively invoke the "Stars and Stripes" or "Old Glory" as the object they are willing to kill and be killed for. Critics of America, at home and abroad, who burn the flag are accused of "desecration"—literally a trampling on the divine.

American presidents have traditionally been viewed as the prophets and priests of American civil religion.[13] The presidency is the only "office" that cannot be left empty—even for one day. Laws are established to ensure instantaneous succession.[14] As commander in chief of the armed services, presidents launch wars and the warrior generals who command them. The United States Military Academy at West Point became, in effect, the first seminary of America's civil religion, later joined by the other service academies.

The locus of American civil religion is not the church or the synagogue or the mosque. Rather, it is the state, which uses sacred symbols of the nation for its own purposes and perpetuation. The appeal proves so powerful and all-encompassing that some contemporary religious critics identify civil religion with idolatry.[15] In a positive sense, scholarly analysts see in civil religion the social and cultural glue that binds a diverse people together and invests them with a collective sense of spiritual unity capable of withstanding internal disintegration.[16]

Civil religion is often associated with, but not identical to, "messianism"—the attribution of sacred status to the place North America.[17]

New World messianism, unlike American civil religion, stretches all the way back to the Puritans. Indeed, historians point to John Winthrop's speech aboard the *Arbella,* "A Modell of Christian Charity," as the first instance of American civil religion, when Winthrop identified New England with Christ's "city upon a hill."[18] And scholars of eighteenth-century colonial society document a pervasive "civil millennialism" in colonial wars.

The rhetoric of messianism or "exceptionalism" is often summarized by the term "jeremiad," which literally refers to a literary work or speech modeled on the Hebrew Bible books of Jeremiah and Lamentations that expresses a bitter lament or prophecy of doom. But because such prophetic warnings were only issued to God's "covenanted" people, the lament actually reinforced their identity as God's chosen people.

In colonial New England, jeremiads were "occasional," or political, sermons, preached during special weekday services of fasting or thanksgiving, or at other times such as on election day. The typical jeremiad began with a paean to the founders' piety as they embarked on an American "errand into the wilderness" and then turned to current sins that imperiled the mission. If unchecked, the sins could lead to doom and defeat. But if the people's sins were reformed, then all could hope to complete the mission of the founders with God's blessing and deliverance. In this rhetoric, defeats and disappointments were never seen as signs of divine desertion but as loving chastisements employed by God to renew His special covenant with His chosen people.[19] This rhetoric would continue to inform the deepest national identities of the Union and the Confederacy in the Civil War.

More meaningful than the rhetorical similarities, however, is a profound distance that separates New England Puritanism from the United States of America. "America" quite simply did not exist. Something decisive happened in 1776 that set American civil religion apart from such earlier outbursts of religious millennialism as Puritan New England or Cromwellian England. After 1776, the new nation inherited the mantle of destiny, and with it, for the first time on American shores, a national patriotism. That patriotism, however, was restrained by pervasive localism and state sovereignty. Only with civil war and a reunified nation-state would "United States of America" enjoy the national significance that it assumes today.

Scholars of civil religion sometimes disagree about whether America's civil religion is understood as "religious" or "ideological," or whether it is defined as "cultural" or "theological." Such debates miss the extent to which it exists in ways that incorporate all the dichotomies. American civil religion is religious *and* ideological, cultural *and* theological. For that reason it exerts enormous power on the loyalties and perceptions of its citizens: a power that can be even greater than traditional theistic beliefs and rituals.

Yet one yawning question remains unanswered: given the existence of an American civil religion that everybody recognizes, *how was it incarnated*? How do we capture the transformation "in the beginning"? Surely the words and some of the symbols appeared with the Revolution. But rhetoric alone cannot create a religion. Neither Puritans' talk of a "city upon a hill" or Thomas Jefferson's invocation of "inalienable rights" is adequate to create a religious loyalty sufficiently powerful to claim the lives of its adherents. In 1860 no coherent nation commanded the sacred allegiance of all Americans over and against their states and regions. For the citizenry to embrace the idea of a nation-state that *must* have a messianic destiny and command one's highest loyalty would require a massive sacrifice—a blood sacrifice.

As I was writing this book and sifting through the enormous body of moral and sermonic literature generated by the Civil War, it became apparent to me (as it had to some of the participants) that something mystical and even religious was taking place through the sheer blood sacrifice generated by the battles. The Revolutionary War, though liberating, had never really shaped a coherent sense of the *nation* as the prevailing object of fealty, over and against local communities and regions. Apart from federal election days and trips to the post office, most antebellum Americans had no real sense of belonging to a vast nation-state whose central government acted directly on its citizens. Their imagined community could not easily stretch beyond their local boundaries. Before the Civil War, Americans would routinely say "the United States *are* a republic." After the war they would instinctively come to say "the United States *is* a republic."

As the war descended into a killing horror, the grounds of justification underwent a transformation from a just defensive war fought out of sheer necessity to preserve home and nation to a moral crusade for "freedom" that would involve nothing less than a national "rebirth," a spiritual "revival." And in that blood and transformation a national religion was born.

Only as casualties rose to unimaginable levels did it dawn on some people that something mystically religious was taking place, a sort of massive sacrifice on the national altar. The Civil War taught Americans that they really were a Union, and it absolutely required a baptism of blood to unveil transcendent dimensions of that union.

As the war progressed, there appeared increasing contemporary references to Union and Confederate casualties as "martyrs." The language of martyrs stands out as religious language. In the case of the Civil War, it is religious language dedicated to political religion rather than to Christianity. By the war's most devastating years in 1863 and 1864, no Americans were said to be dying for their Christian faith, but plenty of "martyrs" were dying for their country. No Christian minister, in the North or South, could self-consciously invoke a civil religion equal to or superior to Christianity for its hold on the American people's hearts and minds. Yet the language of martyrdom reveals how, at least subconsciously, this war was generating through sheer quantity of blood sacrifice a living and vibrant civil religion. By linking patriotism to Christianity and paying lip service to the superiority of the eternal over the temporal, ministers and people could embrace the new faith without fully acknowledging exactly what they were doing.[20]

Tragically, America's civil religion would not include the very freedmen and women so many thousands died to liberate. And here we come to the ultimate moral failure of the war. The historian David Blight marks this as the central "tragedy" of the Civil War: "The sectional reunion after so horrible a civil war was a political triumph by the late nineteenth century, but it could not have been achieved without the resubjugation of many of those people whom the war had freed from centuries of bondage. This is the tragedy lingering on the margins and infesting the heart of American history."[21]

Upon the Altar of the Nation tells difficult stories of unjust conduct on both sides of the struggle. Understandably, most Americans prefer not to face the evidence of an immoral war, especially when the war in question is the American Civil War. But I believe that if we are to understand the meaning of America today, then face it we must. The conclusions I reached at the end were not the assumptions I made at the start, just as for the participants the war meant one thing at the beginning and something entirely different at the end. The Civil War was not a static event, but rather dynamic with ever-changing meanings and transformations as one bloody year moved into the next. Only after vicariously fighting at the battlefronts and imaginatively living on the home fronts did I arrive at the positions I present here. This is the experience I wish for the reader as well: to follow me and fight the battles as they escalate, and as the generals rise or fall to the occasion; to suffer through the prisons as starving men die in lonely and uncelebrated isolation; to witness the sight of once-proud women whose homes and husbands have been destroyed begging for lowly employment; to imagine women and children being physically removed from their homes and placed in prisons; to recapture the faces of farmers helpless before unchallenged armies massed on defenseless populations, in both the North and the South, with the goal of root-and-branch destruction. Only when the reader hears the anguished cries of the suffering—My God, why have you forsaken us?—will the full moral dimensions of "America's costliest war" be revealed for him or her to judge and, in judging, to learn timely lessons for today.

UPON THE ALTAR OF THE NATION

PROLOGUE

The tortured decade of the 1850s began with America's first armed conflicts over slavery and ended with a devastating war between the North and the South. At the outset, bloody engagements over slavery erupted not between soldiers (there were hardly any in the regular army) but among Americans learning to hate Americans. Long before the armies engaged, civilian Americans fought—and killed—one another.

The flashpoint was slavery and the issue of its expansion into the new territories. By the terms of the Fugitive Slave Act passed as part of the Compromise of 1850, federal marshals were required to support slave catchers in apprehending runaways for return to their owners. Enraged abolitionists organized vigilante groups to resist enforcement of the act, by force if necessary. In Boston, Syracuse, and other cities, mobs attacked marshals and marched on courthouses to free captured fugitive slaves.

Others protested with their pens. For years, Boston's ardent abolitionist William Lloyd Garrison had stoked antislavery passions with his national paper *The Liberator*. He was echoed by Frederick Douglass, a self-taught former slave and militant abolitionist orator without peer.

In Cincinnati, Harriet Beecher Stowe, the daughter of the fiery evangelical Lyman Beecher and sister to New York's famous minister Henry Ward Beecher, poured her anger into a bestselling novel, *Uncle Tom's Cabin*, that won immediate acclaim in the North and infamy in the South. More than three hundred thousand copies were sold in 1852, its first year in print. The two-million-plus copies sold over the next decade made it the bestselling novel in American history in proportion to population.

Countless thousands of Americans attended a dramatic stage adaptation of Stowe's novel. Both readers and audiences agonized over the character of

Tom, who is eventually beaten to death by his master, Simon Legree, even as they found inspiration in the escape of Eliza and her five-year-old son through the Underground Railroad. Years later, Abraham Lincoln reputedly greeted Stowe with these words: "So you're the little woman who wrote the book that made this great war."

Ultimately, however, books do not make war. Killing does. As Congress debated the issue of slavery, Americans killed Americans. The violence escalated rapidly between the years 1854 and 1856 in the area that became known as Bleeding Kansas. The trigger was a bill proposed by Stephen A. Douglas, the Democratic senator from Illinois, to organize a large territory to be named Nebraska. To win Southern support for the bill, Douglas agreed to void the Missouri Compromise's prohibition of slavery in the northern part of the Louisiana Purchase and to divide Nebraska into two territories, Nebraska and Kansas. Kansas would be eligible for settlement by Southern slave-holders, despite the fact that it lay north of the Missouri Compromise, in the "free territory" zone.

Douglas's proposal immediately set off a fierce contest over slavery in the Kansas territory, confirming in visceral fashion the inadequacies of "popular sovereignty" as a solution to slavery. Douglas's bill proved to be less a measure for popular sovereignty and order than a pretext for popular anarchy. While Southerners supported the proposal, many Northerners protested vehemently and formed a new political party, reviving the Jeffersonian "Republican" name for themselves.

Predictably, Douglas's compromise proposal succeeded only in generating violence, as Northern and Southern sympathizers flooded into Kansas to determine its status as free or slave. On May 22, 1856, South Carolina congressman Preston Brooks entered the nearly empty chamber of the Senate and caned Charles Sumner, the abolitionist senator of Massachusetts, nearly to death. At the same time, a proslavery mob of seven hundred wantonly destroyed the free-soil town of Lawrence, Kansas, burning down buildings, robbing merchants, and wrecking the town's two abolitionist newspaper offices. In retaliation, a fanatical New York State abolitionist named John Brown, together with his four sons and two sympathizers, murdered five proslavery settlers in cold blood. Brown's "Pottawatomie massacre," as the slaughter became known, provoked further retaliation, initiating a guerrilla war that cost hundreds of lives in 1856, and thousands more before the Civil War ended.

The 1856 election centered around the expansion of slavery. The Republican candidate, John C. Frémont, conqueror of California, vowed to stop the "Slave Power" from expanding. In response, Southern Democrats declared that a Frémont election was grounds for secession. Frémont did not win, but he drew 1.3 million votes to 1.9 million for the Democratic nominee, James Buchanan of Pennsylvania. The Democratic Party had won, but by a slender enough margin to put Southern Democrats on notice that their days of dominance were numbered.

Still, the slave power remained weighty and influential in Congress, and with five Southern Democrats on the Supreme Court, it continued to shape the laws of the land to protect their "peculiar institution." In the 1857 case of *Dred Scott v. Sanford*, Chief Justice Roger B. Taney—a Marylander with Southern sympathies—ruled that blacks had no claim on American citizenship and Congress had no right to prohibit slavery in the territories. Relying on arguments put forward by John C. Calhoun of South Carolina (1782–1850), the redoubtable advocate of states' rights, Taney ruled that the citizens of a territory could prohibit slavery only at the moment of admission to statehood and not before. This decision rendered the antislavery platform of the Republican Party unconstitutional; in effect, the Court had sanctioned the free spread of slavery.

Led by the powerful New York senator William H. Seward, outraged Republicans immediately denounced the decision as a blatant betrayal. Stephen Douglas, who had urged a doctrine of popular sovereignty whereby each territory would determine for itself whether to permit slavery, was also stung. When President Buchanan followed up *Dred Scott* with a recommendation to admit Kansas into the union as a slave state, Douglas formally broke with Buchanan, setting the stage for both a divided Democratic Party and a Republican victory in the 1860 national election.

In 1858 most Republicans assumed their party's nominee would be Senator Seward. But this perception would change rapidly as the nation watched a mesmerizing Illinois senatorial campaign that pitted the popular "Little Giant" Stephen Douglas against an eloquent Republican opponent, the "Rail Splitter" Abraham Lincoln. Although Lincoln lost the Senate contest, the debates had served to thrust him into the national limelight, setting the stage for his election in 1860.

Both candidates—and their parties—believed that America stood in the vanguard of world history. The issue was in what way. In essence, the Lincoln-Douglas debates suggested two conflicting moral visions for America. Douglas's vision privileged democratic local preferences over all else in political decision making. In this context, slavery emerged morally neutral. If the people, territories, and states wanted it, they could have it; if they did not, they could refuse it.

Lincoln's vision subjected local consensus to moral dictates, whether based on history, the Bible, or enlightened rationality.[1] Any democracy worth keeping, Lincoln reasoned, required moral consensus grounded in some higher authority. For Lincoln, that authority was the Declaration of Independence and its ringing affirmation that "all men are created equal." If that declaration was morally right, Lincoln argued, then slavery was morally wrong and therefore could not be allowed to proliferate in the federal territories. Lincoln's idea of the moral consensus was summed up in the party's pithy motto: "Free soil, free labor, free men."[2] By implication, the Constitution became an antislavery document subject to change only by appeal to a higher law than itself. Douglas criticized Lincoln's categorical rejection of slavery in the territories as reckless and an inevitable call to civil war.

Citizen violence again captured the nation's attention in 1859, and again John Brown was its source. In October, Brown, together with his sons and fourteen heavily armed followers, black and white, seized the federal arsenal at Harpers Ferry, Virginia (now West Virginia), hoping to incite a slave insurrection and create a black state within the South. A contingent of U.S. Marines under the Mexican War hero Robert E. Lee easily captured Brown and killed ten of his raiding party. At his hanging, Brown became the contested symbol of America's relentless march to violence. Northern abolitionists deemed Brown a freedom fighter whose execution rendered him a "martyr." In the view of white Southerners, Brown was a fanatical terrorist who embodied the essence of the "Black Republican" Party.

John Brown's raid aroused a sudden tempest at the United States Military Academy. West Point, the nursery of America's military leaders, was destined to play a determinative role in shaping men's minds in the Civil War. Many Southern cadets erupted into violent passion, denouncing the abolitionists and everyone in the North who either shared abolitionist views or supported the Republican Party.

Passions boiled over when it was revealed that a former cadet, George W. Turner (class of 1831), at the time a farmer in Jefferson County, Virginia, was killed in the course of Brown's raid.[3] On a cold December night in 1859, the most famous fistfight in West Point history broke out. Cadet Emory Upton— a self-defined "abolitionist" from Oberlin College who was "shocked" at the profanity he encountered at West Point—took offense when Wade Hampton Gibbs of South Carolina cheered Brown's execution. Abolitionists were few and far between at West Point, but Upton and a small group of sympathizers met for weekly prayer meetings coordinated by the librarian, Oliver Otis Howard. When Upton announced his views to Gibbs, the Southern cadet responded with his fists. Fellow cadets understood "the national significance of the affair" at once and filled the hall to spur on their respective pugilists. Both cadets emerged badly bloodied but unbowed.[4]

On February 27, 1860, Lincoln delivered a lecture at Cooper Union in

New York that he later described as his most important speech. The reasons
are clear. For Northern Republicans, Lincoln declared his antislavery sentiments and offered compelling historical evidence to establish (1) that the
Framers of the Constitution were, in the main, antislavery; (2) that they toler-
ated slavery only with the understanding that it would be extinguished over
time; and (3) that the federal government undoubtedly enjoyed the power to
deny slavery in federal territories *before* they became states.

In other words, the *Dred Scott* decision—not the Republican Party's antislavery platform—was unconstitutional. Furthermore, the "peculiar institution" itself was wrong. To expand slavery into the territories would be a denial
that there was anything morally questionable about it. This, Lincoln hastened to add, did not mean that slavery therefore had to be extirpated by
force where it already existed. Nor did it justify the deliberate cultivation of
slave insurrections. To the South, Lincoln made clear his detestation of John
Brown and his terrorist tactics: "John Brown was no Republican; and you
have failed to implicate a single Republican in his Harper's Ferry enterprise."[5]

On May 18, 1860, Lincoln prevailed over the leading Republican con-
tender, New York's William H. Seward, and captured the Republican Party
nomination. He decided to "make no speeches," letting his earlier positions
stand on their own. Already, a book-length edition of the Lincoln-Douglas debates had appeared in print, and copies of his Cooper Union speech were
widely circulated.

Lincoln faced two Democratic candidates in the November presidential election: the Northern-based Stephen Douglas and the Southern-based
John C. Breckinridge of Kentucky. With a divided Democratic Party, a Republican victory was all but assured. With a plurality of the popular vote and
a majority of the electoral vote, Lincoln would become the next president
without needing a single electoral vote from the South. The prospects for
Southerners were ominous, as they recalled Lincoln's biblically based words,
uttered in his acceptance speech at the Republican National Convention:

"A house divided against itself cannot stand." I believe this government cannot endure, permanently half *slave* and half *free*. I do not expect the Union
to be *dissolved*—I do not expect the house to *fall*—but I do expect it will
cease to be divided. It will become *all* one thing, or *all* the other.[6]

With Republican intentions clear, Southerners turned with alacrity to
their philosopher-statesman John C. Calhoun. According to his argument, the
Constitution not only permitted slavery everywhere but—equally important—
also justified secession. The South was about to put Calhoun's theory to its
ultimate test.

PART I
PREPARATION

PATRIOTS ALL

NOVEMBER 1860 TO JULY 1861

CHAPTER 1

"THE SPIRIT OF THE SOUTH IS RISING"

In November 1860, with Lincoln's "Black Republican" election, South Carolina's forward momentum into revolt was assured. On December 20, a specially selected state convention unanimously adopted an ordinance of secession. At the same time, the rhetoric of self-righteous antagonism between North and South grew steadily hotter.

A national fast day for peace and reconciliation proclaimed by President Buchanan for January 4, 1861, failed miserably. For most Northern pulpits, the fast afforded an opportunity to preach against the sins of slavery in the South and secession in South Carolina. For most Southern pulpits, the fast marked an occasion to preach on ancient themes against the heresies of "Puritan" abolitionism. When not rejecting the immorality of the other, Northern and Southern preachers affirmed the sacred truths, respectively, of "union" and "states' rights."[1] So much for peace and reconciliation.

For the prior thirty years, South Carolina had regularly proclaimed its right to secession. Now it sought fellow slaveholding states to join its cause. From the start of South Carolina's agitation, the issue had never been just about states' rights, but rather about states' rights *and* support for slavery. South Carolina did not appeal to free states to join in secession, because her citizens saw the bond of states' rights and slavery as indissoluble. Nor did they see slavery in any terms other than racial. From John Calhoun's secessionist tract "South Carolina Exposition and Protest" (1828) forward, the most important states' right had remained the prerogative to protect and extend slavery. In words typical of the period, John Townsend, a South Carolina planter, insisted, "The South alone should govern the South, and African slavery should be controlled by those who are friendly to it."[2] Townsend's use of the word "African" confirms how firmly racism would govern proslavery arguments.

South Carolina's slaveholding elites were proud of their leadership role in the cause of secession. From the colonial period on, their state had remained the only one to contain a black majority, and their preoccupation with slavery, coercion, and racial superiority was all-consuming. Not surprisingly, they would lead the way in arguments for states' rights, and their defense would be anchored in the need to defend African American slavery on a self-conscious platform of white supremacy.[3]

South Carolinians prided themselves as well on their "conservatism," a blanket term that encapsulated their differences from the "Unitarian" North. Their America was republican, not democratic, and this meant a society premised on the principle of ordered inequality—aristocratic hierarchy—not equality. In their world, all men and women were created unequal.[4] Such a social order established the planter masters at the top, the slaves at the bottom, and the yeomanry in between. Within the Southern worldview, therefore, slavery constituted a good that protected slaves in a race-based hierarchy of superior and inferior. Slavery appeared as a win-win, both for the black slave and the white owner. Proslavery apologists would argue that any republican society without slavery as its basis could not permanently survive.

Alongside political arguments for an unequal, slave-based republic came powerful religious arguments. Clerical voices—which mattered greatly as moral arbiters and upholders of a virtuous social order—so meshed evangelical Christianity with Southern republicanism that one seemingly could not exist without the other. The historian Stephanie McCurry aptly summarizes Southern planter ideology as "conservative Christian republicanism."[5] In this view, evangelical Christianity, Southern republicanism, and "friends" to slaves existed in a galvanic and ultimately disastrous alchemy.

With the momentous close of 1860, the self-proclaimed "free and independent" state of South Carolina had good reason to believe that this time others would not only embrace their proclamation but also follow their lead. They would not have long to wait. On New Year's Day 1861, the *Charleston Mercury* boldly proclaimed:

> The spirit of the South is rising to meet the great emergency her safety and honor requires; and as State after State withdraws from the Union, the fixed attention which our little State drew upon itself will be turned to the grand aggregation of free and independent Southern states seeking, in a common assemblage, those new means of preserving their liberties and institutions which their separate organization renders necessary.

By February 1861 Mississippi, Florida, Alabama, Georgia, Louisiana, and Texas had joined the "little state" in secession. The seceding states adopted the Confederate constitution on February 8, conspicuously "invoking the favor and guidance of Almighty God" in its preamble. Following these landmark events, Jefferson Davis, a former Mississippi senator and secretary of war, was inaugurated as provisional president of the Confederate States of America and commander in chief of Confederate forces.[6]

At the start, many military officers, Northern opinion shapers, and ordinary citizens were more than willing to let the South secede peacefully. Without ever slackening in their denunciations of slavery and its evils, they nevertheless assumed that under the Constitution, slavery in the existing slave states was up to those states and no one else to abolish. If, instead of abolishing slavery, the cotton states chose to betray the Constitution and leave the Union, that was an evil they would have to answer for; but secession was not a cause for costly offensive military action.

On February 14, 1861, the *Independent*, a nationally influential religious weekly, began a column entitled "What Shall Be Done?" The writers had no doubt what America's course of action should be—let the South leave. Slavery was the major issue dividing the nation, and by allowing the South to leave, "the problem of the perpetuity of slavery is coming to its solution. We have long feared an insurrection of the slaves. We now see an insurrection of the masters." The only thing staying God's vengeful hand from sinful slaveholders, the writers asserted, was their association with the God-fearing North. With secession, God would be freed to exercise "that retributive Providence which is ordering their dreadful destiny."

On March 21, the writers' opinion had not changed: "Let them go! How evident is it that God, for great and beneficent purposes of his own, has permitted this insanity to come upon them! Let them go, to work out their own destiny by themselves!"

In a fast-day sermon delivered on April 4, Zachary Eddy, a Congregational minister in Northampton, Massachusetts, was still not ready for war. Eddy reasoned that the North must let the "idolatrous" South go peacefully. Clearly they were already a new nation. After citing various offenses—including the seizure of federal property, the arming of state militias for self-defense, and the commission of foreign ministers—Eddy concluded that there could be only one response: "I submit that all these facts demonstrate an accomplished revolution—a revolution which will hardly go backward. It is high time to look the melancholy fact full in the face, that the union is actually dissolved."[7]

Some Democratic clergy in the North not only accepted secession but went so far as to say that the abolitionist Northerners were worse than the seceders and should be held primarily to blame. In Bath, Maine, the Congregational minister John Fiske had used the occasion of the January 4 fast to complain bitterly:

There is far more danger to the peace of the country, in my opinion, from the bad, bitter, unscriptural temper with which the institution of slavery has been assailed, than from slavery itself. . . . Party strifes, divisions of opinions, occasional indications of disorder may be expected always to occur. If all slavery were abolished to-day, they would continue to be as many and as violent in the future as they are now.[8]

Other Northern arbiters of morality had their doubts. From their perspective, the Union embodied an idea and a rule of law that was unbreakable. This was precisely President Lincoln's position in his First Inaugural Address:

I hold, that in contemplation of universal law, and of the Constitution, the Union of these States is perpetual. . . . It follows from these views that no State, upon its own mere motion, can lawfully get out of the Union,—that *resolves* and *ordinances* to that effect are legally void; and that acts of violence, within any State or States, against the authority of the United States, are insurrectionary or revolutionary, according to circumstances.

One secession had led to seven. If seven states could secede, why not more? Union was not like marriage, Lincoln asserted; divorce was not an option.[9]

Abolitionists occupied a conflicted position toward secession. Followers of William Lloyd Garrison's American Anti-Slavery Society, founded in 1833, had themselves urged Northern secession from a sinful slaveholding South.[10] After passage of the Fugitive Slave Act, Garrison publicly burned the Constitution. Many other abolitionists had pacifistic principles that discouraged all talk of war as a response to secession. Most doubted the rightness of a war fought solely to preserve the Union. If war were waged for universal and immediate emancipation, that would be just. But in a civil war launched simply for the Union, the cause was territory—not justice—and was therefore wrong.

Rare was the abolitionist who had much good to say about Lincoln. He seemed too timid about slavery. In Worcester, Massachusetts, an ardent abolitionist named Martha LeBaron Goddard made clear in her correspondence her pronounced dislike for President Lincoln and the cause of war. Even before Lincoln's inauguration, she suspected his motives: "I think of nothing but the war, am heart-sick sometimes at the slowness and timidity of men around me—and sometimes fiercely indignant—at

Abe Lincoln, whom I don't trust and don't like—and sometimes, thank God, glad in my soul for a word or act for freedom." One month later, Goddard was willing to let the South go: "The Charleston article in the last *Atlantic* interested me, and made me feel anew how much better it would be to let south Carolina go, and any other states that wish to share her 'outer darkness.' "[11]

Though abolitionists were highly vocal and widely identified in the South as the dominant intellectual and moral influence on the North, the numbers of radical abolitionists were small and not growing. They were more of a symbolic presence than a real numerical force. By 1861 subscriptions to Garrison's *Liberator* had dwindled to twelve hundred.[12] Southerners envisioned abolitionists as all of the North—or at least New England—while Northerners saw them as extreme and hostile to the Constitution and its provisions supporting slavery.

Even if many in the white North were willing to let the South go in early 1861, large parts of the South outside of South Carolina were hesitant to secede.[13] Robert Lewis Dabney, a young Presbyterian pastor who would become Stonewall Jackson's chief of staff and the preeminent champion of Confederate nationalism, feared secession outright.[14] In a letter to Richmond's venerable Presbyterian minister Moses Hoge, written in 1860, Dabney styled himself a "Washington-Madison politician" who feared disunion and the "terrific" consequences of a war setting all adrift in "a sea which has no chart."[15]

On President Buchanan's national fast day in January 1861, Hoge and T. V. Moore—the two most powerful Presbyterian clerics in Richmond—reflected antebellum strictures against "political preaching" and refused to speak to the national crisis from their pulpits. If their integrity as "prophets" was to be maintained, politics would have to be kept out of the pulpit. In a letter to Dabney, Hoge insisted that "Moore and myself do not mean to introduce anything political into our sermons, but wish to direct the minds of the people from man to God. . . . I think of taking for my text: Give us help from trouble: for vain is the help of man."[16] In a letter to Princeton Theological Seminary's Charles Hodge, a conservative former Whig who had voted for Lincoln, Dabney spoke for many in his city when he expressed hope for reconciliation between North and South. In a gracious reply, Hodge asserted that no "sane man" wanted war but preferred instead a "peaceable separation." At the same time, he feared that "forcible separation is inevitably war."[17]

Until the provocative events at Fort Sumter, Lincoln himself did not believe there would be a war or, if there was one, that secession would be permanent or widely supported. Nor did he put much thought into how he might prepare for war. At that point, the newly elected Lincoln wanted desperately to avoid conflict of any kind that would probably lead to more secessions from the upper South.[18] He continued to hope for a redemptive core of "Unionists" who would put down the secession movement and expose a handful of renegade "rebel" planters to be a breed of troublemakers as rare to the South as abolitionists were to the North. Lincoln repeatedly made clear to all sides, from Southern "fire-eaters" to New England "abolitionists," his willingness to entertain compromises that would sacrifice the interests and freedom of slaves for the prospect of saving the Union. He even lent his tacit support to a proposed constitutional amendment that would guarantee the right of the South to their slaves in perpetuity, and he supported colonization for those freed.

Lincoln would not budge on two issues, however: the right of states to secede from the Union and the expansion of slavery into the territories.[19] Neither was allowable or negotiable. Lincoln's patriotism burned deep and informed his morality. Ever since the Senate campaign debates with Stephen Douglas and the presidential campaign that followed, Lincoln had made it plain that there was only one ultimate good that required unlimited loyalty—the Declaration of Independence and the Union that flowed from it. This loyalty was by no means an abolitionist platform, let alone a call for racial equality, but it did have profound implications for the spread of slavery into the vast United States territories.[20]

In his Cooper Union address, Lincoln made it clear that his brief extended only to the territories and fell well short of emancipation in the slave states:

> Mr. Jefferson did not mean to say, nor do I, that the power of emancipation is in the Federal Government . . . as to the power of emancipation, I speak of the slaveholding States only [to emancipate themselves]. The Federal Government, however, as we insist, has the power of restraining the extension of the institution—the power to insure that a slave insurrection shall never occur on any American soil which is now free from slavery.

To fellow Republicans, he insisted, "Wrong as we think slavery is, we can yet afford to let it alone where it is, because that much is due to the necessity arising from its actual presence in the nation."[21]

Lincoln's belief in the Union and American prosperity was confirmed by his interpretation of the Declaration of Independence, which had long since become his political bible. The Constitution might change, and indeed should change through amendments, but the Declaration on which it rested represented its eternal and immutable lodestone. Central to that Declaration, and to the Union, was the universal proposition that "all men are created equal." Using the metaphors, respectively, of apples for the Declaration of Independence and a picture frame of silver for the Constitution, Lincoln argued in 1860 that "[t]he picture was made, not to *conceal*, or *destroy* the apple; but to *adorn* and *preserve* it. The *picture* was made *for* the apple—*not* the apple for the picture."[22]

Lying at the heart of Lincoln's embrace of the Declaration was the abstract *idea* of freedom in a nineteenth-century romantic context. As an idea, freedom would remain forever protean and unbound to time, boundaries, races, ethnicities, or gender. It transcended law and politics, and grounded a metaphysical republic for the ages. In an 1859 letter praising Thomas Jefferson, Lincoln conceded that the Revolution could have been waged without Jefferson's paean to equality, but it would have been merely a political revolt. By including that phrase, Jefferson "had the coolness, forecast, and capacity to introduce into a merely revolutionary document, an abstract truth."[23]

Most Northern Republicans shared Lincoln's hatred for the institution of slavery, yet, as he did, they accepted both Southerners' constitutional right to own slaves and the obligations imposed on them by the Fugitive Slave Law to return, by force if necessary, runaway slaves. Most also shared racist assumptions regarding the inferiority of African Americans, slave or free. But beyond these concessions, they agreed with Lincoln on two points: slavery could not be allowed to spread any further into the territories, and secession was not a moral right but an act of unjust rebellion.

Like Lincoln, Confederate president Jefferson Davis did not expect war. Nor did he prepare for it. Much of his time was spent assembling a government and a military. The numbers of well-wishers and appointment seekers threatened to swamp him. Little around him portended war.[24] Unlike Lincoln, he knew that Northern Union sentiments in the South were weak and ill equipped to spark a move back into the Union. From his vantage point in patriotic Richmond, Davis believed that once Lincoln saw that the Confederacy was intent on creating its own nation, he would have no choice but to let them go.

Throughout the early debates and saber rattling, few asked hard questions about the morality of war should it erupt. The word was constantly on everyone's lips, either as a tragedy to be avoided or an adventure to be embraced. But few explored the moral meaning of war or the "laws of war" with reference to a potential civil war. Their failure to address issues of a just war before hostilities ensued effectively set the stage for Americans to ignore them after hostilities began. For such moral unpreparedness both sides would pay a horrific price.

CHAPTER 2

"LET THE STRIFE BEGIN"

Whatever the expectations of Lincoln and Davis, South Carolina was itching for a fight and would not take its foot off Lincoln's neck. The focal points of pressure were the Federal forts in Charleston Harbor. While Fort Pickens in Pensacola, Florida, was more strategically important to Federal control of the Gulf Coast, the Charleston forts Moultrie and Sumter were more politically important. And so they became all-important.[1]

Better to defend his Federal forces, the commander of the Charleston forts, Major Robert Anderson, a Southerner and friend of Jefferson Davis, spiked the cannons at Moultrie and moved his forces to the more defensible Fort Sumter. Anderson hoped that war could be averted at any cost, but he remained loyal to his commander in chief. Immediately after Lincoln's election, Anderson sent word that Sumter would be almost impossible to defend without substantial reinforcements; supplies were running low as well. Sooner or later the forts would have to be reprovisioned or abandoned. Either way, fateful decisions had to be made.

To South Carolinian sensibilities, reprovisioning of Federal forts in their new nation would constitute an act of war.[2] In fact, they were convinced that the first blow had already been struck when Major Anderson spiked the guns at Fort Moultrie. Neither did it help South Carolinian pride to know that, despite their leadership for secession, theirs was the only secession state besides Florida that failed to seize all Federal properties on its soil.

While loath to be the architect of civil war, Lincoln was not ready to vacate the fort peacefully, despite the advice of General Winfield Scott, the aging hero of the Mexican War. In his inaugural address, Lincoln asserted his intention to "hold, occupy, and possess" Federal properties wherever they be found.[3]

Meanwhile, Major Anderson's plight grew worse by the day. On March 29, after suffering a sleepless night with a migraine headache, Lincoln authorized an unarmed flotilla of supplies to relieve the fort. Most of his advisers pointed out that such an act would be interpreted as an act of war, but Lincoln was not to be deterred. The expedition set sail by April 6.[4] An additional expedition was ordered for Fort Pickens in Pensacola. Nobody knew what the outcome of these resupply missions might be, nor did anyone know what Lincoln would do should South Carolina's response be hostile.

When President Davis received word that Lincoln intended to provision Fort Sumter with nonmilitary supplies, he declared the attempt an "act of aggression." Davis knew that the only way to lend plausibility to a real national independence for the Confederacy in the eyes of England and the uncommitted border states was to make a strong response. Already the *Daily Richmond Enquirer* had responded to Lincoln's inaugural with a vitriolic declaration of war: "Sectional war, declared by Mr. Lincoln, awaits only the signal gun from the insulted Southern Confederacy, to light its horrid fires all along the border of Virginia."[5] To fail to act would be to concede defeat. And in any event, the outraged South Carolinians might attack the fort on their own if they sensed presidential timidity. Davis felt the extreme tension of an ultimatum and went to bed with a migraine of his own.[6]

As the presidents agonized, the people of South Carolina clamored for military action. Their rage for war soon became a paradigm for citizens everywhere. Unlike President Davis and his cabinet, who contemplated armed conflict with trepidation, Charlestonians could scarcely contain their excitement and enthusiasm at the prospect of war. On April 10, the *Charleston Daily Courier* declared defiantly: "Let the strife begin . . . we have no fear of the issue." In the North, Frederick Douglass wrote an editorial in which he said: "Let the conflict come!"[7]

Clearly, the *Courier's* cry of "no fear" referenced manly virtues of martial valor. But it could just as easily have applied to ethics. There was no moral fear of "strife" anywhere. Instead, on April 11, crowds gathered to view the gallantry, only to be disappointed by quiet. A writer for the *Charleston Mercury* expressed the relish for war and sense of corporate disappointment at its delay:

On the battery several hundreds of persons, principally ladies, were promenading until near midnight, anxiously gazing at the dim lights, barely visible through the haze, which indicated the position of the batteries, where fathers and sons, brothers and lovers were willing to sacrifice their lives for the honor of South Carolina. And yet there was but one regret expressed, and that was at the delay and procrastination of hostilities. A detachment of the Citadel Cadets are stationed here for night service, with some heavy pieces of artillery.[8]

At Davis's order, Secretary of War Leroy P. Walker sent Confederate General Pierre G. T. Beauregard instructions to demand the immediate evacuation of the fort. Beauregard duly issued the demand. Despite his Southern friends, Major Anderson refused the order, maintaining his loyalties to the Union.

At precisely 4:30 a.m., on April 12, 1861, Confederate cannons opened fire on the fort. The surprisingly feisty Federal defenders returned fire and held out for hours. But with fires on all sides and depleted munitions, Anderson had no choice but to surrender. From the shoreline, Charlestonians rejoiced to see the Palmetto flag of South Carolina replace the Stars and Stripes over the fortress. In all, one horse was killed.

With the firing on Fort Sumter on April 12, 1861, twenty years of accumulated frustration, occasional violence, and overheated rhetoric at last ignited a war whose outcome was unknown to everyone. Upon receiving word of the surrender, an uncertain President Davis confided that the bombardment would mark "either the beginning of a fearful war, or the end of a political contest."[9] In fact, it brought about both.

Despite the prodigious bombardment of Federal property and the surrender of the U.S. Army, there was no certainty in the seceded South that this would actually lead to a full-scale war. Earlier acts of violence in Kansas and Missouri, to say nothing of John Brown's raid on Harpers Ferry, had aroused fury but had not ushered in war, and nothing overly ominous occurred on April 12. Indeed, as "first shots" go, Sumter was a remarkably banal event, unlike the American Revolution's "shot heard round the world" or a later generation's Pearl Harbor: *no one* died in combat at Sumter. As the "act of aggression" that would eventually create a "just war" on both sides, Sumter was almost trivial. Yet, because the looming war was, like the Revolution, ultimately political and popular, the consequences were anything but trivial.

Following the capture of Fort Sumter, the Confederacy was not about to declare war on the Union. Davis knew that would be an act of aggression entitling the Northern states to take the defensive position. Rather, the Confederates characterized their actions as a simple removal of an unwanted foreign presence from their sovereign territory. As explained by the Confederate vice president, Alexander Stephens, there were occasions when apparently preemptive strikes on one's own territory were just. Offensive wars of conquest were not, he declared, determined by "he who strikes the first blow . . . but the first who renders force *necessary*."[10]

In Washington, D.C., President Lincoln refused to pursue peace at the expense of capitulation, but neither was he willing to call Congress to session for a declaration of war. Instead, he took matters into his own hands and, on April 14, issued a provocative call to arms. With cabinet approval, but without congressional assent, he authorized the procurement of seventy-five thousand volunteers from the free-state militias for a period of ninety days. Their mission was limited: to dismantle "combinations" in Confederate states "too powerful to be suppressed by the ordinary course of judicial proceedings."[11] Lincoln further called for a special session of Congress to meet two and a half months later on July 4. The following day, Lincoln issued a proclamation calling for volunteers and declared that a state of "insurrection" existed, requiring an armed response.

President Davis responded in kind. On April 17 he issued a proclamation calling for thirty-two thousand volunteers. This was necessary, he claimed, because Lincoln "had announced his intention of invading the Confederacy with an armed force, for the purpose of capturing its fortresses, and thereby subverting its independence and subjecting the free people thereof to the dominion of a foreign power."[12] Davis's words and actions, like Lincoln's, amounted to a declaration of war. In fact, both could fairly be charged with starting the war, since neither was at all inclined to back down.[13]

Just as Lincoln wrongly assumed that there was a majority of antislavery Unionists in the South, so too the South was wrong about a majority of abolitionists in the North. In fact, the majority of white Southerners *were* proslavery, while the majority of white Northerners were *not* abolitionists.

Having issued orders for mobilization, both commanders in chief faced the question of whether they would have a viable army. The rage for war in the North and South ensured there would be no lack of volunteers. But who would lead them? For months before and after Sumter, both presidents looked anxiously to the United States Military Academy at West Point and its "long gray line" of graduates, for it would determine, in large measure, the success or failure of their national armies. Indeed, no military institution would be more critical than West Point.

Until 1860 West Point had been able to survive not only external threats but also internal divisions from a diverse corps that represented every state and section in the country, as well as every religion. Its mission was primarily to serve as an engineering school for American armed forces. The Military Academy's location, on the west bank of the Hudson River, was decidedly

"North," but its culture was patrician and equally "South." Honor and duty ruled at West Point and had the nation as their object of devotion.

By training and creed, academy officers and cadets embodied American might and power. A breed apart, they had little in common with the outside world and its preoccupations. Their bond was their honor to one another, and their comradeship larger than life. They eschewed all creeds save America and subordinated all religious observations to the American mission. Alone among American institutions of higher learning, West Point resisted the evangelical revivals of the "Second Great Awakening" as divisive and in bad taste. From its origins, the Military Academy had remained a quasi-Episcopal establishment. Jewish cadets worshipped on Sundays like everyone else, for nothing could transcend the West Point religion. In fact, West Point celebrated the religion of America, and for that purpose trained a cadre of warriors whose divine mandate was unqualified love of country.

With only about seventy students in each class, all the cadets knew one another—a fact that would become extremely important in the emerging Civil War. Students endured a regimen of intense "character formation" that amounted to overwhelming indoctrination. One nineteenth-century teacher commented: "It stands *in loco parentis* not only over the mental but the moral, physical and, so to speak, the official man. It dominates every phase of his development. . . . There is very little of his time over which it does not exercise a close scrutiny, and for which it does not demand a rigid accountability."[14]

West Point cadets and officers were taught also to be "gentlemen." The term "gentleman" carried with it powerful moral imperatives of "honor" and justness in the conduct of war. Through intensive training and indoctrination, cadets imbibed a code that stressed the ideal of a "limited war." The tactics, such as they were, taught by Dennis Mahan, a professor of civil and military engineering, stressed the reserve use of interior lines of operations and campaigns of position and maneuver against armies rather than crushing overland campaigns across civilian populations.[15] This West Point Code demanded that real gentlemen protect the innocents and minimize destruction to achieve desired ends.[16] But this never meant timidity or intimidation in the face of combat against organized armies. Here fearlessness and ruthlessness ruled. Lived experiences in the Mexican War taught officers the superiority of the "tactical offensive"—a tactic that would have devastating consequences in the war to come.

Five hundred and twenty-three West Point graduates fought in the Mexican War, which became a primer for tactics in the Civil War. Under Winfield Scott's command, veteran officers included Ulysses S. Grant (class of '43), William Tecumseh Sherman ('40), Winfield Scott Hancock ('44), George

Thomas ('40), Gordon Meade ('35), Joseph Hooker ('37), John Sedgwick ('37), Joseph E. Johnston ('29), and, most notably, Robert E. Lee ('29). Nearly all were heavily decorated for gallant conduct and imbibed a warrior culture that gloried in the bayonet charge.

The Military Academy's new superintendent, Pierre Gustave T. Beauregard of Louisiana, would serve only five days: on January 28, he resigned his commission, returned to his home state, and went on from there to Fort Sumter. To Southern cadets, who were pulled between loyalty to country and state, he prescribed caution: "Watch me; when I jump, you jump; what's the use of jumping too soon?"[17] Some South Carolina cadets had, in fact, begun jumping sooner and resigned as early as November 1860: the first was H. S. Farley ('62) from South Carolina. Other resignations followed in December and January, but not yet in significant numbers. On the other side, William Tecumseh Sherman resigned as superintendent of the Louisiana Military Academy to attach himself to the North.

In raising an army from the ground up, Lincoln depended heavily on West Point. From 1854 to 1861, the Military Academy had adopted a new five-year course of study proposed by Secretary of War Jefferson Davis and administered by the superintendent, Robert E. Lee. To maximize his officer corps, Lincoln reverted to the old four-year plan and ordered two graduating classes in 1861 with five-year cadets graduating in May and four-year cadets in June. The big question was how many would stay loyal to the Union.

The cadets' response to Sumter would be critical. If only a few followed Beauregard, the South would be deprived of a vital source of skilled lieutenants and captains who could lead untrained volunteers into the mouth of the cannon. If many departed, Lincoln faced a more daunting challenge.

In making their excruciating decisions, Southern cadets found themselves caught between "honor" and "duty to country." Where once these two ideals had forged an indomitable bond of brotherhood in devotion to the shrine of one unified country, they now demanded an unprecedented choice. Duty meant, above all, unquestioned obedience to orders. In defending the integrity of the Military Academy as two nations prepared for war, General John Gross Barnard (class of '33), who would become General George B. McClellan's chief engineer, highlighted duty:

The first duty God requires of man is OBEDIENCE. The first duty the country requires of her people is OBEDIENCE (obedience to her laws). The first virtue of the *Soldier* is *obedience*. The first virtue the system of education at the Military Academy inculcates, the first duty she requires is obedience. . . . The Military Academy has long been recognized . . . as the teacher of the purest patriotism, of the most fervent love of country.[18]

But whose orders would ultimately be honored? They would have to choose whom they would serve. West Point librarian Oliver Otis Howard, who was destined to become one of William Tecumseh Sherman's greatest generals, recognized that "probably no other place existed where men grappled . . . more sensitively . . . with the troublesome problems of secession."[19]

In late April, after Virginia seceded, Ohio cadet Tully McCrea wrote his belle: "This has been an eventful week in the history of West Point. There has been such a stampede of cadets as was never known before. Thirty-two resigned and were relieved from duty on Monday [April 22] and since then enough to increase the number to more than forty. There are now very few cadets from any southern state here."[20] In fact, seventy-four Southern cadets resigned or were dismissed for refusing to take the oath of allegiance to the United States, but twenty-one Southern cadets remained and would eventually follow "duty" and fight for the Union. This was a far higher proportion of loyalists than Southern students at Harvard, Yale, and Columbia. At Princeton, not one Southern student remained at the college.[21]

With Southern cadets resigning and returning home, the time for impassioned fistfights had passed. All realized that soon they would be shooting for real, fighting against former brothers and comrades-in-arms. Rather than making shows of bitterness or violence, departing and remaining cadets expressed sorrow and mutual disappointment.

Cadet George Armstrong Custer ('61 June) recalled walking sentinel duty and seeing fifteen defecting Southern cadets marching toward the steamboat landing:

Too far off to exchange verbal adieux, even if military discipline had permitted it, they caught sight of me as step by step I reluctantly paid the penalty of offended regulations, and raised their hats in token of farewell, to which, first casting my eyes about to see that no watchful superior was in view, I responded by bringing my musket to a "present."[22]

One of the last to leave was the well-liked Fitz Lee from Virginia (not Robert E. Lee's nephew Fitzhugh Lee, who graduated from Harvard in 1856). On the eve of his departure Lee's Northern classmates serenaded him. The next day, as Lee departed, eyes moistened. They were friends after all.

For Tully McCrea, who would graduate in the spring of 1862, the May chapel service was somber. In another letter to his girlfriend he wrote:

I have just returned from church where I heard a sermon from Professor French to the graduating class. It was very eloquent and affecting and a great many realized the truths it contained. . . . There is a certain hymn that is always sung by the choir the last Sunday that the graduates attend church here. It commences "When shall we meet again" and is very appropriate to the occasion. And everyone felt the truth of the concluding words, "Never, no never," for in all probability in another year the half of them may be in their graves, the victims of war or disease. At any rate they will soon be scattered and will never meet together again as a class.[23]

Outside of West Point, partisans on both sides were certain their side would win quickly. The cadets knew otherwise. Besides the defections from West Point, Southern officers and West Point graduates were resigning their commissions in distressing numbers and joining the Confederacy. Having already fought one impassioned fistfight, Cadet Emory Upton foresaw the consequences of a West Point at war with itself. In a letter to his sister he predicted a hard war to come:

If we have war (mark my words), Jeff Davis will be successful in one or two campaigns. He is energetic, and he is drawing all the talent he can from our army. He will enter the war with his forces well organized, and it can not be denied that Southern men will fight well; hence, what is to prevent his success for a time?[24]

Upton's ominous sentiments proved prescient. Little did he realize just how personal they would become for him as he would be wounded in battle three times during the course of the war.

In all, 294 West Point graduates became Union officers and 151 Confederate. Well over half became generals and commanded armies in every major engagement. In fifty-five of the sixty major battles, they commanded both sides. Besides feeding the war machine with aggressive tactics, the West Point generals came to embody the face of American patriotism.

On Friday, April 19, as Federal troops marched south to Washington, riots broke out in Baltimore between Federal soldiers of the Sixth Massachusetts and the pro-secessionist citizens of Maryland. As the soldiers moved through the streets, angry Maryland slaveholders and pro-secessionist citizens rained stones on the soldiers, who returned the action with live fire. At least four soldiers and nine civilians were killed in the exchanges. Hysterical reports of the riots suggested Washington itself might be endangered and have to be evacuated.

In a letter to his fiancée, Therena Bates, written on April 19, John G. Nicolay, Lincoln's chief personal secretary, could not hide his anxiety. As an indication of how frightened the Lincoln administration actually was, Nicolay assured his fiancée: "I do not think any force could be brought against the city to-night, which our men could not easily repel, and therefore do not feel seriously alarmed, although the apprehensions of danger are pretty general."[25]

In a letter to the Reverend Alonzo Hill, written on May 1 on House of Representatives stationery, J. Stewart Brown of the Massachusetts volunteers stationed in Washington reported humorously: "We are comfortably quartered in the Senate Chamber, a curious place I think for military to encamp, but at the same time, residents in this city, who have looked in upon us assert that it presents a more peaceable appearance than ever before." For Brown and his company of volunteers, the overwhelming sentiment was patriotism: "There is but *one* determination, and that is, to stand by our country, to adore the glorious old stars and stripes, and *never* to see them dishonored."[26]

Lincoln by this time was ready for war, and saw in Sumter and the Baltimore riots the perfect opportunity to move beyond his inaugural declaration of "possessing" Federal property to "repossessing" it. When a disconsolate Massachusetts businessman named Gustavus Vasa Fox complained bitterly of the loss of Sumter and the timidity of ranking Republicans, Lincoln wrote him on May 1: "You and I both anticipated that the cause of the country would be advanced by making the attempt to provision Fort-Sumpter [sic], even if it should fail; and it is no small consolation now to feel that our anticipation is justified by the result."[27] In the midst of these events, Lincoln called for a blockade of the Confederate states.

CHAPTER 3

"OUR FLAG CARRIES . . . AMERICAN HISTORY"

In response to armed mobilization, four of the remaining slaveholding states joined the Confederacy: Tennessee, Arkansas, North Carolina, and, most significantly, Virginia. In Richmond, the post-Sumter embrace of secession was electric, and the scene following news of secession bedazzling. Streets were "brilliantly illuminated" by torches and bonfires, signaling with "triumphal acclaim" the birthday of a new nation. Confederate war clerk J. B. Jones, stationed throughout the war in Richmond, described universal enthusiasm: "Ladies everywhere seem embued [*sic*] with the spirit of patriotism." Former president John Tyler delivered a stirring oration invoking "benign providence" to bless the Confederacy's "holy effort," all in the spirit of the "Revolution of 1776."[1]

Certainly in 1860 no one could have predicted that Richmond would become such a vital center for the Confederacy. In contrast to the fire-eaters to the South, Richmond's citizens had not been eager for secession. In 1860 business was booming, and that meant business with the North. With many Northerners living in the city, attitudes toward secession were cautious or opposed. Unlike Charleston or New Orleans, Richmond had much to lose from a Northern invasion and very little to gain. As late as April 4, Virginia's convention voted 2–1 against secession, with Virginia's governor voting with the majority.

Then came Sumter and secession, and Lincoln's summons to the state militias to suppress the rebellion. From the first days of the Confederacy to the last, cannons would sound within Richmond's hearing. The population would increase threefold to more than one hundred thousand. An army was raised so that at any given time ten to fifteen thousand soldiers were stationed in Richmond for training or passing through on battle maneuvers.

Soon they would be joined by thousands of the wounded being treated as hospital patients and, a little later, thousands more prisoners of war.

John Moncure Daniel, editor of the *Richmond Examiner* and destined to be Davis's greatest critic, initially urged action and praised the new president. The even larger *Richmond Daily Dispatch*, with a subscription of eighteen thousand and a reading audience probably double that, also supported the new administration. In 1861 Richmond's secular press represented, in J. Cutler Andrews's words, "the hub of the Confederate news enterprise."[2] The city boasted four major daily newspapers: the *Richmond Daily Whig*, the *Daily Richmond Enquirer*, the *Richmond Examiner*, and the *Richmond Daily Dispatch*. In July 1863 it added another, when the *Alexandria Sentinel* began publishing from Richmond.[3] In addition, Richmond published six denominational religious weeklies with a reading public as great as that of the secular press. Secular and religious leaders, no less than ordinary men and women, participated in the common world of print and would depend on it to shape and disseminate their understanding and interpretation of the war's events.

Virtually no one imagined a war of unprecedented escalation that would soon consume soldier-civilians by the thousands and ravage civilian properties and even lives. Without that "total war" scenario, no one felt the need to launch a moral inquiry into just conduct on either side. All assumed the looming conflict would be brief, clean, decisive, and, above all, defensive.

As presses and politicians fumed, former West Point superintendent and Mexican War hero Robert E. Lee declined Lincoln's offer to take command of the Federal armies. Instead, on April 22, he arrived in Richmond to take command of Virginia troops. On May 20, a grateful Provisional Congress of the Confederacy voted to move the capital of the Confederate nation from Montgomery, Alabama, to Richmond, Virginia—a move calculated to solidify the support of Virginians in all but the pro-North western counties.

From this point on, Richmond, not Charleston, dominated the Southern landscape and represented the single most determined target of the North. No single Northern city occupied the special place that Richmond occupied in the Confederacy as simultaneously sacred site, moral voice, media source, and nerve center of Confederate government and command. If Charleston invented the politics of secession and the ideology of states' rights, the Confederate capital at Richmond invented the ideology and morality of separate nationhood that made those states' rights worth defending to the death. From May 1861, Richmond's destiny as the "Jerusalem of the Confederacy" remained forever fixed in the Confederate imagination. What Charleston had conceived, Richmond delivered.

———

Northern and Southern states rushed to fill their quotas with volunteers brimming for a fight. Hardly anyone now wanted to change the collision course or doubted the righteousness of their respective nation's cause. With the virtue of a just war simply assumed, all that now mattered was the fight.

White Southerners had discovered the awe-inspiring power of patriotism in secession; Northerners would discover it at Sumter. Whatever caution existed before Sumter disappeared after the artillery assault. In both sections, regional patriotism displaced political partisanship. Southern Unionists were effectively silenced, as were Northern peace advocates. There was no room for equivocation.

After a private meeting with President Lincoln, an ailing Stephen Douglas renounced party differences between Republicans and Democrats and threw his support behind Lincoln and the looming war. In words reprinted throughout the nation, Douglas declared: "Every man must be for the United States or against it; there can be no neutrals in this war—only patriots and traitors."[4] Lincoln's secretary John Hay later recalled:

> The day before, we had appeared hopelessly divided. But before the smell of powder disappeared from Charleston Harbor, the flag floated from every newspaper office in the country. From the opposite poles of opinion men thronged to the call of their country. Long-estranged enemies stood shoulder to shoulder. . . . The coldest conservatives sprang forward to the front and the wildest radicals kept time with the new music. Douglas and Lincoln joined hands. Millard Fillmore put on the uniform of a militiaman, and Wendell Phillips stood for the first time in his life under the Stars and Stripes, and "welcomed the tread of Massachusetts men marshaled for war."[5]

Patriotism triumphed with the Civil War. Before then, there were few symbols of national unification. Rather, state and local associations governed American life. In the early Republic, the American flag, the clearest and most literal emblem of patriotism, was barely visible. Flags were limited largely to merchant and naval ships. None flew from homes or churches.[6]

All this changed in 1861. The clearest and most literal emblem of patriotism and resolve was the national flag. Churches, storefronts, homes, and government buildings all waved flags as a sign of loyalty and support. A nation festooned with flags is a nation at war.

On both sides, flags assumed a transcendent significance as symbols of their respective nation's sacred importance. In the North, Henry Ward Beecher, the nation's most famous minister, pointed out the significance of flags:

Our flag means, then, all that our fathers meant in the Revolutionary War; it means all that the Declaration of Independence meant; it means all that the Constitution of our people, organizing for justice, for liberty, and for happiness, meant. Our flag carries American ideas, American history and American feelings.[7]

In the South, ordinary Confederates were the most committed to unfurling banners, first the Stars and Bars, and soon thereafter the aptly named Southern Cross, which became the readily identified icon of the Confederacy and, later, the Lost Cause. On both sides, verse would soon fuse with symbol and produce hundreds of songs directed primarily to the national flags. If West Point became the seminary of America's national religion, then flags would serve as its religion's totem.[8]

To modern readers accustomed to instantaneous news, the most interesting thing to note in the immediate aftermath of Sumter is the absence of extensive news coverage. Soon the press would be transformed no less than the military. But in the beginning, the press had to gear up for an unprecedented war no less than the army. Artists, lithographers, and writers in the field would have to be enlisted for immediate and extensive coverage. The steam-driven press and telegraph would be coordinated for intelligence gathering and dissemination with no clear rules of censure or propaganda.[9]

Soon a syndicate to feed stories nationally—the Associated Press— would be invented in New York City, and Richmond would assume the same dissemination service in the South. Though short on details, the Northern press would not hesitate to bang the drum for war. In fact, the looming war would be a dream come true for Northern newspapers looking for advertising revenue and expanded circulations. For over a generation, the technology of steam-driven presses and the culture of a newspaper-reading public had been moving toward full-blown maturity. Sectional strife and rumors of war would provide the occasion for transforming the penny press into the premier shaper of public information and public opinion.[10]

The *New York Herald*, founded in 1835, boasted the largest circulation of penny papers in the country, with more than seventy-seven thousand daily subscribers in 1860. The paper's publisher, James Gordon Bennett, was no friend of President Lincoln or the abolitionists and initially resisted the drumbeat of patriotism. In the weeks preceding Sumter, Bennett seemed almost more sympathetic with the South than with the Lincoln administration when he praised a speech by Alexander Stephens, the vice president of the Confederate States of America, as "a statesmanlike exposition of the views of the moderate Southern leaders." Of Lincoln's administration, he complained,

"Through lukewarmness, greed of place, and an overweening desire to retain popularity with the ultraists of New England and the Northwest, they also have concluded to take no efficient step towards peacefully solving the difficulties that embarrass the country."[11]

When Sumter fell, Bennett turned, as usual, to the business community for direction. Good money managers that they were, their initial response was caution:

> The leading merchants, traders and professional men of the city of New York intend to hold a private preliminary meeting to-morrow, preparatory to a grand mass meeting, to be held in the park some day during this week, to declare in favor of peace and against civil war and coercion. This will probably be one of the greatest meetings ever held in this city, and its effect on the government at Washington and the government at Montgomery is expected to be very decided.

Still wishing to paint Lincoln into the abolitionist camp of Garrison and other radical abolitionists like Boston's Wendell Phillips, he asserted that "[a]s for Wendell Phillips, he must be fairly exulting over the terrible business. Every boom of the guns from Sumter or Moultrie is sweet music to the ears of the fanatics who have toiled and prayed for years for the destruction of the Union."[12]

The mass meeting in the park never took place. Bennett soon changed his tune as well. Local emotions turned him into a patriot. The symbol of that support was the flag. Those who refused to fly it did so at their own risk. On April 17, after a mob had forced him to fly the American flag over his offices, Bennett went on to show his stripes with provocative rhetoric:

> The people of the North are compelled to accept the dread arbitrament of the sword. They did not seek it. There is no course left for them but an earnest, vigorous, determined support of the government. We have no longer parties, or factions, or cliques. Feeble effort may be made to organize new parties or restore old political attachments, but they will be fruitless. From the Aroostook to the Potomac, from the Atlantic seaboard to the Rocky Mountains, the war slogan has been sounded and responded to with alacrity!"

The *Herald*'s greatest rival and sparring partner, Horace Greeley's *New York Tribune*, proved quicker on the patriotic draw. The first headline ran: "War Begun. The Jeff. Davis Rebellion, claiming to be the Confederate government of the seven States which profess to have seceded from the Federal Union, commenced formal war upon the United States by opening fire on Fort Sumter at 4 o'clock yesterday morning."[13]

Clearly this was not a time for sober moral reflection but for immediate, visceral exclamation. While unable to include an account of the attack for the morning edition of April 12, the paper issued a sensational evening "extra"— the first of many more to come in a society starved for news. Although extras had been issued ever since Bennett first introduced them at the *Herald* in the 1830s, their reach was limited and their appearance rare. The Civil War would transform the extra into a more frequent, electric event beginning with the attack on Sumter.

In an early instance of "making" news, Greeley reported as "news" the great success of his extra in the next morning's edition:

The "extras" issued at 9 o'clock last night, with news from the seat of war at Charleston occasioned the most intense excitement about town. Boys scampered through every part of the city loaded with papers and crying, "Extra!"— "Bombardment of Charleston." From one end of Broadway to the other groups of men were gathered about the most brilliantly lighted windows, reading aloud and discussing the dispatches contained in the extra.[14]

Throughout the following days, the *Tribune* focused on the war effort. On April 15 it read: "South Carolina has thus formally and willfully inaugurated war, and upon no other pretext than that the President desired to save Major Anderson's command from starvation." Four days later, *Tribune* writers called for a massive escalation of forces: "The defection of Virginia shows that little can be hoped for from the loyalty of the dominant party in the Border slave states, and the Government should prepare for a great war. At least 200,000 men should be called out in addition to the regular army."[15] To nineteenth-century readers those numbers would have appeared shocking. Little could they imagine how terribly right Greeley would turn out to be.

There were some hesitant exceptions, to be sure. The Democratic congressman from Ohio, Samuel S. Cox, did not accept secession, asserting, "I call this secession, revolution." But he also stood against Lincoln and the war response, pleading for compromise instead.[16]

An even stronger response appeared on May 4, 1861, when the radical reformer and freethinker Thomas Nichols launched a newspaper in New York entitled *The Age*. The paper would publish only one issue before Nichols fled to England. The religious and political tone of the paper was unusually irenic. Nichols would not be overcome by patriotism; he realized that wars were more easily declared than won.[17] To Northern Republicans filled with unalloyed confidence in their superiority of arms and technology, he issued a sober—and prescient—warning:

> It is easy to clamor for war—but it is wise to count the cost before entering upon such a war as this. Those who think the South is powerless do not understand her. In the Mexican war the Southern States contributed twice as many men as the Northern. . . . In case of civil war, with the North as the aggressor, the whole South would be united to a man, while the North would be divided.

A unified South, Nichols continued, would encompass 560,000 square miles, a territory larger than France, Spain, Portugal, England, Ireland, and Scotland combined. All of this raised ominous questions about the future of America in Nichols's mind. Who was to conquer such a territory? And what would "victory" mean?

> Suppose we were to conquer—burn their cities, waste their fields, introduce all the horrors of servile insurrection, and finally overcome and subdue them. What then? Can one portion of the Union hold the other conquered provinces? Can we hold the South as Austria holds Venetia, or as England holds Ireland? To do this, our Government must become a military despotism. It cannot be done under the Constitution. And if it were, there are four millions of negroes to dispose of. The North, the conquering section, must either govern them in slavery, or take the responsibility of setting them free, and providing for them. Frankly, we see no course for the Government to pursue but to acknowledge the independence of the Southern Confederacy, make equitable treaties, conciliate the Border States, and wait for the developments of the future.[18]

The Charleston press, which had done so much to arouse a war spirit in both the North and the South, was temporarily uncertain how to respond to Fort Sumter. Despite enthusiasm and self-righteous vindication, journalists did not really see the next step. Both the *Charleston Daily Courier* and the triweekly *Charleston Mercury* carried extensive coverage of the attack and surrender. They openly doubted Lincoln's willingness to engage in an offensive war on Southern territory. Yet if war came, they assured their readers, the Confederacy would prevail. The *Mercury*, which for years had served as a clipping service for incendiary editorials against the North, continued the onslaught:

But will not Fort Pickens be held like Fort Sumter? And will we not be compelled to shell them out? Yes! But this will not be war. Will not our coast be
blockaded? Very probably. But this will be war on sea, where we cannot
reach them. But a campaign war—a war of invasion for conquest, by the
North against the South, we do not expect to see. It will be most fatal to
the interest of the North, whilst it may be most beneficial to the South in
uniting them together in one *exclusive* destiny.[19]

The next week the *Mercury* restated the Confederate case for independence. To the question "For What Are We Contending?" the answer was
unequivocal:

The matter is now plain. State after State in the South sees the deadly development, and are moving to take their part in the grand effort to redeem their
liberties. It is not a contest for righteous taxation. It is not a contest for the
security of slave property. It is a contest for freedom and free government, in
which everything dear to man is involved.[20]

It is clear that the Confederates, no less than Lincoln's Republicans,
were fighting for the same thing: the idea of freedom. But their idea of freedom was grounded in the self-evident truth that all men were not created
equal and that therefore white men had a natural and God-given right to own
and expand property in the form of slaves of color. Unlike the Northerners,
moreover, they recognized their hierarchical conception of freedom in their
constitution, whose protections and safeguards they valued over the cavalier
abstractions of their own Thomas Jefferson.[21] The Declaration of Independence was not their apple, nor the U.S. Constitution their frame. Their
frame would be an entirely new republican but stratified society whose fruit
depended on the "peculiar institution."

Religious and moral commentary in the secular press, though evident,
was subordinated to war, honor, and "manliness." One editor, writing from
the aristocratic and honor-bound culture of the planter class, opined, "The
South fights . . . for honor, character, standing, and reputation. She must not
only wipe off the stigma of effeminacy with which Abolition has branded her,
but she must prove that she possesses that high-toned chivalry, that enduring
and indomitable courage that is peculiar to a privileged caste."[22]

Richmond's total newspaper circulation in 1860 was eighty-four thousand, but the reach and influence of Richmond papers expanded greatly during the war.[23] Forty newspapers throughout the South suspended publication
in the first year, and only twenty-two remained by 1865.[24] Five of them would

be in Richmond. The *Richmond Dispatch's* prewar circulation of eight thousand grew to thirty thousand before the war's end (equal to that of its rivals combined).[25] The extra became a staple of journalism in the Confederacy no less than in the North. Often these extras were extracts from newspapers in enemy territory.[26]

Like the *Dispatch*, the *Richmond Enquirer* had supported President Buchanan's fast day in 1861. Significantly, it had also printed Governor John Letcher's letter declining calls from clergymen to proclaim an additional day of prayer in Virginia. Reflecting prewar Southern sentiments against "political preaching," it reminded its readers that the custom in Virginia was to avoid any interference in religious duties, and it repeated Letcher's contention that civil magistrates should have nothing to say about religious matters—that rites of thanksgiving or humiliation were the sole province of ecclesiastical organizations, and not states.[27] This was precisely what Letcher's predecessor, Governor Henry A. Wise, had said in 1856 when he refused to proclaim a day of thanksgiving with this caustic observation: "This theatrical national claptrap of Thanksgiving has aided other causes in setting thousands of pulpits to preaching '*Christian politics*' instead of humbly letting the carnal kingdom alone and preaching singly Christ crucified."[28] In the blink of an eye all this would change, as war challenged ministers to privilege patriotism over spirituality. But not one word on behalf of peace.

CHAPTER 4

"THE DAY OF THE POPULACE"

Leading intellectuals in the North and the South were obsessed by the war and wrote widely to one another and to the press on the subject. In the North, intellectuals and writers participated freely in the patriotic frenzy that raged after the surrender of Sumter. Instead of sober moral reflection, they, like everyone else, stood dazed at the sheer power of patriotism to transform their world overnight. Few literary classics resulted, but letters and speeches abounded.[1]

There was a time when Ralph Waldo Emerson was willing to let the Union dissolve. Then came April 12 with the force of a revelation and an exaltation. In a lecture delivered shortly after Sumter, Emerson told his audience that his life had forever changed. Before the war, "we were very fine with our learning and culture, with our science that was of no country, and our religion of peace." Then came Sumter: "And now a sentiment mightier than logic, wide as light, strong as gravity, reaches into the college, the bank, the farm-house, and the church. It is the day of the populace; they are wiser than their teachers. . . . I will never again speak lightly of a crowd."[2]

Perhaps no writer was more deeply affected by the war than the poet Walt Whitman. Like many other New Yorkers, Whitman first learned of the bombardment from the *Tribune* extra while walking home to Brooklyn. Whitman saw in Sumter a call to American destiny. Already he came closer to sharing Lincoln's deeply moral and millennial view of America than any other intellectual. "I will make the continent indissoluble, I will make the most splendid race the sun ever shone upon, I will make divine magnetic lands," the poet had proclaimed in "Song of Myself" (1855). In the war he would discover his salvation.

Like Lincoln, Whitman regarded the slavery question as secondary. War would be waged for the Union, not only for its own sake but also for the sake of the world. "What we believe in waits latent forever through all the continents," he wrote in "To a Foiled European Revolutionary," but for that to endure, the American Republic had to be preserved—and expanded. For Whitman as for Lincoln, the mission—and the stakes—transcended America to embrace the future of humanity: "Earth's resume entire floats on thy keel O ship, is steadied by thy spars." For the rest of the war he would serve in hospitals and devote himself to the sick, wounded, and dying soldiers.[3]

Intellectuals were proud of their self-control and superiority. Yet they were, in fact, driven mad by Sumter, just the same as ordinary men and women. When word of Sumter reached her, Louisa May Alcott wrote in her diary: "I've often longed to see a war, and now I have my wish. I long to be a man, but as I can't fight, I will content myself with working for those who can."[4] Like Whitman, Louisa May Alcott served in a Union hospital until ill health forced her out.

For elite male intellectuals, the call to war was met with unmitigated "war fever." In a more aristocratic vein than Lincoln, they wondered if they could stand up to the manly challenges of war. Oliver Wendell Holmes Sr. welcomed the call to arms as a tonic to brace the character of his elite colleagues. His son, Oliver Wendell Holmes Jr., dropped out of Harvard and eagerly enlisted in the Massachusetts volunteers. Nathaniel Hawthorne's reaction was identical: "The war, strange to say, has had a beneficial effect upon my spirits, which were flagging woefully before it broke out. But it is delightful to share in the heroic sentiment of the time, and to feel that I had a country—a consciousness which seemed to make me young again."[5]

A younger Charles Russell Lowell enlisted immediately. Fellow Brahmin Henry Lee Higgins also enlisted, observing later: "I always did long for some such war, and it came in the nick of time for me."[6] For Henry Brooks Adams—great-grandson and grandson of presidents, and stationed with his father in England—the impossibility of active service caused extreme frustrations. Even if he were home, a weak physical condition would not have allowed him to serve. In a letter to his brother Charles, he confided: "I feel ashamed and humiliated at leading this miserable life here, and . . . I haven't even the hope of being of more use here than I should be in the army."[7]

Few intellectuals would go as far as the Unitarian abolitionist and soon-to-be commander of African American forces, Thomas Wentworth Higginson, in identifying the war with the moral cause of immediate emancipation. In his essay, "The Ordeal by Battle," published in the *Atlantic Monthly* in July 1861, Higginson challenged his informed readers to see war as a crusade for abolition, not merely for Union:

Either slavery is essential to a community, or it must be fatal to it,—there is no middle ground; and the Secessionists have taken one horn of the dilemma with so delightful a frankness as to leave us no possible escape from taking the other. . . . The watchword "Irrepressible Conflict" only gave the key, but War has flung the door wide open, and four million slaves stand ready to file through. . . . What the peace which the South has broken was not doing, the war which she has instituted must secure.[8]

Northern clergy no less than Northern intellectuals fell victim to the sheer power of patriotism following Sumter. In a sermon preached in Brooklyn's Plymouth Congregational Church during the siege of Fort Sumter, Henry Ward Beecher declared that the only proper response was resistance and patriotism: "Seven States, however, in a manner revolutionary not only of government, but in violation of the rights and customs of their own people, have disowned their country and made war upon it! There has been a spirit of patriotism in the North; but never, within my memory, in the South. I never heard a man from the South speak of himself as an American. Men from the South always speak of themselves as Southerners."[9]

At Roxbury's Universalist Church on April 21, J. G. Bartholomew offered heroic words: "Never before since the days of the Revolutionary memory and fame has there been a call to arms that has so thrilled the great heart of our people, swallowed up all party lines, and set the pulse of patriotic feeling beating in one quick response like this. . . . We stand to-day a band of brothers in a sense we never stood before."[10]

Universalists might have been liberal, but they certainly were not pacifistic. In another Universalist church in Watertown, Massachusetts, the Reverend A. Countryman raised a cry for war: "Already the war is baptized in blood, and from its crimson drops the historic pen has written the inaugural, pronounced on the memorable nineteenth, for the reconstruction of the American Temple, enlarged and improved, to freedom, to virtue, and to God!"[11] The orthodox Presbyterian William H. Goodrich preached the same: "We find our hearts thrilled with strange emotion; at once beating with new impulses of patriotism, and glowing with indignation at those, once our brethren, who are now traitors and deadly foes."[12]

The most important moral authorities for fixing each section's redemptive mission and sacred claims were the ministers with local connections in every community.[13] Both the North and the South would enlist them for the task of the sacred legitimation necessary to mount a mutually "defensive" war. In the North before Sumter, sentiments had ranged from Unionist, to antislavery, to abolitionist. But once Sumter fell, strong Unionist sentiment prevailed in most pulpits and with it the necessity to go to war.

The Sixty-Ninth New York State Militia, 1861. Religion supplied indispensable legitimacy to the war effort on both sides of the conflict. Here the "Fighting Irish" celebrate Mass in the field. Roman Catholics and Jews no less than Protestants proclaimed the holiness of their cause.

In terms of national identity, the North had long adopted the rhetoric of the "New Israel" as its own. By 1861 it was deeply ingrained and as instinctual to elite opinion shapers as to ordinary men and women. The rituals of fast and thanksgiving days, begun in seventeenth-century New England, contin-ued to serve as major occasions to preach righteousness and celebrate chosen peoplehood. They articulated what the intellectual historian Perry Miller dubbed an "American jeremiad" that spelled out America's sacred identity as a "redeemer nation" engaged in a special "covenant" with God to save the world.[14] The Puritan founders and their eighteenth-century Presbyterian cousins in the Middle Colonies had invented the jeremiad in a theocratic context that fused church and state on the model of ancient Israel. Their democratic stepchildren retrieved the rhetoric of most-favored-nation, but in place of theocracy attired it in democratic garb celebrating religious liberty and republican ideology.[15] However they saw the role of slavery in perverting the South, most Northern moral arbiters in 1861 agreed that the ultimate goal of the war was the preservation of the Union.[16] Because of the United States' divine commission to be a redeemer nation, preserving the Union was a suffi-cient cause.

While few Christian moralists in the North favored immediate and universal emancipation for slaves everywhere, many did, like Lincoln, see the system as morally reprehensible and contrary to the Christian gospels. In this vein of thinking, *the* moral cause—preserving the Union—could bring with it the happy by-product of emancipation, or at least limited emancipation. But emancipation could not justify the war. In 1861 slavery had not yet even risen to "a" cause for most white Americans. "The" cause was exclusively the Union. Anything else compromised the Constitution and threatened the national covenant. Before casualties soared, one just cause was enough. And to Union moralists, the guilt was obvious. "Defensive" wars are just and, in the case of the attack on Sumter, the South was undeniably the "original aggressor."[17] As for the North, a just patriotism governed the war mania and gave it saving energy.

The Northern religious press stood alongside sermons as a moral booster for just war. Once a vehicle for religious commentary with extremely limited secular content, the religious weekly was co-opted for political ends virtually overnight. The effects were prodigious and essential to Lincoln's survival and ultimate success.

Already by the mid-nineteenth century, the religious press had become a weekly news medium capable of competing with, and even surpassing in circulation, the secular press. Published in New York, the Congregational *Independent* boasted a circulation of 60,000 as of January 1, 1861. For eight Northern Methodist religious weeklies alone, aggregate circulation averaged 130,000.[18] Where contemporary twenty-first-century religious publications tend to limit their material exclusively to matters religious and spiritual, the nineteenth-century religious press became a polymath production divided among "Religious News," "General News" (politics and war), and commercial advertisements for everything from garden tools to topical application of cocaine for baldness.

Nevertheless, before 1861, religious news dominated the press. Following Sumter, talk of war was irresistible. Beginning virtually to the day of April 12, the ratio of religious to general news shifted decisively to general or secular news and would retain that imbalance throughout the war.[19] Unlike the secular press, moreover, the religious press was almost exclusively Republican and pro-Lincoln—a position that would sustain Lincoln throughout the war.

In the upper Midwest, a Presbyterian newspaper serving the Western Reserve called the *Christian Herald* carried an account of the shelling of Sumter with the following commentary:

War has begun. The North is thoroughly aroused. Millions are being enrolled and drilled for the home defense. We believe that these extensive and thorough preparations for resistance to treason and aggression are the best possible peace measures.

Commentators were prepared to accept the idea of the Union as a just cause. But they understood that cause in the context of a war of limited extent: "We do not yet believe the North can be provoked to invade the South."[20]

In the wake of Sumter, war coverage grew even greater. After canvassing the New York City churches on April 18, the *Independent* reported that "in nearly all the churches in this city—and probably in a majority of churches throughout the country—the sermons of last Sunday were mainly in reference to the War." And what kind of sermons were they? "Many congregations made the day an occasion for patriotic contributions for the outfit of volunteers, or for the support of their families." "The gallant Major Anderson and his wife attended service at Trinity. At Dr. McLane's Presbyterian church, Williamsburg, the 'Star Spangled Banner' was sung. Dr. T. D. Wells preached from the words: 'He that hath no sword, let him buy one.' "[21]

Like all nineteenth-century presses, secular and religious, the *Christian Herald* included skimmings from other presses on its mailing list. The *Methodist of New York* was quoted as saying: "We can sacrifice neither God nor Country even at the demand of a brother."[22] From the *Independent*, the *Herald*'s editors reprinted a justification for war centered on the preservation of the Union: "It is not like our last [Mexican War] a war of conquest and acquisition. It is a war to defend the life of our nationality, the sacredness of our Constitution, the permanence of our Union, and the being of our Government."[23]

In Philadelphia the radically antislavery "New School" Presbyterian minister and editor Albert Barnes wrote in his *American Presbyterian* on April 18: "War Begun . . . Now, treason, hide your diminished head, and the God of our fathers be with the right!"[24] Earlier, Charles Hodge of Princeton Theological Seminary, Barnes's theological adversary, had issued a widely circulated pamphlet entitled *The State of the Country* in which he refused to condemn slavery as, in all instances, a sin. The pamphlet was published in January 1861 and sold in the thousands. Hodge went on in the pamphlet to disapprove of slavery, but urged that, if secession became necessary, it be accomplished peacefully.[25] After Sumter, that sentiment largely disappeared. In Monmouth, Illinois, the editor criticized Hodge for his pamphlet and summoned the readers to war.[26] In time, Hodge would change his mind as well.

No such ambivalence over slavery characterized the black religious press. Their ambivalence was over a "Union" that would not even allow Northern freedmen to fight. Perhaps the most influential African American religious weekly was the African Methodist Episcopal *Christian Recorder*, begun in Philadelphia in 1852 and disseminated widely throughout the African American community.[27] On April 27, the paper carried an editorial on "The Star-Spangled Banner, and the Duty of Colored Americans to the Flag." In it the writer complained of the refusal to enlist black volunteers, but then went on to declare that "if the nation, in its bloody conflict with armed treason, should be so pressed as to have its heart harmonized towards you, and then call upon you for martial aid, you may fly swifter than eagles, stronger than lions, to sustain the national flag."[28]

While Northern moralists uncoupled the campaign for emancipation from the justification for war, they did not hesitate routinely to condemn slavery as a sin. Only abolitionists sought to anchor the moral objectives of the Lincoln administration's war policies and goals in emancipation. Profanity, intemperance, and Sabbath-breaking were also legitimate moral issues and sins, but they could not justify war.

Still, there was also a profound distinction that made slavery different from other sins. In the first place, unlike profanity, it was limited to the border states and the South. Second, despite Southern protests in the name of states' rights, it dictated secession. Moral commentators employed a rhetorical sleight of hand whereby they insisted slavery was *not* the cause of the war. Rather it *was* the cause of *secession*, which *was* the cause of war. This argument, while complex, was not without its own logic. In fact, the issue of secession was *both* about patriotic nation-worship of the Union *and* about the sanctity of a democratically derived commitment to containing the spread of slavery. And in this equation, the moral upper hand was with the containment of slavery (with an eye to ultimate abolition) and not with its growth and infinite perpetuation.

The double-edged argument for Union and the containment of slavery allowed supporters of the war to maintain their stand that the military action was justified. They readily conceded that the slavery issue, more than any other one, fueled sectional animosities and in that indirect sense "caused" hostilities. It was imperative, though, that they cast the issue in a language other than universal abolition, however much they sought it. Otherwise a just war to protect the Constitution and the Union would become an unjust war of aggression and occupation in defiance of constitutional guarantees. For the killing to be just, the Constitution had to be honored. Whatever role slavery may have played in exacerbating tensions and "causing" sectionalism, the cause of war was Southern treason.

In the North and the South, the nation's most respected moral arbiters evidenced little attention to the ethics of looming war. There was no shortage of justifications for war, but virtually no thought was given to how it should be waged or what, if any, limitations ought to be imposed for the sake of a justly fought war. In place of deep moral reflection, each side labeled the other the aggressor and succumbed immediately to the thrill of a "just" war fought, on both sides, for legitimate defensive purposes.

A Northern writer for the Presbyterian Church U.S.A. had no doubt as to who was at fault: "It is not an *aggressive* war on our part. . . . War is offensive, on the part of the power that commits the first act of violence; it is defensive, on the part of him who receives and resists the first act of violence."[29] Immediately upon defending the war as just, the writer proceeded to pillory the enemy with biblical examples of unjust wars:

> I can think of but a single rebellion that will furnish any adequate parallel to the present rebellion of the cotton states of this country in 1861, and that is, the rebellion of the proud, luxurious, lascivious, unprincipled, murderous Absalom, against his noble, unsuspecting, too affectionate and overindulgent father, David."[30]

A Protestant editor in Illinois argued that even if Northern armies entered the South, "[i]nstead of invading the South, they are really repelling an invasion from the South." In these terms, the paper explained, the war's "cause is as righteous as ever summoned a people to arms."[31]

With rhetoric like this, offensive could easily become defensive, so that the whole question of just war could be assumed. Armies could invade the South and claim they were fighting a defensive war. In an argument not picked up by most commentators early in the war but common in the North later, Philadelphia's *Banner of the Covenant* concluded that because of slavery, the South is "the original aggressor" and therefore the "offender" who sets in motion "the lawfulness of defensive war."[32] In other words, slavery itself was the aggressor.

Though unwilling to engage in a moral exploration of just-war theory, or dictate the conduct of a just war, many religious presses were willing to pronounce the war "religious." If the coming war was not a sacred crusade, it nevertheless had religious justifications. In Cincinnati, the writers for *Presbyter* asked the question: "Is this a religious war?" They looked for a moral answer from a most unusual—and arguably secular—source: fund-raising. Many churches were employing Sundays or days of special sermons as an occasion for purchasing equipment for the local militias represented in their congregations: "This movement of churches as such is something quite new, this raising of funds and providing of material equipment on the Sabbath for the war is significant and must certainly be taken as indicating their feeling, that this is a religious war."[33] In mid-nineteenth-century discourse, "religious war" meant a just war.

In the Confederacy, the task of sacralizing a new nation fell with particular weight on the shoulders of the churches and synagogues in the new nation's capital. Without the clergy's active endorsement of secession and war alongside that of the statesmen and generals, there could not have been a Confederate nation. By the 1840s and 1850s, Christianity represented the most powerful cultural system in the Old South. Generations of missionaries and revivalists succeeded in converting the South from a largely unchurched region to a region where evangelicalism triumphed.[34]

To be sure, the Southern culture of "honor" weighed heavily on the master planters, many of whom never bothered to join a church. This culture was constrained, however, by its own aristocratic sensibilities. It could never win popular approval, either among the foot soldiers or on the home front. Independence was painful to contemplate and wrenching to execute, and only the highest ideals could justify it. Those ideals were religious. For men, women, and children, Christianity offered the only terms out of which a national identity could be constructed and a violent war pursued.

In Charleston, the Reverend Thomas Smyth preached a three-part sermon, "After the Fall of Ft. Sumter, 1861." For background, he recalled how, as recently as the advent of the New Year, "this state and city were wholly unprepared to undertake a war. Our forts, our arms, our arsenals were in possession of federal troops. We had no fortification, no organization, no military commander of experience, and but little ammunition." Yet Southern resolve and righteousness ran strong.

In an earlier fast-day sermon, Smyth had made plain that the abolitionists were the root evil behind Northern aggression, and that they dictated Lincoln's politics and pursuit of war. "Black Republicans" were blind to the fact that slavery was a sacred trust imposed on the South by British and Northern slave traders and commissioned by God. Abolitionists forgot that God "ordained" slavery as "a penal infliction upon a guilty race." That was why, in contrast to Northern labor, slaves "have multiplied in a ratio far greater than their masters; that they are healthier and happier than any other laboring class on the face of the earth."[35]

For support, Smyth turned to Augusta's Reverend Joseph Ruggles Wilson. Wilson went so far as to argue that slavery was so central to God's designs that it would persist into the millennium, albeit "freed from its stupid servility on the one side and its excesses of neglect and severity on the other."[36]

With looming hostilities and secession, Smyth continued, the state was transformed. Forces were gathered, siege guns set in place, and the liberation of Charleston accomplished: "The fall of Sumter, and of Sumter's flag, was a signal gun from the battlements of heaven, announcing from God to every Southern State this cause is mine—come ye up, come to the house of the Lord against the mighty, and saying to the North, Thou shalt not go up nor fight against your brethren."[37]

How did this deliverance take place? Here Smyth invoked "the recognition of providence":

> Extraordinary providences are instinctive warnings of great importance in God's government of the world, and to be solemnly considered. The voice of the Lord crieth out unto the city and the men of wisdom shall see his name. . . . In the events connected with the occupation, siege and fall of Fort Sumter, and the unconditional surrender of its garrison, we have a signal display of the powerful providence of God.[38]

At St. Michael's Church (Episcopal) in Charleston, James H. Elliott preached a sermon on *The Bloodless Victory*. The sheer fact of conquest was one thing, but to humble Fort Sumter with no loss of Confederate lives was nearly miraculous. Clearly, Elliott concluded, such a compelling victory could only be ascribed to "the hand of God."[39]

The Confederate religious press, like the Northern religious press, stuck to constitutional arguments, identifying war as a just cause for states' rights. But then, like their Northern counterparts, they went on to address the moral issue of slavery from the opposite side. Southern editors promoted the good of slavery in a "Christian Republic," while denouncing abolitionists as the real enemy manipulating Northern public opinion and riling citizens. By controlling the Republican Party and its president, abolitionists were promoting a war of Northern aggression on innocents.

As in the North, the religious press in the South accompanied the preachers into the fray. Throughout the South, circulation levels were high and destined to grow far higher with the onset of hostilities. Nashville's *Christian Advocate* was the largest, with weekly sales of thirteen thousand already by the 1850s.[40] War would only enhance the news-reading public's appetite for more. Both Northeners and Southerners augmented the reading of their own side's papers with "outside" reading from the New York penny press and Northern denominational papers, although they would have to be smuggled into the South.[41] So effective would the press become that generals on both sides would rely on it for intelligence.

Subject matter aside, Confederate (and Northern) religious newspapers differed in one important respect from the secular penny press: their editors were not professionals. They were not caught up in the journalistic penchant for political infighting and the exposé, nor were they willing to attack the secular press or competing denominational publishers. The religious press had no formal political affiliations and tended to condemn any and all criticisms of duly constituted civil authority. This would prove a godsend to President Davis.

The religious press also differed from the secular press by its explicitly Christian and devotional frame of reference. As summarized by the Episcopal *Southern Churchman*: "It surveys the world not with the eye of the politician, or the merchant, but condenses, arranges, and reports the events of the day, as connected with the religion of Christ."[42]

The *Southern Churchman*, like other religious weeklies, was true to its word. An examination of its contents reveals materials suited for all ages, including children. In many ways, the secular press, with its emphasis on politics, remained a largely male medium. The religious press, on the other hand, appealed equally to men, women, and children, to pious soldiers and politically apathetic civilians. In this sense, it brought the war's ideals and mission to the widest possible audience. When viewed collectively, it is striking how little religious newspapers varied from one to the next. Together they reinforced the rhetoric of the jeremiad and beat the drum for a righteous war.

The circulation of the South's denominational newspapers and religious tracts underwent a phenomenal expansion during the war; the growth of Richmond's secular press was modest by comparison. The Baptists acted first, and their Virginia Sunday School and Publication Board would publish over thirty million pages. The Soldiers' Tract Association of the Methodist Church was established in 1862 and published forty thousand copies of two semimonthly papers (one entitled *The Soldier's Paper*) and various missionary publications. The Evangelical Tract Society, based in Petersburg, Virginia, published more than one hundred tracts and the *Army and Navy Messenger*. In 1864, the *Central Presbyterian* claimed that Richmond alone was sending out ten thousand copies of religious journals each week to the Confederate soldiers, and that religious newspapers had a total circulation of ninety thousand per month in the armies.[43]

With the advent of secession, nationhood, and war, the religious press turned to the preaching of politics. A clerical writer for the *Central Presbyterian* explained that while party politics was best left to others, "there are times when none can be silent." The Methodist *Richmond Christian Advocate* championed the Confederacy's moral patriotism and insisted that it was grounded in "evangelical and vital religion."[44]

Unlike the secular press, religious weeklies explained the doctrinal underpinnings of the Confederacy. In an early editorial, the *Advocate* pointed out the distinction between national covenants and the individual covenant of grace, and the necessity to incorporate the entire "political community" into the national fast. Non-Christians, or those "who make no pretensions to experimental religion," who participated in the sacrament of Communion would be blasphemers, but they *should* participate in the ritual of the national fast and tend to moral reformation.[45] Just as Northern clergy shouted loudest denouncing slavery, so Southern clergy remained staunchly, perhaps uniquely, loyal to the cause of the Confederacy and the Davis administration.

CHAPTER 5

"TO RECOGNIZE OUR DEPENDENCE UPON GOD"

The Confederacy responded in kind to the Northern jeremiad and its historical claims to providential chosenness. But the moral and spiritual creation of a national identity in the South would not be accomplished so readily as in the North. They had no rhetorical heritage that remained solely *theirs*. Instead, a new Confederate jeremiad would have to be invented, or more properly appropriated, from the "heretical" North. The Confederate capital, unlike the Union capital, not only had to invent a nation with a constitution all its own but also invest that new creation with the highest spiritual and moral legitimacy. How else could avowedly Christian citizens be persuaded to kill and be killed?

The Southern clergy's new burden of political preaching was made immensely easier by the new Confederate constitution, adopted on February 8 and ratified on March 11, 1861. Unlike its Federal counterpart, it explicitly declared its Christian identity, "invoking the favor and guidance of Almighty God." The national motto, *Doe Vindice* ("With God as our defender"), added weight to the South's claim to be a uniquely Christian nation.[1]

Now was the time, President Davis proclaimed, to consecrate the new nation and "to recognize our dependence upon God . . . [and] supplicate his merciful protection." This meant that the South was now in a position more analogous to that of ancient Israel with its theocratic constitution or to Puritan New England than to that of the North. The republican Constitution of the Union, after all, failed to invoke—or even mention—God.[2]

The Confederacy was going on record as a Christian nation in a unique covenant with God. Even as the North's claim to political sovereignty was declared null and void, so also were its claims to a covenant with God annulled. The North's Constitution, drafted as it was by "deists and atheists," failed to invoke God's name. Any Northern claims to a special relationship were there-fore spurious. In contrast, God smiled on a Confederacy happy to recognize Him and claim Him as her own.

When Confederate lawmakers introduced God explicitly into their na-tional constitution, they had no idea of the significance this act would later assume. It would not only solidify the South's identity as a Christian republic but also supply a surprisingly powerful critique of a "godless" Northern Con-stitution. It would inspire *Northern* campaigns to get God into their own Constitution and correct the oversight of the Founding Fathers. In the process it would set off a debate that continues to the present over the mean-ing of America. With separation of church and state, and in the culture of re-ligious freedom, could America still be a "Christian nation"? For the South, and most Republicans in the North, the answer was an unequivocal yes.

The premier occasions for articulating the Confederate jeremiad would be the same as those observed in the North: public fast days and thanks-giving days. The mission was to articulate the terms of God's national covenant with the Confederacy and to interpret the meaning of current events within those terms. The special days were proclaimed by nonclerical public officials, chiefly the president, and observed by civil law throughout the land. Although the frequency of fasts ebbed or flowed depending on the state of public affairs, fast days never disappeared. Instead, they stood as ritual markers to proclaim a "peculiar peoplehood" modeled on ancient Israel.[3]

The ascendance of the public fast in the Confederacy, and particularly in Richmond, is truly remarkable. Through all of American history up to 1860, public fasts had been quintessentially Northern and "Puritan."[4] Yet, when se-cession came to war, the Confederacy would employ the public fast *more* fre-quently than the North. In all, Abraham Lincoln would proclaim three national fasts throughout the war while, in the same period, Jefferson Davis would proclaim ten.[5] In addition, multiple state and local fasts were pro-claimed in the Confederacy, as well as fasts in the army.

The novelty and power of these events in the evolving life of the Confed-eracy was large.[6] Lodged within the sense of legitimacy and the yearning for a Confederate identity was a simple notion: the idea of a covenanted—and Christian—nation.

But the realization of this idea required a ritual action—a civil sacrament that conferred legitimacy and sacred meaning upon the evolving nation. In other words, it required an act of collective worship, which the public fast and thanksgiving days became. In town after town throughout the upper and lower South, the ritual of a public fast and the incantation of the jeremiad created a Confederate identity grounded in fundamentally religious values.

For the Confederacy to adopt the public fast day as its own national ritual of self-affirmation, a profound revolution had to take place in a compressed period. Where the Puritans took two generations to invent a rhetoric of nationhood and war around the ritual convention of the fast and thanksgiving days, the Confederacy achieved it in a year, and it grew thereafter until the very last battles were lost—and beyond. The public fast enlisted Christianity for ritual and ideological service to the Confederacy, even though churches for decades had reflexively affirmed the apolitical "spirituality" of the church. While ministers would continue to celebrate the historical spirituality of the Southern pulpit, they would at the same time ring the charges of tyranny against the North and preach political liberty for the South with a ferocity—and frequency—unmatched in the North.

President Davis proclaimed the first Confederate fast for June 13, 1861. Davis's proclamation implored the people to call on God "to guide and direct our policy in the paths of right, duty, justice and mercy; to unite our hearts and our efforts for the defense of our dearest rights; to strengthen our weakness, crown our arms with success, and enable us to secure a speedy, just, and honorable peace."[7]

Clergymen throughout the Confederacy rallied to make the religious grounds of political union explicit. O. S. Barten's fast-day sermon for June 13, 1861, preached at St. James Church in Warrenton, Virginia, and published in Richmond, noted that the new Confederacy promoted a close relation between religion and government. The biblical grounding and constitutional circumstances of the Confederacy's founding pointed to a glorious future and announced the birth of a unique Christian nation. Great nations, Barten argued, display a distinctive character: Judea exemplified divine unity; Rome, political power; England, constitutional liberty; the United States, human rights. The Confederate States could become the greatest of all as the embodiment of the Christian rights and liberties derived from God and confirmed in Jesus Christ. The North had some Christians, and was once part of a divine commission that issued in independence. But it was now run by infidels and fanatics under a godless government. The South had Christian men in a Christian government presiding over a Christian people. Therefore, Barten concluded, as the South struggled "to *become* a truly Christian confederacy, even then God's purposes are bound up with us as a nation!"[8]

For the Southern clergy, as for the Northern clergy, the war proved to be irretrievably costly. As clergy rushed headlong to promote the war effort and the president who conducted it, they found themselves simultaneously liberated and co-opted. They would be freed to expand their pulpit commentary and religious press from "spirituality" to politics and support for the war.[9] But in that very liberation, they would be captured by the state and its political agenda. Once set, it was a trap they never escaped for the duration of the war.

To appreciate the novelty and power of Barten's words, we must hear them as his Confederate audience heard them, almost for the first time. And we must hear them in a Southern setting deeply religious but previously alien to national fasts and thanksgivings. Whether they could articulate it or not, Southern audiences were experiencing a new ritual of social order. Through words like Barten's, repeated in similar settings throughout the Confederacy, a nation was being born.

Perhaps in South Carolina clerics like James Henley Thornwell had glimpsed the new birth months earlier, even before the old nation had been dissolved. But in Richmond and other Southern locales, where many had resisted secession and had been wary of war, the sheer fact of the victory at Sumter validated all the hopes for the emergence of a righteous Christian nation in the South.[10] Now the Confederate nation had a "history"—however brief—of her own, as a newly constituted, divinely ratified, and victorious covenant nation. Preachers could now freely adopt the language of the Hebrew prophets for their own without it being the "political preaching" they had condemned for so many years. It would be God speaking. If the language they used sounded remarkably like that of the Puritans of old, that fact was never announced. Confederate clergymen spoke as if theirs were the first truly legitimate, God-honoring political fasts and thanksgiving days observed in America since the Revolution. This was not merely a rhetorical move of convenience, but a new affirmation of national identity that vaulted the Confederacy into the sublime status of a New Israel.

With military mobilization moving rapidly forward, and young men rushing to arms, most of those listening to sermons delivered in local churches were female, who found in them a powerful source of their fierce and self-righteous involvement in the war and their growing sense of political involvement in the struggle. *Their* morality and *their* covenant-keeping, no less than the men's, would hold the key to success or failure in the looming conflict. Card-playing, profanity, usury, and drinking were standard male sins cited in fast-day sermons. But covetousness, pride, excessive attachment to worldly apparel, gossip, and "loose-talking" were clearly directed at females. These themes loomed large in Confederate jeremiads.

For many women religion "opened an avenue into the male world of politics and public action." Certainly, the new politicized fast and thanksgiving sermons—recorded in print and repeated to female-centered congregations throughout the land—accelerated that transformation.[11]

The language of the covenant was hardly limited to the clergy. Indeed, the power of the jeremiad lay in its flexibility and its inclusivity. Statesmen and generals, intellectuals and journalists, housewives and children could invoke it no less than pastors. For the jeremiad to work as a ritual of social order, all had to be true believers. This is precisely what happened as the language took on the status of deep national myth.

O. S. Barten explained that God recognized the collective nation as a "moral person" and rewarded or punished it in *this* world because—like all nations—it would have no existence in the afterlife: "Nations are but aggregates of individuals who compose them, and what God requires of one in his individual capacity, he demands of the whole in their associated character."[12] Battlefield defeats were God's punishments for the sins of the Southern people, while victories were signs of God's pleasure.

The rhetoric of the Confederate jeremiad, like that of its Northern counterpart, was as amenable to print as to speech. Literacy rates were no higher in the nineteenth-century Confederacy than they were in colonial New England, where the jeremiad was first voiced. The volume of printed addresses, however, was much higher, extending the influence of the form and, in some ways, making it more powerful than its Puritan predecessor. Protestants had always been pioneers in the utilization of mass media, and Confederate Protestants were no exception.[13]

Throughout the lifetime of the Confederacy, nearly three-quarters of all printed sermons would be public fast or thanksgiving sermons or similar political and war-related sermons preached on other days. Once a rarity in Southern print, these sermons became a staple religious product of the Confederate press. Religious publications as a whole, excluding periodicals, would amount to more than 40 percent of the unofficial imprints appearing in the Confederacy.[14] Of course, printed sermons represented only a small fraction of the total fast and thanksgiving sermons preached in the Confederacy during the Civil War. But they remain a useful index to what was heard publicly throughout the Confederacy in churches and synagogues of all faiths and denominations—and to what was preached to soldiers in the army.

By June, the triumph of the Confederate jeremiad was complete, and Southern secular editors and magistrates, no less than their Northern counterparts, preached "Christian politics" alongside Christ crucified. The *Richmond Daily Dispatch* hailed the Confederacy's first fast-day proclamation for June 13, 1861, as an outgrowth of the sentiments of the people, and spent nearly two columns reporting the activities at St. John's Episcopal Church and summarizing other local sermons.[15]

Once the Confederacy was educated in the moral logic of the jeremiad through sermons, newspaper comments, and presidential proclamations,

Southerners truly internalized the message. Each victory would be interpreted as God's work, a gracious favor just short of the miraculous that signified a triumph of divine justice. A defeat, however, was never a sign that the cause was not righteous, or that God had deserted His chosen people, but rather that God was purifying His people through the fires of adversity so that they would come to depend only on Him. At that point, victory would be granted.[16]

CHAPTER 6

"THE CHURCH WILL SOUND
THE TRUMPETS"

As armies massed and generals plotted, politicians, editors, and clergymen on both sides stoked the fires of self-righteous hatred and resolve by denigrating the other and promoting the virtues of their "just cause." In what would soon prove to be a very nasty surprise, both sides found that the citizens were even more bloodthirsty than their military counterparts. Hardly anyone thought out loud about rules of engagement or codes of behavior, for which all would pay dearly as this first "modern" war evolved. Just as neither side's moral arbiters could even conceive of the modern war that they would do so much to incite, neither could they credit the other as anything but evil. Guilt and innocence were absolute and mutually exclusive. One side must be entirely just, the other entirely unjust.

In defending the righteousness of their causes, both Northern and Southern commentators transformed their nations from political compacts into moral imperatives. President Lincoln set the tone. The United States, he argued, was not derived from rational expediency, but rather stood as a sacred trust—a "political religion"—whose sacred text was the Declaration of Independence and whose eternal flame was its dictum that "all men are created equal."[1]

In his debates with Stephen Douglas, Lincoln had made plain his empathy with the Southerners' plight: "I think I have no prejudice against the Southern people. They are just what we would be in their situation. . . . When Southern people tell us they are no more responsible for the origin of slavery than we; I acknowledge the fact." Even after Sumter, Lincoln's view had not changed. The moral issue at hand was Union and not slavery.

In addressing Congress on July 4, Lincoln reaffirmed the South's constitutional right to its slave property and insisted that constitutional protections,

including the Fugitive Slave Act, would not be abrogated once the states returned to the Union. But then he repeated what he had steadfastly insisted:
the Union would not be compromised, nor would the spread of slavery into
federal territories be allowed. The Union was not simply one more political
union or imagined community, but its own self-evident moral cause. As such
it embodied a sacred mandate of *chosenness* to save the world for freedom
and democracy, no matter what the cost. Referring to himself in an almost
messianic third-person voice, Lincoln concluded prophetically, "He had no
moral right to shrink; nor even to count the chances of his own life, in what
might follow."[2]

Southern commentators saw in Lincoln's Union-worship rank idolatry.
Stephen Elliott, an outspoken secessionist bishop from Georgia, preached
adamantly in *God's Presence with the Confederate States* that God was on the
side of the Confederacy. But the central goals of Confederate nationalism,
according to Elliott, did not include either global influence or the civil religion of patriotism. Rather, the South fought

> for great principles, for sacred objects . . . to prevent ourselves from being
> transferred from American republicanism to French democracy . . . to res-
> cue the fair name of our social life . . . from dishonor . . . to protect and pre-
> serve a race who form a part of our household, and stand with us next to our
> children . . . to drive away the infidel and rationalistic principles which are
> sweeping the land and substituting a gospel of the stars and stripes for the
> gospel of Jesus Christ.[3]

For their part, Northern Christian moral arbiters were certain that secession was not only politically untenable but also ultimately a sin against God.
By thus presenting the Union in absolutist moral terms, Northern voices im-
puted the same moral urgency—and global redemption—to political union
and "democracy" that abolitionists had injected into universal emancipation.[4]
It was this very absolutism for Union among Republicans, and emancipation
among abolitionists that made it difficult for either to support the other's
moral platform. Moral certitude and patriotism blocked all reflection and
ethical analysis on moral issues of just conduct in the looming war. Confederate moral critics, in contrast, perceived from the outset how Unionism
and abolitionism could be fused into one moral absolute with devastating
consequences—consequences that would dictate a total war for unconditional surrender and involuntary reconstruction. Indeed, by overestimating
the strength and numbers of Northern abolitionists, Confederates assumed
such a fusion from the start, so that when emancipation was eventually pro-

claimed by Lincoln, no Southerner was surprised or aroused in any way as were many Northerners.

Most Northern secular newspapers, and virtually all religious weeklies, reflected the prevalent absolutist Unionist sentiments of the Union majority. Horace Greeley's *New York Tribune* stated the moral issue in terms identical to Lincoln's:

> The question is whether the Union, through the baptism of blood, shall re-turn to the spirit of Washington, or, like the South American Republics, be changed into an arena of endless struggles, wherein the banner of Freedom shall become a mere plaything, to be passed from hand to hand, through a succession of adventurous generals.

In one prophetic respect, Greeley differed from Lincoln: "The Southern press really speaks the truth (an accident for which it is not blamably respon-sible) when it declares that there are very few men in the South who would now, even if it were safe, advocate the restoration of the Union."[5]

The antislavery religious press, meanwhile, backed off its identification of the war with abolition in the immediate aftermath of Sumter. It joined the Northern consensus to portray the war as one for the Union with a moral am-plitude of its own. The *Christian Instructor* commented simply: "It is not an aggressive war on our part. . . . War is offensive, on the part of the power that commits the first act of violence; it is defensive, on the part of him who re-ceives and resists the first act of violence."[6] In similar terms, the *Independent* boldly proclaimed the "moral uses of the war," assuring its readers "that blood is not worth the having which is not worth the spending."[7]

In the South, a similarly reflexive patriotism prevailed. Charleston's Thomas Smyth preached a jubilee celebration sermon at the Second Presbyterian Church on the theme "Our Fathers." The point was to invoke the spirit of Washington and Jefferson as patriotic Southern voices who embraced the same spirit of independence that their Confederate descendants proclaimed in 1861: "They have ever and every where been found firm, faithful and true, honest and honorable, indomitable in will, uncompromising in principle, and clinging to their rights with unconquerable tenacity."[8]

Sympathy for Southern nationalism led the Southern-raised William J. Hoge to resign one of the most prestigious Northern pulpits at Brick Presby-terian Church in New York City. When Hoge prayed publicly for the rulers of the Confederate States, as well as the Union, he knew he was on bor-rowed time and announced his intention to return to the South. On July 21 he delivered his farewell discourse to Brick Church, confessing that: "Ever since the beginning of this national conflict, my heart has yearned towards my beloved South, and especially the dear Commonwealth of Virginia. I have longed to share their privations, their dangers, and their destiny, whether of humiliation or triumph."[9]

The *Charleston Daily Courier* used the Fourth of July to tout the glories of the new Confederacy: "These are stormy times indeed. In addition to the reported fighting on the Potomac, and the invasion of the Old Northwest, we have intelligence of a glorious victory of the Confederacy in Western Virginia, and another by the Confederates in Missouri. Can it be that Providence designs that we shall rejoice over the simultaneous fall of Washington, Wheeling, and St. Louis?"[10] Of course, Charleston's intelligence was flawed, and the "victories" were not forthcoming. But such were the vainglorious hopes and self-righteous certainties that would fuel the bloodlusts on both sides as they prepared to do battle.

Without knowing exactly where the first great engagement might come, all realized that it would be somewhere in Virginia on a route to Richmond. For the soldiers, excitement came mingled with fear. On the eve of battle, a young soldier wrote a worried letter to his pastor, asking him to help in the disposition of his "personal effects" in the event of his death. Like many soldiers who had not yet seen "the elephant" (combat), premonitions of death haunted him:

> In the next fight I shall not escape [death]. Not my dear pastor because I distrust the Power that has hitherto kept me from all harm, not that I think that our Heavenly Fathers arm is shortened so that he cannot save, not that I lack *faith* in his mercy and goodness to me, Oh no, none of this. I know he is good to me and blesses me richly every day and hour, but yet how can I hope to have such loving kindness as has been shown me continued when in every fight, better men than I go down and fall before my eyes in every battle. Oh remember if I do fall I have met with a cheerful spirit and say "gods will be done" and I do assure you dear friend I shall go to my duty with a cheerful heart and *with no regrets* that I am here trying to save my country.[11]

Confederate resolve was no less assured. In a sermon preached in June 1861 to Savannah's Pulaski Guards, who were about to join the army in Virginia, Stephen Elliott urged boldness: "Ye may go to battle without any fear, and strike boldly for your homes and your altars without any guilt. . . . The Church will sound the trumpets that shall summon you to battle."[12] In hopeful terms he assured the soldiers that with a proper relationship to

"God's word," victory would be assured.[13] With moral counters and assurances like these, all the pieces were put in place for the bloodshed to come.

As Davis moved to secure Richmond, Lincoln attended to his Maryland border in order to protect his capital. With the Baltimore riots as a powerful reminder of how vulnerable Washington was, Lincoln quickly ensured that Maryland would never again threaten Washington. This meant a "root-and-branch" extraction of all outspoken Confederate loyalists in public places.

The most draconian measures Lincoln took—and a hint of things to come—were to suspend the writ of habeas corpus from Philadelphia to Washington, effectively erasing civil liberties, and to place Maryland under martial law. When Chief Justice Roger B. Taney opined that only Congress had the constitutional right to suspend habeas corpus, Lincoln—who had despised Taney ever since the *Dred Scott* decision—issued orders (never served) for Taney's arrest. Secretary of State William Seward followed with the arrests of thirty-one proslavery Maryland legislators together with the mayor of Baltimore. From the start, Lincoln knew in essence where he was headed and was clearly prepared to take whatever steps were necessary to crush resistance, without waiting for Congress or the Supreme Court to oppose him.[14]

On the Northern and Southern home fronts, news of episodic exchanges and skirmishes filled the press with foreboding and declarations of crisis but not many reports of casualties. The most serious fighting was occurring in the West. In western Virginia, a Union army under General George B. McClellan occupied the mountain counties of western Virginia and pursued a successful campaign to drive Confederate forces out of the newly created pro-Union state of West Virginia. Meanwhile, in Missouri, Governor Claiborne Jackson, the pro-Confederate "border ruffian," refused Lincoln's call to raise state militias and kept his militia in spring quarters at Boonville, near St. Louis.

Under Lincoln's authorization, a small Union regiment led by the highly volatile and possibly insane Nathaniel Lyon compelled Jackson's proslavery militia to surrender their arms. Soon a sympathetic crowd gathered around Jackson, shouting insults. In an impetuous move, Lyon opened fire and killed twenty-eight civilians in cold blood. He was never charged by the Lincoln administration.[15] This "victory" helped the Union control the Missouri River, but at the cost of unending internecine disputes and guerrilla warfare that resulted in even higher civilian casualties.[16]

Ongoing violence in Missouri, pitting neighbor against neighbor, would only grow more savage as time passed. In effect, a civil war was erupting within its own borders. Lyon declared war on Sterling Price, commander of the pro-Southern militia, and chased him to the southwest corner of the state. In the process, Price set in motion pro-secession guerrilla bands—little more than common criminals—who ambushed and murdered anyone in their path, including women and children.

Three-fourths of Missouri residents were Unionists, and the guerrillas would stop at nothing to intimidate and terrorize these private citizens. In the process, they pushed the region into a virtual state of anarchy. Under their reign of violence, blood revenge trumped all sane considerations on both sides. Pro-Southern "bushwhackers" like William Quantrill, George Todd, "Bloody Bill" Anderson, and brothers Jesse and Frank James faced off against Unionist "Jayhawkers" (also guerrillas) like Charles Jennison, James Montgomery, and James Lane. In the orgy of killing that followed, there were no innocents and no limits on the extent of depredations they would enact. More than any other state, Missouri offered a chilling preview of what would happen if guerrilla warfare were to erupt on a grander scale.

Though strategically important, none of the spring encounters in the West had, in West Point terms, "risen to the dignity of a battle." As in most wars, the shooting would come first and the war plans would follow. With the exception of Winfield Scott, no American commander on either side had any experience commanding a brigade of two or more regiments in the Mexican War (about eight hundred men). And no one had commanded units as large as divisions (about five regiments) or corps (consisting of three divisions).

Based on modest experiences, initial military objectives were also modest. Northern generals strove to fight a traditional campaign on land and sea designed merely to force Southerners to accept the legitimacy of the Union government and come back into the Union with slaves and property intact. Winfield Scott's noncombative "Anaconda" strategy sought gradually to blockade the entire South, cutting off their access to ports and strangling them into early submission. Like Lincoln, Scott presumed a strong Unionist presence in the South that would soon sue for peace.

On the other side, Confederate leaders planned to march on Washington, picking up supposed legions of Maryland loyalists along the way. In time it would become clear that Maryland would not flock to the Confederacy any more than supposed masses of Southern Unionists would flock to the Union. But in 1861 hopes burned bright on both sides and promised quick victories. A "clean" and decisive Confederate victory in the field would win European recognition, which meant Northern blockades could not stand, and Lincoln would have to let them go.[17]

PART II
ROMANTICIZATION

THE MAKING OF HEROES

JULY 1861 TO MARCH 1862

CHAPTER 7

THE BATTLE OF BULL RUN: "A TOTAL AND DISGRACEFUL ROUT"

The Civil War began with the attack on Fort Sumter, but the first significant battle would wait three long months.[1] In the interim, armies had to be raised, logistical infrastructures created, munitions manufactured, officers commissioned, and battle plans laid. Neither the Union nor the Confederacy was prepared for war, and while everyone knew war had begun, no one knew what it meant. The ninety-day enlistment periods confirm that most leaders assumed the war would be brief and the costs minimal. Northerners, confident in a strong Unionist yeomanry, assumed the planters would capitulate without popular support. Southerners, well aware of Northern Whig opposition to the Mexican War and of abolitionist pacifists like Wendell Phillips, assumed the North would cut and run once the bullets flew. Hardly anyone thought a war would last longer than six months. Patriots on both sides remained confident that triumph would soon be theirs and victories glorious. Armies passed in review, volunteers lined up to fight, and civilians mixed easily with the commanders and local soldiers around the camps.

The politics of this war—aimed at reunion and reconciliation—dictated minimal civilian deprivations and fair fights by armies in the field. Leaders on both sides assumed that civilian property would be protected and, of course, civilians left untouched in any way. Above all, the code of *jus in bello*—just conduct—gave highest priority to the protection of innocents and civilians, even at the cost of heightened risk for the combatants.

By June Confederate soldiers were guarding the three major invasion routes into Virginia. Brigadier General Joseph E. Johnston's forces stood at the mouth of the Shenandoah Valley; Brigadier General Pierre G. T. Beauregard remained just above Manassas guarding the railroad; and Colonel John

("Prince John") Bankhead Magruder guarded the Peninsula between the James and York rivers. All were West Point graduates with experience in the Mexican War. Faced with the lack of a general in chief, President Davis assumed both the title and the responsibilities of commander in chief. The decision would prove costly.

In Washington, D.C., one thing was clear. Lincoln intended to fight rather than let the South go peacefully. And he would not wait for congressional consultation to increase the size of the regular army. When he assumed office, the professional army numbered under 20,000, spread out over seventy-nine frontier outposts. By July 4, when Congress was called into session, Lincoln had increased the Union forces to 235,000 men. Virtually all of the troops were already under arms—volunteers spoiling for a fight and a quick victory. There was a general staff and commanding general, the tall and imposing Winfield Scott. Scott had led America to victory in the war with Mexico. While a cadet at West Point, a young Ulysses S. Grant had stood in formation while Scott passed in review. Now at the head of the Union forces, Scott had one overarching objective: "Forward to Richmond."[2] The North, he knew, enjoyed an enormous advantage in sea power and shipbuilding capacity. But that would not immediately help a land campaign, which this war threatened to be.

Many voluntary companies were led by incompetent amateurs who would factor largely in early battles. But looming over them were the professional soldiers who had fought in Mexico and graduated from the service academies. Campaign strategies began to take shape immediately after Sumter. Both armies were served by the hundreds of talented West Point graduates trained both to command the armies and to lead by courageous example. Their powers in the field were virtually unchallenged. In the calculus of this looming war, the importance of generals would be difficult to overestimate. Civil War generals fought at the front and their instantaneous and instinctive decisions literally meant victory or defeat. Raw physical courage also determined outcomes. This was a time when generals still *fought,* unlike modern wars in which commanding generals function more like congressmen than warriors immediately in harm's way.

The key to the offensive was, in the Swiss tactician Antoine-Henri Jomini's term, "vivacity"—a single spirited charge of such intensity that the intimidated defenders, trapped in their inadequate entrenchments, would be rolled over and destroyed. Along with vivacity came romance. The greatest "art" of the offensive was the bayonet charge, a romanticized moment of individual—up close and personal—bravery and glory. One Confederate manual carried as its motto: "The bayonet is the weapon of the brave."[3] If forced to take a defensive position, commanders were trained to return to the offensive as fast as possible, preferably with a bayonet charge. These tactics had proved irresistible in the Mexican War. The question was not raised as to whether they would succeed in the coming war.

But times had changed greatly since the Mexican War. By the mid-1850s, old smoothbore muskets had been replaced by expandable minié balls that were easier to load, more accurate to fire, and capable of killing at much greater ranges. When placed in strategic defenses alongside heavy artillery with canister and heavy entrenchments, they allowed defenders to destroy attacking enemies massed in close-order formations before they ever reached defended lines.

Northern and Southern commanders understood the new technology, to be sure, but traditional West Point culture blinded them to the need to alter battlefield tactics. The vast majority of amateur non–West Point officers knew even less about technology and tactics, and had only the dimmest idea of how to manage combat under fire.[4] They did not anticipate the scope or duration of the burgeoning conflict. Nor, at first, did they contemplate a war on civilian populations. They knew only that armies had to be destroyed in the field en masse for the war to be deemed successful.[5] Technological advances, however, rendered tactical offenses meat grinders. Fueled in no small measure by the vivacity of a West Point education, the commanders had to see thousands of lives slaughtered before finally drawing the appropriate tactical lesson: in this war, the side that mounted the most effective *defense* against frontal assaults ultimately won.[6]

By mid-July, General Irvin McDowell's grand army of more than thirty thousand Federal troops advanced on Virginia soil and prepared to attack Brigadier General P. G. T. Beauregard's Confederate force of over twenty thousand rebels. To civilian and soldier alike the spectacle of a massed army was sublime. One eyewitness described the advancing Federal army in characteristically romantic terms: "The stirring mass looked like a bristling monster lifting himself by a slow, wavy motion up the laborious ascent."[7] The citizen spectators were even more excited about the coming battle than the citizen soldiers. But soldiers and observers alike were struck by the sheer, animal majesty of an army in the field.

For Northern newspapermen in the field, such as E. C. Stedman of the *New York World,* the whole affair took on the air of violent entertainment. In a letter to his wife he wrote: "We had a perfectly magnificent time to-day. I never enjoyed a day so much in my life. Was in the van throughout, at the head of the army, and it was exciting and dramatic beyond measure."[8] Right down to the last moment, the thrill of battle outweighed any sense of horror. Even religious newspapers such as the *Christian Instructor* could not help but marvel: "An army is truly a great machine. A locomotive; all its varying parts, living, intelligent, and working in harmony with one another. . . . Never has it been my lot to witness so general a display of order and strength, beauty and romance, as to-day."[9]

As the "great machines" faced each other by the town of Manassas, thirty miles southwest of Washington, crowds of spectators dotted the hillside with picnic lunches. McDowell signaled his intent to end the war in one decisive blow leveled against outnumbered and undersupplied rebel troops. So confident was he in his own superiority that he hardly bothered with a comprehensive plan of battle, nor did he consider the possibility of Confederate reinforcements that might overwhelm his army. Presidents Lincoln and Davis were likewise naive, fancying themselves accomplished military minds with overarching strategies in hand for a speedy resolution to the conflict.

But McDowell and Lincoln were in for a cruel surprise. In a pattern that would plague Union forces in the bloody years to come, Confederate commanders had closely followed newspaper accounts and intelligence reports documenting the exact progress of McDowell's advance and prepared to surprise the invading foe.

If any commander could calmly and forthrightly survey the fray and stand his ground, the battle would be his. Sadly for the Union, that leader stood on the other side, among General Johnston's reserves. As Union forces advanced ragtag on the Confederates at the Warrenton turnpike on Sunday, July 21, a brigade of rebels massed at Henry House Hill and stood their ground under the command of a dyspeptic former Virginia Military Institute professor-turned-general named Thomas J. Jackson.

As Jackson ordered "no retreat," General Barnard Bee of South Carolina looked to Jackson at Henry House and rallied his troops, (supposedly) crying out: "There is Jackson standing like a stone wall! Rally behind the Virginians!" Jackson's brigade stopped the Union assault in its tracks and, in the process, established the legend of the indomitable "Stonewall" Jackson.[10] The war's first warrior hero had been incarnated.

When a Confederate shell hit a wagon on Cub Run Bridge, blocking the Federal retreat, Federal troops panicked and soon became ungovernable. Soldiers mingled with congressmen and sightseers in a frantic retreat. Only a spirited rearguard defense, hastily organized by a grizzled Mexican War veteran and former banker, Colonel William Tecumseh Sherman, prevented a wholesale rout of Federal forces. Unlike the "political" generals with no formal training, the West Point–hardened Sherman held on. In doing so, his brigade suffered higher casualties than that of any other Union commander.[11]

A jubilant President Davis turned up on horseback at the battlefield to witness the capture of hundreds of Union prisoners and savor "his" victory. Instead of celebrating victory (and in the process setting off a fight for bragging rights with General Beauregard), Davis should have been urging his soldiers on. But that would have required an experienced military mind that Davis only thought he possessed. Fortunately for the Union, the Confederates were equally unprepared for a real battle and failed to pursue and destroy McDowell's army. Davis's failure to order a night pursuit into Washington cost him the Confederacy's best opportunity to end the war on Confederate terms. The Confederate army was as disorganized by its victory as McDowell's was by its defeat. Heavy rains the next day erased all opportunity for a Confederate knockout victory, and Washington, D.C., remained safely in Federal hands.[12]

In the North, the shame of defeat proved bitter beyond anticipation. The disappointment was all the more galling, following as it did the premature news of victory. By late afternoon, John Nicolay observed, "The President has been receiving dispatches at intervals of 15 minutes from Fairfax station. . . . For half an hour the President has been somewhat uneasy as these reports seemed to indicate that our forces were retiring."

Awakened from his nap, General Winfield Scott assured the president that this could not be the case, and Lincoln went out for a ride. The rest is described dramatically by Nicolay:

At six o-clock, the President having in the meanwhile gone out to ride, Mr. [William] Seward came into the Presidents room, with a terribly frightened and excited look, and said to John [Hay] and I who were sitting there
"Where is the President?"
"Gone to ride," we replied.
"Have you any late news?" said he.
I began reading [Simon P.] Hanscom's [optimistic] dispatch to him.
Said he, "Tell no one. That is not so. The battle is lost. The telegraph says that [General Irvin] McDowell is in full retreat, and calls on General Scott to save the Capitol" &c Find the President and tell him to come immediately to Gen. Scotts.
In about half an hour the President came in. We told him, and he

started off immediately. . . . It is now 8 o'clock, but the President has not yet returned, and we have heard nothing further.

Besides capturing the pain of defeat, Nicolay's account provides an early illustration of the indispensability of the telegraph in this civil war. With generals, statesmen, and journalists all crowding telegraph offices, it was not always clear who got the news first. But in the next several days, the whole country knew, with one side left deliriously joyful and the other disillusioned, grief stricken, and profoundly embarrassed. A dispirited Nicolay was forced to concede that "[o]ur worst fears are confirmed . . . a total and disgraceful rout of our men. The whole army is in retreat." As for President Lincoln, an assistant described a conversation with the goverment printer John D. Defrees in which an agitated Lincoln exclaimed: "John, if Hell is [not] any more than this, it has no terror for me."[13]

Lincoln would soon enough see more hell than he ever imagined, but the first cut was the deepest. When General Scott learned that McDowell had been defeated and that his army was in full retreat, he imposed a strict censorship on the telegraph so that word would not go out over the wires until Monday morning.

With news of the victory at Manassas emanating from Richmond, predictable jubilation and self-righteousness erupted. On July 24, the *Charleston Mercury* brought the glad tidings of victory and confidence: "The battle of the 17th, at Bull's Run, has inspired the greatest confidence in the superiority of our generals and their troops, and our power, with decent executive energy in receiving enough for the field, to defeat the mercenary hordes of the North; and compensates for our losses west of the mountains."[14]

Ecclesiastical reports invoked battlefield successes to proclaim the divine truth of the Southern jeremiad's message. The Presbyterian Synod of Virginia's annual report in 1862 would identify the public fast as the cause of victory at Manassas: "At first God did not seem to smile on our defensive operations. . . . Then God put it into the heart of [President] Davis to call for a day of fasting, humiliation, and prayer. . . . The united supplication of the whole people went up before the God of battles and was graciously accepted through the intercession of our great High Priest. . . . We were wonderfully delivered out of the hands of our enemies."[15]

The toll from Bull Run seemed incredible enough at the time, and to disbelieving eyes lined up at telegraph offices and reading newspapers probably had greater effect than later battlefield reports that would yield far larger numbers. Citizens on both sides were startled to learn that for the Federals 460 were killed, 1,124 wounded, and 1,312 missing, for a total of 2,896 casualties.

Confederate casualties included 387 killed, 1,582 wounded, and 13 missing for a total of 1,982. The shock lay in the fact that almost as many Americans had been killed in the entire Mexican War.

In a collective ritual that would repeat itself throughout the war, newspapers and telegraph offices recorded the names of the dead, wounded, and missing with updates that listed ever "more names of the killed and wounded."[16] In Worcester, Massachusetts, Martha LeBaron wrote to her friend Mary:

> This morning seems a week ago. I went down [the] street early, before I had seen a newspaper, and in the Post-office a young clerk with wet eyes, held out to me a list—of our dead officers. A few minutes after at the Station, the ticket master said to me, with tears raining down his face, "Ah, Miss LeBaron, I thought of you as soon as I heard this, and of how grieved you would be." Wasn't that strange in him? for he knows that no one *near* to me was in danger—and he felt only how my whole heart is in the war. Then I met other friends, and the hand-pressure was very close before a word could be spoken. People choked when they tried to talk, and attempted smiles ended in starting tears.[17]

If Sumter prompted Northern moderates to support war rather than secession, the bloodshed at Bull Run prompted them to hate the enemy as malicious and effective killers who, without formal recognition as a nation, nevertheless fought as a nation—and savagely at that. No moral reflection on the rules of war surfaced, even in the religious press—only a demand for blood revenge:

> We are now opening our eyes to the unwelcome fact that they are enemies of the country, and must be dealt with as TRAITORS. This once settled, scruples fast vanish about the mode of conducting the war. We feel bound to use every means in our power to put down a rebellion which is striking at the very life of the nation.[18]

At the same time that the *New York Evangelist* advocated using "every means in our power," it issued a bold and prescient proposal, certain to support a total war:

> When hundreds and thousands of our brave young soldiers are brought home from the bloody field; when there is a cry in the land, like the wailing in Egypt, because in every house there is one dead, the question will be

asked: why not make a speedy end of this dreadful business by at once pro-claiming freedom to the slaves? . . . Whatever rights they [Southerners] had before as loyal citizens, they have forfeited by their treason and rebellion.[19]

The South, too, saw the prospect of total war in Bull Run. On September 26, a day that Northern churches spent in fasting, the *Charleston Mercury* car-ried an ominous report titled "Negro Slaves Contraband of War":

> These virtuous Abolitionists of New England, when they can steal or get into possession of the negro slaves of Maryland and Virginia, no longer talk of emancipation. They take possession of them as property. . . . It is not enough that we arm and go forth to battle—we must do so with the desperate con-viction that we fight along the edge of the precipice. We must hurl the enemy over; or he will hurl us. We must not suffer ourselves to be beaten. There must be, in every soul, a personal passion—an individual resolution—enforced by the most vindictive determination—to send our weapons home to the heart of the enemy. We must smite unsparingly, with sweeping vengeance, and not merely conquer, but destroy! It is our homes that are in-vaded by the robber and the outlaw—our firesides, our wives, women and children. Sons of the South, be men! Be men![20]

Of all the news reports, the one most eagerly awaited by Northern and Southern readers alike was that of William Howard Russell, correspondent to the *Times* (London). The *Times* was perhaps the most influential paper in the world and spoke widely for British sentiments. Confederates had long hoped that their profitable cotton trade with Britain would draw England into their camp, or at least force the great nation to recognize the Confederacy as legiti-mate belligerents. They had good reason to be hopeful. British papers, on the whole, evidenced scant appreciation for Lincoln or the Republican Party.[21]

When Russell's column finally reached American papers, weeks after the battle, Northern readers were devastated. Russell began by invoking the jovial scene where "[e]very carriage, gig, wagon, and hack has been engaged by people going out to see the fight. The price [of carriage] is enhanced by mysterious communications respecting the horrible slaughter in the skir-mishes at Bull Run."

Russell then made clear that Northern civilian naïveté was equaled by that of their military. At the very moment that he listened to Northern re-porters crowing about victory, Russell was witnessing a wholesale panicked retreat of Yankee forces: "The drivers spurred and whipped and urged the horses to the utmost of their bent. I felt an inclination to laugh which was overcome by disgust and by that vague sense of something extraordinary taking place which is experienced when a man sees a number of people acting as if driven by some unknown terror."[22]

To Northern readers, hoping to leave Bull Run behind, Russell's delayed account threw salt into still raw wounds and raised anew worries about England's neutrality. Henry Brooks Adams raged at the defeat in a letter written to his soldier brother Charles Francis Adams from London, where Henry served as amanuensis to his father:

> After studying over the accounts of the battle and reading Russell's letter to the [London] *Times*, I hardly know whether to laugh or cry. Of all the ridiculous battles there ever were fought, this seems to me the most so. . . . But the disgrace is frightful. The expose of the condition of our army is not calculated to do us anything but the unmixed harm here. . . . If this happens again, farewell to our country for many a day. Bull's Run will be a by-word of ridicule for all time.[23]

Military defeats require a scapegoat, and General McDowell easily fit that bill, both at the popular level and with the president. On the day following Bull Run, Lincoln removed his general from command and appointed the impressive thirty-five-year-old General George B. McClellan as commander of the newly dubbed "Army of the Potomac."

Through summer and autumn, "Little Mac" worked tirelessly to increase and organize his new army, bringing in ten thousand soldiers a week until the army swelled to more than one hundred thousand men. McClellan had graduated second in his class at West Point and served with distinction both in the war with Mexico and in the Ohio Valley–western Virginia campaign. All indications in the North were that he would conquer Richmond by December, and the war would be over in time to celebrate a proper Christmas.

McClellan, however, was a Democrat and a firm advocate of the West Point Code. He evidenced a strong reticence to any plan resembling total war, especially if it involved noncombatant suffering.[24] Such a strategy, in his view, would only render reunion more difficult. In time, McClellan's reticence would prove his downfall, but for the time being Lincoln was pleased with McClellan's formidable organizing skills and the respect he commanded from the soldiers.

In the wake of Bull Run, Northern clergymen faced the difficult task of balancing a just cause with a disastrous defeat. Somehow the two had to be kept simultaneously in view if the right lessons were to be learned. God favored the North, but besetting sins obviously had led Him to chastise the North before He would grant them deliverance.

What were these sins? Evangelical Sabbatarians immediately noted that Bull Run took place on the Sabbath. They saw in Bull Run "a timely warning against the tendency in the army to disregard the Sabbath."[25] Profanity was also cited as a cause. One chaplain present at Bull Run attributed the defeat to "officers swearing at the men and the men cursing each other." Drinking was also a grave problem: "Let those who send us tracts, send us a large supply in the evils of profanity and intemperance, and they will do a good work."[26]

Other more sophisticated seers disregarded Sabbatarian explanations, intemperance, or profanity, and instead sought to divine deeper meanings. In Hartford, Connecticut, the Reverend Horace Bushnell, perhaps second only to Henry Ward Beecher as the voice of the white Protestant North, preached a sermon on the Sunday following Bull Run entitled *Reverses Needed*. The sermon was widely circulated and excerpted in the religious and secular press.[27]

The reasons for the sermon's importance are not hard to discover. From the start, it offered an apologia of suffering that would transcend trite appeals to Sabbath observance and address the very meaning of America. Bushnell's question was not original to him and it would never disappear from American public discourse: was the nation merely a political republic or was it a *Christian* republic, conditioned by its Puritan legacy to be a self-consciously covenant people? For the Confederacy, as was already evident, this was not an issue. They cast themselves from the start as an indissoluble Christian republic. But for the North, an ambiguity existed that could, in Bushnell's view, prove fatal to the Republic.

Bushnell was angry, and not only at the slaveholding South. He was angry at the fact of defeat, and he was angry with his nation's secular evolution, which, he believed, had prompted it. The Confederate cause was evil, but the rhetoric of being a Christian nation was correct. This was what God wanted to see for the righteous North. For Bushnell, this meant that Americans must recognize the mistakes and shortcomings of the Founding Fathers. And not only them, but also any present politicians who accepted the Fathers' secular sentiments uncritically, including President Lincoln. The greatest transgression was neither petty sins nor poor leadership, but bad philosophy. Bushnell's idea of freedom was not grounded in Lockean and Jeffersonian epistemology nor the naturalistic premises of the Declaration of Independence, but in the Puritans.

Whose fault was the Civil War? Thomas Jefferson's. "He had no conception of any difficulty in making a complete government for the political state by mere human composition. . . . Going never higher than man, or back of man, he supposed that man could somehow create authority over man; that a machine could be got up by the consent of the governed that would really oblige, or bind their consent."[28] Without ever mentioning Lincoln by name, Bushnell complained:

> Our statesmen, or politicians, not being generally religious men, take up with difficulty conceptions of government, or the foundations of government, that suppose the higher rule of God. . . . Our political theories never gave us a real nationality, but only a copartnership, and the armed treason is only the consummated result of our speculations. Where nothing exists but a consent, what can be needed to end it but a dissent?[29]

Left only with Jeffersonian categories and Lincoln's "political religion" of republicanism, no transcendent ground remained to oppose secession, for there was no higher cause superintended by a higher power. In this case, the success or failure of secession rested solely on coercion and superior firepower, not morality. Republicanism without God—and a non-Christian Constitution—was immoral. The perpetuation of a truly providential government, as distinct from an "abstract" government grounded in natural-law theories of contract, was its own moral imperative for a just war. To signify this, Bushnell added his voice to the clamor for a constitutional amendment invoking God, although he conceded that "this is no time to agitate or put on foot political reforms of any kind."

Bushnell's sermon illustrates perfectly the different moral groundings that Northerners could bring to justify war. For some—including the early Lincoln—securing a Lockean and Jeffersonian republic, grounded in natural law and self-evident truths, was a sufficiently moral end to justify the war. For others, like Bushnell and most Protestant and Catholic clergy, mere natural law could not legitimize a nation or justify a war to suppress secession. Ultimately, the moral meaning of America had to be about something more than a simple experiment in republicanism; it had to be about the Puritan "errand into the wilderness."[30]

In Bushnell's sermon, we see a tension between Christian republicanism and Jeffersonian republicanism. It lay at the heart of Northern Republican ideology, and had no real equivalent in the South. In fact, Republicans in the North encompassed three ideological groups, all opposed to the South and supporting the war, but grounded in very different presuppositions: Jeffersonian Republicans like Lincoln and his cabinet, Christian Republicans like Bushnell, and abolitionist Republicans like Garrison and Douglass. Ultimately, the tensions would only be resolved by a total war for abolition and the creation of a full-blown nondenominational civil religion, existing alongside of and equal in power to Christian and Jewish denominations. All three ideologies would become constituent strains that would find a way to coexist. In time, Lincoln would move increasingly to a transcendent understanding of the war and the nation, even as Bushnell and Unitarian abolitionists would move increasingly to a blood-sanctified American Republic existing as a model of freedom and equality.[31] But before that could be fully incarnated, there would have to be a horrific baptism in blood.

CHAPTER 8

TRIUMPHALISM: "ADORNED BY THE NAME OF GOD"

For the Boston Brahmin author/editor Charles Eliot Norton, Bull Run ensured a long campaign with death and glory enough for all. The nation, in Norton's view, should not blanch at the prospect of a long war, even "if a million men should die on the battlefield."[1]

In contrast to the Unionists, Confederates had no bifurcated and conflicted take on the righteousness of their nation. At least publicly, skeptics were silenced, and Protestants and Catholics alike knelt at the feet of a suffering Savior and a Christian nation. Since God—not Christ—was invoked in the Constitution and national motto, Confederate Jews could also embrace their Confederate "New Israel."

As part of a self-confessed and constitutionally explicit covenanted nation, Confederates could expect special mercies. Manassas would be their indispensable evidence. In a letter to his wife, written two days after the victory at Bull Run, Stonewall Jackson described a wound to his finger that could have been to his heart. But it was not, prompting him to conclude: "My preservation was entirely due, as was the glorious victory, to our God, to whom be all the honor, praise and glory. . . . Whilst great credit is due to other parts of our gallant army, God made my brigade more instrumental than any other in repulsing the main attack."[2]

West Point graduates did not ordinarily speak this way, but Jackson was an exception. A Presbyterian elder and frequent Sunday school teacher, he brought a prophetic rage to the battlefield that was fearless in the face of death and sought not only to conquer his—and God's—enemies, but to annihilate them. As God's first warrior hero, Jackson's embrace of wholesale violence and Christian faith embodied the civil religions of both nations' leaders and commanders.

In a thanksgiving sermon celebrating the victory at Bull Run, William C. Butler, Richmond's Episcopal rector, declared that the Confederacy had received a divine commission—calling—when the people ratified the Confederate constitution with public prayers and national benedictions. But that commission did not come without its religious requirements. The constitution was a piece of paper, a mute document; only time would tell if it meant anything. Happily, God ratified the Confederacy by bestowing the remarkable victory at Manassas. That astounding victory proved that the South fought for principles that were congruent with God's "Divine government":

> God has given us of the South to-day a fresh and golden opportunity—and so a most solemn command—to realize that form of government in which the just, constitutional rights of each and all are guaranteed to each and all. . . . He has placed us in the front rank of the most marked epochs of the world's history. He has placed in our hands a commission which we can faithfully execute only by holy, individual self-consecration to all of God's plans.[3]

On behalf of a chosen people, Confederate theologians and moralists had no need to justify the war—or its conduct—according to the secular "law of nations." Ancient Israel provided a better model for righteous war. Nor were Confederate moralists willing to invoke Jefferson's "spurious" claim that "all men are created equal." They were Bushnellians all, grounding their identity and war around sacred texts and transcendent commissions.

Confederate preachers and moralists continued to celebrate the inclusion of God in their constitution.[4] In his thanksgiving sermon preached at Flat Rock, South Carolina, Edward Reed reiterated that the Federal Constitution was flawed:

> Whether through inadvertence, or, as is unfortunately more probable, from infidel practices imbibed in France by some members of the Convention . . . it contained no recognition of God. Our present Constitution opens with a confession of the existence and providence of the Almighty.[5]

This, Reed exulted, continued in the aftermath of Bull Run: "To see the supreme legislature of a people, in the first moment of decisive victory, turning its hall of legislation into a temple, returning solemn thanks to almighty God, and then adjourning for the day is a spectacle which fills the heart of the Christian patriot with the liveliest joy."[6]

Confederate intellectuals echoed the clergy. John Esten Cooke was one of the South's greatest novelists. He was a soldier as well. At Manassas, Sergeant Cooke served in the infantry and later became a first lieutenant with J. E. B. Stuart's staff, living to witness Lee's surrender at Appomattox. Writing for the *Southern Illustrated News*, Cooke reflected on Manassas and the changes it wrought:

> What dreamer ever fancied its future—ever thought it possible that this summer land, all flowers and sunshine and peace, would become as Golgotha, "the place of skulls"—a Jehoshaphat full of dead men's bones? . . . The old era of tranquility was to pass away, and a hideous spirit of destruction to rush in. The war dogs, held in leash with difficulty at Washington, were to circle and trample and hunt for their prey—until they found the Southern wolf at Manassas and were torn by him![7]

Writing from Charleston to his New York writer friend James Lawson, William Gilmore Simms confided, "I am literally doing nothing in letters, I am so much excited in the present condition of things that the labour of the desk is irksome." Simms had good reason to be distracted; things looked promising for the Confederacy. Although he had sought peace rather than war, as he reminded Lawson, once war came he knew the Confederacy would prevail:

> By this time your thinking men see the sort of game that is before them. Let them grow wise before it be too late. Every battle, thus far, has resulted in Southern Victory.—Sumter, Bethel, Bull Run, Manassas, Harper's Ferry and Missouri,—all tell the same tale. Your Generals are cashiered. Your army demoralized. Your papers are at a loss where to cast the blame. They will be at no loss before long. They will see that their cause is bad.[8]

On August 10 2,330 Union and Confederate troops lay dead or wounded in the bloody battle of Wilson's Creek, Missouri. In response, President Lincoln proclaimed a national fast day for the last Thursday in September. In it, Lincoln employed providential language to urge all Americans to:

> pray that we may be spared further punishment, though most justly deserved; that our arms may be blessed and made effectual for the reestablishment of law, order, and peace throughout the wide extent of our country; and that the inestimable boon of civil and religious liberty, earned under His guidance and blessing by the labors and sufferings of our fathers, may be restored in all its original excellence.[9]

By September, much of the shame of Bull Run had passed, and Northern triumphalism was securely back in place. The *Banner of the Covenant* printed "A National Fast Day Hymn." The poem closed with a note of global imperialism:

> *Unsheathe the gleaming sword, and lead*
> *Our loyal armies on,*
> *And smite the rebel bands, until*
> *Of traitors there are none.*
> *And then to greater conquests led*
> *By thine exalted Son.*
> *May we march o'er earth's bloodless fields,*
> *Till all the world is won.*[10]

Secular papers were as global in claiming international influence for America, but not always as pious. On September 23, the *New York Tribune* announced the fast day, though without the reverential tones of the religious press: "The National Fast Day . . . The devoutly inclined will find the places of public worship open to-day almost without exception." For the less devout: "In the afternoon, several boat and horse-races are announced to come off, and most of the places of amusement hold out extra attractions to the public in the evening."

By contrast, the *Boston Telegraph* proved as heavenly minded as the religious press when it proclaimed: "The National Fast Day will be observed to-morrow throughout New-England with utmost solemnity. In Boston business will be entirely suspended, even to the closing of the offices of the ferry and railroad corporations. The daily newspapers suspend publication from Thursday morning until Friday noon. Divine services will be held in all the churches."[11] New Englanders knew how to honor a fast.

New York never did have Boston's piety for the fast day, and other considerations prevailed there as churches proclaimed fasts. Money always mattered, and in the aftermath of Bull Run, it mattered more than ever. Happily, the *Tribune* reported:

> The stock market this morning was without any important features. It opened dull and rather heavy, excepting for Governments. . . . There was no disposition on the part of either bulls or bears to operate with any vigor. . . . These figures show an entire recovery from the panic which followed the disaster at Bull Run, and evince the confidence of capitalists in Government stocks.[12]

Many Northern moralists and editors wished to put the debacle of Bull Run behind them, but fast-day preachers did not.[13] The day provided an occasion to refight the battle, but this time on the moral battlefield of sins and punishments. By September 26 ministers had had ample time to reflect on the spiritual dimensions of defeat and draw appropriate lessons.

With Confederate sanctimoniousness in mind, Northern evangelicals rehearsed the case for a constitutional amendment in the North that would invoke God. Echoing Bushnell, they argued that America should be a Christian and not a Jeffersonian republic. Ezra Adams condemned as "monstrous" the Confederates' invocation of God in their currency and constitution, and urged that the *real* chosen people acknowledge Him: "We therefore intensely desire that God might be acknowledged in the Constitution of the United States. That the temple of national existence . . . might be adorned by the name of God."[14]

Desperate to find something of God in the government, many ministers and religious newspapers saw, in the ritual of the fast, the equivalent of a constitutional invocation of God. When Lincoln proclaimed a fast day "to be observed by the people of the United States with religious solemnities and the offering of fervent supplications to Almighty God," he was saying, in effect, that the United States was a Christian nation as much as if it had been written in the Constitution. Lincoln's proclamation, they argued, "is part of our more recent national history. Its record will be found in the archives of our Republic in the form of a Congressional vote and an executive proclamation."[15] The North might not need the fast to create a new nation, but it did require it to sacralize a republic whose Constitution never mentioned God.

Fast-day services were held in the army as well as local churches and synagogues. The Unitarian chaplain William Scandlin kept a diary throughout his time in the Union army and recorded the following entry for September 26: "Our service was to be at 11 and I was to preach extempore." Scandlin's evident satisfaction in preaching "extempore" reflects how unusual it was for a Unitarian to preach in such a way. Following the fast, Scandlin wrote to the Unitarian Autumnal Convention and expressed his sense of the justness of the cause and the shame of compromise:

> For enshrined within the civil and religious liberties of this nation, are the highest and brightest hopes of the world. Hence our duty is to preserve this Christian legacy in a Christian spirit to reveal our conscious appreciation of its value by a sacrifice commensurate with its worth. Less than this is

treason to the country, humanity and God. The thought of peace and its accustomed prosperity fills us . . . with a joy beyond description. But the demand for peace must come from those who have heaped injury upon insult.[16]

Not all states were as comfortable as the insulated Northeast with the justness of the war. Missouri's experience with a savage civil war waged indiscriminately on civilians dispelled all romantic and world-regenerative illusions. R. H. Weller's fast-day sermon to Christ Church, in St. Joseph, Missouri, contained no patriotism, and is illustrative of what other ministers *could* have said, but seldom did.

In the face of mounting terrorist attacks fought in the name of patriotism, Weller assigned equal guilt and culpability to the North and the South: "Is it not a repetition of the sad calamity that befell Israel of old,—a disrupted country, with rival capitals, and the hands of brethren embued in brethrens blood?" Though nominally Christian, "our practice has given the lie to our pretensions, and practically we are a nation of infidels." Such words, he knew, would not endear him to those aching for a fight. Talk of peace was downright offensive "amidst the heat of passion, and the lynx-eyed gaze of partisanship."

In contrast to Northern preachers who would declare that "law is vengeance," Weller preached reconciliation. In place of patriotism, he proclaimed peace: "Let us strive to lay aside passion and prejudice—to hold fast to charity—to covet the good things of God's blessing, the things which make for peace."[17] The paucity of sermons like Weller's reveals the real object of fasts: to promote patriotism; but the effect was self-righteousness, not humility before God.

Two other extremes provided exceptions to the main fare of the jeremiad. One was the abolitionist contingent. In preaching to the Church of the Puritans in New York, George B. Cheever, founder of the Church Anti-Slavery Society, invoked the revolutionary actions of the very John Brown whom Lincoln repudiated as the true paradigm of a just warrior:

In this war, in the putting down of this rebellion, the conscientious Abolitionists are the truest, incorruptible, unchangeable patriots, because their fire of soul and body is not only the common love of country, but the fire of heaven against a rebellion that has in it more of the element of hell than any rebellion ever organized . . . this eternal love of freedom for all, this irresistible sentiment of justice and hatred of all injustice, is the permanent, inexhaustible, incorruptible material on which the government and the country must rely.[18]

Cheever's just war was so just it effectively acknowledged no restraints. With Brown as his prototype, Cheever could claim that preemptive wars and assaults on civilians were righteous and just, as long as the end was abolition. In time, Cheever's—and not Lincoln's—model would become policy on both sides of the conflict.

The other exception to the standard jeremiad fare came out of the Unitarian camp. While it is true that the Civil War did not produce one theoretical advance in just-war theory, and indeed took it several steps back, one intriguing effort at originality appeared in a fast-day sermon delivered by the Unitarian minister Orville Dewey in the Church of the Messiah in New York.

In an unusual turn, Dewey frankly examined the case for a just preemptive war on the South. Shedding the flimsy pretense of fighting a defensive war, Dewey contemplated offensive assault and occupation. If the notion of a "first shot" defensive war was a patent invention in a world where Northern cities lay virtually immune to invasion, how *could* the war be justified? Conventional Christian just-war theory allowed only wars of "self-defense." Hence the desperate—and often ridiculous—efforts of moralists on both sides to appear pacifistic and defensive. But Dewey had other ideas:

I doubt whether this limitation [of self-defense] can be defended. . . . I am struck at the outset with this potent fact,—that war seems to have been a part of the normal condition of nations. . . . It is computed that more than six thousand millions of the human race have perished in battle,—about seven times the present population of the earth.

With so many wars, "[h]ow could it be so, if all war, or all but defensive war, is contrary to the will of God?" Citing "Mr. [Pierre-Joseph] Proudhon, the French writer," Dewey wondered if "there is a 'right of war,' founded on the 'right of force'; that is to say, that any nation, deprived by another, or conceiving itself to be deprived, of what is lawfully its own,—a fishery or territory, a fort or arsenal,—has a perfect right to reclaim it by force."

In this amoral assertion, Dewey anticipated Realpolitik arguments for war based on self-interest:

I believe that there is a conscience on both sides, always, at the bottom of every war; for war is not robbery or piracy, where the marauder knows that he has no right, but a solemn levying of the national force. I do not believe that nations fight but upon the ground that they have the right upon their side. The greatest mystery,—if I sought to find one,—in the system of Providence, is this difference of opinion, with all its consequences; and yet I see,

The American Patriot's Dream. This early Currier & Ives lithograph praises the patriotism of Federal soldiers and explicitly links battlefront and home front in patriotic unity.

that among imperfect beings, it is inevitable; that it was, in the nature of things, impossible to constitute a race of moral and imperfect beings, without this element of trouble.

Northern self-interest justified the North's invasion of the South according to Dewey's logic. His just war would not be defensive, but offensive, grounded in strategic and moral right: "To us this is a holy war. Religion—in the highest and widest view of it—commands us to do what we are doing."[19]

Good and bad, right and wrong; the terms flowed on all sides so easily and logically and self-righteously that one suspects they masked a deeper-seated animal lust for battle. The historian Michael Fellman has talked about this in the context of "blood sport."[20]

J. Glenn Gray, reflecting on his wartime experiences in World War II, speaks of war as "spectacle" and the "lust of the eye"—a "secret attraction." To clarify his meaning, Gray invokes Robert E. Lee's famous observation about war:

If we think of beauty and ugliness without their usual moral overtones, there is often a weird but genuine beauty in the sight of massed men and weapons in combat. Reputedly, it was the sight of advancing columns of men under fire that impelled General Robert E. Lee to remark to one of his staff: "It is well that war is so terrible—we should grow too fond of it."[21]

Both of these writers are concentrating on soldiers at war "without their usual moral overtones" and the irrational transformations they experience in becoming warriors. Yet that soldier mentality of irrational obsession and demoralized "beauty" could and did infuse the whole society in this citizens' war.

Beneath all the rationalizations and moral affirmations, Manassas and its aftermath showed a deeper irrational strain impelled by the almost intoxicating sight of massed armies in the field and on parade. Any society at war finds itself in an unnatural and evil state. It may be a necessary evil, as most non-pacifists agree, but it is nevertheless evil. But in the crucible of war, that fact is easily lost sight of. After Manassas, "manliness," "spectacle," and "patriotism" were the only facts that mattered, from the highest executive to the lowliest soldier and the youngest child.

CHAPTER 9

"WILL NOT THE MARTYRS
BE BLESSED . . . ?"

While the Northern secular press raged against incompetent generals and panicked soldiers, other moral critics took different meanings from the ongoing defeats. Some of the strongest responses to Federal defeats came from abolitionists who saw in reverses divine confirmation of the moral inadequacy of preserving the Union as a sufficient justification for war.

Nonclerical abolitionists echoed clerical abolitionists like George B. Cheever. In Worcester, Massachusetts, Martha LeBaron Goddard wrote to her friend Mary that battlefield casualties could be accepted if the cause of abolition was embraced:

> Yet . . . from men and women whom I have seen, has come the same thought over and over again—"It is terrible; but *defeat* and suffering will *force* us to do right: and the administration will be beaten into doing justice." And so forever behind the clouds, is the heaven bright—and if we learn by the dead faces of our white brothers, to put joy and life and power into those of our black ones—will not the martyrs be blessed indeed?[1]

The language of "martyrs" had been used by the abolitionists to label fallen comrades as far back as the abolitionist editor Elijah Lovejoy, who was murdered in 1837, and John Brown. They were willing to transform death into martyrdom *if* it was grounded ethically in abolition. In time, as casualties mounted to unprecedented levels, all battlefield fatalities on both sides of the conflict were termed martyrs to their respective causes. What began as a political war was being transformed, in effect, into a moral crusade with religious foundations for which martyrs would willingly sacrifice themselves on their nations' altars. Inevitably, such language absolutized the war on both sides and reinforced the demand for self-righteous blood revenge. In the North and the South, the clergy were more than willing to comply.

In 1861 most Northerners were not prepared to see the war in abolitionist terms. Nor were they certain that the North was morally superior in its treatment of blacks. In an editorial on the "Object of the War," one clerical writer exposed racist hypocrisies in the North, observing that in 1850, "colored membership of the different churches, south, was one out of every twelve of the colored population. With us, it was one out of fifty-six." These statistics, the writer concluded, were "not pro-slavery arguments," but they did put into question the sincerity of Northerners claiming to have the souls of slaves uppermost in their thoughts. Concerned that Lincoln did too much to accommodate slaveholders, the *Banner of the Covenant* criticized his "excessive sensibility in regard to slavery, when it is considered that it has been the chief cause of the war."[2] Others assured their readers that "God will never give victory to our arms" until slavery was ended.

Many Northern soldiers were also disillusioned, but not over the slavery issue. On November 9, as reports of the disaster at Ball's Bluff circulated, Private Franklin Bullard wrote an embittered letter to his uncle, complaining of incompetent commanders. But of the cause itself, he still remained hopeful:

> I don't want to come home before these Southern Rebels are whiped out of their hides although I am pretty well satisfied with the luck I had at Balls Bluff in having the satisfaction of knowing that I killed one rebel and did not receive even a scar the bullets came thick and fast all round the house Colonel Devins . . . I heard him say never mind the bullets give it to them boys he is a lucky boy Captain Philbrick is a great and honest man and he is not afraid to die in this holy cause he is a man we will follow even unto death in this cause. To die in a good cause is an honor to die a traitor is a disgrace give me liberty or death is what patrick henry said and I say it and I will have liberty.[3]

In the South, news of the rout at Ball's Bluff again swelled Confederate hearts. The South Carolina aristocrat Mary Chesnut recorded in her diary: "At Bonney's store heard that at Leesburg, Shanks Evans had defeated Yankees, taken three hundred prisoners, and they left five hundred dead on the field. Besides a great number who were drowned. Allowing for all exaggeration, it must be a splendid victory."[4]

Even the *Richmond Daily Whig* celebrated victory by joining the religious press in invoking Providence alongside patriotism: "We have to felicitate the country this morning upon another signal and cheering evidence of the courage and devotion of our patriot troops, and to continuing favor of Heaven. Victory has again perched on the Confederate banners."[5]

Like Private Bullard in the North, Savannah's Charles C. Jones was not afraid "to die in a good cause." A Princeton-trained lawyer and Confederate civil officeholder, Jones could have avoided the army, but instead he enlisted in the Chatham Artillery Cavalry as an officer. In a letter to his father, C. C. Jones, the Presbyterian minister and "slave evangelist," he explained why:

> Above all, as a matter of personal duty and of private example, I think I ought to render service in the field. Were I to consult my own private incli-nations as based upon principles of comfort, considerations of interest, and prospects of gain, I would not go. The service will be arduous, involving sac-rifices great in their character; but I am of opinion that my duty requires it, and I will go.[6]

By October 26, Jones was stationed at Camp Claghorn, Georgia, enjoy-ing "our pure white tents" and preparing for battle. His mother, Mary, wrote, urging him to "[r]emember the Sabbath Day to keep it holy!" While conced-ing that she knew none of his company personally, "I pray for them all, from your captain down." Lest there be any doubt about where Southern women stood in the conflict, Mary assured her son that whether he lived or died, the cause was just:

> I know that you are now every moment exposed to the attack of our perfidi-ous and merciless enemy; but your sword will be drawn in a righteous cause, and I fervently implore my God and Redeemer to protect and save you in the day of battle, and to encourage your heart and the hearts of our commander and of all your noble company, and to strengthen your arms for the conflict, that in your full measure you may be enabled to repel the infidel invaders who are now at our own doors with their work of ruin and destruction.

With an ailing husband and many slaves on the plantation, Mary closed her letter on a more ominous note shared by many Confederate women fearing slave insurrections: "Their intentions are now openly declared, and nothing but Omnipotent Power will keep them from making this not only a civil but a servile war."[7]

In Richmond, Mary Chesnut experienced similar fears on a much more personal level. On September 21, 1861, she wrote in her diary that while reading her husband's mail for him she came across a letter from her cousin Mary Witherspoon: "I broke down. Horror and amazement was too much for me: poor Cousin Betsey Witherspoon was murdered! She did not die peacefully, as we supposed, in her bed. Murdered by her own people. Her negroes . . . Horrible beyond words."[8]

In the roller coaster this war would become, Southerners barely concluded their celebrations over Ball's Bluff when their euphoria came painfully down to earth with news of bitter disappointments for the Confederate armies and painful reminders of the all-powerful Federal navy. No coastal location was safe from naval bombardments and amphibious invasions. Most devastating was the capture of Port Royal Sound, South Carolina, and the nearby town of Beaufort, which gave the North a toehold between Savannah and Charleston and helped secure their blockade of the East Coast.

A month earlier, Mary Chesnut had reveled in victory at Ball's Bluff. By November 8 the tide had turned: "The Reynoldses came, and with them terrible news. The enemy are effecting their landing at Port Royal. I ordered the carriage and rushed off to Camden to hear the worst. . . . Utter defeat at Port Royal. [William] DeSaussure's and [Richard] Dunovant's regiments cut to pieces."[9] But God was still present: "Not one doubt is there in our bosoms that we are not the chosen people of God. And that he is fighting for us."[10]

President Davis agreed. Having just been formally elected president of the Confederate States of America, Davis wasted no time in calling for another day of fasting. The proclamation was reprinted in virtually every Confederate paper. It would be observed on November 15, when "the Reverend Clergy and the people of these Confederate states . . . [repair] to their usual places of public worship; and to implore the blessing of Almighty God upon our arms; that He may give us victory over our enemies; preserve our homes and altars from pollution, and secure to us the restoration of peace and prosperity."

As in the North, Confederate fast and thanksgiving days offered unique opportunities for civilians and soldiers to come together as full coparticipants in the war. Supplicating an overseeing Providence alone would determine the outcome of hostilities. Civilians could think of themselves (for a little longer anyway) as noncombatants and innocents, but their holy days belied them. Noncombatants, yes, but innocents, no. On both sides the people were soldiers all. As soldiers fought and prayed, so would the home front fight the war with their prayers and fasts.

Local papers reprinted Davis's proclamation and promoted the occasion almost universally. In Charleston, the *Daily Courier* even printed a recommended prayer for the collect (one of the few surviving prayers):

O let not our sins cry against us for vengeance; but hear us Thy servants begging mercy and imploring Thy help against the face of our enemies. We implore Thy protection and power against those who have invaded our soil and our homes. We humbly look up to Thee, oh God, and say that we have done them no wrong. Defend, O Lord, and establish our cause. Endue us with power and strength; give us victory over all our enemies and make it appear that Thou are our Savior and mighty Deliverer, through Jesus Christ Our Lord—Amen.[11]

Not every secular press was as compliant with the fast as Davis hoped. In an ominous portent of looming divisions between the press and the Davis administration, the *Richmond Daily Dispatch* ruefully acknowledged a "Puritan inconsistency" in fasting. Nevertheless, it bowed to public pressure: "In conformity with the recommendation of the President all business will be suspended in the office of the *Dispatch* to-day, and consequently, no paper will be issued tomorrow."[12] This was the peoples' war as well as the soldiers', and the people fought with prayers and fasts that permitted no cynicism—even to journalists.

Despite its editorial view on fasting, the *Richmond Daily Dispatch* took up a defense of military chaplains, arguing that the payment of chaplains at a private's rate was an insult to the office.[13] They were not alone. Ministers and religious presses throughout the Confederacy pointed to the inconsistency of a "Christian" nation that treated its clergy as mere privates entitled to only one ration per day and assigned no uniform (in contrast to Union chaplains who received an officer's rank and pay).[14]

In fact, the Confederates' professed spiritual superiority did not entirely offset a lingering anticlericalism in the military and in the government's condescending treatment of chaplains. Not surprisingly, the chaplains felt discriminated against in a "manly" military culture that responded apathetically to the high turnover in Confederate chaplaincies.[15]

While West Point culture may have bred "gentlemen," manliness was a separate matter, and one not easily reconciled with evangelical piety. In North and South alike it referred to the powerful bonding of men in the ranks as they prepared for battle. Often it would be associated with "manly" activities like drinking, gambling, and fighting—activities far removed from the restraints of evangelical culture. "Pride of manhood" steeled soldiers to combat and countered their greatest fear, the fear of cowardice. The ultimate "test" of manhood came in combat, but feistiness in the camp characterized soldiers' poses as well. As the human destruction of war magnified in the coming years, manliness would come to be coupled with evangelical Christianity, especially in the South, but in the beginning the tensions between the two were more typical.[16] The wonder is that so many chaplains served at all. One of the strongest indexes to the power of religion in the Confederacy (and the army) is that anywhere from six hundred to eleven hundred chaplains served actively during the war (though fewer than fifty served through the entire war). In time, manly generals who derided chaplains as "effeminate" would have opportunity to revise their estimations.

If men were supposed to be men, women were supposed to be women, but not in God-offending "luxurious" ways. The Southern religious press warned women about the limits of femininity, in particular during time of war. In preparation for the November fast, the Methodist organ *Southern Christian Advocate*, "a Religious Family Newspaper," urged women in particular to dress modestly as befits their superior piety and patriotism:

> Women may be adorned, but let them wear the ornaments of a meek and quiet Spirit, with modest apparel, rather than those of a foolish and fashionable world. . . . The fashions of the world—and insane love of dress and outward adornment—has destroyed—to use no stronger term—both the church and the world together, and the devil has become almost absolute monarch of all he surveys.[17]

Richmond's Thomas Moore preached to the First and Second Presbyterian churches praising the purifying effects of war on the sins of materialism and "effeminacy."[18]

The November fast-day sermons echoed the already familiar themes of the jeremiad, punctuated with a more sober this-worldly realism. Preaching at Christ Church in Savannah, Stephen Elliott warned that the heady days of Manassas were gone: "We are only at the beginning of a long and bloody conflict, and it is the duty of everyone to consider it so and prepare himself for such a contingency." Recognizing that Davis and Beauregard were still feuding over the honors of Manassas, and that the citizenry was joining in the debate, Elliott enjoined all to honor the administration or deliverance would not be granted.[19]

In a fast-day sermon addressed to the Georgia state legislature, Mercer University professor Henry H. Tucker spoke on *God in the War*. His theme was Providence and divine protection. The South was innocent, he reiterated, and "thus, the guilt of those who wage this diabolical war on the unoffending people of the Confederate States, finds no apology in the providence of God."[20]

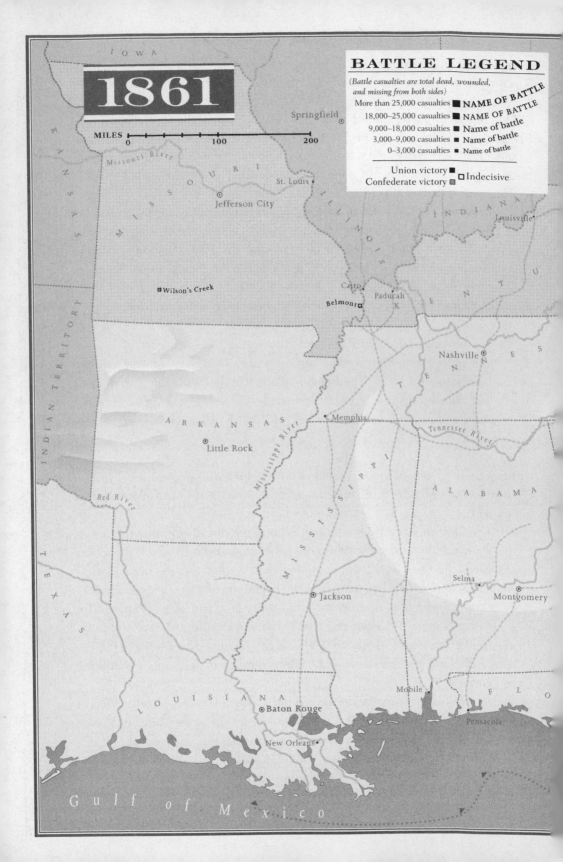

1861

MILES

0   100   200

BATTLE LEGEND

(Battle casualties are total dead, wounded, and missing from both sides)

More than 25,000 casualties ■ NAME OF BATTLE
18,000–25,000 casualties ■ NAME OF BATTLE
9,000–18,000 casualties ■ Name of battle
3,000–9,000 casualties ■ Name of battle
0–3,000 casualties ■ Name of battle

Union victory ■   □ Indecisive
Confederate victory ◩

IOWA

KANSAS

Missouri River

Springfield

St. Louis

MISSOURI

Jefferson City

ILLINOIS

INDIANA

Louisville

Cairo

Paducah

Belmont

■ Wilson's Creek

INDIAN TERRITORY

KENTUCKY

Nashville

TENNESSEE

ARKANSAS

Memphis

Mississippi River

Little Rock

Tennessee River

Red River

ALABAMA

TEXAS

MISSISSIPPI

Selma

Jackson

Montgomery

LOUISIANA

Mobile

FLO

Baton Rouge

Pensacola

New Orleans

Gulf of Mexico

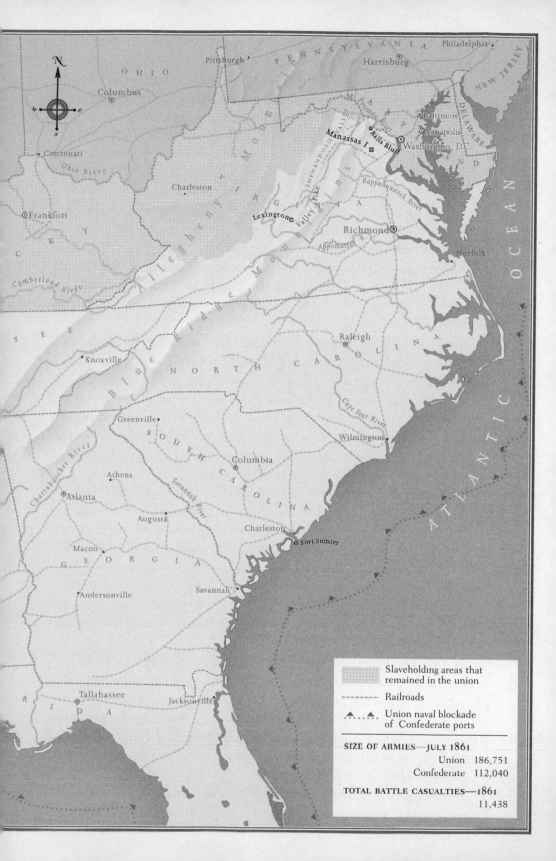

N

OHIO

PENNSYLVANIA

Philadelphia

Pittsburgh

Harrisburg

NEW JERSEY

Columbus

DELAWARE

Baltimore

Potomac River

Annapolis

Cincinnati

Balls Bluff

Washington, D.C.

Ohio River

Manassas I

MARYLAND

Charleston

SHENANDOAH VALLEY

Rappahannock River

Frankfort

VIRGINIA

Lexington

Valley Pike

Richmond

Appomattox R.

Norfolk

Cumberland River

OCEAN

TENNESSEE

Blue Ridge Mountains

Raleigh

Allegheny Mountains

Knoxville

NORTH CAROLINA

Cape Fear River

Greenville

SOUTH CAROLINA

Wilmington

Chattahoochee River

Columbia

Savannah River

Athens

Atlanta

Augusta

Charleston

ATLANTIC

Macon

Fort Sumter

GEORGIA

Andersonville

Savannah

FLORIDA

Tallahassee

Jacksonville

Slaveholding areas that
remained in the union

Railroads

Union naval blockade
of Confederate ports

SIZE OF ARMIES—JULY 1861

Union   186,751

Confederate   112,040

TOTAL BATTLE CASUALTIES—1861

11,438

Fast-day worship services were held in all Southern churches and incorporated large congregations. Even Mary Chesnut backed away from her occasional skepticism to endorse the fast. On November 16 she entered in her diary: "We fasted and prayed—and we think our prayers are answered, for lo! good news has come. Another ship with ammunition and arms has slipped into Savannah. If our prayers are to be so effective, let us all spend our days and nights on our knees."[21]

The South's lament was the North's joy and an occasion for thanksgiving services that would unite soldiers and citizens in praise to God for victory. By late autumn, traditional thanksgiving days would be observed with cautious celebration. Although President Lincoln did not proclaim an official Thanksgiving observance until 1862, the tradition was so strong that Northern churches and states observed self-proclaimed days of thanksgiving for Thursday, November 28, 1861.

Unlike abolitionist radicals, the main body of ministers agreed with statesmen, journalists, and generals that the preservation of the Union was a sufficient cause to wage war against the Confederacy, and that victory would confirm its divine justness. While most ministers claimed to avoid "political preaching" in their Sunday worship services, all knew the fast and thanksgiving weekdays marked the occasion for explicit moral and spiritual reflection on the war. Not surprisingly, the war dominated these pulpit performances, and all understood what God's intentions would be.

Encouraging reports of a successful naval blockade and the capture of Port Royal lent a more optimistic air to the thanksgiving occasion. Also encouraging was the founding of the Christian Commission by the YMCA in November 1861, designed to serve as an evangelical alternative to the more secular and professional Unitarian-based Sanitary Commission. The Christian Commission could work with chaplains to minister to ailing soldiers, provide needed supplies, and Christianize them with tracts and testimony. The commission also began efforts to educate former slaves wherever they encountered them.[22]

In New York Henry Ward Beecher mounted his esteemed pulpit and reiterated the global stakes attached to this fratricidal war: "A battle on the Potomac for our Constitution, as a document of liberty, is the world's battle. We are fighting, not merely for our liberty, but for those ideals that are the seeds and strength of liberty throughout the earth." The word "liberty" was important to Beecher as a code word for the hidden cause of emancipation that many Northern clergy had long harbored.

Beecher hoped a way could be found to emancipate slaves in the South, but without usurping protections granted by the Constitution. Though strongly

Slaves standing in front of buildings on Smith's Plantation in Beaufort, South Carolina. Once liberated, many of these slaves disproved their owners' racial prejudices by their aptitude for literacy and skilled labor.

emancipationist, he was no abolitionist in the strict sense of the term. To betray the Constitution by making abolition in the South the war's formal end might actually imperil the cause and its justness. If choices needed to be made, the Constitution and not emancipation must be honored: "If there be given to us no right by our Constitution to enter upon the States with legislation subversive of their whole interior economy, not all the mischiefs [sic] of slavery, and certainly not our own impatience under its burdens and vexations, should tempt us to usurp it. This conflict must be carried on *through* our institutions and not *over* them."[23]

If there was good news, there was still ample cause to be nervous. This was precisely the message of Gardiner Spring, pastor of Brick Presbyterian Church of New York City and a former friend of the South, who, despite his support for the Union, had little good to say about American character and its misplaced global pretensions: "Instead of moving on in our course courageously and faithfully . . . our hearts have been lifted up, we have walked loftily, rushing in the pursuit of greatness, reckless and extravagant, and confident of our resources."

Such language might sound disloyal, but to congregations attuned to the logic of the jeremiad it was just the opposite—a confirmation that God was still on the side of the North, awaiting repentance and reformation as prelude to ultimate victory. Despite her flaws, America still remained the world's best hope because America was favored by God. For this transcendent reason, rebellion against America and its Constitution was not just a political violation but a "sin against God and man." In the end, the political issues came down to morality: "The simple question is, Is this secession of the South morally right?" Of course the answer was no. Therefore, while war is an evil, "a Southern Empire, extending to Cuba and Mexico, with the slave-trade as its basis, is . . . a greater evil."[24]

In the South, jeremiads appeared in the secular press no less than the religious. On January 10, 1862, in an editorial mixing judgment with bravado, the *Richmond Daily Dispatch* assured its readers that Lincoln would be held accountable for his sins:

> Wo, then, wo the usurper who has forced this war upon an unoffending people. The maledictions of Eternal justice rest upon the tyrant's soul. There is blood upon his hand, blood upon his garments and upon his threshold; the blood of the innocent and the just. Let the thought inspire the hearts and nerve the arm of all true patriots . . . this particular war is not an unmixed evil. War elevates and expands the heroic part of man's nature: "The nations most favored by God have been baptized in the crimson laver of battle, and the holiest of saints have not worn the crown until they have borne the cross."[25]

Chaplain Robert Bunting, who served with the Texas Rangers, described the battle scene in a letter to the *San Antonio Herald*: "Surely ours is now a peculiar lot. . . . Whilst but a short distance below us the enemy's ships are blockading our river and his dreaded guns of war are booming out a salute over the ruins of a sister city, laid half in ashes by the incendiaries torch. Surely we live in stirring times. Strange scenes all around us. But God reigns, therefore will we not fear."[26]

The logic of the Northern and Southern jeremiads made it virtually impossible for preachers and moral savants to register judgments of uncertainty or ambiguity. No moral spokesman could attribute victory to the mendacity and immorality of his generals and soldiers just because they had more guns, and no savant could attribute defeat to, say, a sudden upsurge in religious revivals.

The rhetoric was pat, the originality nil. Speakers and writers employed stock arguments to draw on reflexively, depending on immediate events. Vic-

tories brought out the language of selfless humility, prayer, godly conversation, and revival that pleased the divine deliverer, while defeats brought out
the language of pride, effeminancy, greed, and materialism that exposed a
people not right with God, and in need of the loving discipline of defeat. Like
death itself and the funeral sermons that followed, the jeremiad allowed no
room for rhetorical creativity. Only a traitor would violate the conventions
of the jeremiad or invoke nonprovidential explanations like "luck," "fate," or
"incompetence."

Already in 1861, the jeremiad established a clinching of the rhetorical war
knot, closing off alternatives or compromises. Were leaders in power able to
see both sides as right and wrong, then alternatives to war might be explored.
But in an atmosphere of absolute right and wrong, with God in control and
demanding the total surrender of sin and evil, few could escape the trap. In
fact, one of the few who could was in the White House. Lincoln did perceive
right and wrong on both sides and did seek to explore alternatives to war. But
the populace was rapidly losing the capacity to listen.

In one of the greater ironies of wartime rhetoric and morality, the very
universality and inclusiveness of the jeremiad undermined itself and effectively removed all restraints from the war's brutality. As a widely held Christian doctrine that dated back to Augustine and the apostles, the providential
worldview was intended to personalize theology to inculcate a sense that God
was present in the saints' lives overseeing their eternal destiny.

But as it emerged in the Civil War, providentialism did the opposite, generating a de facto fatalism. When Providence explains everything in absolute
categories, it explains nothing at all in particular. If victories and defeats, life
and death, good times and bad times are all caused equally and decisively by
divine Providence, then nothing can explain particular events or experiences.
Fate takes the place of a biased deity—*my* survival or *my* destruction happens
independent of *my* prayers or *my* failure to pray. Whether I live or die is "in
the cards."

Even worse, on a commonsense level, fatalism became ingrained so that
nothing was unacceptable; it just *was*. No destruction could be too great because God, not man, was orchestrating affairs. All one could do was mouth
the proper rituals, beat the drum of patriotism, and keep on fighting, confident in the right and ultimate vindication.

Unlike the earlier fast-day rhetoric of the Seven Years' War or the American
Revolution, that of the Civil War generated relatively little millennial specu-
lation about living in the "end times."[27] The reason is to be found in the language that Northerners and Southerners used to describe their ultimate
enemy. In the Seven Years' War and the American Revolution, the ultimate

enemy was clear: the Antichrist foretold in biblical prophecy. But in the Civil War, both sides appeared curiously reluctant to label their war a war against the Antichrist. Nor was the Antichrist identified with Abraham Lincoln or Jefferson Davis the way he had been with George III. Instead, less ultimate name-calling labeled the foe as "tyrants," "traitors," "blasphemers," "Black Republicans," or "slave drivers."

In both sides' refusal to paint the other with the apocalyptic degradation of Antichrist, we gain important clues into the unique nature of the Civil War. Two reasons stand out for the curious silence. First, and more obviously, every American Protestant knew the Antichrist was the pope. Yet with Catholics fighting on both sides for their separate causes, the pope could hardly be blamed, thus providing no Antichrist. With Catholics no less loyal to their sides than Protestants and Jews, satanic plots were harder to discern.

When accused of persecuting fellow Catholics in the South and permitting the slaughter of Irish Catholic troops in his own army, a combative Archbishop John Hughes of New York wrote to his counterpart, P. N. Lynch of Charleston, South Carolina. In a blistering response, he denied any possibility of peace without surrender: "Since violence, battle and bloodshed have occurred, I dare not hope for peace unless you can show me a foundation of rock or solid ground (but not quicksand basis) on which peace can be reestablished." As for the accusation he was abetting the slaughter of Irish troops, Hughes replied curtly, "If this end were a deliberate policy of the North, I should scout and despise it." But as things stood, Hughes's loyalties remained with the North rather than with fellow Catholics in rebellion.[28]

A second explanation for the rhetorical restraint is more apparent in retrospect. Protestants, Catholics, Jews—temporarily divided into two "Americas" and eventually reunited—were Americans all. America's incarnating civil religion would appropriate Christian and Jewish rhetoric and make it American, so that Christianity and Judaism would never become an enemy or a false god (hence the efforts to put God into the Federal Constitution). Rather, the language of "liberty," "martyrdom," "baptism," and "redemption," when added to the sheer military might consecrated by America's armies, blocked the all-out demonizaton of the enemy. At the same time, as we will see, it pointed the way to ultimate reconciliation of "Americans" and "Confederates" under a common American faith. As explained by one religious editor, a "national religion" was reasonable, and not inconsistent with the separation of church and state: "National church establishments are very different things from national religion; which is simply the profession and practice of obedience to the law of Christ in their public policy, by the representatives of the nation."[29]

CHAPTER 10

"TO HUMBLE OURSELVES BEFORE GOD"

Despite strategic breakthroughs in Kentucky and on the coast, Lincoln's winter was no happier than Davis's. The navy might be indomitable, but the soldiers were not. Frustrated with the lack of movement in his armies, especially in the East, Lincoln took the unprecedented step of issuing Presidential Order No. 1 on January 27, 1862, commanding all of his generals to move immediately "against the insurgent forces." Lincoln was particularly frustrated with the reticent General McClellan's Army of the Potomac and, on January 31, issued a separate Special War Order No. 1 ordering McClellan to seize Confederate territory south of Manassas Junction. But McClellan, by now implacably opposed to Lincoln's aggressive war policies, simply dug in his heels.

In the West Lincoln's orders bore more fruit. In early February, fifteen thousand troops under a then relatively unknown General Ulysses S. Grant marched on Fort Henry and Fort Donelson on the Tennessee River with a view toward attacking them the following day. If Fort Donelson could be taken together with Fort Henry, major invasion routes along the Tennessee and Cumberland rivers could be organized in ways that would "turn" General Albert Sidney Johnston's army from its position south of the forts near the Tennessee border. To carry the forts, Grant and Flag Officer Andrew Foote planned a coordinated land and sea attack for February 6. Foote's specially designed ironclad riverboats, with their large siege guns, would cover Grant's soldiers for an overland assault.

When faced with a costly siege, Confederate General Simon Bolivar Buckner proposed a negotiated surrender to Grant, from one West Point gentleman soldier to another. When asked for terms of surrender, Grant replied in curt terms that would soon be broadcast in every Northern newspaper:

The Storming of Fort Donelson. Featuring a "terrific bayonet charge," triumphant flags, and surging Federal troops, this Currier & Ives lithograph typifies the romantic renderings of early Civil War battles that give little sense of the war's savage reality.

"No terms except unconditional and immediate surrender can be accepted. I propose to move immediately upon your works." With that, the North had control of two strategic rivers and a new hero general in U. S. "Unconditional Surrender" Grant.

News of the capitulation of Fort Donelson reached Richmond just as the recently elected president of the Confederacy prepared his inaugural address. In a separate message to Congress on February 25, Davis joined the public outcry over Donelson, expressing amazement that a Confederate army would surrender without a real fight. Like many of his listeners, he openly feared that this was more an issue of character than command.

Lacking confidence in his commanders' character, Davis turned to Providence. In his inaugural address he reiterated the rightness of the Confederate cause, which he likened to the "patriots of the Revolution," and confidently called on God for deliverance:

My hope is reverently fixed on Him whose favor is ever vouchsafed to the cause which is just. With humble gratitude and adoration, acknowledging the Providence which has so visibly protected the Confederacy during its brief but eventful career, to thee, O God, I trustingly commit myself, and prayerfully invoke thy blessing on my country and its cause.[1]

In the midst of growing dismay, the Confederate Congress anticipated the possibility of domestic unrest and granted President Davis the power to suspend the writ of habeas corpus. According to war clerk J. B. Jones, the measure was principally aimed at Richmond, and—more ominously—"at some few other places."[2]

By 1862 the time for serious weighing of options seemed to have passed for good. Moral "reflection" abounded, to be sure, but only in ways that reinforced the "right" side. Despite unprecedented losses, hard questions of cause and conduct were seldom raised. Moral arbiters on both sides fell back on stock rhetorical affirmations coming dangerously close to clichés. From the start this had been a political war that proceeded not from moral cause to military consequence, but rather from military offensives to unquestioned moral validation on both sides. Once the sequence was established, it did not matter how horrendous the slaughters might rise; like forward-moving troops and John Brown's soul, the rhetoric marched on.

On February 22, the day of his formal inauguration, one of Davis's first proclamations was for a public day of fasting. The secular press printed his call dutifully, while the religious press eagerly promoted it. The cause, they repeated with drumlike regularity, was just. War came, the Southern Baptist *Richmond Religious Herald* argued, "from infidel humanitarians who . . . have labored to pervert the Union into an instrument of abolition." God, who had ordained or at least permitted slavery, would never bless the Christ-denying, humanistic North. Therefore, the only thing preventing success had to be domestic sin: "If we truly renounce iniquity, the days of this distress will be shortened."[3]

Once again the Confederacy used the occasion of Davis's inauguration and the formal establishment of government to underscore their superiority as the only truly Christian nation. In a letter to his father, Lieutenant Charles C. Jones Jr. described how the fast was observed in his company and then went on to drum the familiar refrain:

No God was ever acknowledged in the Constitution of the old United States. We have acknowledged "the Almighty God" in our Constitution—the God of the Bible, the only living and true God—as our God; and we take Him as the God of our nation and worship Him, and put our nation under His care as such. . . . And moreover, under the old Constitution of the United States we never had a Christian President—never a man who in the Presidential chair openly professed the orthodox faith of the gospel and connected with that profession an open communion with the Lord at His table.[4]

The Confederacy changed all of that. It would be Christian.

Confederates continued to hold up the inclusion of God in their consti-
tution and national motto as a sort of talisman because they knew Northern
Republican Christians felt vulnerable. Throughout the first year of war, the
Northern religious papers continued to complain about the absence of God
in their Constitution and called for a constitutional amendment invoking
God. Failing, they also moved for the inclusion of "Jesus Christ" alongside
"God" in official fast and thanksgiving proclamations: "All Christian men are
grieved to observe how universally and industriously the name of Christ,
through whom alone our prayers are accepted, has been omitted from these
proclamations."[5] Surely this would equal the score with the Confederacy,
which, like the Union, mentioned only God in its proclamations.

Not to be outdone, evangelical Confederate moralists pressed for the
same language—also without success. What they could not see taking shape
was a Christian-like civil religion that could not officially mention Christ lest
it lose inclusiveness, even though it identified the cause—and its patriotism—
with "Him."

In Montgomery, Alabama, Basil Manly, the venerable Baptist pastor and
former University of Alabama president, delivered a fast-day sermon explaining how evil reverses were not signs of divine desertion. By the time of his
sermon, Manly had served as a chaplain and buried scores of Montgomery
soldiers killed in the recent battles.[6] But, employing the logic of the jeremiad,
Manly demonstrated how even defeats were a divine test to see if God's people would remain loyal.

On paper, the prospects for the North never looked brighter than in the
spring of 1862. But beneath the serene military surface, strong undercurrents
of dissent pulled the North in conflicting directions. Unlike the Confederacy,
which, in 1862 anyway, had one party and one mind, the North was bitterly
divided, with Lincoln trying to hold the center. On one extreme were "peace"
Democrats who had seen enough bloodshed and wanted a negotiated treaty
that would allow the South to go and the war to end. These were held in tension by "war" Democrats who rejected secession but favored a negotiated
peace based on the shared ideology of white supremacy.[7] On the other extreme were antislavery and abolitionist radicals who wanted to broaden the
war's goals to include universal emancipation. Such a move would inevitably
strengthen Confederate resolve and transform the war into a "total war"
aimed at the social and political reconstruction of the South.

To appease the antislavery wing, Lincoln reiterated his preference for aid
to all states who would adopt the gradual abolition of slavery in their territo-

ries. On the other side, he continued to favor a policy of colonization of free blacks in Central America and Africa, and a graduated payout of compensated emancipation for loyal slave owners. This was precisely the sort of language that could not penetrate public discourse of the North and South, dominated as they were by the rhetoric of Providence. Lincoln's frame of reference allowed him to think nonconventionally. But his thoughts would lead to nothing in the face of an implacable North and South, each certain that God and global destiny dictated events.

Left ideologically adrift, Lincoln had to gain military victories, no matter how bloody. Otherwise, the Democrats would wrest power on the premise that victory over so vast a region was impossible—a premise Confederates also embraced.

Spring thaw brought renewed opportunities for new battles. On both sides, the anticipation was suffused with dread and excitement. In what was to become characteristic of the Civil War, battles were fought on so many fronts that civilians had to depend on the press to sort them out. On March 7, General Sam Curtis's eleven thousand Yankees defeated General Earl Van Dorn's seventeen thousand Confederates in the snow at Pea Ridge, Arkansas.

No sooner was Pea Ridge concluded than a stunning naval battle erupted at Hampton Roads, Virginia, between two ironclad juggernauts, the USS *Monitor,* with its single revolving turret gun, and the CSS *Merrimack* (officially *Virginia*). Shells bounced off the armored titans, and each ship alternately rammed the other and withdrew. When neither side could gain the advantage, both retreated. Most Americans did not realize at the time that they were gaining a preview of modern naval warfare. Henceforth, wooden vessels of the fleet would stand by helplessly as the new era rendered them obsolete.

Whatever uncertainties plagued both sides in the early spring of 1862, one fact seemed inescapable. This war, expected initially to be done in a year, was far from over. In a letter to his soldier son, the Reverend C. C. Jones conceded that predictions of early success were naive. "We are engaged in a long and desperate war, and our only hope is in the Lord and in the wise, energetic, and determined use of every means in our power to obtain our independence."[8]

Despite disappointments at Donelson and Pea Ridge, Confederates continued to trust in God and their cavalier "manliness." The river war, though disappointing, was not yet over and spring was coming. To buttress the war effort the Southern Congress enacted conscription and martial law. In the North confidence burned bright and the end was in sight—or so they thought.

CHAPTER 11

"IS IT NOT GRAND . . . ?"

In June 1862 the *Christian Herald and Presbyterian Recorder* ran a "Children's Corner" with "Talk about War" led by a Federal chaplain known as "Uncle Jessie." Uncle Jessie sought to describe battles in realistic scenes for the children, but first he needed to set the stage by explaining why the war was necessary and just. Uncle Jessie's young readers soon learned that one side in the struggle was entirely right and the other entirely wrong. Because the enemy was evil, no level of destruction could be too much. With "Christ's sword" in hand, Uncle Jessie was now ready to get down to the business of describing the macabre details of an actual battle:

> I must describe a battle to you as well as I can . . . we met men running like frightened sheep . . . they became panic stricken—that is crazy from fear. . . . All this while we heard the roar of cannon and the rattle of musketry. . . . Soon we began to meet the wounded, as they were carried, or dragged themselves away from the road. Some had bullets through their limbs, some through their bodies, some through their faces. I saw men with their legs shot off, others with their arms shot off, others with parts of the jaw, or one of the cheeks shot off. . . . We were hurried on. . . . In half an hour one-fifth of our soldiers were either killed or wounded.[1]

Other religious newspapers soon picked up on the same series. On October 2, 1862, the *Presbyter* interrupted its series on Uncle Jessie to observe that "Uncle Jessie had to be *in* the war again last week, and had no time to talk about it." But the next week Jessie was back from the war to talk to the children about "Picket Guard."[2]

This war that was fast becoming a citizens' war inevitably meant a children's war as well. In a letter to her husband soldier, George Frederick Jourdan, Nancie Jourdan wrote: "Albert went to bed tonight crying for me to read Papas letter. I had just got him undressed and commenced reading, he was just as interested as could be when William drove up. I did not finish it, of course, and when he saw Emily put it into her pocket he could stand it no longer. I finally soothed him by telling him I would go up and get it for him."[3]

For children to be co-opted into the war effort there had to be an all-encompassing indoctrination on both sides of the struggle. By spring of 1862 the work was virtually complete. Awed children learned to revere the war and the warriors of Christ who prosecuted it. No lessons emerged on minimizing casualties or the virtuous protection of innocents. Only a romanticized glory endured.

Children's literature echoed the same themes as adult moral commentary and propaganda. Published often by the American Tract Society or religious newspapers, it was far more patriotic than ethical. In one poem published in the aftermath of Bull Run, the patriotic story of "Charlie the Drummer-Boy" is recounted. In the poem, Charlie serves bravely on the battlefield and loses an arm. The scene then shifts to the reunion as an old Union veteran delivers his drummer boy home. Bowed but not broken, Charlie comforts his mother with this:

> It might have been worse too—the right arm instead.
> I'm glad for my country I've suffered and fought;
> I'll try to be brave now, and bear as I ought
> This little misfortunate that Providence sent
> You will not mind, mother, if I am content.[4]

Music was also employed to instill patriotic fervor and martial glory in the children of the North and South. War songs like the "Star-Spangled Banner" and "Battle Hymn of the Republic" ("Glory, Glory, Hallelujah") were sung in school and performed in public. Playgrounds became parade grounds and children learned to imitate soldier fathers and brothers.[5]

Recent studies have shown that children were assimilated early in the war effort and encouraged to wear uniforms and play war games, turning chairs into ambulances and imagining themselves without a limb like Charlie the Northern drummer boy. Parents would have photographs taken of their children with guns and swords. Alongside the games, patriotic songs and "panoramas" brought home the nobility of war to children on a dramatic scale. One broadside for the Tremont Temple in Boston advertised a "[p]anorama or, gigantic illustrations of the war" that would include musical

A photographic portrait of a boy soldier. The war reached all ages of Americans in both the North and the South. Children not old enough to volunteer dressed up like soldiers and imitated their actions in heroic battles waged against imagined dastardly foes.

accompaniment and paintings of all the major battles through the Peninsula campaign against Lee in Virginia.

The broadside promoted a reduced admission for children and promised a thrilling experience: "In the Battle Scenes is heard the Rattle of Musketry— the Booming of Cannon, mingled with the tumultuous noise of the deadly conflict. The Storm effects at Sea are wonderful and sublime, filling the beholder with awe. You see the vivid flash of the lightning, you hear the terrible roar of the tempest, and above it all, now more distant—now more near— peal on peal, the thunder rolls."[6]

The degree of "realism" in these activities varied, but all shared a lack of any real moral grounding. They simply boosted the relatively new commercial distribution of toys. In fact, most war games abandoned any attempt to encourage moral improvement. The object, in part, was to make war entertaining and fun, hence marketable.[7] Beyond that, the clear purpose of panoramas, toys, and music was martial and patriotic, not moral or cautionary.

In a column for children, the New York Evangelist described the war in exalted terms: "We are waiting for the thunder from Richmond. When two clouds charged with electricity approach each other in midheaven, we look to see the angry bolts leap from the black driving mass. So when two great armies stand in the presence of each other, we know that a collision cannot long be delayed." To "the children at home," the Evangelist provided a "Chapter about Heroes" that begins:

"Is it not grand to hear about all these brave men? I am so glad that I live in these war times!" said George. "So am I," said his brother William. "We did not think that the men who live now-a-days could be such heroes. It seems like reading the histories of old times." "Don't you wish, Will," said George, after a pause, "that we were men and could do such things?"[8]

The opposite of manliness, of course, was cowardice, and the religious press often addressed the duty of courage together with assertions that Christians make braver soldiers because they have heaven in view. Children learned that the worst shame was cowardice. A "Sunday School missionary" for the *Christian Herald* told young readers the story of "The Soldier Boy who was a Coward." Young female readers were taught to despise such a soldier: "And as for little girls, would they waste their bright glance and sunny smiles upon a boy who was a coward? . . . the more of a Christian a boy was, the better soldier he would prove."[9]

Letters from the battlefront to children or younger siblings often included horrific details of battles. In some cases the letters also employed the horror of war and death as a not-so-subtle enjoinder to behave at home so that God would look kindly on their fathers in time of battle. The historian James Marten quotes Private Henry Abbott's letter to his children: "Now you must be good all the time & remember, when you get mad & begin to cry, it makes the rebel bullets come a good deal nearer to me." Two other children, Hilga and Edmund Heg, worked hard to be good and keep their father and brother alive; unfortunately, Marten concludes, "they may have paid a huge psychic price when [their father] Colonel Heg was killed at Chickamauga."[10]

In the South, children learned the same lessons. War stories proved especially popular, and no one was more revered than Stonewall Jackson. In *Boys and Girls Stories of the War*, Edward Boykin recounted the battlefield heroics of Jackson and then went on to describe the people's veneration, both free and slave. Echoing the familiar myth that slaves preferred their servile but protected status to unprotected free labor in the North, Boykin worked up a dialogue between "Uncle Ned," a slave who hated the Yankees for robbing his house, and a mysterious soldier. Uncle Ned asked the stranger: "Is you a Confed. Or a Yank?" "I am a Confederate officer," replied the soldier in the gray coat, with stars on his collar:

> "Well den marster I will tend to you right 'way. But stop, who is at de head of all dese men. Is it old Stonewall?" "Yes," said the officer, "I am Stonewall." "Hooray" cried uncle Ned, "hurray! I goes wid you ober de Blue Ridge! Hurray!" and he swung his old hat in the air. . . . So the faithful negro shut the

window, locked the door of his cabin and was soon seen guiding the army through the mountain pass.[11]

For years, white Southerners had chafed at their dependence on Northern presses—steeped, as they supposed, in "abolitionism"—for so much of their literature, including primers and textbooks.[12] With the onset of war, they determined to produce their own children's textbooks. Although that meant that they had far fewer children's books or magazines to choose from, it enabled them to retrofit schoolbooks for the war effort and a partisan indoctrination. In many instances, Southern publishers simply took existing textbooks and added "Confederate" instead of "American." In terms of nationalism, textbooks contained more of what the historian George Rable terms "negative nationalism"—or the excoriation of the Northern enemy—than constructive discussions of Confederate nationalism.[13]

Talking about a Confederate textbook, however, and producing one were two different things, as the South quickly learned. Some texts, such as *The First Confederate Speller*, came out at the start of war in 1861. But the great majority of Confederate texts did not appear until the last two years of the war.[14] By then a significant enough time had elapsed for young readers to learn the "history" of the young nation and its just war.

A *Geography for Beginners* articulated the just cause of the war and its divine destiny:

In 1861 the Government of the Confederate States was duly established at Richmond, Va. . . . Every effort that human ingenuity could contrive, or immense resources of money and vast armaments on sea and land could accomplish, was made by the Northern government to capture the capital and other important plans, and break up the political organization of the Confederacy. But by the constant, evident and acknowledged aid of the God of Battles and King of Nations, these efforts have all failed; and, at vast expense of suffering and blood, the people of the Southern States have fought their own way to political independence and the respect and amity of the great nations of the world.[15]

Beyond patriotic pride and celebration of leaders, the texts offered little moral commentary on the war. Military themes and history predominated. For example, children learned math by computing company and brigade size and armaments. The *Dixie Speller* explained to its young readers that "[a] *Battery* is used in war to protect the gunners. *Cavalry* are soldiers who fight on horseback, and *infantry* are those who travel on foot." The effect, as the historian Rachel Stillman has pointed out, was to "emphasize the manhood, bravery, loyalty and sometimes the invincibility of Confedcrate soldiers."[16]

Although patriotism dominated commentary on the war in Confederate textbooks, moral commentary did appear in two forms. The first was unstinting loyalty to Christian orthodoxy as the foundation of the nation. Children were enjoined to read the Bible as the inspired Word of God and to have daily devotions. "Bible morality" became the watchword for daily behavior and the Ten Commandments were recited in classrooms daily. Mathematics textbooks included exercises utilizing Bible texts and chapters.[17]

The second moral theme developed in Confederate texts was the rightness of slavery. Children would be taken through the same Bible texts adult theologians argued to justify biblical precedents for the institution. But alongside these standard defenses and denigration of abolitionists were enjoinders to treat the slaves as human beings with moral dignity. God would not rain defeat on the Confederate cause for slavery, but He would punish the South if they refused to see His image in the slaves' souls.

Marinda B. Moore's *Primary Geography* insisted that slavery was not sinful, as the North wrongly claimed, but that the slaves' common humanity needed to be respected: "Let all the little boys and girls remember that slaves are human, and that God will hold them to account for treating them with injustice."[18] Texts told stories of slaves who were "liberated" by Union soldiers only to return to the safety and security of their masters. This happened, children learned, because good masters treated their slaves well and took care of them. Children too must be "kind" to their "servants" or God would hold them accountable.

Ironically, amid all the defenses of slavery in white textbooks, the Civil War marked one of the first times that Southern educators talked seriously about educating blacks. Ministers—especially Baptist ministers—pushed their conventions to pass resolutions that would promote the repeal of laws banning slave literacy. To this end, the resolutions would encourage church members to urge their legislators in that direction. Clearly worried that God's favor depended on just treatment of the slaves, Confederate moralists sought to expand slaves' opportunities in ways that would encourage God to smile on His Confederacy. In so doing, proslavery leaders recognized they needed to appear more humanitarian in the eyes of a larger world—especially Britain.

Among Presbyterians, the moderator of the Southern Presbyterian Assembly, James A. Lyon, pastor of the First Presbyterian Church in Columbus, Mississippi, placed at the top of his priorities "a manifesto on slavery and the religious instruction of negroes." Though emphatically proslavery, Lyon was intent on reforming the institution, particularly in regard to education. He even went so far as to recommend mixing whites and blacks in existing public schools. Although his clerical peers supported him in the general assembly, the laity balked and the reforms were put on hold.[19] The laity understood only too well what *they* were fighting for, and it was not to affirm the humanity of the Negro.

Clearly Northern and Southern children could have been spared the raw details of battles. Neither did they have to wallow in pools of patriotic romanticization. But this war would rapidly become a total war, and that dictated that children, no less than adults, would experience it directly. It also required that restraining moral considerations not be allowed to silence the drumbeat for ever-greater battles, and glory for all.

Throughout the war much of the child-rearing and household maintenance fell perforce on the women. As accounts of battles reached every town and city, the pressures on the home front could prove intolerable. Historians are only now comprehending and chronicling the toll on wives and children. In her December 1861 letter to her husband, George Frederick, Nancie Jourdan included entries from her diary to convey to him the effects of war at home:

> Nervous illness. "27th Thanksgiving. . . . came home and went to bead after having something like a fit. Had the Doctor at about 7 oclock. I trembled all over so badly I could not get my things off when I got home but cannot account for it. The Doctor called it a neuralysis of the nerves. I thought I should never see daylight again. I think my blood did not serculate around my heart, for I had such bad feeling there, and my limbs were allmost inirely useless. I continued to be weak for a week or more, could not go up and down stairs without a great deal of exertion. Am well now hope to remain so until your return. . . . I will now close please accept this from your affectionate and lonely.
> Nancie.[20]

The toll was equally steep, and far more direct, in the South, where rich and poor women alike suffered. The derogatory term "refugee" was first applied to wealthy planters who, when faced with invading Federals, fled with their slaves, sacrificing patriotism for possessions. But soon the term took on a more gendered meaning as the majority of dispossessed were female. Although often resented for their class and aristocratic attitudes toward work and station, many women were left penniless and forced to throw themselves on the mercy of the state.[21]

An especially poignant window into white Southern women's experience in the Civil War are the letters from them seeking employment with the Confederate States Treasury office "for signing and numbering Confederate notes."[22] Applicants were instructed to write to Christopher Gustavus Memminger, secretary of the Confederate Treasury, with assurances that priority would be given to those with the greatest need (and acceptable handwriting).

In a letter to Treasury Secretary Memminger seeking employment with the agency, L. E. Hughes captured the plight of rearing children with a husband in the field:

> My object in getting employment is to support myself and three children, all under eleven years of age, while my husband is in the army: and I wish to make a permanent arrangement for a year. I have no means of support and no near relation living, having lost my only brother in one of the battles before Richmond. I am perfectly willing to give my whole time to business and to work faithfully with a determination to give satisfaction. I shall anxiously await your answer, which I earnestly hope may be favourable, and until that time I remain very respectfully yours.[23]

Many of these letters describe the immediate suffering imposed by the loss of a husband or sons. On October 3, 1862, Eugenia Hyde wrote: "I am a widow, with three sons in the army, and finding that a prolonged exile has contracted seriously my former income, I venture to apply for a situation as clipper of Treasury notes, such as I understand you have already bestowed on many in similar circumstances." An accompanying letter of reference from George Woodbridge read: "Mrs. Hyde is a lady of great worth and excellence of character. She belongs to the old Fairfax family, one of the first families in the state. Her home has been entirely destroyed by the enemy, and her three sons now in the war, are unable to render her any assistance. If there be a situation to confer upon any lady now, it could not be conferred upon one more deserving or more destitute."[24]

From many of the petitions it is clear that the war devastated all ranks of Southern society. However much troops might complain about a "rich man's war and a poor man's fight," there was more than enough suffering among all classes. When Mary Gifford applied for work with the department, her reference, W. M. Tucker, told the following story:

> She is the widow of Mr. A.F.D. Gifford, lost in his return to this country with a cargo, to fill a contract with the government. She is the daughter of the late Chapman Johnson, one of the greatest lawyers of Va. She is the guardian and protector of two little orphan children of her late brother Dr. Curtis

Johnson, lost in the arctic. Upon the death of her husband, his affairs being settled left her dependent. She joined her brother in teaching a school in Fredericksburg on the 1st of October last. But she is driven here by our Public Enemy. . . . To see her in such a state as she is, is as painful almost as I would be to see my sister so. I am much attached to her . . . and her appointment would be a real personal favor to me.[25]

Husbands in the field often complained about the delays or infrequency of letters from home. When placed in the context of Southern petitioners it becomes clear that the war had become as much a war of civilian suffering as military. The same was true in the North. Assuming that 30 percent of Union and Confederate soldiers were married, the number of women widowed by the war would be at least 108,000. Still, the momentum for war ran strong in the civilian populations as both the North and the South contributed and received patriotic reinforcements on all sides.[26]

If women at home were praised for their virtue, women on the other side were villanized even more than the men. This was particularly true of Southern women who far more frequently came into direct contact with enemy soldiers. When not excoriating soldiers' sins in the South, many Northern moralists fixed a damning eye on Southern women. In a sermon delivered on the anniversary of the surrender of Fort Sumter, Henry Ward Beecher seared the Confederate woman:

Consider, again, the strange part that has been played in this conflict by Southern women. A woman always goes with her whole heart, whether for the good or for the bad. Women are the best and the worst things that God ever made! And they have been true to their nature in this conflict. Southern men have been tame and cool in comparison with the fury of Southern women.[27]

The exalted role of woman provided a powerful national emblem or symbol in both the North and the South (as did the denigration of the enemy's women). A column for the *New York Times* on "The Women and the War" opened:

Whatever folly our public declaimers may have uttered year after year on "Women's Rights," practically, the women of America have "rights and privileges" in all that man does, and feels, and possesses, through the best medium—her sympathy. . . . The women far more than the men in the North, have always been, in feeling and instinct, opposed to the Southern "sacred institution."

The same editorial accused the women of the South of "amazing ferocity and bitterness," and traced it to the same source:

We believe it but a corresponding part to what we have been describing at the North. The American woman shares all things with the man. If he is a rebel and a barbarian, she will be so, too. If he hates the flag, she will hate it also. If he drinks from Yankee skulls and plays tattoo with Northern tibia, she will display barbarism in her own way—by weak insults, by bitter taunts, by spitting in the faces of those who, as gentlemen, cannot protect themselves, by vulgar gestures and coarse abuse of the suffering. And inasmuch as in sympathy with the man's ferocity she has violated her own nature, so will she be ten times as much of a devil as he.[28]

CHAPTER 12

"THE POPULAR HEART"

Even as soldiers, statesmen, mothers, and children geared for a rapidly escalating war, artists were more than willing to lend their hands to the cause. The arts proved as captive to the war as print and oratory, and they were boxed in the same rhetorical traps. In both the North and the South, music had long thrived. So a citizens' war was inevitably a patriotic musical war on the battlefront no less than the home front. Lydia Maria Child, the staunch abolitionist and writer, recognized that "nothing on earth has such effect on the popular heart as Songs, which the soldiers would take up with enthusiasm, and which it would thereby become the fashion to whistle and sing. . . . Old John Brown, Hallelujah is performing a wonderful mission now."[1]

In his history of music in the North, Kenneth A. Bernard estimates that during the first year alone, at least two thousand compositions were produced, and "by the end of the war more music had been created, played, and sung than during all our other wars combined."[2] Despite Southern shortages of paper and printers, this was as true in the South as in the North. Patriotic songs aligned martial spirit and sectional loyalties to become anthems of war. In the North, "Hail, Columbia," "Yankee Doodle," the "Star-Spangled Banner," and Henry C. Work's "Marching through Georgia" would give voice to the Union cause. In the South, it would be Daniel Emmett's "Dixie," "Maryland," and Harry Macarthy's "Bonnie Blue Flag."

These popular standards betrayed all the same preoccupation with patriotism and glory seen in popular literature and the press. Nowhere to be found are the issues of war, the mystery of death, or conduct unbecoming a true soldier. Rather, the horror of war was subsumed under romantic themes of nostalgia, sentiment, bravery, and noble death. With music such as this, inspired

The band of the Eighth New York State Militia, 1861. Military bands played indispensable roles in inculcating the patriotism that fueled soldiers' and civilians' participation in and support of the war.

soldiers could ride full fury into the fray in ever greater numbers, certain that family members at home revered their bravery and honored their memory.

Soldiers carried military tunes into the field and paraded to the airs of regimental bands. By 1861 military brass bands had become prevalent and displaced the earlier drum and fife corps. Wherever the military went, from recruiters to warriors, the bands followed. On November 20, 1861, a great mass of people converged at Bailey's Cross Roads, near Fairfax, Virginia, to hear fifty regimental bands perform patriotic music. Of the one hundred thousand present, fifty to seventy thousand were soldiers ready to march with the regimental bands to such classics as "The Standard Bearer Quickstep," or George F. Root's "Tramp, Tramp, Tramp, the Boys Are Marching."

The large-scale review was a spectacular and inspiring sight to soldier and citizen alike. Thousands of soldiers marching with military precision, hundreds of artillery pieces drawn by horses, and bands by the dozens appeared in order that the commanders and the public might view the immense military machine rendered even more dramatic by the stirring music. The massive procession stretched on for over a mile. As commanders rode by in review, a particular unit with attached musical organizations would proudly render their best selection from such national airs as "America," "The Marseillaise," or "Red, White, and Blue."[3]

In the parade at Bailey's Cross Roads, emotions peaked as General McClellan appeared with a cavalry escort. Soon he was joined by President Lincoln and Secretary of War Simon Cameron. Reporting on the regiments marching in review, a writer for the *New York Times* commented: "What strength was slumbering in that mighty host, and what death and carnage lay before it, when it should move on the foe. When the question of union and disunion was so glibly discussed by politicians on the stump, who ever dreamed he should live to behold such a sight as this?"[4]

On the home front, local and military bands provided public concerts that attracted enthusiastic audiences. Although the vast majority of Northern songs identified the preservation of the Union as the cause of war and ignored emancipation, one abolitionist songbook was put together by John Hutchinson of New Hampshire. Hutchinson built on abolitionist songs like Whittier's "Hymn of Liberty" to equate the war with emancipation. One, entitled "Coming Right Along," closed with the triumphant theme:

> *No longer shall the bondman sigh beneath the galling fetters—*
> *He sees the dawn of freedom nigh, and reads the golden letters.*
> > *Coming right along,*
> > *Coming right along,*
> *Behold the day of freedom is coming right along!*

Not to be outdone, the New York abolitionist James S. Gibbons wrote "We Are Coming, Father Abraham"—a tribute to Lincoln with strong abolitionist sentiments.

While popular with abolitionists, such music was not preferred in the North, where slavery was subordinated to patriotic love of Union. At one concert in Fairfax, Virginia, soldiers from New Jersey incited a riot when Hutchinson's band played "Hymn of Liberty." Only the intervention of two chaplains prevented the destruction of the band's equipment.[5]

As with jeremiads, identical themes embodied the music of the Union and the Confederacy, revealing how much common ground they continued to share. Two songs' sheet music sold by the millions in the North: "Yes, We'll Rally 'Round the Flag, Boys" ("The Battle Cry of Freedom") and "We Are Coming, Father Abraham." Such was the popularity of "Rally 'Round the Flag, Boys" that the Confederacy sang the same song with their own lyrics.

Much Union sheet music written before emancipation ignored slavery and concentrated on patriotism and loves left behind. In the North and the South, in music and art, the flag was ubiquitous. As national totem, the flag would also serve as a fierce catalyst for triumph. The flag song was a fight song:

We're in the right, and will prevail, the Stars and Stripes must fly;
The "Bonnie Blue Flag" will be hauled down and every traitor die,
Freedom and Peace enjoyed by all, as ne'er was known before,
Our Spangled Banner wave on high, with stars just Thirty Four.[6]

The theme of "Thirty-four Stars" became the subject of a song praising Union commanders and set in opposition to the Confederate "Bonnie Blue Flag":

The Rebels sing the "Bonnie Blue Flag" but we the "Stripes and Stars,"
  Our Union Flag we love so true,
Will conquer their Stars and Bars;
  Their Seceshairs, their Marylands,
Are contraband of war;
  Our cause is right and the Flag for the fight,
Is one with thirty-four stars.

Chorus:
Hurrah! Hurrah! For equal rights Hurrah! Hurrah!
For the dear old Flag, with ev'ry Stripe and Star.

Another common song set to different lyrics by the North and the South was the anthem "Battle Cry of Freedom." The Union chorus refrain, written by George F. Root, focused on Union and the flag:

The Union forever, Hurrah, boys, hurrah!
Down with the traitor, up with the star; While we rally 'round the flag, boys
Rally once again, Shouting the battle cry of Freedom.

The Confederate lyrics written by W. H. Barnes adapted it to an idea of freedom that emphasized "Dixie" and Christian faith:

Our Dixie forever, she's never at a loss
Down with the eagle, up with the cross, We'll rally 'round the bonnie flag
We'll rally once again, Shout, shout the battle cry of Freedom.[7]

Of course, the mounting killing could not be ignored. But rendered in song, death like war became either sentimental or glorious. One of the most popular songs, also sung on both sides of the conflict, was "All Quiet Along the Potomac Tonight." In the North it was published as "The Picket's Last

Watch." Its closing chorus told the story of a picket's love and death at the hands of a sniper:

> Hark! was it the night wind that rustled the leaves?
>   Was it the moonlight so wond'rously flashing?
> It looked like a rifle! "Ha! Mary, good-bye!"
>   And his life-blood is ebbing and splashing.
>
> All quiet along the Potomac to-night,
>   No sound save the rush of the river,
> While soft falls the dew on the face of the dead,
>   "The Picket's" off duty forever.[8]

Cowardice was every soldier's greatest fear and a theme in many a letter, as well as in much of the music.[9] In this citizens' war, no one wanted to retreat or be shot in the back. In "Let Me Die Face to the Foe," the last words of Brigadier General James C. Rice, Army of the Potomac, signaled the theme of bravery transcending death:

> I am wounded, soldiers, dying,
>   Send this word unto my wife
> "I've been true unto my country
>   In her cause I yield my life."
> Hark! the drums beat—victr'ys ours!
>   Let me ask you ere I go
> Comrades "turn me t'wards the traitors!
>   Let me die face to the foe!"

Even more than Northern music, Confederate songs offered no sense of moral ambiguity or irony, but instead celebrated the war without restraint. With the homeland under attack, the identification of war and the land assumed greater emphasis than in Northern music. In "The War Song of Dixie," the theme of country, flag, and arms reaches a stirring crescendo:

> Southrons, hear your country call you,
>   Victory soon shall bring them gladness,
> To arms! To arms! To arms! In Dixie!
>   Exultant pride soon banish sorrow;
> Smiles chase tears away tomorrow,
>   To arms! to arms! To arms! In Dixie![10]

The one prominent exception that proves the general rule of musical medioc-
rity appeared first as a poem in the February 1862 issue of the *Atlantic
Monthly*. The poem was composed by Massachusetts abolitionist Julia Ward
Howe and titled "The Battle Hymn of the Republic." In fact, the poem had
been written three months earlier on a sleepless night in Washington, D.C.

Howe visited the capital as part of a group that included her husband,
Dr. Samuel Gridley Howe, together with Governor John A. Andrew of Massachusetts and the Reverend James Freeman Clarke. The party had been
granted a personal visit with President Lincoln at the White House, and later
observed hundreds of soldiers in their lighted campground singing "John
Brown's body lies a-moldering in the grave." Clarke asked Howe if she could
write a poem with some more appropriate, uplifting words.

Later, Howe recalled that night in the Old Willard Hotel, when her sleep
was interrupted:

> I awoke in the gray of the morning twilight, and as I lay waiting for the dawn,
> the long lines of the desired poem began to twine themselves in my mind.
> Having thought out all the stanzas, I said to myself, "I must get up and write
> these verses down, lest I fall asleep again and forget them." So with a sudden
> effort I sprang out of bed and found in the dimness an old stump of a pen
> which I remembered to have used the day before. I scrawled the verses
> almost without looking at the paper. I had learned to do this when, on previ-
> ous occasions, attacks of versification had visited me in the night and I
> feared to have recourse to a light lest I should wake the baby, who slept near
> me. . . . At this time, having completed my writing, I returned to bed and
> fell asleep, saying to myself, "I like this better than most things that I have
> written."[11]

Howe's modesty produced an understatement. "The Battle Hymn of the
Republic" became widely sung in Union armies, especially after Gettysburg,
and eventually enjoyed unrivaled status. During the war, Howe's hymn never
displaced "John Brown's Body" as the soldiers' favorite song. But in American
memory, "Battle Hymn of the Republic" better served America's future by
linking the war less to patriotism than to abolition, in part reflecting the fact
that Howe and her husband were abolitionists.

The early verses of the "Battle Hymn" bask in a martial glory common to
many songs of the time. But in her triumphant conclusion, Howe reaches a
transcendent identification of Christ's sacrifice with emancipation: "As He
died to make men holy, let us die to make men free." As with the words of

other abolitionists, Howe's anthem helped transform the war's meaning into a moral crusade of freedom that would outlive its creator. In American memory, the hymn would virtually define the war's final meaning. For Lydia Maria Child, the "Battle Hymn" was an answer to her abolitionist prayer: "If the soldiers only *had* a Song, to some spirit-stirring tune, proclaiming what they went to fight for . . . and indignantly announcing that they did *not* go to hunt slaves."[12]

Precisely because of her transcendent moral gravitas and abolitionist subtheme, Howe's "hymn" to America has remained *the* American song to emerge from the Civil War. More than any other song, it turned the war into something holy, hence beyond moral critique. In this regard, her earlier stanzas stand as more representative of the norm:

> *Mine eyes have seen the glory of the coming of the Lord:*
> *He is trampling out the vintage where the grapes of wrath are stored;*
> *He hath loosed the fateful lightning of His terrible swift sword:*
> *His truth is marching on.*

In his insightful analysis of this national hymn, Edmund Wilson observes that Howe's God was not the gentle Christ of the lilies of the field (he was "born across the sea"), but the vengeful God of the Hebrew Bible ready to wreak vengeance on His enemies. The hymn is an urgent call to arms and promises victory over the enemies of Israel.[13]

In the North and the South, the dramatic performing arts evidenced a predictable moral avoidance. After an exhaustive review of Civil War–era plays, Rosemary L. Cullen discovered that during the war relatively few plays dealt with the subject of war at all. The closest was the 1852 dramatic rendering of Harriet Beecher Stowe's celebrated novel *Uncle Tom's Cabin*, which was wildly popular on the stage during and after the war.

For the most part, however, the offerings were escapist and took on any theme *but* the war. As summarized by Cullen: "It became evident that audiences preferred rousing patriotic and military spectacles of a noncontroversial nature to any mention of the real causes of the conflict."[14] Plays like Harry Seymour's *The Battle of Booneville* or Charles Gayler's *The Stars and Stripes* celebrated heroic generals and battles in a virtual sea of patriotism unconnected to the war. In the Confederacy, where paper was scarce, few plays were published. Those that found their way into print celebrated martial valor or pilloried Lincoln's public and (supposed) private life.

Like the general public, President Lincoln was a great fan of the theater and attended Grover's Theater and Ford's Theater frequently. And like them, he had no interest in stage productions on the theme of the war. He preferred Shakespeare or comedy. It is perhaps ironic that before the war ended, one of his favorite actors, John Wilkes Booth, would carry the war directly into the theater to find and shoot Lincoln himself.[15]

CHAPTER 13

"RELIGION HAS GROWN WARLIKE"

The battles of 1861 proved only one thing: despite its feeble origins, this war was destined to last a long time and become far more desperate. Between July 1861, when the first Battle of Bull Run was fought, and March 1862, Union and Confederate armies grew from a combined total of roughly three hundred thousand to more than one million.[1] Inevitably the collisions would turn ever more brutal.

The spring campaigns of 1862 marked the last days of the West Point Code and of its unrepentant embodiment, General McClellan. Added to the sheer growth in numbers of troops were new weapons. Armies on both sides carried rifled muskets with conical bullets designed to increase distance, accuracy, and hitting power. At the same time tactics remained depressingly traditional, with both sides stubbornly employing close-order frontal assaults on entrenched defensive positions. Such was the power of culture—even military culture—that commanders resisted change, even though "tactical offenses" rarely carried well-placed entrenchments and invariably ate up casualties by the thousands.[2]

Just as tactics failed to keep pace with military technology, so also did medical technology fail. Ever larger and larger armies camped in close and often unsanitary winter quarters, prisons, and hospitals. Such conditions spread diseases so viciously that they took a third more lives than the battlefields themselves. In a letter to his wife, Private William Willoughby observed: "Our Regt is perhaps as healthy as any other yet we lose a man almost every day by disease. . . . We had when we left hartford some 800 or 900 men on dress parade we now scarsly [sic] number 400 the rest are all either killed wounded died or sick."[3]

With McClellan playing it safe in Virginia, the next significant action took place in the western theater of the war. In Tennessee, Grant's Federal army was still celebrating capturing Forts Henry and Donelson. They were unaware that a new Confederate line was forming farther south in Corinth, Mississippi, to attack Grant's army in force and retake Tennessee. A Confederate army of twenty-seven thousand, under the command of Albert Sidney Johnston and P. G. T. Beauregard and reinforced by fifteen thousand additional troops from Braxton Bragg's army in Mobile, Alabama, planned to strike Grant's army before he could be reinforced by Don Carlos Buell's Army of the Ohio, which was temporarily blocked by flooding rivers and by Buell's McClellan-like caution. Widely regarded as one of the best and most intrepid commanders in the Confederate army, Johnston ordered a morning attack, hoping to catch the Yankees by surprise.

The gamble paid off, at least in the short run. Not expecting an attack, Grant had organized his army for convenience rather than a strategic defense. He would pay a stiff price. On the morning of April 6, as Yankees lingered over coffee and breakfast, rebel forces burst through the blooming peach trees at Pittsburg Landing and, to the rebels' astonishment, caught Grant's forces almost totally by surprise. To green troops still unaccustomed to "modern" warfare and massive assaults, the surprise unsettled the entire Union army. Grant himself was nine miles below the point of engagement and his disjointed and still untested Federal unit commanders failed to communicate and support one another, allowing the initial momentum to swing decisively in Johnston's direction.

The most exposed northern position was near Shiloh Church, about three miles southwest of Pittsburg Landing. Here an unlikely hero saved the day for the Union. Discredited and overly timid in Kentucky, General Sherman returned to active command with a vengeance to serve under his friend Grant.[4] He received the full force of Johnston's assault but held the line for four exhausting hours, "sometimes gaining and at others losing ground." But stand he did.

Shiloh proved to be Sherman's redemption. Terrified troops, some of whom had just received their muskets, ran panic-stricken, unable to fight. But despite being slightly wounded himself, Sherman rallied his troops up and down the line, providing the critical assistance Grant needed to save the day and extend the fight.[5] Shiloh marked the cementing of a partnership between Sherman and Grant that grew stronger with each passing battle.

That night torrential rains pounded the battlefield, compounding the suffering of ten thousand wounded soldiers lying exposed on the killing fields and awaiting the next day's battle. Sensing blood, Grant launched a massive counterattack at 7:30 the next morning, with fresh divisions aching for payback against the unsuspecting rebels. Again the battle seesawed back and forth around a focal point several hundred yards from Shiloh Church, the two armies slugging it out at the crossroads. At one point Sherman ordered a regiment to "stand fast" even though they were out of ammunition because, as he later explained, "to retire a regiment for any cause, has a bad effect on others."[6] With Sherman at his soldiers' backs threatening to shoot any who cut and ran, the rebel offensive bogged down. A dispirited Beauregard disengaged his losing forces and retreated unmolested to his starting point in Corinth.

The day belonged to Grant and Sherman, and it marked the Union's conquest of the Tennessee River. But the real news of Shiloh was not the outcome of the battle; it was the carnage. Neither army was decisively defeated and both would live to fight another day. What changed permanently was the scale of combat. From this point on, "proportionality" mattered in command decisions. As news of Shiloh spread, readers in the North and South were staggered at the butcher's bill. Of 42,000 Federal "effectives" (participants), 1,754 were killed, 8,408 wounded, and 2,885 missing, for a total casualty list of 13,047. For the Confederate army of 40,000, 1,732 were killed, 8,012 wounded, and 950 missing, for a total of 10,694. Included among the killed was General Albert Sidney Johnston. The combined losses at Shiloh totaled 24,500 and rivaled casualties in all previous battles combined. It still stands as the costliest battle ever fought in the western theater, before or after.

Such was the devastation unleashed at Shiloh that a new industry soon proliferated by the battlefield sites—caskets. Increasingly, ads for embalmment and caskets filled the pages of the religious and secular press. One typical advertisement from John Good, Undertaker, No. 921 Spruce St., Philadelphia, notifies readers of a new "branch" office close to the Virginia battlefields:

> To the friends of our Patriot Dead. Repeated applications having been made to the subscriber to establish a branch of his business in the vicinity of the late battlefields, with a view of reducing the cost of bringing home the bodies of the dead, he respectfully announces that he has now established a branch at Hagerstown, Md. . . . Orders from a distance promptly attended to. The BURIAL CASKET furnished by me is equal to any other in use with regard to security, economy, and entire absence of any of the unpleasant circumstances which generally surround similar articles.[7]

Good repeated his advertisements in subsequent editions and was soon joined by three other undertakers receiving orders. Despite the presence of embalmers, soldiers frequently had to take the remains of their comrades

Embalming building and morgue near Fredericksburg, Virginia. An embalming surgeon at work on a soldier's body. One of the grimmer aspects of the war was handling bodies of the dead hundreds of miles from home. Many dead soldiers never made it home and instead were buried on the battlefields.

into their own care. In a letter home, Yankee Private Edwin Wheelock wrote, "The bodies of the two that were killed of our company exhumed day before yesterday . . . were put in boxes ready to send home. Their parents were anxious to have the bodies sent home. The bodies were packed in lar[d]."[8]

Further defeats followed the Confederates in the West as General Henry Halleck's Army of Missouri followed up on Grant's success at Shiloh and marched on Beauregard's shattered army in Corinth. Like McClellan, General Halleck was, in 1862, still a believer in the West Point Code. In pursuing Beauregard's forces to Corinth, he refused to "invest" (besiege) the town, which would risk soldiers and civilians alike. Instead he allowed Beauregard an avenue of escape—an option the badly outgunned Beauregard was more than eager to take. Halleck gained control of the strategic territory he sought on the Mississippi without bloodshed.[9]

But strategies that sought to avoid bloodbaths if strategic gains could be had in other ways would not survive the war. In fact, neither McClellan's nor Halleck's strategies would gain favor with Lincoln and his newly appointed secretary of war, Edwin M. Stanton, or even with some of McClellan's own soldiers. In time, Halleck would change as well.

One Northern soldier recalled that despite McClellan's orders to avoid civilian goods, "the officers found it impractical, and next to impossible to observe . . . as our soldiers could not understand how that we were ever to whip the Rebels without hurting them."[10] Increasingly the more offensive and violent tactics advocated by Clausewitz and determinedly pursued by

Grant, Lee, and Jackson would characterize Civil War battles, transforming a "traditional" and limited war into a "modern" war.

At the same time that Halleck dispatched with Beauregard, Union General John Pope's Army of the Mississippi—some twenty thousand strong and protected by Admiral Foote's fleet of gunboats and mortar-boats—moved down the Mississippi and captured Island No. 10, again without bloodshed. Included in the fortress were five thousand prisoners and considerable artillery and ammunition. Pope was not a believer in the West Point Code and proceeded to revile the "enemy" in terms broad enough to include anyone— soldier or civilian—who got in his way. Back in Washington, Lincoln liked the reports that arrived. It also did not hurt that Pope, unlike McClellan, was a Republican.

But as gratifying as the victories on the Mississippi were, they were not the prize Lincoln most coveted. Whether or not Richmond deserved to be the obsessive strategic point of attraction it became in the North was beside the point. When not worrying excessively about the safety of Washington, Lincoln was micromanaging the war in Virginia, looking closely over his generals' shoulders and generally not approving of what he saw. In contrast, Lincoln left his generals in the West to their own devices, and they learned how to fight a new war on its own terms. They would fare better without the president's close oversight and, in time, bring the lessons they learned back to the East.[11]

Not everyone was thankful for the course of the war. Ever since Lincoln's March 6 report to Congress proposing gradual emancipation and compensation for slave owners, *The Liberator* had issued unrelenting criticism: "His message is wholly destitute of sympathy for the enslaved, of any recognition of the injustice or wrongfulness of slavery, of all moral principle; it is based upon selfish considerations alone."[12] *The Liberator* followed this up by reprinting Thomas Vickers's April 10 sermon to Meadville Theological School on the subject of a just war:

> Tell me not of victories over Southern rebels! I am sick at heart over these victories. I would to Heaven that they had conquered the rebellious North,—rebellious against the law of God. The North is not yet worthy of victory—*not morally ready for it.* And I pray that God may not withhold his hand, that disaster on disaster may come upon us, until we are ready, nay anxious, to do the right.[13]

Vickers's sentiments were echoed by nonclerical abolitionists. In a letter to her friend Mary Johnson, Martha LeBaron Goddard excoriated the Northern leader's performance to date:

Well! The summer gets on and I wonder whether each day brings us nearer to salvation or ruin. What utter blindness and weakness prevail in high places. Government seems to *earnestly love* nothing but slaughter: and I don't wonder enlisting is so backward while men can't tell whether they are going to fight for Jeff. Davis or against him.

Later in the letter she reflected on the perils of a nonabolitionist command: "I do think the greatest curse we have had is McClellan—and I am fast growing to think Lincoln is almost a match for him. War meetings as they are called are stupid and heavy and spread-eagle and vain attempts to create enthusiasm for the war merely."[14]

The abolitionist chaplain Horace James took these thoughts further. For such a "baptism of blood," the war ought to have larger moral goals than simply the preservation of a large nation-state. It is not enough, he argued, "to bring this country to its position just before the breaking out of the rebellion." Only a war for abolition would justify the bloodshed. The stakes, James concluded, were global: "The present country has seen no such opportunity of blessing the world, no such opportunity of kindling a new light in the moral heavens to shine as the stars forever and ever, and may we not lose it by our driveling unbelief."[15]

Despite pockets of criticism, after more than a year of fighting, the mobilization of two massive armies with complex chains of command and coordination was virtually complete. Already in 1862, most citizens on both sides of the conflict knew family or friends called to service. Churches, schools, and town meetings could talk of little but war. Religious press editors feared their papers would not be read (or subscribed to) if the war was not elevated to supreme status and with a patriotic and supportive spin.

A surprised writer for Philadelphia's *Banner of the Covenant* observed:

Among the revolutions of this year, that of the literary world is remarkable for its belligerent drift. The press teems with Manuals of Tactics. . . . Religion has grown warlike. Men have discovered the Book of the Wars of the Lord, and congregations are chanting the war psalms now in all their majesty, that would have been shocked a year ago to hear anything stronger than Watts' dilutions.

The writer went on to note disapprovingly how even religious publications were festooned with "the stars and stripes in gorgeous red, white and blue."[16]

In the South, a writer for the *Richmond Daily Dispatch* quoted a Methodist minister hoping that the war would last "ten to fifteen years" so that the South would be forever purged of Northern dependence.[17] Patriotism and Christianity were becoming interleaved and virtually inseparable, with patriotism leading and Christian ministers and churches in tow. In fact, Americans of the North and South were discovering a new appetite for war.

PART III
DESCENT

HARD WAR, SPILLED BLOOD

APRIL 1862 TO OCTOBER 1862

CHAPTER 14

"WHAT SCENES OF BLOODSHED"

W hile Union navies and western armies moved relentlessly on Confederate defenses, General McClellan continued to dawdle in Virginia. Even with a massive army of one hundred thousand soldiers, McClellan claimed to be woefully undermanned and requested reinforcements from Lincoln for a show of overwhelming force. In reality, only fifteen thousand Confederate forces under General John Magruder were holding an eight-mile front. Instead of attacking Magruder's undermanned forces and smashing through to Richmond, McClellan ignored Lincoln's orders and laid siege to Yorktown from April 5 to May 5.[1]

McClellan's timidity bought precious time for Lee and Davis to bring their numbers closer to parity with McClellan's. Concurrently, General Joseph E. Johnston redeployed his army from Manassas in a superior defensive position closer to Richmond. Confederate generals were more than willing to grant McClellan his bloodless success while they planned something far more bloody and daring.

Throughout the spring, Stonewall Jackson's hard-driving infantry had been busy tearing up Federal forces in the Shenandoah Valley and striking terror everywhere. In a rash decision, Lincoln redirected General McDowell's corps from McClellan's Army of the Potomac to the valley, hoping to catch Jackson by surprise. Instead, Lincoln and McDowell played right into the rebels' hands. Jackson's "foot cavalry" was simply too elusive and fast to be caught. But by sequestering McDowell on a fruitless chase, the Army of the Potomac was left at reduced strength. To compound the problem, Lincoln's excessive estimation of Jackson's prowess led him to withhold forty-five thousand men to protect Washington, D.C., from an attack that would never come.

With Robert E. Lee still in the shadows as a military adviser to President Davis, there was only Jackson. Richmond newspapers, which were read throughout the Confederacy, led the way in praising their native son.[2] Southern evangelicals and the Richmond religious weeklies also cooperated in the mythmaking that focused on Jackson's all-consuming personal faith and his acknowledgment of God as the giver of victory to his troops at Manassas.

Confederate soldiers, sensing another side to Jackson, admired his stated preference for "taking no prisoners" and absorbed his almost manic obsession with destruction and glory even at the cost of unprecedented casualties. Jackson's imperious style took in generals no less than soldiers. He had General Richard Garnett, commander of the "Stonewall Brigade," arrested in the Shenandoah Valley for not charging Union General James Shields's victorious army with the bayonet when his ammunition ran out. Garnett was later released only to die in Pickett's charge at Gettysburg. Jackson also had Provost Marshall General Charles Winder arrested and, amazingly, arrested the veteran commander General A. P. Hill twice (with whom Jackson eventually reconciled only after Lee's intervention).

In her diary, Mary Chesnut quoted a frank assessment of Jackson's fiery character by General Alexander Lawton, who served under Jackson in the Shenandoah Valley. Lawton noted that Jackson rarely slept. To train his troops for battle, he would wake them at all hours, send them out marching for a few miles, and bring them back. "All this," said Lawton, "was to make us always ready, ever on the alert." Jackson never asked for his men's love, only their respect. "He gave his orders rapidly and distinctly and rode away. Never allowing answer nor remonstrance . . . When you failed, you were apt to be put under arrest. When you reported the place *taken*, he only said 'Good.'"

Lawton continued:

He had no sympathy with human infirmity. He was a one-idea'd man. He looked upon broken-down men and stragglers as the same thing. He classed all who were weak and weary, who fainted by the wayside, as men wanting in patriotism. If a man's face was as white as cotton and his pulse so low that you could not feel it, he merely looked upon him impatiently as an inefficient soldier and rode off, out of patience. He was the true type of all great soldiers. The successful warrior of the world, he did not value human life where he had an object to accomplish. He could order men to their death as a matter of course.[3]

In the spring of 1862, Jackson embodied all that Sherman would eventually become.

Even Lincoln and Northern soldiers were awed (and intimidated) by Jackson. Jackson himself remained resolutely Calvinist. In his eyes, the glory of the coming of a vengeful Lord was before him. In time, he was certain, his ravaging army would be moving north. In a letter to the Reverend Robert Dabney, who had joined Jackson's army as a preacher and staff member of the adjutant general, Jackson wrote: "In God's own time I hope that He will send an army North and crown it with victory, and make its fruits peace, but let us pray that He send it not, except he goes with it."[4]

By the end of May 1862, McClellan's moment of absolute superiority had passed. Confederate reinforcements continued to pour into Virginia, narrowing the odds between the two armies. A writer for the *Richmond Daily Dispatch* commented on May 21: "The Critical Moment. The enemy is near the city. . . . Let us bear it like a people conscious of right and relying implicitly upon that Providence which fails not in the end to secure the triumph of justice."[5]

The first "critical moment" occurred on May 31 at Seven Pines (Fair Oaks), Virginia, outside of Richmond. There, Johnston's forces were driven back toward Richmond and Johnston himself was wounded and relieved of command. Though a great general, Johnston, like Beauregard, never got along with Davis. As cadets at West Point, Davis and Johnston got into a fistfight over a belle and Davis lost. Johnston would pay a stiff price thereafter. President Davis replaced him with General Robert E. Lee, a choice that would soon mythologize the "saviour" of the newly designated "Army of Northern Virginia."

At first Lee was not a popular choice with the officers. When Lee was appointed commander of the Army of Northern Virginia, one of Jackson's aides complained that he was "slow." To this Jackson replied: "General Lee is not slow; He is cautious. He ought to be. General Lee is a phenomenon. He is the only man I would follow blind-fold."[6] For three long and bloody years, the Army of Northern Virginia—and its commander—would stand as the virtual embodiment of the Confederacy.

As Lee assumed command of Richmond's defense, McClellan added a division of McDowell's corps (previously held in reserve to protect Washington) and more confidently moved his expanded army south of the Chickahominy River. He did not realize, however, that his was not the only expanded army. By June Jackson was through the Shenandoah Valley and joined up with Lee's forces to face McClellan and the Army of the Potomac. The two created a combined force of eighty-five thousand, the largest Confederate force yet, and they were fighting in their own backyards.

With Jackson at his side, Lee wasted no time planning coordinated attacks between Jackson and his other top generals: A. P. Hill, James Longstreet, John B. Magruder, and Benjamin Huger. From June 25 to July 1, some of the greatest feint-and-maneuver movements in military history would take place. Collectively, they would become known as the "Seven Days' Battles."

In early fighting the North prevailed, but a cautious McClellan again failed to follow up on the advantage with a counterattack and instead moved his army to Harrison's Landing on the James River south of Richmond. Not only was Lee spared to fight another day, but the siege of Richmond was effectively lifted before it ever began. Seldom was defeat snatched from the jaws of victory in a more stunning fashion.

On June 27, the third of the Seven Days' Battles was fought at Gaines' Mill between Cold Harbor and Seven Pines, where the Union had set up a new defensive position. A. P. Hill led the assault followed by Longstreet, while an uncharacteristically tardy Jackson was late to the fight. The Yankees fought well. But finally, after multiple charges across rugged ravines and swamps by commander John Bell Hood's Texas brigade and George E. Pickett's Virginians, the Union line broke, leaving behind nearly three thousand Federal prisoners. Gaines' Mill marked one of the few instances in which a tactical offensive succeeded. When the armies clashed in the same locale two years later with defensive entrenchments that were far deadlier, the offensive failed miserably.

Again the costs of victory were horrendous, with the North taking sixty-eight hundred casualties and Lee sacrificing close to nine thousand. Lee's losses were steep, but the blow to Northern pride was even steeper. Insisting that he was outmanned and outgunned, McClellan withdrew his army to the James River under the rubric of a "change of base." No one in the North or South bought the rationalization, and Richmond celebrated its relief from the siege.

From his new headquarters at Harrison's Landing, McClellan prepared for yet another encounter at Malvern Hill, north of the James River.[7] In this last of the Seven Days' Battles, fought on July 1, an overconfident Lee suffered a nasty reversal. Wrongly assuming that McClellan's soldiers were as timid as McClellan, Lee again employed a tactical offensive. But this time McClellan's veteran soldiers were set up in strong defensive positions and could not wait to fight Lee. Unknowingly, Confederate General D. H. Hill initiated a suicidal frontal assault along the Willis Church Road and across open fields and a steep embankment. Union General Fitz-John Porter's well-equipped Fifth Corps—with 250 artillery pieces covering all enemy approaches—rained canister upon oncoming Confederates at point-blank range. The result, as Hill would later charge, "was not war—it was murder."[8] This would not be the last time such words were uttered.

Whether he knew the terminology or not, Hill was raising the moral issue of "proportionality" or acceptable losses among the soldiers.[9] In all wars, it is not enough merely to spare noncombatants. Strategic planners should have to weigh their own probable casualties against the gains against the enemy. But in this war, considerations of proportionality were fast becoming subordinated to blood revenge.

Meanwhile, Richmond's citizens "soldiered" on with the constant sound of cannons in their ears and accepted whatever devastations Providence exacted. As forces in the field groaned, so appetites at home grew insatiable for the shedding of more blood. The secular press in Richmond did not back down from the threat of imminent battle and local bloodshed. In an essay on "War and Peace," printed on June 26, the *Richmond Daily Dispatch* observed: "War, then, has within it seeds of good, seeds which must be fertilized by blood to bring forth a harvest of blessings. And if there ever was a war that demanded at once the energies of the patriot and the benediction of the Christian, it is a war in defense of homes and altars, of civil liberty, of social virtue, of life itself, and of all that makes life worth having."[10]

Unaware of McClellan's near paranoia, the Northern religious press continued as well to support the war effort—and McClellan's handling of it. Apparently many agreed with McClellan that he was vastly outnumbered. The *American Presbyterian* reported: "Events of a most important character have transpired during the past week in the vicinity of Richmond. A series of desperate and bloody contests, all of them of the proportions of great battles, has been fought between our forces and vastly superior numbers of the Rebels."[11]

The Seven Days' Battles settled nothing, except to set a new standard in casualties. Lee's army succeeded in temporarily driving the Federals away from Richmond at a combined cost of twenty thousand casualties to the Federals' sixteen thousand. But Lee failed to defeat McClellan. In all, the Seven Days' casualties exceeded all the battles in the western campaign, including Shiloh. From this point on, the greatest slaughters would take place under Lincoln's and Davis's noses between the Army of Northern Virginia and the Northeast-fed Army of the Potomac.

Proportionality meant nothing to the civilian audience. As with Shiloh in the West, citizens on both sides of the conflict were appalled at the level of destruction, even as they approved the destruction's moral legitimacy. Richmond's Mary Williams Taylor, daughter of the prominent Baptist minister James Barnett Taylor, kept a diary. On June 27, she recorded the anguish "this cruel war causes." Two days later she brooded: "While I am seated here in this quiet country home on this holy day, what scenes of bloodshed are being enacted near my own loved home. I shudder to think of it. . . . For three days the battle has raged. . . . O that it may be the means of driving our enemies far from us. O God spare us and save our beloved city."[12]

In the end, nothing strategic was achieved by the destructive campaign, but few were willing to speak out or question the "proportionality" of the losses and instead sat back in numbed silence. Southern cheerleaders screamed "Victory!" and Lee and Jackson began their rise to mythic glory.[13] The real lesson in these battles should have been tactical. Frontal assaults should never be undertaken when it is possible to turn the enemy's position. Strategic offensives in the face of entrenched positions and modern weaponry amount to virtual suicide. When green troops and inexperienced commanders were thrown into the mix, the futility grew exponentially. Still, nothing changed. Sadly, the adrenalized "charge" of a frontal assault was simply too intoxicating to abandon any time soon.

Suicidal or not, the military action also captured the imagination of non-combatants who were remarkably well informed about the battles. Foreign wars were often fought in a fog of home front ignorance, but Americans on both sides of this civil war knew what was happening, and often in sensationalist terms. "Yellow journalism" may have been the creation of the Gilded Age, but its roots reach back to the Civil War. Writing of the Richmond campaign, the *Philadelphia Inquirer* screamed its headline: "Scene of the Present Terrible Conflict in Front of Richmond." Then followed a series of "bullets": "Latest War News!" "Great Battle on Friday." "Evacuation of White House." "Onward to Richmond!"

On the next page, readers were provided with lists of the names of Pennsylvania soldiers killed or wounded, together with the plaintive note, "There are two here who are unable to give their names or any information respecting themselves. They will both die and remain unknown!"[14] Four days later the news continued, with "slaughter" being the favorite adjective: "The Terrific Battles in the Peninsula Great Slaughter of Rebel Soldiers!" "Arrival of Wounded and Sick Soldiers. Gloomy Day in Fredericksburg, Va."[15]

News of McClellan's retreat was greeted in Richmond with the sort of joy that comes to a people literally under siege. Confederate nationalism would come to reside in Lee's army, and, by extension, Lee himself embodied the savior, both to his own men and to the Confederacy as a whole.[16]

In an address to the Army of Northern Virginia, President Davis invoked manliness and Providence:

Soldiers: I congratulate you on the series of brilliant victories which, under the favor of Divine Providence, you have lately won. . . . Let it be your pride to relax nothing which can promote your future efficiency, your one great object being to drive the invader from your soil and carry your standards beyond the outer boundaries of the Confederacy, to wring from an unscrupulous foe the recognition of your birthright, community independence.[17]

Like so many proclamations on both sides of the conflict, references to death and suffering were absent. Instead, all was "death-defying valor." Davis left unsaid the matter of thousands who defied death—and lost.

Victory might be glorious, but the civilians in Richmond tasted battle to an unsettling degree. It should be no surprise then that they were among the first to become true believers. The themes of the jeremiad dominated local unpublished oratory as well as printed sermons and official pronouncements. Few unpublished sermons remain from the midst of war, but one remarkably complete selection survives from Richmond's Jeremiah Bell Jeter, who was pastor of the Third Baptist Church, a cofounder of the Southern Baptist Convention, a teacher at Richmond College, and a "reluctant" slave owner.

Throughout the war, Jeter preached weekly in Richmond at the Grace Street Baptist Church. At the front of his sermon booklet he wrote: "This volume of notes was prepared during the war. Many sermons I prepared during that trying period with the roar of battle in my ears."[18]

When word reached Richmond that Lee had attacked on the Peninsula and pushed McClellan's powerful army away from the city, Jeter promptly penned a thanksgiving sermon "on the occasion of the national victories." The coincidence of victory with fast was to Jeter's eye clearly causal. At first, "it was a dark day for the Confederacy." But then the Confederacy knelt in national humiliation, and in response God smiled upon His people. Apart from some naval defeats, victory occurred on almost every front. "The siege of Richmond has been raised"; the enemy was on the defensive. What meaning should be taken from this? Victories "are not to be ascribed to the number or skill of our troops—not to the superiority of our generals—but to the divine hand."[19] Like virtually all of his Northern and Southern peers, Jeter had no moral commentary on the scale of carnage. Throughout the war, this subject would remain taboo.

With commentary such as this, it is not surprising that the fast was rapidly becoming a martial totem. Through their prayers, ministers and people could share in the glory for "their" victory. Theologically, ministers agreed that fasts or thanksgivings could not magically ensure earthly triumphs. But when victories came, they simply could not resist the assumption that their piety had commended—or at least cajoled—God's orchestration of events in the field. Had a defeat followed the fast, ministers would either say nothing or complain that the people were not sufficiently sincere. In the inclusive world of the jeremiad, "incompetence" in the field was not a sufficient explanation for defeat. In this sense the home front could also share in the shame of "their" common defeat.

In the Confederacy, criticisms of Davis focused both on his strategy and initiative and on his appeals to heaven. The secular press, traditionally less than pious, openly wondered whether Davis's newfound religiosity might represent a feminizing agency that weakened his army's manhood. Already in February 1862, following the loss of Fort Donelson, the *Richmond Daily Whig* had openly questioned whether "more energetic men might not have effected far more important results."[20] War clerk John B. Jones observed, "Our army has fallen back to within four miles of Richmond. Much anxiety is felt for the fate of the city."[21] Faced with this threat and mindful of Davis's recent baptism and private confirmation at St. Paul's, the secular press questioned policies founded on piety and fasting.

President Davis knew that he depended on the churches for support. On May 3, he once again proclaimed a fast day for May 16. The tone was as somber as anything he ever wrote:

Recent disaster has spread gloom over the land, and sorrow sits at the hearthstones of our countrymen; but a people conscious of rectitude and faithfully relying on their Father in Heaven may be cast down, but cannot be dismayed. They may mourn the loss of the martyrs whose lives have been sacrificed in their defense, but they receive this dispensation of Divine Providence with humble submission and reverend faith.[22]

Davis understood the sacred language of "martyrs" and was nothing if not persistent. Barely three months earlier, the Confederacy had observed a national day of fasting for deliverance. Then came Pea Ridge, Shiloh, and Corinth. Clearly, one fast was not enough.

But this time a growing divide existed between Davis critics in some secular papers and the religious press. Where religious presses continued to endorse observance of the day and praised Davis's leadership without qualification, others demurred. The *Richmond Examiner* was especially harsh as news of one more fast reached their offices. John Moncure Daniel had had enough:

Never has any one year seen so many of these affairs. It is hoped that the latest is the last. The country has had quite enough of them. . . . In truth, these devotional proclamations of Mr. Davis have lost all good effect from their repetition, are regarded by the people as either cant or evidence of mental weakness and have become the topic of unpleasant reflection with intelligent men.

Not content to blister the fast day, Daniel went on to pillory the president: "When we find our President standing in a corner telling his beads, and relying on a miracle to save the country, instead of mounting his horse and putting forth every power of the Government to defeat the enemy, the effect is depressing in the extreme."[23]

The editorial was more than another of the *Examiner's* political attacks upon the Davis administration. It was an expression of grave misgivings about the state of the Confederacy's civil religion, and about the effect of its central ritual, the fast day, upon Southern morale. The editorial signaled the first explicit break between Richmond's pulpits and secular press over the religious meaning of the Civil War. As internal strains, mounting casualties, and battlefield defeats tore apart the superficial unity shaped by the flush of early success, the secular presses of Richmond, the news hub of the South, increasingly avoided what the *Examiner* would call the pulpit's "sanctimonious terminology" when discussing the deeper meanings of the war. Newspaper pundits attacked even the Confederacy's ritual bows to God as another failed policy of an ostentatiously religious Davis administration.

There was no question that the war was taking its toll on Confederate unanimity, which depended on victories for its united front. In time the divide between the religious and some secular newspapers (though by no means all) widened as ministers remained ever loyal to the cause and administration, while secular editors throughout the Confederacy questioned Davis and his war policy. These divisions were never strong enough utterly to defeat morale or to create a surrender mentality on a popular level, but they did signal strains in the fabric. Even as faith in fasts was challenged, and the press criticized the Davis administration, public faith in the army and its generals remained high.[24] Only time would tell how they would respond to even greater escalations of war and civilian suffering.

While no other writers assumed as caustic a stand as Daniel, a noticeable lack of enthusiasm for prayer prevailed in the secular press in 1862. In this dynamic war, attitudes would be transformed yet again in the war's last and bloodiest year. But in 1862, Southern "manliness" was preferred among some secular writers to piety. This stood in sharp contrast to the belief of the pulpit and religious press and Christian generals like Stonewall Jackson who argued just the opposite, that pious Christians made the best soldiers. Earthly confidence in armies and generals without true piety, they maintained, was a formula for disaster, and the recent defeats confirmed it. In Richmond, ministers preached to filled congregations.

The Confederate press, though willing to endorse fast days, was not as certain as pastors, presidents, and generals that fasts won battles. In a "Lay Sermon" printed in early 1862, the *Examiner* mentioned Providence, but then proceeded to dwell on the lessons of "natural philosophy." The "philosopher learns that the world is like a great mart of commerce, where Fortune exposes various commodities, some good and some bad."[25] In a portent of what was to come, the *Examiner* began to complain that after a defeat too many people imagined that "the only course left is to grovel in the dust and beg, like whipped curs, for mercy."[26] Seven months later, as yet another fast approached and ministers were trying to read the will of God in the signs of the times, the paper declared that "[w]ar is a game of chance; and in all games of chance there are unaccountable runs of good and bad luck."[27] Even more than the clergy and religious press, secular presses were miles from expecting or accepting moral accountability in any recognizable form. By their telling, blood and luck would run their course until both ran out.

In April 1862 the Presbyterian minister Robert Dabney resigned his Richmond pulpit and his professorship at Union Theological Seminary in order to accept an offer from Stonewall Jackson to serve as chief of staff of his army. Dabney's motives, unlike those of the secular press, were religious and patriotic. In a letter to the board he confessed:

> If any modern nation can possibly be placed in the situation of Judea when oppressed by Antiochus, when the Maccabees, although priests, judged it their religious duty to take up the sword, our people are now in a case equally urgent. But my main object . . . is to exercise a religious influence among my brethren and fellow-citizens now acting as defenders of our country. . . . Moreover, the most of our students of divinity are already in Gen. Jackson's army . . . I propose to set out today for his army.[28]

Dabney's forthright behavior typified the responses of many ministers, even if few enlisted for combat.

Though unable to take Richmond, General McClellan was unwilling to deviate from the limiting goals of the West Point Code, taking the moral high ground of honorable victory with minimal casualties. In a June 23 letter to his wife, Mary Ellen, written from his headquarters at Harrison's Landing, Mc-Clellan confessed: "[E]very poor fellow that is killed or wounded almost haunts me! My only consolation is that I have honestly done my best to save as many lives as possible [and] that many others might have done less towards it."[29] If John Moncure Daniel blistered President Davis for his religious softness, General McClellan condemned his commander and chief for his religious harshness. Shortly after the Seven Days' Battles, McClellan, by then well aware of Lincoln's taste for blood and the country's broad base of support for such a war, urged restraint and respect for the innocents. McClellan objected to a strategy of total war in terms of both military casualties (proportionality) and civilian suffering (discrimination).

In a letter on July 7 to Lincoln written from his headquarters at Harrison's Landing, McClellan insisted that "our cause must never be abandoned." Nevertheless, there needed to be clearly articulated rules of engagement for armies in the field because "this rebellion has assumed the character of war." This meant that the Confederates had to be treated less as criminals or rioters than as citizens and soldiers of a hostile state in which the conduct of war would be governed by the international rules of engagement.

As commander in chief, Lincoln was responsible for determining such "a civil and military policy," and, in McClellan's view, that policy should invoke the highest principles to ensure the speediest and most amiable reconciliation:

> [The war] should be conducted upon the highest principles known to Christian civilization. It should not be a war looking to the subjugation of the people of any State in any event. It should not be at all a war upon population, but against armed forces and political organization. Neither confiscation of property, political executions of persons, territorial organization of States, or forcible abolition of slavery should be contemplated for a moment. In prosecuting the war all private property and unarmed persons should be strictly protected, subject only to the necessity of military operation.

To achieve victory, McClellan urged Lincoln to appoint a commander in chief of the army and, in not very subtle terms, implied that he might be just the man. God was never far from McClellan's thoughts and he closed the letter: "I may be on the brink of eternity and as I hope for forgiveness from my maker I have written this letter with sincerity towards you and from love for my country."[30]

For all its nobility, McClellan's West Point Code did not extend to slaves. But equally tragic, few voices were willing or able to pick up McClellan's call for a war of "highest principles." When Northern Democrats echoed McClellan's theme, the bedrock of their appeal lay less in "Christian civilization" for all than in a white Christian civilization, grounded in both North and South upon the central cultural principle of white supremacy and the politics of apartheid.[31]

Two days after receiving McClellan's letter, a frustrated and disappointed Lincoln paid a personal visit to the general at his headquarters. When forced to choose between a principled war and victory, Lincoln chose victory. He removed McClellan from command, appointing Henry Halleck general in chief of the army, with headquarters in Washington. Lincoln then brought fiery General John Pope from the West to command the armies of John C. Frémont, Irvin McDowell, and Nathaniel P. Banks in the new Army of Virginia, and ordered McClellan to withdraw his army from the Peninsula and join Pope. After spending three weeks in Washington, D.C., with Lincoln and Stanton, Pope clearly understood the new course his commander wanted him to take. In a word, escalation—a war that would unavoidably carry deep into the lap of the enemy, impacting civilians as well as soldiers.

Pope immediately alienated his own troops and McClellan in an impudent address to the soldiers of the eastern army: "Let us understand each other. I have come to you from the West, where we have always seen the backs of our enemies." Having thus humiliated the eastern soldiers, he went on to describe the kind of war he favored. Not surprising for a tough talker, he chose the tactical offensive:

> I desire you to dismiss from your minds certain phrases, which I am sorry to find so much in vogue amongst you. I hear constantly of "taking strong positions and holding them. . . ." Let us discard such ideas. The strongest position a soldier should desire to occupy is one from which he can most easily advance against the enemy. . . . Let us look before us and not behind. Success and glory are in the advance, disaster and shame lurk in the rear.[32]

McClellan protested Pope's appointment in vain. In a letter to his wife on August 8, he reflected on Pope's reputation for cruelty and confided that if he were still commander, he would "give directly the reverse instructions to my army—forbid all pillaging and stealing and take the highest Christian ground for the conduct of the war—let the Govt [i.e., Lincoln] gainsay it *if they dare*."[33] McClellan was not heeded (losing generals seldom are), and "the highest Christian ground" was lost forever.

CHAPTER 15

"GOD WILLS THIS CONTEST"

The summer of 1862 would mark the end of the West Point Code. As the fact of nearly unanimous Southern belligerence became undeniable, Lincoln came to understand, in advance of most of his generals, that if his aim of preserving the Union was to be achieved, the war would have to be escalated to a total war on both citizens and soldiers. And that meant unavoidably a war that no longer exempted civilian suffering.[1] When Unionists in New Orleans protested Lincoln's war policy he replied:

> What would you do in my position? Would you drop the war where it is? Or would you prosecute it in future with elder-stalk squirts charged with rosewater? Would you deal lighter blows rather than heavier ones? Would you give up the contest, leaving any available means unapplied? I am in no boastful mood. I shall not do more than I can, and I shall do all I can, to save the government, which is my sworn duty as well as my personal inclination. I shall do nothing in malice.[2]

In the early period of the Civil War, instances existed of "hard" war, to be sure. Even assaults on innocent civilians occurred. These, as we have seen, appeared especially in the Missouri territories, where civilian bushwhackers plundered and killed at will on both sides of the conflict. But these were not officially sanctioned acts by armies in the field; they were more like mob rioters and criminals, repudiated by both Presidents Lincoln and Davis. Indeed, Federal soldiers in Missouri served, in part, specifically to stop the terrorist war on civilians.[3] No one in 1861 or 1862 could imagine that such acts of civilian barbarism would become paradigmatic for an invading army

commanded by West Point graduates and a president who began with a conciliatory strategy.[4]

President Davis faced similar challenges in the Confederacy and met
them with similar responses. Wherever he could wage a total war he would,
and he too would leave no card unplayed, including, most ominously, guerrilla warfare in the event his armies were defeated. Earlier than Lincoln's proclamation of September 24, he suspended writs of habeas corpus. And, like
Lincoln, his actions met with strident opposition in state governments. But
he, like Lincoln, recognized that the cause required draconian measures.[5]

Sadly for Davis, he was in no position to mount a hard overland campaign
into the North. By spring 1862, with crushing defeats at Forts Henry and
Donelson, Pea Ridge, Shiloh, Corinth, New Orleans, and Memphis, he was
approaching a physical and mental breakdown. More bad news came from
the newly created Trans-Mississippi Department, where his new commander,
Major General Thomas C. Hindman, abruptly declared martial law, alienating
the local population and his own officers. On top of everything else, Davis's
poor judgment of men came to the fore when he replaced Hindman and appointed Theophilus H. Holmes, his incompetent friend and West Point
classmate, as the new commander of the Trans-Mississippi Department.[6]

Faced with his own embarrassing defeats and unimaginable losses at
First Bull Run, Shiloh, and the Seven Days', Lincoln and his Northern commanders came to the shared understanding that limited war would not work.
With reluctance, but before most others, Lincoln abandoned his earlier presumption of a strong corps of nonslaveholding, small yeomen Unionists in
the Confederacy. Like it or not, the Confederacy looked like a nation,
thought like a nation, and fought like a nation. Lincoln could call them
"rebels" as much as he wanted (and he never thought about them in any
other terms), but nothing short of total war could break their will to fight and
coerce them back into an abolitionist Union they despised.[7]

Total war meant a war that would put civilians immediately at risk. Total
war to transform society meant conquest and occupation by a president who,
in 1848, had vigorously protested the Mexican War because, in his own
words, it was a "war of conquest" that "places our President where kings have
always stood."[8] A mere fourteen years later, Lincoln was placing himself in a
similar position for a different cause.

The conventional dating of the beginning of total war is usually marked by
President Lincoln's appointment of General Grant as commander of the Federal armies, and the subsequent appointments of Sherman and Philip Sheridan to key commands in 1864. The decision itself actually came earlier, in

July and August 1862, at the same time Lincoln was drafting his Emancipation Proclamation. It was made not by commanding generals, but by their commander in chief, President Lincoln.

In his brief tenure as commander of the Army of the Potomac, Major General John Pope, with Lincoln's approval, passed general orders directing the Army of the Potomac to live off the land (General Orders No. 5) and requiring that "all villages and neighborhoods through which they pass will be laid under contribution."[9] Lincoln allowed his military champion a free hand to wage war. Between July 18 and 23, 1862, Pope ordered the punishment of civilians—including the destruction of their homes and the forced payment of indemnities—living in areas where his army suffered the effects of guerrilla warfare or sabotage. Since any citizen *could* be a guerrilla, the Union army effectively carried a blank check to deal with civilians as they pleased, short of rape or murder.

The effects of Pope's orders were predictable. Soldiers on both sides and civilians in occupied areas reported widespread marauding and cruel destruction. No one was immune from Pope's concept of total war. Writing from Corinth, Mississippi, where he was stationed with the Ninth Brigade, Twelfth Illinois, Private A. W. Bill described the new license afforded by General Orders No. 5:

> All the soldiers are rejoiced at the new orders that are being issued [and] every day they all want to go forward and burn and destroy all rebel property and kill every [rebel] we meet till the rebellion is crushed we have got entirely out of patience with the way the rebels have been treated heretofore instead of being treated like enemys they have been treated as if they were the best friends the government had . . . [the soldiers] hail with joy the late orders concerning rebel property and we all hope to close the war before June.[10]

In New Orleans General Benjamin Butler, the Federal military governor, ruled the city with an iron fist that gave no succor to civilians and earned him the sobriquet "Beast" Butler. Already an incompetent (political) general who lost battles, he knew how to alienate. In May 1862 Butler had issued an order that any woman caught insulting Northern soldiers "shall be regarded and held liable to be treated as a woman of the town plying her avocation." Butler later had a civilian named William B. Mumford publicly hanged for pulling down a United States flag.

In response, an outraged President Davis issued a general order declaring "the said Benjamin F. Butler to be a felon deserving of capital punishment. . . .

I do order that he be . . . considered . . . an outlaw and common enemy of mankind, and that in the event of his capture the officer in command of the capturing force do cause him to be immediately executed by hanging." Beyond Butler, Davis also declared all commissioned officers in Butler's command outlaws and "criminals deserving death, and that they and each of them be, whenever captured, reserved for execution."[11] Predictably, Davis's General Order did little more than render Butler a hero in the North.

Few Republicans or soldiers objected to the new rules of war. But some voices were heard. C. C. Coffin, a correspondent for the *Boston Journal*, wrote a letter to Governor John A. Andrew of Massachusetts from Hilton Head, South Carolina, marked "private and confidential." In it he wrote: "I am sorry to say that the Mass. 24th has been acting outrageously here, robbing, burning houses, killing cattle, etc.—ravishing negro women—beating their husbands who attempted protection."[12]

The Union chaplain William Scandlin made known his objections to the new war. Scandlin would be captured at Gettysburg and spend several months in Richmond's Libby Prison, where he would condemn Confederate mistreatment of prisoners of war. But in 1862, he concerned himself with his own soldiers' conduct.

In an unpublished sermon delivered in the field at Camp Charlestown, Virginia, Scandlin used John 21:22 to confirm the moral call of a higher law than military orders and condemn what he termed the "apparent sanction" of Pope's general order to plunder and destroy civilian property: Even if other soldiers "trample upon human rights and . . . the sacred sanctity of other homes, what is that to thee? Follow thou me." The present behavior of Union troops was unjust:

> Glance with me over the history of our forces in this vicinity for the past week. 1 the shelter of home no protection 2 private property ruthlessly plundered 3 churches used for stables and dwellings. And some of you had a part in our portion of this evil guilty of what I blush to think of. Think of our feelings when we read the history of the British action in Boston. We are doing the same for others to read. . . . Men of New England as you respect yourselves and have the culture and affection of our dear old Commonwealth discountenance and condemn all such action. Remember that the evil course of this is nothing to them and that trampling upon the laws of honesty and right to uphold the authority of the nation is a complete burlesque. Leave all who have rebelled to the laws they have violated and follow thou Christ.[13]

Such words undoubtedly did not endear Scandlin to officers and soldiers bent on destruction, but they do confirm that moral conscience was not wholly absent. That confirmation condemns the conduct of the majority who celebrated the new policy. For most, no moral restraints remained short of murder. The midwestern *Christian Instructor and Western United Presbyterian* recognized that "the people are becoming somewhat restive, thoroughly roused, and in certain quarters a little desperate, and are demanding of the Administration to do what it has to do quickly."[14] The Northern press greeted the general orders with glee and headlines celebrating, "The Kid Glove Policy Abandoned."[15]

Pope issued the orders, but it is clear that he himself was under orders. Lincoln willingly sacrificed traditional moral restraints to strike fear in the heart of the enemy and to protect his soldiers from hostile civilians and guerrillas. General Halleck disagreed with the severity of Pope's new policy, but he did not protest because he knew it had the president's approval. In fact, Lincoln followed up Pope's orders with an executive order of his own permitting commanders to seize or destroy civilian property as long as such activity was not wanton or malicious. Lincoln issued the executive order the same day in July that he read his preliminary Emancipation Proclamation draft to his cabinet. The coupling of orders on the same day perfectly symbolized the conjunction of emancipation and total war in Lincoln's mind.[16]

However necessary the removal of McClellan to achieve Lincoln's war objectives, the appointment of Pope proved to be a disastrous miscalculation. Lincoln liked the confident and aggressive swagger of Pope's language in the West and in his testimony before the Committee on the Conduct of the War. There, Pope openly disparaged the West Point Code and bragged that he would win if granted the license to promote a total war. But Lincoln knew nothing of Pope's tactical skills or his capacity to command and coordinate a large and complex army in the field—particularly when that army faced the strategy of Lee and the tactics of Jackson.

To his dismay, Lincoln soon learned that tough rhetoric alone could not produce victories. In a remarkably short period, Pope revealed his rank incompetence. Lee and Jackson had no more respect for Pope than they had had for McClellan. Indeed, Pope's insistence that Southern civilians would feel the cold hand of war so infuriated Lee that he referred to Pope in uncharacteristically demeaning terms as "that miscreant."

Operating in familiar terrain around Richmond, Lee and Jackson imaginatively employed risky flanking movements to achieve complete surprise and victory over Pope's numerically superior Union forces. Every time Pope moved to shift his armies, Lee and Jackson anticipated him and confidently divided their army, allowing Jackson the advantage of surprise behind enemy lines. With the intelligence support of Jeb Stuart's cavalry, Jackson knew Pope's every move and was able to rejoin forces with Lee before a punch-drunk Pope could recover and smash Lee's undermanned and divided positions.

Despite glaring weaknesses in Northern command, the Yankee soldiers continued to remain confident in their superiority. On August 27 a cocky Private Dickinson wrote to his brother: "I do not believe any danger is to be apprehended from the Rebs being [that we are] in superior numbers." But just in case, "this letter will be put in the hands of one of our band who are going home. Give my love to all, your affectionate brother, Fred."[17]

Two days later, Dickinson was killed in yet another Union fiasco in the battle of Second Bull Run, fought on August 29 and 30. With McClellan rushing reinforcements to Pope, and with Pope's army already outnumbering Lee seventy-five thousand to fifty-five thousand, Lee launched the bold (and highly risky) tactic of dividing his smaller army between Longstreet's thirty thousand soldiers west of the Bull Run Mountains and Jackson's twenty-four thousand soldiers at Manassas. Between these contingents stood Pope's massive army. Had Pope known of Lee's strategy, he could easily have smashed each wing of Lee's army in succession, leaving Lee utterly destroyed and Richmond within Pope's grasp. But Lee appropriately counted on Pope's indecision and made up in speed and effective command what he lacked in concentrated forces to achieve victory.

In all, Pope suffered 16,000 casualties to 9,100 for the South. He lost as well two of his best commanders—Isaac Stevens (in line to become the next commander of the Army of the Potomac) and Philip Kearny.[18] The reversal of fortunes had an electric effect on the Confederacy. For President Davis, the victory confirmed his confidence in Lee, even at the risk of leaving Richmond temporarily unprotected. Instead of standing at the gates of Richmond, the Army of the Potomac lay in rout, and Lee stood poised to invade Maryland and even the capital.

Despite the victory, many in Richmond mourned the heavy casualties the city's defense exacted. Churches witnessed countless rituals of funeral sermons, celebrating the heroism of fallen members and hoping their destination was heaven.

In a funeral sermon for Roswell Lindsey, recorded in his private sermon notebook, Jeremiah Bell Jeter grieved with the parents and then praised the son's patriotism: "[He] was a brave soldier beloved by his comrades . . . and his body sleeps on the gory field. He died at the post of duty—offered his life on the altar of his Country—and there is hope concerning his future estate."[19]

In Savannah the Methodist pastor George G. N. MacDonell memorialized two members of his congregation who fell in battle "near Richmond." One eulogy, for Captain Jonathan Ethridge, delivered on June 8, took for its text Revelation 21:3–4 and developed the doctrine that "[m]an [is] subject to the laws of suffering and death." A month later, in a sermon for the Reverend Robert Jones, MacDonell delivered a gentler sermon on the same text, this time with the doctrine "no death in heaven."[20]

In New York the religious press issued a rare denigration of Lincoln following Second Bull Run when "the sun seems to rise and set in blood." In the end, they would counsel loyalty, but not veneration:

> A year and a half of very difficult administration has shown our President to be a plain, good man, honest in heart, pure in intention, but certainly *not* those rare geniuses, who are born to "ride in the whirlwind and direct the storm." We have taken a plain country lawyer out of his village and placed him at the head of the Government, and imagined him to be a great man, and because he does not quite measure to the character, were ready to censure and complain. Might we not rather reprove ourselves for our unreasonable expectations?[21]

The secular press paid less attention to Lincoln and more to sensational headlines. On August 18, 1862, the *Philadelphia Inquirer* front page included: "News of the Repulse of Breckinridge at Baton Rouge," "Gen. Williams' Head Shot Off by a Cannon Ball," "The Recent Demonstrations of the Negroes," and "Outrages of the Guerrillas along the Mississippi." In contrast to the religious press, the *Inquirer* had far less sympathy with the plight of the slaves and instead denigrated the "poor deluded creatures" who thought that invading Yankees would bring them their freedom.[22]

A deeply frustrated Lincoln questioned himself and turned for direction to his God. Like Davis, Lincoln was becoming steadily more spiritual, although without compromising his unshaken resolve. Along with spirituality came a sort of mystical fatalism. Increasingly he sensed that something more than a mere civil war was going on in this conflict, and that it transcended the rightness or wrongness of either side. Northern clergy and opinion shapers might be certain that God was on their side, but Lincoln, almost alone, was not convinced. He too had a growing sense of Providence, but without the self-righteous evangelical piety that went along with so much patriotism in the North and the South.

In a moment of disturbed meditation, he reflected on just whose side God was really on:

The will of God prevails. In great contests each party claims to act in accordance with the will of God. Both *may* be, and one *must* be wrong. God can not be *for* and *against* the same thing at the same time. In the present civil war it is quite possible that God's purpose is something different from the purpose of either party—and yet the human instrumentalities, working just as they do, are of the best adaptation to effect this purpose. I am almost ready to say this is probably true—that God wills this contest, and wills that it shall not end yet. By His mere great power on the minds of the now contestants, He could have either saved or destroyed the Union without a human contest. Yet the contest began. And having begun, He could give the final victory to either side any day. Yet the contest proceeds.[23]

Here we see the first premonitions of a sense of destiny that would lift Lincoln above the rank partisanship of virtually everyone else. It could allow him to glimpse a divine purpose to the war that transcended section and ultimately helped him escape the rhetorical cage of the jeremiad. In life, this provided for Lincoln a Christlike compassion for his foes; in death, it would render him a Christlike messiah for the reconstituted American nation.

Lincoln was unusual in questioning the ironclad logic of the jeremiad that promised success, but he was not alone. Princeton's Charles Hodge came to a similar conclusion, and called into question the entire moral logic of the jeremiad: "The distribution of good and evil in this world to individuals, churches, or nations is not determined by the principles of justice, but according to the wise and benevolent sovereignty of God . . . the orderings of his providence are not determined by justice, but by mysterious wisdom for the accomplishment of higher ends than mere punishment or reward."[24]

But the Lincolns and Hodges were lone wolves. Most clergy embraced the contractual logic of the jeremiad and sought in it formulae for victories. In casting about for explanations of why victories were not forthcoming, abolitionist clergy saw in slavery the hidden cause of defeat. In a sermon delivered to the First Congregational Church of Leavenworth, Kansas, James D. Liggett used the case of the ten tribes of Israel to underscore the point that defeat did not mean that God's "favor is even temporarily with his enemies, and against his own people." What then did God intend? In a word, Liggett asserted, God wanted the Civil War to become an abolition war, and only then would victory be granted to the North:

The question is now, whatever it may have been twelve months ago, no such thing as "the restoration of the Union as it was." Let that most stupid and transparent of all fallacies . . . be abandoned. Let us break away from the fallacies and prejudices of the past . . . and in manly strength grapple with the living issue of the agonizing Present. That issue is Liberty or Slavery. The rebels have resolved to destroy the nation that they may establish Slavery. Shall we hesitate to destroy Slavery that we may preserve the nation?[25]

Other less abolitionist preachers explained defeats with reference to the traditional jeremiad sins of pride, materialism, profanity, and Sabbath-breaking. Added to these universal sins were others peculiar to the North. Again the question of God in the Constitution was raised as a sort of mantra. For Philadelphia's Henry Boardman:

There is one feature of our government too closely connected with this question [of defeat], and too conspicuous, to be passed by in silence. I refer, as you will readily suppose—for the topic is a familiar one—to the absence of any adequate recognition of the sovereignty of God, and the religion of which he is the author and object, in our Constitution. . . . Our national charter pays no homage to the Deity.

As if the constitutional oversight were not enough, Boardman also divined that God was angry because He was missing from the coinage of the nation. This absence, Boardman insisted, "is not a trivial matter . . . [for] the entire absence of all such emblems and legends from the coins of a nominally Christian nation, must be taken to indicate as much a want of reverence for the Deity, as a want of respect for the common religious sentiment of mankind."[26]

On September 4, a triumphant President Davis proclaimed a national thanksgiving day for September 18. The fast days had done their job and now the time had arrived for measured thanksgiving: "Once more upon the plains of Manassas have our armies been blessed by the Lord of Hosts with a triumph over our enemies. It is my privilege to invite you once more to his footstool, not now in the garb of fasting and sorrow, but with joy and gladness, to render thanks for the great mercies received at his hand."[27]

This time, with victories to count, the secular press was more willing to concede efficacy to religious observances. The *Richmond Daily Whig* enjoined all to observe the occasion: "To-day all the people of our fair land, which He has given us for a heritage should approach His footstool with joy and thanksgiving, and pour forth their hearts in praise and gratitude to Him who hath given us the victory."[28]

Richmond's Jeremiah Bell Jeter celebrated the thanksgiving with an unpublished sermon on "The National Victories." His text, from Psalm 126:3 ("The Lord hath done great things for us"), yielded a classic jeremiad. In developing the parallel between ancient Israel and God's new Confederate Israel, Jeter explained that both had experienced crushing defeats, but then turned to their covenant God and were delivered: "The Jews rejoyced in their restoration to their own land and well they might. Have we not cause to rejoice in our deliverance?" The recent victories around Richmond confirmed God's presence with the Confederacy:

> The enemy has been defeated in a succession of battles—the siege of Richmond has been raised—the foe has been almost entirely driven from Confederate soil—is dispirited—demoralized. Fleeing. Thousands of them have been slain or taken prisoners. In every conflict, apart from the gunboats, they have been beaten. Meanwhile our victorious armies have pushed forward their successes, invading territory that heretofore [lay] in the undisputed possession of the enemy. Truly our deliverances have been wonderful.[29]

Of the many published sermons following the September thanksgiving, one delivered by Henry Allen Tupper, pastor of the Baptist Church in Washington, Georgia, stands out. Tupper had the distinction of also serving as a chaplain of the Ninth Georgia regiment and delivered a sermon to his home congregation. His text, from Psalm 124 ("the snare is broken") had been a highly favored scripture during the American Revolution. From start to finish, Tupper's sermon offered a vitriolic attack on the "Northern rapacity," as only a chaplain involved in combat could produce. If the South had its "peculiar institution," Tupper countered, the North had its "peculiar sentiment"—a sentiment so hateful to Southern sensibilities and life that nothing short of "monstrous barbarities" against the South can satisfy its bloodlust. In response to this apostasy, God blessed the South with "many providences," so that "since our escape, how merciful has God been to us, as a Government, a people, and an army!"

By locating the Southern struggle in the American Revolution and invoking its rhetoric, sermons like Tupper's grafted the short history of the Confederacy onto the long history of the American Revolution and, through that, to ancient Israel. On that rhetorical foundation, Tupper could conclude with a confident benediction: "Oh God, look down upon our bleeding country— hear the cries of our distracted mother—and arm her sons with hearts of fire, and sinews of steel, and let future ages know, in our rescue from the jaws of ruin, the glory of thy mercy, and the terribleness of thy wrath."[30] In September 1862 Tupper had confidence that just as Americans looked back to the

Revolution for present history and comfort, so "future ages" would look back on these revolutionary years as the beginning of a very old and distinguished history.[31]

Meanwhile, in the Confederacy, President Davis passed the Second Conscription Act on September 27, authorizing the government to call out men between thirty-five and forty-five years of age. A million soldiers in arms was clearly not enough. Total war meant entirely new proportions of soldiers, which meant disproportionate carnage. By the end of the year, soldiers in uniform would number 918,121 for the North and 446,662 for the South, for a total of nearly 1.4 million men.[32] With ever-increasing levies, and no end in sight, there was no room to think of exits or peace. It was a fight to the death and at the end only one would prevail.

CHAPTER 16

ANTIETAM: "THE HORRORS OF A BATTLEFIELD"

Pope had to go. But Lincoln saw no clear successors. Where were his Lee and Jackson? At the moment, and unbeknownst to Lincoln, Grant and Sherman were in the western theater. But in the all-important East, with no obvious candidate in view, Lincoln went back to the soldiers' choice and reinstated the popular McClellan. One soldier's song captured the respect the general still commanded with the soldiers:

> Give us back our old Commander, Little Mac, the people's pride,
> Let the army and the nation, In their choice be satisfied.
> With McClellan as our leader, Let us strike the blow anew,
> Give us back our old Commander, He will see the battle through.[1]

McClellan returned to a hero's welcome among the soldiers of the Army of the Potomac, but no one was more pleased than Robert E. Lee, who was presently entertaining thoughts of bringing Maryland into the Confederacy, and from there moving north to Washington. With McClellan effectively immobilized Lee would be free to maneuver at will and offset numerical shortcomings to his advantage.

By fall Lee had Davis's complete trust and proceeded virtually unchecked. On September 5, 1862, Lee pressed the offensive, crossing the Potomac near Leesburg and occupying the town of Frederick, Maryland, two days later. This represented the first Confederate invasion of the North, and hysterical officials and journalists feared for Baltimore and Washington. Even Philadelphia was not considered safe before the menace of Lee's bold tactics, Stonewall Jackson's mysterious wanderings, and a flashy cavalry led by Jeb Stuart.

To secure his line of communications as he headed north, Lee again divided his army and sent Jackson's six divisions to capture Harpers Ferry and secure supply lines to the Shenandoah Valley. Again, Lee's gamble paid off. On September 15, Jackson captured Harpers Ferry, taking with him an astounding eleven thousand prisoners. Meanwhile McClellan's massive army of nearly ninety thousand remained safely and predictably cautious before Lee's nineteen thousand effectives.

In what would stand as one of the most colossal overlooked intelligence finds of the war, Union Corporal Barton W. Mitchell discovered a copy of Lee's orders wrapped around three cigars. "The Lost Order of Antietam" plainly showed how precariously Lee's army was divided into four parts—McClellan's army was actually closer to each Confederate wing than the wings were to one another.

Had McClellan acted decisively on this intelligence, he could easily have destroyed the Army of Northern Virginia in detail, by first smashing Lee's army with overwhelming force and then turning on Jackson with similar results. In yet another instance of pathological caution, however, McClellan divined that the intercepted order must be a ruse planted by Lee to trap McClellan's outnumbered army, so he held back for eighteen critical hours.[2] Such are the contingencies of war, that with that fatal miscalculation, the moment to crush the Army of Northern Virginia, and quite probably the Confederacy with it, passed.

But a battle still remained to be fought. Lee's newly combined force of forty thousand stood before an Army of the Potomac almost twice its size. But Lee had long since learned that raw numbers did not win battles—at least not in 1862—and decided to take his stand. Lee did not hesitate to divide his army and dramatically increase his hitting power. Of course the risks were enormous. If the Yankees ever had an inkling of a divided army, they would simply mass on one side and destroy it in force, then turn on the other and complete the destruction of Lee's army. But that would require superior intelligence, and in the early years the Confederates—particularly Jeb Stuart's cavalry—had the advantage. Lee knew exactly how strung out the Federals were and therefore where they were most vulnerable to flanking movements. With the Army of Northern Virginia reunited, the stage was set for the most horrific battle yet fought in the Civil War, and the single bloodiest day in American history.[3]

At daybreak on September 17, 1862, before the morning mist had burned away, Federal General Joseph Hooker's First Corps engaged Stonewall Jackson's seventy-seven hundred men in Miller's cornfield along the Hagerstown Pike toward Dunkard Church. At the same time, Union General Edwin

The "Sunken Road" at Antietam. This photographic print on stereo card reveals the horror of the Civil War in a way that no other medium could convey to contemporary viewers. The Antietam photographs taken by Alexander Gardner and James Gibson were exhibited a month later at Mathew Brady's studio in New York City.

Sumner led five thousand men of General John Sedgwick's division of Second Corps directly into a well-placed ambush by Confederate troops at West Woods just north of Dunkard Church. In twenty minutes, 40 percent of Sumner's division was lost. Included among the wounded was Oliver Wendell Holmes Jr., who had been shot through the throat and left for dead.

Soon fighting broke out among other units, rapidly intensifying the engagement to the level of a battle. Battles, unlike skirmishes, involved units of tens of thousands rather than thousands. This meant, necessarily, casualties in tens of thousands rather than thousands. Rare was the commander who could simultaneously envision and assess fights across multiple fronts—each of which would have constituted a full-fledged battle a year earlier—and calmly deploy his legions. At Antietam, Northern commanders once again proved that they lacked that imperturbable vision.

Still the battle roared. Another battle raged just south of West Woods along a wagon-rutted old road known as Sunken Lane, but forever after remembered as Bloody Lane. There, two of Sumner's divisions had marched south to attack Lee's center. The rebels set their defensives in the hollow of the sunken lane where they were virtually impregnable. Wave after wave of General O. O. Howard's famed Irish Brigade sought to breach the lines, leaving behind what the historian James McPherson describes as "a carpet of blue-clad corpses strewn across the fields northeast of the sunken road and a carpet of butternut and gray-clad corpses in the appropriately named Blood Lane."[4] Before the fighting around the road concluded, three thousand

Union soldiers and twenty-five hundred Confederate soldiers lay stacked in rows, dead or waiting to die.

Despite heavy losses, McClellan's brave infantry continued to pound Confederate positions furiously, and by midafternoon were well on their way to winning a battle of annihilation that could end the war. But as the critical moment to throw all into the wager arrived, McClellan once again lost his nerve, holding back nearly two full corps of reserves—over twenty thousand men—for fear of a Confederate counterattack.

One member of McClellan's reserve force was Sergeant Major Charles Ward of the Thirty-second Massachusetts Volunteers. In a letter to his brother, written under live fire while the battle was raging, he described the frustration of hearing shattering gunfire, with needy comrades gone before, and simply jotting letters and "waiting for our time."[5] Ward was not alone in his frustration. When informed of McClellan's timidity, Lincoln reportedly remarked: "He is an admirable engineer, but he seems to have a special talent for a stationary engine."[6]

By midafternoon, Union General Ambrose Burnside finally crossed Antietam Creek over a stone bridge that has since borne his name and threatened to overwhelm Lee's right flank. All appeared lost for the Southern contingent until, at the last moment, A. P. Hill's division reached the battlefield from Harpers Ferry. Though exhausted by the forced march, Hill's soldiers delivered a crushing counterattack that caught Burnside totally by surprise and saved the Army of Northern Virginia.

With no conclusive victory, Lee withdrew his army to Virginia, believing that he could yet strike Northern targets and terrify Northerners as far north as Philadelphia. In his wake, he left behind the worst wreckage of human lives in one day that America would ever see. Antietam implicitly rewrote the rules for acceptable losses in war, and no one protested. Twelve thousand four hundred Federals were killed and wounded alongside 11,724 Confederates for a total of 24,000 casualties in little more than twelve hours.[7]

Immediately after the battle, a writer for the *Philadelphia Inquirer* described rebel dead in characteristically lurid detail:

So sultry had been the atmosphere that decomposition had been making rapid progress. All countenances had swollen beyond point of possible recognition. Features had become one dark purplish mass of putridity. . . . Here lay a Rebel, still living, with introverted eye, but with warm, pulsating heart. His brain was oozing slowly, by a disgorging process, from a bullet hole on either side of the head.[8]

Though sensational, the *Inquirer's* account was not fictitious. Two weeks after the fighting, Union Private Franklin Bullard was still in shock at the enormity of the collision. In a letter to his aunt he recounted his experience:

Now about the fight which occurred the 17 day of September 1862 which will be put down in history as the bloodiest battle of the war. Where thousands yielded up their lives to his holy cause. My wound was slight. I was in the hospital 2 days and then rejoined my reg I was lame for several days after a piece of shell struck me in the thigh. But thank god I am now safe and well. How I escaped the many bullets that showerd down upon me god only knows the bullets came a whining by my face and cutting down right and left poor fellows following thick and fast around me. You cannot realize the horrors of a battle field to see the dead and wounded some with arms and legs off and cut up in every shape. It is awful the 15th reg is now a mere corporals guard to what it was before the fight.[9]

For surgeon Daniel Holt of the 121st New York Volunteers, the aftermath was equally grim as he prepared bodies for burial. In a letter to his wife he described the scene:

I have seen, stretched along, in one straight line, ready for interment, at least a thousand blackened, bloated corpses with blood and gas protruding from every orifice, and maggots holding high carnival over their heads. Every house, for miles around, is a hospital and I have seen arms, legs, feet and hands lying in piles rotting in the blazing heat of a Southern sky unburied and uncared for, and still the knife went steadily in its work adding to the putrid mess.

Largely because of McClellan's failure to bring up his fresh reserves, neither side could claim victory in tactical terms. Five Federal drives were repulsed at horrendous costs, with no victorious outcome. Bitterly disappointed, Holt wrote to his wife: "I am loosing [sic] all confidence and respect for McClellan—a man who a year ago I verily believed to be an agent of God to put down the rebellion. . . . Well, I only feel sad and disgusted, and not only I but almost the entire army, for we all believed that we had the rebels in the tightest spot they ever were."[10] Holt might have been a surgeon, but his military assessment was correct.

In terms of morale, Lee's audacity stood as the antithesis of McClellan's caution. President Davis praised the Army of Northern Virginia for heroic deeds "which have covered our flag with imperishable fame." But in strategic terms, Antietam represented a stunning Northern achievement, in spite of the North's ineffective command. By forcing Lee to retreat south, the Union ensured that Virginia, and not Maryland or Washington, would remain the center of war in the eastern theater. Just as portentously, the retreat from Antietam meant that European nation-states would not rush to recognize the Confederacy. Most historians agree that Antietam was not only the bloodiest single day in American history but also the single most significant battle in the Civil War.

In the West, meanwhile, General Sherman was learning his second lesson—to abandon the West Point Code and take the war to civilians. In October 1862, while on duty in Memphis, Tennessee, Sherman sustained a series of guerrilla attacks on his gunboats. In retaliation, he destroyed the town of Randolph, Tennessee, and issued orders to expel ten families for every boat fired upon. When the next attack came, Sherman immediately expelled ten of the city's residents and destroyed all houses, farms, and crops along a fifteen-mile stretch of the Mississippi south of Memphis. When a Memphis woman objected, Sherman replied that God Himself had destroyed entire populations for far lesser crimes. Until Confederate leaders returned to their true faith, he declared, the destruction would continue. Then, ominously, he added that she (and he) were seeing "how rapidly war corrupts the best feelings of the human heart."[11]

CHAPTER 17

"BROKEN HEARTS CANNOT BE PHOTOGRAPHED"

Besides being the bloodiest battle of the Civil War, Antietam also represented the first widely photographed in American history.[1] The major catalysts in bringing photography to the battlefield would be the well-established New Yorker Mathew Brady and his younger Scottish partner, Alexander Gardner. They were joined initially by perhaps two hundred other photographers, mostly in the North. Having already achieved fame as "Lincoln's Photographer," Brady saw with the onset of war the potential to record history in the making.

Prior to the Civil War, no one thought of photography as a form of outdoor journalism but rather as an indoor medium for portraiture. Photographic portraits imitated the painter's canvas and tended to romanticize subjects in the same way that painted portraits did. With the onset of war, soldiers of all ranks flocked to studios to have their portraits shot. With sidearm usually included, the poses were heroic and the visages clean—literally pictures of confidence and resolve. Portraits of generals and statesman also sold well and frequently appeared in woodcut reproductions in magazines and newspapers. When Gardner joined Brady, their portrait business boomed. Gardner ran a second studio in Washington and introduced Brady to the enlargement process. With the war's commencement, the two soon made a fortune selling "Imperial Photographs" for as much as seven hundred dollars apiece.[2]

But if portraits provided Brady an income, the battlefields called to his muse and imbued him with a self-proclaimed destiny. That destiny would, in the end, bankrupt him, even while it brought him immortality. Brady saw earlier than most how the camera could offer at least an indirect sense of action: "I know well enough that I cannot take a photograph of a battle, but I can get a little glimpse of some corner somewhere that will be worth while. We are making history now, and every picture that we get will be valuable."[3]

Mathew Brady's portable lab in front of the trenches at Petersburg, Virginia. By 1864 Brady had battlefield photography down to a science.

Through 1861 and to the spring of 1862, Brady trained and outfitted twenty assistants. These trainees were eventually assigned to thirty-five theaters of the war and prepared "Brady" photographs wherever the war erupted. To each operative, Brady assigned a horse and wagon, which amounted to a movable darkroom. Though the most famous, Brady and Gardner were hardly alone as field photographers. By the war's close, at least fifteen hundred photographers worked the war as field agents or portrait makers, generating well over a million images, the vast majority of which were portraits of soldiers. Hundreds of thousands survive to the present, making the pictures proprietors of the face of civil war in American memory.

As long as Gardner worked for Brady, his photographs, like every other Brady employee's, were identified as taken by Mathew Brady. In fact, however, it was Gardner and his assistant, James Gibson, who rushed to Antietam the day after the battle in time to catch the carnage before the burials were complete. Gardner took the camera from the wagon and then removed the cap from the lens, all the while surveying the gruesome scenes to fix in collodion.

Using a wet-plate process that would take ten minutes to print and ten minutes to develop into negatives, Gardner managed to produce seventy images in four days. The herculean effort included fifty-five stereo negatives, or stereoviews, and eight large eight-by-ten-inch plates.[4] With Lee moving the Army of Northern Virginia back to Virginia, most of the still-unburied bodies that Gardner was able to photograph were Confederates. Arguably, even if Yankee bodies were available, he would have less interest in "shooting" them for fear of censorship and the dampening effect such images might have on Northern morale.

Mathew Brady's new photographic gallery at the corner of Fulton and Broadway in New York City. Thousands of horrified viewers lined up in 1862 to view Brady's exhibition "The Dead of Antietam."

Contrary to most modern presumptions, Civil War photographs were not reproduced in the penny press. But, though unable to reproduce Gardner's photographs in the press as news, or what we would call photojournalism, Brady and Gardner could mount exhibits of the images at their studios in New York and Washington.

Gardner first exhibited "The Dead of Antietam" at Brady's gallery in New York one month after the battle. Viewers lined up on the streets of New York and pressed up against the gallery windows to stare. For the most part, the viewers were limited to New Yorkers and Washington residents—significant in numbers to be sure, but still only a small slice of the American people. Ordinary people on farms throughout the Midwest and South would not have had access. Nor would soldiers in the field.

All who witnessed the exhibits left profoundly moved. These pictures captured what no other art form could: the individual soldier at war. Warrior generals might have battles named after them, but at their most elemental, wars are about individuals locked in mortal combat with other individuals. One lives to fight again, another does not. Throughout this civil war, killing remained up close and personal, and nothing could capture the horror of tens of thousands of individual dances with death like photographs of the dead.

The photographs gave the public their first look at war—and their *reactions* became news as reporters struggled to describe to the absent nation the simultaneous allure and horror that drew crowds to the viewing. For a public accustomed to romantic sketches and bloodless victories the sight could be profoundly unsettling. Viewers saw bloated bodies with missing limbs and bodies contorted in frozen distension, eyes overly wide open and mouths puckered out. Dead horses lay everywhere.

For Oliver Wendell Holmes Sr., who had been at the battlefield searching for his wounded son, the sight of Gardner's photographs stirred painful memories. "It was so nearly like visiting the battlefield to look over these views," he wrote, "that all emotions excited by the actual sight of the stained and sordid scene . . . come back to us. We buried them in the recess of our cabinet as we would have buried the mutilated remains of the dead they too vividly represented."[5]

Never again in the Civil War would photographs of the battlefield dead have the shocking power that those of Antietam brought. The reason had less to do with the fact that Antietam was America's costliest single day of war than because it was the first to be widely photographed. A writer for the *New York Times* caught the pathos of the moment well as he walked by the studio and reflected on the long lines one late October day:

[T]he dead of the battle-field come up to us very rarely, even in dreams. We see the list in the morning paper at breakfast, but dismiss its recollection with the coffee. There is a confused mass of names, but they are all strangers; we forget the horrible significance that dwells amid the jumble of type. . . . Mr. Brady has done something to bring home to us the terrible reality and earnestness of war. If he has not brought bodies and laid them in our door-yards and along streets, he has done something very like it.[6]

"Something very like" was still an imperfect representation of real battle. Although employing relatively new technology, photographers nevertheless remained artists, and photography an art form. The images and objects it captured were necessarily filtered through the eye of the artist-photographer. This meant that photography, no less than the more inexact arts, could be vulnerable to ideology—and distortion. The same prescient reporter went on in his account to point to the limits of art—even photographic art: "[There is] one phase that has escaped photographic skill. It is the background of widows and orphans, torn from the bosom of their natural protectors by the red remorseless hand of Battle. . . . Homes have been made desolate, and the light of life in thousands of hearts has been quenched forever. All of this desolation imagination must paint—broken hearts cannot be photographed."[7]

Gardner left Brady soon after Antietam and created his own business out of a Washington, D.C., studio two blocks away from Brady's studio on

Pennsylvania Avenue. The two remained amicable, but their differences in approach and philosophy overrode their partnership.[8]

Photography's origins in portraiture meant that the intellectual meaning and interpretation it brought to the war were perceived by the public less as "news" or current events than as historical preservation. In American memory, Brady's and Gardner's Civil War photographs stand as the epitome of war art and photojournalism. But they were not widely viewed at the time.[9]

For photographers no less than other artists, Civil War images focused primarily on the patriotic and the promotional. That meant that if patriotism required it, the camera had to "lie." When publishing his battlefield photographs, Gardner composed deceptive captions using the same corpses to represent Confederate soldiers desolated by defeat or Union soldiers heroic in self-denying victory. On occasion photographs could be doctored. When photographing the "Devil's Den" at Gettysburg a year later, Gardner's assistant Timothy O'Sullivan planted a dead body from another location on the scene and placed a rifle in his hand to represent "Dead Confederate soldier at sharpshooter's position in Devil's Den."[10]

Northern photographers showed a decided preference for Confederate over Union corpses. Similarly, Brady shot photographs of emaciated Northern and Southern prisoners of war, but only the Northern prisoners were exhibited publicly. Photographs of the Confederate prisoners of war suffering in the Union prisons would not be available to Northern (or Southern) viewers until after the war.[11] Clearly in photography as everywhere, realism and criticism were subordinated to patriotism and the "imagination" of art. Photographs that might conjure self-censure were simply dismissed.

Like photography, paintings would endure and shape America's Civil War memory more than they informed contemporary news. With few public spaces to exhibit them, their production was slow and uneven. Artists accustomed to painting landscapes adjusted with difficulty to capturing scenes of war. No artistic renderings of note would appear until after the great battles of 1862 and 1863.[12]

Of all the great American painters, Winslow Homer emerged as the most important oil painter of the Civil War. The timing was right—he was in his early twenties when the conflict began, and as the war matured, so did the artist. The great seascape artist of the future first encountered his destiny in battle scenes from the Civil War.[13]

Homer's access to the Civil War came mainly through his attachment to the Army's Second Corps, including, most importantly, the Sixty-first New York Infantry Regiment. By April 1862 Homer obtained passes to follow the troops into Virginia, where he completed several on-site sketches and paintings. On April 5, 1862, he drew *The Ocean Queen with Irish Brigade on Board Going Down the Potomac*. On April 6 he drew *Assault on Rebel Battery at Lee's Mill*.

Homer's first battle scene appeared in the July 1862 issue of *Harper's Weekly* and featured a bayonet charge at the Battle of Seven Pines (Fair Oaks). Rendered as a lithograph for *Harper's Weekly*, the print shows a massive scene of close combat but little blood or "patriotic gore." In a romantic departure from the facts of the battle, the Union was depicted routing the enemy in a blur of charging energy at the very time when, in reality, Union troops were hastily retreating on the Peninsula.

The following week another Homer wood engraving entitled *The Surgeon at Work at the Rear during an Engagement* appeared in *Harper's*. Again the theme was more denial than encounter. The view from Fair Oaks was meant to assure Northern audiences that wounded soldiers were immediately attended to by caring physicians. The reality, however, was different, as the wounded soldiers lay overnight in the rain awaiting railroad transport behind the lines.[14] In a letter to his mother written from Harrison's Landing, one Union soldier wrote: "The surgeons don't know or care whether a man is sick or not and have so little care for patients in the hospital that it is the last place a man wants to see."[15]

Four months later, following the Seven Days' Battles, on November 15, *Harper's Weekly* again printed a Homer painting, *The Army of the Potomac—A Sharpshooter on Picket-Duty*. The bold portrayal of a Union sharpshooter introduced a stark and difficult dimension of the war, namely the targeting of officers by snipers. The first organized use of snipers occurred during the Peninsular campaign, when Union marksmen organized in two specialized regiments known as Berdan's Sharpshooters, after Hiram G. Berdan. Their prize possession would become their Sharps rifles, symbolizing their status as individual killers free to attach themselves to any line as needed.

In his romantic account of the Berdan's Sharpshooters, Captain C. A. Stevens nevertheless conceded unpleasant side effects of the "license" snipers were given. He told of one unsavory soldier who "carried a stick, and whenever he shot a man he made a notch in it. He would sit for hours behind a stump or clump of earth until he got sight of a rebel's head, when bang went the rifle, and down dropped the rebel, and out came the stick to receive its notch."[16]

Snipers took advantage of cover and long distances to shoot unaware soldiers in cold blood. To modern sensibilities, snipers, like civilian casualties, are a part of war. But to a society in transition from a professional's war to

modern warfare, they offended the sense of fair play. Homer himself understood the morally ambivalent nature of his subject. Several years later, he described looking through the scope of the sniper's rifle: "As I was not a
soldier—but a camp follower and artist, the above impression struck me as
being as near murder as anything I ever could think of in connection with the
army and I always had a horror of that branch of the service." According to
Christopher Kent Wilson, many soldiers believed it to be:

> an unceremonious and vicious tactic that amounted to nothing more than
> murder . . . sharpshooting never affected the outcome of a major battle but
> instead only killed individual soldiers for no real gain . . . when not perform-
> ing an important [military] role, the sharpshooters would often kill not for
> tactical advantage but for the sake of killing.[17]

The observations of Wilson and Homer span a century but share the horror of war's escalating effects. What neither of them recognized is that by late
1862, snipers differed very little from regular soldiers in a furious modern war
in which killing increasingly existed "for the sake of killing."

In time, the photograph would become the staple of war art, but not in the
Civil War. America's quintessential nineteenth-century democratic art form
was the stone-engraved lithograph. Not surprisingly, the Civil War would
mark a high point of lithographic art and probably extended its life for a
decade.

When James Merritt Ives joined the shop of Nathaniel Currier, an
American institution was born.[18] In all, the partners created more than seven
thousand prints that sold in the "uncounted millions of copies"—at one
point, 95 percent of all lithographs in circulation in the United States.

The nonverbal information contained in a lithographic print, when combined with verbal description underneath, created "news" about America at
its most basic. With photojournalism still in the future, lithographs were the
most important source of large-scale visual images in the mass media. They
put images where before had been only names, places, and events described
in words and disseminated through print. These images were not intended to
be "art" in the formal sense of the term, nor were they designed to be literal
or objectively "real" in the vein of the photography soon to come. Rather, they
reflected what the consumers wanted to imagine about their democratic
America and its citizens' war.

In all, Currier & Ives produced more than two hundred lithographs of
the Civil War that sold in the thousands. Later there would be a comparable
market in Lincoln prints, especially after his assassination.[19] Two qualities

are especially striking about them. First is their preoccupation with heroic battle scenes. While the occasional camp scenes or cartoons appeared, the big battles predominated. Ordinary Northern Americans apparently wanted a war they could visualize. Second is the extent to which the lithographs avoided visualizing the war too graphically. People wanted *imagined* battles, and no one could create these better than lithographic artists, freed as they were from the facts to present poses and gallantry as they wished.

Consequently lithographs, no less than speech and print, avoided any sort of moral commentary on war, nor did they attempt to bare its violent soul. Civilian sufferers are never present in the pictures, nor is excessive brutality. Instead, all is charging horses, fixed bayonets, and always, everywhere, battle flags and "Old Glory." Where political cartoons could be vicious in their dehumanization of the enemy, Currier & Ives tended, in the historian Bryan LeBeau's words, to avoid "the sordid realities of battle . . . retaining the romance and glory of the war." They were reluctant to dehumanize the Southerners, who would one day return as fellow citizens and, they hoped, as customers.

In a word, their art was comforting. Currier & Ives provided moral reassurance that Union sacrifices were for a righteous cause without demonizing the enemy.[20] These prints portray plenty of emotion, especially a sort of sentimentalized loyalty to the cause, but they lack the passion of moral inquiry or anomie of war that might have derailed 100 percent support for the war effort, no matter where it led.

In many instances, lithographic prints were not only romantic but downright deceptive. Battles that turned out to be devastating losses for the North, like First and Second Bull Run, Antietam (really a draw), or Fredericksburg, emerge in prints as outstanding Federal victories. Triumphant Union soldiers were depicted overwhelming Confederate defenses, even as the reality of the battles pointed in the opposite direction.

In *The Battle of Mill Spring*, a bayonet charge is depicted with the caption: "Terrific bayonet charge of the 9th Ohio Volunteers and total defeat of the Rebel army under Gen. Zollicoffer." In fact, there was a bayonet charge at Mill Springs, but General Zollicoffer was hardly a dominant presence. Badly nearsighted and disoriented, Zollicoffer mistook Federals for Confederates and rode right into their ranks, where they promptly shot him dead. Bayonet battles were rare in the Civil War, but the vast majority of battle lithographs figured swords and bayonets in close combat situations.[21] They captured the war as seen from West Point manuals, not the war as it was actually fought.

With the public clamoring for visual images from the front, major American illustrators such as Alfred and William Waud, Edwin Forbes, Winslow Homer, and Thomas Nast journeyed to the front and sketched the battles around them. Teams of artists and craftsmen worked for the larger news-papers, as well as for illustrated weeklies such as *Frank Leslie's Illustrated Newspaper*, *Harper's Weekly*, the *New York Illustrated News*, and, in the Con-federacy, *Southern Punch* and the *Southern Illustrated News*. With as many as fifty artists at the front, prints could be rendered within less than two weeks of their occurrence. As "action images," the sketches were superior to photo-graphs and presumed to be just as accurate.

Reality, of course, is in the eye of the perceiver, and what the images re-vealed was a reality the producers assumed their viewers wanted to see. In time, the public's interest became more visceral and violent so that field artists grew increasingly realistic in their action sketches. But in the first year of the war, avoidance was the rule.

When sermons, newspapers, and public art and music are put together and examined for their critical perspective, a static picture emerges in an ever-changing dynamic war. Even as battles loomed ever greater and closer to noncombatants, the commentary remained fixed. It did not matter what the photographs showed as Americans sang their patriotic songs and clung to their romantic images. Love of country and irrational fascination with war's glory brought reality and illusion together in deceptive ways. Commentators everywhere looked to an uncharted future without scruples.

PART IV
JUSTIFICATION

THE
EMANCIPATION WAR

OCTOBER 1862 TO MAY 1863

CHAPTER 18

"ALL WHO DIE FOR COUNTRY NOW, DIE ALSO FOR HUMANITY"

In reflecting on those dark days of 1862, Lincoln later explained: "Things had gone on from bad to worse, until I felt that we had reached the end of our rope on the plan of operations we had been pursuing . . . that we had about played our last card, and must change our tactics, or lose the game!"[1] By Lincoln's calculation, the killing must continue on ever grander scales. But for that to succeed the people must be persuaded to shed the blood without reservations. This, in turn, required a moral certitude that the killing was just. Only emancipation—Lincoln's "last card"—would provide such certitude.[2] In so doing he counted on a rising tide of antislavery sentiment in the North, an even greater tide of hatred for the "enemy," and a mounting desire to hurt the South where they would feel it most.

In April 1862 Lincoln had approved the joint resolution of Congress calling for gradual emancipation of the slaves by the states. At the same time, Congress passed a measure abolishing slavery in the District of Columbia, with compensation to the owners. On June 19 Lincoln signed into law a measure prohibiting slavery in the territories of the United States, without compensation. But he could not keep up with a Republican-driven Congress that was hastening along an antislavery agenda of its own.

In July Congress enacted a new militia act, the Second Confiscation Act, expanding the legal basis for freeing slaves of all "disloyal" owners. The act effectively freed all fugitive slaves escaping to Union lines from their Confederate owners. The Militia Act, passed the same day, permitted the employment of blacks in any capacity "for which they may be found competent."[3] Northern soldiers saw in this act the potential to substantially build up their military might, even as Confederates lost theirs.

With some reservations, Lincoln signed both congressional acts.[4] At the same time, he revealed his own ideas on the subject in a meeting with his cabinet. There, on July 22, Lincoln proposed a limited Emancipation Proclamation and read a preliminary draft to the gathering. Limited emancipation was a risky business, virtually certain to raise the stakes of war. It was a risk Lincoln was willing to take. After Lincoln had shared the draft with his cabinet, Secretary of State Seward urged him to wait for a military victory before announcing his policy. Otherwise it might look like a desperation measure to disguise losses on the battlefield.

Both Lincoln and Republicans in Congress realized that by their combined actions, they—the Federal government—were serving notice that the meaning of the war had changed dramatically. No longer would the war be fought just to preserve the Union, and certainly not the "Union as it was." Henceforth, it would be a much bigger war—one that would reweave the South's social fabric in a revolutionary way and ensure that postbellum America would be radically different from antebellum America. Both the North and the South would feel the tremors. The slaveholding class would exist no longer, and they would react strongly as they recognized that their very way of life was at issue. With tens of thousands of bodies already in the grave, they would most likely call for total war on all fronts—no matter what the consequences, no surrender. Lincoln was prepared to take this risk because he had already himself determined on a course of total war as the only solution to entrenched Confederate nationalism. In these terms, emancipation decisively furthered the draconian military course he had already set.

As ambiguous a "victory" as Antietam was, it sufficed for Lincoln. Indeed, he perceived it as a providential signal to act.[5] On September 22, 1862, he announced his Emancipation Proclamation, effective January 1, 1863. The message was brief and lacked Lincoln's customary sense of literary style. But the substance said it all. After establishing the context for his proclamation "as a fit and necessary war measure for suppressing said rebellion," Lincoln went on to declare, "that all persons held as slaves within said designated [rebellious] States, and parts of States, are, and henceforward shall be free; and that the Executive government of the United States, including the military and naval authorities thereof, will recognize and maintain the freedom of said persons."[6] With that proclamation, the war assumed a double significance for the North as a war for union and a war for freedom. For the South, the proclamation also confirmed a double significance: to protect a sovereign nation's right to self-defense against an outside invader, and to protect that nation's white population from slave insurrections and disloyalty.

At the same time that Lincoln targeted the rebellious states for emancipation, he also called for congressional approval of gradual, compensated
emancipation for slaveholders in the border states. If the border states could
be convinced, it might even turn the Confederacy and end the war at a much
cheaper price. To prepare the way, he met with a congressional delegation
from the border states to persuade them of the wisdom of his plan. In that
meeting, he pointed out that antislavery sentiment was growing so strong in
the North that he doubted the institution would survive the war. Instead of
losing all their value with a constitutional amendment and coerced emancipation, why not gradually free slaves over the next decades with compensation of $400 per slave? To those in the border states, and even more, the free
states, who objected to the staggering costs of such compensation, Lincoln
replied that it was far cheaper than war and coerced emancipation. Even
more important, compensated emancipation saved lives that coerced emancipation wasted.

However logical the argument, Lincoln's appeal fell on deaf ears. Two
days after the meeting, twenty of the border-state congressmen formally rejected Lincoln's proposal, and a minority of eight approved.[7] Freedom for
slaves would not appear on any slaveholder's agenda until coerced by force of
arms or law.

Despite its place in American memory as America's abolition declaration,
the Emancipation Proclamation was hardly an abolitionist document. Nor
did it represent any change in Lincoln's war aims (at least none that he could
admit to publicly). But that did not stop either side in the conflict from effectively and intentionally misreading the proclamation as a new and revolutionary document. In that deliberate misreading, Northern abolitionists created a
self-fulfilling prophecy.

The proclamation reaffirmed Lincoln's stated war purpose as the restoration of the Union and reaffirmed his intention still to strive for compensated
emancipation. He reiterated that abolition was not a war aim of the North. If
the Confederacy came back into the Union before January 1, the proclamation provided that the institution of slavery might continue in those states.
Yet, as the historian J. G. Randall shrewdly recognized, "[t]he truth of the
matter was that the proclamation became a species of slogan or shibboleth;
its dramatization in the popular mind was of more effect than its actual provisions. . . . [I]t came to be pretty generally assumed that in September of 1862
the war somehow took a new turn, and that thenceforward it was being
prosecuted as a war against slavery."[8]

Whatever the popular interpretation, coercive universal emancipation
was not what Lincoln intended by his proclamation. In his annual message to

Congress on December 1, 1862, he reiterated his favored solution of a constitutional amendment implementing compensated emancipation through the issue of Federal bonds to be completed by 1900. This would be expensive, but less expensive than war: "The war requires large sums, and requires them at once. The aggregate sum necessary for compensated emancipation, of course, would be large. But it would require no ready cash; nor the bonds even, any faster than the emancipation progresses. This might not, and probably would not, close before the end of the thirty-seven years." Left unsaid by Lincoln was the fact that in compensated emancipation, abolition would come gradually, not immediately.

Along with this proposal, Lincoln also took the occasion to reiterate his preference for voluntary colonization of freedmen: "I cannot make it better known than it already is, that I strongly favor colonization." As for Northern freedmen, "I wish to say there is an objection urged against free colored persons remaining in the country, which is largely imaginary, if not sometimes malicious."[9]

The failure of compensated emancipation to win any support from any quarter provides an important insight into the war. Try as he might to popularize a morally acceptable and diplomatically expedient solution to the war and slavery, Lincoln would not be heard. In 1863 hardly anyone was ready to quit the killing. Nevertheless, Lincoln's efforts to arrange for a compensated emancipation, though unsuccessful, should not be overlooked. They reveal Lincoln to be one of the few principals in the war capable of transcending the prevailing rhetoric of absolute right and wrong.

For any kind of compromise to work, both sides had to be able to see ways in which guilt resided on all sides. Northern abolitionists could countenance this no sooner than could Southern fire-eaters. From the abolitionists' stance of moral superiority and absolute identification of God with His Northern New Israel, the slaveholding sinner should not be compensated for his sin, even if it saved lives and ultimately cost less. Why? Because the North was utterly right and the South utterly wrong. Such moral high ground was, as Lincoln recognized, sheer hypocrisy that ignored the utter complicity of Northern traders and consumers in the "peculiar institution."

Reverend Moses Smith of Connecticut agreed: "We invented the machinery and opened the [slave] markets. We took mortgages on southern property, and became *owners of men*. We fitted out the ships and became the slave traders of the land. Northern men voted in the Fugitive Slave Bill."[10] Both Lincoln and Smith were correct. It was not morality that blocked the acceptance of compromise of any sort, but rather a self-interested rewriting of history.

The proclamation came as no surprise to the Confederates. A writer for the *Richmond Daily Dispatch* insisted "Lincoln's proclamation changes nothing; this has been an abolitionist war from the beginning."[11] But they howled at a codicil that declared that "the Executive Government of the United States . . . will do no act . . . to repress such persons . . . in any efforts they may make for their actual freedom." Confederates interpreted these words as an incitement to servile insurrection, dubbing Lincoln's proclamation the "Insurrection Proclamation."

Southern reactions to the Emancipation Proclamation were generally flat except for the implied call to slave insurrection, which they read into it. Confederates had assumed from the very start of hostilities that the war of "Northern aggression" was a thinly disguised, New England–driven abolitionist war.

President Davis's first inclination (never implemented) was to hand over all Union officer prisoners to state civil authorities so that they would be tried and executed according to capital laws covering incitement to servile insurrection. Later, Davis insisted that the proclamation "affords to our whole people the complete and crowning proof of the true nature of the designs of the party which elevated to power the present occupant of the Presidential chair at Washington and which sought to conceal its purpose by every variety of artful device."[12]

On October 9, the *Richmond Religious Herald* echoed Davis's outrage in a column titled "The Proclamation of Abolition." In it, the editor pointed to the revolutionary effects of this document, if implemented: "The sudden revolution would break the whole fabric of society in pieces, and slaveholders and non-slaveholders, of the present generation at least, would struggle hopelessly to extricate themselves from the universal wreck of financial interests and domestic institutions. . . . If successful, it would create a new Pariah race to curse the world, and to be itself accursed of God and man."

Others were less offended and downplayed the proclamation. The *Southern Illustrated News* saw in Lincoln's proclamation "a state of desperation" that had little immediate effect on anyone, while the *Augusta Weekly Constitutionalist* likened the futility of Lincoln's aspirations for the South to "the Pope's Bull against the Comet."[13] In fact, the South had promulgated the myth that the Civil War was waged solely for emancipation so vigorously that Lincoln's Emancipation Proclamation did not have quite the symbolic effect on them that it did in the North. But it did mean an all-or-nothing war.

Confederate fears of widespread slave insurrections diminished as it became clear that life for most slaves went on as usual. Occupied places, such as New Orleans or Port Royal, South Carolina, where slaves ran to freedom, were the exception. In 1863, with no Federal troops yet in view, slaves continued to work the plantations and armories and to support the army from behind the lines. The buying and selling of slaves remained as robust as ever, with prices ranging from $3,000 to $5,000.[14]

In the North, African Americans recognized the futility of insurrection once the war began. In an editorial for the African Methodist Episcopal *Christian Recorder*, the writer wrote that no Northern statesmen counseled insurrection before the war. Now, the writer continued:

> [T]hat same people want the slaves to rise up and fight for their liberty. Rise against what?—powder, cannon, ball and grape-shot? Not a bit of it. They have got too much good sense. Since you have waited till every man, boy, woman and child in the so-called Southern Confederacy has been armed to the teeth, tis folly and mockery for you now to say to the poor, bleeding and downtrodden sons of Africa, "Arise and fight for your liberty!"[15]

If Lincoln employed emancipation as a ground for total war, Southern voices employed emancipation as a ground for attacking the group they hated most: evangelical clergy. Southern observers exposed the utter captivity of the Northern churches to the patriotic cause and to the lawyer-politicians who orchestrated it. In a column printed in the *Southern Illustrated News* on "Odium Theologicum," the Richmond-based editors focused on the Northern church as the embodiment of "servile" political preaching:

> And when we say "the Church," we use the term in no restricted or sectarian sense . . . but as embracing all who acknowledge the Christian faith, in any manner, Trinitarians or Unitarians, Protestants or followers of Rome, from the disciples of Theodore Parker to the brethren of the Pennsylvania Conference bordering on the Pan-Handle, and from the applauding audience that attends the performances of Beecher to the devout flock that awaits the benediction of Archbishop Hughes. Not only are the religionists of the North unanimous in their support of the war, but they far outstrip the politicians in the rancor and hatred they exhibit.

If the same warlike sentiments appeared in the Southern pulpits, which they certainly did, that did not mark hypocrisy, the editors argued, because the South's cause was utterly just. And because secession was just, the Southern cause was purely self-defense:

If it be said that it is natural that the feelings of Christians should be with their country in time of war, that patriotism is a high Christian duty, and that our own clergymen are actively engaged in the cause of the Confederate States, many of them being in military command, we could answer that there is all the difference conceivable between an offensive and defensive war. The Southern people have never desired hostilities. They have only taken up arms to protect their altars and fire-sides.[16]

Here, in the deafness to one's own "applauding" and blindness to the pulpit of hatred, appears a compelling illustration of the "servile" cultural captivity of the churches, North *and* South, to their nations.

Responses in the North rang predictably strong on all sides. Northern white abolitionists, slaves, and freedmen all adjudged the proclamation good but insufficiently strong. Only universal emancipation, they believed, would satisfy God's will. In its September 26 issue, *The Liberator* reprinted the Emancipation Proclamation and remarked:

Though we believe this Proclamation is not all that the exigency of the times and the consequent duty of the government require,—and therefore are not so jubilant over it as many others,—still, it is an important step in the right direction, and an act of immense historic consequence, and justifies the almost universal gladness of expression and warm congratulation which it has simultaneously elicited in every part of the Free States.

In an important concession, *The Liberator* added: "In view of the fact that the old Union has literally ceased to exist and cannot be restored, we think that the Abolitionists who may be drafted, and who are not committed to radical peace principles, will be justified in standing loyally by the government as such, on the battle-field or in any other capacity."

One such nonpacifist abolitionist was William R. Williams of New York, whose abolitionist thought piece entitled *Of the Birth and Death of Nations* arrived at a justification for total war solely on the foundation of abolition. Where most Republicans were willing to escalate war on civilians for the preservation of the Union, Williams would only accept as morally just a total war that sought immediate and universal emancipation. The pretenses of a war merely to preserve the Union must be dropped and the war fought as an abolition war: "There is then no alternative for this nation; either its own original, divinely endowed life must be surrendered up, or it must conquer and destroy its unappeasable enemy, slavery."

From there Williams moved to an explicit analysis of the general "laws of war" in terms that justified a turn to total war. Quoting an unnamed source, he wrote:

[S]ince the object of a just war is to suppress injustice and compel justice, we have a right to put in practice against our enemy every measure that will tend to weaken or disable him from maintaining his injustice. To this end, we are at liberty to choose any and all such methods as we may deem most efficacious.

Not content with total war to end slavery, Williams concluded by urging the Union government not only to free the slaves and employ them behind the lines but also to arm them for frontline combat. By dying in battle they too could share in the nation's sacred atonement: "If, in the present supreme hour, 'there can be no salvation without the shedding of blood,' they also should have the privilege of making the great sacrifice. It is the needed discipline and necessary preparation for the possession of freedom, that they who seek it, should be willing to die for it. It is for you to give them the opportunity."[17]

Lincoln refused to bargain with God on the basis of his moral superiority over the enemy. He knew there was more than enough guilt on all sides. But not so abolitionists. In a note of moral hubris distinct to the North and especially abolitionists, Israel E. Dwinell dared to see the war in global terms: "It seems to me that the world—and I say it knowing the danger and the sin of presumption, but I say it not as an American, but more, a man regarding the interests of the whole race,—*that the world* cannot afford to spare us." Obviously not entirely at ease with his world-regenerative creed, he quickly backed off: "This is a dangerous point, and I leave it."[18] But the point *was* made. In a sort of providential blackmail, Dwinell implied that by holding up the trump card of abolition, God would be forced to give the North victory and allow America to save the world.

In an address delivered at Boston's Faneuil Hall on October 6, Massachusetts's abolitionist senator Charles Sumner made plain his support for the Emancipation Proclamation as a "war measure" and "not as an abolitionist." With that token disclaimer for pretext, Sumner pronounced the remainder of the oration not as a Union warrior but in the clear language of an abolitionist, and speculated on the implications of emancipation for America's world-regenerative mission:

But, fellow-citizens, the war which we wage is not merely for ourselves; it is for all mankind. . . . In ending slavery here we open its gates all over the world, and let the oppressed go free. Nor is this all. In saving the republic we shall save civilization. . ... In such a cause no effort can be too great, no faith can be too determined. To die for country is pleasant and honorable. But all who die for country now, die also for humanity. Wherever they lie, in bloody fields, they will be remembered as the heroes through whom the republic was saved and civilization established forever.[19]

Although antislavery sentiment spread in the North, ultra-abolitionist senators like Sumner still remained a minority, and abolitionist ministers did not necessarily speak for the congregations or even their profession. Many Northern ministers remained antislavery but not abolitionist. Princeton Theological Seminary's venerable Charles Hodge evidenced a clear grasp of just-war theory and where abolition fit in it. In terms similar to those of Lincoln and other antislavery Republicans, he made a strong moral case for civil war justified solely by the preservation of the Union.

War, he began, is a "tremendous evil." To kill fellow human beings on battlefields, "there must be a moral obligation on a people to make war, or the war itself is a crime." To fight an offensive war for abolition would be a "crime":

Now it cannot be asserted that the abolition of slavery, however desirable in itself, is one of the ends for which our national government was instituted. We are not bound to abolish slavery by war, as we should be bound to resist invasion, or as we are bound to suppress rebellion by force of arms . . . to make such abolition the end of the war, is a plain and palpable violation of the oath of allegiance to the Constitution, and of the law of God.[20]

In terms of just-war theory and the stated goals on which war was predicated *in 1861*, Hodge was right. But by 1863 there were more than enough Northerners willing to transform emancipation from a means to an end, and deliberately overlook the constitutional limitations, if it would sustain the war on a sufficient scale to destroy the Confederacy. In fact, Hodge himself would eventually reform and declare, with his denomination, that the sin of slavery was "the" cause of the war.

Other Northern Unionists—including many soldiers—agreed with Hodge's initial position and believed that the proclamation had wrongly changed the cause of the war from the Union to emancipation, and from defensive war to protect the Union to an offensive war to occupy the South and transform it through force of arms. In New York, William Shedd, the Old Light pastor of the Brick Presbyterian Church, evidenced long-standing hostility toward abolitionists and coercive emancipation and recommended instead a gradualist emancipation:

> The American people and Government have not been able to see that an instantaneous emancipation of the four millions in bondage would be best either for them or for the nation. . . . On the contrary, they look to a gradual method, that shall prepare them for freedom and self-government. . . . A compulsory reform, even if it is possible, is undesirable.

As for the war, "let it be confined strictly to the restoration of the authority of the Constitution over all parts of the land."[21]

In the political arena, both "War" and "Peace" Democrats were unalterably opposed to the Emancipation Proclamation. In every congressional vote that concerned slavery, they united in their opposition. And they were temporarily successful. Five of the North's largest states who went for Lincoln in 1860 turned in the fall by-elections of 1862 and returned Democratic majorities to Capitol Hill. The linchpin of their strength remained white supremacy.

In a speech to the Anti-Slavery Society in Philadelphia, Frederick Douglass recognized that race-based slavery defined the very identity of the Democratic Party:

> The Democratic party is for war for slavery; it is for peace for slavery; it is for the *habeas corpus* for slavery; it is against the *habeas corpus* for slavery; it was for the Florida war for slavery; it was for the Mexican war for slavery. . . . It has but one principle, one master; and it is guided, governed, and directed by it.[22]

Few Democrats disagreed with Douglass. In a speech before the House of Representatives of Maine in February 1863, Moses Page complained:

> The people are getting weary. They see that this war is being perverted from its true and legitimate purpose of restoring the Union as it was, and upholding the Constitution as it is, to a war upon the institutions of States in rebellion. The soldiers, too, are getting uneasy; they are unwilling to endure the vicissitudes of battle and the privations of the camp, for any other purpose than to defend and maintain the supremacy of the Constitution, and to preserve the Union.[23]

Other political critics feared the effects of a black influx into their states. In an address to the U.S. House of Representatives, Ohio's Samuel Cox employed racist humor to signal his grave reservations:

If the rush of free negroes to this paradise continues, it would be a blessing if Providence should send Satan here in the form of a serpent, and an angel to drive the descendants of Adam and Eve into the outer world. If it continues, you will have no one here but Congressmen and negroes, and that will be punishment enough. [Laughter.] You will have to enact a fugitive slave law, to bring the whites to their capital. [Laughter.] . . . It is a practical question as the war is already throwing them within our borders in great numbers.[24]

One Southern Unionist, Bryan Tyson, who was forced to flee Moore County, North Carolina, for Washington, D.C., wrote for Northern Democrats and the white race. Though in favor of the Union, Tyson opposed Lincoln's proclamation because it had no one's best interests at heart, including the slaves'. Because "the negro is an inferior species of the human race," he declared, liberation would simply leave him vulnerable to superior and exploitive whites. Instead of coerced emancipation, "I am for first applying to them the anointing oil of learning and Christianity; and, whenever it shall have been clearly demonstrated that they are in a fit condition to take care of themselves, I am then for their going out free."[25]

Soldiers were also divided. In a letter to his mother, Private Henry Joslin, destined to die in battle one year later, reflected on emancipation and *his* civil war in terms that could not have been more starkly opposite of the abolitionists':

You may depend that after the "boys" get into Massachusetts again they will not sit where he does now. There are a good many voters learning something (as well as I am) who did not come out here to fight on the nigger question but for the Union of the U.S. and the protection of the Capital and the Constitution.[26]

Lincoln's Illinois, whose black code set the standard for Northern racism, was equally indignant. Its legislature issued a resolution opposing the proclamation as "unwarranted in military as in civil law; a gigantic usurpation, at once converting the war, professedly . . . for the vindication of the authority of the constitution, into the crusade for the sudden, unconditional and violent liberation of 3,000,000 slaves."[27] The midwestern soldiers who would fill out Sherman's army—and Sherman himself—were also largely disinterested or hostile to slaves.[28] One western officer in Sherman's army linked blacks with Indians (especially detested on the Midwest frontier) and declared in a vitriolic speech in Columbia, South Carolina, that the Union existed solely for the white man: "the Indian, as well as the Negro had to be . . . exterminated."[29]

The Confederacy's concerns with emancipation focused more on the practical and political than on the moral. Not least of these was the effect of the Emancipation Proclamation on England's recognition of the Confederate cause. From the start of the war, the British press had shamelessly supported the South and advocated recognition of the Confederacy. With a circulation of sixty-five thousand, the *Times* of London harshly criticized Lincoln and sympathized with the Southern cotton exporters on whom England's textile economy depended. But all of these influences were rendered moot by the prospect of emancipation. Writing from London, Henry Brooks Adams gloated: "The Emancipation Proclamation has done more for us here than all our former victories and all our diplomacy. It is creating an almost convulsive reaction in our favor all over this country."[30]

European—especially British—commentators recognized the politics of Lincoln's Emancipation Proclamation and resigned themselves to the consequences but remained cynical about the morality of Lincoln's act. In a caustic editorial, the London *Spectator* declared: "The [moral] principle is not that a human being cannot justly own another, but that he cannot own him unless loyal to the United States."[31] Other English observers echoed the *Spectator*, searching the document in vain for any principled antislavery statement that would declare the institution of slavery itself everywhere immoral and unjust.

Obviously African Americans, and slaves in particular, felt the greatest impact of the proclamation.[32] For the most part, they determined to see the promise of emancipation rather than its limitations. Frederick Douglass recognized Lincoln's motives: "In a word, in all that he did, or attempted, he made it manifest that the one great and all commanding object with him was the peace and preservation of the Union, and that this was the motive and mainspring of all his measures."

Yet at the same time Douglass could not constrain his excitement at the prospect of movement forward toward the all-consuming goal and motive of universal and immediate emancipation. In an address delivered in Rochester, New York, on December 28, 1862, Douglass exulted: "We stand to-day in the presence of a glorious prospect. . . . It is difficult for us who have toiled so long and hard to believe that this event, so stupendous, so far reaching and glorious is even now at the door."

Later, he recalled the mood when he first saw the news on the wires:

The effect of this announcement was startling beyond description, and the scene was wild and grand. Joy and gladness exhausted all forms of expression from shouts of praise, to sobs and tears. My old friend Rue, a colored preacher, a man of wonderful vocal power, expressed the heartfelt emotion of the hour, when he led all voices in the anthem, "Sound the Loud Timbrel O'er Egypt's Dark Sea, Jehovah Hath Triumphed, His People Are Free."[33]

The African Methodist Episcopal *Christian Recorder* responded to Lincoln's proclamation with a blistering jeremiad of its own. It began in classic language: "God has a controversy with this nation. He is chastising us severely, by civil war. We have tried to humble ourselves; have fasted and prayed . . . but his wrath is poured out still." Why, the writer continued, "does not his anger subside?" The answer: because limited emancipation such as what Lincoln proposed was not enough. The only means to peace is "Universal Emancipation." With ongoing violence in view, the editorial continued its jeremiad: "God sometimes so leads men, and so hedges up their way, as to make his will most plain—so plain that their refusal to do it he regards as unpardonable obstinacy, which he beats with many stripes, if he does not avenge it with unquenchable anger."

The war rages on because peace and slavery cannot coexist. God "makes them incongruous, incompatible." Then, speaking for God, the editorial concluded: "These are my children, made of the same blood with yourselves, they are no longer to be your slaves. They have served you many generations. They have now attained their majority—to a state of manhood. I demand their freedom."[34]

For those African Americans who, for the first time in their New World experience, were slaves no more, the effects of Lincoln's emancipation were electric. In innumerable ways overt and subtle, they had risked all for freedom and finally saw their Day of Jubilee. With news of the Emancipation Proclamation, New Orleans slaves asked General Nathaniel Banks to permit a day of celebration for January 1, when the law went into effect. Their letter expresses the intensity of the moment:

We The members of Th union association Desir Th & Respectfully ask of you Th privirliges of Salabrating Th first Day of January th 1863 by a Large procesion on that Day & We Wish to pass th Head quarters of th union officers High in a authority that is if it Suit your approbation & We also Wish to Give a Grand union Dinner on the Second Day of Januay that is if it so pleas you and th profit of th Dinner Will Go To th poor people

in the Camp th Colour Woman & children. Your Most Homble obedien
servant

    J M Marshall, th president of th union association.[35]

The deferential tone of the letter cannot disguise the ecstasy of the moment for these people and *their* union.

Though no abolitionist, General Banks did allow former slaves to enjoy their de facto freedom and approved of subsequent celebrations. The observances, he concluded, were wholly salutary:

> They occupied the streets and the squares the whole day, and not a disorderly act, not an uncivil word was heard; not a white person, as far as I know, received or gave offense, and nothing was witnessed during the day but the most perfect sobriety and order. Orations were delivered in French and English that would have done honor to any assembly.

Banks offered paid employment, in place of unpaid servitude, to all able-bodied former slaves who wished to work and achieve self-sufficiency as well as "education for the young."

The "experiment" to see if agriculture could exist without slavery proved to be a "complete success."[36] Colonel George Hanks of the Fifteenth Regiment, Corps d'Afrique, issued a formal report to Secretary of War Stanton in which he summarized the results of the experiment in similarly glowing terms:

> The negroes came in scarred, wounded, and some with iron collars round their necks. I set them at work on abandoned plantations, and on the fortifications. At one time we had 6,500 of them; there was not the slightest difficulty with them. They are more willing to work, and more patient than any set of human beings I ever saw . . . the negroes *willingly accept the condition of labor for their own maintenance, and the musket for their freedom.*[37]

Despite the capacities of African American freedmen to stand on their own, white Americans posed serious problems, even with emancipation. In a column on "Slavery and the Negro," a writer for the *New York Evangelist* pointed out that the challenge of dealing with the "Negro" problem only began with emancipation:

> It is well therefore, while the public mind is absorbed with the question of slavery, to look ahead to that other question which may soon be upon us, and

to consider the magnitude of the work which we have to do—a work which concerns nothing less than the destiny of a whole Race, and which will task all the wisdom and philanthropy of the country for a half century to come.[38]

That "destiny," tragically, would not soon be glorious.

CHAPTER 19

LINCOLN, EMANCIPATION, AND TOTAL WAR

How did Lincoln understand his proclamation? Lincoln took a broad view of his constitutional powers in time of war and saw emancipation in that context. He knew that this idea had been broached before by President John Quincy Adams as a legitimate war measure that could bypass traditional constitutional restraints in the interests of pressing national security.[1] Lincoln also appreciated the many practical advantages to be gained by such an act. Preventing England from recognizing the Confederacy was surely one pressing motive in his decision. Maintaining the loyalty or at least the neutrality of the border states was another. But the most important consideration was pragmatic: winning the war.

In fact, Lincoln was no more supportive of slave insurrections than he was of John Brown.[2] Both he deemed terrorists attacking noncombatant populations in preemptive acts of war. Lincoln reaffirmed this position in his final proclamation on January 1, 1863, when, in the same codicil, he added: "I hereby enjoin upon the people so declared to be free to abstain from all violence, unless in necessary self-defense." The opposition of Lincoln, his generals, and his administration to the rhetoric of slave insurrection offers perhaps the strongest confirmation that, contrary to American memory, the Civil War was not at all an abolitionist war, let alone a war for racial equality. Most Northern intellectuals agreed. New York's Presbyterian pastor William R. Williams asked the rhetorical question: "Do we anticipate or desire the excesses of servile revolt?" His unabashed response: "God forbid! But the very presence of two contending armies, Northern and Southern, will serve as an alarmed police to restrain such excesses, were they otherwise probable."[3]

Lincoln was emphatic that his act be seen as a measure of war enacted "by virtue of the power in me vested as commander-in-chief of the army and navy . . . and as a fit and necessary war measure." Any other terms would be opposed to the Constitution he was pledged to uphold.[4] His proclamation included no pleas for congressional approval or recommendations for a constitutional amendment abolishing slavery everywhere. In this sense, his act was more analogous to his orders to blockade the enemy's coast than it was to England's emancipation in 1833 or the subsequent constitutional amendments ending slavery in the United States in 1865.[5] In 1863 Lincoln's position coincided with Charles Hodge's. Limited emancipation was a means to total victory, not a moral end in itself. The moral end remained the Union.

But also like Hodge, Lincoln changed over the last and bloodiest years. Lincoln was an abolitionist at heart in his personal views ("If slavery is not wrong, nothing is wrong"). He detested the ownership of one human being by another. And with emancipation as a war measure, he could at last bring his personal views more in line with his public executive self. Lincoln was also a pragmatist who wedded emancipation to his other certainty—the resort to total war if necessary to preserve the Constitution and the Union. As a war measure, the Emancipation Proclamation carried the further practical benefit of enlisting black soldiers into Union armies.[6] And with black enlistments, Lincoln would never again mention colonization as a solution to the race problem.

Nevertheless, slavery and emancipation did not bring out Lincoln's rhetorical genius during the war in the way the Union did. Lincoln knew that total war would demand even more blood on the fields and far more suffering in the civilian homesteads, and this realization incarnated in him a growing mystical reverence for the Union as itself something sacred and worthy of sacrificial worship. Lincoln's sacralized interpretation of the Union's meaning led to a level of humility not seen in most of the Northern and Southern moralists. Lincoln's God would not be bound by self-righteous claims to moral superiority by one side or the other. God, in other words, could not be contained in human rhetorical traps. And, almost alone in the war, neither could Lincoln.

Still, Lincoln's hatred of slavery fell far short of guarantees Garrisonians and black abolitionists demanded on the subject of racial equality. On September 18, 1862, in a meeting with a large delegation of Northern clergymen from Chicago, Lincoln had hidden his intention to issue a proclamation. In response to the clergy's plea that he transform the war into an abolition war, Lincoln had made plain that whatever he might do or not do about slavery in the Confederate states would be in response not to moral imperatives or personal opinions but to the exigencies of war.[7] As reported by *The Liberator*,

Lincoln informed the delegation: "I view the matter [of emancipation] as a practical war measure, to be decided upon according to the advantages or disadvantages it may offer to the suppression of the rebellion."

In the same spirit, he sent a public letter to Horace Greeley, printed first in the *New York Tribune* on August 22, 1862, and widely reprinted thereafter:

> My paramount object in this struggle *is* to save the Union, and is *not* either to save or to destroy slavery. If I could save the Union without freeing *any* slave I would do it, and if I could save it by freeing *all* the slaves I would do it; and if I could save it by freeing some and leaving others alone I would also do that. What I do about slavery, and the colored race, I do because I believe it helps to save the Union; and what I forbear, I forbear because I do *not* believe it would help to save the Union. . . . I have here stated my purpose according to my view of *official* duty; and I intend no modification of my oft-expressed *personal* wish that all men every where could be free.[8]

It is important also to remember that his proclamation did not include slaves in the loyal border states. Furthermore, hatred of slavery did not translate into the higher moral imperative of hatred of racism, though all abolitionists recognized it was a necessary starting point. Frederick Douglass recognized this tragic limitation even as he praised emancipation. As long as the Union was the nation's ultimate priority and not abolition and racial equality, racism would endure:

> The law and the sword cannot abolish the malignant slaveholding sentiment which has kept the slave system alive in this country during two centuries. Pride of race, prejudice against color, will raise their hateful clamor for oppression of the negro as heretofore. The slave having ceased to be the abject slave of a single master, his enemies will endeavor to make him the slave of society at large.[9]

Speaking to his white congregation in Plainville, Connecticut, the Reverend Moses Smith issued a bold and parallel judgment on race in the North:

> [A]s to the black man, he is as really, and I have sometimes believed more terribly, enslaved at the North than at the South. He knows that he is a slave there, and expects a slave's reward. But here he is tantalized with the name of freedom, but denied its privileges. . . . Do what he will and be what he will, he is hated everywhere at the North, banished from society, denied often so much as a seat in the cars. . . . We talk of liberty? Of all galling

bondage, this bondage to social feelings, this servitude to caste, this being a "nigger" in society, and "a nigger" at the communion table is probably the most heartless and unrelenting slavery beneath the skies. It may not shackle the body, but it crushes the mind and kills the heart.[10]

Douglass and Smith saw the future.[11]

Lincoln could escape the rhetorical trap of the self-righteous jeremiad and see his way to a newly sacralized republic. But he could not escape the culture of racism and white supremacy of which he was a product. Besides favoring colonization of slaves before emancipation, he expressed no abhorrence about the racist laws in his native Illinois, nor condemned their even more racist denunciations of Indians. When, in August, Lincoln convened a delegation of African American leaders to discuss his interests in colonization, he was disappointed at the stridency of their opposition. "This is our country as much as it is yours, and we will not leave it," an outraged delegate from Philadelphia wrote.[12]

In like fashion, the African American bishop Daniel A. Payne wrote a note for the *Weekly Anglo-African* questioning "the opinions of the government [that] are based upon the ideas, that white men and colored men cannot live together as equals in the same country."[13] To a person the delegation made plain that they were, after all, fully and equally American—a fact that Lincoln's buoyant but racist nationalism could not embrace. An angry editorial in *The Liberator* castigated Lincoln's words and behavior at the August meeting: "What could be more undeserved, or what more insulting, than the remark of President Lincoln to the committee whom he was addressing, 'But for your race among us, there could not be a war . . . it is better for us both therefore, to be separated.' "[14]

If the Emancipation Proclamation did not render Lincoln the "Great Emancipator" in any immediate sense, what was his motive? Emancipation legitimated—and promoted—an escalation of the war on the battlefields and the Southern home fronts like no other action could do. Just as Southern secession cannot be understood without understanding its symbiotic connection to slavery, neither can Lincoln's Northern Emancipation Proclamation be understood without understanding its symbiotic connection to a commitment to total war as the only means to preserve the Union. In moral terms, Lincoln repeatedly made it quite clear that he did not need emancipation to fight a just defensive war.[15] But in practical terms, emancipation was necessary as a means to total war.

When Democrats (and some Republicans) accused Lincoln of shifting a war for Union into a war for abolition, Lincoln denied the charge, but then, in a telling concession, explained that emancipation was his "lever" for a total war that would engage freed black soldiers. The war, Lincoln explained, was not "for the sole purpose of abolition. It is . . . for the sole purpose of restoring the Union. But no human power can subdue this rebellion without using the Emancipation lever as I have done."[16]

However much his Republican citizens clamored for Confederate blood and civilian suffering, Lincoln did not easily come to total war. It was he, after all, who would have to answer for it both to history and to God. But decide he did, and in terms far harsher than the "Christian civilization" McClellan argued for in his Harrison's Landing letter.

On this issue, Lincoln would differ significantly from the Republican theologian Charles Hodge. In Hodge's widely circulated moral reflection on the war, he turned from questions of just cause (*jus ad bellum*) to just conduct (*jus in bello*), and here he remained a West Point Christian. From credible sources, Hodge had learned "that men and women [in the North], professing to be Christians, have been so demoralized or demented by passion, as to maintain that it would be just to visit the South with the fate of the Canaanites." That would be wrong, Hodge asserted, a "sin, a violation of the law of God, for our government to disregard any of the established laws and usages of modern warfare in its efforts to suppress the rebellion."

In time of civilized war, wrote Hodge, "the lives of non-combatants [must] be regarded as sacred." Besides protecting the lives of noncombatants, "it is one of the humane regulations of modern warfare that private property is entitled to protection. Robbery or marauding, on the part of soldiers, is punishable with death." Hodge conceded that sometimes food for men and horses must be taken in enemy territory, but that was a far cry from "the doctrine that the private property of non-combatants is a lawful prize in war."[17]

Lincoln did not agree with Hodge nor with McClellan and the Democratic Party, which was even more adamant on limiting the scope and conduct of the war. His sense of just means was considerably wider and grew more so with every passing battle. But unlike Hodge's vengeful countrymen, his motives were more pragmatic and "prudential" than blood revenge.[18] Almost alone among his American contemporaries, Lincoln evidenced an almost otherworldly capacity to prescribe hard actions "with malice towards none."

Lincoln's strategy worked nearly perfectly. Far more than the Confiscation Act, Lincoln's proclamation encouraged black enlistments in the army and

A group of "Contrabands" (former slaves) standing outside a shanty. Many would go on to work actively for the Union both on the battlefront and behind the scenes.

freed all slaves in secessionist states, those of secessionists and loyalists alike. And with emancipation, a policy of total war enjoyed an unprecedented moral stature, allowing the Northern public to fasten on the "good" of emancipation without ever inquiring into the "bad" of unjust conduct in a total war.[19] From the very inception of the war, Northern clergy had focused their moral commentary on the sin of slavery to the virtual exclusion of all other moral considerations—including *jus in bello* and (with prominent exceptions) Northern racism. Emancipation merely reinforced their unrestrained cheers and unacknowledged silences. On the subject of slavery and emancipation, the clergy insisted loudly through all media that it was their right and moral obligation to "preach politics" in a cause so just that the world would be transformed. On the subjects of *jus in bello* and total war, they retreated to the "spirituality" of the church and said nothing.[20]

Behind this moral silence, which featured the clergy but also included intellectuals and artists, lay a disturbing fact. The war was steadily becoming its own end. Daily battlefield accounts, graphic in detail, accompanied by lithographs, music, art, drama, and, after Antietam, photography, instilled an irrational, but insatiable, fascination with war that fed off its own energy. Many Northerners recognized a revolution brought on by the Emancipation Proclamation that highlighted emancipation as the true cause of the war and its intended effect. That revolution, from military campaign to moral "crusade," meant new limits would be implemented in the execution of the war.

For their part, the Confederates were more than prepared to respond in kind. Nobody could avoid the subject of war as a focus crowding into all aspects of life, religious no less than social. This obsession had its roots less in moral introspection than in sheer preoccupation with battles and destruction.

Emancipation put to final rest any thoughts of a negotiated peace by which the South would be permitted to leave the Union or, conversely, to return with slaves and existing leaders intact. As long as Lincoln and the Republican Party were in power, the Union would stand and slavery be put on notice. With slavery—not Union—as the focal point, commentators could accept the escalation of war virtually without restraint.

From the issuance of Lincoln's Emancipation Proclamation on, Americans in the North and the South would not look back to restrained codes or charity. Total war, with emancipation as the inner accelerator, meant articulating a war ethic in which civilian suffering could be presumed and morally justified. By the spring of 1863 Lincoln's legal scholar, Francis Lieber, would complete a rationale for total war that would stand as a new American foreign policy.[21] If enough attention could be paid to emancipation, however minimal the actuality might be, no one would ask hard questions about the moral implications of either a turn to total war or enduring white supremacy. The slippery slope began.

Northern thanksgiving sermons happily endorsed the new terms of war. In his thanksgiving "discourse" denouncing Northern racism, Moses Smith also picked up the Bushnellian theme of a Christian (Puritan) America. Despite pretensions to being a "Christian nation," the Lincoln government "[has] resounded with sneers against any law higher than the Constitution. . . . [O]ur honored President, with all his praise-worthy efforts for the oppressed, and with all his appeals to praying people for God's direction and assistance, not so much as recognizes the idea, that God and righteousness have anything to do with the deliverance of 4,000,000 bondsmen." But happily, Smith concluded, Lincoln's Emancipation Proclamation set the nation on a reforming course and established that "our nation is not forsaken." With that proclamation, victory could be assured.[22]

Philadelphia Presbyterian Albert Barnes agreed with Smith. It was not enough to restore the Constitution: "I believe that mistakes were made in framing that constitution . . . there are evils contained in the constitution which it is possible still to remedy and remove."[23] Chief of these evils was, of course, slavery, and if coercive emancipation was the only way to change the Constitution, then, Barnes concluded, so be it.

In the Dutch Reformed Church of Stapleton, New York, Thomas H. Skinner undertook to examine the nation "from the stand-point of Eternal Providence," and, in effect, speak for God's global intentions in the war. Clearly God was only on the side of the North, and the South was "simply demonic."[24] America, Skinner concluded, and not Christ's return to earth, would lead the world into millennial glory.

In such nationalistic millennialism, the historian James Moorhead discerns a "dangerous substrate" that identifies Providence with "the idealistic conception of American destiny." Such identification minimizes moral restraints or adherence to international standards of war common to all civilized nations. Instead, it can legitimate excesses and raw terrorism. By linking emancipation and the "crusade" against slavery to total war and a "crusade" against the Confederacy, Lincoln's administration watered the seeds of an American-led Christian imperialism that was not without costs in later American history.[25]

On December 1, 1862, President Lincoln delivered his State of the Union message to the Thirty-seventh Congress. The news for the Union was good. Europe remained out of the war and refused to recognize the Confederacy. Despite the enormous costs of war, Federal receipts were satisfactory and "the public credit has been fully maintained." Bloody Indian wars might be avoided through forced relocation of warring tribes. If colonization would not work with African Americans, forced relocation and confinement on Federal "reservations" would, Lincoln asserted, work for Native Americans.[26] Most important, a way eventually to abolish slavery was found.

With the moral good of emancipation on the floor, Lincoln turned to national ends. Questions of just conduct and habeas corpus were not raised. "Honor" would be invoked, but not the honor of the West Point Code. Only emancipation was referenced as the tag for a stirring conclusion that would introduce phrases for an American scripture:

> Fellow-citizens, we cannot escape history. We of this Congress and this administration, will be remembered in spite of ourselves. . . . The fiery trial through which we pass, will light us down, in honor or dishonor, to the latest generation. . . . We know how to save the Union. . . . We—even we here—hold the power, and bear the responsibility. In giving freedom to the slave, we assure freedom to the free—honorable alike in what we give, and what we preserve. We shall nobly save, or meanly lose, the last best, hope of earth. Other means may succeed; this could not fail. The way is plain, peaceful, generous, just—a way which, if followed, the world will forever applaud, and God must forever bless.[27]

Total war was regrettable, but not as regrettable as sacrificing the world's last best hope. When white Unionists in New Orleans protested Union policies of emancipating slaves in occupied territories, Lincoln responded: "I am a patient man—always willing to forgive on the Christian terms of repentance; and also to give ample time for repentance. Still, I must save the government if possible. . . . [And] it may as well be understood, once for all, that I shall not surrender this game leaving any available card unplayed."[28] Soon enough all would learn that Lincoln meant exactly what he said.

CHAPTER 20

FREDERICKSBURG: "SO FOOLHARDY AN ADVENTURE"

Lincoln's decision to wage total war meant that he was prepared to obliterate prior rules and that, in turn, meant that more and more attention inevitably had to be given over to the question of non-combatant immunity. Lincoln's executive order permitting commanders "to seize and use any property, real or personal" that would further the war effort, issued on July 22, 1862, together with General Orders Nos. 5, 7, 11, and 13, allowed the Army of the Potomac to "subsist upon the country." The army could also hold rebel civilians responsible for attacks on army personnel in their region. Any civilian who refused to swear an oath of allegiance to the United States—in essence every white Southerner—would be liable to be turned out of their homes and sent within rebel lines.

With these orders, issued at the highest level, the war now descended directly upon the homes, farms, and lives of Southern civilians. Clearly any war on civilian populations rendered questions of just conduct acute in the minds of those responsible for setting orders in motion and the soldiers who would carry them out. Where were the answers? Incredibly, there existed no English-language handbook on the code of war. When asked how soldiers had been guided in the Mexican War, Winfield Scott had to concede that they operated only from an "unwritten code." In December 1862, with emancipation and total war looming, Lincoln commissioned a board to draw up, for the first time, a code of just conduct in time of war. The only civilian on the board, Francis Lieber, turned out to be the chief architect and author of the resulting code.

Lieber had personal and intellectual interests in the project that made him ideally suited for the task at hand. Despite spending sixteen years teaching in South Carolina before moving north to the Columbia Law faculty,

Lieber had no sympathy with either secession or slavery. His experience as a young German soldier fighting at Waterloo convinced him that states required strong central governments to rein in secessionist impulses. In his view, the Union must be preserved. But also weighing on his personal positions was the fact that all three of his sons were fighting in the Civil War. Hamilton Lieber fought for the Union and lost an arm at the battle of Fort Donelson. Norman Lieber, also a Union soldier, fought against his rebel brother, Oscar Lieber, at the battle of Williamsburg (May 1862), where Oscar was killed, cursing his father and the North as he lay dying.

Lieber completed his work in April 1863, noting in a letter to Henry Halleck, "I had no guide, no groundwork no textbook. . . . Usage, history, reason, and conscientiousness, and a sincere love of truth, justice, and civilization have been my guides." Lincoln approved the document immediately and distributed it to his commanders as General Orders No. 100.

The manifest object of Lieber's Code was to limit the abuses of total war described generally as "savagery." The reason for laws of war, Lieber recognized, was moral: "Men who take up arms against one another in public war do not cease on this account to be moral beings, responsible to one another and to God." Offenses of "wanton violence against persons in the invaded country," wrote Lieber, "all destruction of property not commanded by the authorized officer, all robbery, all pillage or sacking, even after taking a place by main force, all rape, wounding, maiming, or killing of such inhabitants, are prohibited under the penalty of death, or such other severe punishment as may seem adequate for the gravity of the offense." While conceding that "the citizen or native of a hostile country is thus an enemy . . . and as such is subjected to the hardships of war," it was also advisable that "the unarmed citizen is to be spared in person, property, and honor as much as the exigencies of war will admit."[1]

But all this attempt at humane treatment was undermined by the higher duty to win the struggle no matter what the cost. By identifying the national cause with the war and valuing the survival of the nation over all competing considerations, anything could ultimately be justified under the rubric of what Lieber termed "military necessity":

Military necessity, as understood by modern civilized nations, consists in the necessity of those measures which are indispensable for securing the ends of the war. . . . Military necessity admits of all direct destruction of life or limb of armed enemies, and of other persons whose destruction is incidentally unavoidable in the armed contests of the war. . . . [I]t allows of all destruction of property, and obstruction of the ways and channels of traffic, travel, or communication, and of all withholding of sustenance or means of life from the enemy, of the appropriation of whatever an enemy's country affords necessary for the subsistence and safety of the Army.

What Lieber contributed to restraint under the duty of humane treatment and protection of private life on the one hand, he removed with the other as "military necessity." Lieber's Code effectively gave commanders a blank check for operations in the field. As the ethicist James Turner Johnson recognizes: "Where the difference between private and public is hard to discern, or where the aims of war are so broadly defined as to do away with that difference, then it is difficult to see how Lieber's argument for protection of noncombatants can have any restraining force at all."[2] Lincoln could not have asked for any more.

"Military necessity" supplied the moral cloak permitting war on civilian populations. In effect, civilians were transformed from "noncombatants" to "the enemy" of the nation state. The code protected American officers and soldiers from virtually any reprisal. While a few soldiers were tried and executed for rape during the war, there would be no trials for destruction of civilian property or lives.[3]

Union generals showed scant interest in the code and soldiers none. Confederates probably studied it more closely for its vagueness in preventing "retaliation" or revenge on enemies and its wide-open definition of "military necessity" that, if necessary enough, could justify just about anything. But Lieber's Code gave Lincoln and his generals what they needed as they contemplated a new war that would deliberately invade civilian lives and properties.

Besides a liberal code of military conduct, Lincoln desperately needed his own Lee or Jackson to win major battles in the East, where voters and the media were concentrated. Lieber's Code would mean little if there were no commanders willing and able to implement crushing overland campaigns with strategic sensibilities. Already Democrats had seized on unprecedented carnage and unfulfilled war goals to make sizable inroads in state and Federal midterm elections. Without victories, Lincoln stood no chance of reelection, and without great warrior generals there would be no victories.

McClellan was not such a general, and on October 1, 1862, an angry Lincoln visited McClellan in the field and again expressed his frustrations over McClellan's failure to pursue Lee's retreating army. When McClellan continued to pursue the cautious path of limited war instead of crossing the Potomac while the November roads were still passable, Lincoln once again relieved McClellan of his command on November 5, and replaced him with Major General Ambrose Burnside.

On paper, Burnside looked good. An 1847 graduate of West Point and a veteran of the Mexican and Indian wars, he had resigned from the army to form a business manufacturing firearms and had invented the breech-loading rifle. But his performance in commanding massive and complex armies in the field, where outcomes were determined by contingency and improvisation, was untested. He twice refused offers to command the Army of the Potomac, and his listless performance at Antietam, when he let Lee escape, suggests that he knew himself better than Lincoln did. But Lincoln could not stick with McClellan. The only other possible candidate, Joseph Hooker, was widely disliked by his fellow officers. So Burnside reluctantly took command of the most powerful army on the continent, if not in the world.

In the next six weeks, Burnside confirmed his inability to command a large army with stunning finality.[4] Instead of decisively moving his massive army of 122,000 south to strike Lee's divided army on their unprotected wings and destroy them in detail, Burnside shifted his lines east and confronted Lee's army at the hilly town of Fredericksburg, fifty miles north of Richmond alongside the Rappahannock River. The ground behind the town was ideal for strategic defensive placements, as it rose high in the air, peaking in an area known as Marye's Heights. Soldiers could lie six deep in a sunken road behind the stone wall, creating a virtually impenetrable barrier that, with artillery behind, could withstand any frontal assault.

And frontal assault was exactly what Burnside planned.[5] On a chilly Saturday, December 13, just as the morning fog gave way to startling sunlight, Confederate defenders, heavily fortified with artillery of their own, watched the oncoming Army of the Potomac with awed anticipation. Thousands of Yankees with battle flags streaming marched rank upon rank up the hill in a desperate bid to dislodge Confederate defenders from their nearly perfect defenses.

The assault was hopeless. Despite heroic charges by Burnside's divisions, Longstreet's line held and repulsed the Federals. None even made it to the stone wall. With inestimable bravery, if not wisdom, Federals continued to charge until nightfall, leaving behind a field stacked three deep in casualties. Finally, after fourteen separate brigade-size attacks, the Federals retreated, leaving piles of their dead in front of the stone wall.

Still unable to accept the full horror of his failed assaults, Burnside contemplated renewed assaults the next day. His officers persuaded him to revoke the orders. On the other side, Lee wisely resisted the temptation to carry a counteroffensive into well-entrenched Federal artillery aching for a payback, and held his soldiers back. The ratio of losses between North and

Bombardment and capture of Fredericksburg, Virginia. Despite the fact that General Ambrose Burnside (seated on his noble steed) and his Federals lost miserably at Fredericksburg, Currier & Ives chose to portray a heroic victory for Northerners on the home front.

South ranked Fredericksburg among the most one-sided battles in the war: in all, Burnside lost 12,600 men to Lee's 5,300.

Only in the gruesome aftermath would common soldiers recognize the slaughter they had wreaked upon each other. Fredericksburg itself was destroyed, though most of the civilians had escaped before the battle. The night after the battle, screams punctuated the dark as wounded men pleaded for assistance.

The dead received no respect. For Confederate forces, undersupplied and bitterly cold, the temptation to ransack Federal dead for clothing, shoes, and food proved irresistible. Starlight brought with it the haunting landscape of pale naked Yankee corpses lying in frozen suspended animation before the stone wall. They looked, one soldier later recalled, "like hogs that had been cleaned."[6] A disbelieving Robert E. Lee looked at the carnage and muttered the famous words, "It is well that war is so terrible—we should grow too fond of it."[7]

Private John E. Anderson arrived at Fredericksburg from Belle Isle Prison the day after the battle to rejoin his unit, only to find them decimated: "Thomas Plunkett has lost both arms. Hugh Gallagher has lost a finger. The rest are dead or on detached duty at the hospital. . . . I see many new faces, and look in vain for any of the old ones."[8]

After initial reports of a stunning Federal triumph, Lincoln and the War

Department in Washington soon learned otherwise and were aghast at the enormity of the defeat. Besides the military setback, the political ramifications were devastating. Northern morale would plummet, and political support for the war and the party that fought it would drop still further.

To minimize the damage, Burnside imposed an immediate gag on the press, blocking all access to the telegraph wires and forbidding anyone—especially reporters—from leaving the scene of the battle. For several days, the North stood in ignorance both as to the scope of the defeat and the names of the casualties.

The same was not true in the South, where commentators mocked the stupidity of Union commanders. One writer expressed the general opinion that:

> The Yankees had essayed a task which no army could have accomplished. To have driven our men from their position and to have taken it, was a work compared with which the storming of Gibraltar would be as child's play. . . . No other man than Burnside would have attempted so difficult or so foolhardy an adventure.[9]

When word of the extent of defeat finally reached the Northern public, fury was unleashed both on Union commanders and on the press for supposedly suppressing the tragic news. The press immediately exonerated themselves, leaving the commanders to absorb the full rage of public sentiment. According to Murat Halstead, editor of the *Cincinnati Commercial*, who had earlier accused Sherman of being "gone in the head," Burnside was even worse:

> It can hardly be in human nature for men to show more valor, or Generals to manifest less judgment, than were perceptible on our side that day. . . . We did not take a battery or silence a gun. We did not reach the crest of the hights [sic] held by the enemy in a single place. . . . The occupation of Fredericksburg was a blunder.[10]

While pro-Republican papers like the *New York Tribune* or *Chicago Tribune* tried to minimize the disaster, opposition papers—most notably the *New York Herald*—had a field day criticizing the War Department and General Burnside. Burnside was so incensed by the blistering account registered by William Swinton in the *New York Times* that he summoned him into his tent and threatened to shoot him.

Sid Deming, chief correspondent of the Associated Press, was arrested for breaking the gag and removed to Washington for his printed account of plummeting morale in the army. It did not help Deming that he was a champion of McClellan and an enemy of Halleck. To blunt criticisms of Lincoln for adopting a suicidal total-war strategy, Burnside issued a public apology to the Associated Press, taking sole responsibility for the debacle.[11]

While quick to criticize Northern leadership for the defeat at Fredericksburg, no public commentators remarked on the level of slaughter. In fact, Lee's lament came too late. The two nations had already grown far too fond of war to give up on it anytime soon. The infantry of patriotism, reinforced with the artillery of mounting hatred, rendered both sides mindless killing machines bent on destruction.

One Confederate chaplain wrote in the *Central Presbyterian*: "We should add to the prayer for peace, let this war continue, if we are not yet so humbled and disciplined by its trials, as to be prepared for those glorious moral and spiritual gifts, which Thou designest it should confer upon us as a people, and upon the Church of Christ in the Confederacy, and upon mankind."[12]

Meanwhile, in the days following Fredericksburg, Burnside's public acceptance of blame reaped a whirlwind of public rage in the press and in the War Department. Again, Lincoln faced the prospects of incompetent command and mounting criticism at home. A scathing cartoon in the *New York Illustrated News* depicted Secretary of War Stanton and Lincoln garbed in country dresses with the caption: "This is old mother Lincoln explaining to old mother Stanton how the slaughter of our troops at Fredericksburg reminds him of an anecdote he heard out west."[13]

From the trenches, James Gassner wrote to his mother:

What do the people up North think about Burnside now? Do they think he can do just as he pleases with the Rebs? Perhaps they will want little Mac. To save the Capitol again and their played out President [Lincoln] and the rest of his gang. I'll tell you what it is; little McClellan knows more in one day than all the rest of our Generals in three weeks. I think if McClellan had had command of us we never would have had to retreat.[14]

Left out of this ordinary soldier's perception from ground level was the tactical truism that McClellan would never have had to retreat because he would have never advanced.

Not all fatalities were on the battlefield. For Henry Joslin, a baker with the Union army, death came slowly by disease. In letters to his mother in

January 1863, he described problems with scurvy that placed him on light duty. By February he asked for a furlough to heal but was denied. In March he wrote his mother, "I have taken out a bunk in the hospital tent where I can have better care and rations then in the Co. quarters where I have been." But it would not help. His final letter, written near Potomac Creek, Virginia, was a last-ditch plea for his mother's help:

> Dear Mother, Captain Eager said that he was going to have you send for me or come and get me and the quicker you come the better. I think I can start right off with you as the surgeon told me to write for where to come for me. My appetite is good and I feel first rate only weak yet. You will find me at 2nd Div. 2nd Corps Hospital Potomac Creek Bridge. Come and God speed you to your soldier boy, Henry Joslin.[15]

By the time his mother arrived, Henry Joslin, "soldier boy," had died.

On December 22 Lincoln conferred in Washington with Burnside and congratulated the army for its bravery at Fredericksburg, publicly labeling the defeat an "accident." Despite the good face, Lincoln was desperate for leadership that could expend lives but at the same time win victories.

CHAPTER 21

"GOD HAS GRANTED US A HAPPY NEW YEAR"

While the Army of the Potomac licked its wounds in the East, Lincoln's eventual redeemers Grant and Sherman continued to tarnish their reputations in the West, both on and off the battlefield. In Grant's case, criticism surrounded his infamous General Orders No. 11. Concerned over exploitative peddlers and speculators preying on Union camps, Grant pointed the finger at all Jews with the following order: "The Jews, as a class violating every regulation of trade established by the Treasury Department and also department orders, are hereby expelled from the department within twenty-four hours from the receipt of the order."[1]

Though never put into effect and eventually rescinded by Lincoln, the order did its damage. Grant added to the stigma of alcoholism the opprobrium of anti-Semitism. But neither of these dark marks dislodged Lincoln's confidence in Grant's military abilities. Given the way the war was going, a world of sins could be forgiven by one victory.

In Richmond, the *Daily Dispatch* exploited Grant's attempted expulsion of Jews from his department as "all in keeping with the professed religious toleration of the puritans." In contrast, they held up Judah Benjamin, their Jewish secretary of state, as an example of superior toleration. The paper went on to defend religious toleration as a sacred principle and blasted "Yankee historians" who traced intolerance back to the South.[2] The editors seemed to make a point of welcoming Jews and Catholics into the Southern tent as they published commentaries by rabbis and bishops who supported the Confederate cause.[3] They also explained how Irish Catholics were being duped into fighting for the North, and later defended the Jews when they were singled out in the war as extortionists.[4]

At the same time, tolerance had its limits. Virtually all Confederates agreed that Northern-only movements such as Mormonism and Spiritualism did not deserve the term "religion." Instead, these movements must be viewed as evil outgrowths of a deeply rooted, Puritan-derived fanaticism that had taken a religious form.[5] The *Richmond Daily Dispatch* printed a letter on "Thoughts for Soldiers" that contrasted the piety of the Christian South to the heresies of the North: "Hence the materialism of Practical Phrenology, the irresponsibility from Mesmeric Influences, the ridiculous revelation of Mormonism to Joe Smith, the ascension robes of Millerism, the seven spheres of Spiritualism, etc." Only secession could save the continent for Christ, "as the consequence of the foregoing God cut us off from the North, not only to save us from this contamination, but to save to the cause of Christ one branch of the church as yet unshaken. Mark! not for our merit, or because we were without fault, but as the Jews were often saved because 'to them were committed the oracles of god.' "[6]

On the battlefield, General Sherman suffered another ill-advised Federal defeat when he took an expedition down the Mississippi from Memphis to Chickasaw Bluffs north of Vicksburg. On December 29, in a movement reminiscent of Fredericksburg, he advanced on General John Clifford Pemberton's well-entrenched forces and was soundly beaten back. Out of 31,000 effectives, Sherman lost 1,776 compared to only 207 Confederates.[7]

Meanwhile, Confederate civilians continued to feel the brunt of battle in their home lives. Letters to the Confederate Treasury Department continued to overwhelm Secretary Christopher Gustavus Memminger. One particularly poignant appeal to President Davis came from Julia Williams of Petersburg, Virginia. Williams's husband had been killed at Malvern Hill even as Yankee forces were destroying her home. Davis forwarded her appeal to Secretary Memminger with the note "widow of Lt. Williams killed at Malvern Hill." Her story speaks for itself:

> Servants and everything else we possess have long since been in their possession. All this I cheerfully resigned, while I had the aid and comfort of my patriotic and devoted husband, But alas! The time had come that he too had fallen as a noble martyr upon the altar of his country. . . . Consequently I am deprived by the chances of war of his aid and forced to surrender the resources on which I have hitherto relied for support. I am left entirely dependent therefore and present myself as an humble supplicant. . . . I do sincerely hope I shall not be compelled to return to my desolate home unprotected and unprovided for. I am indeed in a lamentable situation.[8]

Behind the suffering lay a mounting fury that generated blood appetites that could not be satisfied. These sentiments found their most strident voice in the clergy and their calls for blood revenge. In a funeral sermon "for Lieutenant Abram Carrington of the CSA," reprinted in the *Central Presbyterian* of Richmond, the firebrand Robert Dabney preached an incendiary sermon condemning the North for an "aggressive war," which, in moral terms, "is wholesale murder."

Lieutenant Carrington, a close friend of Dabney's, had become the most recent victim of the conflict. After extolling Carrington's courage at the battle of Frayser's Farm on June 30, 1862, Dabney took aim at the hearts of his congregation's young men:

> Surely [his] very blood should cry out again from the ground, if we permitted the soil which drank the precious libation, to be polluted with the despot's foot! Before God, I take you to witness this day, that its blood seals upon you the obligation to fill their places in your country's host, and "play the men for your people and the cities of your God," to complete vindication of their rights.[9]

The language of blood as a "precious libation" could not go unnoticed by Dabney's young hearers as they prepared themselves for sacrifice.

The effect of joining emancipation and total war assumed an eerie confirmation when New Year's Day newspapers presented coverage of both the Emancipation Proclamation and a frightful new battle with horrific casualties. This time the center of attention shifted to the western theater. There Confederate forces in retreat from Perryville, Kentucky, under the command of General Braxton Bragg, met advancing Federal forces under General William Rosecrans near the town of Murfreesboro, Tennessee. Both commanders were hot-tempered and eventually lost their commands, but not before clashing in a full-fledged bloodbath.

On December 31, forty-four thousand Yankees faced off against thirty-eight thousand rebels just west of Stones River. That night, with battle looming, the contending bands played their rival national tunes. Then in another poignant moment of American fellow feeling, both bands and armies joined together in singing "Home Sweet Home." Two armies, one home. The next day they met in battle.

Ironically, both generals planned to attack the other's right flank and get into his rear, cutting his army from its base.[10] General Rosecrans ordered his attack to start at daybreak after breakfast. But as at Shiloh, the Confederates

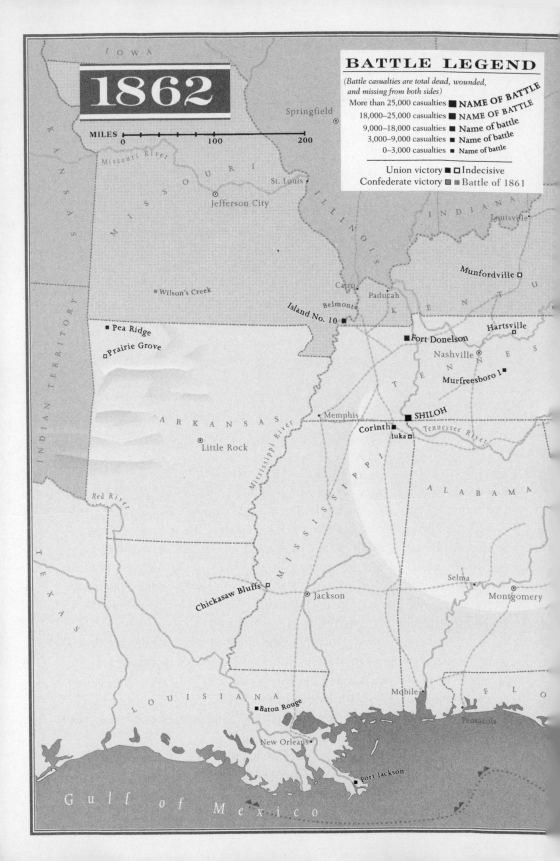

1862

MILES
0   100   200

IOWA

KANSAS

Missouri River

Springfield

St. Louis

MISSOURI

⊙ Jefferson City

ILLINOIS

INDIANA

Louisville

Cairo

Paducah

■ Wilson's Creek

Belmont

■ Island No. 10

Munfordville □

KENTUCKY

INDIAN TERRITORY

■ Pea Ridge

□ Prairie Grove

■ Fort Donelson

Hartsville

Nashville ⊙

TENNESSEE

Murfreesboro I □

ARKANSAS

Mississippi River

Memphis

■ **SHILOH**

■ Corinth

Iuka □

Tennessee River

⊙ Little Rock

ALABAMA

Red River

Selma

Chickasaw Bluffs □

⊙ Jackson

MISSISSIPPI

Montgomery

TEXAS

LOUISIANA

Mobile

FLO

■ Baton Rouge

Pensacola

New Orleans

■ Fort Jackson

Gulf of Mexico

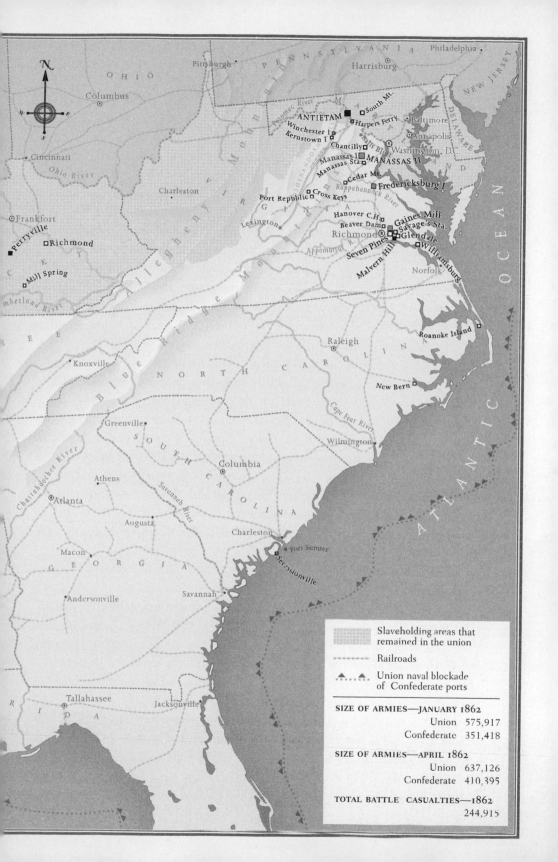

N

OHIO

Columbus ⊙

W ● E
S

N

Cincinnati ●

Ohio River

Charleston ●

⊙ Frankfort

Perryville ●

□ Richmond

Mill Spring □

Cumberland River

Pittsburgh ●

PENNSYLVANIA

Harrisburg ●

Philadelphia ●

NEW JERSEY

M A R Y L A N D

ANTIETAM ■   South Mt.

Harpers Ferry □

Baltimore ●

Annapolis ●

DELAWARE

Winchester I □

Kernstown I □

Chantilly □

Bull Run

Washington, D.C. ⊙

Manassas I □   MANASSAS II ■

Manassas Sta. □

Cedar Mt. □

Fredericksburg I □

Rappahannock River

Port Republic □

Cross Keys □

Hanover C.H. □

Beaver Dam □   Gaines' Mill ■
Savage's Sta. □

Richmond ⊙   Glendale □

Seven Pines □   Williamsburg □

Malvern Hill ■

Norfolk ●

OCEAN

V I R G I N I A

Lexington ●

Appomattox R.

Shenandoah

Potomac River

Blue Ridge Mountains

Allegheny Mountains

Knoxville ●

Raleigh ⊙

Roanoke Island ■

N O R T H   C A R O L I N A

New Bern ■

Cape Fear River

Greenville ●

Wilmington ●

S O U T H
C A R O L I N A

Columbia ⊙

Savannah River

Chattahoochee River

Athens ●

⊙ Atlanta

Augusta ●

Charleston ●

Fort Sumter ■

Secessionville ●

G E O R G I A

Macon ●

Andersonville ●

Savannah ●

ATLANTIC

ATLANTIC

Tallahassee ⊙

Jacksonville ●

F
L
O
R
I
D
A

Slaveholding areas that
remained in the union

••••••••• Railroads

▲▲▲ Union naval blockade
of Confederate ports

SIZE OF ARMIES—JANUARY 1862
Union   575,917
Confederate   351,418

SIZE OF ARMIES—APRIL 1862
Union   637,126
Confederate   410,395

TOTAL BATTLE CASUALTIES—1862
244,915

caught the coffee-sipping Yankees by surprise. With a burst of bloodcurdling rebel yells, the Confederates advanced and drove the Federal right flank back three miles before they were finally stopped. A fierce holding action and counterattack by the young and extremely gifted General Philip Sheridan bought sufficient time for the Federals to regroup. In the course of a furious four-hour firefight, Sheridan lost one-third of his men and all of his brigade commanders. But the imperiled flank held, and with it Sheridan's reputation.

By noon, the Union line had regrouped in a precarious position likened by military historians to a "jackknife with its blade nearly closed." If the Confederates could break the Federal line anywhere along the Nashville turnpike, the blade would snap shut and the Union army would be destroyed.[11] The crucial angle where the blade joined the handle lay in a four-acre oak grove named Round Forest, but which the soldiers would rename "Hell's Half Acre." Confederate corps commander and former Episcopal bishop Leonidas Polk ordered his Mississippi rebels to charge across an open field to attack the Round Forest.

On the other side, General George Thomas—who enjoyed the distinction of never leaving the battlefield through four years of war—had placed lines of heavy artillery in the paths of the charging Confederates. In a single salvo of shattering noise, the artillery opened up and tore the advancing Confederates to shreds. The noise was so intense that it reportedly drove the rabbits mad, and they tried to crawl under prostrate soldiers for protection. A second charge penetrated the Union line west of Round Forest and succeeded in capturing one thousand prisoners and eleven guns. But still the midwesterners held Round Forest as a cigar-chomping General Rosecrans, in rumpled hat and bloodstained overcoat, rallied his forces up and down the line.

Bragg was so certain Rosecrans would retreat, weighed down as he was with many Union casualties and Confederate prisoners in tow, that he sent a victory message to President Davis: "God has granted us a happy New Year." But Bragg's God proved to be a New Year's angel of darkness. Instead of retiring, Rosecrans decided to remain in the field overnight, moving his army from the Round Forest to higher ground perfectly situated for a strategic defensive position. There the Federals launched a fierce counterattack that claimed seventeen hundred casualties in little over an hour.

With a third of his troops dead, wounded, or missing, Bragg could neither follow up his tactical victory with an attack on Rosecrans's larger army nor drive it back. Instead, badly intimidated, he called off the attack and retreated to a new position south of Murfreesboro, leaving a bloodbath behind. Clearly Lincoln was not the only president dealing with incompetent generals. Federal losses totaled 12,906 of 41,400 engaged. In proportional terms, this would prove to be the deadliest battle the North would fight. The Confederates lost 11,739 out of 34,739 engaged.

As Rosecrans's equally savaged army fell into Murfreesboro to recover, Lincoln confronted serious problems of his own, both within his cabinet and within his eastern army. A cabinet split between Seward and Secretary of the Treasury Salmon Chase threatened to undermine Lincoln's authority and respect. Radical Republican senators, working with Chase, sought to remove Seward from office and push Lincoln into total emancipation alongside total war. After listening to the senators and to his cabinet, Lincoln determined to retain both cabinet members and refuse each of their resignations. Nor was he yet ready for total emancipation.

The military leadership crisis continued. In the Army of the Potomac, Lincoln's generals were alternatingly hesitant and arrogant at the most inopportune times, thus squandering their numerical and material superiority. Burnside was clearly incompetent, but his most likely successor, Fighting Joe Hooker, evidenced an excess of ambition and a shortage of discretion. Nevertheless, Lincoln felt he had no choice, and, on January 25, 1863, he replaced Burnside with Hooker. Knowing the disaffection that Hooker's fellow officers felt for him, Lincoln followed up his promotion with a blistering letter of "fatherly" advice to the arrogant general:

> You have confidence in yourself, which is a valuable, if not an indispensable quality. You are ambitious, which, within reasonable bounds, does good rather than harm. But I think that during Gen. Burnside's command of the Army, you have taken counsel of your ambition, and thwarted him as much as you could, in which you did a great wrong to the country. . . . I have heard, in such a way as to believe it, of your recently saying, that both the Army and the Government needed a Dictator. Of course it was not for this, but in spite of it, that I have given you the command. Only those generals who gain successes, can set up dictators. What I now ask of you is military success, and I will risk the dictatorship. . . . Beware of rashness, but with energy, and sleepless vigilance, go forward, and give us victories.[12]

The soldiers were not happy with the turnover in generals. For John Emerson Anderson, recently released from a Confederate prison, the verdict remained uncertain: "You may think my patriotism is shaken but I tell you no, I think if we cannot find any leader to take command of us that will lead us on to victory, there [is] little use in continuing the war. However we cannot tell what Hooker will do."[13] Other soldiers extended their criticisms to the entire officer corps. In a letter to his wife, William Willoughby of New Haven complained:

> I have just been out for Regimental Inspection by our beautiful Colonel who was beautifully drunk and who had a beautiful fight last night with one Captain Quinn of Company "G" over three or 4 W.——s [whores] who they got to quarter in their Barracks through the night. . . . In the fight "pistols" was cocked and swords drawn. Other officers had to interfere and separate before order could be restored. A good portion of the company and Regimental Officers are a poor drunken sett of fellows wholly unfit for the position they hold. And it is not very encouraging to go into battle with such men to lead us.[14]

Lincoln's problems with the press would not go away either. Criticism of his generals and plans abounded, but often on the basis of rumor and unsubstantiated reports. The press of daily issues frequently led to incomplete and even misleading accounts of key battles. In an effort to harness irresponsible and sensationalist reporting, Hooker ordered all dispatches to be signed by their writers. But still the scurrilous reporting continued.

Because the religious press appeared weekly and was written by ministers rather than journalists, it promoted itself as superior in terms of sober reflection and accuracy. On January 8 the *New York Evangelist* carried an account of Murfreesboro under the "Course of Events" column. In the following week's issue, three editors pointed out the advantages of a weekly print: "We think weekly papers have an advantage over the Daily. Conflicting rumors have time to be compared, and the truth to be sifted out from them all. Many of our readers have told us that they get a better idea of the General Progress of the War from the 'Course of Events' . . . than from all the daily papers put together."[15] But whatever truth was sifted out by virtue of delay, the avoidance of moral commentary was as characteristic of the religious press as of the secular.

Late January and early February 1863 saw one of the worst winters on record, and left both Union and Confederate armies resting and nursing their wounds. In the East Hooker was preparing his Army of the Potomac for a major spring campaign, while in the West Grant was still indecisive around Vicksburg. Moral commentary was absent, but not the commerce of war. For some time, the secular and religious press had been filled with advertisements for caskets. By 1863 another item increasingly appeared in the press:

mourning clothes. Philadelphia's *American Presbyterian* advertised that "families about putting on Mourning will find it to their advantage to examine our stock before purchasing elsewhere."[16]

On the home front, Confederate sermons continued to impress on listeners the consolation of God's sovereignty and the demands of duty. In a thanksgiving sermon preached to the First Methodist Church in Austin, Texas, the pastor, W. Rees, spoke on the theme of divine Providence, enjoining all his hearers to depend on God rather than armies or foreign deliverers.[17]

In the North, sermons on Washington's Birthday began, for the first time, to liken Lincoln to the Founding General-Father of the nation. In a Washington's Birthday sermon on "Loyalty," Horace C. Hovey conceded that at the moment Lincoln was no George Washington. But emancipation represented a noble moment:

We cannot but wish that in all points there was a closer resemblance between him and the illustrious Washington. Yet coming generations may have as much occasion to bless Abraham Lincoln, as we have to bless George Washington; and the muse of History may record with equal pride his name who broke the yoke of Slavery, and whose strong arm struck off the chains of British tyranny.[18]

On a more ominous note, Northern citizens were beginning to learn about life in Confederate prisons. In another Washington's Birthday sermon, the Reverend Samuel Spear reported on a returning prisoner of war who had been imprisoned in Richmond. The prison, he noted, was

about one hundred feet in length and thirty-five feet in width, and containing in a single room some two hundred and thirty men . . . furnished with no beds or blankets, and [who] live on a pint of soup salted with saltpeter and a small piece of bread, supplied twice a day. The prison is literally alive with vermin. . . . Such facts stir my blood. They arouse my indignation against this wicked rebellion, and against the men who are its leaders.[19]

As bad as that sounded, it was nothing compared to what was coming in both Northern and Southern prisons.

While the battlefields returned a mixed verdict for the Confederacy, internal divisions caused increasing concern and represented a turning point in Confederate morale that only a military victory could offset. Davis, no less than Lincoln, desperately needed battlefield triumphs. The notion that a single party could transcend internal divisions and contentions was, by 1863, a bad joke in Southern circles. The conflicts were especially sharp in Richmond where the national government interacted with local government and Richmond's citizenry. Everywhere there were divisions: rich and poor, pro- and anti-Davis factions, local versus Confederate governments, religious versus secular press. All began to fray under the pressure of relentless war and increasing shortages for the military and the home front.[20]

Class conflict grew especially intense as currency inflated at a staggering rate, driven by speculators who profited at the painful expense of ordinary men and women whose savings dwindled in value and soon disappeared. The historian William J. Kimball observes that "by the end of 1862 there were obviously two distinct classes of people in wartime Richmond . . . the haves and the have nots."[21] These class tensions exacerbated tensions raised by military defeats and would only grow worse.

Dissent and contention did not signal an erosion of Confederate nationalism or capitulation to Unionist sentiment as some historians have claimed.[22] But they did eliminate the myth that one party could preclude deep divisions or that the Confederacy could transcend politics and stand as a model of unity. Just as the Davis administration could no longer speak for the people at large, or even the state and local governments, so neither magistrates nor ministers could any longer claim to speak for the poor in all their interests.[23] As scarcity fell unevenly on the population, many laborers sank into a depression that questioned the Confederacy.

Economic tensions further strained Richmond society and prompted ethnic discrimination. Wages did not keep up with inflation, even while the salaries of city officials increased by a total of more than 200 percent. Despite their self-righteous criticisms of Grant's anti-Semitism, the South was no better. Judah Benjamin was Davis's most loyal cabinet member and a model of religious tolerance for Southern Christian apologists. But his appointment did not prevent Jew-baiting among the general populace.

With spring, an exasperated and wildly anti-Semitic war clerk, J. B. Jones, exclaimed: "Oh the extortioners! General Winder has issued an order fixing the maximum price of certain articles of marketing, which has only the effect of keeping a great many things out of market. The farmers have to pay the merchants and Jews their extortionate prices. . . . It does more harm than good." Elsewhere Jones observed, "The president is thin and haggard; and it has been whispered on the street that he will immediately be baptized and confirmed. I hope so, because it may place a great gulf between him and the [Jewish] descendants of those who crucified the Saviour."[24] Clearly Jones wanted Jews to go away from Richmond as badly as Grant wanted Jews expelled from contact with the Northern armies.

Jones observed that after January 1863 Davis was "rarely seen in the streets now." Instead Davis frequented St. Paul's, leading Jones to conclude: "I am rather inclined to credit the rumor that he intends to join the church. All his messages and proclamations indicate that he is looking for a mightier power than England for assistance."[25] In fact, Davis did convert, and the conversion was a sincere search "for a mightier power." Like many of his generals and his Northern counterpart, Abraham Lincoln, Davis found religion increasingly significant as the battles raged on. In all these cases, conversion was preparation for martyrdom and death, and it translated into terms of "no surrender."

CHAPTER 22

"AS SAVAGE AS SAVAGES"

Nationalism endured in the Confederacy, but the optimism contained in the Confederate jeremiad could no longer hold the unquestioned loyalty of the secular press and politicians as the suffering continued. Although the ministry invented a rhetoric of sacred nationhood around the ritual conventions of the fast and the thanksgiving day, they could not fix its meanings nor shape a cohesive and consensual Confederate ideology that automatically absorbed alternative visions. Defeats and disappointments inevitably strained unanimity among the populace and challenged the unquestioned supremacy of the clergy as moral authorities.

At the beginning of the war, Southern pulpits and the secular press had been engaged in a common enterprise: banging the drum for a "Christian" and "manly" war effort. But the strains on the Confederate government in the midst of total war and the social stresses upon a rapidly transforming capital city could not smooth over ideological differences among various factions for long.

For some, "Christian" and "manly" became separated. The new political function for the church and religious role for the state, especially in times of military defeat or internal discord, did not ring true. Vicious political battles over Confederate policy, public discontent over the moral decline of the wartime Confederacy, economic profiteering, hoarding, social breakdown—all flagrantly contradicted the spiritual and national consensus called for on fast days.

In Richmond the jeremiad offered a prescription for success in the face of defeat. A cavalier ethic of masculine nobility and war for war's sake could not easily keep company with public humiliation, moral reformation, and exaltation of God over the works of men. In place of consensus, conflicting strains between the secular and religious press, and even within the secular press itself, emerged. The new and immensely popular magazine *Southern Illustrated News*, published in Richmond and intended to displace *Harper's* magazine, made virtually no reference to religion, instead highlighting (and canonizing) the Confederate generals.

Political attacks on Davis increased, and so did contention between the Confederate and state authorities in Richmond. Political adversaries confronted each other anew as they coalesced into pro- and anti-Davis factions. One especially contentious issue was Davis's suspension of habeas corpus, received as coldly in the South as Lincoln's act had been in the North. The normally moderate *Richmond Daily Dispatch* urged resistance in defense of "the great bulwark of freedom": "If Congress would be so wanting in spirit— so derelict in duty—let Virginia Senators at least be committed to present uncompromising resistance to this surrender of all our liberties."[1]

In a similar vein, the *Richmond Examiner* continued its attacks on Davis. "Our politics are now an unknown, because unexplored sea," they lamented. "We have lost sight of all the ancient landmarks, and the old charts are known to be fallacious."[2] As in the North, the secular press was not one press but many, and in its midwar divisions, multiple and contending themes appeared that distraught Confederates confronted amid the din of nearby battles. Still, a fearfully militant nationalism endured.

Discussions in the secular press that shifted from "Providence" to "fate" or "chance" were meanwhile denounced in the Confederate religious press and pulpit as disloyalty and creeping atheism. The *Central Presbyterian* was especially perturbed when the *Daily Dispatch* characterized Stonewall Jackson as "a fatalist." Southern pulpits and religious publications also expressed outrage over the signs of defeatism they detected in some Confederate newspapers.

As bodies continued to be sacrificed on the altars of their nations, citizens on the home front absorbed the blows of sorrow and despair with unbowed faith. In Kentucky the Union Baptist preacher B. F. Hungerford kept a diary of events. On March 4, 1863, he wrote:

Have just received a communication from Bro. A Cook of Pigeon Fork requesting me to visit him on the morrow, as his son is about to die. He is a member of an Indiana Regiment but has come home to die. Oh! War! How insatiable thou art! And still it rages. God surely has forsaken this people. Given them over to destroy one another![3]

In a lecture to the Richmond YMCA, John Randolph Tucker, attorney general of the state of Virginia, justified the Confederate cause and then proceeded to pillory the Yankees for their conduct in the war:

No war in modern times, among Christian nations, has been marked by such ferocity—such disregard of private rights of persons and property—such assaults upon the liberty and conscience of private citizens—such atrocities towards non-combatants, men, women and children—and such wicked violations of all sanctions of our Holy religion. In the estimate of international law, our enemy must stand for condemnation in the Pillory of Nations.[4]

In this contentious atmosphere President Davis called for a fast day on March 27, 1863. A disillusioned war clerk, J. B. Jones, could not conceal his sense of irony: "This is the day appointed by the President for fasting and prayers. Fasting in the midst of Famine! May God save this people!"[5] The reactions of the press were more supportive. The *Richmond Daily Whig* supported the fast and urged attendance: "The religious portion of the community and the Pharisees [Jews] too will attend the various places of public worship. We trust that the congregations will be large."[6]

Among the clergy there was no ambivalence. The war was just, but only insofar as the Confederacy remained a Christian nation dependent on God. A writer for the *Central Presbyterian* was explicit on the necessity of a fast:

One or two of our newspapers have at times not obscurely, hinted their approbation of a maxim Napoleon is reported to have sanctioned that God was always on the side of the strongest regiments and the heaviest artillery. The remark . . . is an atheism our Christian nation will disdain to take upon its lips. Our people do believe that the Almighty God holds our destiny in the hollow of his hand. . . . If he casts us down, our sins have deserved it; if he lifts us up, it is the hand of mercy that does it.

The essay closed: "We trust that the day appointed will be more generally and sacredly kept than any before it."[7]

From the start the clergy had been among Davis's most faithful and enthusiastic supporters and on March 27 they would not disappoint him. In Savannah, Georgia, the Reverend George G. N. MacDonell delivered an unpublished fast-day sermon on Matthew 22:21 ("Render unto Caesar what is Caesar's and unto God what is God's") and outlined "the respective claims of God and Caesar." In the end, he concluded, the claims were separate as to sphere but united as to their common end: a "Christian Republic."[8]

Following the March fast, the *Richmond Christian Advocate* added its own complaint against those "who have written in bitter terms of denunciation against various chief men—especially against the President." Such criticism, the editorial continued, was traitorous: "Every man who contributes to depress the public heart helps the enemy." The clergy may have been late-comers to the Confederate cause, but, like their Northern counterparts, they proved its most loyal supporters. With unbroken confidence in God's cause and no comment on man's conduct, they probably extended the war by a year—the bloodiest year, as it turned out.

Printed sermons also appeared. In Savannah's Christ Church, Stephen Elliott, a bishop of Georgia, published a sermon, *Sampson's Riddle,* that confirmed that a people's strength came from God.[9] On the same day, Bishop George Foster Pierce and Benjamin Palmer delivered addresses to the General Assembly at Milledgeville on God's blessing of the Confederate cause.[10] Similar assertions were put forward wherever people gathered, whether at schools, in army camps, or in hospitals throughout the Confederacy.[11] In Richmond, Maximilian J. Michelbacher preached at the German Hebrew synagogue, Bayth Ahabah. At St. John's Church in Richmond the Reverend William Norwood spoke from Psalm 103:19 on the subject of "God and Our Country."[12]

While happy to complain about Davis, the secular press was unwilling to take on the clergy and their large popular following. Instead the press praised the fast and the wide participation it attracted. A writer for the *Southern Illustrated News* reported that "[t]he day of fasting and prayer was generally observed throughout the Confederacy, and we trust that the Almighty will answer the contrition and prayers of the people."[13] In Charleston, the *Daily Courier* recognized that

[w]e are at last awake to the fact that we have to depend upon the means and instruments which Heaven has conferred upon us for the achievement of our independence. In the course of this conflict it has been demonstrated that, with the blessing of God, we are equal to the work in which we are engaged.

Central to that "work" was the preservation of slavery. Thus on the very day set aside for fasting, the *Daily Courier* followed a call for a "Union Prayer Meeting" with the announcement: "James Grant sold at auction on Thursday, a field hand, about 17 years old, for $2320."[14]

After pleading for a sincere fast-day observance, the *Central Presbyterian* was pleased to report that "[t]here is reason to believe that this day was observed with uncommon solemnity over our entire country. Blessed be God whose spirit prepared the hearts of the people!" Besides "the people," the generals and their armies increasingly embraced the fasts. In the same editorial, the paper went on to observe that alongside the fast observances of churches throughout the nation had been a fast day in Lee's army: "The order of General Lee, suspending all duties in the Army of Northern Virginia, save those of necessity, concludes with a stirring address to the soldiers."[15]

Lee no less than Davis was getting religion. He sounded ever more evangelical as time passed, locating his—and his army's—fate in God's hand, not his own. In a letter to his ailing wife he reflected on marriage and Providence:

> I will not let pass the day devoted to thanksgiving to Almighty God for His mercies without holding communion with you. . . . I know that in Him is our only salvation. He alone can give us peace and freedom and I humbly submit to His holy will.[16]

One striking example of fast-day observances in the Confederate army survives in the sermon book and diary of Robert Bunting, chaplain to the Eighth Texas Cavalry, which was known as Terry's Texas Rangers in honor of plantation owner and commander Benjamin Terry.[17] Though born in Pennsylvania and educated at Princeton Theological Seminary, Bunting considered himself a "Southern by conviction." Against the wishes of his Northern abolitionist father-in-law, Bunting worked actively at the Presbyterian assembly in Augusta, Georgia, to form the Southern Presbyterian Church, and then enlisted in the Rangers in November 1861. His diary reflects a daily routine of prayer meetings, mail delivery, extensive letter writing on behalf of soldiers, Bible study, and attendance on the sick.

Readers in his hometown of San Antonio received regular reports from Bunting in their newspapers. Bunting tracked Terry's Rangers as they fought at First Manassas and then returned to Texas, eventually to join fellow Texan General Albert Sidney Johnston's Army of Tennessee. Later Bunting would participate in battles at Shiloh, Perryville, Murfreesboro, and Chickamauga, Georgia.

Bunting was a rigorously Calvinist Presbyterian who made no concessions to ecumenism among his troops or to bland patriotism as a substitute for religion. Repeatedly he insisted that patriotism and religion were essential sentiments for the Confederacy, but clearly separate. One involved earth and history, the other heaven and eternity. In a sermon series on "Tekel" from the prophet Daniel's vision of the "handwriting on the wall" (Daniel 5:25), Bunting brought home the haunting theme that "thou art weighed in the balances and art found wanting." This text, directed to the "fools" in Babylon who turned their backs on the true God, was delivered with modern "fools" in view. Chief of these were Northern "atheists" and "infidels" who "disbelieve the inspiration [of scriptures], and teach that Hell is a fable." These very people would suffer in hell "irrespective of virtue or morality or character or social position." His words, he was pleased to observe, inspired a "very strict attention" from the brigade numbering one thousand men. Indeed, he was pleased to observe that "all attend save about a dozen who are busily engaged gambling near by—this is being now a crying sin in the Regiment."

In the meantime, spring brought a new intensity to the suffering in Richmond. The capital city simply could not accommodate the vastly expanded populations of government workers, soldiers, and, increasingly with the breakdown of exchanges, prisoners of war. The winter of 1863 had been severe and set in motion real deprivations. While balls continued to sparkle for the wealthy, the poor only grew poorer.[18]

Richmond's *Central Presbyterian* ran a series of essays on extortion throughout the winter and spring, strongly hinting that greedy fellow Confederates were as threatening as the enemy outside the gates. Capitalist greed could not supersede Christian charity: "The undue stress laid by Adam Smith upon the cost of production, as the controlling regulator of prices, has been the means of misleading the public mind until the present."[19] Only by controlling prices and eliminating extortion could the public will be maintained.

A beleaguered Jefferson Davis seldom appeared in public and remained badly out of touch with the people. On April 2 a crowd of more than a thousand angry men, women, and children, led by Mary Jackson, a housepainter's wife, and Minerva Meredith, brandishing a pistol, massed in Capitol Square to cry hunger. Soon the crowd grew from hundreds to thousands. By midmorning a "mob" marched down Ninth Street and across Main Street looking for "something to eat." According to war clerk J. B. Jones, "They impressed all the carts and drays in the street, which were speedily laden with meal, flour, shoes etc."[20] The mayor appeared and called out troops, who read the Riot Act and threatened to fire into the crowd. Only the appearance of President Davis prevented carnage upon the Confederacy's once proud own. Davis himself was unmoved by the citizens' plight and later addressed the Confederate nation with blatantly unrealistic censure.

> Is it not a bitter and humiliating reflection that those who remain at home, secure from hardship and protected from danger, should be in the enjoyment of abundance, and that their slaves also should have a full supply of food, while their sons, brothers, husbands and fathers are stinted?[21]

Sallie Putnam, one of the "haves," reflected her own distant and aristocratic biases as she witnessed the "disgraceful riot." The "rioters," she noted,

were "a heterogeneous crowd of Dutch, Irish, and free negroes" who soon
went beyond bread for dry goods and clothing. As the women sought food,
"men carried immense loads of cotton cloth, woolen goods, and other articles, but few were seen to attack the stores where flour, groceries, and other
provisions were kept," thus calling into question the starvation motive. While
conceding that the "want of bread" was "too fatally true," she noted that most
of the rioters were not among the sufferers. All their actions succeeded in doing, she complained, was to add propaganda grist to Northern papers who
promptly printed "highly colored accounts of the starving situation of the inhabitants of Richmond."[22]

While Sallie Putnam wished to downplay the seriousness of Richmond's
civilian population distress, her telltale concession that bread shortages were
"too fatally true" belied the indignation she expressed. In fact, many Confederate women of means suffered in Richmond alongside their poorer compatriots. This was especially true of nonnative refugees fleeing battlefields for
the capital city. On the same day that rioters demonstrated in Richmond, the
aristocratic Ann Grymes of King George County penned the following letter
to President Davis:

> Dear Sir, I am a widow of seventy two years of age. My home . . . has been
> desolated by the Yankees, and my negroes, mules and horses stolen by them.
> I fled from the destruction that surrounded me there, and took refuge in
> Fredericksburg, with a daughter that resided in that place. I had to leave
> there a few days before the Battle, and I went to Dinwiddie Co. where I
> spent the winter. My means being nearly exhausted, I came to Richmond to
> seek employment whereby I could support myself during the few remaining
> years of my life, and will be truly thankful for employment in any of the de-
> partments where ladies are employed.[23]

Outside of Richmond, the devastations wrought by Union armies were as apparent to Northern soldiers as to the victims. In a letter to his wife, Philo B.
Buckingham, commander of Company H of the Twentieth Connecticut Volunteers, described the destruction from his vantage point in Stafford Hills,
Virginia, directly across the Rappahannock from Fredericksburg:

> Any one seeing the country last fall when we arrived here and looking at it
> now would hardly know it to be the same place. The houses formerly occu-
> pied by the chivalry about here are all desected [sic] and occupied by the
> general officers or have been burnt up. . . . There is an air of general desola-
> tion and what miserable people there are left here . . . their niggers gone

with every thing else by the greed of the rapacious soldiers either of the Rebel army or of our own.[24]

On a more personal level, Buckingham described an old man from a wealthy family, worth $250,000 before the war, who had been reduced to two pigs. These too soon fell victim to hungry Union pickets who "actually took them killed and cooked them before the old mans eyes." When the old man complained to Buckingham that he was a noncombatant in duress, he received a response that did not bespeak an officer and a gentleman: "The moral is that those who dance must pay the fiddler, those who *rebel* must take the consequences." In time, General Sherman would refine this logic to a science; civilians, no less than soldiers, must feel the hard hand of war. And overseeing all was President Lincoln and Lieber's Code.

Life was not much better in the Army of Northern Virginia than in Richmond. Lee's ill health grew worse, even as his undermanned army of 50,000 faced Hooker's 122,000 infantry and 12,000 cavalry. With Longstreet still detached, all Lee could do was wait for Hooker to make the first deployments and then depend on contingency and ingenuity to win the day. Fortunately for Lee, Hooker accommodated him by wasting his vast superiority and deploying his line of seven corps stretching all the way from Fredericksburg to the Rappahannock and Rapidan rivers fifteen miles to the west. By April 30 Hooker's objective became clear as three Federal corps under General Henry Slocum, a roommate of Philip Sheridan's at West Point, massed on Lee's flank.

On the very day that Hooker planned to attack, the North was observing a fast. Most Northern newspapers promoted the fast and underscored Union goodness, but one demurred. In terms that would anticipate Lincoln's famous Second Inaugural Address, a writer for the *New York Evangelist* reflected on the meaning of the war:

> The war has been permitted as a punishment to both the North and the South. Both have been guilty, though in different ways and in different degrees. We trust that God will overrule it for good to both, but it will not be because either deserve it. . . . There is one sin the North is committing *toward the blacks,* that needs to be repented of. It is not slavery, but it is *the denial of the rights of men to the poor unfortunate negroes who are among us* . . . we *are* called as a people to acknowledge the full manhood of the negro race.[25]

Words like this stand out for their relative scarcity in the rhetoric of war, reinforcing *The Liberator*'s demand for equality as a "reparation" for "the awful sin and injustice to them which lies at our door."26 To a culture unwilling to think of blacks as "men" as opposed to "boys," such sentiments must have appeared oddly alien. For appearances' sake, most Northern citizens involved in fast services were willing to confess stock sins of envy, greed, materialism, and so forth. They acknowledged the *South's* sin of slavery. But they would not concede racism in their own backyard, or even, for that matter, in the South. It simply did not register. Few white voices asked the one genuinely comprehensive moral question that could justify a war and reconstruction. Racism was a sin to which they did not confess, let alone concede as the primary cause of war.

The *Evangelist*, however, did not stop with African Americans but went on to extend racism to include injustices to Indians. In the same issue, the paper included a column for "the children at home" that told the story of wars fought against Indian men, women, and children. In the story, one child asks in regard to an Indian woman seeking a burial space for her grandson:

> "Are they allowed to come here?" "No, but they do come." "Well," he replied, "if *we* should see one of them in *our* streets, we would shoot her." That is the way multitudes of our good people feel towards these poor miserable natives, and that is the way they express their sentiments. It seems to me that they are almost as savage as savages. I don't think our Saviour is pleased to see such feelings in the heart. I hope your readers will pity and pray for them.27

Finally, pulling no punches in anticipating the sins of the fast day, the *Evangelist* took issue with the conduct of the war—again a rare occurrence. In a second "children at home" column, the paper explored "A Story of Fredericksburg." It was not a story of heroes and just war. Rather it told the story of houses shelled by Northern artillery with only a doll to salvage by "the despoiling hand of war":

> For doubtless what the shot and the shell had left was soon spoiled by the ruthless hand of [Federal] soldiers. For it is a fact that the most indiscriminate plundering took place as soon as our soldiers entered the town. Feather beds were turned inside out the most costly furniture was broken up and thrown into the streets. . . . Children you cannot be too thankful for your peaceful homes.28

In a sixty-two-page handwritten fast sermon, Worcester's Reverend Seth Sweetser reiterated the myth of American origins in "the Mayflower brought over [by] men who sought a refuge from the oppressed faith," and who proceeded to lay the foundations for a Christian republic. This continued through the Revolution, Sweetser claimed, and now reappeared in the war: "There has been a wonderful revival of patriotism. . . . The people were astonished at the resurrection of a spirit, which many thought had long since been buried in the sepulcher of the past."[29]

In another unpublished fast sermon, Abijah Marvin, a Worcester minister, took note of the slaughter of the war. He predicted that, if nothing else, it would discourage any future civil wars: "If peace were restored today on the old footing, it would be a long time before another rebellion would occur. . . . The South remembers that the Revolution was successful, and that it did not cost them much. But their children will remember that this rebellion, whether it proves successful or not—was carried on at a frightful expense of life."[30] Little did he know that at that very moment, carnage loomed with dire consequences.

PART V
TRANSFORMATION

HEARTS INVESTED

MAY 1863 TO APRIL 1864

CHAPTER 23

CHANCELLORSVILLE: "THE CHAMBER OF DEATH"

As Northern churches fasted for victory, Hooker set up headquarters around the Chancellor family house, known as Chancellorsville. His plan was simple. He would advance on Richmond, using sheer superiority of firepower to turn Lee's left flank and rout his army from the rear. Because of his numerical superiority, Hooker believed he could break his army up into three units. One, led by General John Sedgwick, would feint an attack on Fredericksburg, drawing Lee back toward the town where he had been so successful months earlier. Then the other two units would crush Lee's undermanned army in a converging vice grip, leaving Lee no choice but surrender or destruction. For weeks Hooker savored the sweet revenge his plan would inevitably bring and boasted of imminent victory. Like many other generals of both the North and the South, he was fast becoming a legend in his own mind. But he forgot his commander's dictum that victories had to be won on the field before they could be celebrated in talk. And his pride blinded him in respect to the general opposing him, who spoke very little indeed.

Like McClellan and Pope before him, Hooker badly underestimated both Lee's intelligence resources and his audacity. By late April Lee knew what Hooker's intentions were and had determined a counterresponse.[1] With only sixty thousand effectives, Lee faced a daunting challenge. But Jeb Stuart's cavalry had informed him that Hooker was advancing in force through the isolated and densely wooded area of second-growth forest known as the Wilderness to strike Lee in the rear. This was territory Lee knew well and Hooker knew not at all. As before, Lee determined to divide his outnumbered forces, gambling on the power of surprise and the effective use of his interior convex lines for rapid redeployment. Hooker expected Lee either to retreat or to face annihilation. Instead, Lee planned the unthinkable: to take the offensive in a savage attack that so surprised Hooker that numerical inequities no longer mattered.

On the evening of May 1, soldiers on both sides knew they were in for a battle. John Emerson Anderson of the Second Massachusetts Volunteers Infantry was not fooled by Hooker's bravado and described the scene of anticipation:

> As we waited for the morning dawn of the Sabbath there seemed to be an unusual soberness take possession of each one as if the soul was trying to look into its future. If we had occasion to speak to one another it was done in that low hushed voice that is used in the chamber of death.[2]

At the same time, Lee and Jackson met that night in a scene romanticized in thousands of lithographs as *The Last Meeting between Lee and Jackson*. They agreed to send Jackson and three divisions southwest and then north to hit Hooker's isolated flank and get in the rear of the Federal army.

The next day, Jackson moved six of his fifteen brigades in position to storm General O. O. Howard's exposed west (right) flank. He got away with it because Howard and Hooker were certain that Jackson was retreating. Military historians hold up Jackson's successful movement as one of the most daring—and dangerous—maneuvers in war: a flank march across Hooker's entrenched front. Should Howard discover the movement, Jackson's widely strung-out column would be exposed and raked with artillery fire. Everything depended on coordinated timing, nerves of steel, and the element of surprise. There could not be a moment's hesitation or all would be lost.

The gamble worked. Lee later summarized Jackson's actions in a letter written after the war to Jackson's widow: "General Jackson, after some inquiry concerning the roads leading to the terrace, undertook to throw his command entirely in Hooker's rear, which he accomplished with equal skill and boldness, the rest of the army being moved to the left flank, to connect with him as he advanced."[3] Jackson, like Lee, counted on Hooker to do nothing. As usual, "Fighting Joe" Hooker's battle-eve bravado gave way to crunch-time caution. It cost him dearly. His exposed right flank was now Jackson's for the taking.

With two hours of sunlight left, Jackson's exhausted but manic army stormed the unsuspecting and relatively untrained German regiments in Howard's Eleventh Corps and a rout ensued. Rebel yells and heavy musketry ripped through the Federal lines and, despite stiff resistance from "Howard's Dutchmen," the line crumpled. Though overrun, the troops did not turn tail in panic and thus cause the Federal defeat. The fault was Hooker's. Though relatively untrained and less than stellar, Howard's soldiers fought bravely, but in a hopeless cause. By evening, Hooker's right wing was blown to pieces with twenty-four hundred Yankees killed or wounded in little over two hours of desperate combat.[4]

On the night of May 2, most soldiers wanted to stop fighting. Except one. Stonewall Jackson furiously pushed ahead of his troops to scout areas around the Rappahannock where he might move his troops at night and destroy Hooker's army the next morning. While riding ahead to look for roads, he placed himself in front of a North Carolina regiment. Seeing Jackson and mistaking him for Yankee cavalry, they opened fire and shot Jackson off his horse.

"Friendly fire" inflicted a wound that would never heal. Two bullets tore into his left arm, requiring that it be amputated. As happened to many amputees, Jackson's wound became infected, throwing him into a battle for his life that he could not win. On May 10 Stonewall Jackson died, the first warrior general destined to live not on the battlefield but enshrined in sacred mythology. A disconsolate Lee had earlier written Jackson as he lay dying: "Could I have directed events, I should have chosen for the good of the country to have been disabled in your stead."[5]

With Jackson's mortal fall, Lee immediately reorganized his Second Corps, placing cavalryman Jeb Stuart in temporary command. The two generals carried their wings into the Wilderness, fighting vicious battles in the woods west of Chancellorsville. By noon on May 3, they had pushed the Federal line back far enough to reunite their two wings. As Hooker surveyed the battlefield from his headquarters at the Chancellorsville house, an artillery shell exploded near him and temporarily stunned him. But it did nothing to his senses that Lee had not already done.

On May 4 Sedgwick's imposing army finally overran Jubal Early's undermanned holding action at Marye's Heights, but not before the Mississippi volunteers held off four Federal assaults, buying precious time for Lee to hammer an utterly confused Hooker one more time. As Sedgwick began driving his army to the Wilderness to envelop Lee's army from the rear, Lee saw the new threat and completed his masterpiece—one that is still studied by military strategists. In a dizzying back and forth movement of his interior lines, Lee created the illusion of a force double his actual strength.

The reunited wings did not remain together long. Again Lee divided his army, this time leaving Stuart's Stonewall brigade with twenty-five thousand men to contain Hooker's immobile seventy-five thousand Federals, and marched the remaining twenty thousand to reinforce Early. Faced with enemies that suddenly appeared from nowhere on three sides, Sedgwick was forced to retreat across Banks' Ford, taking heavy casualties along the way and leaving Lee once again to unite his divided army and turn back on Hooker's well-entrenched defensive position. On May 6, a thoroughly whipped Hooker withdrew his forces to Falmouth.

Chancellorsville represented the first large battle in which both sides built substantial field fortifications that furthered the already definitive superiority of the strategic defense. The destruction was multiplied geometrically, and it was a chilling preview of a new era of horror.

At first the Northern papers minimized the defeat, preparing the country gradually for the shock to come. But by May 7, the country knew what Washington knew. Again the Army of the Potomac had been driven back across the Potomac with numbing losses. In all, 11,116 Yankees lay dead or wounded alongside 10,746 Confederates. Neither blood count was reasonable. Even the loyal Republican Horace Greeley sought to muzzle his reporters and protect Hooker. But he could not prevent Josiah Sypher from writing the blunt truth that "there was no time from Friday morning to Monday night but what Hooker could have attacked and defeated Lee's army, but he lacked the ability to give the order."[6]

Meanwhile hundreds of thousands of newly created widows, desolate parents, and loved ones gathered at the telegraph offices, unable to comprehend the extent of death and suffering. For Union officer Philo Buckingham, who earlier conveyed the destruction of civilian property to his wife, the battlefield's aftermath was almost indescribable:

It seemed more like a dream than anything else and yet the hospitals full of wounded men [gave] sad evidence that it was not a dream but a terrible reality. On Sat night the scene was wonderfully grand and yet hideous beyond description. Our men constantly being carried to the rear with almost every conceivable kind of wound with blood streaming down their faces arms shot off legs shot off some holding their own bowels in their hands which had been let out by the explosion of a shell, horses rushing about the fields riderless and perhaps with a leg or legs shot off others with the blood streaming from holes.

Two weeks later, it still was not clear to Buckingham who had won: "The army feels it has not been defeated and yet it has not won a victory, although the rebels without doubt lost in killed and wounded 3 times as many as we did. What will be done next I do not know."[7]

Though soldiers' letters in the immediate aftermath of battles virtually never discussed the morality of the war or the ethics of battle, they did invoke themes of sin and salvation as they faced death. Thomas Sherman of South Abington, Massachusetts, was also at Chancellorsville where "maney of my comrades fell on Sabbath morn May 3." His thoughts turned to conversion: "God onely knows how thankfull I am to Him, that my life was spared once more. I pray that all this present disciplin may draw me nearer to my Saviour."[8]

When Lincoln learned the full extent of defeat on May 6, he reportedly turned "ashen" and, asking no one in particular, moaned, "My God! my God! What will the country say?"[9] Lincoln did not have to wait long. While Lincoln grieved, the country raged. As Lincoln ruminated once again over his generals, Democrat "Copperheads" and peace Democrats gloated, seeing in Chancellorsville the possibility of their own victory at the polls. Armchair generals throughout the Union marveled at Lee and Jackson almost as much as their countrymen did. Detailed battle maps refought the battles and highlighted Federal incompetence.

Again Northern censorship withheld news of the disaster for several days, but ingenious reporters circumvented the censors and published their accounts. The *New York Times* led the way with reports from William Swinton and Lorenzo Crounse. When Horace Greeley learned the extent of defeat, his face turned gray as he exclaimed, "My God! It is horrible—horrible; and to think of it, 130,000 magnificent soldiers so cut to pieces by less than 60,000 half-starved ragamuffins."[10]

In fact, Lincoln's Republicans worried prematurely. "Lee's masterpiece" at Chancellorsville represented a Pyrrhic victory that marked the beginning of the end of the Confederate army. Without Jackson, Lee never replicated the brilliance of Chancellorsville. Even with Jackson, the odds of future victories were slim. The logic of Lincoln's "awful arithmetic" continued to wear down the limited resources of the South. And though a marvel of military strategizing and pinpoint execution, Chancellorsville settled nothing in an ultimate strategic sense. Hooker was still at large with his massive Army of the Potomac, and Richmond still lay under its menacing cloud. Indeed, within days of his victory, Lee was imploring Davis for reinforcements. Without them, he would have to retreat to Richmond. In the West Grant was making more progress in his campaign for Vicksburg than anyone knew.

On May 12 Jackson's coffin returned to Richmond. The Baptist *Richmond Religious Herald* reported: "The sun arose yesterday upon a mourning city . . . it beamed upon a nation to whom its light, brilliantly and beautifully as it shone, became suddenly veiled and opaque, shedding gloom instead of gladness."[11] Thousands flocked to observe the ceremony in numbed silence.

Leading the procession was Jackson's riderless horse led by a black servant. Behind it were fellow general officers and President Davis, looking worn and haggard. Later, while standing over Jackson's casket, a tearful Davis murmured to a fellow mourner, "You must excuse me, I am still staggering from a dreadful blow. I cannot think."[12]

Despite the great victory, the whole city was shut down for religious services and a review of Jackson's coffin. In their minds and words, Jackson was not only a heroic general, but a "martyr" to his cause. A writer for the *Richmond Daily Dispatch* grieved, but not without hope: "All has been against us save our own innate vigor, and a just and righteous cause with God to aid."[13] In Richmond Sallie Putnam described the procession of the "hero-idol of the South" in its "metallic coffin" to its conclusion at the hall of the House of Representatives, where the coffin was placed "on an altar covered with white linen." Crowds estimated at upwards of twenty thousand lined and stood patiently despite sweltering heat to view the remains. Not until Abraham Lincoln's assassination two years later would there be a comparable sense of loss. And, as with Lincoln, the loss would be interpreted in terms that would pave the way for a civil religion, in this case a Southern civil religion.[14] Sallie Putnam concluded her description of a man who was not only a great general but Christlike in his death:

> When we reflect upon his stainless reputation, we feel that he was one of whom the world was not worthy,—that "he walked with God, and was not, for God took him." With us, Jackson can never die. The mouldering remains that lie where he wished them, in the beautiful village of Lexington, in the Valley of Virginia, are not all of him; there is an immortal part to which all the South, all the noble, good and true of all lands lay claim,—the spirit of patriotism in Stonewall Jackson,—that can never die! In our souls he lives; in our hearts is graven the name whose destiny is a glorious immortality. Though dead, he yet lives—shall ever live![15]

In similar terms, Attorney General John Randolph Tucker described the general's legacy in terms that fused Christian piety with patriotic nationalism:

> Among the clouds which hung about the dawn of the war, the sun of Jackson arose from obscurity. . . . Christianity may well cherish the memory of this holy hero, as the noblest example of pious patriotism; and appeals to his name, as an imperishable proof, that the devout conscience of the South, in the fear and love of God, is constrained to yield up life, a bleeding sacrifice upon the altar of its country's independence![16]

Tucker turned from Jackson's piety to a spirited defense of "the institution" of slavery—an institution ordained by God for the transformation of the African race:

We are a superior race, with an inferior race to deal with. We are its guardians, and it is our pupil, and all this under God's good providence. . . . God put the negro here, and placed us in authority over him—to regulate him—to make him useful, instead of being unthrifty—industrious and not idle—Christian and not savage. This work we mean to do despite the efforts of our foes in arms, and the revilings of ignorant fanaticism throughout the world.[17]

In the public response to Jackson's death we see a concrete illustration of the process by which a Confederate civil religion was incarnated through a violent atonement. Themes of Christian faith, righteous cause, white supremacy, martial valor, and a "martyr's" immortality all intermingled, creating a powerful national faith with the soul of a church. Christianity and Confederate nationhood became impossible to separate. And in Jackson, the citizens discovered a messianic figure who "can never die."

Surprisingly, the Northern press was as obsessed with Jackson as the Southern. The *Christian Instructor and Western United Presbyterian* wrote an account of "How Gen. Jackson was wounded" without any criticism or even outspoken wishes for his death.[18] Their reaction to his death was not unusual. Instead of berating him as a devil or murderer, they evidenced respect. In like manner, the *New York Evangelist* wrote:

General Jackson was perhaps the most brilliant executive officer which the present war has brought forward. . . . His exploits are too fresh to need recapitulation. He was, too, a man of undoubted piety, long an Elder in the Presbyterian Church, and one who took a lively interest in her councils. He opposed secession until Virginia was forced into the movement, when the Southern doctrine of States Rights carried him off. His death will be an irreparable loss to the enemy.[19]

Meanwhile, Northern armies were active on two of the three major fronts. Hooker's Army of the Potomac remained positioned at Chancellorsville in the Wilderness of Virginia, and a portion of his army under Sedgwick threatened the Confederates at nearby Fredericksburg. In the West the earlier frustrations of laying siege to Vicksburg began to yield results as Grant now lay below the city on Mississippi soil. Confederate General Joseph Johnston saw the situation as desperate and hoped to relieve General John Pemberton to save the city. On the third front in Tennessee, Rosecrans and Bragg continued to recover and build their armies back to fighting strength. There was not yet a Union general with the prescience to mount a massive campaign on all fronts simultaneously, but in the West Grant and Sherman were learning rapidly and would soon improve on those lessons.

As the war entered its third summer, both sides focused their attention on the West. For Confederates, fresh off their stunning victories at Chancellorsville and Fredericksburg, anxiety rose as Pemberton's army and Vicksburg's citizens braced for a long siege and the relentless artillery of Grant's big guns. For the North, stung by surprise defeats and inferior command, hopes rose with Grant and his army.

As for Lee's Army of Northern Virginia, nobody knew where the next campaign would ensue, but by June 3 Lee's army was on the move again. In a crucial strategy meeting with President Davis on May 15, Lee had dissuaded Davis from sending reinforcements to Vicksburg, despite Davis's strong loyalties to his native state and the pleas of General Johnston. Instead Lee held forth the glittering prospect of a Northern offensive, this time to Pennsylvania, where a victory would terrify Northern cities and lead to a negotiated peace for the Confederacy. In the heady days of post-Chancellorsville, Davis and his cabinet were prepared to believe that Lee's charm would never end. More tellingly, so was Lee.[20]

Union commanders and soldiers felt certain that Lee was preparing just such a desperate maneuver and remained alert to all movements north. In a letter on June 6 written from Ellis Ford, Virginia, Private Howard Prince of Pennsylvania described the readiness of Union troops and, along the way, provided a glimpse into the strange and ironic fraternization between enemies that took place between the battles:

> We are very pleasantly encamped in a hardwood forest a short distance from the river, and near us the 16th Mich. The rest of our brigade is a half mile back in reserve. We can see the enemy's pickets plainly at a few rods from our camp. . . . The pickets at both places are very social, swimming across, exchanging papers, and trading tobacco for coffee.[21]

Yet the decision to invade the North a second time had been made and it was only a matter of time before the clash. Although nobody knew it at the time, the Gettysburg Campaign had already begun.

CHAPTER 24

GETTYSBURG: "FIELD OF BLOOD, AND DEATH"

Lee's chances for a successful Northern campaign looked good. His reorganized Army of Northern Virginia included First Corps, still commanded by James Longstreet, Second Corps commanded by Stonewall Jackson's successor Richard Ewell (returning from Second Bull Run with a wooden leg), and Third Corps under the veteran A. P. Hill, with Jeb Stuart's cavalry as his intelligence. Lee's total strength, expanded to three infantry and six cavalry brigades, was 75,000. True, they faced a formidable buffer between Virginia and Pennsylvania with the Army of the Potomac and its seven infantry corps of 122,000 effectives. But a smaller army was nothing new to Lee. Nor was his confidence in his own abilities to take his battle-hardened veterans into the jaws of hell, if that was what victory required.

In addition, Lee faced a familiar Union general in tough-talking Fighting Joe Hooker. From Chancellorsville, he knew that tough words rarely translated into tough stands. In fact, ever since Chancellorsville, General Hooker had been on thin ice and he knew it. His fellow officers distrusted his abilities, and his commander in chief doubted he could navigate the rough waters generated by Lee's legions. Hooker himself had lost something at Chancellorsville that he never regained—his confidence.

On June 3 Lee's audacious move north commenced, to the horror of Pennsylvania residents and the unrestrained joy of Virginians, thankful at last to have the war in the lap of the enemy. Mindful of Northern papers and public opinion, Lee forbade all pillaging in hopes of a counterexample to the behavior of invading Union armies. At Chambersburg Lee declared: "No greater disgrace can befall the army and through it our whole people, than the perpetration of barbarous outrages upon the innocent and defenceless. Such proceedings not only disgrace the perpetrators and all connected with them, but are subversive of the discipline and efficiency of the army, and destructive of the ends of our movement."

While these orders undoubtedly had a restraining effect, in practice he was no more able to prevent random soldiers' raids on Northern property than were Union officers. Lee succeeded in saving towns from the torch, however, and prevented wanton theft and destruction of civilian property.[1] Lee's army considered railroads and former slaves fair targets, and black escapees (free and former slaves) in Pennsylvania were forcibly sent back to the South. One Confederate officer, William Christian, confessed that despite his orders to protect property, "there is a good deal of plundering going on, confined principally to the taking of provisions. No houses were searched and robbed, like our houses were done by the Yankees." As for blacks: "We took a lot of Negroes yesterday. I was offered my choice, but as I could not get them back home I would not take them." Then, in an odd moment of compassion, he added: "In fact, my humanity revolted at taking the poor devils away from their homes. They were so scared that I turned them all loose."[2]

When Hooker learned of Lee's movement north, he began to position his army in Lee's rear around Frederick, Maryland, to prepare an attack on undefended Richmond. The plan made sense. But a skeptical General Halleck, lacking all confidence in Hooker, countermanded his orders. Betrayed and humiliated, Hooker had no choice but to proffer his resignation on June 28, which President Lincoln accepted on the spot. General George Gordon Meade, the battle-hardened former commander of Fifth Corps, assumed command of the Army of the Potomac at its most critical hour and reversed course to engage Lee in Pennsylvania.

Deprived of his usual intelligence by a stymied Stuart and marching in unfamiliar terrain, Lee was surprised to learn in late June that Hooker had been replaced by Meade. He learned, too, that Meade had abandoned his base south of the Potomac to close in with his army. By sheer coincidence, the two armies arrived around the farming village of Gettysburg, Pennsylvania, on July 1. Immediately it became clear to both commanders that this quiet village offered ideal terrain for a pitched battle. The ground sloped and rose in valleys and small hills strewn with heavy rocks and caves that afforded perfect defensive protection. Added to these formidable defensive positions were open fields begging for heroic frontal assaults. The stage was set for a perfect battle.

At 10:00 a.m. on July 1, scattered fighting began outside of Gettysburg. Several skirmishes had already been fought and it was not immediately apparent to commanders on either side that this one would be any different. But as

"Field Where General Reynolds Fell." This photograph taken by Alexander Gardner, originally titled "A Harvest of Death," shows the bodies of Federal soldiers killed on July 1, 1863, near the McPherson Ridge, on the first day of the Battle of Gettysburg.

both sides rushed to secure strategic defensive positions from which they could launch offensive thrusts, the stakes quickly grew higher. Knowing Lee's location, Meade appointed his best young general, John F. Reynolds, to command the left wing of the army with trusted veterans from the First Corps (the Iron Brigade of midwesterners), Oliver Howard's Eleventh "Dutch" Corps, and Daniel Sickles's Third Corps. Immediately they established a strong defensive position near the town of Emmitsburg, just west of Gettysburg.

Events quickly took on a momentum of their own. General John Buford's Federal cavalry encountered heavy resistance from two divisions of A. P. Hill's Third Corps advancing rapidly on Gettysburg. Recognizing immediately the strategic location of the junction at Gettysburg, Buford dismounted his cavalry and ordered them to hold McPherson Ridge, on the route to Seminary Ridge, "at all costs" (meaning no retreat, no surrender). Reynolds bravely led his First and Eleventh Corps in to reinforce Buford, but was promptly shot dead, leaving command of the wing to Abner Doubleday, who continued the attack. Soon Ewell's powerful Second Corps arrived to support Hill and the Battle of Gettysburg was launched.

As the second day dawned, Lee's extended lines were spread thin around the outside of Meade's defenders with Ewell to the north, Hill in the center, and

Longstreet to the south. Despite the Union's formidable defenses, Lee did not intend to be denied. The burden of attack fell on Lee's least enthusiastic but most valuable "Old War Horse," General James Longstreet, who faced Sickles's Third Corps. Assuming that the greatest Federal strength lay alongside the Emmitsburg Road, with its flank near the Wheat Field, Lee ordered Longstreet to hit the flank with two divisions and then turn north to roll up the supposed enemy strength along the road.

Battles raged up and down the entrenched Federal line as Lee probed for weak spots to strike and vanquish. The perfect spot of attack, of course, was the disconnected Union line at Little Round Top, still miraculously unoccupied. If Longstreet could get artillery to the top of that mound, the entire Union left would be exposed to a withering crossfire and the battle determined. But Lee, bent on massive destruction, had other ideas, and assigned only a token force of five hundred men from the Fifteenth Alabama to take Little Round Top.

Five hundred men were not many, but still the strategic position would have sufficed had not Meade's chief of engineers, General Gouverneur K. Warren, spotted the unprotected hill. Instantly he recognized the mortal danger that Confederate artillery on Little Round Top would pose to exposed Federal lines. Without delay he rang the alarm to the Federal Fifth Corps commander General George Sykes, and elements from the First Minnesota and Twentieth Maine were immediately dispatched to save the hill. The Twentieth Maine, led by the former Bowdoin College professor of rhetoric, Colonel Joshua L. Chamberlain, held the extreme left of the line with orders to hold the position "at all costs."

For nearly two hours, Chamberlain's down-easters held off desperate assaults from the Fifteenth Alabama. No sooner would one charge cease than another began. With one-third of his men down and ammunition all but out, Chamberlain made one of the most intrepid moves in Civil War annals. Instead of retreat or surrender, he ordered his men to fix their bayonets sans ammunition and charge down the hill into the teeth of the Alabamians. Unnerved by the savage roar of the oncoming troops and unaware of their desperate straits, the Confederates surrendered en masse, leaving Little Round Top in Federal hands.[3]

In a later memoir, Chamberlain described the successive attacks in words befitting a professor of rhetoric:

All around, strange mingled roar—shouts of defiance, rally, and desperation; and underneath, murmured entreaty and stifled moans; gasping prayers, snatches of Sabbath song, whispers of loved names; everywhere men torn and broken, staggering, creeping, quivering on the earth, and dead faces with strangely fixed eyes staring stark into the sky. Things which cannot be told—nor dreamed. How men held on, each one knows,—not I. But manhood commands admiration.[4]

With the Round Tops secured, a Union line now extended without gaps. While nothing was settled after the second day, the losses were enormous. Each side suffered nine thousand casualties, bringing the two-day totals to thirty-five thousand—far more than any previous two days in the war. Lee's prospects for victory were bleak. But that was nothing new, and the outcome was still at issue. For a supremely confident Lee, that meant one more throw of the dice.

Having already struck unsuccessfully at both of Meade's flanks, Lee determined that night, again over Longstreet's vehement but loyal objections, to attack the center in a frontal assault. Again Lee selected Longstreet to lead the assault, augmented with a fresh third division under the recently arrived General George Pickett and his five thousand Virginia veterans—all, Pickett bragged, aching for a good fight. The historian Bruce Catton described the scene:

> Then out of the woods came General Lee's assaulting column, like actors in some unimaginable drama coming at last onto the stage—rank after rank, Pickett and [General James] Pettigrew and [General Isaac] Trimble and their divisions and when they got into the open the men halted and dressed their ranks as carefully as if they were going on parade. They were worth looking at. Their line was a mile wide from flank to flank, Pickett's division on the right, Pettigrew's beside it, Trimble's in close support, general officers mounted, battle flags overhead, sunlight glinting off of the rifle barrels. They perfected their alignment, finally, and when the line began to roll forward it looked irresistible.[5]

The sight did not deceive the Yankees. General Winfield Scott Hancock's Second Corps held their fire, patiently awaiting the lambs about to be sacrificed. Many must not have believed what a perfect target Longstreet's courageous divisions made. Perhaps they thought back to their own annihilation at Marye's Heights. Sergeant John Dunn of the First Delaware later recalled: "This would be our Fredericksburg, and it required no effort on our part to hold our fire until they crossed the [Emmitsburg] road."

Pettigrew's and Pickett's divisions converged at "the angle" near the center

Confederate dead at Gettysburg, 1863. Northern photographers Alexander Gardner and Timothy O'Sullivan took these photographs on July 5, three days after the soldiers had been killed, and just hours before burial crews began the grisly task of burying the bloated corpses.

of Meade's line. At two hundred yards, artillery and infantry fire erupted frontally and on both Confederate flanks. As the rebels continued to advance closer, Federal artillerymen switched their ammunition from case shot and shell to murderous canister and then to golf ball–sized double canister. Longstreet's brave soldiers fell in waves. Pettigrew's already mauled division actually led the legendary Pickett's charge and took the hardest hit. Confederate infantry pulled down their caps over their eyes and bowed their heads, in one observer's words, "as if meeting a hail storm."[6]

For the oncoming Confederates, the choice was stark: retreat and possibly survive or move forward and die. Amazingly, many continued to press forward over the bodies of their fallen comrades. A few hundred actually breached the Federal line and engaged their foes in close combat. Confederate General Lewis Armistead led the advance through the angle and fell mortally wounded over the muzzle of a Federal cannon, ironically marking "The High Tide of the Confederacy."

John Emerson Anderson of the Second Massachusetts retraced the battlefield the following day. The sight filled him with an odd sympathy:

Many hundreds of the enemies dead were still lying where they fell. As we passed over that field of blood, and death, in thoughtful silence, we looked on those upturned youthful faces, and as we saw no trace of passion, or of hate, our minds would wander unbidden away off to that Southern home, and picture a fond Mother, who on bended knees is fervently asking Gods blessing to rest on her darling soldier boy. And as we spread our mantle of charity over them we murmur, "my brother rest in peace."[7]

As great as the hatreds were, they could not extend to dead, wounded, and helpless soldiers, who were "brothers" once more.

Northerners died no less grimly than Southerners. One destined to die at Gettysburg was Sergeant Charles Ward of the Thirty-second Massachusetts Volunteers. Like many soldiers, Ward had written, "I hope I may come home again but life here is uncertain," and wondered "how I shall conduct myself if called to fight." He found out soon enough as his brigade charged the wheat field and absorbed 50 percent of the casualties. Sergeant Ward fell, wounded by a sharpshooter. After lingering for seven days, he died on July 9. In his last letter to his mother, written after he was wounded, he wrote: "Dear Mother, I may not again see you but do not fear for your tired soldier boy. Death has no fears for me. My hope is still firm in Jesus. Meet me and Father in heaven with all my *dear friends*. I have no special message to send you but bid you all a happy farewell. Your affect and soldier son, Charles Ward."[8]

For the Confederates, devastation prevailed. Longstreet had predicted the disaster and consoled himself with the knowledge that he had minimized the numbers of soldiers committed to the assault (to the criticism of later Lost Cause Confederate historians). But Pickett would not be consoled. As he watched the butchery from Emmitsburg Road, tears filled his eyes as he cried, "Great God, where, oh! Where is my division?" Pickett never forgave Lee. Later he claimed, "[T]hat old man had my division slaughtered." Lee did not disagree, and in a letter to President Davis accepted full responsibility and offered to resign. Davis refused to accept Lee's resignation. Nevertheless, the commander of the Army of Northern Virginia would never again go on the offensive.

CHAPTER 25

"FOR THE SAKE OF THE CAUSE"

The final assault of the three-day Battle of Gettysburg lasted little more than half an hour. Of the fourteen thousand Confederates who braved the assault, only half returned. Pickett lost 42 percent of his men and all of his senior officers. The heaviest casualties in Longstreet's advance occurred in General Richard B. Garnett's Brigade (65 percent, including Garnett), including the Eighth Virginia's astounding 92 percent casualty rate. One eyewitness account described the final day's battle in stark terms:

> I have heard more noise, louder crashes, in other battles, but I never saw or heard of such desperate, tenacious fighting as took place on this [left] flank. . . . Never was there a more vigorous and deadly assault than that made on our centre by Longstreet. It was a death struggle on the part of the enemy to break our lines, repeated and renewed a half-dozen times during the afternoon, in which they were as often repulsed and driven back with a loss of life unparalleled by any previous battle. . . . The country around Gettysburg is crowded with wounded men. Every house and barn is a hospital. Probably, in the aggregate of both armies, at least 50,000 have been placed *hors du combat*.[1]

The numbers proved accurate. After three days of battle, Federal losses totaled 23,049 and Confederate losses 28,063. Depending on whether the three days are counted as three battles (in which case the Confederacy arguably won two) or one, the Confederacy had reached its high-water mark and never returned to the North in force.

Nothing illustrated more starkly the symbolic quality of the war than

Newspaper vendor and cart in camp, 1863. Newspapers became a fixture for both sides on the battlefields and were often exchanged by Union and Confederate soldiers during times of inactivity. The governments provided horses and wagons to transport the papers, and allowed journalists an "embedded" presence with armies in the field. This vendor prepares to distribute papers to General George Gordon Meade's Army of the Potomac.

flags soaked in blood.[2] Reports circulated throughout the North about "Rebel Battle Flags": "Thirty-one new rebel flags, captured by the Union forces in the recent battle at Gettysburg, have been deposited in the War Department," wrote one reporter. "Most of them were much torn by balls, and many are very bloody."[3]

Both Northern and Southern presses continued to monitor the enemy's papers very closely and comment on them. Of these, none were read more closely than Richmond's papers. Hence it was with some glee that one Northern writer observed how "[t]he Richmond papers are terribly doleful over the recent disasters."[4] Horace Greeley confidently predicted that Lee would soon be vanquished: "We ought now to be near the end of our great struggle, and our Government may, without compromising its dignity . . . openly invite proposals from North Carolina, Georgia, Texas, and other revolted States, for a peaceful restoration of the Union."[5]

Contrary to Greeley's optimism and much to Lincoln's dismay, Lee lived to fight another day—indeed another year and a half. With inclement weather and a badly mauled army of his own, Meade failed to press his advantage with a wholesale pursuit of Lee's fleeing forces. The Army of Northern Virginia remained formidable, and Lee himself maintained his mythic status, minus the air of invincibility that had carried the South through earlier battles.

With minds set like flint on the task at hand, no question arose of proportion or acceptable losses. One suspects that the casualties could have numbered one hundred thousand instead of fifty thousand and the response would have been the same. One writer for the *Independent* noted how numbed Americans had become to bloodshed. In the opening, relatively benign, military encounters, "every early dash in the war was turned into fame. . . . Our first defeats threw the whole community into panics, for men were then unused to stern times." But that changed profoundly for the worse: "We have since become so familiar with war, that Gettysburg, a greater battle than Waterloo, made no such impression upon the popular mind as the first few flashes of powder from [Fort] Moultrie, at daybreak of April 19, 1861."[6] The moral brake linings had sheared, leaving only reflexive endorsements of a cause that knew no limits.

In the North, Fourth of July celebrations extended into the following week. Washington was giddy with excitement. One account described the scene: "Bells are ringing wildly all over the city. Citizens grin at one another with fairly idiotic delight."[7] Reports blended fact, rumor, and talk of greatness to the exclusion of any serious inquiry or chronicle. The *Philadelphia Inquirer* exulted: "Waterloo Eclipsed!!" adding, "The Rebel Loss Truly Frightful . . . General Lee reported in full retreat, pursued by Gen. Meade's Forces."

Elsewhere, the *Inquirer* speculated on the "reported deaths of Hill and Longstreet" and praised the bravery of the soldiers: "It would take reams of paper and more time than we have at present writing, to tell of the gallant deeds done by detached bodies and individuals. Let it suffice to say that all did well and nobly, and fought with the desperation of tigers. Never were troops so well handled—neither have they ever gained for themselves so much glory and renown." Throughout, the tones were dramatic and mythic in recounting "lightening" raids and "trembling" earth. Confederate losses were staggering, while "our loss was comparatively small."[8]

Glory could not compensate the emptiness for individuals who lost loved ones. One especially emotional account was provided by *New York Times* correspondent Samuel Wilkerson. After earlier describing the magnitude of the battle, he eventually reported the battle's aftermath alongside the body of his dead son. In words almost too pure to bear, he wrote:

Oh, you dead, who at Gettysburg have baptized with your blood the Second birth of Freedom in America, how you are to be envied! I rise from a grave whose set clay I have passionately kissed, and I look up and see Christ spanning this battlefield with his feet and reaching fraternal and lovingly up to heaven. His right hand opens the gates of Paradise—with his left he beckons to those mutilated, bloody, swollen forms to ascend.[9]

Music, while it could not capture the morality of war, effectively embraced the suffering. In the popular "Angel Mother I'm Coming Home," the writer explained that the inspiration for the song was a soldier's letter from Gettysburg: "A sweet smile o'er spread his features, his lips moved, and he whispered George I am dying, tell the boys we shall meet again where parting does not come." Again he spoke of his happy childhood, his brothers, sisters, and his mother, who had died since his enlistment. His last words were, "Angel mother I'm coming home! After which he sunk back to rise no more."[10] In song no less than speech, war's horrors were submerged in a sea of romanticization that hid the starker realities from citizens in the North and South who did not want to know.

In response to a serenade on July 7, President Lincoln evidenced the germs of ideas he developed more fully at Gettysburg Cemetery in December. First Lincoln repeated the scripture on which his faith rested. July Fourth, he argued, was of unparalleled importance, because "for the first time in the history of the world a nation by its representatives, assembled and declared as a self-evident truth that 'all men are created equal.'" For this reason, he continued, the date assumed a mystical significance, confirmed by the deaths of Adams and Jefferson on that date, and "another president, five years after, was called from this stage of existence on the same day."

Now, in the midst of civil war,

> on this last Fourth of July just passed, when we have a gigantic Rebellion, at the bottom of which is an effort to overthrow the principle that all men are created equal, we have the surrender of a most powerful position . . . and not only so, but in a succession of battles in Pennsylvania, near to us, through three days, so rapidly fought that they might be called one great battle . . . and on the 4th the cohorts of those who opposed the declaration that all men are created equal, "turned tail" and ran.

But then he stopped: "Gentlemen, this is a glorious theme, and the occasion for a speech, but I am not prepared to make one worthy of the occasion."[11] Five months later he would be prepared, and on that occasion, he solidified Gettysburg's reputation as the apotheosis of the Civil War and made his speech America's greatest sermon.

In the weeks following, Lincoln's ebullience waned as the failure of Meade's army to seal the victory set in. By failing to pursue Lee, Meade had rendered Gettysburg inconclusive, a tactical success but a strategic bust. In a moment of unrestrained anger and frustration, Lincoln drafted (but wisely never mailed) a stiff rebuke to his general of the Army of the Potomac:

> You had at least twenty thousand veteran troops directly with you, and as many more raw ones within supporting distance, all in addition to those who fought with you at Gettysburg, while it was not possible that he [Lee] had received a single recruit, and yet you stood and let the flood run down [the Potomac], bridges be built, and the enemy move away at his leisure without attacking him. . . . I do not believe you appreciate the magnitude of the misfortune involved in Lee's escape.[12]

Others, lacking Lincoln's grim appetite for greater short-term casualties in the interests of long-term ends, were more forgiving of Meade. After describing the glorious Northern victory, a writer for the *Christian Herald* praised all of the generals unstintingly and reprinted General Meade's congratulatory address to the troops, in which he acknowledged God's providential assistance to the Union cause. "It is right and proper," he asserted, "that we should, on suitable occasions, return our grateful thanks to the Almighty Disposer of events, that in the goodness of His providence, He has thought fit to give victory to the cause of the just."[13] Whatever the personal religious convictions of the generals, they contributed to their sacralization with purple providential prose claiming a God who smiled on the justness of their devastation.

Despite Lee's escape, morale among Northern soldiers was high, and most supported Meade. As the ones slated to do the actual fighting and dying, many did not agree with Lincoln's harsh assessment of Meade's failings as general. John Emerson Anderson, who had earlier toured the desolate battlefield, considered the toll staggering and the idea of pursuit something only critical "northern newspapers" would entertain: "Without doubt if General Meade should advance now, we should be checked or repulsed, owing to our weakness in numbers and the advantage General Lee would have by placing himself on the defensive."[14]

In a letter to his father, Union soldier John Francis Gleason revealed that Confederates were not the only soldiers lacking shoes. Yet Union spirits were high: "We have now been on the move for fifty days, and six of those have been fighting days. . . . Human nature can endure wonderfully when inspired by an idea. . . . It was rather hard for some of the boys to travel over those macadamized turnpikes barefoot—the route was marked with their blood— but they did it cheerfully for the sake of the cause."[15]

At the same time that Gettysburg came to its strategically inconclusive end, a far more decisive campaign was winding down in the western theater. There U. S. Grant staged one of the most brilliant and definitive victories of the war at Vicksburg, Mississippi. Although not destined to live like Gettysburg in American memory, the Vicksburg campaign far eclipsed the eastern action in actual strategic significance by controlling the Mississippi River and dividing the Confederacy in two. It also provided a classic instance of patient but forthright command tactics maintained over a sustained period of time, beginning in November 1862 and not concluding until July 1863. After months of unsuccessful feints and engagements, Grant hit on the bold plan to march his army into the heart of Mississippi, even if it meant separating from his supply lines and living off the land.

On May 7 Sherman's corps linked up with Grant, and the forty thousand Union troops prepared to attack General Joseph E. Johnston in the field at Jackson, Mississippi. They hoped to draw General Pemberton's army out of its Vicksburg fortress. Pemberton's twenty-five thousand men and Johnston's army of about the same number were unable to unite against Grant and Sherman. Grant lodged his army between the two rebel contingents, allowing him to do to the rebels what Hooker could not do to Lee at Chancellorsville. By isolating Johnston and Pemberton and imaginatively shifting his interior lines, Grant was able to attack each wing in succession—a classic Napoleonic divide and conquer.

On May 12 Grant ordered one wing of his army under General James B. McPherson to attack Johnston at Jackson. By May 14 the capital city belonged to Grant. Then Grant wheeled west and routed Pemberton's hapless forces as they attempted a rescue at Champion's Hill on May 16. Beaten but not surrendered, Pemberton retreated to the fortress.

On May 19 and again on the twentieth, Grant unsuccessfully stormed the fortress, taking heavy casualties along the way. Unable to carry the assault, Grant laid siege to the Confederate "Gibraltar." Every day, artillery shells rained down on the fortress's soldiers and civilians alike. One Union lady living in the Vicksburg fortress through the siege described the terror that accompanied Union shelling:

A shell burst right outside the window in front of me. Pieces flew in, striking all around me, tearing down masses of plaster that came tumbling over me. When H. rushed in I was crawling out of the plaster, digging it out of my eyes and hair. When he picked up a piece as large as a saucer beside my pillow, I realized my narrow escape. . . . Another [shell] came crashing near, and I snatched up my comb and brush and ran down here. It has taken all the afternoon to get the plaster out of my hair, for my hands were rather shaky.[16]

Eventually the starving inhabitants could hold out no longer. Just as Grant was planning another assault, Pemberton surrendered his army on the unfortunate date of July 4. Unlike Gettysburg, the victory was complete. Between March 29 and July 4, Grant defeated an army of forty thousand, won five battles, captured twenty-nine thousand Confederates, and destroyed hundreds of artillery pieces and munitions. Four days later, the final Confederate fortress on the Mississippi at Port Hudson surrendered to General Nathaniel Banks, leaving the Federals in control of the river and effectively dividing the Confederacy in half.

Grant's relentless spring campaign that set up the siege of Vicksburg stands as one of the greatest offensives in the war and established Grant's reputation as a strategist on par with Robert E. Lee. One writer at the time observed, "The capture of Vicksburg is the most staggering blow that has yet been dealt to the Confederacy, and reflects the highest credit on the skill and energy of General Grant."[17] Following the victory, the *Inquirer* ran a portrait of Grant under the headline, "The Hero of the South-West."[18] Grant himself supposed the surrender "sealed" the fate of the Confederacy. For his part, Lincoln (who had not yet met Grant) believed that at last he had found his general.[19]

To Northerners, the recent victories seemed irresistibly providential. Surely God had orchestrated the triumphs to fall on the Fourth of July as a signal that America was His chosen nation. The *New York Evangelist* gloated, "God Our Deliverer. Good news thick upon us. At last the Gibraltar of the Mississippi has fallen."[20] This was not the last providential signal to fall on a sacred day, as Lincoln's assassination on Good Friday would tragically exemplify, but it was surely the brightest. In one fell swoop, Gettysburg and Vicksburg secured the North and the Mississippi, creating an apparently overwhelming advantage for the Union cause. Richmond and surrender were imminent.

Of all the smaller civil wars within America's Civil War, that of the African American would prove most just. If anyone had a "cause" that could meet all the moral scruples of a just war, it was the slaves and freedmen. W. E. B. DuBois would later go so far as to argue in the extreme that even in palpably unjust wars—or battles—African American soldiers should not be held culpable:

He [the African American] cannot be blamed for them so far as they were unrighteous wars (and some of them were unrighteous), because he was not a leader; he was for the most part a common soldier in the ranks and did what he was told . . . he believed that by fighting for America he would gain the respect of the land and personal and spiritual freedom . . . always fought for his own freedom and for the self-respect of his race. Whatever the cause of war, therefore, his cause was peculiarly just.[21]

DuBois made an important point, but one that could also be extended to white soldiers following orders.

Nineteenth-century African Americans' victimization became dramatically evident in a series of draft riots in New York that particularly targeted blacks for violence. In March 1863 the Lincoln government passed a national conscription law and, on July 12, posted the names of the first Northerners drafted into the Union army. Democrat speakers and newspapers whipped up a rage of working-class discontent over the exemption and substitution provisions of conscription, which created the appearance of a rich man's war and a poor man's fight.

Along the way, the Democrats singled out African American targets—hardly rich, but, just as polarizing, black. The tensions soon escalated into ethnic and racial bitterness as a civil war within the Civil War broke out in New York City on July 13. The rioting persisted through four days of dark violence. Mobs of predominantly Irish rioters rampaged through the city, burning the homes of prominent Republicans and lynching innocent blacks. Chanting "kill the naygers," they burned the Colored Orphan Asylum down and roamed the streets seeking out more black victims. At least six African Americans were hanged and burned.[22]

Women no less than men participated in the mayhem. In a report entitled "Great Riot," the *Christian Intelligencer* observed how "[t]he fury of the mob was directed . . . to negroes who were found in the streets." Republican newspaper reporters were also targeted: "A young man near the spot was taken for a reporter of the *Tribune*. He was kicked and beaten until nearly dead."[23]

As the violence threatened to overwhelm the police, an incensed President Lincoln called troops from the battle of Gettysburg to put down the rioters. When news of the riots reached Philo Buckingham, he wrote to his wife "after the fight at Gettysburg, Penn": "How I wish I could take this division . . . to New York for a week. . . . Our troops here would just like the job of putting down such a riot. It would be play in comparison to some of the battles in which they have been engaged."[24]

In a letter to his parents, John Emerson Anderson brought the surprising news that instead of chasing Lee, he was close to home to "enforce" the draft:

> Our regiment is quartered in barracks on city hall park. A battery belonging to our brigade has the muzzles of their Napoleons pointing down two of the streets where the rough element has held the sway of late. Those guns are slotted for close actions, and the men that handle them are in the habit of obeying the orders of their officers without asking questions. Indeed we are all united in this sentiment namely that the enemies of our flag must be conquered wherever met.[25]

And conquer they did, killing more than one hundred (largely Irish) rioters before the city was finally brought under control.

George Templeton Strong, treasurer of the United States Sanitary Commission, was horrified at the targeting of innocent blacks, the "unspeakable infamy of the nigger persecution. They are the most peaceful, sober, and inoffensive of our poor, and the outrages they have suffered during this last week are less excusable . . . than St. Bartholomew's or the Jew-hunting of the Middle Ages. . . . How this infernal slavery system has corrupted our blood, North as well as South!"

One female eyewitness to the rioting, Maria Daly, was no less offended at the violence, but considerably less sympathetic to the plight of the blacks:

> Three or four Negroes were hung and burned; the women assisted and acted like furies by stimulating the men to greater ferocity. . . . Although very sorry and much outraged at the cruelties inflicted [by the rioters] . . . I hope it will give the Negroes a lesson, for since the war commenced, they have been so insolent as to be unbearable. I cannot endure free blacks. They are immoral, with all their piety.[26]

The draft riots provide a unique window into the violent tensions that boiled beneath the surface of Northern society and the complex relationships binding outraged Republicans and African American "natives" against Democratic Irish "foreigners." In this cauldron of racial and ethnic hatreds it is clear that hatred of "the enemy" could spill internally as well as outwardly. Newspapers were unstinting in their criticism of the rioters. At first many papers blamed Southern sympathizers and Democratic Copperheads for inciting the mobs as a "diversion" from Confederate military defeats. But soon other more nativist theories prevailed.[27] The fact that so many of the rioters were Irish Catholics—and Democrats—was not lost on the overwhelmingly Protestant religious press.

A writer for the *Evangelist* who long championed against slavery, contextualized the violence in nativist terms that privileged black victims over immigrant white rioters:

> In looking over the long list of killed and wounded we find scarcely an American name . . . they are almost all Irishmen. . . . They were especially conspicuous in the hunting, burning, and hanging of poor negroes. . . . At such times we cannot forget that these Irish who thus attack a part of our population, are all foreigners, while the negroes whom they hunt like fiends, are natives of the soil—Americans by birth, that have a far better right here than this scum of a foreign population.[28]

As news of the atrocities spread, support for emancipation grew steadily. Instead of denigrating African Americans, the draft riots helped transform public opinion into an increasingly supportive identification of the war with abolition.

In tabulating the costs of the riot, the *Philadelphia Inquirer* put the total figure from damages at over one million dollars, not including "the expenses of suppressing the riot." And for what, it asked? "Not even an escape from the Conscription Act, for the draft is to go on."[29]

CHAPTER 26

"A POLITICAL WORSHIP"

In contrast to the Confederacy, the Union called for no more fast days in 1863. Instead, two joyous thanksgiving days were observed, one on August 6 and the other in November, marking a premier "national" holiday. At the August 6 thanksgiving, many orators and newspapers contrasted the present happy state of the war with the dark days of Chancellorsville and Fredericksburg. They celebrated faith in God as well as the elevation of General George Meade, who acknowledged divine deliverance. This was in contrast to his predecessor, Joe Hooker, who offered a "profane boast" before Chancellorsville "that he should capture or destroy the rebel army in spite of Providence." The ensuing "disaster" and "retreat" proved that God was on the side of the pious and not the boastful.[1]

In Philadelphia, extreme heat kept people off the streets, but flags flew everywhere and all the churches held services. In excerpting sermons preached in the area, the *Philadelphia Inquirer* fastened on the theme of history and bloodshed. Nobody rehearsed the numbers of casualties; only the baptism in blood.

By 1863 political preaching in the North and South had virtually completed the apotheosis of "patriotism" into a full-blown civil religion. "Martyrdoms" became a major theme in 1863 fast sermons. Even as the North won, the costs mounted to staggering levels, and the only accolade that seemed to work for most were "martyrs" sacrificing themselves upon the "altar" of their country.

At the Church of the Intercessor, the Reverend William Carden looked to the history of early Christian martyrs and asked, "Was the Church established without blood and slaughter?" The answer, he continued, was no: "Past history records too faithfully the terrible trials and privations of the first ambassadors for Christ. . . . It was something to be a Christian then. It called for honesty, and manliness, and self-sacrifice—nay, death." It did not stop there. "After the Church had passed through her early baptism of blood . . . did no more baptisms of blood await the people of God?" Again, the answer was no: sufferings continued to the present centuries. Then, in a rhetorical shift that had become commonplace, Carden substituted the American nation for the Christian church, and raised the same questions, with the same sacred stakes. Apparently, by Carden's reckoning, the two were interchangeable.[2]

Among the ranks of Northern patriotic clergy, none perceived the sacred dimensions of America more clearly than Horace Bushnell. From his opening salvo in 1861 on "Reverses Needed," Bushnell revealed that he perceived in bloodshed something mystically religious and moral that was creating a nation where only inchoate states and loose confederations had previously existed. And the source of that mysticism was divine Providence—a force that superceded natural law and a mere consent of the governed, burnishing all into a holy communion. Neither slavery nor the "North" nor the "South" defined the war for Bushnell so much as the fruition of a providential Christian state, conceived by the Puritans, rearticulated in the Declaration of Independence, and actualized through civil war.

Lincoln himself was moving toward Bushnell's position through a fatalistic route of his own. Lincoln's vision of the Last Best Hope of Earth, however, was not *necessarily* Christian. For Bushnell and many other American Protestants, only a Christian state would make America into God's own nation—a Christian state whose convictions included democracy and religious liberty for all. Thankfully, the Civil War was moving America in that direction: a nation wrought in the fires of war upon the anvil of blood sacrifices under the hammer of a providential God.[3]

Blood recurred as a theme in Bushnell's meditations as the necessary and sufficient condition for nationalism. The shed blood of soldiers, North and South, white and black, would stand as the vicarious atonement for the newly realized, organic Christian nation-state. This was not simply a metaphorical atonement, but quite literally a blood sacrifice required by God for sinners North and South if they were to inherit their providential destiny. By late 1863 this war that was not self-consciously fought *for* the creation of an American civil religion was unintentionally becoming *about* the creation of an American civil religion that would grow as the killing endured.

In an essay on "The Doctrine of Loyalty," written shortly after Gettysburg, Bushnell identified the war with the ultimate loyalty usually reserved for faithful martyrs, sacrificing their lives for a larger cause:

Virginia Soldiers' Cemetery in Alexandria. All across the country, granite and marble markers, wooden crosses, and national flags marked row upon endless row of the "martyrs" who died to save their nation's life.

How far the loyal sentiment reaches and how much it carries with it, or after it, must also be noted. It yields up willingly husbands, fathers, brothers, and sons, consenting to the fearful chance of a home always desolate. It offers body and blood, and life, on the altar of its devotion. It is a fact, a political worship, offering to seal itself by a martyrdom in the field. Wonderful, grandly honorable fact, that human nature can be lifted by an inspiration so high, even in the fallen state of wrong and evil![4]

In similar terms, the Swiss-born American theologian and church historian Philip Schaff located the mystical animus of the war not in slavery (for which he found some biblical precedent), nor in abstract claims to nationalism on European models he knew so well, nor even on freedom and democracy, but rather in providential destiny. The war, he concluded, was "a very baptism of blood [entitling] us also to hope for a glorious regeneration."[5]

Christian ministers—especially Protestant ministers—were predisposed to see transcendent signals in history and to claim to know their meaning. Others were less certain, but this did not eliminate the power of the war in shaping a religious national consciousness. In ways few could perceive, blood *was* becoming a sacrifice, if not for a demanding God, then certainly for a sanctified nation with a sacred destiny of its own.

Confederates were slow to realize the enormity of the loss visited at Gettysburg and the defeat at Vicksburg. Newspapers, particularly outside of Richmond, often relied on Northern papers for news, especially from Democratic publications that could be skewed to place the South in the best possible light. On July 7, for example, Raleigh's *North Carolina Standard* reported, "We think it clear, from the Northern account that the Confederates achieved a victory at Gettysburg." From reading the *New York Herald*, the report concluded, as well, that "Vicksburg can never be taken by assault." Two days later, Richmond's *Central Presbyterian* reported, "Everything yet received [from Gettysburg] indicates an overwhelming defeat to our enemies."[6]

It would be two weeks before the full extent of Gettysburg and Vicksburg reached Southern newspapers, often with the embarrassed confession that earlier issues "gave an exaggerated account of General Lee's success at Gettysburg" and bemoaning "the Fall of Vicksburg."[7] But even this news was often obscured by denial. On August 1, well after the battlefield defeat, the *Southern Illustrated News* simply glorified Pickett's suicidal assault: "It is believed that a more gallant and heroic charge was never made on this continent. . . . The division went in from five to six thousand strong. Three days after the battle but fifteen hundred reported for duty. Well done, noble heroes, officers, and men."[8]

In its July 9 issue, obviously written earlier, Richmond's *Christian Observer* described a "Great Battle at Gettysburg," noting that "the Confederates Hold the Field," even as the Confederate positions "furnished a play for artillery like that of Marye's Hill." Complementing this distorted account was a column on "Great News from the West" reporting "that Grant has been defeated by Johnston, and his army cut to pieces."[9]

The rhetoric of "gallantry," like the rhetoric of the jeremiad, was impervious to defeat—and to the future. With discourses like these, the fighting could continue indefinitely until there were no more souls to slaughter on the altar of their nation. At the same time, the rhetoric of gallantry signaled an important transformation in Confederate morale as the Confederate soldiers embarked on their long, sullen descent into bloodshed, with only the dimmest prospects for victory. Increasingly "duty" would augment gallantry as the operative goal rather than triumph. Fighting on to keep deaths from being in vain is different from fighting to win. And in the denial of late 1863 we see a cause blinded to its failure but determined to honor duty and let the destruction go where it may.

By July 10 reality set in throughout the South, as news of the double defeats arrived. The *North Carolina Standard* lamented, "Our worst fears are realized. The [Vicksburg] garrison has made a most heroic and glorious defense, but nothing could avail against the storm of shot and shell which poured into the city from all sides, and the constantly encroaching forces of Grant." As for Gettysburg, "We fear this news [of victory] is unfounded. If General Lee is retreating towards Hagerstown, the inference is that the tide is against him. . . . The heart bleeds and the tear unbidden starts from the eye, when we think of the noble and gallant thousands of our countrymen who went down in the fiery vortex."[10]

Throughout the South, July was wrapped in gloom. Writing from Georgia to her son in the army, Mary Jones asked: "How long will this awful conflict last? It does appear that we are to be brought very low. May the Lord give us such repentance and humility before Him as shall turn away His wrath and restore His favor, through the merits and intercession of our Divine Redeemer!"

In response, Colonel Charles Jones replied, "The heavens above us are indeed dark; but although for the present the clouds give no reviving showers, let us look and pray earnestly for His favor who can bring order out of chaos, victory out of apparent defeat, and light out of shadow."[11]

In opposition to secular editors and critics of Davis who rose up from the ashes of defeat, the Confederate religious press proved to be the truest believers—and perpetuators—of the sacred Confederacy and its civil religion. They almost unanimously praised the cause of the war, in defeat no less than victory, and honored its political and military leaders.

After Gettysburg, the *Christian Observer* turned to reporting on the sorrow in England that greeted the news of Stonewall Jackson's death. The account described Jackson's international appeal as soldier and Christian and the grief God-fearing Christians experienced universally in England. The internationalization of Jackson was one more piece of his mythologization.

Even as losses mounted and the memories of Chancellorsville and Fredericksburg faded, the cult of Jackson grew steadily in the Southern secular and religious press. The Episcopal *Southern Churchman* had no real affinity with Jackson's Calvinistic Presbyterianism but nevertheless continued to sing his praises in biographical sketches written by ministers such as Moses Hoge and Robert Lewis Dabney, and in accounts of impending honors.[12] Other papers captured "a scene in the Life of General Jackson," highlighting his piety and Christian manliness.[13] Both secular and religious writers fused Jackson's military prowess with his staunch Presbyterianism and implied that each was inextricably tied to the other.

From his position in the field near Rome, Georgia, with the Texas Rangers, Chaplain Robert Bunting wrote an uplifting letter that effectively denied the enormity of July's defeats and promised ongoing divine deliverance. Dated July 30, 1863, the letter insisted that defeats at Gettysburg and Vicksburg were "not so severe a blow as the evacuation of Bowling Green and Nashville . . . or the loss of Fort Pillow and Memphis, or New Orleans and the lower forts." Nor did they signal divine disfavor with the cause. In words also offered to the casualty-riddled soldiers in his brigade, Bunting affirmed:

> We may lose all of our sea-board, and control of the Mississippi and Richmond itself, and yet we are neither undone or conquered. It matters not, although the *New York Herald* may declare that "the rebellion is already crushed," and propose terms for the reconstruction of the Union, yet that does not make it so . . . No! this people are not yet conquered. And more—I have faith enough left to believe they never will be overrun and subjugated. Such people have never yet been enslaved. Search the pages of history, and you will fail to find a people recognized so clearly in their struggles for freedom—for the possession of their Canaan of earthly hopes, by the Court of Heaven, as this bleeding Confederacy.[14]

Words like these could easily lead to a moral case for guerrilla warfare.

On July 27, 1863, a disheartened war clerk, J. B. Jones, contextualized the setting for another fast-day proclamation:

> Nothing but disasters to chronicle now. Natchez and Yazoo City, all gone the way of Vicksburg, involving a heavy loss of boats, guns, and ordnance stores; besides the enemy have got some twenty locomotives in Mississippi. Lee has retreated as far as Culpepper Court House. The President publishes another proclamation, fixing a day for the people to unite in prayer. The weather is bad.[15]

Two days later, bad weather led a despondent Jones to question his cause: "Still raining! The great fear is that the crops will be ruined, and famine, which we have long been verging upon, will be complete. Is providence upon us for our sins, or upon our cause?"[16]

That Jones would ask such a question reveals how devastating Meade's and Grant's victories were. But few went so far as to question the morality of the South's cause. Instead, the answer, as it emerged from virtually every pulpit and religious publication in Richmond, and then broadcast abroad, was that the Confederacy's cause was just and God's punishment a purification for sin.

Pulpits and presses throughout the land cited instances of punishment and salvation from the Old Testament to assure their audiences of divine favor. The most often cited example was Nineveh, which was spared when the ancient inhabitants turned to God in fasting and repentance. In a column asking, "Is the Lord on Our Side?" the *Southern Churchman* responded in the affirmative and castigated those who "nor for the first time . . . ask 'can the Lord be on our Side?' "

Equally certain was the culpability of the North. In his fast sermon to the Centenary Church in Lynchburg, Virginia, the Reverend Leroy Lee pointed toward the enemy's intention to "exterminate the white population of these states." But, he insisted, this would not come to pass because "we have strong grounds to trust that God will hear our prayers, and interpose for our deliverance."[17]

With some exceptions, the secular press concurred. A writer for the *Richmond Daily Whig* pointed out: "No man or woman in the Confederacy who is familiar with the doctrines or commandments of the Inspired Word can be greatly surprised at the present state of affairs. Have not the people everywhere devoted themselves to the worship of Mammon? Have they not all practiced extortion?"[18]

Fast-day preaching might be losing "its good effect through repetition" among many observers in the government and the secular press, yet a flood of religious print continued to drape the carnage with spiritual significance. Denominational newspapers trumpeted the "Christian heroism" of generals like Stonewall Jackson and Robert E. Lee, effectively fusing patriotism with the same Christian legitimation that prevailed in the North. By August 1863 the war had created and consecrated two American civil religions, mortally opposed, but both Christian and both "American."

In a letter to the *Houston Tri-Weekly Telegraph*, written on August 23, 1863, Chaplain Bunting described the scene at a fast-day church service in Rome, Georgia, led by the Confederate firebrand Benjamin Palmer of New Orleans. Midway through the service, Union artillery began bombarding "hundreds of non-combatants [who] were in the different houses of God for worship." For Bunting, this bombardment bore a dual significance. It underscored both the unjust tactics of the "fiendish" enemy in attacking innocents, and the bravery of the worshippers who refused to leave despite the bombardment:

Yet the mass remained in their places, and the man of God continued in his prayer. There he stood, this noble Ambassador of Christ from the far South, with eyes and hands raised to Heaven, not a note altered, not a sign of confusion, excitement or alarm, naught but the calm, Christian face, uplifted and full of the unconsciousness to all save its devotions, which beam from the soul of true piety.[19]

Eventually, as the shelling continued, services concluded and congregations dispersed, having learned the lesson that "[t]he enemy may burn our churches; he may exile our people, with his cannon pointed against the place of prayer . . . but he cannot seal the lips of the believer, nor yet prevent the heart from sending forth its petitions to the 'Father of Mercies.' "[20]

To clergymen and religious publishers who recognized the power of the press to mold opinion, however, a more immediate danger than the bombardment appeared as the war continued. The shifting tone they detected in the mainstream secular press and the increasingly harsh criticism of the Davis administration in the opposition papers threatened a disillusionment that could very well erode the faith of the people in both their cause and their prospects for success. Here too an evolving civil war within a civil war appeared, as journalists criticized leadership and clergy criticized journalists for bad faith. To counter what they perceived as a more secular nationalism promoted in some newspapers, religious editors identified patriotism without piety as the "defective patriotism" that was drawing God's chastisement.[21] In one soldier's tract, a Virginia chaplain wondered why this patriotism seemed more motivating than the cause of Christ.[22]

In fact, not all secular newspapers were critical of the war effort; some stood resolutely beside a virtually unanimous religious press. A few even succumbed to pure blood revenge. The *Richmond Daily Dispatch* recognized with a sort of helpless resignation that "the taste for blood grows with the indulgence, and men become every day more like wolves, as they give way to the growing appetite. . . . We are getting savage, with the rest of our countrymen, and we confess to a special delight in hearing of Yankee corpses." In such a mentality, no contradiction existed between revenge and just war: "Adversity will bring out only in bolder relief the virtues of the people of the South—the virtues of courage, constancy, and faith in a Just Cause and a Just Providence."[23]

But the political and military leadership was another matter. Following the defeat at Gettysburg, the *Richmond Daily Whig* continued to invoke religion, but turned from Israel to place a far greater emphasis on secular history and antiquity:

The glory of Athens and the strength of Sparta were acquired by making every man a soldier, and considering non-combatants as drones in the national hive. . . . No nobler principle, no dearer homes, no fairer land were ever fought for, bled for, died for than hang upon the issue of this conflict. Natal rights and native land, hereditary titles to property, the immunities of free citizenship, the sanctities of the hearthstone, the appealing voice of innocent and helpless womanhood—all that can touch the heart or nerve the arm, cry trumpet tongued to all brave and true men to fight this fight out to victory or death.[24]

The point was clear. Religion might be enough to justify the war, but the bracing tonic of ancient warriors made victory sweeter.

As pro-Davis "political preaching" escalated in the churches, secular criticism of the clergy's preaching grew fierce in some corners. The *Richmond Examiner* gave very clear advice to the clergy that reflected a return to the antebellum doctrine of "the spirituality of the church." It was time for the clergy to preach Christ and, by implication, get out of politics where they were doing no good: "[I]t is rather their duty to soften the passions aroused in the contests of the world, and withdraw our thoughts from their fevered excitement, than to stimulate them by passionate discourse."[25]

The North and South were now headed in opposite directions, the *Examiner* claimed: the North was rapidly becoming more radical, the South more conservative and more attached to its institutions.[26] The South's unique social organization made it special: "We are the only religious and conservative people in Christendom. . . . It is nothing but our social institutions and our domestic slavery that distinguishes us from the rest of the nations of Europe." *Because* of slavery, the South escaped "the moral and political evils that afflict other countries." Christian morality was natural to a slave society but impracticable in a free land, "where all men are equals, [and therefore] all must be competitors."[27] Clearly, if it was left to the South, slavery would not disappear anytime soon.

On August 6, 1863, after the humiliations of Gettysburg and Vicksburg, the *Richmond Examiner* bitterly declared that defeat came in no small part because of the persistence of the "Southern Government" in fighting a just war: "There is neither Christianity nor religion of any kind in this war. We prosecute it in self-defense, for the preservation of our liberty, our homes and our Negroes." This statement grew as much out of frustration with Davis's policies and his outspoken clerical defenders as from philosophical commitment. If the conduct of Confederates at war was more just and humane (and Lee's orders in Chambersburg, Pennsylvania, reinforced that image), it was time to change and grow more savage, like the North.

The *Examiner* never denied that Christianity was at the core of Southern society (hence its moral superiority), only that religion—and its gentle ethics—had no place in war. The paper's editors had no further patience with religion being mixed up with politics, public occasions, or national policy. This, despite the blatant fact that Southern religious leaders were anything but gentle.

The paper's editor, John Moncure Daniel, mercilessly criticized Davis's government for "what might be called the white-cravat policy; the practice, in a deadly struggle with the devil's own brood, of the Christian precept of doing good for evil, of turning another cheek when smitten."[28] Politicians, in their public and political capacities, should stay away from religion, and clergymen, like women, should avoid politics. "That in times of high excitement the clergy should share the feelings of the community, is natural; and it may be difficult to prevent all confusion of earthly and heavenly considerations in pious discourse, yet the nature of our Government, widely adverse to the union of the secular and the sacred arm, forbids it."[29]

For the *Examiner*, separation of church and state also meant a more rigid separation of religion and politics than Davis, his generals, and many other journalists were willing to employ. While Confederate advocates of the jeremiad could not see the contradictions between their fast days and jeremiads and the antebellum tradition of the spirituality of the church, Daniel saw it all too clearly. The Confederate nation under Davis was becoming dangerously "Puritan," thus subverting the very cause of separation:

Fast days and Thanksgiving days strike the Southern ear with a puritanical sound, always disagreeable, and, now, pre-eminently hateful. They smack of Latter Day sanctity; savor of the nasal twang and recall disagreeable reminiscences of Praise-God-Barebones, the Pilgrim Fathers, and their Yankee descendants.

Public trust in "Divine aid" was one thing, Daniels continued, but still,

it is to be regretted that the phraseology we use should be unfortunately associated with all that is repugnant to our taste and our feelings. . . . This revolution should secure us social as well as political independence. We should get rid of Yankee manners as well as of Puritan laws; and one of the most obnoxious is the vice of political preaching. Let the Southern clergy, then, be assured that they will win more lasting respect, and exert more legitimate influence, in abstaining from a custom discordant to our manners.[30]

For all of his fulmination against churches and fasts, Daniel never attacked the religious press nor did he criticize denominational statements supporting the Confederacy. Nor did he question the cause. He attacked fast-day preaching and the president who called for it. And he questioned a military ethic of just conduct that placed the unjust conduct of Northern troops at an advantage. Indeed, for a Christian republic, these were all good, pure traditions. His criticisms were reserved for political sermons and, in particular, fast-day sermons uttered from the ashes of defeat. These departures from the rigid separation of church and state, he believed, promoted a supernatural fatalism that placed the chief burden for victory on God rather than Confederate guns.

In words bristling with bitter irony, Daniel observed that the North—the originator of fasts—had itself outgrown them, while the South foolishly picked them up: "They by the way do not seem now to rely on fasts and humiliation. They have recently indulged in thanksgiving for victory, but their panacea for defeat seems to be fresh levies of men, more ironclad and additional fifteen-inch guns."[31]

The implications of Daniel's perspective were obvious. Only by duplicating the North's civil religion, at the expense of traditional Christianity, could the Confederacy adopt a tough-minded, patriotic savagery capable of defeating the North on its own terms. But this would not happen. Confederate Christianity was simply too powerful a cultural system to discard. Instead, Confederate Christians would grow even tougher and embrace the savagery.

CHAPTER 27

"THE ROCK OF CHICKAMAUGA"

T hroughout the war, Jefferson Davis took the high moral ground regarding the conduct of soldiers in the field. Despite the heavy destruction wrought on Federal armies at Gettysburg, no widespread pillaging occurred, nor destruction of Pennsylvania towns. Neither were civilians harassed with a view toward destroying their morale. This, he asserted, was in sharp contrast to the hard-war policy condoned by the North.

In a letter to President Lincoln, drafted on July 2, 1863, Davis addressed himself to the issue of just conduct: "I have to complain of the conduct of your officers and troops in many parts of the country, who violate all the rules of war by carrying on hostilities not only against armed foes but against non-combatants, aged men, women, and children." Assaults on property were not solely to support armies in the field but also to destroy civilian life. Union soldiers "not only seize such property as is required for the use of your forces, but destroy all private property within their reach, even agricultural implements." Furthermore, Northern armies sought "to subdue the population of the districts where they are operating by the starvation that must result from the destruction of standing crops and agricultural tools."[1]

Davis did not mention particulars (implying they were too universal to be itemized), but examples of unjust conduct multiplied. One, reported in a letter by Robert Gould Shaw, commander of the first Northern black regiment, the Fifty-fourth Massachusetts, described the actions of Colonel Montgomery in the abandoned town of Darien, Georgia, in June 1863. After bombarding the town with artillery, Montgomery landed boats and confiscated all the furniture and movable property. Then, "in a very low tone, and . . . [with] a sweet smile," he informed Shaw, "I shall burn this town."

Though "not a shot had been fired at us," Montgomery ordered Shaw and other officers to burn the town. When Shaw asked for an explanation, "the reasons he gave me . . . were, that the Southerners must be made to feel that this was a real war, and that they were to be swept away by the hand of God, like the Jews of old." Personally, Shaw did not like "being made the instrument of the Lord's vengeance," but fearing that if he reported the destruction it would do more harm to the reputation of his black soldiers than to Montgomery, Shaw said nothing, while conceding "this makes me very much ashamed of myself."[2]

In accusing Lincoln's troops of unjust conduct, Davis was especially concerned that Lincoln, as commander in chief, refused to "disclaim having authorized them," thus raising the haunting specter that such actions were approved at the highest levels of Union government. If this was the case, Davis averred, a price would be exacted: "I have, notwithstanding, refrained from the exercise of such retaliation, because of its obvious tendency to lead to a war of indiscriminate massacre on both sides, which would be a spectacle so shocking to humanity and so disgraceful to the age in which we live and the religion we profess that I cannot contemplate it without a feeling of horror that I am disinclined to doubt you would share."[3]

Significantly, Lincoln did not reply.

While correct that Lincoln had authored the hard-war policy on civilian populations, Davis could not substantiate the innocence he claimed; in fact, both armies were descending into an ethical gray zone. Davis did not raise the subject of "irregular" Confederate assaults on innocent civilians, nor the Partisan Ranger Act of April 1862, and for good reason. By this act, the Confederate government, in effect, legitimated guerrilla organizations and produced local heroes such as John Mosby, the "Grey Ghost" who terrorized Union soldiers in the Shenandoah Valley, or Nathan Bedford Forrest, "the Wizard of the Saddle," or John Hunt Morgan. But at least these were under orders and paid by the Confederate government. In the language of Lieber's Code, they were partisans.

Meanwhile, an entirely different category of guerrillas arose: unsupervised "freebooters" and criminals who preyed on innocent populations at will. The most infamous was the former Ohio schoolteacher William Clarke Quantrill. Quantrill's murderous band, bent on robbing and killing unarmed civilians, included Frank and Jesse James.[4]

On the very day (August 21) that churches and armies fasted throughout the Confederacy, a dark event was playing itself out in "Bleeding Kansas." Quantrill and his "rangers"—minus sixteen-year-old Jesse James, deemed too young by the gang—entered the "abolitionist" town of Lawrence, Kansas, with cold-blooded murder on their minds. As the rioters shouted, "Kill! Kill!" they rounded up the local population and killed 150 unarmed men and boys in a senseless display of wanton violence. They then torched the town, leaving it in ashes.

Northerners and Southerners condemned the attacks. One Northern account informed readers:

> We learn from Leavenworth, Kansas, that a band of rebel guerrillas made a descent on Lawrence on the night of the 20th instant, murdered the inhabitants, and pillaged the town finally setting it on fire and destroying it. . . . The list of killed and wounded is said to number one hundred and eighty . . . the loss at Lawrence, it is estimated, will amount to about two millions, which will fall heavily on New York as well as Lawrence merchants.[5]

If anything, the Confederacy condemned the attack more than the Union. General Lee prevailed on President Davis to repeal the Ranger Act that gave "irregular" partisans liberty without discipline or order.

Northern commanders used the massacre as a rationale to ratchet up the war on the South to a more total form of war directed against civilians—enemies all—as well as armies in the field. Key Union commanders, including Grant, Sherman, Halleck, and Sheridan, had all experienced guerrilla opposition of a less murderous variety than seen in Lawrence, and one directed at soldiers, not innocent civilians. But they nevertheless lost whatever qualms they felt about civilian suffering in the aftermath of Quantrill's raid and parallel "irregular" attacks on Union forces. From the experience of rebel guerrilla action, now expanded to include civilians in general, the "strategy of exhaustion" that marked the campaigns of 1864 and 1865 emerged.

In response to Lawrence, Federal forces now turned reciprocally vengeful in an escalating rain of horror on (mostly) innocent civilians. The turn to total war on civilians began with General Orders No. 11. These authorized Federal forces first to drive from their homes ten thousand Missouri citizens in suspected guerrilla territories that bordered Kansas, then commanded them to burn to the ground the homes of suspected abettors.[6] The orders were followed to the letter, leaving as many dead civilians in their wake as Quantrill had murdered. The Civil War's version of "war crimes" had now moved into high gear.

Aware of public criticisms of total war, particularly emanating from the Democrats, Lincoln defended civilian suffering—short of massacre—as common to war. In a letter to James C. Conkling, his lawyer friend from early days, written on August 26, Lincoln summarized his view of a just war: "Civilized belligerents do all in their power to help themselves, or hurt the enemy, except a few things regarded as barbarous or cruel. Among the exceptions are the massacre of vanquished foes, and non-combatants, male and female."[7]

Besides taking the war more directly to civilians and the partisans hidden among them, Lincoln continued to defend his suspension of habeas corpus when dealing with disloyal and traitorous citizens. The decision was difficult, he conceded, and "I was slow to adopt the strong measures." But military necessity required it:

> Civil courts are organized chiefly for trials of individuals, or, at most, a few individuals acting in concert—and this in quiet times, and on charges of crimes well defined in the law. . . . Habeas corpus does not discharge men who are proved to be guilty of defined crime; and its suspension is allowed by the Constitution on purpose that men may be arrested and held who cannot be proved to be guilty of defined crime, "when, in cases of rebellion or invasion, the public safety may require it." This is precisely our present case—a case of rebellion wherein the public safety does require the suspension.[8]

While the war escalated to new levels of civilian involvement, Confederate revivals soared and news of "the spirit of the Army" inspired civilians at home. As one writer observed, "The Southern army is in fact the Southern people. It contains the cream of chivalry, the patriotism, the physical stamina, and the moral worth of the land."[9]

As Lee's badly mauled army licked its wounds, a recovered Confederate Army of Tennessee, under General Braxton Bragg, engaged General William Rosecrans's Army of the Cumberland (supported by Ambrose Burnside) for a rematch, this time across the Tennessee River at Chattanooga.

Preliminary engagements on September 18, 1863, set the stage for a pitched battle the next day at Chickamauga, Tennessee, between Federal forces totaling sixty-two thousand and Confederate forces numbering sixty-five thousand.[10] With Longstreet present on loan from Lee, and avoiding offensive charges wherever possible, Confederate generals improved their chances. Instead of open-field charges, they chose densely wooded areas and swamps that maximized the advantage of local knowledge and allowed for little tactical control of units in the field. In large part because of the thick woods, neither the Southern nor the Northern commander knew exactly where either the enemy or his own units were.

For two hours, the Federal left commanded by General George Thomas held off heavy attacks with their unyielding defenses. But Longstreet was not to be denied. By exploiting a temporary gap in Federal lines, Longstreet's trusted subordinate, General John Bell Hood, crashed through the lines, leaving the Union army dangerously divided.

In a monumental miscalculation—or loss of nerve—Rosecrans assumed his entire army had been destroyed and fled to Chattanooga, leaving Thomas and what was left of the Army of the Cumberland alone in the field to block Longstreet's advance. One unwitting participant in Rosecrans's retreat—a runaway slave named Thomas Cole—was picked up by Northern troops just in time to join the battle. In his later account, he recalled his first moments in battle assigned to support a cannon: "Finally they . . . puts me to work helping with the cannons. I feels 'portant then, but I didn't know what was in front of me, or I 'spects I'd run off 'gain."

Unable to run, Cole stayed for the first day's fight, and afterward surveyed the horror of the dead and wounded, "blood running out them and the top or sides their heads gone, great big holes in them." The next day was a rout: "The Rebels 'gins shooting and killing lots of our men, and General Woods ain't come, so General Rosecrans orders us to 'treat and didn't have to tell me what he said, neither. The Rebels comes after us, shooting, and we runs off and leaves that cannon what I was with setting on the hill, and I didn't want that thing nohow. We kept hotfooting till we gits to Chattanooga, and there is where we stops."[11]

Abandoned by Rosecrans, Thomas, who never left a battlefield throughout the war and never lost a battle, held his position with scant ammunition and fixed bayonets until help arrived from the Army of the Kentucky. Thomas was not always the fastest commander in a fight, but his bulldog tenacity at Chickamauga earned him the moniker "The Rock of Chickamauga."

In what was becoming a numbing ritual, both sides suffered 28 percent casualties, including four thousand killed. In tactical terms, Bragg's plan worked and gave him a decided victory. But with no reserves to exploit Longstreet's success, the strategic objective was lost. The North's superior numbers grew yet larger. This would mark the last Confederate victory in the western theater. Meanwhile Thomas's unbowed troops heaped acclaim on their fearless general.

Back in both the Union and the Confederate camps, recriminations flew in all directions. Lincoln thought Rosecrans "confused and stunned like a duck hit on the head" and relieved him of command, together with two of his commanders, for leaving the field while others fought.[12] Lincoln then created the Division of the Mississippi under the command of his new hero, U. S. Grant, and rewarded General Thomas with command of the Army of the Cumberland.

In the Confederacy, the already heavily criticized Bragg underwent the humiliation of a council of war with President Davis and his generals, where every subordinate commander urged Bragg's dismissal. Lacking any viable alternative, and still close friends with Bragg, Davis turned a blind eye to reality and refused. One obvious replacement for Bragg was General Longstreet, but in a remarkable testimony to the power of generals to negotiate their fate, Longstreet declined, preferring a different command or a return to Lee and the Army of Northern Virginia. Eventually Bragg would be relieved by General Joseph E. Johnston and reassigned to Richmond as a military adviser to Davis. But by then the damage was done, facilitated in no small measure by Davis's inability to rise above friendships (and enmities) to make disinterested judgments.[13]

As soon as the Federal soldiers garrisoned in Chattanooga were relieved of a possible Confederate siege, Grant went after Bragg's ill-led army. General Halleck ordered General Hooker to seize control of the imposing Confederate defenses at Lookout Mountain, due south of Chattanooga. To most observers, the steep cliffs appeared impregnable. But in another of his mindless miscalculations, Bragg posted only two thousand soldiers on the mountaintop. With surprising ease, Hooker's ten thousand men seized control of the mountain on November 24, in what later became known as the "Battle above the Clouds."

The next day, General Thomas's divisions attacked remaining Confederate strength at Missionary Ridge, Tennessee, and without orders, his troops spontaneously continued on shouting "Chickamauga! Chickamauga!" until the entire ridge was theirs. This unauthorized "soldier's battle" effectively sealed the fate of the Confederacy in Chattanooga. With the vital communications center now in Federal hands, the stage was set for Sherman's legendary march to the sea.[14]

The "miracle of Missionary Ridge" was cheered by the Yankees and a nightmare for the Confederates. The retreating rebels seemed to have lost their nerve. How else to explain the almost uncontested abandonment of a strong fortified position? Bragg was done; Johnston would soon replace him. As 1863 drew to a close, the despondency of the South could find no solace save in the heart of their downtrodden army.

CHAPTER 28

"IN THAT IMMORTAL FIELD"

T hough strategically inconclusive, and not the critical turning point that Antietam represented militarily and politically, Gettysburg stands in American memory as the greatest battle of the war and Pickett's charge as the embodiment of noble sacrifice, North and South.[1] Just-war questions of proportionality were not raised then, or later. Instead, American memory of Pickett's charge as a romantic turning point would be immortally captured in William Faulkner's oft-cited musings from his novel *Intruder in the Dust*:

> For every Southern boy fourteen years old, not once but whenever he wants it, there is the instant when it's still not yet two o'clock on that July afternoon in 1863, the brigades are in position behind the rail fence, the guns are laid and ready in the woods and the furled flags are already loosened to break out and Pickett himself with his long oiled ringlets and his hat in one hand probably and his sword in the other looking up the hill waiting for Longstreet to give the word and it's all in the balance, it hasn't happened yet, it hasn't even begun yet, it not only hasn't begun yet but there is still time for it not to begin against that position and those circumstances which made more men than Garnett and Kemper and Armistead and Wilcox look grave yet it's going to begin, we all know that, we have come too far with too much at stake and that moment doesn't need even a fourteen-year-old boy to think *This time. Maybe this time* with all this much to lose and all this much to gain: Pennsylvania, Maryland, the world, the golden dome of Washington itself to crown with desperate and unbelievable victory the desperate gamble, the cast made two years ago.

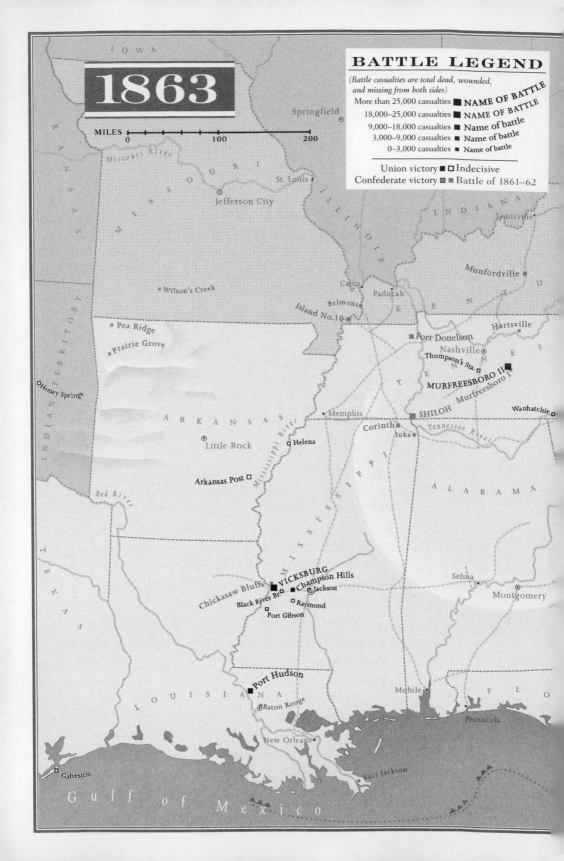

1863

MILES
0 ———————— 100 ———————— 200

IOWA

Springfield

Missouri River

KANSAS

St. Louis

MISSOURI

Jefferson City

ILLINOIS

INDIANA

Louisville

Munfordville

Wilson's Creek

Cairo

Paducah

Belmont

KENTUCKY

Hartsville

Island No.10

Fort Donelson

Nashville

Thompson's Sta.

MURFREESBORO II

Pea Ridge

Prairie Grove

Honey Springs

INDIAN TERRITORY

ARKANSAS

Little Rock

Memphis

Corinth

Iuka

SHILOH

Murfreesboro II

Wauhatchie

Tennessee River

TENNESSEE

Helena

Mississippi River

Arkansas Post

ALABAMA

Red River

Selma

VICKSBURG

Champion Hills

Chickasaw Bluffs

Black River Br.

Jackson

Raymond

Port Gibson

Montgomery

TEXAS

LOUISIANA

Port Hudson

Baton Rouge

Mobile

FLO

Pensacola

New Orleans

Fort Jackson

Galveston

Gulf of Mexico

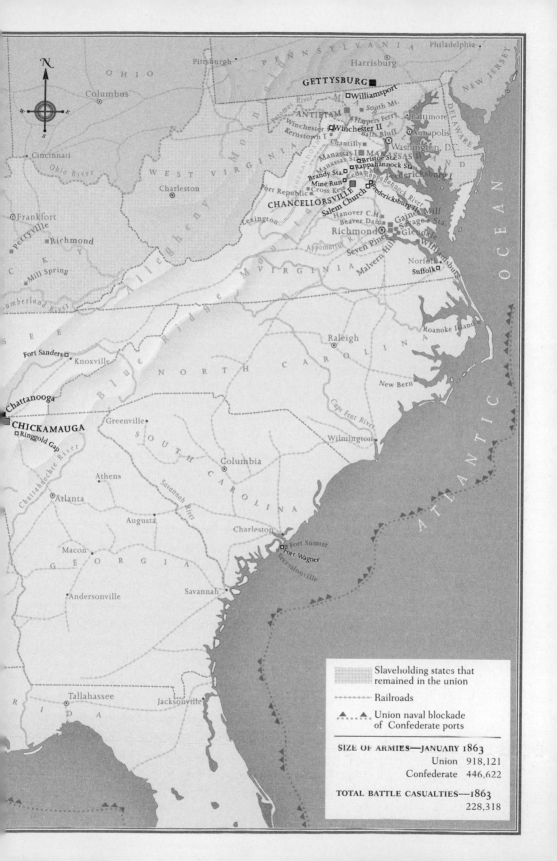

N

OHIO

Columbus ⊙

Pittsburgh •   PENNSYLVANIA   Philadelphia •

Harrisburg •

GETTYSBURG ■

□ Williamsport

ANTIETAM ■   ☐ South Mt.
Winchester □   Harpers Ferry
Kernstown I   □ Winchester II   Balls Bluff
Chantilly   Baltimore
Annapolis ⊗

Cincinnati •

Ohio River

Manassas I ■   MANASSAS II
Manassas Sta.□   Washington, D.C.
Brandy Sta.□ □ Bristoe Sta.
Mine Run ■ □ Rappahannock Sta.
Cross Keys   Cedar Mt.   Fredericksburg I
Port Republic   Rappahannock River

WEST VIRGINIA

Charleston •

Frankfort ⊗

Petersville
Richmond ■

K   Y

Mill Spring •

Cumberland River

CHANCELLORSVILLE
Salem Church   ■ Fredericksburg II
Hanover C.H.   ☐ Gaines' Mill
Beaver Dam   Savage's Sta.
Lexington   Richmond ⊙ ■ Glendale
Appomattox R.   Seven Pines   Williamsburg
Malvern Hill   ■ Yorktown
Norfolk ■
Suffolk □

VIRGINIA

Fort Sanders □
Knoxville •

Chattanooga ■

CHICKAMAUGA
□ Ringgold Gap

Chattahoochee River

Greenville •

Athens •

⊗ Atlanta

Augusta •

GEORGIA

Macon •

• Andersonville

Savannah •

Raleigh ⊙

NORTH   CAROLINA

New Bern •

Cape Fear River

SOUTH
CAROLINA

Columbia ⊙

Wilmington •

Charleston •
□ Fort Sumter
□ Fort Wagner
Secessionville

Roanoke Island

ATLANTIC   OCEAN

Tallahassee •

Jacksonville •

F   L   O   R   I   D   A

Blue Ridge Mountains

Savannah River

☐ Slaveholding states that
remained in the union

••••• Railroads

▲   ▲ Union naval blockade
of Confederate ports

SIZE OF ARMIES—JANUARY 1863
Union   918,121
Confederate   446,622

TOTAL BATTLE CASUALTIES—1863
228,318

The Battle of Gettysburg. Heroic prints like this one by Currier & Ives helped preserve the place of Gettysburg in American memory as the Civil War's greatest battle.

As heroic as Faulkner's account is, it only described the Southern memory of Gettysburg. Something besides its romanticization emerged from Gettysburg that would become forever etched in the American imagination. A sacralization of this particular battlefield would mark it forever after as the preeminent sacred ground of the Civil War—and American wars thereafter. Such lasting reverence had less to do with the battle itself than with what happened there four months later on November 19, when President Lincoln returned to the battlefield to participate in the dedication of the national cemetery.

Edward Everett delivered the main oration in standard Ciceronian eloquence and duration (two hours). Lincoln added a three-minute address of his own. It met with scant immediate enthusiasm and was actually belittled by his political detractors. Clergymen, put off that no ministers were asked to speak at the dedication, little realized that America's greatest sermon had just been preached by a politician rather than a preacher.

Lincoln's comments would become immortalized as the Gettysburg Address, yet most religious presses failed even to note the occasion. The speech was not issued by a minister, and thus unworthy of note. In one writer's view: "The whole affair had well nigh been a failure from the absence of many of those large-hearted, conscientious, religious men, from whom this war receives its moral dignity." Everett was a "true patriot . . . but there is in the production little of that breadth of vision which will give it power in the future."

As for Lincoln, his address was summarized in one paragraph and "had none of the manner of an Orator," despite the fact that "his unselfish and generous devotion to the country had given to him the hearts of the people."[2]

One exception was the *Presbyter*, issued out of Cincinnati, which included the text of Lincoln's address, followed by an account of its reception by an adoring audience: "The president's address was received with long and loud demonstrations of applause, all assenting that it was the right thing in the right place and a perfect thing in every respect."[3]

In England, where the press often showed itself hostile to the North and to Lincoln, garbled and distorted reports of the Battle of Gettysburg implied a Southern victory. As for Lincoln's address, it was met with either silence or derision. The London *Times* provided a contemptuous account:

> The inauguration of the cemetery at Gettysburg was an imposing ceremony only rendered somewhat flat by the nature of Mr. Everett's lecture, and ludicrous by some of the luckless sallies of that poor President Lincoln, who seems determined to play in this great American Union the part of the famous Governor of the Isle of Barataris.[4]

What American memory has since elevated to the status of national scripture evoked hardly a ripple in the national consciousness of 1863. Ironically, in an earlier issue, the *Banner of the Covenant* identified the difficulty in perceiving historical legacies in immediate events:

> As the newspaper records events as they *occur*, all the interest of the reader is likely to be concentrated upon the events themselves, whilst their meaning and connections are liable to pass unregarded. . . . The newspaper, again gives its facts without selection, whilst well composed history is distinguished as much by the character of the matter it embraces, as by the elegance and truthfulness of the narrative . . . it is by studying the records of the past, that we learn to read, with the highest intelligence and profit, the transactions of the present.[5]

Even Lincoln was unaware of the legacy his words would imbue to later generations, both at the time he delivered the address ("The world will little note nor long remember what we say here") and in its immediate aftermath. In a letter to Edward Everett, written the following day, Lincoln praised Everett for his speech, in particular, "the tribute to our noble women for their angel-ministering to the suffering soldiers." In response to Everett's earlier praise

("I should be glad if I could flatter myself that I came as near to the central idea of the occasion in two hours as you did in two minutes") Lincoln replied, "I am pleased to know that, in your judgment, the little I did say was not entirely a failure."[6]

Never in American oratory has there been a greater understatement than this. Lincoln's rhetoric would connect forever after with Americans seeking a common meaning for their collective experience, and that meaning was, the literary critic Edmund Wilson later recognized, "quite mystical."[7] A Christlike tolerance appeared in his meditations as he reflected on the war's innermost meaning—not the "Union" triumphing over an evil Confederacy, but a common sacrifice that, in God's time, would deliver a united redeemer nation. In his address, Lincoln refused to condemn his enemies, as Everett had done so ruthlessly moments before. But neither had he yet reached the all-embracing "charity for all" that would come only with victory in sight.

Scholars have rightly praised the literary qualities of Lincoln's brief address at Gettysburg as a new sound in American rhetoric.[8] But in American memory, it became much more. It became the sacred scripture of the Civil War's innermost spiritual meaning. Central to that meaning was the revolutionary principle, always in need of implementation, that "all men are created equal." By linking past ("four score and seven years ago"), present ("these honored dead"), and future ("a new birth of freedom"), Lincoln presented a redemptive republic wedded to an idea ("that all men are created equal") in timeless form. As long as the idea survived, so too could America be assured that this "government of the people, by the people, for the people, shall not perish from the earth."

If the white Northern press exhibited a muted response to the dedication speech, the African Methodist Episcopal *Christian Recorder* proved more enthusiastic. The November 28 issue carried a complete description of the setting, a verbatim transcript of the address "amid a scene of wild and lengthened excitement," and the prayer of dedication by the House chaplain "delivered in the most impressive manner, and . . . listened to with breathless attention." Two weeks earlier, the *Recorder* perceived in Gettysburg and Vicksburg the death knell of slavery and a "new life": "with the removal of slavery . . . we may reasonably anticipate the decline of sectional jealousies, until in the future we shall know no North, no South—we shall all be Americans."[9] Tragically, while right on a common white America, they could not perceive that many African Americans would be left out of the new nation.

While the South fasted for its autumn defeats, President Lincoln issued a national thanksgiving proclamation on October 3, 1863, for the last Thursday of November. He thus set in motion the ritual machinery that would become America's national Thanksgiving Day, a time to reflect on the sacred destiny of America. In his proclamation, Lincoln recited the blessings of international peace and victory: "They are the gracious gifts of the Most High God, who, while dealing with us in anger for our sins, hath nevertheless remembered mercy . . . and fervently implore the interposition of the Almighty Hand to heal the wounds of the nation and to restore it as soon as may be consistent with the Divine purposes to the full enjoyment of peace, harmony, tranquility, and Union."[10]

The use of "Union" is significant here, but equally significant is the fact that it appears in the context of "healing" and not retribution, and "Divine purposes" rather than divine right. Conspicuous by their absence are references to "freedom" and emancipation, ideals more apt to divide Northern audiences and congregations than to unite them.

Upon receiving news of the national thanksgiving, a writer for the *New York Evangelist* traced the long history of thanksgiving days in New England and then went on to contrast them to Lincoln's proposed national day of thanksgiving, which "of course . . . will supercede the State Thanksgivings." The writer was confident that "the people of New England and of the older states, will be pleased to see their ancient custom thus honored, [and] will cheerfully accept the day designated by the President, and will gladly merge their usual celebrations in this more general observance."[11] Even as the national government was creating a Union that would supercede particular states, so too was the nation's sacred identity increasingly defined and "merged" in national rather than sectional or state holy days.

The November thanksgiving prompted widespread pulpit commentary on America's mission not only to its own or their regions but to the world. In a thanksgiving address to his Baptist congregation, Henry Clay Fish looked out upon two thousand hearers and described the "Grand Issues of the War" from God's vantage point. Emancipation clearly held a central position: "Freedom for the *enslaved blacks* on our own soil is *one* of the things involved, and a very important one." But most important was the promise of global freedom that would only be possible if the Union persevered: "For if we fail here, and above us darkness gathers, what star of hope remains in the whole horizon? I said rightly, then, that in this struggle we stand for the world, we represent the world. *For the world freedom lives or dies here and now!*"[12]

In Chester County, Pennsylvania, near where the Battle of Gettysburg had raged, the Reverend John M'Leod preached at a "Union Meeting" to local Baptist and Presbyterian churches. M'Leod began by recalling the recent dedication of the Cemetery of Gettysburg, which "will be a memorial to coming ages that there were patriots in 1863, who felt they belonged to a country worth dying for."[13]

With all of the bloodshed in the past year, one principle remained unmistakably clear to M'Leod: "We are a Nation. . . . The rebellion makes it clear to ourselves and to all foreign powers that we are a nation." Throughout his address M'Leod ridiculed those European skeptics who believed democracy could not survive a massive convulsion such as civil war. Luckily for them, M'Leod continued, they were mistaken, because American success was for *their* good as well as for the good of the Union. Europeans needed America more than America needed Europe. In fact, the world needed America. Emancipation was important, and a black soldier "makes a good soldier," but ultimately, the Civil War fulfilled "the mission of America." That mission, in brief, was messianic: "God in his providence, we believe, is preparing this nation for a high service of Christian influence through the world."[14]

The common lesson to be taken from the Gettysburg Address and Lincoln's Thanksgiving Day proclamation was the expanding scope of freedom. The same writer for the *Banner of the Covenant* who witnessed the Gettysburg Address came back to that theme in quoting a thanksgiving sermon whose central argument was that "[o]n Cemetery Hill, now consecrated forever to the memory of valor and sacrifice, were conquered more fears, prejudices, political obstinancies, and schemes of treason, than ever fell before in one single conflict. A dead revolution lies in that immortal field."[15]

That themes of union could prevail amid the most bitter of hostilities confirmed to many spectators that divisions would end with the war's end. In preaching a thanksgiving discourse to St. Paul's parish in Brookline, Francis Wharton looked to war's end and restoration on two fronts. First, and most obviously, was restoration between the two sections—one "community" after all. But second, and hardly self-evident, was reconciliation between emancipated slaves and their white brothers and sisters. Political freedom was not enough. There must also be a moral shift that removed "that prejudice which in the North, and particularly at the North-West, refuses to receive the negro as part of the industrial energies of the land."

If, Wharton continued, "in view of the liberty we are giving to so large a part of the negro race, and the military debt we are accumulating to them, we do not remove this prejudice . . . we shall, I think, be eternally branded as a nation dead to generous impulses, and unfaithful to the most sacred trusts."[16] Since the elimination of racial prejudice was never a war theme or a political goal, racial prejudice would arguably grow stronger rather than weaker as a consequence of the war. There in a nutshell lay the moral critique that would dim emancipation, however noble it was, and "eternally brand" the nation.

Another issue that never went away in the aftermath of reconciliation had to do with the essential nature of the nation itself. Would the reconstructed nation be a Christian republic or would it take the form of a Lockean-Jeffersonian secular state? Again, the issue of a godless Constitution came into play, as clergy and evangelical moralists promoted an explicitly Christian America. With victory on the horizon, the time for resolution and remembrance was at hand. For the Reverend A. Cleveland Coxe, this meant: "When peace shall come, let us not forget what was so fatally forgotten by our fathers, to inscribe the Constitution of our regenerated country with the name of Him without whom we are nothing."[17]

Union thanksgiving sermons were as notable for what they did not address as for what they did. Conspicuous by its absence was any commentary on the war itself. Generals could be praised, victories savored, and "the cause" affirmed, but of the conduct of the war, there was only silence. In a time when censorship away from the battlefields was virtually unknown, and mass media prevailed as the most widely published and read in the world, the silence had to have been self-imposed. Forgiveness of the South and emancipation of the slave were laudable goals, but questioning the means to reach them remained off limits.

Some speakers went so far as to praise the means. In Freeport, Illinois, home to the famous Lincoln-Douglas debates, the Reverend Isaac Carey established the principle that "God is on our side," and, therefore, destruction was a "power" working on God's side. Because Union power resided "on the side of freedom," and the South wielded "a power on the side of wrong and oppression," Carey could say:

I rejoice to think of a million bayonets every one of which means universal liberty—bayonets wielded by patriot soldiers, every one of whom is a freeman, and fighting for freedom. I rejoice in our iron-sided vessels of war, whose defiant look has so much of admonition and warning to despotic powers. I rejoice in the ponderous guns, that can throw their crushing missiles for a distance of five miles—I rejoice in them . . . I rejoice . . . because they represent the eternal right and justice and the eternal law.[18]

In contrast to most moral commentators who saw in war a bracing moral tonic uplifting the soldiers and citizenry, Baltimore's border-state pastor N. H. Schenck saw this war bringing out the worst in American society. The voice is rare, but needs to be heard as an evidence of what *might* have been said. In a near perfect reversal of the vast majority of moral commentary in the North and South, Schenck concentrated on just war conduct and resolutely ignored patriotism—and emancipation. The war, he observed, represented a great "unmasking" of base motives and the "masquerade" of virtue on both contending sides. Nations did not deserve to be worshipped, and war did not produce martyrdom, only slaughter and immorality: "When victories mean nothing but wholesale slaughter and no great or permanent advantage secured, the victory mainly ascertained by measurement of blood and calculation of corpses, I fail to see in it the occasion of thanksgiving to God."

Far from perceiving a cause for thanksgiving, Schenck witnessed a "tragical era"—human life itself devalued in the mindless pursuit of war. But in the grip of patriotism, he declared, the truth became almost impossible to glimpse:

> The ranks thinned to-day are filled to-morrow and the mournful dead march is directly changed into the gleeful quickstep. And as we grow indifferent to the value of life, we become proportionately indifferent to those great moral interests attached to life. . . . It is very difficult for us fairly to realize that we are making for history the bloodiest record which has ever crimsoned its scroll. It is very difficult for us to appreciate the fact that we have suddenly become not only a military, but a warlike people. But difficult as it is, the mind must open for the entrance, and widen for the embrace of these tragical ideas.[19]

There would be no civil religion in Emmanuel Church, Baltimore.

The last nationwide fast day in the Confederacy in 1863 took place on August 21. After the debacles at Gettysburg and Vicksburg, the *Richmond Daily Whig* eagerly complied with Davis's proclamation. Rejecting the notion that God rained defeat on them for their cause, the *Whig* instead singled out sins. These were not the sins of pride or profanity or Sabbath-breaking—the stock-in-trade general sins applicable to all peoples at all times—but the sins of materialism and hoarding, particularly acute in Richmond. "No man or woman in the Confederacy," wrote one commentator, "who is familiar with the doctrines or commandments of the inspired Word can be greatly surprised at the present state of affairs. Have not the people everywhere devoted themselves to the worship of Mammon? Have they not all practiced extortion?"[20]

In South Carolina Benjamin Palmer preached a state fast sermon on December 10 that was later printed and widely circulated. The sermon outlined the Confederacy's civil religion. All hint of separation of church and state disappeared. As Palmer observed from the start, because the state called the fast, "it is the nearest approach which can be made to an act of worship by the State, as such . . . the state is, in some clear sense, a sort of person before God."

Having justified the holy stature of the Confederacy, it remained only for Palmer to worship. Like countless of his Northern counterparts, Palmer plunged into nation worship. Even as loyal soldiers were martyring themselves, "undergoing the fearful baptism of blood," so must all Confederates realize the sacred stakes at issue: "The offering which patriotism renders to country, a sovereign state, on bended knee, with sacramental fervor, dedicates to God. Lift up the right hand to Heaven, as the grand oath rolls up above the stars, that you are prepared for death, but not for infamy."[21]

New Year's opened in Richmond with optimism. Likening the South to David battling a Northern Goliath, the *Richmond Daily Dispatch* promised deliverance: "The little South, not one fourth her [the Union's] size, has been chosen the instrument of puncturing the colossal gas bag of Unshaken self-conceit of the enemy."[22] Providence had a "beneficent design" in protracting the war, and for that reason the people should not despair. Citing one of the most favored texts in the American Revolution ("A Nation Born in a Day"), the paper went on to comment: "The American Revolution was mere child's play compared to the gigantic struggle which is being waged on this continent. . . . A nation has been born in a day, and at the instant of its birth, it has been called upon to do the work of a giant."[23] Nevertheless, as long as God was trusted and President Davis supported with love and respect, victory would be sure.

But not everyone in Virginia supported the Davis administration, and even fewer outside of Virginia did. The criticisms of the ambitious governor of Georgia, Joe Brown, were deemed especially dangerous by advocates of the Confederate government. The "peace editors" of the Georgia press pushed for a peace that Davis was unwilling to pursue on any terms other than Confederate independence.[24] The *Atlanta Daily Register*, in a particularly offensive editorial, recommended a return to the independence states had enjoyed before 1772 and secession from the Confederacy.[25]

Richmond's newspapers responded defensively with a shift of editorial direction. In 1862, the *Examiner* had opined that "the Confederate Ship of State is drifting toward the rock of consolidation, the same rock on which the Union split and went to wreck." But by April 1864, in a column significantly titled "The Principles of 1776," the paper criticized Brown and narrow Confederate claims to states' rights over and against the centralizing needs of the nation: "It is an effort to defeat the object for which we are fighting:

which is the nationality of 'the Confederate States of America,' and not the independence and sovereignty of Virginia, North Carolina, South Carolina, etc. etc."[26]

Richmond could more easily remain hopeful because they had been *in* war for three and a half years and had grown accustomed to its hardships. Other Confederates lacked their perspective—and their optimism, as war encroached directly upon their borders. In Charleston the bombardment of Fort Sumter was by this time only a memory. As the tables turned under constant Federal bombardments, however, sentiments shifted decisively toward despair, albeit still short of defeatism.

Charleston's *Daily Courier* saw the full consequences of war:

> There are no signs of peace visible to our gaze. . . . We have ceased to expect help or justice from the nations across the sea. . . . How many born to fortune, and brought up in the lap of luxury, after enduring numberless and great hardships and sufferings, will lie down in unmarked graves, and no one will be able to tell the spot where those uncoffined bodies repose? The prospect is gloomy, revolting, terrible! "What a fearful scourge war is!" When will this dreadful contest have an end? Exclaim thousands whose hearts are bursting with grief, or beclouded with anxiety.[27]

CHAPTER 29

"THE PRESENT UNHOLY WAR"

I n the North Lincoln was winning bloody battles but under fire from angry Democrats warming up for the national elections in November 1864. Some "Peace Democrats," most notably the Ohio congressman and gubernatorial candidate Clement Vallandigham, urged peace immediately no matter what the cost. When Vallandigham cleverly arranged his own arrest for "disloyalty," Lincoln commuted his sentence from imprisonment to banishment. While in exile, Vallandigham ran in absentia on the Ohio Democratic ticket, where he was soundly defeated by the Republican candidate, John Brough.[1] Vallandigham was marginalized by the taint of disloyalty, especially in the context of stunning victories at Gettysburg and Vicksburg. The "War Democrats," on the other hand, posed a more serious threat.

American memory, as the historian Joel Silbey demonstrates, has viewed the war years through what he describes as a "Republican prism," effectively sidelining the Democratic Party.[2] But in reality, the Democrats remained a potent political force substantially represented in the legislature and governors' mansions. Since the midterm elections of 1862, the party had grown increasingly powerful. By the summer of 1863 their opposition had intensified as emancipation became law, battlefield deaths mounted, and President Lincoln acted to limit disloyalty and run a war through the draft, income tax, and military tribunals. Though challenged in regard to their "loyalty" because of their criticism of Lincoln's handling of the war, most Democrats remained loyal to the Union. They also served in the armed forces and, for the most part, supported a war fought to reestablish the Union. That did not prevent them, however, from differing profoundly over presidential acts and the conduct of the war.

On the surface, the Democratic opposition to total war rested on a moral critique grounded in just-war theory. For Democratic leaders such as Congressman Samuel C. Cox of Ohio, the only just cause for war was the preservation of the white Union and a lenient peace that left "the Union as it was." That single end, in turn, required a limited war seeking neither social revolution, total extermination, nor widespread civilian suffering.

When faced with the prospect of emancipation and the seizure of Confederate "property," Cox demurred, citing Swiss jurist Emmerich de Vattel and the "laws of [civil] war as between nations." In an address to Congress, he argued from Vattel's classic just-war treatise that civil war must be a civilized war, which meant a limited war:

> It was urged to soften the horrors of war, to save mankind from cruel and unjust violence, to limit war and its horrors to the combatants, to reduce the conflict to a duello between armies, and to save the sea, as the land was already saved by law, from being the theatre of cruel, predatory, and barbarous practices. The reason urged for this doctrine is that it enables men to make peace, lasting and fraternal, unembittered by cruelties to helpless women and children, to non-combatants, and men of productive industry and peaceful occupations in private life. It is the doctrine of the Saviour of mankind.[3]

In praising General McClellan's principled opposition to Lincoln's total war, Cox again cited Vattell: "I affirm on the best human and divine authority, that all objects of human effort, even war, should contribute to human happiness and peace. If this war have any other object, then it is abhorred of God and man; and every dollar and life sacrificed would be a criminal waste." If rules of clemency and protection of innocents were not rigidly observed, there would be no effective limits:

> As well fire the hospitals of the sick, and the libraries of the learned; as well pillage the homes of the widow and the hermitage of the orphan; as well refuse the flag of truce or the exchange of prisoners; as well fire upon the former and hang the latter. . . . Nay, by the same reason that we would abstain from these horrible means which intensify sectional hate, and reinvigorate rebellion, we must leave open the same means which two nations at war ever have, for the restoration of peace.[4]

Sadly, Cox's grim visions would take form soon enough on both sides of the conflict.

The Democratic opposition was based on pragmatic considerations, including fears that foreign-born soldiers and citizens would bear a disproportional share of the dying (not true), an underlying sympathy with the white South, and a sense of political defeatism (that the war was not winnable).[5] Democrats observed correctly that the war had not continued as it began, but rather had become a "holy crusade" to remake Southern society and rewrite the Constitution—first as a "war measure" for emancipation and second as a constitutional amendment. They pointed to a vastly expanded Federal bureaucracy with unprecedented powers to draft, tax, and impose martial law. And they vigorously protested Lincoln's "unconstitutional" reaches, most egregiously his Emancipation Proclamation.

All of the Democratic principles were legitimate and arguable within the context of a loyal opposition. But in looking for moral significance, the end to which they pointed must be judged. And that end was, bluntly, hardly moral. Essentially, Democratic opposition to Lincoln and the Republican Party found its grounding less in a prophetic critique of the Union military machine than on the creation of an apartheid state built on the social and political reality of white supremacy. This all-encompassing mission dictated virtually every Democratic response to Lincoln's party and Lincoln's conduct of the war.

The racist goals of Peace Democrats ensured that they would win no loyalty among the relatively small number of American pacifists in the North. The largest peace party—the American Peace Society—refused to condemn the war at all, interpreting it as a police action rather than a war between nations. Other, more radical "perfectionist" pacifistic organizations, like Alfred Love's Universal Peace Union, agreed with Peace Democrats that the war was a sin and that therefore the Confederacy should be acknowledged as a legitimate nation, but they refused any cooperation with the Democrats because their "motives" were diametrically opposed. As the historian Thomas F. Curran recognizes, "The perfectionists perceived nothing but insincerity and hypocrisy in the Democrats' call for peace."[6]

In contemplating the rise of the Republican Party and the evolution of the war, Democratic leaders suspected a conspiracy that had nothing to do with constitutional principles of Federal rule versus states' rights, and everything to do with abolition. In a speech before Maine's House of Representatives, Moses Page raged against "the fiddling Neros of the Republican Party." By "trampling" on the Constitution, Lincoln was betraying his office with mindless bloodshed. In response, Page concluded:

I see but one way left open for us to prevent it [disunion], and that is to grant to our wayward sisters the rights which belong to them under the Constitution, and let the nigger alone; then, I have no doubt, we could conclude an honorable peace with the South in less time than Mr. Seward declared he would, when he got the reins of government. . . . I think this country was destined for one people, and would have remained ok, had not the fell spirit of abolition crept in and overturned the work of our fathers. . . . Mr. Lincoln and Mr. Seward are in a great measure responsible for the present unholy war, which has sacrificed so many of the young men of our country, and wasted so much treasure.[7]

As war deaths mounted, Democratic critics condemned Lincoln for deceiving the American people with a premeditated plot to transform the war into an abolition war. Like their white Confederate enemies, they insisted that Lincoln's end was not the preservation of the Union after all, but the creation of a mixed race society that would undermine white supremacy. They recited a checklist of Lincoln's policies, including the Emancipation Proclamation, the repeal of the Fugitive Slave Act, congressional recognition of "the Negro" Haitian Republic, opposition to slavery in the territories, and abolishment of slavery in the District of Columbia. It all pointed inescapably to one fact: Republicans were conspiring to "Africanize" the nation by privileging the interests of blacks over whites. It would be race—and not moral arguments over just war—that set the defining context for the coming national elections in 1864.

When faced with the issue of recognizing Haiti in 1862, Congressman Cox had objected on the grounds that America should not recognize Negro ministers of state from a nation whose constitution barred whites from office. The United States should do the opposite, Cox argued, and bar blacks from holding public office. This, he averred, exemplified the innermost meaning of America: "I have been taught in the history of this country that these Commonwealths and this Union were made for white men; that this Government is a Government of white men; that the men who made it never intended, by any thing they did, to place the black race on an equality with the white."[8]

Elsewhere Cox praised Lincoln's state of Illinois for refusing to allow blacks full citizenship, and insisted on the rights of the states, including his own, Ohio, to determine residence and the voting franchise for themselves:

The right and power to exclude Africans from the States North being compatible with our system of State sovereignty and Federal supremacy, I assert that it is impolitic, dangerous, degrading, and unjust to the white men of Ohio and of the North, to allow such [black] immigration. . . . As a general thing, they are vicious, indolent, and improvident.[9]

What appeared humanitarian and pacifistic on the surface turned out on closer examination to be a clarion call for white supremacy and a Jim Crow society. Indeed, midwestern states with large Democratic constituencies succeeded in passing segregationist legislation that the postwar South would later emulate.[10] To the Republican credo "Free Soil, Free Labor, Free Men," Democrats replied: "The Constitution as it is, the Union as it was, and the Negroes where they are."

Democrats had their heroic generals who fought loyally even as they opposed Lincoln's policies. Most notable was McClellan, the "Christian General." His behavior in the field comported with the limited goals of Democratic politicians. He tried to enforce Sabbath observance and strove to avoid belittling and vilifying the enemy.

McClellan's "humane" voice stood in stark contrast to the crude and sometimes profane utterances of Grant or Sherman, but it did not extend to slaves and Northern freed blacks. Their humane "place" was the inhumane condition of enslavement. In an earlier address to the House of Representatives, Congressman Cox praised McClellan and condemned Republican moves toward escalation. Lincoln's removal of McClellan "was a sacrifice to appease the Ebony Fetich."

Other Democratic generals evidenced similar reservations as the move toward total war gained momentum. For Winfield Scott Hancock, a gifted general but like McClellan a Democrat, the command of the Army of the Potomac held no appeal. In a letter to his wife written soon before Gettysburg, where he would be severely wounded, he wrote: "I have been approached again in connection with the command of the Army of the Potomac. Give yourself no uneasiness—under no conditions would I accept the command. I do not belong to that class of generals whom the Republicans care to bolster up."[11]

Democratic racist rhetoric was hardly limited to the leaders in Congress and the military. They merely echoed their rank-and-file constituency in towns and cities throughout the North and in the army. Besides mob violence directed toward African Americans, popular entertainment reinforced racial phobias.[12] As a form of popular entertainment in the North, minstrelsy had no rival, particularly among the urban and immigrant working classes who filled out so much of the Democratic electorate.[13] Minstrel shows embodied and dramatized the abstract prejudices that Northern whites, particularly Democrats, absorbed. Chief among these was the bestial inferiority of the black race, captured in virtually all minstrel shows and in the lithographs that advertised them. The historian Jean H. Baker shows how

> minstrelsy simply placed blacks in nonhuman roles: the hair of Negroes was like sheep's wool, their faces and features resembled monkeys, their feet

were those of elephants, their eyes like "de coon," their skin tough as animal hide, their arms strong as "the smell of de pole cat," and their hearts bigger than the biggest raccoon.[14]

During the Civil War, minstrel shows featured black "Zip Coons" dancing with white partners at "Emancipator Balls," signaling white fears of both miscegenation and Republican abolitionists, who were supposedly promoting interracial marriage.

Hysterical Democratic fears of a Republican-incited campaign for racial miscegenation became one of the great rallying cries of Democrats in the 1863 and 1864 elections. For Congressman Cox, the real issue was race. "The irrepressible conflict is not between slavery and freedom," he wrote, "but between black and white." The Republican party sought miscegenation, which, Cox continued, "was another name for amalgamation." From science, it was clear to Cox and his fellow Democrats that this could never work: "The physiologist will tell the [abolitionist] gentleman that the mulatto does not live; he does not recreate his kind; he is a monster. Such hybrid races, by a law of Providence, scarcely survive beyond one generation."[15]

The same racist themes appeared in other popular art forms, most notably the music of outspoken Democrat Stephen Foster and the lithographs of Currier & Ives. Popular cartoons also contributed to the perspective of white supremacy, stereotyping Lincoln as an African-like baboon or a monkey, cementing the Democratic identification of Republicans with those who would "Africanize" America.

For sheer race-baiting, it is virtually impossible to distinguish Democratic cartoons in the North from their Southern counterparts. In contrast to most clergy and some newspapermen, no abolitionists existed among lithographic journalists. The Civil War of Currier & Ives was not an abolitionist war. Their audience was white, usually middle-class, and predominantly female, and they had no use for black subjects except to degrade and humiliate them. In one lithograph, *The Irrepressible Conflict or the Republican Party in Danger*, Currier & Ives pictured the major Republican figures of the day with a black man who was trying to keep their boat from capsizing by tossing the radical William Seward overboard and giving the more moderate Abraham Lincoln the helm. Depicted standing on the bank, Uncle Sam recommended that they "heave that Tarnal nigger out" instead.[16]

Like northern Democratic politicians and their constituencies, "Christian" (clerical) Democrats insisted on retaining a strict separation of church and state, in keeping with their Jacksonian origins. They maintained the silence of ministers in the pulpit on purely political matters—most notably party politics—opposed preaching social reform, and rejected Federal intervention as an agency of social transformation.[17] If they were not as explicitly racist in their pulpit discourse as their party's pols, their silence on the subject nevertheless identified them with the cause.

Clerical Democrats provided their party with the biblical exegesis that supported the proposition that slavery was not a sin.[18] As late as 1864, they continued to produce treatises "proving that the institution of slavery was not abolished by the Gospel." These they often coupled with critiques of Lincoln's appeal to equality.

The Reverend John Henry Hopkins of Vermont asked, "In what respect are men 'created equal,' when every thoughtful person must be sensible that they are brought into the world with all imaginable differences in body, in mind, and in every characteristic of their social position?" Nor, Hopkins continued, were there any "unalienable rights," for "they are all alienated, forfeited and lost through the consequences of [Adam and Eve's] transgression." As for Christian Republicans, they were anything but Christian: "Here, then, we have a full display of the new revelation—the gospel of ultra-abolitionism which anticipated our mournful war as the true means to emancipate the negro, and seeks to accomplish this favorite object through a deluge of blood, and at any sacrifice of life and treasure."[19] While unwilling to comment on political parties in print, Christian Democrats would address the issue of slavery in writings like "Why Christ did not proclaim emancipation."

For all intents and purposes, most Northern Protestant pulpits and publications espoused Republican views, a fact not lost on those Christian Democrats who were denied a voice in all publications save those in the border states. Clerical Democratic dissenters spoke at their own risk, vulnerable to denominational discipline and dismissal. Nevertheless, a small minority of clerical voices did call the Republican Party into question, and with it the conduct of the war and the bald "political preaching" of Northern evangelical Protestant denominations.

Emancipation did not stand as Lincoln's only war measure. Earlier he had established his right under the war powers of the presidency to suspend writs of habeas corpus (which enables a citizen who has been detained by government officials to seek a judicial determination on the legality of that detention). Two days after announcing his Emancipation Proclamation Lincoln issued another proclamation suspending the privilege of the writ of habeas corpus. At the same time, he established extrajudicial military tribunals for trying all those "affording comfort to Rebels against the authority of the United States." It would be left to the Lincoln administration and the

War Department to determine who those "disloyal" citizens were. Just as the war on rebellion was being transformed in military tactics and objectives, so also was the war on insurrectionists in the border states and among disloyal Northerners raised to accommodate the totality of the new situation.

Most Republican suppression of civil liberties was justified in a war emergency and fell within acceptable limits. Federal arrest records confirm that the arrests had less to do with mere dissent or loyal opposition and more to do with actual treason. Outside of government, however, other more extragovernmental avenues of suppression were blatantly political and designed to intimidate Democratic voices. These were especially egregious in the powerful Northern Protestant denominations.[20]

It is difficult to ascertain the number of clerical Democrats, in part because so many feared reprisals and a loss of their living. Furthermore, their strictures against "political preaching" discouraged any public statements from the pulpit (though not in their opinions as private citizens). In any case, civil liberties did not extend to them any more than freedom of speech extended to loyalists in the American Revolution. When New York's Democratic minister Henry J. Van Dyke attacked abolitionists in print for their moral arrogance and suprascriptural appeals to "higher law," a Republican mob threatened him with physical attack. Other Protestant ministers—notably Charles Hodge—also hedged on the sin of slavery, but their civil liberties were protected because they were Republican.

Methodists and Presbyterians, especially conspicuous as articulate Democratic proponents of peace, paid stiff penalties for their beliefs. Many Democratic Methodist clergymen were suppressed by their congregations and, more significantly, by their denominational boards and agencies.[21] Methodist Episcopal Church officials insisted that Northern clergy subscribe to the proposition that slavery was the "cause" of the war; those who demurred risked losing their pulpits and livelihoods. When the Reverend William C. Howard of the Moawequa Circuit (Shelby County, Illinois) failed to pray for Abraham Lincoln and stated his preference for Clement Vallandigham in the Ohio gubernatorial election, he was hauled before the conference assembly, "tried" outside of a formal church trial, and dismissed.

Even as Christian Democrats accused fellow churchmen of being politically partisan, clerical Republicans did more than live up to the accusation—indeed they carried it as a point of pride. The Republican religious press, like the denominations that sponsored it, continued to be proudly partisan and supportive of the president and the cause. In their view, the war had been transformed with the Emancipation Proclamation into an antislavery war, and therefore an unremitting good that required no hard ethical questions, only victory.

The idea that God would not grant the North victory until slavery was reduced occurred to evangelical clergy far earlier than to political or military leaders. Already in 1862 radicals had prepared for midterm elections by persuading their churches to vote only for antislavery candidates, i.e., Republicans. The Methodists carried a column in the *Ladies' Repository* urging Christian women to spy on neighbors and weed out opposers to war: "Detect and expose the covert traitors in your neighborhood. . . . Hunt them out."[22]

When Democrats announced a platform calling for negotiated peace with compromise, evangelical denominations, led by seven Methodist annual conferences and eleven Baptist associations, condemned the proposal and urged their congregants to vote Republican. They were soon followed by Congregational associations and Presbyterian synods.[23] Throughout the Union the cause of abolition was praised as the real cause of the war, while the topic of just conduct in the field toward soldiers and noncombatants never came up.

In a perverse jumble of conflicting agendas, the nation was convulsed by war between a white, slaveholding Confederacy and a Northern Republican administration promoting emancipation to justify total war. For the administration, total war was the regrettable end and emancipation the means, while Democrats promoted conciliation with slavery and white supremacy as the end and peace the means. In a profound sense, white America was getting what it deserved.

CHAPTER 30

"FROM HEAD TO HEART"

R eligious life in the Confederacy closely resembled that of the Union at the start of the war. But by 1864, material destruction and crushing defeats were taking their toll on the local churches and the denominations that integrated them. Even before the war, membership rates had fallen lower in the South than in the North, and "unchurched" constituted the largest category of membership.[1] With the war, matters only worsened. Many church buildings were destroyed, others deprived of members and money. In its annual report to the denomination, the Lexington, Virginia, presbytery stated, "That religion is generally reported to be on the decline is a fact which some of us are beginning to accept as indubitable."[2]

Elsewhere news was also grim. After reporting on the sixty-seventh commencement at the University of North Carolina, the *North Carolina Standard* noted that enrollments had shrunk from eighty graduates to seven, with the remainder all in the army. One in five faculty members had been killed; it remained the only university running continuously. As for the general mood: "How to escape present troubles . . . both temporal and spiritual, are the main questions before the public now. Hence politicians and preachers are the only speakers who can find hearers."[3]

In this barren spiritual environment, faith continued to burn bright in the Confederate armies and hospitals. Abstract warnings of death became chillingly immediate in the aftermath of Antietam, Gettysburg, Chickamauga, and the battles to come in the spring of 1864. Throughout the winter, an increasingly desperate President Davis urged his soldiers on, placing confidence in Providence even as might of arms and tactics suffered. In an address to the armies he cited revivals to press the point: "Soldiers! Assured success awaits us in our holy struggle for liberty and independence. . . .

When that success shall be reached, to you, your country's hope and pride, under Divine Providence, will be its due."[4]

Already by 1863, the Southern pulpit and religious press increasingly addressed the public heart rather than the public mind. Reasoned arguments could articulate issues and generate debate and conflict, but they could not sustain courage in the face of the bloodbaths of this war.

Reason could not motivate suicide, but faith could.[5] Nor could reason cross the divide from public, civil religion to private, experiential "saving faith." Sentiments of the heart would take over and push the drumbeat harder. Justifications for the cause shifted from a legalistic list of "principles" (which, after all, had changed as the war progressed) to an assessment of the "sentiments" motivating each side.

While some angry editors dissembled, Davis and his universal phalanx of clerical supporters and generals asserted that God was precisely the point of the war. The tendency of some secular presses (though by no means all) to denigrate the fast days and their sacralized rhetoric amounted to rank disloyalty and blasphemy. As the church was sacred, so also was the Confederacy; neither could be worshipped without invoking the other.

The Confederate shift in rhetorical strategy from head to heart can be seen in two sermons preached and published by D. S. Doggett, then pastor of Richmond's Broad Street Methodist Church. The first, delivered in September 1862, reasoned from a list of "facts" revealing that God was interested in the struggle. Doggett went on to define the war as a defense of "the rights asserted by our forefathers, in the immortal Declaration of Independence; the rights of self-government, self-protection, and of conscience."

In his second sermon, preached in the spring of 1864 and published by the Soldier's Tract Association in Richmond, Doggett argued that the war received its moral character by the passions and fundamental convictions of each side. It was a war of Southern truth and justice against Northern lust and prejudice—a war of Bible believers against heretics and infidels.[6] If rationalizations became tangled and confused as the war progressed, a Christian's heart could still be in the right place. If God's designs for the South seemed less clear in 1864 than in 1862, then trust in Him became all the greater an act of faith.

Meanwhile, alongside the religious press's relentless support of Davis and the war came a significant shift in rhetorical focus of the fasts that exemplified the advent of increasing rather than decreasing religiosity. Where the object of earlier fasts was social reform, the focus of new fasts shifted to revival and preparation for eternity. The locus of these revivals also shifted decisively away from the churches to the army. Things looked bleak under the harsh light of the secular press, and churches steadily surrendered their property and members to destruction and spiritual depression, but the army revived.[7]

The *Christian Observer* asked, "Is Religion Declining?" in response to the assertion "that religion in the church is in a low and sickly condition." The answer was yes. In response the paper turned to the army for hope.[8] Accounts of "Revival among the Texas Rangers" or "Revival in the Army of Northern Virginia" filled newspaper columns with space freed by the lack of victories in the field. From the "army in the west," the "news" shifted from battles to revivals: "There is a mighty work of the Spirit going on now in the camps of this regiment and brigade."[9] Like crusaders of old, Confederate soldiers could find an antidote to fear in saving faith and garner a "triumph" over sins that military triumphs were not providing.

For many in the Confederacy unwilling to embrace journalistic cynicism, the army now became *the* spiritual hope of the land, displacing a dispirited and demoralized populace as vehicles of saving grace. Church societies directed thousands of conversionist pamphlets and tracts toward every Southern town, hospital, and Confederate army tent. In Richmond colporteurs worked feverishly with the armies and in the greatly expanded hospitals to urge the soldiers on to revival.

Mary Jones reported eagerly the happy news that "revivals in our army are certainly the highest proofs we can possibly desire or receive of the divine favor."[10] A revitalized Southern spirituality, concentrated on individual salvation, along with the logic of the Confederate jeremiad, which sanctified the entire South, would shape the perceptions of white Southerners long after the fall of Richmond and the surrender at Appomattox.

It would be hard to exaggerate how totally news of revivals began to fill the pages of religious and secular presses following Gettysburg and Vicksburg. The *Richmond Religious Herald* devoted space in virtually every issue to revival. From army missionary A. Broaddus, readers learned of a "regimental revival" where "the chapel has been well filled and frequently crowded." Soon other reports detailed "Revival in Wilcox Brigade" and "Revival in Mahone's Brigade."[11] From Tennessee, readers of the *Southern Churchman* learned of "immense congregations assembled to hear the word . . . and many sinners led to cry for mercy; a chaplain informed me that 1,000 men in his division had professed the faith."[12]

Emphasis on the heart did not mean that the "Christian manliness" of Stonewall Jackson declined, only that it became romanticized. Calls for blood revenge continued to sound in the religious no less than the secular press. In a column on "The Voice of Southern Blood," one writer for the *Religious Herald* assured his hearers that "in good season, He will speak for [the innocent dead]. . . . When He speaks, He will avenge it. . . . [Let us] wait remembering that 'the righteousness of God' has said, 'Vengeance is *mine*—I will repay!' "[13] Of course, the "I" in this affirmation was also the army, sacralized to the task of a redeemer nation.

In his earlier diary entries at the start of the war, the Texas Ranger chaplain Robert Bunting complained that soldiers seemed hardened to his conversionist preaching. But now, as lights faded on the battlefield, revivals proliferated in the camp: "The camp was filled with the presence of 'the Lord of Hosts.' It is a second pentacostal season upon the earth. Thousands are being born again." By war's end, two-thirds of Bunting's regiment would be dead. For the third who survived, religion proved indispensable.

Bunting's own role in the revivals was considerable. Together with "an old friend and classmate," J. H. Kaufman of Georgia, Bunting took over a church building and began holding meetings for the soldiers:

> For twenty days we have carried it on. We preach morning and night daily. We are assisted by the resident ministers of Rome occasionally. God was with us from the beginning. A deep solemnity pervaded the congregation and the work first began on the church membership. They were greatly revived and comforted. Some who have been very much backslidden tell me that they now live over again the joys of their first conversion. In the meantime the impenitent were being convicted, and first one came forward and said "Brethren pray for me."[14]

In the context of such sentiments throughout the winter of 1864, revivals proliferated to a far greater degree in the Confederate army than in the Union.[15] More significantly, they became even more the subject of news in the demoralized daily papers. Unlike in the North, where army revivals were less widespread, churches went unharmed, and revivals tended to be reported only in the religious weeklies, in the South army revivals became secular news.

Throughout the winter and spring of 1864, it was the rare newspaper that did not feature revivals in the Confederate army. What began as a wave in 1863 following Gettysburg and Vicksburg steadily swelled and showed no signs of abating. On January 29, the *Richmond Daily Dispatch* reported "From General Lee's Army" that "the religious interest in the army is unchilled by the cold weather. Meetings are still held in every part of the army; and in many, if not all the brigades, meeting-houses have been constructed for their own use, and faithful chaplains nightly preach to large and deeply attentive congregations."

Following the Confederate defeats at Gettysburg and Vicksburg, nobody dwelt on the battle or on Lincoln's subsequent commemoration at Gettysburg Cemetery. Instead the news ran: "Revival in Longstreet's Army" or "religion in the army." One writer from the Army of Tennessee described "revivals in nearly every brigade in Hood's Corps. . . . The same great work is spreading through Hardee's Corps." A soldier wrote in the same paper that "during the [revival] meeting a number professed faith in Jesus."[16]

By April, as the spring campaigns drew ominously near, all eyes were on Virginia. There, Lee's legendary Army of Northern Virginia stood between Grant's and Meade's Army of the Potomac and the city of Richmond. A form of fatalism now prevailed and discouraged the earlier fascination with battles and wars. Death and suffering had become too random and unpredictable to savor. War coverage shrank as moral and religious uplift blossomed.

Revivals depended chiefly on evangelical sermons delivered by chaplains or local clergy. In a revival sermon preached frequently to Confederate regiments in February and March 1864, Chaplain William Baker pointed to the dreaded coming season of war: "We are now approaching a crisis in public suffering. We are looking forward to a campaign which will probably be stirring and decisive. . . . Has not the church a work of preparation to do as well as Congress and the army?"

Besides news of spiritual laxity in the churches, "we hear not of revivals or missionary enterprises" in occupied areas of the South. The implication was clear: the army must step into the moral and spiritual void to "save" the South and, in the process, "win" the battle with Satan. It *might* even win battles on the battlefield.[17]

After intoning the standard Protestant orthodoxy that revivals were purely spiritual affairs that could not necessarily cause "temporal victories," Baker made an immediate about-face. In the next breath, he promised the troops: "If we are zealous for his cause, he will be zealous for our cause. If we make his ordinances effective for spiritual victories, he will make our muskets and cannon effective for temporal victories." While conceding that battles were about contingency—"the mysterious panic, the swollen river, the apparently accidental position"—contingency itself was ultimately providential. Cynics missed precisely that when they ascribed purely natural causes to battles. Likening Generals Lee and Johnston to the Old Testament warriors Gideon and Barak, Baker assured his hearers that as God gave these ancient warriors victory, so also would He reward Confederate Christian generals.

Of course, casualties would inevitably mount in the spring, even as victory ensued from God's ultimate will: "How appalling the thought that in a few months, thousands—the bravest and the strongest—who are now in the flush of health and in the glory of their manhood, will be struck down." To vivify death for the soldiers in attendance, Baker evoked a scene that to modern sensibilities seems melodramatic but that spoke with power to the soldiers facing imminent battle:

> Alas many bitter tears will be shed before another summer brings in its harvest—Many who found it hard to say goodbye to him who was more than half their life, will find it harder to hear the tidings that he is never more to return. That parting scene, how can even the stranger ever forget it! How she stood under the car window and took the hand which he held out to her. How she lingered until the moving train tore him away. Every thoroughfare is full of such scenes. . . . God help the mourners who already mourn and help us all to attain such nearness to him—such conformity of desire and thought and will, that when our time comes, we may be able at once and without a moment's bitter rebelliousness of heart to cry "thy will, my God, thy will be done, and let that will be mine."

Revival sermons were augmented by religious tracts and newspapers to promote revivals in the army. In one popular tract entitled *The Soldier's Aim by a Charleston Pastor*, the anonymous preacher strove, in the most romantic terms, to assure Confederate soldiers that saving faith would quell all fears and quiet all anxiety: "The pious man has a mind freed from the passionate conflicts and terrors of the wicked. He is not distracted by the struggle between the Creator and the creature, between the conscience and the life. . . . To him the weary march is bright with visions of a heavenly home and cheerful with the sound of holy voices that come to him upon the winds."[18]

Soldiers in 1862 may have found sentiments like these a bit much to swallow. By 1864, they overlooked the hyperbole and embraced the message as virtually the only hope in a world rapidly closing in on them.

For the South, the dark side of revivalism was Puritanism. Many writers justified the righteousness of their cause by contrasting the evangelical Christianity of the revivals with the "Puritan" spirituality of the North. In a column titled "Does God Favor the North," a writer for the *Richmond Religious Herald* replied that the North had sacrificed its faith for a Puritan-based abolitionism: "Federal infamy will not be veiled by triumph. . . . They have bartered the true principles of Christianity for sectional conquest—and the prize they have coveted will elude them." As for slavery: "Our enemies make slavery the central question of the war. But no one at the South doubts the Divine Sanction of slavery."[19]

Revival sermons were augmented among the soldiers by spontaneous prayer meetings. One letter, written by a chaplain to the *Religious Herald* predicted the future impact of Confederate army revivals:

> I know young men to whom this war has been a real blessing in this respect; and if they live to see it close, their churches at home will mark what I say. Sometimes in thinking over this matter, and seeing such striking examples of Christians improved by being soldiers, I have almost come to the conclusion that the war is not such an unmitigated evil, after all. . . . Men who have come out of this war Christian soldiers, will not be apt to desert the standard of Christ afterward.[20]

The chaplain was right. These were the very men who, with the war's end, would lead mighty evangelical revivals that would transform the postwar South from Episcopalian and "Spartan" to "converted" evangelicals.

No one in 1861 could have predicted that ministers would claim war—and defeat—as a moral and religious good that made men Christians. Yet, by 1864, that was indeed their claim. Just as white Christian apologists in the antebellum South had praised slavery as a converting institution for the slaves from paganism to Christ, so these Civil War apologists now praised war as a converting institution for white soldiers and, in turn, white society.

In this madness, we see the seeds of what would become the postwar "Religion of the Lost Cause" and the triumph of evangelical Protestantism. Where the antebellum evangelical was tarred with the label of "dissenter" and, worse, "effeminate" postwar evangelicals and itinerants would be reared in the armies and hardened in the battles. In the new South, to be evangelical and "born again" would come to signify the Confederate army as well as the Southern pulpit. It would mean pride and manliness, humility and submission. The "Lost Cause" of the white Christian South would constitute a self-contained region—and religion—isolated from the international community of believers that preserved the sacred memories of the war and the revivals its army produced.[21]

PART VI
PROPORTION

THE SOLDIERS' TOTAL WAR

MAY 1864 TO AUGUST 1864

CHAPTER 31

"I CAN ONLY THINK OF HELL
UPON EARTH"

No moral category of the Civil War received more attention in 1864 than the treatment of prisoners of war. What began as a humane affair with adequate accommodations and generous exchanges degenerated with the war's progress into a living hell. In all, approximately 194,743 Union soldiers languished in Confederate prisons, and 30,218 died. Northern prisons took in 214,865 Southern prisoners, and 25,976 died.[1] Newspapers regularly denigrated the sadism of the enemy with sensational headlines like this from *The Liberator*: "Brutal Treatment of Union Prisoners in Richmond: How They are Starved to Death."[2] Lithographs and drawings portrayed starving wretches under headings like *Let Us Forgive, but Not Forget*.

Years later, soldiers could forgive many episodes of the war, but not the prisons. A wave of barbarous accounts written after the fact by former prisoners of war did not help. Both during the war and after, the central themes were sensationalist: thrilling escapes, heroic confrontations, and barbarous guards. Wholesale death by pestilence and malnutrition, though depressingly real, were generally avoided in the press because they offered neither heroism nor romance—only the banality of death.[3]

Photographs of emaciated Union prisoners returning from the South shocked Northerners precisely because they had no analogue in the viewers' experience. To twenty-first-century eyes, the men look eerily like the sunken, skeletal survivors of Nazi death camps. But in 1864, only one unseen analogy came to mind: hell.

In May 1864 a delegation from the committee on the conduct of the war visited the camp at Annapolis and photographed eight prisoners who were emaciated and on the verge of death. The sight outraged Northern viewers,

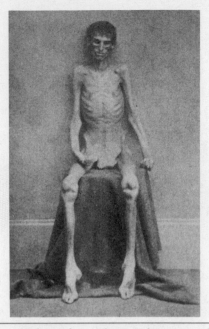

Federal prisoner seated, nude, facing front. Photographs were used to reinforce Northern beliefs that Confederates were seeking to exterminate Union prisoners, though in fact, conditions were also horrendous in Federal prisons.

who assumed these prisoners were typical victims of deliberate Confederate sadism. Confederate accusations that photographers deliberately selected the worst cases to stoke hatreds, and that comparable cases could be discovered in Northern prisoner-of-war camps, held no sway. The committee concluded that a conspiracy existed on the part of Confederate commanders to murder Federal prisoners.[4]

For generations to come, volumes of survivors' recollections from both armies would appear in waves, stoking bad memories and renewing hatreds that would not go away. Predictably, citizens on both sides pilloried the evil of the "other's" camps. *Their* prisons were as humane as possible. *Their* treatment of prisoners was as respectful as could be. It was the *others* who were monsters.

But from a larger perspective, what moral conclusions can be drawn about the history of prisons in the Civil War? That prisoners suffered endlessly is beyond debate. Was "wrong" done? Mistreatment of prisoners was deliberate, so the soldiers claimed, and intended ultimately to "exterminate" prisoners in their control. Only in the twentieth century, thanks in large measure to the pioneering scholarship of the historian William Hesseltine, has the accusation of deliberate murder been put to rest.[5]

Of the degrading and momentous loss of life among prisoners on both sides there can be no doubt. As prison populations began to mount, it became painfully clear that neither side had really thought about or prepared a plan for dealing with prisoners. Of the two, the North would respond more humanely, but less from superior motives than from superior resources. As a rule—both on principle and, as much as possible, in practice—neither side sought to be barbarians, as each was routinely accused by the enemy.

In moral retrospect, what is most surprising is that "retaliations" and "atrocities" were relatively minimal. The worst abuses tended to come from noncombatants or home guards who had little martial discipline or restraint. *No* officers were bent on extermination and murder. All were subject to the gruesome givens of a war that no one planned with contingencies that no one anticipated. They faced the unforeseen consequences of a war whose larger moral limitations had blown dangerously out of control, which is to say that the *war* was to blame, and, by extension, those who purposefully escalated it. It was for this reason that the only Confederate officer executed for war crimes was the commander of the infamous prison at Andersonville, Georgia, Henry Wirz.

At the start of the war, prisoners and the prisons to hold them were not a great issue. From careful study of government records and soldiers' memoirs, Hesseltine showed how prisons in both the North and the South in the years 1861 and 1862 generally adhered to the accepted rules of war. Both allowed prisoners basic rights of dignity and provided the same rations to prisoners as were available to soldiers in the field.

Even as battles grew larger, numbers of prisoners did not swell because both sides agreed to a cartel of prisoner "exchanges" based on a complex formula that relied on numbers of prisoners and their ranks. Captured officers would be "paroled" with the understanding that they would not rejoin their units until "exchanged" with a prisoner of comparable rank, at which point both would be free to reenter their units.

The foundation of the exchange was honor.[6] Paroled officers would pledge: "We and each of us for himself severally pledge our words of honor as officers and gentlemen that we will not again take up arms against the United States nor serve in any military capacity whatsoever against them until regularly discharged according to the usages of war from this obligation."[7] Here, as in other places, the Civil War appears as the last romantic war, where honor was a category worthy of recognition.

But prisons changed dramatically in 1863 when Lincoln and Grant discontinued the exchange for moral and strategic reasons. On moral grounds,

they canceled the exchange because Confederate authorities refused to recognize black prisoners as equal to whites and therefore equally eligible for pa-
role. Although instances of Confederate authorities selling black prisoners
into slavery are rare, they did prohibit black prisoners from the exchanges
and allowed recaptured slaves to be returned to their masters.

In a letter to Robert Ould, Confederate agent for exchange, Lieutenant
Colonel William H. Ludlow protested the Confederacy's planned discrimination against black troops in the strongest terms, arguing "you have not a foot
of ground to stand upon in making the proposed discrimination among our
captured officers and men." If the discrimination were implemented, Ludlow
continued, the cartel would be endangered and "the United States Government will throw its protection around all its officers and men without regard
to color, and will promptly retaliate for all cases violating the cartel or the
laws and usages of war."[8]

When the Confederacy refused to alter their policy, the inevitable breakdown occurred. As it continued, families of prisoners on both sides pleaded
for resumption of exchange, but the Confederacy would not yield on the subject of returning recaptured slaves to their owners. In a letter written to
Robert Ould on August 27, 1864, General Benjamin Butler, Union commis-
sioner for exchange, again engaged the subject of "colored" prisoners of war.
Given that prisoners on both sides were in extremis, Butler assured Ould that
he would do anything to resume the exchange—anything, that is, "except to
barter away the honor and faith of the Government of the United States,
which has been so solemnly pledged to the colored soldiers in its ranks."

With that as a given, Butler sought to find a way to encourage the Confederacy to revise its policies on their own terms to win the release of black
prisoners. Even if one assumed that slaves were merely property—the Southern definition of slaves—they still deserved to be returned because they had
become the property of the United States who, by its sovereign right, determined to free them: "All are free men, being made so in such manner as
we have chosen to dispose of our property in them which we acquire by
capture."

Then, with bitter irony, Butler continued: "Will you suffer your soldier,
captured in fighting your battles, to be in confinement for months rather than
release him by giving for him that which you call a piece of property, and
which we are willing to accept as a man? You certainly appear to place less
value upon your soldier than you do upon your negro."[9]

The Confederate response was predictable. Insofar as their entire society
rested on the institution of slavery, and inasmuch as that institution considered slaves as property, there could be no proper exchange of a black soldier
for a white soldier, a black human for a white human. For Confederate Agent

of Exchange Robert Ould, this meant that the North pressed an "inadmissible claim" that "recaptured slaves shall be treated as prisoners of war."[10]

Compounding the moral issue of race was the issue of honor. When Grant discovered that paroled Confederate soldiers from Vicksburg were fighting in Tennessee without mutual agreement, he viewed that as a loss of honor.

Strategic reasons existed as well as to why a refusal to exchange would work better for the North than for the South. In his letter to Ould, Butler pointed out that Confederates supporting the resumption of exchange were motivated "by the depleted condition of their armies, and a desire to get into the field . . . the hale, hearty, and well-fed prisoners held by the United States, in exchange for the half-starved, sick, emaciated, and unserviceable soldiers of the United States now languishing in your prisons."[11]

While wrong about the "hale and hearty" Confederate prisoners, Butler was right about the Confederacy desperately wanting to bring prisoners back to serve in the army. Strategically, Grant also realized that he more easily than the Confederacy could afford the lost manpower of inactive prisoners. The prospects of a quicker victory and fewer lives lost in the field made the breakdown of "exchange" worthwhile and, in Grant's eyes, even moral.

Living conditions in Confederate prisons were unarguably harsher than in Union prisons, but so were living conditions in the Confederate army and Confederate society in general. Most Northern camps, such as Elmira, Douglas, Morton, Butler, Johnson's Island, and Alton, had barracks. Most Confederate prisons—especially prisons for enlisted soldiers—offered only partial shelter or mere tents.

If Yankee prisoners were fed and clothed less than prisoners held by the North, so were Confederate soldiers. Even as the women of Richmond rioted for lack of bread, so Federal prisoners at Libby Prison and Belle Isle suffered food shortages and poor diet. Only the worst cases who were sent to the hospital received two meals a day, the rest only one of diminishing nutrition.

In a statement on conditions in Richmond prisons and hospitals, Thomas James, a hospital steward, described the suffering, in particular of the prisoners in Belle Isle, who lacked the shelter afforded Union officers in Libby Prison. One surgeon was a "brute" to the very ill prisoners sent to the hospital, but "others were very kind to the men and did all in their power, but the material to prescribe from was so limited they were unable to accomplish much good." Diseases ran rampant: "The principal diseases were typhoid fever, typhoid pneumonia, chronic diarrhea, and dysentery, but the two last mentioned was the cause of death in the majority of cases."[12]

Northern writers, cartoonists, and even General Grant assumed the

North would never mistreat prisoners and that all were healthy and well fed. Nothing could have been farther from the facts. While certainly better supplied and maintained than their counterparts in the South, Northern prisons were also overcrowded and unsanitary death camps. Examination of the higher mortality rates in Confederate prisons, while important, must be weighed against the fact that "lower" mortality rates in the North were still astounding. Nothing could match the 29 percent mortality rate at Andersonville (thirteen thousand of forty-five thousand) except for Salisbury Prison in North Carolina, whose rate was even higher. But the overall mortality statistics—15.5 percent of Northern prisoners and 12 percent of Southern prisoners—were scandalous on both sides.[13]

Salisbury inmates were mostly political prisoners and Yankee deserters, with POWs added only after October 1864. From October 1864 to February 1865 (when exchanges were resumed), 3,479 of Salisbury's 10,321 prisoners died—a higher rate than at Andersonville. In Northern prisons, the highest mortality rates for POWs occurred at Rock Island, Illinois (77 percent); Elmira, New York (32.5 percent); Alton, Illinois (21 percent); and Camp Butler, Illinois (20 percent).[14]

Clearly prisoner-of-war camps were a tragedy. But were they immoral, as the participants claimed? Insofar as morality refers to intent and not unintended consequences, it is hard to affix guilt on either nation for deliberately plotting to starve or murder innocent prisoners. The historian James M. McPherson rightly concludes that "the treatment of prisoners during the Civil War was something that neither side could be proud of."[15] No evidence exists, however, of a program of cruelty and extermination aimed at white soldiers on either side.

But if the macro world of prisons and prisoners was more victim than perpetrator of evil, micro stories exist that point to the moral consequences of inhuman enslavement, whether of slaves on the plantations or of prisoners in the camps. Most glaring was Confederate mistreatment of black prisoners. By an act of the Confederate Congress, black prisoners had to be named in local newspapers and their status as prisoners or recaptured slaves revealed for their owners to claim them. The majority who remained in prison suffered even harsher conditions than those endured by their white counterparts. While languishing behind Confederate lines, they were frequently employed like slaves in hard labor on Confederate railroads or fortifications around Mobile, Alabama.[16] While wasting away in Andersonville, Union Private Robert Knox Sneden observed that "the Negroes do all the hardest work of course. They often get lashed by their masters or overseers, as we can hear their cries of pain plainly on still nights."[17]

Related to the deliberate mistreatment and exploitation of black prisoners was the use of them as human shields. In July 1863, following the defeats at Gettysburg and Vicksburg and during the siege of Charleston, Colonel John L. Branch conceived the idea of placing enemy prisoners of war under fire of their own siege guns to discourage Federal bombardments. The plan was to include all Yankee prisoners, officers and enlisted men alike: "these prisoners to be exposed during our operations."[18] But black prisoners bore a disproportionate amount of the danger and hard labor. The same was true at Richmond, where black prisoners were placed on the city's fortifications under direct Federal fire. The practice continued until Northern generals placed an equal number of Confederate prisoners at Union fortifications under fire.[19]

A more general moral issue developed around stealing from guards and from fellow prisoners. The rules of war recognized by both sides forbade stealing from the prisoners. But among both hungry Confederate prison guards and cold Federal guards, the pillage of prisoners was rife. Food, clothing, cash, and valuables of any sort were in play.

No good prisons existed in the South or North. In July 1864 Confederate prisoners were transferred from Point Lookout to vacant barracks at Elmira, New York. Familiar problems of sanitation and disease appeared, augmented by a rash of scurvy caused by no-vegetable diets. By the end of August, more than seven hundred cases of scurvy had been reported. In October word emerged from Camp Douglas of a rapid increase of fatalities, and Elmira health officials concluded that based on mortality rates in August and September, the entire prison would be depopulated within a year.[20]

The worst prison conditions of all existed at the infamous Camp Sumter in Andersonville, Georgia. With the rapid rise of prisoners on both sides, and with Grant's army marching on Richmond, Belle Isle could no longer hold the bulk of prisoners, and new facilities had to be constructed. In October 1863 Lee recommended moving prisoners away from Richmond to Danville, Virginia. But Danville proved inadequate, and in November, Andersonville, Georgia, was selected as the site for a new prison.

The site seemed ideally isolated from Confederate cities and invading armies. But tragically, no one recognized that those very advantages would prove disastrously disadvantageous for the prisoners. There were simply no real provisions to build a protected environment. Basic staples such as nails and rope could not be found to build shelters.[21] Shortages of lumber meant no buildings and, by spring, no coffins.

The first prisoners began arriving at Andersonville from Richmond in

Andersonville Prison, southwest view of the stockade showing the "deadline." Close to thirteen thousand Union prisoners of war lost their lives there. Thousands more perished in other camps, both Federal and Confederate.

February 1864 and continued at a rate of four hundred per day. Since shelter was not available, prisoners had to survive on their own, often with little more than a blanket to provide warmth or protection from the sun. The prison contained no cells, but all inmates had to live within the brutally enforced boundaries—the original "deadline"—with guards ordered to shoot any and all who crossed them.

By May the bakery was completed and prisoners received the same rations as guards. But the only stream into the camp was polluted by refuse from the bakery. Already weakened from their stay in Richmond, prisoners died steadily from disease—especially bowel diseases like diarrhea and dysentery, combined with scurvy. Survival and recovery were hindered even more by the widespread presence of what psychologists today would term clinical depression. When Captain William Chauncey arrived as a prisoner at Andersonville on May 29, he wrote in his diary: "No shelter, or rations except corn meal. Water insufficient for the number confined here. No conveniences for washing or in fact for living at all. I can only think of hell upon earth."[22]

"Sergeant" Henry Wirz in Richmond's Belle Isle was transferred to command the interior of the prison in Andersonville as "Captain" Wirz (the exterior guard force was commanded by Colonel A. W. Persons). Of Wirz, one prisoner would write: "The half-mocking respect which the [Union] officers in the Richmond prisons had for the bustling efficiency of Sergeant Wirz . . . was changed in the new prison to bitter hatred. The fact that he was a foreigner and spoke with [a German] accent militated against his making a good impression." Rumors abounded that Wirz personally shot soldiers and that guards were given furlough time for each Yankee they killed. Had Union officers been present at Andersonville, some marginal improvement might have been achieved, but officers were confined at Macon, Georgia.

In a state of complete demoralization, prisoners fought with each other. By August the prison designed to hold only ten thousand reached a population of nearly thirty-three thousand men, making Andersonville the fifth largest "city" in the Confederacy. The prisoners defecated in a swamp, which in turn bred maggots. One prisoner recalled: "The largest crawled out in the hot sand, shed their tail-like appendages; wings would unfold, and an attempt be made to fly; and thousands were clumsily dropping all over the camp. They tumbled into our mush, bedding places, and on the faces of the sick and dying." Wirz permitted aid from the Sanitary Commission, but it arrived irregularly and did nothing to prevent the spread of disease.

One remarkable account of prison life in Andersonville appears in the diary of Sergeant John L. Ransom, the brigade quartermaster of the Ninth Michigan Calvary.[23] On November 6, 1863, Ransom was captured in east Tennessee and taken to Belle Isle Prison just as prisoner exchanges were being discontinued. From there he was transported to Camp Sumter, Andersonville. On March 14 Ransom arrived at the camp, where the prisoners were left out in the open air, surrounded by a wooden stockade and the ubiquitous deadline of boards running around the inside of the stockade. The lack of cover led Ransom to the immediate understanding that "it is going to be an awful place during the summer months here, and thousands will die no doubt."

He was right. Invariably, the prisoners' despair turned to rage against their captors. Their rage also focused inward in self-destructive patterns generated by depression. Worse yet, furies were directed at one another in shameful displays of theft, brutality, and even murder. As spring moved into "the summer that killed thirteen thousand men," the prisoners escalated the fighting among themselves, responding with violence to trivial arguments or interservice brawls between soldiers, sailors, and marines. There were no officers to intervene. Morale reached so low a pitch that prisoners often refused to take care of themselves, making a bad situation worse: "Many have long hair, which, being never combed, is matted together and full of vermin. With sunken eyes, blackened countenances from pitch pine smoke, rags and disease, the men look sickening. The air reeks with nastiness, and it is wonder that we live at all. When will relief come to us?"

With thousands of new prisoners swelling the already putrid and overcrowded camp, spirits plummeted still further: "New men are perfectly thunderstruck at the hole they have got into. A great many give right up and die in a few weeks, and some in a week." But Ransom was not one of them: "Could give up and die in a short time but won't. Have got living reduced to a science."

Where soldiers could maintain their morale and love of Union, prisoners could not. The fault, Ransom concluded, was not only with the Confederates who were too poor to properly feed and clothe their own soldiers but more with the Union leaders who canceled the exchange cartel. By March 30 Ransom was willing to concede that "our government is at fault in not providing some way to get us out of here. The hot weather months must kill us all outright."[24]

Outside of Andersonville, Union officers urged the government to act as Ransom requested. In a letter written on August 14, 1864, by Federal officers in Charleston Prison to President Lincoln, on behalf of enlisted prisoners in Andersonville, the officers pleaded with the president "to use every honorable effort to secure a general exchange of prisoners, thereby relieving thousands of our comrades from the horrors now surrounding them."

Chief of the horrors was starvation: "Nothing more demoralizes soldiers and develops the evil passions of man than starvation . . . the terrible condition of Union prisoners at Andersonville can be readily imagined. They are fast losing hope and becoming utterly reckless of life. Numbers crazed by their sufferings wander about in a state of idiocy; others deliberately cross the dead-line and are remorselessly shot down. In behalf of these men, we most earnestly appeal to the President of the United States."[25]

If the exchange of slaves was the only issue preventing the cartel, the officers continued, "we beg to suggest some facts bearing upon the question." In a calculated willingness to betray black prisoners for the sake of whites, the officers proceeded to suggest that blacks were actually better off: "It is true they are again made slaves, but their slavery is freedom and happiness compared with the cruel existence imposed upon our gallant [white] men. They are not bereft of hope, as are the Union soldiers dying by inches. Their chances of escape are tenfold greater than those of the white soldiers, and their condition, viewed in all its lights, is tolerable in comparison with that of the prisoners."[26] While sympathetic, Lincoln remained unmoved, citing the moral obligation incurred by promises to black soldiers. By this point, Lincoln was playing all sides of the moral card, while bearing a large portion of the responsibility for unimaginable suffering and death.

In contrast to soldiers embracing religion, many of the prisoners around Ransom lost their faith. While some continued to pray, "very many too who have been heretofore religiously inclined, throw off all restraint and are about the worst." God did not deliver them or grant them laurels from the battlefield when they died. God must have died or deserted the cause.[27]

By June, fellow prisoners—"raiders"—were robbing and killing weaker mates at alarming rates: "Raiders kill some one now every day. No restraint in the least. Men who were no doubt respectable at home, are now the worst villains in the world." Only after the prisoners threatened Wirz with a full-scale riot did he consent to allow them to organize a police force of "Regulators" and supply them with clubs to apprehend the leading raiders. Soon "arrests" were made: "The raiders fight for their very life, and are only taken after being thoroughly whipped." Once rounded up, fellow prisoners trained in law established criminal trials on charges ranging from theft to murder. Six gang leaders were sentenced to be hanged for murder, and another eighty-six sentenced to "run the gauntlet" inside the stockade. Although too weak to join in the gauntlet, Ransom could scarce contain his excitement at the prospect of hangings.

On July 11 the convicted murderers were led to the hastily constructed gallows and allowed last words. Most blamed starvation or "bad company" for their actions. One "spoke of his mother and sisters in New York, that he cared nothing as far as he himself was concerned, but the news that would be carried home to his people made him want to curse God he had ever been born." The hangings themselves were received by the prisoners as long overdue justice. As the condemned prisoners (now doubly so) made their confessions, others shouted and interrupted them, eager to see justice—or revenge—executed. Ransom wrote:

> I occupied a near position to the hanging and saw it all from first to last, and stood there until they were taken down and carried away. Was a strange sight to see and the first hanging I ever witnessed. The raiders had many friends who crowded around and denounced the whole affair and but for the police there would have been a riot; many both for and against the execution were knocked down. . . . Have got back to my quarters thoroughly prostrated and worn out with fatigue and excitement, and only hope that to-day's lesson will right matters as regards raiding.[28]

The hangings did diminish the killing but not the theft. With order restored "the men have settled right down to the business of dying, with no interruption." Each day as many as 220 died in the stockade and the camp hospital. By the end of July, Ransom could not walk and "am trouble with poor sight together with scurvy and dropsy. My teeth are all loose and it is with difficulty I can eat." The daily presence of death and dying inured all to the decencies of life:

> There is no such thing as delicacy here. Nine out of ten would as soon eat with a corpse for a table as any other way. In the middle of last night [July 18] I was awakened by being kicked by a dying man. He was soon dead. In his struggles he had floundered clear into our bed. Got up and moved the body off a few feet, and again went to sleep to dream of the hideous sights. I can never get used to it as some do. Often wake most scared to death, and shuddering from head to foot. Almost dread to go to sleep on this account. I am getting worse and worse, and prison ditto.

On July 30 Ransom could write "hang on well, and no worse." Finally, at death's door, he was transferred to the Marine Hospital in Savannah.

Ransom's experience reveals the degradations of war wrought on soldiers who would never die heroically in battle. Contained in their experiences is the story of a living hell in which neither side was morally "right" or morally "wrong," but rather both sides, without evil intent, inadvertently created a horror pit whose losses were horrendous, yet without glory or pride. It is revealing that in recounting the horrors of Andersonville, Ransom never perceived or described systemic evil or extermination. Even Wirz, though he emerged as despicable and the hated authority figure, never was portrayed as demonic or criminal. When he was later tried for war crimes, nobody could provide the name of a single prisoner that Wirz supposedly murdered in cold blood.

For many prisoners, heroism died in the prisons, as did religion, camaraderie, patriotism, and a young man's will to live. But not for all. In order to earn some extra bread, Ransom was aided by a prisoner named Battese, "the Minnesota Indian." As Ransom's conditions worsened, Battese stayed at his side, and when Ransom was too weak to move, Battese nursed him. "Battese is an angel," wrote Ransom, "[and] takes better care of me than of himself."

In September the glorious word spread that prisoners would be transferred. But "all who cannot walk must stay behind." Ransom confessed, "Am worried fearful that I cannot go, but Battese says I shall." True to his word, Battese saved Ransom's life at risk to himself: "Battese picked me up and carried me to the gate." Once at the gate, Battese and a sergeant propped Ransom up, but not before he was spotted by one of the guards. The guard "tried to stop us, but my noble Indian friend kept straight ahead, hallooing: 'He is all right, he well, he go!'"

If nothing else, the record of prisoner-of-war abuse on both sides confirms that bad things did indeed "just happen." They were, in fact, part of an overall pattern of moral avoidance and, for the most part, unexamined prejudices erasing all the "right" side's faults and exaggerating the evil of the "enemy." In the South, no one protested accounts of Northern atrocities and Southern honor. In the North, some Democratic voices protested the dehumanization of the Confederacy only as something that would make peace (with white brothers and sisters) even more difficult to attain. And Lincoln himself would affirm "malice towards none" in his Second Inaugural Address. But these voices were drowned out in a roar of self-righteous denunciation of a perfidious foe.

CHAPTER 32

"NO PLEDGE TO MAKE BUT ACTION"

As war measures, the Second Confiscation Act and the Emancipation Proclamation carried the further practical benefit of making black soldiers available to Union armies. The first five regiments were authorized to be raised by General Rufus Saxton, the military governor of the South Carolina Sea Islands. The First South Carolina Volunteers were officially mustered by November 7, 1862, under the command of Thomas Wentworth Higginson.

The advantage would prove immense. Abolitionists and most religious presses enthusiastically supported black mobilization as a far superior alternative to colonization. In a column titled "Don't Colonize, But Arm!" a writer for the *Banner of the Covenant* urged the North to "cease our colloquies on the subject of colonizing people that may be made so useful in its defense; let us openly and everywhere summon them to arms."[1]

A writer for the *American Presbyterian* saw beyond the practical benefits of enlisting blacks a strong moral opportunity. The effect of black mobilization "would be to recognize his brotherhood and to sacrifice the wicked prejudices against mere color of which the Northerners are so guilty. It would be acceptable to a just God, and, so far, a new ground of hope for success in a cause which loudly vaunts its justice."[2]

Black mobilization was also good news for Northern soldiers, including many who had little sympathy for abolitionism, let alone black equality. One letter from Iowa governor Samuel J. Kirkwood to General in Chief Henry W. Halleck clearly articulated the pragmatic (and racist) views on blacks in the Federal army:

> I have now *sixty men on extra duty* as teamsters &c whose places could just as well be filled with *niggers*—We do not need a single negro in the army to

African American soldiers with rifles. These troops served as provost guard of the Fourth U.S. Colored Infantry at Fort Lincoln, charged with the defense of Washington, D.C. Other "colored" regiments served closer to the front as part of every Union army save General Sherman's.

fight but we could use to good advantage about one hundred & fifty with a regiment of teamsters & for making roads, chopping wood, policing camp &c. *There are enough soldiers on extra duty in the army to take Richmond or any other rebel city if they were in the ranks instead of doing negro work.* I have but one remark to add and that in regard to the negroes fighting—it is this— When this war is over & we have summed up the entire loss of life it has imposed on the country I shall not have any regrets if it is found that a part of the dead are *niggers* and that *all* are not white men.[3]

Like Kirkwood, many Northern military officers saw plainly the advantages to be gained by enlisting freedmen and slaves into the conflict. Every slave enlisted for the Union was one less slave enlisted for the Confederacy, and, in more racist terms, every black man in harm's way took the place of one white man. Union General Sherman was no friend to abolitionists, but he did see the utility of employing fugitive slaves behind the lines and worked to actively promote their service (albeit not in combat).[4]

Lincoln did not have to wait long to see if slaves would enlist. The answer was yes, in droves. To Lincoln's delight, the most striking candidates came from the border states. Forty-two thousand black men from the border states served in the army and 2,400 more in the navy. The historian Ira Berlin shows that black enlistees amounted to 25 percent of eligible black men in Delaware, 28 percent in Maryland, 39 percent in Missouri, and a whopping

57 percent in Kentucky.[5] In all, 180,000 to 200,000 black soldiers fought for the North, with killed and wounded totaling 68,178, or more than one-third of the total engaged.[6]

Ever since the Militia Act of July 17, 1862, black enlistments had been officially sanctioned and enlisted slaves freed immediately. Despite this, they were denied appointments to officer's rank and received less pay than white soldiers of comparable rank. Northern blacks were slower to enlist than their Southern counterparts, citing discrimination and the thinly veiled threats of Confederates to murder black prisoners of war or sell them into slavery.

Nevertheless, leading black figures urged their people to enlist in the cause of freedom for their race. When two of Frederick Douglass's sons enlisted in New York (the first black recruits in that state), Douglass implored others to swallow their pride and fight:

> Shall colored men enlist notwithstanding this unjust and ungenerous barrier raised against them? We answer yes. Go into the army and go with a will and a determination to blot out this and all other mean discriminations against us. To say we won't be soldiers because we cannot be colonels is like saying we won't go into the water till we have learned to swim. A half a loaf is better than no bread—and to go into the army is the speediest and best way to overcome the prejudice which has dictated unjust laws against us. To allow us in the army at all, is a great concession. Let us take this little the better to get more.[7]

Northern antislavery officers saw the new enlistments in more idealistic terms than Sherman did. In November 1862, before the proclamation formally took effect, Thomas Wentworth Higginson was invited to take command of the first slave regiment. Higginson trained his regiment—known as the First Regiment of South Carolina Volunteers—and led it in raiding operations up the St. Marys and Edisto rivers. The soldiers, most of them freedmen, fought bravely.

In a letter written on November 24, Higginson described his troops to his old company:

> Give my hearty love to the Company. Tell them I have hardly even a mulatto, that is not as black as printer's ink, with the coats and red legs—but they have stood fire splendidly in two expeditions. . . their marching is very good for some reason. The first words I exchanged with them were good. I was introduced to one, wounded in two places in the late expedition—"Did you

think that was more than you bargained for?" said I—"Data's just what I went for, masta" was the plucky response—a good beginning.[8]

But when Northern free blacks inquired about volunteering, Higginson was cautious. In a letter to William Brown, a Worcester, Massachusetts, upholsterer, Higginson warned:

Dear Sir: If you would like to come and join me, I should be happy to have you. I can secure you a Sergeant's place and pay . . . or possibly a first sergeant. Or if you prefer, I might have you for my personal attendant in which case you need not enlist. Otherwise you enlist for 3 years. My greatest objection to your coming here is this. *If taken prisoner by the Rebels at any time, you would probably be sold as a slave.* This being the case, I do not think it your absolute duty to leave your family and come. But if you wish to come, and have made up your mind to do it, you can be very useful to us, as there are but few in our regiment who can read and write with ease. We have now 733. I advise you by all means, to come out as Lieut. Thomas Earle's servant. It will spare you discomfort and annoyance on the way. I will send the news to him, which will bring you both on the boat from New York. Truly your friend, T.H. Higginson.[9]

Apparently Brown took Higginson's warning to heart for there is no record of him serving.

In Louisiana, the abolitionist writer and general John Wolcott Phelps organized four black regiments before the Emancipation Proclamation went into effect. By order of the Confederate government he was declared an "outlaw" for having "organized and armed Negro slaves for military service against their masters, citizens of the Confederacy." Massachusetts abolitionist Robert Gould Shaw took command of the first black regiment from a Northern state to go to the war. Shaw's Fifty-fourth Massachusetts realized heroic recognition at the ill-fated assault on Battery Wagner, Charleston Harbor, on July 18, 1863.

In 1864 Lincoln would announce that nearly 150,000 blacks were under Union arms. In separate actions, black regiments would fight in Louisiana, South Carolina, Florida, and Virginia, at Port Hudson, at Olustee, and at Petersburg. By New Year's 1864, African American soldiers had become an established presence in the Union armies and heroic in the eyes of abolitionists and fellow African American slaves and freedmen. At a New Year's celebration of the first anniversary of emancipation, held in Beaufort, South Carolina, the cold weather could not stifle a wide turnout of freedmen proudly watching a "civic and military procession . . . under the command of Col. T. W. Higginson, 1st S.C. Vols."

The address was delivered by the Reverend James Lynch, an "educated colored preacher of Baltimore, Missionary to the Freedmen on St. Helena." Lynch made his principal subject the African American soldier at war for Union and freedom, who, like the white soldier, was fighting ultimately not only for America but for the world:

> This stream of loyal blood which is flowing in mighty current—strong, pure and noble like the fount from which it bursts—shall bear this nation with all its inhabitants to a height of moral and political grandeur that shall be the standard for an advancing world—combining the excellencies of ancient civilization with all the desirable elements and characteristics of modern— throwing out the golden cord of assistance to every political element of the globe.

As for the black soldier, in particular, Lynch concluded, "Our race have no pledge to make but action. Put the nation's uniform upon them—they will never disgrace it."[10]

In moral terms, the most significant battles were not always the biggest. Port Hudson, Milliken's Bend, and Fort Wagner were all relatively small battles but carried huge symbolic significance for the North and the South. Confederate slaveholders and Northern Democratic white supremacists assumed that blacks could not or would not fight under "the black flag" as the equals of whites. The African American's manliness and honor were denied in the classroom and at voting polls, just as his humanity was denied on the battlefields. Black leaders such as Douglass recognized that only action would dispel such racist myths.

Colonel Higginson's regiment fought well in isolated skirmishes but had not participated in battles significant enough to win the attention of skeptics. In contrast, the brave but unsuccessful assault on Port Hudson in May and June 1863 (later won by siege) received widespread publicity and praise. Faced with the imposing riflepits and heavy guns of Port Hudson on the lower Mississippi, black soldiers from New Orleans had fought bravely, if unsuccessfully. In crossing open ground under murderous fire, they had continued until sheer futility called their charge to a halt. One participant observed:

> No matter how gallantly the men behaved, no matter how bravely they were led, it was not in the course of things that this gallant brigade should take

these works by charge. Yet charge after charge was ordered and carried out under all these disasters with Spartan firmness. Six charges in all were made. . . . The self-forgetfulness, the undaunted heroism, and the great endurance of the negro, as exhibited that day, created a new chapter in American history for the colored man.

In his official report, a previously skeptical General Nathaniel P. Banks concurred, noting that "the severe test to which they were subjected, and the determined manner in which they encountered the enemy, leaves upon my mind no doubt of their ultimate success."[11]

On June 7, 1863, at Milliken's Bend north of Vicksburg, black soldiers evidenced the same tenacity and courage. Although the black soldiers were armed with antiquated weapons, their bravery caught the attention of the North. The hatred on both sides led to a relatively rare (at the time) hand-to-hand engagement with bayonets in place and rebel cries of "no quarter" to the black soldiers.

Later reports described the murder of captured blacks. In a letter to his aunt, Captain M. Miller of the Ninth Regiment of Louisiana Volunteers of African Descent described the heroism displayed that day:

We were attacked here on June 7, about 3 o'clock in the morning, by a brigade of Texas troops about 2,500 in number. We had about 600 men to withstand them—500 of them negroes. . . . Our regiment had about 300 men in the fight. . . . We had about 50 men killed in the regiment and 80 wounded; so you can judge of what part of the fight my company sustained. I never felt more grieved and sick at heart than when I saw how my brave soldiers had been slaughtered. I never more wish to hear the expression, "the niggers won't fight." Come with me 100 yards from where I sit, and I can show you the wounds that cover the bodies of 16 as brave, loyal and patriotic soldiers as ever drew bead on a Rebel.[12]

Fort Wagner proved to be the most important battle for black soldiers in the Civil War. As Gettysburg and Vicksburg raged in the momentous month of July 1863, yet another major battle erupted in which African American volunteers played the leading role. For some time soldiers and commentators alike had praised the use of black soldiers in the field. One writer for the religious press observed that black soldiers from the Fifty-fourth Massachusetts were as fit for service as any white men: "They accept discipline; they make great proficiency in soldierly attainments; they submit to all the recognized restraints of civilized warfare. And what is more *they fight,* and fight bravely too."[13]

The reference to "recognized restraints of civilized warfare" represented an important commentary on African Americans and just conduct. Racist white America perceived them as "bestial," so that their conduct became as important an issue as their bravery. By lining up the black soldiers on the side of "civilized warfare," commentators established their common humanity and their common Christianity. This was precisely the identification most feared in the Confederacy and the Democratic Party, where stereotypes of black "cannibalism" would serve as a rationale for the mass butchery of black troops and their white commanders whenever they were defeated.

In May the Fifty-fourth was transported to Beaufort, South Carolina, and from there fought their way to Fort Wagner near Charleston. By July 18 they were at the gates of Wagner. But standing between them and victory were formidable defenses, including heavy fortifications, an intervening ditch filled with four feet of water, and a steep sloping parapet.

An undeterred Shaw requested and received permission to lead the charge. He and his men met the full fury of concentrated fire from the Charleston Battalion and the Fifty-first North Carolina. Predictably, the charging soldiers fell in droves; Shaw himself died with a bullet to the heart. The failure of reinforcements to arrive forced the brave soldiers to retreat, but not before suffering 50 percent casualties. In a final insult, the Confederate commanders refused to give Shaw a traditional officer's burial space and threw him in "the common ditch with the Negroes that fell with him."[14]

One black participant from New Bedford, Massachusetts, Corporal James Henry Gooding, described the bravery of his fellow soldiers under fire:

At the first charge the 54th rushed to within twenty yards of the ditches, and as might be expected of raw recruits, wavered—but at the second advance they gained the parapet. The color bearer of the State colors was killed on the parapet. Col. Shaw seized the staff when the standard bearer fell, and in less than a minute after, the Colonel fell himself. When the men saw their gallant leader fall, they made a desperate effort to get him out, but they were either shot down, or reeled in the ditch below. One man succeeded in getting hold of the State color staff, but the color was completely torn to pieces.[15]

Later, Gooding further commended them: "The men of the 54th behaved gallantly on the occasion—so the Generals say. It is not for us to blow our horn; but when a regiment of white men gave us three cheers as we were passing them, it shows that we did our duty as men should."[16]

Later still, an aggrieved Gooding wrote "his Excellency," President Lincoln, to protest unequal wages. Despite bravery under fire and the fact that "all we lack is a paler hue and a better acquaintance with the Alphabet," wages are unequal: "We have done a Soldier's Duty. Why Can't we have a Soldier's pay?"[17]

Gooding survived the fight but would later perish as a prisoner of war in Andersonville. The man who seized the flag, Sergeant William Carney, though severely wounded, planted the flag on the fort's parapet and remained there flattened against the wall for half an hour. Later, he brought the flag to the rear with the words, "Boys, the old flag never touched the ground." For his bravery Sergeant Carney became the first African American soldier to be awarded the Medal of Honor.[18] African American soldiers no less than their white comrades rallied to the American civil religion. For them, however, its sacredness came from freedom and emancipation first, and Union second.

In the weeks following Fort Wagner, word of black bravery reached African American churches throughout the North. The *Christian Recorder* printed a letter from James Lynch, their correspondent in South Carolina, who visited the wounded "colored heroes" in the hospital and proudly reported: "I never saw men so cheerful in suffering in my life. It seems as though every man had counted the cost and fought and bled from the deepest inwrought convictions of duty." As for the commander, Robert Shaw, he "was buried in a pit with twenty-five of his men. The Colonel if he had chosen wouldn't chose another grave. This young hero—though fallen in battle, has written his name on the hearts of the colored race, and his deeds of valor—his zeal in the cause of liberty will give the historian of this war his brightest page."[19]

In American memory, as shaped by Augustus Saint-Gaudens's magisterial memorial on Boston Common, the Fifty-fourth is the most famous colored regiment to fight in the Civil War. But they were not alone. Corporal Henry S. Harmon of the Pennsylvania Third United States Colored Troops described the role his regiment played at Wagner, digging trenches under intense enemy fire right up to the parapet of the fort.

The regiment was "backed by the 54th and the 2nd South Carolina Volunteers [Colored]." Aware of white racist criticism, Harmon wrote the citizens of Philadelphia, informing them of the troops' bravery: "When you hear of a white family that has lost father, husband, or brother, you can say of the colored man, we too have borne our share of the burden. We too have suffered

and died in defense of that starry banner which floats only over free men."
He then closed on a providential note: "We expect some warm work here before long, but with the help of the God of battles, who knows the justice of our cause, we hope to go through without wavering, and though many of us must find graves in this land, I feel assured that the name of the colored soldier will stand out in bold relief among the heroes of this war."[20]

When the Union War Department informed Lincoln that some of the captured black soldiers were sold as slaves, he promised retaliation in kind on Confederate prisoners.[21] Fortunately, the black soldiers of the Fifty-fourth Massachusetts eluded capture, or their fate would have been the same as those captured at Milliken's Bend.

In a letter to his future wife, Frederick Douglass's son Lewis, a sergeant in the Fifty-fourth, described the fight at Fort Wagner and the bravery of the troops: "This regiment has established its reputation as a fighting regiment not a man flinched, though it was a trying time. Men fell all around me. . . . How I got out of that fight alive I cannot tell, but I am here. My Dear girl I hope again to see you. I must bid you farewell should I be killed. Remember if I die I die in a good cause."[22]

Fort Wagner persuaded many racist and skeptical white Northerners that African Americans could fight well and bleed for their country alongside whites. Soon after the war was concluded, a writer for the *New York Tribune* looked back on that day as pivotal:

> It is not too much to say that if this Massachusetts Fifty-fourth had faltered when its trial came, two hundred thousand colored troops for whom it was a pioneer would never have been put into the field, or would not have been put in for another year, which would have been equivalent to protracting the war into 1866. But it did not falter. It made Fort Wagner such a name to the colored race as Bunker Hill had been for ninety years to the white Yankees.[23]

The analogy to Bunker Hill is not overdrawn. The only way to know if armies can fight is to let them fight. What white Americans learned at Bunker Hill, African Americans learned at Wagner—or, more accurately, relearned, for they too fought nobly alongside white patriots in the Revolution.

General Grant perceived the strategic value of black soldiers as clearly as anyone. In a letter to Lincoln he observed: "This [arming of black soldiers], with emancipation of the negro is the heaviest blow yet given the Confederacy. . . . They will make good soldiers and taking them from the enemy weakens him in the same proportion they strengthen us."

While Grant referred primarily to the military and strategic consequences of arming black soldiers (most former slaves), the ideological consequences were, if anything, even greater. Perhaps even more than Lincoln's
Emancipation Proclamation, the willingness of black soldiers to fight and die
helped to transform the moral meaning of the Civil War from a war for Union
to a "crusade" for freedom. With black soldiers under arms, white Northern opposition to emancipation (in particular Democratic opposition) now
meant opposition to the Northern army—a box not easily escaped. This vulnerability was not lost on the Republicans, and it would further the drumbeat
for African American participation in the war. Resounding Republican victories in the 1863 elections, including, most dramatically, the trouncing of Vallandigham in Ohio, confirmed the political capital to be gained by enlisting
black soldiers.

On the home front, Northern sermons moved beyond their praise of
emancipation and commentaries on the issue of slavery and the Bible to
comment on black soldiers' admirable qualities as warriors. In his Thanksgiving Day sermon to the First Congregational Church of Albany, Ray Palmer
spoke of the change in sentiments accompanying black soldiers in the field:

> To a great extent, to our shame it should be spoken, they have lived among
> us as under band. But at last their manhood has been recognized. They have
> been summoned, as men, to go forth for the defence of our common coun-
> try; and they have not only bravely fought beside our sons and brothers in
> the field, but have dared with them the deadly breach and mingled their
> blood with theirs on the fiercely contested height.[24]

On the battlefront, African American soldiers participated eagerly in
Thanksgiving. Among them was Corporal James Henry Gooding, who had
fought bravely at Fort Wagner. With Charleston now under siege he had occasion to describe the religious observance:

> The air was just cool and keen enough to make one feel that it was a genu-
> ine old New England Thanksgiving day. . . . It was a scene long to be
> remembered—a grand army assembled on the verge where old ocean roars,
> to render homage and thanks to the Great Giver of victory. The gilded star
> and waving plume of warring chief stood side by side with the humble citi-
> zen soldier or quondam slave! The famed cathedrals of the Old World never
> presented a scene more grand, majestic, and impressive than the volunteer
> soldiers of a great and powerful Republic, gathered in a solid mass, with the
> arching dome of heaven for their temple, acknowledging their dependence

on the mighty King of kings. We had no rich toned and powerful organ to lull the warring passions into submissive reverence; but the waves on the sea-beat shore seemed to partake of the majesty of the hour, and in low and gentle ripples made music on the sands. Every head was bared as the Post Band commenced to play some of the good old Orthodox airs of home—no doubt reminding many there assembled, of the day as observed at home.[25]

On February 20, 1864, black regiments again distinguished themselves in another noble but losing cause at Olustee (Ocean Pond) in Florida. From their base in Jacksonville, General Truman Seymour's Tenth Corps, which included several black regiments led by the Fifty-fourth Massachusetts, moved inland to Baldwin, where they were surprised by a Confederate counterattack. In a desperate holding action, the Fifty-fourth maintained their position "at all costs," waiting until dark to allow for an orderly Federal retreat to Jacksonville. The Eighth U.S. Colored Infantry also fought and suffered more than three hundred casualties.

For Sergeant Major Rufus S. Jones of Pittsburgh, Pennsylvania, the battle again proved black bravery under fire as only fire can prove. The Confederate attack came so suddenly that sergeants had no time to take off their sashes, making them sitting ducks for Confederate fire. For the first time, black soldiers faced white soldiers eyeball to eyeball on common ground.

Unfortunately for Seymour's army, the attack came so suddenly that only half of his men were loaded with ammunition. When their top two officers and many soldiers fell, the Eighth moved to the rear of the Fifty-fourth and helped them hold their position. After the battle, surgeons picked up wounded black soldiers before white, fearing what would happen if they were captured. For Jones, "it looked sad to see men wounded coming into camp with their arms and equipments on, so great was their endurance and so determined were they to defend themselves till the death. I saw white troops that were not badly wounded, that had thrown away everything."[26] A former slave, Susie King Taylor, labored as an unpaid and untrained nurse among wounded black soldiers and, in her memoir, described how she overcame the horrible sights of the battle:

It seems strange how our aversion to seeing suffering is overcome in war,—how we are able to see the most sickening sights, such as men with their limbs blown off and mangled by the deadly shells, without a shudder; and instead of turning away, how we hurry to assist in alleviating their pain, bind up their wounds, and press the cool water to their parched lips, with feelings only of sympathy and pity.[27]

New York was the last Northern state to actively enlist black recruits, the lateness stemming from the resistance of its Democratic governor, Horatio Seymour. But by March 1864 three black regiments enlisted as the Twentieth U.S. Colored Troops and paraded through New York City as "white and colored ladies wave[d] their handkerchiefs." The irony did not escape a writer for the *Christian Recorder*:

> I think that some of the same rabble, who were in the pro-slavery melee of July 13, 1863, were made to shed tears of repentance on beholding the 20th regiment of Colored Troops off Riker's Island, as they marched through the streets of this great city in glorious array, onward to the defence of their country, God, and the right, notwithstanding the outrages they suffered a few months past at the hands of the . . . copperheads.[28]

By 1864 Confederates were also aware that black soldiers performed admirably. The response was predictable. On April 12 the intrepid and brutally racist slave trader Nathan Bedford Forrest led a Confederate cavalry division on a mission to reduce Fort Pillow, Tennessee, and block Federal navigation along the Mississippi. The fort was defended by 262 black soldiers from the Eleventh U.S. Colored Troops and 295 whites. Together they were no match for the superior numbers and tactical genius of Forrest.

By afternoon, Forrest had his fifteen hundred men in position and took the fort with light casualties. Despite Confederate denials at the time, evidence has since shown that many Federal troops, and in particular the black troops, were murdered after they had surrendered and laid down their arms. In later congressional testimony, eyewitnesses described rebel troops shouting, "No quarter! No quarter! Kill the damned niggers; shoot them down!" Claims of black soldiers buried alive may have been inflated, but it is clear that scores of black soldiers and some white compatriots were "massacred" after their surrender—an act of cold-blooded murder.[29] Forrest himself avoided censure because he "neither ordered nor condoned the massacre." Left unsaid was the fact that he did not need to. What he needed to do was order the protection of prisoners. It was a lesson in moral avoidance that Northern generals would also learn perfectly.

On June 12 Sergeant Ransom recorded in his prison diary that some new "negro soldiers" arrived at Andersonville from the Eleventh U.S. Colored Troops. They told "hard stories," he wrote, against the Confederacy at Fort Pillow: "Many were wounded after their surrender."[30]

After the murder of black prisoners at Milliken's Bend and Fort Pillow, black soldiers vowed "no quarter" on their own part and fought under the banner "Remember Fort Pillow." With black soldiers now in combat, and no quarter given on either side, the Civil War had turned the corner toward a race war. At the battle of Brice's Cross Roads on June 10, Federal forces were routed by Forrest's corps. The white Yankees ran in defeat, but the black soldiers refused to surrender, emptying all their ammunition and then engaging the Confederates with bayonet and clubbed muskets.[31] As hatreds seethed in both directions, Confederate troops shrank from combat against black soldiers just as much as black soldiers dreaded to be captured. The war within a war pitted blacks against Confederates, both uncertain of any mercy in defeat and desperate to avoid surrender. Both, in the words of black soldier Joseph T. Wilson, "accepted the portentous fiat, victory or death."[32]

The race issue existed not only between Confederate and black Union troops but within the Northern armies themselves. Commissary Sergeant Richard W. White of the Fifty-fifth Massachusetts Infantry described how, en route to Florida in March 1864, a white Irish soldier "took on himself the prerogative of calling one of our men a nigger" and prompted a near riot. With memories of the New York draft riots freshly in place, the enraged black soldiers sought to teach "Pat" a lesson. But violence was avoided when the Fifty-fifth's protective commander, Colonel Fox, ordered the white soldier arrested and sent to the provost guard. A relieved White concluded, "A few cases like this will teach these fellows to attend to their own business and let other folks alone."[33]

At the same time, Northern outrage at Fort Pillow was immediate and, ironically, did much to win white sympathy for black soldiers under arms. In a letter to "My Dear Mr. Bradlee," Luis Endicott expressed the opinion of many when he observed, "What a dreadful thing the Fort Pillow affair was. It only shows us, what this horrid war will eventually run into. I think if after a thorough investigation of the facts on this case, the killing of the negros and whites after surrender is fully confirmed, Mr. Lincoln should certainly retaliate—two for one."[34]

CHAPTER 33

"THE MOST INTERESTING MEN IN THE COUNTRY"

By 1864 both North and South had acknowledged that generals stood as a breed apart, as "brilliant" in the business of killing as philosophers with ideas or painters on canvas. They stood as the warrior priests of America's dawning civil religion, entrusted with making the sacrificial blood offerings that would incarnate the national faith. The generals joined Lincoln and Davis as subjects of songs. Given their respective changes in fortune, attention shifted from McClellan to Grant. One triumphant song sheet, "All Hail to Ulysses!" was printed with a lithographic portrait of Grant on the cover. The stanzas were reverential:

> All hail to Ulysses the patriot's friend,
>   The hero of battles renowned
> He has won the bright laurel,
>   Its garland he wears,
> And his fame thro' the world we will sound.
>
> Chorus:
> Yes, hail patriot soldier, we'll welcome you home,
>   When strife and rebellion are o'er
> When terror shall cease
>   And our land be at peace,
> And the war shall be heard of no more.[1]

Likewise in the Confederacy, the "Beauregard Manassas Quickstep— A beautiful edition, with an accurate lithographic likeness of Gen. Beauregard" became a musical composition of choice.[2] Virtually every issue of the

Southern Illustrated News featured a lithograph and biographical sketch of Confederate generals. Not even defeat could dull their aura.

While the lauds were certainly extravagant and widely distributed, the actual number of truly great commanders was limited. By New Year's 1864, Northern and Southern armies combined approached 1.5 million soldiers. On such a vast scale, commanding generals oversaw units that exceeded their entire armies of two years earlier.[3] Battle decisions spanning troop deployments over miles had to be made in minutes, inevitably saving or destroying thousands of lives. In such battles, individuals mattered and one great commander was literally worth a corps.

General Meade's aide, Lieutenant Colonel Theodore Lyman, a Harvard graduate and an "unpaid volunteer," observed Meade and Grant and their corps commanders in their eastern campaigns and understood their rarity. "To be a good officer requires a good man," Lyman noted. "Not one man in ten thousand is fit to command a brigade; he should be one who would be marked anywhere as a person (in that respect) of superior talent. Of good corps commanders I do not suppose there are ten in this country, after our three-years' war. Of army commanders, two or three."[4]

Few doubted the capacity of Stonewall Jackson or Robert E. Lee to command armies in the heat of battle. But no such persons had appeared in the North. Only in 1864 did Lincoln finally believe that he had found his own Lee in General Grant, and he promptly commissioned him general in chief of the Union armies.

On the evening of March 24, President Lincoln met Grant for the first time. The two plain-speaking midwesterners conferred at the White House. Grant's mission was clear to both: "Get Lee." Lincoln expressed frustration at the "procrastination on the part of [earlier] commanders," and Grant assured him that he would "avoid as far as possible annoying him or the War Department." Two days later Grant was back in Virginia, putting together "the plan" that would bring decisive Northern victory.

On the recommendation of Lincoln's advisers—and Lincoln himself—Grant did not share his plans with Lincoln. The reason was simple. "He was so kind-hearted," Grant would later recall, "so averse to refusing anything asked of him, that some friend would be sure to get from him all he knew." For good measure, Grant also refused to share his plans with Secretary of War Stanton or Chief of Staff General Halleck, confirming just how autonomous commanding generals were.

While unwilling to hear Grant's plan, Lincoln was only too eager to share his own military thoughts on the situation. According to Grant:

A large wagon park at Brandy Station, Virginia (December 1863–April 1864). The logistical challenges to supplying large armies in the field were immense. These wagons stand ready to feed and provision Union soldiers in winter quarters.

> [Lincoln] suggested that the army might be moved on boats and landed be-
> tween the mouths of these streams. We would then have the Potomac to
> bring our supplies, and the tributaries would protect our flanks while we
> moved out. I listened respectfully, but did not suggest that the same streams
> would protect Lee's flanks while he was shutting us up.[5]

Grant's presence in the field, meanwhile, compromised the authority of
General Meade, the titular commander of the Army of the Potomac. It be-
speaks all the more the quality of Grant's leadership that the two worked
hard to avoid a rupture. But Grant's two most valuable warrior priests were
not with the Army of the Potomac. One, the redeemed General Sherman, advanced to Grant's former command in the West. The other, the youthful
Irishman General Philip Sheridan, had command of the cavalry in the
Shenandoah Valley and was already the stuff of legend.

Grant's strategy was brutally simple. In the past, Union armies had operated independently, allowing Confederates to shift defenses to trouble spots
as needed. Under Grant, "concentration of force" on all fronts would be the
order of the day. In a communiqué to Sherman, written on April 4, Grant
confided, "It is my design, if the enemy keep quiet and allow me to take the
initiative in the spring campaign, to work all parts of the army together, and
somewhat towards a common centre."[6]

That center, of course, would be Richmond. The Army of the Potomac under Meade's and Grant's command would dog Lee's army: "Wherever Lee goes, there you will go also." Sherman would march into Georgia against the formidable General Joe Johnston and reduce Atlanta. Sheridan would operate in the Shenandoah Valley, checking Forrest's equally legendary cavalry, and razing the land to cut off Lee's food supply and demoralize the citizenry.

Alongside these central campaigns, Grant intended to see every other major Confederate army pinned down and unable to assist Lee and the Army of Northern Virginia. Grant's lesser (political) generals—Nathaniel P. Banks, who moved from the Red River campaign in Texas (which he badly mishandled) to Mobile, Alabama, and Franz Sigel (appointed to appease German Americans)—were to march south in the Shenandoah. Grant appointed the ineffective Benjamin Butler, a political Democrat whom Lincoln felt he had to retain until the national elections, commander of the Department of Virginia and North Carolina with orders to move against Richmond from the south side of the James River.[7]

To this bold but simple strategy Grant applied tactics intended to be equally direct—and harsh. For these armies to succeed, the Confederate will to fight must be crushed so completely that Davis and his generals would finally recognize the futility of continuing the war. Lincoln and Grant realized that in this newly escalated citizens' war, the people must be engaged and crushed. Otherwise the armies could fight forever.

That the back had not yet been broken on Confederate morale appeared on many fronts. Sheet music, for example, continued to thrive in the dying Confederacy, often in denial of realities. In "Wait 'Till the War, Love, Is Over," one stanza glossed war and the home front:

'Twas gentle spring the flowers were bright,
    The bird's sweet song was lonely,
I wander'd in the moon's pale light,
    With her I loved so fondly,
Her face with smiles shone cheerfully,
    My heart with joy ran over,
As tenderly she whisper'd me
    Wait 'till the war, love, is over.

In fact, many Confederate brides were not telling their soldier men to wait but to come home now. This was especially true for wives separated from battlefields—and from the sight of occupying Federal forces. For them (unlike wives closer to war zones), need and grief displaced rage and revenge. What began as a united home front and war front had, by 1864, extended too long for many women to tolerate. They began to launch their own private moral crusade questioning the war's integrity. In a letter to her husband, George, Martha Fort angrily asked: "How many lives are to be laid on the alter of ambition of men. I look on this war as nothing else but to gratify unholy ambition."[8] Yet the Confederates were far from ready to capitulate. Lincoln and Grant intended to change that.

In 1864 civilian suffering did not mean mass murder of innocent civilians (that would wait for another century) nor rape. In fact, such tactics would backfire by stiffening enemy civilian resolve and eroding Union soldiers' discipline. Starvation, destruction of homes and property, and widespread marauding, however, were a different story.

Here the Federal commanders engaged a moral gray zone. Generals could not command rapine to get their wishes. That would not look good in subsequent review. Instead, they had only not to discourage it with mass courts-martial or executions. Already by 1863, Sherman had noted the fact that generals "make feeble efforts to stay the disorder, but it is idle." The fact was that war—or at least this war—could not be controlled: "You cannot help yourself, and the only possible remedy is to stop war." This, in turn, required Sherman "to destroy both the rebel army and whatever of wealth or property it has founded its boasted strength upon."[9]

With sentiments like these, generals could rely on the soldiers to follow their instincts, steeled by three years of war and unremitting civilian hatred. Whether this civilian suffering should be termed "hard" war, "destructive" war, or "total" war is a scholar's game. The point was that citizens must suffer. This, in turn, meant an irrevocable end to the ideals of "Christian civilization" touted by McClellan and the Democratic Party for their own racist ends. With Lieber's Code at the ready, the justification for waging a war of deprivation on civilians was in place. And with the leadership of Lincoln, Grant, Sherman, and Sheridan, the men to accomplish it were assembled and in place. Each general had dealt directly with guerrilla and "irregular" warfare in the West and border states, and each had lost whatever vestiges of the West Point Code they originally harbored.

Clearly Grant had a draconian plan. But would it work? For three years the two armies had dueled with severe casualty rates, but neither could achieve a decisive victory. In fact, soldiers on both sides questioned "which would whip" in the event of a final showdown.

Grant, however, knew he would whip—as long as the press and people supported him. His orders—and inclinations—were to promote a final engagement from which there would be no retreat, no matter what the casualties. No proportionality of losses could mitigate against this end—moral reflection about acceptable losses could not even be part of the equation. Instead, pragmatism must define the line between acceptable and unacceptable losses, and the cost would be high indeed. Grant understood that to annihilate Lee he would have to engage in "as desperate fighting as the world has ever witnessed."[10]

Perhaps more than any other battles, the spring 1864 campaigns of Grant and Lee highlighted the nearly mythical status of generals and their people's loyalties. Lee's veteran lieutenant James Longstreet summarized the situation on the eve of the battles:

> The commanders had chosen their battle after mature deliberation. They knew of each other's numbers and resources before they laid their plans, and they had even known each other personally for more than twenty years. Each had the undivided support and confidence of his government and his army, and it was time now to leave the past and give attention to the future.[11]

Predictably, as massive battles loomed, Congressman Samuel S. Cox again urged restraint and conciliation. In a congressional speech delivered on May 4 he insisted:

> History teaches in vain, if it does not contain lessons of moderation in civil wars. . . . Will our rulers heed these lessons in time? Will they return to the purpose of the war, as declared by General McClellan, for the sole great object of the restoration of the unity of the nation, the preservation of the Constitution, and the supremacy of the laws . . . let them remember, also, that all our labors to rebuild the old fabric will fail, unless out of the "brotherly dissimilitudes" of section and interest, we evoke the spirit of fraternity, which has its true similitude in the perfect spirit of Christian fellowship![12]

Though eloquent in his compassion, Cox left unsaid the underlying reality that his "spirit of fraternity" and "Christian fellowship" was a whites-only fraternity, and its "fabric" woven with the racist thread of white supremacy.

Meanwhile, Lincoln fretted that a lack of convincing victories would cost him the 1864 election to McClellan. Yet his party remained overwhelmingly supportive of the war, not only in the army, but among the rank and file. The exception was John C. Frémont, the disgruntled general who was deprived of a high command by his humiliation in Missouri. Frémont tried to create a third party composed of Republican abolitionists and radical German Ameri-

cans with a platform that was nearly the mirror opposite of Cox's. Cox
branded Lincoln with the icon "nigger lover"; Frémont accused Lincoln of
being a rebel lover, unwilling to extract the last measure of blood revenge.
Frémont intended to be God's self-proclaimed enforcer, with radical congressmen as his henchmen. The tragedy of the Civil War's legacy would be
the triumph of both: white supremacy and vengeful reconstruction.

But in 1864, Frémont attracted little support. Frémont's strongest sup-
porter, the radical anti-Lincoln abolitionist Wendell Phillips, represented an
alliance sure to win more enemies than friends. Few Republicans or Democrats expressed much interest. At the nominating convention on May 31 in
Cleveland, the "Radical Democratic Party" denounced Lincoln's softness on
abolition and reconstruction. They further advocated that Congress, not the
executive, set plans for reconstruction that included the confiscation of rebel
land for redistribution. But they garnered little national support.[13]

For Martha LeBaron Goddard, an admirer of Wendell Phillips, the
prospects did not look good: "I was dreadfully disappointed in the Cleveland
convention, for I had hopes that the opposition to Lincoln might accomplish
something. Now I despair—Fremont is my man, but his party looks forlornly
weak to me, so far as I know anything about it; and I suppose we and the
poor negroes must suffer another 4 years of Abe's slowness and feel guilty
and mean explaining and apologising for every decent thing he has done."[14] If
Lincoln failed to impress Goddard, the generals were a different story: "This
last month of fighting has told upon the Worcester soldiers, and some of our
best and bravest soldiers have fallen. . . . Grant and Lee are by far the most
interesting men in the country to me now."[15]

Abijah Marvin, an abolitionist minister, also evidenced concern over a
war fought for war's sake. Citing earlier American barbarities in the Seminole
War and Mexican War, he wondered if the present war was any different:
"When I picture to myself two armies composed of such profane men rushing into deadly conflict, the idea of humanity seems to be withdrawn, and to
my mind's eye, two armies of incarnate fiends are venting the rage of hell itself. O what a terrible necessity is war!"[16]

In the Confederacy President Davis continued to do battle with the Carolinas and Georgia over his policy of centralization and conscription, but the
army seemed in good spirits.[17] Longstreet's corps returned to Lee's Army of
Northern Virginia, ready to help "Marse Lee" beat off a Union attack. And
General P. G. T. Beauregard was reassigned from Charleston to lead the Department of North Carolina and Southern Virginia, with responsibility for defending Richmond and North Carolina against Butler's threatened invasion
from the South. While no large battles had taken place since the fall of 1863,

the pieces were falling neatly into place for destruction of military and civilian lives and property on an unprecedented scale. A shaken writer for the *Richmond Daily Whig* recognized that "upon the eve of a momentous campaign, within the period of which lie undisclosed events, inscrutable to the most earnest gaze, affecting the destiny—the very existence perhaps—of our people as a free people."[18]

In his classic treatise *On War*, Carl von Clausewitz defined war as "politics by other means," and so it had begun with the Civil War. But by 1864, as battles resumed, war was becoming its own end. Richmond's papers could print little else than news of the war—and with it stories of the generals who dueled like industrial knights commanding engines and explosives alongside horses and sabers. Headlines fed the public lust for new conquests. Civilian anticipation for massive battles would not wait long to be satisfied. If Antietam stands as the military and political "crossroads" of the war, 1864 would stand as the moral crossroads of a war pursued with unprecedented violence on soldier and civilian alike. By 1864 even Lincoln was through with efforts at compromise and conciliation. With black soldiers under arms, there would be no further talk from Lincoln of colonization or compensated emancipation. Instead, it was all-out war.

CHAPTER 34

"IF IT TAKES ALL SUMMER"

Shortly after midnight on May 4, 1864, Grant began the dreaded spring campaign by posting the Army of the Potomac across the Rapidan under cover of darkness. On the other side, Lee waited patiently in his command headquarters at Orange Court House with his veteran army of just under sixty-five thousand loyal disciples willing to sacrifice themselves for their master. Instead of challenging Grant's invasion at the Rapidan, Lee posted his army north of Richmond in the thick and familiar tangle of trees and undergrowth that was the Wilderness.

The choice was brilliant. Rather than confront Grant's superior numbers in a frontal assault, Lee would force Grant to come to him on his turf, just as he had done with Hooker at Chancellorsville, five miles to the north. In the Wilderness, there would be no massed army to flank—or even to see. Artillery, which had proved so devastating at Fredericksburg and Gettysburg, would be of little use. Lee hoped that by effectively silencing Federal artillery and capitalizing on the advantages of terrain and local knowledge, he might once again humble the Goliath from the North.

Winslow Homer's painting of the Wilderness captured the haunting, almost surreal quality of the terrain where the two armies would soon grapple in a desperate battle. The dark forestation was so thick with small pines and scrub oak, cedar, and dogwood that visibility all but ended beyond ten yards, making coordination between large military elements virtually impossible.

Though fighting without Stonewall Jackson and unhappy with Longstreet's tardiness at Gettysburg, Lee still enjoyed a general corps roughly the equal of Grant's in terms of ability and experience. Such were the talents of the battle-hardened commanders on both sides that none would flinch or

"Bones of Dead Soldiers in the Wilderness." This photograph of skeletons in the woods captured the tangled morass of the Wilderness, where some of the war's fiercest fighting took place.

run. Neither would the equally hardened soldiers, Darwinian survivors all. Great commanders and veteran soldiers ensured great battles—and great losses.

Grant thought he knew all about the terrain from reports about the debacle at Chancellorsville. Hoping to get through the Wilderness as quickly as possible, he divided his forces into two columns marching in two directions. But his hopes were not realized.[1]

Like Gettysburg, the Battle of the Wilderness began accidentally with a chance early-morning encounter on May 5 between Gouverneur K. Warren's Fifth Corps and Richard Ewell's Second Corps on the Orange Turnpike. Warren was ordered to attack what he believed to be no more than a division. When it became apparent that Ewell's entire corps was on the road before him, Warren realized that this attack would soon rise to the dignity of a full-fledged battle. Fierce fighting broke out on Orange Plank Road between Confederate A. P. Hill's advancing Third Corps and Winfield Scott Hancock's Second Corps. Though outnumbered forty thousand to fifteen thousand, Hill fought a brilliant and successful holding action by shifting his interior lines to concentrate his limited forces against the specific points of Federal attack.

In the immediate aftermath of the battle, Hill was so exhausted and weakened from the day's fighting that he failed to adequately reorganize his front, which remained scattered and unprepared for renewed fighting the next morning. At the same time, Lee worried about Ewell's health and resolution in the face of battle. Lee could ill afford to lose any of his depleted warrior priests. Fortunately, he still had Longstreet, who was moving rapidly to join up with him.

By morning Longstreet had still not arrived, leaving Lee shorthanded and desperate. But timing is everything in battles, and just as hope was waning, Lee spotted approaching soldiers. He asked where they were coming from. When the answer came back "Texas," he knew that Longstreet had arrived.

With uncharacteristic glee, Lee left his position and rode to meet the loyal Texans. For their part, they were no less moved by the sight of "Marse Robert" in the field. One courier cried out, "I would charge hell itself for that old man." Caught up in a frenzy of his own, Lee assumed a position as if to lead the charge until cries of "Go back!" "Lee to the rear!" rang through Longstreet's corps. When, at length, Lee's staff officer caught the bridle of Lee's mount Old Traveller and turned Lee back, the rebels followed Longstreet with renewed passion into the fray.

The moment was indeed Longstreet's, and he never shone brighter. The energized rebels pushed Hancock's Yankees hard down the Orange Plank Road and single-handedly turned the tide of attack. With room to breathe, Hill's units reordered and reconnected with Ewell as the new center of the Confederate line.[2] Later, Longstreet praised the intrepid courage of his men "at the extreme tension of skill and valor."

As Longstreet pushed forward down the Orange Plank Road, the Federals fell back, leaving Lee's forces in place to turn Grant's left flank at Brock Road and roll up his army. But just as rapidly the tide turned again. At the critical moment of attack, Longstreet was struck by a volley of fire issued by his own pickets and fell, badly wounded in his neck, coughing blood and unable to continue. The "Old War Horse" had fallen at the hands of his own men, just as Jackson had fallen in the Wilderness a year before.

Longstreet would live to fight another day, but his glorious moment was lost. Still, this would not be Lee's last thwarted opportunity. At the other end of Lee's line, General John B. Gordon's scouts informed him that, incredibly, Union General John Sedgwick's right flank was exposed and "in the air." A skeptical Gordon crawled past his lines toward the end of Grant's breastworks, where he beheld the most amazing sight: "There was no line guarding this flank. As far as my eye could reach, the Union soldiers were seated on the margin of the rifle pits, taking their breakfasts."[3]

Ecstatic at the sight, Gordon proposed that he attack at once. His immediate superior, timid Jubal Early, refused permission to make the assault. When apprised of Gordon's intelligence hours later, Lee immediately countermanded Early's orders and sent Gordon forward in the waning daylight.

The surprise was total as wave after wave of Gordon's rebels rolled back entire regiments of stunned Yankees.

Throughout the day, men fought in clumps of desperate engagement that became lonely worlds unto themselves. Lacking any visibility or contact, soldiers sometimes fired on their own men. Worse, in the dense and dry underbrush, artillery and musketry ignited fires up and down the line. Dead trees burned like kindling as two hundred wounded Union and Confederate soldiers and their fallen horses suffocated or burned where they lay. Victory could not be seized; precious daylight waned and rebel soldiers got caught in crossfire from their own troops. As later summarized by a recovered Longstreet: "Thus the battle, lost and won three times during the day, wore itself out."[4]

Grant knew he had not taken the day, but was consoled by the fact that Longstreet was removed. His loss, Grant observed, "was a severe one to Lee, and compensated in a great measure for the mishap, or misapprehensions, which had fallen to our lot during the day."[5] Grant determined nevertheless that Lee's entrenched defenses were too powerful to carry. The next morning, May 7, both armies remained in their respective positions along the five-mile line from Germanna Plank Road to Spotsylvania Court House. With Lee well entrenched in the Wilderness, any offensive would have to originate with Grant. He was not yet ready to roll the dice again, and with good reason. The losses from the Wilderness fight were staggering on both sides. Of 115,000 Federals engaged, 17,666 were killed, wounded, or missing; of Lee's 65,000 Confederates, the combined casualties stood at more than 7,500. Furthermore, Lee had lost the services of two of his three commanders. In addition to Longstreet, A. P. Hill was too ill to continue in front of his army and had to be replaced by Jubal Early.

Amazingly, despite the losses on both sides, neither commanding general was deterred. As Grant smoked a cigar and whittled wood, preoccupied with his next move, Lee correctly ascertained that Grant was neither a retreating McClellan nor a rash Hooker, but rather a general of grim determination. As Grant's army slid past Lee's army and moved south, Lee also deduced that his destination was Spotsylvania Court House, a small village where a number of roads converged with vital strategic implications for command and communications.

For the first time, Lee faced a general who would press on the offensive no matter what the cost in human sacrifice. No moralists moved to caution Grant. To the contrary, the people cried for more. Grant's strategy left no room for nuance. "It was my plan, then, as it was on all other occasions," he would later write, "to take the initiative whenever the enemy could be drawn from his intrenchments if we were not intrenched ourselves."[6] At that moment in the Wilderness, with Grant's decision to press on, the fate of the Army of Northern Virginia was sealed. But not even Grant could estimate the butcher's bill that Lee would extract.

On the evening of May 7, Grant issued the fateful orders to Meade, directing him to move Warren's Fifth Corps overnight to Spotsylvania Court House, twelve miles away. Having anticipated this aggressive movement, Lee was already marching in the same direction. General Richard Anderson, temporarily replacing Longstreet in command of First Corps, was ordered to lead the race to Spotsylvania. When Meade's infantry and Sheridan's cavalry got entangled and clogged the road south, Lee's more nimble troops took advantage of interior routes and arrived at the crossroads first. Immediately they began digging for their lives to construct stout entrenchments.

In his memoirs, Grant later described Lee's anticipation and pointed to the irony of cause and effect in time of war. Despite the best-laid plans of men, Grant conceded, "accident often decides the fate of battle."[7] Anderson entrenched his corps immediately across Warren's front and beat back initial assaults. Aware of the full strength of the enemy before him, and leery of suicidal offensive charges, Warren established a position at Lee's front, which he too immediately fortified with formidable entrenchments.

Fortifications had reached new levels of sophistication in these spring campaigns of 1864. Already past masters of their craft, Lee's soldiers constructed a deadly matrix of breastworks with trenches behind, artillery emplacements, traverses, and abatis of spikelike trees felled toward the enemy. General Meade's staff officer, Lieutenant Colonel Theodore Lyman, observed with wonder how the rebels could put together earthworks:

> Hastily forming a line of battle, they then collect rails from fences, stones, logs and all other materials, and pile them along the line; bayonets with a few picks and shovels, in the hands of men who work for their lives, soon suffice to cover this frame with earth and sods; and within one hour, there is a shelter against bullets, high enough to cover a man kneeling, and extending often for a mile or two. . . . It is a rule that, when the Rebels halt, the first day gives them a good rifle pit; the second, a regular infantry parapet with artillery in position; and the third a parapet with an abatis in front and entrenched batteries behind. Sometimes they put this three days' work into the first twenty-four hours. Our men can, and do, do the same; but remember, our object is offense—to advance.[8]

While the tactical defensive often determined the outcome of individual battles in the Civil War, Lee recognized that purely defensive wars would ultimately end in submission. Sooner or later Lee would have to catch Grant in a fatal mistake and switch to a counterattack or the game would be up. In a message to President Davis, Lee summarized his strategy by observing that Grant's entrenched army was virtually impregnable: "We cannot attack it with any prospect of success without great loss of men which I wish to avoid if possible." But then Lee concluded on an offensive note: "I shall continue to strike him whenever opportunity presents itself."[9]

Had Grant seen Lee's determined message, he might not have continued to underestimate his adversary—which led him to miss the determined warrior lurking within the gentleman. Colonel Lyman overheard Grant say with confidence that a bloodied Lee would retreat south. Lyman feared otherwise: "[Lee] will retreat south, but only far enough to get across your path, and then he will retreat no more, if he can help it."[10] Lyman was correct. In fact, General Grant still had much to learn about General Lee.

Across the extended lines, Grant faced the similarly hoary specter of massive blood sacrifice, but was willing to trade a "great loss of men" in return for steadily eroding Lee's dwindling army. Had the soldiers sensed that millions back home would have been morally aghast and outraged at the looming slaughter, desirous only of peace, neither Grant, nor Lincoln, nor all the statesmen on earth could have impelled the soldiers forward. In this war, however, citizens on both sides cried for no surrender.

As Grant faced Lee at the strategic crossroads at Spotsylvania Court House, he faced two options: either flank the defenses as he had done earlier at Vicksburg and as Sherman would do so successfully against Johnston in Georgia, or attempt another frontal assault along Lee's five miles of defensive works. He would try both, and both would fail. The assaults would come first.

On the morning of May 8, elements of the Union Fifth Corps engaged the Confederate First Corps at Spindle Farm, along the Brock Road. The fighting lasted all day. Additional troops arrived on both sides with neither able to force their way through the other's defenses. By nightfall, parallel fieldworks faced each other across the Brock Road. The battle of Spotsylvania Court House would grind on for two weeks from May 8 to 20. By the fifth day, Grant was farther south than ever, with no intention of letting up. At the end of six days of constant engagement, he signaled his resolve to finally defeat Lee in a famous memo to General Halleck that closed: "I am now sending back to Belle Plain all my wagons for a fresh supply of provisions and ammunition, and propose to fight it out on this line if it takes all summer."[11] In fact, it would take all summer—and more. In the process, it would lead to the most desperate fighting ever visited in the war.

Grant and Meade believed that a massive assault on one Confederate soft spot would split the Army of Northern Virginia and win the battle. The spot selected was "the Mule Shoe," a U-shaped salient in advance of Lee's main line, about a mile deep and a half-mile wide. If enough concentrated force could be brought to bear on that soft middle, Grant reasoned, the seam of Lee's army could be rent and the battle won. But it would not be easy. Confederate commanders also understood the vulnerability of their principal salient at the Mule Shoe, and battle-savvy rebel soldiers redoubled their efforts, digging even deeper entrenchments and denser abatis. They had no place to retreat; they would have to stand and fight.

At 4:35 a.m. on May 12, the Federal Second Corps, commanded by General Winfield Scott "The Superb" Hancock, moved forward and struck the apex of the salient.[12] The initial assault was a staggering success. Before Confederate artillery could be brought to bear, the enemy was already in their rear demanding surrender. In a mere thirty minutes, Hancock informed Grant that three thousand soldiers from Ewell's "Stonewall Brigade" had been taken prisoner.

Thinking Lee whipped, Grant's staff burst into applause—except for Meade and Lyman, whose "own experiences taught me a little more skepticism." Sure enough, the determined rebels hit back as John B. Gordon, sensing the fate of Lee's entire army in the balance, re-formed a line midway down the salient between Brock Road and Harrison House.

Gordon knew that his forces could not dig in and hold their position forever. They would have to counterattack. As soon as Lee arrived on the scene, Gordon proposed another audacious plan that Lee immediately approved. Once again Lee appeared to head his horse to lead the advance. And once again he was turned back as worshipful troops called "Go back!" "General Lee to the Rear!" At last Lee relented and Gordon turned to his electrified troops, fixing the order, "Forward! Guide-Right!"[13] As the rebels yelled and the line surged, Gordon's division, reinforced by North Carolinians, clawed and hacked their way through the mud, rain, and chill, pushing the enemy steadily back traverse by bloody traverse.

Badly surprised and bloodied by the counterattack, Hancock's line buckled, but it would not back down. The Federals retained a strong toehold at the northeastern tip of the Mule Shoe, and all day, infuriated soldiers fought eyeball to eyeball, each trying to overwhelm and destroy the other. Before this, relatively few battlefield casualties had come from bayonets and hand-to-hand combat. Where such encounters emerged, they had seldom lasted for more than an hour before one side or the other retreated. But in an unprecedented reach, soldiers who had already been fighting nonstop for days literally lost all respect for life—theirs or the enemy's.

In what would prove to be the longest sustained hand-to-hand action of the war, the soldiers clawed, bit, and stabbed at each other in a fifteen-hundred-yard killing pit known variously as the "Corner," "the Death-angle," or, later, the "Bloody Angle." In that agonizingly small space, two entire corps piled in and stood facing each other at fifty yards. Large trees were cut in half, severed by musket fire coming from both sides. For twenty-three hours, from dark to dark, soldiers threw themselves at one another in a savage death dance during which communications were impossible, lines unformed, and men fighting desperately for their lives.

All discipline broke down as the soldiers devolved into wild men. When ammunition ran dry, they threw bayonets like spears or used their rifles as clubs to beat the enemy senseless. Even the dead were reenlisted in this fight as soldiers shaped the hands of their dead and dying comrades to hold cartridges, so that as those fingers stiffened in a cupped position, they would provide ready access to the ammunition. Union Major General Lewis A. Grant described the fatal intimacy of the battle: "Many were shot and stabbed through crevices and holes between the logs; men mounted the works, and with muskets rapidly handed them kept up a continuous fire until they were shot down, when others would take their places and continue the deadly work."[14]

As afternoon passed into night, no relief arrived. Exhausted Confederate troops at the apex were ordered to hold the line "at all costs" until a new line could be entrenched at the base of the salient. Finally, at midnight, the exhausted rebel survivors fell back, wild-eyed and mad with the horror of nonstop killing. More than five thousand Confederates lay dead or wounded, alongside six thousand Yankees, many of them pressed so deep in the mud by the feet of their comrades that their features could not be discerned.

The next day Lieutenant Colonel Lyman walked the battlefield. In a letter to his wife, he described the scene: "The bodies of friend and foe covered the ground. Some wounded men were then taken out from under three or four dead ones. One body, that lay exposed to the fire, had eighty bullets in it."[15]

Still the fighting pressed on as the warrior priests prepared for new sacrifices. The next day, both armies withdrew and re-formed their lines north of the salient along Fredericksburg Road. On May 19, Ewell assaulted Grant's right flank but was stopped at Harris Farm by a former artillery company pressed into service as infantry under General Robert O. Tyler. The fighting was brief but intense, leaving fifteen hundred Union casualties to nine hundred Confederates. Though small by Bloody Angle standards, Harris Farm marked the end of the Battle of Spotsylvania Court House.

CHAPTER 35

"JUNE 3. COLD HARBOR. I WAS KILLED."

In the aftermath of Spotsylvania, even Grant was stunned by the carnage. By the time the two armies finally broke off on May 20, they left behind eighteen thousand Federal casualties to Lee's ten thousand. In little over twelve days, the Army of the Potomac had lost thirty-two thousand men. Northern reporters, and not a few Democrats, branded Grant a "butcher," and some of his own soldiers agreed. Nothing before had equaled the sheer intensity of killing. Yet even as the mounting death reports hit home, thoughtful men and women did not raise serious questions of scale and proportionality. Grief and sorrow mixed aplenty, fueling new levels of hate and fury. The bottom line was: more.

As Northern readers groaned, Southern readers thrilled to heroic accounts of Confederate bravery. A writer for the *Mobile Daily Advertiser and Register* described the scene in characteristically purple prose:

> The battle was soon fully joined, and for nine hours it roared and hissed and dashed over the bloody angle and along the bristling entrenchments like an angry sea beating and chafing against a rock bound coast. The artillery fire was the most sustained and continuous I have ever heard for so long a time. . . . The rattle of musketry was not less furious and incessant.[1]

Readers of the *Advertiser* could exult in a battle that "roared and hissed" without ever having to reflect on the lives lost at the Bloody Angle and the blood shed obscenely on both sides.

The religious press, no less than the secular press, filled its columns with live reports on the progress of the war. On May 19, as the battles raged, a writer for the *American Presbyterian* wrote: "While we write there is a lull in the fearful storm of battle raging for eight or ten consecutive days in Virginia.

It is but for a moment, doubtless; and soon the strife will recommence; and a contest which is accepted as final by the rebels . . . will go forward to the dire conclusion."[2] One thing had become clear to Lee and to Grant, and eventually to the entire citizenry: There would be no spending limit on this butcher's bill.

From the first battles, civilians on both sides knew a surprising amount about battles and generals. For Richmond's diarist Sallie Putnam, the spring campaign proved that Lee's army, though "barefooted, ragged, ill-fed," was not demoralized, so that "Grant and his friends were alike astonished." Still, she could not help but be impressed by Grant:

> The most striking feature in the character of this distinguished commander of the Federal army, seems to be quiet determination, and indomitable perseverance and energy. Under similar disappointment, another would have had his courage so shaken that he would gladly have foregone an undertaking that promised so little fulfillment in success. The saving of his army appeared not to have been with him an object, if by it he should lose an advantage.[3]

Another diarist, Martha Wayles Robertson, who lived just north of Petersburg, heard the din of cannon and prayed for deliverance. As guns fired only five miles distant, she prayed that the "noble Beauregard" and Lee would repel the evil invaders: "Oh give them the victory. They are both Christians!"[4]

In the field after the battles around Spotsylvania Court House, Lieutenant Colonel Theodore Lyman observed the curious fraternization taking place between the warring armies:

> To-day has been entirely quiet, our pickets deliberately exchanging papers, despite orders to the contrary. These men are incomprehensible—now standing from daylight to dark killing and wounding each other by thousands, and now making jokes and exchanging newspapers! You see them lying side by side in the hospitals, talking together in that serious prosaic way that characterizes Americans. The great staples of conversation are the size and quality of rations, the marches they have made, and the regiments they had fought against. *All sense of personal spite is sunk in the immensity of the contest.*[5]

Herein lies the central paradox of the Civil War: the soldiers' awe at the scale of conflict and destruction eventually transcended personal "spite"; in the very act of annihilating one another, they recovered the fact that they really were Americans all.

The destructions wrought in 1864 were unique and pivotal in the Civil War. As the spring campaigns raged, prospects of death displaced romantic love as the soldier's central obsession. On May 22, Private William Willoughby wrote: "The Rebs now hold the R. Road from Petersburg to Richmond. We have been here 16 days and we have had 12 or 13 days hard fighting. Almost a constant roar of Cannon and rattle of Musketry and it is astonishing to me how a man escapes alive." Whatever the fears, Willoughby resigned himself to a Providence that none could foretell: "I submit to the will of God. Let him do as seemeth him good."

While duty and Providence justified the war, they did not steel Willoughby in the face of battle. In responding to a letter from his wife, Willoughby wrote:

> You say Eliza thinks I was foolish in going with the Regt and you write as though you regretted it. Now you would not want it said your Husband was a coward nor would Eliza care to have it said she had a cowardly Brother in the Army. Neither would Raymond a few years hence should he live, care to hear his Father was a Shirk or Flunkey. My attachments for home and Friends are as Strong as any ones Yet to come home disgraced I should not care to do. I shall not of course expose myself unnecessarily, and shall try to take care of my self the best I can.[6]

John Emerson Anderson had no doubt what he was fighting for. This he defined simply: "Patriotism as I understand it, is, to be willing to sacrifice something to promote any good cause for our common country. It is not in words, that great things are accomplished but in deeds, and in actions . . . continue to pray Mother for our common cause and I have the best assurance that you will not pray in vain." Of the justice of his cause, Anderson had no doubts. Emancipation had rendered it a "holy war," so that Union soldiers who were killed in action were nothing less than "martyrs" who died that slavery might end:

> May they realize that the sacrifice of our brave and noble comrades who have fallen in the struggle are every one of them martyrs. Justice demands at our hands that they shall not have fallen in vain, but that every vestige of the great National Sin, slavery, shall be washed away with their blood, that future generations may look back upon the records of these times and say with pride as well as with reverence these men were our preservers under God, for they saved our Republic. I believe God is certainly with us. And if so who can prevail against Him.[7]

Many went so far as to draw analogies between the soldiers' deaths and the atoning work of Christ on the cross. In the North, at a funeral for James T. Stebbins and Myron E. Stowell, the pastor cried out: "We must be ready to give up our sons, brothers, friends—if we cannot go ourselves—to hardships, sufferings, dangers and death if need be, for the preservation of our government and the Freedom of the nation. We should lay them, willing sacrifices, upon the altar!"[8]

By 1864 the language of martyrdom and sacrificial altars was instinctual and, through sheer repetition, forming a national consensus and literally incarnating a powerful new religion of patriotism. After rehearsing the lives of Albany's "martyrs" who died for their nation, Pastor Rufus Clark closed: "A republic for which such sacrifices have been made, and upon whose altar such noble and precious lives have been laid, must live, must triumph over all its foes, and shine with new splendor in the ages yet to come." In all seriousness, one minister consoled grieving parents with the words that their son "laid himself cheerfully upon the altar, and gloried to be there."[9]

Of course soldiers did not cheerfully do any such thing. But interestingly, many did not wish to lay their enemies on the altar either. Unlike American armies trained after World War II—programmed to instinctively shoot to kill—many soldiers, though patriots and nonpacifists, could not bring themselves to kill another human being in the heat of battle.[10] This understandably concerned commanders, but not as much as did the deserters or "skulkers" who were also part of every battle. They were the ones who would feign injury or illness or effect labors to save wounded comrades—anything that would take them behind the lines.

This could prove to be devastating. Soldiers had to know they could count on their comrades. To ensure this, the commanders instituted the ultimate penalty for desertion. On both sides, soldiers who deserted their comrades in time of battle were put to death by execution. Lieutenant Colonel Lyman observed how in the recent battles "stragglers have committed great outrages" in the cause of victory. Worried that Lincoln might later manumit the sentences, Lyman was in favor of hanging deserters on the spot in full view of their advancing comrades. Desertions continued, he believed, because of "the uncertainty of the death penalty through the false merciful policy of the President. It came to be a notorious thing that no one could be executed but poor friendless wretches, who had none to intercede for them . . . there was no certainty in punishment, and certainty is the essence of all punishment."[11]

On this score, Lee was similar to Lincoln. He lacked the stomach to execute Confederate deserters. In practice, this meant officers would rely not on civil process to punish deserters and stragglers but on the point of their own swords in the back of the offenders.

Sporadic skirmishing continued for several days after Spotsylvania, but neither general itched for an immediate replay of "the game." The most significant engagement took place on May 11 at Yellow Tavern, Virginia, just six miles north of Richmond. There Philip Sheridan clashed with Lee's flamboyant cavalry officer Jeb Stuart. Both generals shared a fearlessness in battle that energized their soldiers. When Sheridan's twelve thousand troops met up with Stuart's five thousand cavalrymen, Sheridan assumed the offensive. He was repeatedly beaten back until Brigadier General George A. Custer's brigade broke through the line. In the process, the charismatic Stuart was felled by an unmounted Michigan cavalryman and died the following day in Richmond. Again the capital city was devastated.

As the Confederacy mourned its heroic general, Sheridan rejoined Grant and prepared for the next assault. Despite the exhaustion of both armies, Grant and Lee understood that they could not stand still. If Grant was not to retreat—which he certainly was not—then he must resume the battle, or Lee would hit him first. Likewise, if Lee was to avoid open contact or costly offensive assaults, he would have to remain far enough ahead of Grant's omnivorous army to entrench strongly and nullify his inferior numbers, which grew more diminished by the day.

From the start of the campaign, Grant had hoped to close Lee in a vice between Meade's Army of the Potomac and Butler's Army of the James, which presumably was coming from the south to get into position around Petersburg. But the incompetent General Butler had his hands full with Confederate General Beauregard. Worse, he was hamstrung by his own timidity and indecisiveness. Through a series of disastrous moves that even an amateur map reader could have avoided, Butler managed to hem himself into his own trenches between the James and Appomattox rivers. Incredulous, General Beauregard took his small army into entrenched lines that sealed Butler off, rendering his thirty-thousand-man army, in Grant's words, "in a bottle strongly corked."[12]

Now on his own, Grant once again confronted an experienced and determined foe. In the last week of May, he began moving on Richmond, knowing Lee would have to follow.

The two armies next dug in with entrenchments and abatis in the tightly confined fields around the intersections at Cold Harbor. The site was near Gaines' Mill field where, two years earlier, Lee had defeated McClellan. But much had changed in two years. Gaines' Mill offered only picket fences for cover. At Cold Harbor, Lee could forge a battle line with tangled abatis and field guns supporting entrenched positions. The line extended from Bethesda Church on the Mechanicsville Turnpike south along Bethesda Church Road to the Chickahominy River below Cold Harbor and Gaines' Mill.

Lee left no reserves behind and no option for retreat. With local knowledge, skilled engineers, and veteran soldiers, his entrenchments were cunningly designed to provide maximum defensive support as well as fields of fire that would take advantage of ravines and tree lines to create murderous crossfire from which no escape, forward or backward, would be possible. Nature and logistics together were impregnable. Amazingly, neither side appeared to be discouraged or demoralized.

If Grant and Meade were confident in their superior numbers and willing to put the men to the task, the troops were less certain. Having already borne bloody battles for a month straight, a sort of mad fatalism permeated their conversations and actions. In an unusual gesture, many soldiers wrote out their names and addresses on slips of paper and pinned them to their hats or shirts so that kin could be notified of the fact that "June 3. Cold Harbor. I was killed."[13]

For Charles Washburn of the Thirteenth New Hampshire, the work of music continued in or out of battle, rain or shine. The bands usually played in the morning as marches began, and one or two pieces again in the evening after supper. Funerals were also fit for music and became increasingly common. To Washburn, a funeral dirge represented "the most beautiful and affecting music ever written." Grant was about to provide him with all the beauty he could desire.

Although Grant (who would assume formal responsibility) has often been solely credited for the assault about to happen, he actually shared the decision with Meade. For some time, Meade had been concerned that Grant was getting all the attention for commanding what was, in fact, *his* Army of the Potomac. In a gesture of reconciliation, Grant had ceded operational control to Meade, who bragged openly: "I had complete and entire command on the field all day." He would later rue his words of dismissive pride.[14]

At 4:30 a.m. the tragically brief and criminally expensive assault began. The worst destruction hit Union Brigadier General John H. Martindale, whose division had to pass through a ravine that was murderously swathed by crisscrossing lines of fire. The first line approached the Twentieth South Carolina, where the rebels waited patiently, sighting their targets. The Yankees never had a chance as the first line "reeled and attempted to fly the field, but were

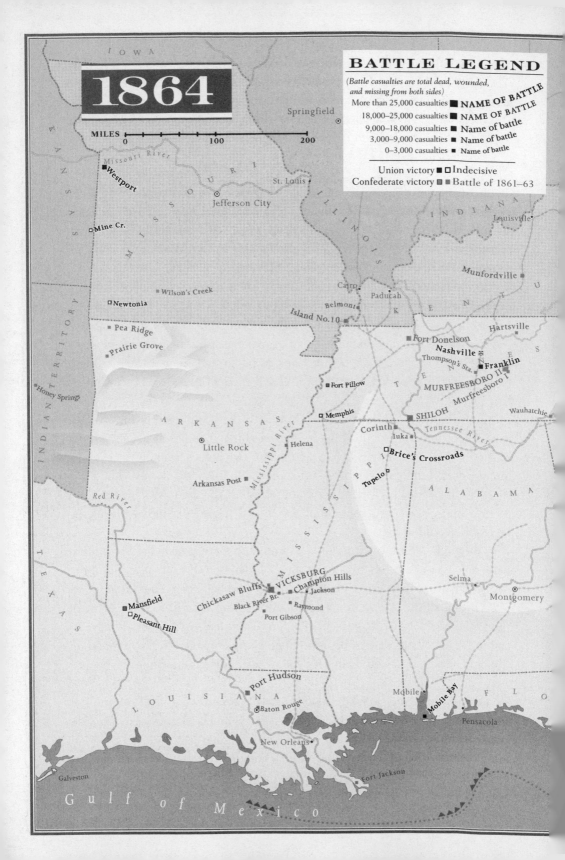

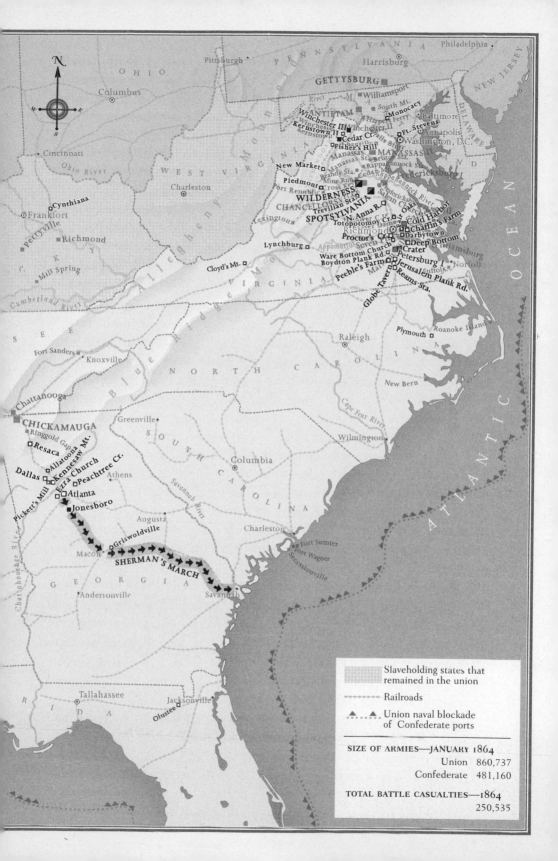

N

OHIO

Columbus

PENNSYLVANIA

Pittsburgh   Harrisburg   Philadelphia

GETTYSBURG

Williamsport

Cincinnati   South Mt.   NEW JERSEY

WEST VIRGINIA   ANTIETAM   Monocacy

Winchester III   Harper's Ferry   Ft. Stevens   Baltimore

Winchester II   Winchester   Annapolis

Kernstown II   Cedar Cr.   Falls Ch.   Washington, D.C.

Charleston   Fisher's Hill

Kernstown   Manassas   MARYLAND

New Market   Manassas Sta.   Bristoe Sta.

Cynthiana   Piedmont   Brandy Sta.   Rappahannock Sta.

Frankfort   Cross Keys   Mine Run   Fredericksburg I

Richmond   Port Republic   Cedar M.   Rappahannock River

Perryville   WILDERNESS   Trevilian Sta.   Salem Ch.

K Y   CHANCELLORSVILLE   Fredericksburg

Lexington   SPOTSYLVANIA   Seven Pines

Mill Spring   N. Anna R.   Savage's Sta.

Lynchburg   Totopotomoy Cr.   Cold Harbor

Cumberland River   Richmond   Chaffin's Farm

Cloyd's Mt.   Proctor's Cr.   Darbytown

Appomattox River   Seven   Deep Bottom

Ware Bottom Church   Crater   Williamsburg

Boydton Plank Rd.   Petersburg I   Norfolk

VIRGINIA   Peeble's Farm   Jerusalem Plank Rd.   Suffolk

Globe Tavern   Reams Sta.

Raleigh   Plymouth   Roanoke Island

Fort Sanders   NORTH CAROLINA

Knoxville   New Bern

Chattanooga   Cape Fear River

CHICKAMAUGA   Greenville

Ringgold Gap   SOUTH CAROLINA   Wilmington

Resaca   Columbia

Allatoona   Savannah River

Dallas   Kennesaw Mt.   Athens

Pickett's Mill   Ezra Church   Peachtree Cr.

Atlanta   Charleston

Jonesboro   Augusta   Fort Sumter

Griswoldville   Fort Wagner

GEORGIA   Macon   SHERMAN'S MARCH   Secessionville

Andersonville   Savannah

Tallahassee   Jacksonville

F   R   I   D   A

Olustee

OHIO RIVER

ATLANTIC OCEAN

Slaveholding states that
remained in the union

Railroads

Union naval blockade
of Confederate ports

SIZE OF ARMIES—JANUARY 1864

Union 860,737

Confederate 481,160

TOTAL BATTLE CASUALTIES—1864

250,535

met by the next column, which halted the retreating troops with the bayonet, butts of guns, and officer's sword." As rebel soldiers fired methodically and relentlessly from their impregnable entrenchments, Union soldiers funneled like pigs into a slaughter pen. They had no choice but to press on, pushed forward as they were by their own men.

The next line fared no better, "rear rank pushing forward the first rank, only to be swept away like chaff." Rebel soldiers laughed and joked as they poured lead into the hapless Yankees. The carnage was total.

When Captain Thomas Barker of the Twelfth New Hampshire was ordered to re-form his lines for another massed assault, he "declared with an oath that he would not take his regiment into another such charge, if Jesus Christ himself should order it."[15] In little over an hour, all three assaulting Federal corps were repulsed with staggering losses that totaled seven thousand. In comparison, rebel casualties were meager, under fifteen hundred.

When Charles Washburn had arrived at Cold Harbor, he had found it "a very unsafe place to be." After the assault, he was immediately enlisted at the field hospital to help with the wounded. He would later write: "It was there I experienced, or realized the awfulness of war . . . the wounded were everywhere, under every tree and bush where they could be partially sheltered from the hot rays of a June sun. . . . Holes were dug in the ground near the tables, and I saw them actually filled, with amputated limbs."[16]

In the battle's aftermath the warrior priests communicated directly. Hundreds of dead and wounded soldiers lay side by side in the field between the two armies. The two generals negotiated the fate of their soldiers, each interceding for his charges. Grant began with a letter to Lee, noting that unless a temporary cessation of hostilities was effected, the wounded could not be gathered up for care. Would Lee agree to such a truce immediately, selecting any three-hour block he liked?

For the victorious Lee, who had already recovered most of his wounded soldiers, honor and the "rules of war" required a formal flag of truce initiated by the vanquished, which Grant refused to permit. Although Lee's sense of just conduct could sometimes minimize civilian suffering, as on the march to Gettysburg, it could work in the other direction on the field of battle. In his view, honor dictated that the vanquished should not claim equality or moral superiority to the victor, even if wounded soldiers were dying and suffering.

Left with little choice, Grant finally acquiesced and raised the flag, and on June 7 all the living Federal wounded were finally gathered up—both of them. The rest had died where they lay on the battlefield. Grant would not forget the humiliation of this day. In the not too distant future, he would dictate the terms to Lee, and it would be permanent.[17] For now, however, some of Grant's officers were not humiliated but furious that the wounded had

African Americans collecting the bones of soldiers killed in the battle of Cold Harbor, Virginia. This photograph by John Reekie portrays the grisly aftermath of General Grant's ill-fated charge against Confederate defenses.

been left to die for the sake of "honor" and the "rules of war." Colonel Francis Walker issued a harsh judgment of his commander:

> If it be asked why so simple a duty of humanity as the rescue of the wounded and burial of the dead had been thus neglected, it is answered that it was due to an unnecessary scruple on the part of the Union commander in chief. Grant delayed sending a flag of truce to General Lee for this purpose because it would amount to an admission that he had been beaten on the 3d of June. It now seems incredible that he should for a moment have supposed that any other view could be taken of that action. But even if it were so, this was a very poor way of rewarding his soldiers who had fallen in the attack, or of encouraging their comrades to take similar risks.[18]

Clearly, the South was not the only side to venerate "honor" at the expense of morality. On both sides, the West Point generals understood honor only too well.

Grant would later reflect on the battle of Cold Harbor and would concede profound "regret" for his (and Meade's) command decisions. As he wrote:

> At Cold Harbor no advantage whatever was gained to compensate for the heavy loss we sustained. Indeed, the advantages other than those of relative losses, were on the Confederate side. Before that, the Army of Northern

Virginia seemed to have acquired a wholesome regard for the courage, endurance, and soldierly qualities generally of the Army of the Potomac. They
no longer wanted to fight them "one Confederate to five Yanks . . ." This
charge seemed to revive their hopes temporarily; but was of short duration.[19]

Grant's concession suggests that he had a moral sense of the war and an understanding of when the moral brake linings sheared. But even Cold Harbor
could be morally justified by his commander in chief, who kept closely to his
awful arithmetic.

Grant's reference to lopsided losses resonates well with Lincoln's overall
moral calculus that the prodigious deaths on the Cold Harbor battlefield
shortened the war and prevented higher ongoing death rates in prisons and
winter camps. For the most part, American military historians agree, chalking
the episode up to bad judgment, forgiving Grant because he admitted his
mistake, and then moving on to the next great battle. In this way, Americans
past and present manage to record and solemnize battlefield deaths without
judging them. Somehow, in ways they could not explain then or now, Americans accepted the levels of destruction as secondary to the work of national
redemption America's God required.

When the losses at Cold Harbor were factored into the combined casualties from the rolling battles of May to June 3, 1864, the totals were stunning
and widely broadcast in the North and South. In less than one month,
Grant's Army of the Potomac had lost fifty thousand men—virtually the same
number as Lee's entire Army of Northern Virginia. Even for battle-hungry
civilians and statesmen, these figures were shattering—nearly half of the total Federal casualties for the entire three years prior. Shiloh, Antietam, Gettysburg, and Chickamauga had served as mere dress rehearsals for spring
1864. Lee's losses of thirty-two thousand were equally devastating, represent-
ing in proportional terms half of his Confederate Army. Neither general
would order a frontal assault again in the war.

For once, civilians, no less than soldiers, became sickened by the river of
blood. Newspapers and ordinary people again labeled Grant the "butcher."
His own soldiers picked up the label and evidenced telltale symptoms of
what today would be called post-traumatic stress disorder. Having lived
through the Wilderness, Spotsylvania, and Cold Harbor, they were physically
and psychologically shot. No commander—not even Grant—could get them
to do it again. In fact, Grant *had* underestimated Lee, and Cold Harbor became his painful classroom. A vindicated Meade, who earlier had to listen to
Grant belittle Union fears of Lee, wrote, "I think Grant has had his eyes
opened." Still, the campaign to "get Lee" would not miss a step.

For embalmers and coffin manufacturers, business was good. As the battles peaked in the overland campaign, notices for "Undertakers" appeared regularly in the newspapers. From a location near the Federal hospital at City Point, Virginia, in July, an embalmer carried a drawing of a coffin with the words:

> The subscribers being located by the proper authorities near the Army of the Potomac, would respectfully offer their services to the friends and relations of deceased soldiers, as Embalmers of the Dead bodies procured from the field and hospital grounds when practicable, disinfected and expressed home with promptness properly encased and securely packed.

Meanwhile, in Philadelphia, William Moore advertised "metallic coffins constantly on hand. Particular attention paid to persons desirous of purchasing ground in Woodland Cemetery."[20]

Again Lee was victorious tactically, but his army was too devastated to take strategic advantage of his position and launch a devastating counterattack on Grant and Meade. To all intents they were locked into the strict defensive mode that Lee had sought desperately to avoid. Unless Richmond could be conceded, which Davis was loath to do, there would be no more offensive victories for the Army of Northern Virginia. For his part, Grant understood that Lee could not afford to attack and so altered his strategy from a war of maneuver to one of siege.

"The plan" continued as ever to pursue Lee and flank him out of his defenses, but now a new three-pronged strategy would replace the frontal assaults.[21] The army in the Shenandoah Valley commanded by General David Hunter moved south through the valley, destroying railroads and supplies, and continued east toward Richmond where they would converge with Grant. Sheridan was ordered to enter the Shenandoah Valley from the north and meet in the center with Hunter. Grant and Meade meanwhile slid past Lee at Cold Harbor and seized Petersburg, the last railroad link between Richmond and the South. With Richmond isolated from railroads and communications, and the valley also deprived of railroads and foodstuffs, the Army of Northern Virginia had to either surrender Richmond or starve. In the end they would do both.

PART VII
DISCRIMINATION

A CIVILIAN WAR

AUGUST 1864 TO FEBRUARY 1865

CHAPTER 36

"THE PIOUS MEN WILL BE HELD UP AS THE GREATEST OF PATRIOTS"

With Grant laying siege to Petersburg, Virginia, and with Lee having no viable plan to engage Grant's army in battle, attention shifted to the Shenandoah Valley. Grant's Virginia strategy was sound, but the execution would require one more bloody year and many false starts before it could finally annihilate the enemy. In the Shenandoah Valley, Union commander David Hunter's troops succeeded in small skirmishes but encountered no open battle. Instead they were beset by "partisans"—guerrillas who dressed in civilian clothes, hit the enemy hard, and then melted back into the population. Again armies were reminded that in this new kind of war there were no innocent civilians.

Fed up with the guerrilla tactics, Hunter's men (with his acknowledgment) foraged with impunity from the local farmers, destroying what they did not consume, and leaving the population of some of the country's finest farmland to starve. Property was also fair game. With the destruction of railroads as a genuine military objective, the troops freely savaged everything around them. On June 12 Hunter's marauding soldiers entered Lexington and burned the governor's home and Virginia Military Institute, whose "boys"—literally—had earlier put up a brave charge at New Market. Only Jubal Early's timely arrival with the remnants of the famed Stonewall Brigade prevented the destruction of Lynchburg.

In cutting Early free to reinforce the rebels in the vital farming areas of the valley, Lee hoped that Early would counter Hunter and threaten Washington, forcing Grant to lift his siege and cross the river in defense. Lee's strategy brought some Confederate gains on June 17 and 18, as Early disgraced the numerically superior Hunter by driving him across the Allegheny Mountains in retreat. With Hunter out of ammunition and forced to flee,

Early's army of thirty thousand had the valley to themselves and, more important, the means to plan an audacious raid on Washington.

With Hunter in hiding in West Virginia, Washington stood dangerously exposed, and Early nearly made it. Only a desperate holding action by General Lew Wallace bought Grant a precious extra day to funnel reinforcements from the Army of the Potomac into the capital city. Still, Early's troops reached the outskirts of Washington before they were repulsed. From there they returned to the valley, continuing their hit-and-run attacks on transportation and supply centers that were designed to terrify the soldiers and weaken northern morale.

With only a ghost force of twenty-five hundred to defend against Grant, General Beauregard fought the greatest battle of his career at Petersburg. By placing his men well behind strongly fortified defenses and imposing walls, Beauregard held Grant's forces at bay, buying critical time for Lee to arrive with reinforcements. On June 15 Union forces under General William F. "Baldy" Smith attacked the outer defenses of Petersburg. The assault succeeded in destroying the outer lines, thanks in large measure to a regiment of black troops who attacked with vigor and gained distinction in the Northern press. But again the Union losses proved substantial and prolonged the war by months. The "back door" to Richmond had closed.

As the dreadful warfare continued in Virginia, Confederate moralists praised ongoing army revivals. In desperate times, even the skeptical *Richmond Examiner* joined in praise for the "untiring exertions of [religious] associations, whereby a vast number of chaplains and missionaries have permeated through the refreshing stream of spiritual inspiration. They have succeeded in making the army of Virginia respectful acknowledgers of the Divine Director, if not devout and pious disciples of the Redeemer."

Throughout the war, the *Examiner* had praised "the more chivalrous spirit of the Cavaliers" over the "bigoted descendants of the Puritans" and its tendency to "prevent us, by instinct, from making war on women and burning their homesteads over their unshielded heads." But in this fierce war, Cavalier manners might not survive or suffice. Religion was also required:

> But if the natures and dispositions of man be not cultivated in the same degree as the mind, even the manly and chivalrous instincts of the Cavaliers will degenerate into the savage. The religious communities have foreseen this danger . . . they have endeavored to instill a religious sentiment in the minds of the army. . . . There may be a time when the praying man . . . will be considered as great a general as those in the fields. There may be a time when the pious men . . . will be held up as the greatest of patriots.[1]

Once again the secular press flip-flopped its position in this dynamic war. For the *Examiner* to come this far toward piety reflects just how desperate the Confederate cause had become in this ever-changing war.

Religion blossomed as well in Northern prisoner-of-war camps. This account is from Elmira, New York:

About ten thousand prisoners are under confinement at the Rebel Camp in Elmira, New York. They are supplied with preaching by the local clergy, and are allowed to choose, from time to time, whom they will hear, the only limitation of choice being that none but ministers of undoubted loyalty should be invited. Strange to say, they have never asked for a man of questionable patriotism. Thomas K. Beecher is quite a favorite among them. Their preaching audiences sometimes number more than two thousand. They have prayer meetings every morning and evening, on the open green, where it is affecting to witness often large masses kneeling in solemn supplication to heaven.[2]

Meanwhile, in a speech to the U.S. Senate, Senator Benjamin Brown of Missouri fulminated at Lincoln's refusal to lay out a plan of radical reconstruction, but then went on to note how important religion was becoming in the North: "The nation is putting on its Puritanism. Thanksgivings appoint themselves unitedly. Days of supplication are become somewhat more than holidays. The bowing down has ceased to be a mockery in the presence of the multitudinous remembered dead; and even they who heretofore have been accounted most indifferent begin to hold to a realizing conviction that God does direct the affairs of nations by His special providences."[3]

Back on the fields of battle, Lee's army began filing into the Petersburg trench works with a determination to halt Grant once again. By the time the Federals finally mounted a massive assault on June 18, Lee had dug in; the Yankees were unwilling to face another Cold Harbor. After a couple of token raids, in which it became clear that the Yankees would not fight suicidally any longer, Meade called off the assaults. Grant decided that Petersburg would have to be invested (besieged). Once again the opportunity to smash Lee's army came and went, leaving Lincoln frustrated and Grant more determined than ever. By retaining control of the railroad to Richmond, Lee avoided a full-scale siege of starvation and could communicate with the rest of the Confederacy. But he lacked all room and resources for maneuver in the face of Grant's superior numbers.

After June 22 battles ceased for the summer and the war deteriorated into a duel of trench systems where snipers ruled. Lee worried less about

Grant, whom he felt confident he could withstand, than about food. In a message to President Davis on June 26, he declared:

> I am less uneasy about holding our position than about our ability to procure supplies for the army. I fear the latter difficulty will oblige me to attack Genl Grant in his entrenchments, which I should not hesitate to do but for the loss it will inevitably entail. A want of success would in my opinion be al- most fatal, and this causes me to hesitate in the hope that some relief may be procured without running such great hazard.[4]

Petersburg, in other words, was in danger of becoming Lee's own Andersonville.

Petersburg afforded a glimpse of the future, in which trench warfare would replace frontal assaults. Every day was potentially a soldier's last, as snipers took aim at close range from trench to trench. George Elsworth de- scribed the new realities: "We are on pickett every other day and only about thirty yards apart. I had 6 of my Co. kild last night. . . . I wish to be remem- bered by all and tell them I have seen the Elephant. I have been in twenty two battles and only was wounded once in the left wrist slightly. I have never seen a day in the first 3 years but what I should do duty and not one in the last [year]."[5]

Again, when not engaged in the business of killing, soldiers engaged in conversation across the line. In a letter written in August, Union Private Blynum described picket duty: "We are now picketing the extreme left near Petersburg. Our line is within speaking distance of the 'Johnies' and yesterday we exchanged papers with them."[6]

Besides unveiling a new type of war, battles around Petersburg greatly en- hanced the reputation of African American soldiers fighting on the outskirts. African American troops were assigned the hardest fighting against forts near Petersburg. A white officer attached to the Twenty-second U.S. Colored In- fantry described their triumphant charge up "an almost impassable ravine" that led to a rebel "skedaddle" (retreat). Their performance left no doubt in his mind: "The problem is solved. The negro is a man, a soldier, a hero."

Then, with Fort Pillow in mind, the officer added a moral of his own:

> Our men, unfortunately, owing to the irregular feature of the ground, took no prisoners. Sir, we can bayonet the enemy to terms on this matter of treating colored soldiers as prisoners of war far sooner than the authorities at Wash- ington can bring him to it by negotiation. This I am morally persuaded of. I know further that the enemy won't fight us if he can help it. I am sure that

the same number of white troops could not have taken those works. . . . The real fact is, the rebels will not stand against our colored soldiers when there is any chance of their being taken prisoner.[7]

While Petersburg lay under siege, Richmond nervously awaited its fate. Davis made clear that "we have no friends abroad," but still retained hope in Johnston's army to escape Sherman's snare, aid Lee, and deliver up the Federals.

Newspapers on both sides continued to print rumors and declare victories prematurely. On June 18 the *Philadelphia Inquirer* ran front-page headlines on "The Capture of Petersburg." The news was spectacular: "Baldy Smith Attacks Petersburg," "The Rebel Fortifications Carried," "The City Now Held by U.S."[8] The problem, of course, was that the assault had failed, and, on that very day, Grant determined to invest the city and begin a siege.

While Confederate currency was rapidly reduced to near-worthless paper, the Northern stock market, strong for a while, showed signs of panic. In another signal of mounting desperation, the price of gold surged. Northern audiences were meanwhile shocked by the scale of destruction launched by Grant's armies. After the loss of fifty thousand boys, Grant was—on paper anyway—no closer to Richmond than McClellan two years earlier. And the bodies continued to pile up. Democratic pleas for a negotiated settlement were stronger than ever. What victories there were lost their luster as life in some communities rent by the war became one continuous funeral procession. Casualties that took only weeks to multiply would require years to recover from.

In response, Lincoln proclaimed a fast day for August 4. Word of Lincoln's proclamation quickly reached the Southern papers and excited much religious response. The secular *Richmond Daily Dispatch* had, by 1864, become as religious as the religious press had become worldly. On July 16 a writer commented, "A despot humbles himself because his bloody crimes have not yet produced their desired result. Can anything more shockingly blasphemous be imagined?" Clearly both sides thought the other reprobate (regardless of soldierly respect).

The following week, another shot was lodged at the fast day. Conveniently forgetting that the Confederacy had long-since been "Puritanized" with its observation of civil fast days, the paper accused the North of a "blending of politics and religion . . . a distinctive characteristic of Puritanism." Without religion, the writer declared, the evil war could not continue. But Lincoln's proclamation for a fast day and the churches' willing acquiescence proved that "[t]he Puritan pulpit is the big drum for the Yankee war, calling sinners to the battlefield instead of to repentance."[9]

While on the losing side more often than not, Southern opinion was not as sour as that in the North. In part, they were encouraged by a Northern Democratic resurgence. And in larger part, they were encouraged by Lee. That his forces could fight to the death and, at the same time, turn to Christ in record numbers provided a mighty inspiration. Americans have always loved an underdog, and in that role Lee and his army held uncontested sway over the Confederate public imagination. As long as Lee stood, so did the Confederacy.

Although loath to assault Lee's impregnable fortifications at Petersburg, Grant was not one to sit idle. In late June he hatched a brilliant scheme to employ a regiment of coal miners from Pennsylvania to dig a five-hundred-foot tunnel under the Southern trenches and pack it with an immense eight-thousand-pound load of gunpowder to blast the rebels into oblivion.

The engineering and the explosion on July 30 were nearly textbook perfect, but the follow-up proved to be yet another Federal slaughter. It began when Meade countermanded Burnside's orders to lead the assault with a division of black veterans led by an experienced commander and instead chose a white division with a green commander chosen by drawing straws. Worse, the commander, James H. Ledlie, failed to appear at all, staying behind the lines drinking rum. The blast was so enormous that it created a crater twenty-five feet deep and two hundred feet wide and momentarily stunned the rebel defenders.

But then the plan ran awry. Instead of exploiting the gap created by the explosion and running around the crater as he was ordered, Burnside, in Grant's words, "seemed to have paid no attention whatever to the instructions and left all the obstruction in his own front for his troops to get over."[10] The Yankees flooded *into* the crater instead of *around* it, where, to their horror, they soon found themselves entombed by recovered Confederates. What was forever after known as the Battle of the Crater became a shooting gallery as the Confederates sealed the breach and then proceeded to virtually murder the targets massed beneath them.

Again Grant looked incompetence and destruction in the eye. He later complained, "The effort was a stupendous failure. It cost us about four thousand men, mostly, however, captured; and all due to inefficiency on the part of the corps commander and the incompetence of the division commander who was sent to lead the assault."[11] James H. Payne, an African American quartermaster sergeant, agreed:

How easily Petersburg could have been taken on the 30th of July, had the white soldiers and their commanders done their duty! But prejudice against colored troops prevented them. Instead of a general effort being made, as was contemplated, only a few men were taken in to be slaughtered and taken prisoner, which is the equivalent of death, for no mercy is shone to them when captured.[12]

Though defeated, the division of African Americans commanded by General Edward Ferrero showed their courage and determination in action. When the rebels re-formed and counterattacked, they encountered the black division left behind. For Lee's soldiers, who had never seen African American troops, the sight was enraging. Not content to simply shoot at the Yankees, the rebels charged into the fray, killing five hundred black soldiers and taking only two black prisoners. Many of the blacks were shot in cold blood after surrendering. Lee had observed the carnage from only five hundred yards away and obviously knew of the murders taking place. In yet another searing enactment of the inhumane racial civil war within the Civil War, he made no comment, then or later.[13]

CHAPTER 37

"IF THEY WANT PEACE THEY . . . MUST STOP THE WAR"

As Grant invested Lee's troops at Petersburg, a very different war emerged in Georgia. Sherman had built his army less for brute strength than for maneuverability and rapid flanking movements. For John Emerson Anderson, who had fought with General Banks in the Shenandoah, suffered as a prisoner of war at Belle Isle, and then been reinstated with Sherman's army, the first impression of the army in formation was overwhelming:

> When we awoke on Monday May 9 1864, thousands upon thousands of our union boys had been collected here from all parts of the lines east, and west, organized in six army corps each one commanded by men that were a host within themselves, and the whole commanded by General W. T. Sherman whose very appearance denoted a giants strength of intellect, force and physical endurance. As we stood and gazed on the magnificent host in our sight, who were formed in mass, in the order of rank in which the columns would move at the word of command, our faith in the final triumph of the union arms was quickened.[1]

In all, Sherman's army consisted of three departments or armies: the Department of the Ohio, commanded by General John Schofield and numbering fifteen thousand; the Department of the Cumberland, commanded by General George Thomas, the Rock of Chickamauga, consisting of fifty thousand; and the Department of the Tennessee, commanded by the youthful but brilliant General James B. McPherson, consisting of fifteen thousand. Ill and wounded soldiers were left behind. With this "compact army," Sherman set out to destroy General Johnston's army located in Dalton, Georgia, between Chattanooga and Atlanta.

Even as Grant kept Lee in his sights at all times, Sherman aimed to hound the "army of Jos. Johnston" to prevent Johnston from coming to Lee's rescue. The key cities of Atlanta, Augusta, and Savannah mattered only insofar as they might harbor Johnston's army.[2]

In a letter to General Grant on April 10, Sherman outlined a plan for provisioning his army by living off the land: "Georgia has a million of inhabitants. If they can live, we should not starve. If the enemy interrupt our communications, I will be absolved from all obligations to subsist on our own resources, and will feel perfectly justified in taking whatever and wherever we can find."[3]

Grant threw his full support behind the plan, having employed similar tactics in the Vicksburg campaign. At the time, Sherman still had supply lines, but when he later decided to cut those communications, the plan of "taking whatever" was already in place. To further assist him, Sherman gathered census tables for every county in the state of Georgia, listing local population figures and farming acreage.

On May 5, as Grant was crossing the Rappahannock, Sherman's "great campaign" was launched with his lead army moving out toward Atlanta. Sherman proved himself to be the brilliant tactician Grant had partnered with in the West. Instead of direct assaults on well-entrenched positions, Sherman continually flanked Johnston's army, threatening his rear and forcing him to slowly but steadily drop back toward Atlanta. Bloody engagements took place along the way, but by successively turning Johnston out of his positions, Sherman generally avoided direct assaults and casualties were kept to a minimum.

On the other side, Johnston was second only to Lee as a tactician and avoided being drawn out into costly assaults with his smaller army. When Sherman got in his rear or threatened his flanks, he steadily fell back to strongly fortified defensive positions.

The cat-and-mouse pursuit continued through Georgia, much to the chagrin of Southern editors and politicians who craved a bloody, Lee-style open engagement. But Johnston had other ideas. The longer he retreated to well-fortified positions, the more he knew his detachments could thrive even as Sherman was forced to expend his peak strength on detachments to repair and guard railroads and supplies. Bemused by "the newspapers of the South," which criticized Johnston, Sherman praised Johnston's tactics, all the while fulminating over the lack of a "grand battle," which he knew his armies would win.

As news of "bloody and desperate battles" between Grant and Lee in the Wilderness reached Sherman, he continued his relentless pursuit, resolved to give Johnston's army no rest or hope of linking up with Lee to attack

Grant. With Thomas's army in the center as his "column of direction," Schofield on the left, and McPherson on the right, Sherman moved inexorably toward Atlanta. He encountered elements of Johnston's army along the way, but drove him steadily from strong positions at Dalton, Resaca, Cassville, Allatoona, and Dallas. Fighting was continuous, with poor visibility among trees and bushes. Daily casualties numbered in the dozens and sometimes the hundreds. All along the way, Sherman's soldiers killed farm animals, ransacked houses, and put unoccupied buildings to the torch. For Georgia's terrified citizens, the unimpeded course of Sherman's army did more psychological damage than a pitched battle.

Observing the effects of destruction on civilian morale, Sherman confided in a letter to his wife that "all the people retire before us, and desolation is behind. To realize what war is one should follow our tracks."[4] In all, Sherman would absorb 5,393 casualties in the month of May—a significant number to be sure, but nothing like the destruction taking place at the same time in Virginia, sometimes on a daily basis. Employing his own calculus of war, Sherman observed: "I always estimated my force about double his, and could afford to lose two to one without disturbing our relative proportion."[5]

As a rule Sherman was determined to avoid tactical offenses against fortified positions. The exception came on June 14, when Johnston's army was spread among three hills—Kennesaw, Pine Mountain, and Lost Mountain. The positions were well fortified with fresh lines of parapets and heavy infantry. But in Sherman's view, Johnston had finally made a mistake by spreading his lines too thin. Sherman had been to Kennesaw in 1844 on a survey mission and knew the terrain well. After careful study he determined that Johnston was vulnerable to a concentrated assault in the gap between Kennesaw and Pine Mountain.

On June 27 Sherman determined to advance on Johnston at Kennesaw, "the key to the whole country." Johnston was indeed spread thin but was so well entrenched that he stayed in place, forcing Sherman to attack his fortified lines. At 9:00 a.m. the Union troops moved forward to assault with supporting artillery and musketry all along a ten-mile line. McPherson's Fifteenth Corps was assigned to feint a major assault at the base of Little Kennesaw, while the main attack was shouldered by two divisions of Thomas's Army of the Cumberland.

Sherman underestimated Johnston's defense and battle savvy. General William J. Hardee's well-entrenched Confederates were not fooled by Union feints and with well-placed fields of fire for artillery and musketry waited patiently for the main assault. To further defend themselves, the rebels had concealed artillery pieces that were deliberately kept silent in earlier exchanges.

The main attacking columns fell under a murderous artillery barrage. The fire was so intense that troop discipline broke down and the attacking divisions lost their concentrated focus. In place of companies and regiments, isolated groups of men swarmed the hill in a desperate attempt to scale the ridge and mount the summit. When it became obvious that the summit would not be gained, the attack turned into a pell-mell retreat. Officers and flag bearers were murderously mowed down as vengeful rebels shouted "Chickamauga" and "Come on."[6]

By 11:30, the assault was over. The rout was complete. That night regimental bands played patriotic music to soothe the bloodied soldiers and inspire their confidence. Two days later, under a flag of truce, Federal soldiers gathered their badly bloated dead comrades for burial and chatted idly with Confederates. Soldiers who days earlier were pitched in a murderous rage shared newspapers and whiskey, traded for coffee, and even shared autographs.

But all knew it could not last. Though momentarily stunned and concerned that some of his troops were openly complaining of suicidal assaults, Sherman was not through with Johnston by a long shot. Even as Kennesaw was lost, Schofield's Army of the Ohio succeeded in gaining ground on Johnston's left, threatening his rear. By July 2 McPherson's Army of the Tennessee was marching toward the Chattahoochee River. Once again Johnston was blocked as Sherman contemplated a flanking movement, and once again he escaped to the Chattahoochee on July 3. Sensing blood, Sherman commanded an all-out pursuit of Johnston's retreating army but could not catch him before he once again ensconced his army behind murderous entrenchments on the west bank of the Chattahoochee. This time Sherman did not assault, but rather returned to his flanking movements, forcing Johnston to withdraw ever closer to Atlanta.

An important, if largely overlooked, episode in Sherman's Atlanta campaign occurred in early July at two mill sites located near Johnston's fortified army at Roswell. In his memoirs, Sherman later noted innocently: "I ordered Garrard's division of cavalry up the [Chattahoochee] river eighteen miles, to secure possession of the factories at Roswell, as well as to hold an important bridge and ford at that place."[7]

Contained within the Roswell "possession," though, was a frightful story, seldom told in the North or the South.[8] In fact, Sherman took possession of not one but two small factory towns, Sweetwater or Factory Town and

Roswell. Both of these mill towns produced cotton yarn for Confederate uniforms and were operated primarily by women serving in the place of the men who had been conscripted into the army.

As Sherman's army swooped in to destroy the mills, Sherman issued, and then repeated, a remarkable accompanying order to a stunned General Kenner Garrard on July 7:

> I repeat my orders that you arrest all people, male and female, connected with those factories, no matter what the clamor, and let them foot it, under guard, to Marietta, whence I will send them by cars to the North. Destroy and make some disposition of all mills save small flouring mills manifestly for local use, but all sawmills, and factories dispose of effectually, and useful laborers excused by reason of the skills as manufacturers from conscription, are as much prisoners as if armed.

Sherman closed the order with the observation:

> The poor women will make a howl. Let them take along their children and clothing, providing they have the means of hauling or you can spare them. We will retain them until they reach a country where they can live in peace and security."[9]

Later, in explaining his actions to General Halleck, Sherman remarked, "They were tainted with treason. . . . I will send all the owners, agents, and employees up to Indiana to get rid of them there. I take it a neutral is no better than one of our own citizens engaged in supplying a hostile army." For Sherman, in fact, there were no "neutrals" in the Confederacy, and what he did or did not do was his decision to make. He could deport civilians or ignore them, but either way he deemed all white Southerners guilty traitors. There were no innocents, not one.

Sherman's orders were duly carried out. After the mills were destroyed the female workers were arrested, charged with treason, and sentenced to be deported with their children to the North under Federal guard. Sweetwater would never be rebuilt. In fact, the women never made it north but wound up in a Female Military Prison constructed just for them in Louisville, Kentucky, where they remained with their children until the end of the war.[10]

The charge Sherman invoked to justify the mass arrests and trials was "treason." The justification for this removal, in Lieber's terminology, was "military necessity." Since the factories lay near the river site where Sherman intended to cross his army, and since the presence of one thousand women around a Union army was certain to be a "distraction," Sherman felt comfortable with the orders he issued. For the sake of his army, the "traitors" were to be deported from their homes and country for the "crime" of laboring in factories left vacant by their soldier husbands and fathers. It was an evolving logic that would grow ever darker through his Southern campaigns and into the campaigns of Indian extermination in the 1870s and 1880s (when he replaced Grant as commander of American armies). In Sherman's view, his coercive actions were not "punitive" or brutally intimidating but strategic and merciful—a favor to the stranded women and an act that helped to end the war sooner.

In responding to the removal, one Confederate writer complained: "It is hardly conceivable that an officer wearing a United Sates commission of Major General should have so far forgotten the commonest dictates of decency and humanity, (Christianity apart), as to drive four hundred penniless girls hundreds of miles away from their homes and friends."[11]

The *Milledgeville* (GA) *Confederate Union*'s assault on Sherman was reprinted in the *New York Commercial Advertiser* (never a friend of Sherman's), but the forced removal attracted little attention in the North, and where it was noticed, provoked little commentary. A correspondent for the *New York Tribune* observed simply:

The refugees from the Sweetwater Factory and from Roswell are going North by train as fast as transportation can be afforded. Meanwhile, Major Tompkins, of General Sherman's staff, who is charged with the care of these multitudes of homeless people, is looking after their comfort.[12]

When it became clear that the "refugees" or "prisoners" were not being moved to Indiana after all, but to Louisville, the *Tribune* cited military necessity, but then went on to concede the brutality of it all: "Only think of it! Four hundred weeping and terrified Ellens, Susans, and Maggies transported, in the springless and seatless Army wagons, away from their lovers and brothers of the sunny south, and all for the offense of weaving tent-cloth and spinning stocking yarn! However, I leave the whole business to be adjudged according to its merits by your readers."[13] All understood the severity of the measure, but none wanted to make "judgments."

A patient commander, Johnston continued his deliberate retreat, waiting for Sherman to make a fatal mistake that would allow him to go on a rapid counteroffensive. But much to the dismay of Johnston in particular and the South in general, Sherman did not slip. On July 17 Johnston was relieved of command by a frustrated Davis and replaced by the feisty Texan John Bell Hood.

Lee was not pleased. In a telegram to President Davis, he noted simply:

"Hood is a bold fighter. I am doubtful as to other qualities necessary." In a follow-up message, Lee made clear his preference for William J. Hardee, should Davis persist in his conviction that Johnston had to be relieved.[14] A war reporter for the *Richmond Daily Whig* (already critical of Davis) agreed with Lee, adding a prescient observation of his own:

> General John B. Hood's promotion to the command of the army in Georgia excites much surprise. Few are willing to believe that the appointment is permanent. As a division commander, Hood was eminently successful, but his successes were not achieved without the assistance of the Texas brigade. . . . Other division commanders have been as successful as Hood, and as the commander of a corps, Hardee is surely entitled, both by seniority and greater experience, to the promotion.[15]

Grant and Sherman both agreed with Lee, as have subsequent military historians. But by then, the moral continuum was beyond proportionality and prudent calculation. President Davis misjudged Johnston's strategy, which was correct for the situation. The Confederacy wanted action, however, and Atlanta's civilians were getting nervous at the prospect of a Federal siege.

Once he learned of the command change from the Confederate press, Sherman sought out more information on his new adversary and did what any general would do; he checked Hood's West Point connections. General McPherson, a classmate, remembered him as "a born fighter, a perfect animal organism without knowledge of fear." General Schofield also briefed Sherman, who "learned that he was bold even to rashness, and courageous in the extreme; I inferred that the change of commanders meant 'fight.' "[16] And "fight" was precisely what Sherman's superior army wanted.

Sherman did not have to wait long. On July 20, with Sherman's three armies converging on Atlanta, Hood's forces burst on Thomas's Army of the Cumberland at the Peachtree Creek. General Joseph Hooker's corps caught the brunt of the attack and fought bravely in hand-to-hand combat. Hooker, who could lead a corps if not an army, then brought artillery fire to bear on the Confederates, driving them back to their trenches. Hooker suffered fifteen hundred casualties, but Hood's losses were far greater, numerically and strategically. Having failed in his first great test as a commander, Hood obliged Sherman by trying again on July 22. A desperate battle ensued throughout much of the day, swinging back and forth from a Confederate advantage to a Federal advantage. But again Hood stumbled badly, and before he retreated to Atlanta, more than ten thousand Confederates lay dead or wounded, alongside only thirty-five hundred Federals.

Despite the victory, disaster struck in the Union general corps. While riding to the front to inspect the enemy's works, James McPherson, Sherman's protégé and best general, was shot off his horse and died shortly thereafter. Sherman had shown an enormous professional and personal respect for McPherson. When he had offered McPherson a promotion to major general in the regular army, McPherson refused the honor, believing it should be held up as a prize for the most distinguished commanders in action.

The loss of a genius general—Stonewall Jackson, James Longstreet, John Reynolds, or James McPherson—was a devestating blow for both sides. Federal generals Thomas and Schofield were solid, but McPherson was special and had the same commanding presence that Grant saw in Sheridan, and Lee saw in Jackson. As they left the battlefield, Sherman remarked to an aide:

> The army and the country have sustained a great loss by the death of McPherson. I had expected him to finish the war. Grant and I are likely to be killed, or set aside after some failure to meet popular expectation, and McPherson would have come into chief command at the right time to end the war. He had no enemies.[17]

Sherman's comments are revealing. As warrior priests, these military leaders faced their own deaths unafraid, and even expected it. But even warrior priests had to answer to the pressure of public opinion.

With McPherson's death, General O. O. Howard assumed command of the Army of the Tennessee. When later accused of favoring West Point graduates, Sherman responded, "I was not intentionally partial to any class. I wanted to succeed in taking Atlanta, and needed commanders who were purely and technically soldiers, men who would obey orders and execute them promptly and on time." Then, in a swipe at the critical officers, Sherman argued, "I regarded both Generals [John] Logan and [Francis] Blair [political generals] as 'volunteers,' that looked to personal fame and glory as auxiliary and secondary to their political ambition, and not as professional soldiers." But that still left Hooker to contend with. Upon learning that he had been passed over for Howard, Hooker indignantly applied to be relieved of his command, which General Thomas "*heartily* recommended." Sherman agreed as well and replaced Hooker with General Henry Slocum, feeling a distinct "sense of relief" that Hooker was gone.[18]

With Howard in command of the Army of the Tennessee, Sherman's relentless war machine was ready to march on Atlanta. Unwilling to waste time on a siege, Sherman began shelling the city into submission with two thirty-pound Parrotts able to hit any target at will. Yankee artillerists would, Sherman assured General Henry Halleck, quickly turn Atlanta into a "used up community." By this time Halleck too had abandoned not only the West Point Code but, worse, even Lieber's Code, which stipulated that "[c]ommanders, whenever admissible, inform the enemy of their intention to bombard a place, so that the non-combatants, and especially the women and children, may be removed before the bombardment commences." But of course all laws were negotiable and subject to "military necessity." The shelling continued for three weeks, as often as not over the heads of Hood's soldiers into the town's houses and stores. Terrified citizens hid in dugout caves or "bomb proofs" in their backyards, sometimes receiving direct artillery fire.[19]

At the gates of Atlanta, facing a running army, John Emerson Anderson exulted in the terror his forces struck:

> A shell was thrown into the city from these guns once in five minutes day and night. . . . We sometimes watched the shells as they sped on their way, and when we saw the splinters flying from the roof, or the gable end of a building on Whitehall St. or a fire kindled by their explosion in a store or warehouse in the center of the city, we knew the owners thereof would become anxious to have the war cease just in proportion to the blows dealt them.[20]

Forced to choose between flight or fight, Hood withdrew his forces from the garrisoned city, allowing Sherman to occupy it unopposed on September 2. In reporting to an ecstatic President Lincoln, Sherman announced, "Atlanta is ours, and fairly won." Summarizing Sherman's achievement, his commander and friend General Grant observed: "The campaign had lasted about four months, and was one of the most memorable in history." Beyond military annals, Grant realized another consequence of Sherman's victory. It "probably had more effect in settling the election of the following November than all the speeches, all the bonfires, and all the parading with banners and bands of music in the North."[21]

For the citizens of Atlanta the bonfires were quite different. In his photographic history of Atlanta's destruction, the photographer George Barnard documented the utter desolation left behind. What Sherman's shells did not destroy his troops did as they filed into the city (and later out of the city), blowing up houses, public buildings, and rail lines. On Atlanta's main thoroughfare, Whitehall Street, only one building was left standing. Throughout

Boxcars loaded with civilian "refugees," 1864. As part of his campaign to "break the will" of the South, General Sherman expelled Atlanta's citizens from the city.

the city up to five thousand buildings were destroyed with only four hundred houses left intact. These damages could one day be repaired; the civilian casualties could not. No exact figures survive, but in a letter to General Hood, Sherman estimated that five hundred "rebel" civilians were killed and twenty-five hundred wounded. Given the source, one can assume these figures are significantly understated.[22]

Atlanta represented Sherman's first great conquest, and he was not done. With the city captured, there ensued one of the most morally fraught decisions of the war. Unwilling to either feed civilians or protect himself from them, Sherman determined to turn Atlanta into a military base. He ordered all the citizens to leave the city and go either north with his support or south on their own. All the still-standing houses of Atlanta would be used for military storage and occupation.

In a letter to General Halleck announcing his purpose, Sherman concluded: "If the people raise a howl against my barbarity and cruelty, I will answer that war is war, and not popularity-seeking. If they want peace, they and their relatives must stop the war." By considering Southern civilians as, in effect, belligerents, Sherman could proceed "with the absolute certainty of its justice." Furthermore, he asserted, "I knew that the people of the South would read in this measure two important conclusions: one, that we were in earnest; and the other, if they were sincere in their command and popular clamor 'to die in the last ditch,' that the opportunity would soon come."

In the ensuing days, more than 700 adults and 860 children were "sent south" with as many of their belongings as Hood could accommodate. The sight was pathetic, the event dangerous. In most cases, these were Atlanta's young, females, and elderly, and many had no place to go.

Sherman's order would spark controversy for a century and longer. While actions against civilian "irregulars" or bushwhackers could be justified by the laws of war, no immediate attacks on Federal forces in Atlanta had occurred to justify forced expulsion of an entire population who surrendered to the invader. In a plea for mercy, Atlanta's mayor begged Sherman to reconsider because "it will involve in the aggregate consequences appalling and heart-rending . . . we know of no such instance ever having occurred—surely never in the United States—and what has this helpless people done, that they should be driven from their homes, to wander strangers and outcasts, and ex-iles, and to subsist on charity?"[23]

Sherman was unmoved and lectured the town fathers on the nature of war: "You might as well appeal against the thunder-storm as against these ter-rible hardships of war. They are inevitable, and the only way the people of Atlanta can hope once more to live in peace and quiet at home is to stop the war."

Hood was outraged. In the letter war that followed between the generals—reprinted in both Southern and Northern presses—each spoke on behalf of his nation and lectured the other on the morality of the war's con-duct. For his part, Hood saw in Sherman's expulsion of every citizen regard-less of age, gender, or health an unspeakable outrage on a civilian population. Sherman's sole purpose was national self-interest at the expense of any moral standard: "You announced the edict for the sole reason that it was 'to the in-terest of the United States.' This alone you offered to us and the civilized world as an all-sufficient reason for disregarding the laws of God and man."[24]

For Hood, Sherman's decision to expel civilians and destroy property was made by a general who deliberately sought to terrorize innocents: "And now, sir, permit me to say that the unprecedented measure you propose tran-scends, in studied and ingenious cruelty, all acts ever before brought to my attention in the dark history of war. In the name of God and humanity, I protest, believing that you will find that you are expelling from their homes and firesides the wives and children of a brave people."

Outraged himself by Hood's "impertinence," Sherman made his case in equally strong moral terms. By positioning his interior lines near Atlanta's civilians during the bombardments of the city, Hood was, in effect, using his own civilians as human shields: "You defended Atlanta on a line so close to

town that every cannon-shot and many musket-shots from our line of investment, that overshot their mark, went into the habitations of women and children." As for invoking God:

> I ask you not to appeal to a just God in such a sacrilegious manner. You who,
> in the midst of peace and prosperity, have plunged a nation into war . . . ex-
> pelled Union families by the thousands, burned their houses, and declared,
> by an act of your congress, the confiscation of all debts due Northern men
> for goods had and received! Talk thus to the marines, but not to me. . . . If
> we must be enemies, let us be men, and fight it out as we propose to do, and
> not deal in such hypocritical appeals to God and humanity. God will judge
> us in due time, and he will pronounce whether it be more humane to fight
> with a town full of women and the families of a brave people at our back,
> or to remove them in time to places of safety among their own friends and
> people.

For Sherman, God had long ceased to be the governor of this war. The
cause was just and indeed holy, but the conduct profane and disconnected to
God and the Suffering Savior. Sherman's religion was America, and America's
God was a jealous God of law and order, such that all those who resisted
were reprobates who deserved death. To make this war work, Sherman argued in a follow-up letter to Assistant Secretary of State Charles Dana, "We
must and will harden our hearts. Therefore when preachers clamor, and san-
itaries wail, don't join in, but know that war, like the thunderbolt, follows its
laws, and turns not aside even if the beautiful, the virtuous and charitable
stand in its path."[25] Thus absolved of all responsibilities or accountability,
Sherman could blame the enemy for anything and everything that happened
to them. They deserved it.

While Southerners were horrified to read Sherman's callous words,
Northerners thrilled to the rhetoric and cried for more. It has often been said
by scholars and writers who wish to absolve Sherman of moral culpability
that he talked tougher than he behaved. But that is irresponsibly evasive.
Sherman did have a cadet's sense of honor and integrity, and his word was his
bond. Take Lincoln's words at Gettysburg at face value, then take Sherman's
words at Atlanta—and Sweetwater, and Roswell Mill, and numerous stops to
come.

In response to Sherman's claim that citizens were used as human shields,
Hood pointed out what everyone who knew Union armies understood:

> There are a hundred thousand witnesses that you fired into the habitations
> of women and children for weeks, firing far above and miles beyond my line

of defense. I have too good an opinion, founded both upon observation and experience, of the skill of your artillerists, to credit the insinuation that they for several weeks unintentionally fired too high for my modest field-works, and slaughtered women and children by accident and want of skill.[26]

Whether shields or innocent targets, it did not matter to Sherman. There were no innocents anymore, and everyone got what they deserved.

Both generals had legitimate moral complaints to make, but they came far too late and too little to matter. Halleck, Grant, and Lincoln all signed off on Sherman's proposal and heaped praise on him. Civilians were not innocents in this citizens' war and their nerves had to be shattered if their will was to be broken. But this did not include deliberate "slaughter" of women and children, as Hood accused. Even Sherman had his strict limitations. By adhering to the letter of the law and avoiding, for the most part, violent crimes of rape and murder, Sherman could defend his actions as just.

In fact, both generals were disingenuous, preferring a massive destructive war, no matter what the consequences. And both generals were right. By holing up in the city and exposing civilians to the risk of artillery assaults, Hood was, in effect, using them as human shields. And in pursuing his "hard" war, Sherman was right that there were no "innocents" in this citizens' war. Even old people and children must feel its hard edge.

In Washington Lincoln was far less concerned with Sherman's conduct of the war (which he approved) than with the implications of the Atlanta victory for the coming national election. Before Atlanta, Lincoln had been certain he would lose. He drew up contingency plans for a massive escalation in the time he had left before the inauguration of his rival. But, like Grant, he now imagined that victory would be his, as did ordinary citizens. In a letter from John M. Howe to his brother, Howe wrote: "Our glorious old ship Constitution and Union must and will be preserved by electing Abe for the presidency. . . . I well know and so do you that there is a party composed of bloodlessness and ignorance with a few traitors at the head that are bound to break up the Union. But the God on high has flanked them in giving the union army the victory at Atlanta."[27]

Confederate critics of Northern fasts and religiosity had a point when they accused Northerners of trusting in guns more than God. As citizens of Virginia and Georgia reeled from the massive destruction unleashed by Grant and Sherman and sought the face of God, Northerners thought ahead to summer vacations in August. On the day of the Northern fast, the *American Presbyterian* issued an editorial, complaining, "It is to be regretted that the very general scattering of church-going people, with their pastors, in pursuit of health and recreation, will interfere with the public celebration of this day."[28] In Branford, Connecticut, the Episcopal rector Frederick Lewin complained that as the South starved, the "sins of the north" multiplied in extravagance and materialism. People were getting wealthy! Women were dressing up! Reform must begin with the individual: "The Sabbath-breaker and the profane swearer, the drunkard and the profligate, the skeptic and the infidel, and all who forget God and break his laws . . . are real enemies to this country—strong obstacles in the way of lasting peace and prosperity."[29]

On the same fast day that the *American Presbyterian* decried the lack of public following for a fast in summer vacation months, it again gnawed at the bone of God in the Constitution. In contrast to the inclusivity of America's civil religion, premised on the separation of church and state, these clergy wanted something explicitly Christian. In an editorial titled, "Shall we be a Christian nation," the editors argued for a constitutional amendment whose preamble would explicitly mention God, Jesus Christ, and the scriptures as "supreme authority." This they posed in opposition to "this senseless clamor about church and State. It is an old stager—a fogy of the fogiest kind."[30]

Although unwilling to proclaim America a Christian nation on the grounds of the separation of church and state, and aware of the Confederacy's boasted Christianity, Lincoln agreed to a compromise that would strengthen the links between Christianity and America's civil religion, while keeping each distinct. Without seeking to amend the Constitution to create a Christian republic, he would create a national motto invoking trust in God and have it struck on the nation's coinage. On April 22, the first coins were struck with the new Federal motto, "In God We Trust," a calculated response to clerical and evangelical demands for a Christian Constitution. Given the materialism condemned in Northern pulpits, Lincoln could not possibly have picked a more ironic symbol to represent Christianity than the nation's cash.

Where Lincoln thought he was Christianizing the Republic, one fast-day preacher argued the reverse. Though he lacked the contemporary terminology of "civil religion," Worcester's James Cruickshanks did perceive that the war was elevating America as its own religion. In words that captured the transformations wrought by the war, he asked: "If indeed God be a God of peace, and he is Almighty, we ask, why is war, with its untold evils, permitted to brood over this fair land?" The answer—instead of trusting in God, the people placed their faith in armies, scanning newspapers daily, looking at little else but the movement of armies: "In a word, the army is the people's God. They idolize it—they worship it." Besides armies, they worshipped "some military leaders." Too much "hero-worship" of generals prevailed:

The American people are given in a peculiar manner to the indulgence of this spirit. The General—whoever he may be—who is on the crest of popularity is, for the time being, the demigod of the nation. If his reputation has been established as a military leader, he becomes the idol of the nation. The people accord to him every attribute except that of deity, and even this— blasphemous as it appears—seems not to be withheld when the people are glutted with the successes of their deified hero.

Faced with such powerful nation worship, Cruickshanks could draw only one conclusion: "We are then as a people a nation of idolaters. We are at once, the most religious, and the most idolatrous people on the globe."[31] Significantly, Cruickshanks did not move from condemnations of nation worship to moral questions about the war itself.

CHAPTER 38

"RED OCTOBER": "THE WORK OF DESTRUCTION"

O n May 15, 1864, at Chambersburg, Pennsylvania, the Reverend F. W. Conrad of the English Lutheran Church delivered a Thanksgiving sermon blasting the Confederate army for unjust conduct: "They have shot down our pickets, fired into our hospitals, bayoneted our wounded, and dispatched our soldiers without quarter. . . . They have seized noncombatants and imprisoned them . . . they have neglected our wounded, amputated their limbs unnecessarily, and maltreated our sick." The conclusion was obvious: "The pages of history are examined in vain, to find examples of meanness and infamy, of cruelty and barbarity, comparable with those inflicted by the rebels."[1] Little could Conrad have realized how prescient he was. Even as he preached, Jubal Early contemplated a direct retaliatory attack on innocent civilians—Chambersburg's civilians.

On July 30 Confederate forces under General John McCausland approached the defenseless town of Chambersburg, Pennsylvania. In retaliation for General David Hunter's tactics in the Shenandoah Valley, McCausland (under Early's orders) imposed an impossible demand on the citizens of Chambersburg: come up with a cash payout of $500,000 specie in compensation for Hunter's destruction of VMI and the governor's mansion, or see their town burned to the ground. Unable to raise the money, and disbelieving the threat as too callous even for men at war, the citizens waited. A reluctant McCausland, on orders from Early, then put the inner city to the torch, leaving only the home of a respected veteran and the Masonic Temple standing. Before the fires subsided, 278 houses, factories, and businesses lay in rubble.

Though later uneasy with his actions, McCausland claimed the work as "fair retaliation" for Hunter's destruction of VMI (his alma mater). An outraged President Lincoln—who had no qualms about destroying Confederate property—ordered Grant to move on Early, which he did by sending his most trusted general, Philip Sheridan, into the valley with orders to "follow Early to the death."

As the generals held sway in their relentless grip, the conflict rapidly degenerated into a war of raids on civilian properties in both the North and the South. Years later, Early remained unrepentant. The act was "just" because "retaliation" was part of the "laws of war." Writing in 1887, Early recalled that it "afforded me no pleasure to subject non-combatants to the rigors of war, but I felt that I had a duty to perform to the people for whose homes I was fighting and I endeavored to perform it, however disagreeable it might be."[2]

Based on this form of just-war theory, fully articulated as well in the North, the way was clear for Southern citizens to celebrate the destruction as just and estimable. In an editorial from the *Charleston Courier*, reprinted by an equally vengeful *New York Times*, the writer asserted: "If our Government is unable to protect their property and the persons of those most dear to them, it should permit them and their comrades to strike avengeful blows, to burn, devastate and destroy."[3] President Davis also approved of the raid and endorsed subsequent assaults on civilian property, even as this citizens' war careened increasingly out of control.

Predictably, Northern generals responded to Early in kind, continuing the spiral of attacks on civilian property. On August 1 Sheridan assumed command of the newly commissioned forty-three-thousand-man Army of the Shenandoah with Grant's orders to hunt down Early's sixteen-thousand-man army: "Wherever the enemy goes let our troops go also."[4]

Grant commanded Sheridan to take all able-bodied men under fifty as "prisoners of war" and to "take all provisions, forages and stock wanted for the use of your command. Such as cannot be consumed, destroy." Grant's orders specifically exempted buildings from the swath of destruction, but with no food, the buildings meant little. Still, in Sheridan's view, this was a sound strategy, both in retaliation for Chambersburg and for civilian demoralization. "Reduction to poverty," he later claimed "brings prayers for peace more surely and more quickly than does the destruction of human life."[5]

Here, in a nutshell, was the essence of the new Northern strategy of hard war—a strategy that encompassed soldier and civilian alike and that treated all as the "enemy." For John Emerson Anderson, attached to General Banks's corps in Tennessee protecting railroad lines, it was appropriate to deal summarily with the "bushwhackers or guerrillas" who attacked innocent civilians in Tennessee: "As they have shown no mercy to their victims they are quietly turned over to the guard with the remark from the presiding officer of the court to take them away to the mountains and not bring them back again."[6]

Generals on both sides liked to talk about the army as the people. When President Davis was considering reinstituting the patrician and socially divisive Society of the Cincinnati, Lee warned him not to: "I think it important to unite as closely as possible the interests of the army with the interests of the citizens. They are one in reality and all for the Country."[7] But when the people were treated as the army, moral issues arose that none were prepared to recognize.

Critics of retaliatory war were relatively rare when speaking of acts done by their own soldiers, as distinct from acts done to their own by the enemy. With absolute moral right on each side, both possessed a blank check for just retaliation. The prominent exceptions, of course, were Northern Democrats who questioned whether General Hunter had done the things he was accused of and blamed Northern Republicans for pursuing a war in which they got in kind what they deserved. In Chambersburg the Democratic organ, *Valley Spirit*, blamed Republicans and specifically Horace Greeley (who had criticized the people of Chambersburg for cowardice) for the burning:

> The conduct of Mr. Greeley is the more inexcusable for the reason that the burning of Chambersburg was the indirect result of his barbarous teachings. From the very beginning of this war a certain class of fanatical men in the north, of whom Mr. Greeley is chief, have urged a system of warfare against the South totally inconsistent with the civilization of the age. To burn and destroy, lay waste and make desolate the Southern territory was their theory of war. They never seemed to dream of [Confederate] retaliation.[8]

When General McClellan received the nomination at the August convention in Chicago, hopes ran high. Democrats no less than Republicans revered generals, and in "Little Mac" they believed they had found the winning formula. But when Peace Democrats demanded a plank for armistice inserted into their platform, they were only one Union victory away from disaster.

In September disaster happened. With Sherman's occupation of Atlanta and Sheridan's movements in the Shenandoah Valley, the tide suddenly swung in Lincoln's favor. The ill-fated insurgency of John C. Frémont did not amount to anything, and Lincoln was easily renominated in September, with victory now in his grasp. The Republican platform endorsed all of Lincoln's war measures, demanded the unconditional surrender of the Confederacy, and proposed a constitutional amendment to abolish slavery. To emphasize the mandate to restore Union, the party temporarily renamed itself the National Union Party and nominated for vice president Andrew Johnson, a Tennessee Democrat who had remained loyal to the Union and stayed in the Senate.

Besides endorsing all of Lincoln's policies, the Republicans had no comment on the conduct of the war or the ways in which Sherman and Sheridan were treating noncombatants. The streams of homeless refugees multiplied and the historian James M. McPherson estimates that as many as fifty thousand Confederate civilians probably perished.[9] Still, no one asked hard questions.

That the Republicans remained quiet and incurious may be predictable, especially in an election year. The Democrats' blind eye is more surprising. Democratic critics adamantly opposed emancipation and decried the Republican administration's constitutional abuses, but they said little about the conduct of the war, even as it moved into its "hard" phase against Southern civilians. It may be overstated to claim that this joint avoidance was a "conspiracy of silence." Yet it is certainly the case that neither side evidenced the least desire to question the conduct of their generals in the field, who as often as not commanded as many Democratic soldiers as Republican soldiers.[10]

While slow to comment on the conduct of the war, Democratic boosters did not hesitate to step up their racist platform. At every opportunity, Democrats pumped up their racist denunciations of African Americans and almost paranoid fears of miscegenation. Music, incorporated in the struggle for the North's political soul, featured the same racist themes, often to the tunes of the classics. In place of the "John Brown Tune," they sang:

> Tell Ole Abe to let the nigger be;
> We don't want the darkies free—
> Glory, glory, Hallelujah!

And in place of the traditional "We Are Coming, Father Abraham," they sang:

> We are coming, Father Abraham,
>   Two millions strong I'm sure,
> To drive you from the White House;
>   Abe, your acts we can't endure.
> You suppressed the habeas corpus, Abe;
>   You imprisoned without cause,
> And trampled on our sacred rights
>   The constitution and laws.[11]

By fall it became clear that public reactions to the Emancipation Proclamation would determine the election.

Meanwhile, on the battlefield, Lincoln continued to roll out his agenda for total war. With Grant investing Petersburg for the winter, the principal theaters of action shifted to the Shenandoah Valley and Georgia. Like Grant and Sherman, Sheridan was attacking not only an army but also a symbolic legend in Jubal Early, whose raid on Washington's outskirts had terrified the nation even as his wanton destruction of Chambersburg enraged them.

When word reached Sheridan that two of Early's divisions were sent back to Petersburg, he employed his numerical advantage immediately and, on September 19, routed Early's smaller forces at the third battle of Winchester. The losses on both sides were heavy, with Sheridan losing 4,018 and Early 3,921.

With a characteristic arrogance that Northerners loved and Confederates hated, Sheridan brazenly announced: "I attacked the forces of General Early on the Berryville Pike at the crossing of Opequon Creek, and after a most stubborn and sanguinary engagement, which lasted from early in the morning until 5 o'clock in the evening, completely defeated him, and driving him through Winchester captured about 2,500 prisoners, five pieces of artillery, nine army flags and most of their wounded."[12]

These were the sorts of boastful and destructive words Northern audiences (and Lincoln) wanted to hear. Others were more humble. For the surgeon Daniel M. Holt, physician to the 121st New York Volunteers attached to Sheridan's army, the victory was divinely ordained: "I cannot sufficiently extol and magnify His name, nor with sufficient humility prostrate myself before Him. Forgive me, oh my savior for ever distrusting Thy power, or ever rebelling against Thee."[13]

The news for the Confederacy was not good. Sheridan's victory virtually restored Union control of the lower valley from the Potomac to Strasburg, effectively securing Pennsylvania and Maryland from any further incursions. Following the victory Sheridan wasted no time in pursuing Early's fleeing army up the valley and, on September 22, inflicted another grave blow on Early's rebels posted on Fisher's Hill. Overwhelmed by Union soldiers, the Confederates broke in what Sheridan later sketched as an "indescribable panic." Although not the total defeat that Sheridan hoped for, the results were encouraging.[14]

Sheridan's Shenandoah campaign would put the death knell to Democratic hopes for the 1864 election, which, as late as August, ran high. Whatever distant possibilities persisted after Atlanta were now utterly lost. Lincoln and his Republican Party would rule four more years—more than enough time to subdue the rebellion by force of arms and restore a united Christian America.

When, on October 3, Sheridan's engineer officer, Lieutenant John R. Meigs, was reportedly murdered by three men dressed in Union uniforms, Sheridan's response was swift and harsh. The people must suffer:

> The fact that the murder had been committed inside our lines was evidence that the perpetrators of the crime, having their homes in the vicinity, had been clandestinely visiting them, and had been secretly harbored by some of the neighboring residents. Determining to teach a lesson to these abettors of the foul deed—a lesson they would never forget—I ordered all the houses within an area of five miles to be burned. General Custer . . . was charged with this duty, and the next morning proceeded to put the order into execution.[15]

Earlier, in May and June, Hunter had employed identical tactics against supposed abettors of John Singleton Mosby's irregular rangers, ordering that "the houses and other property of every secession sympathizer residing within a circuit of five miles from the place of outrage, shall be destroyed by fire."[16]

Left unsaid by Sheridan was the obvious fact that many innocents suffered alongside those guilty of harboring saboteurs. Even more disturbing is the fact that he wrote this years later, by which time it was well known that Lieutenant Meigs had not, in fact, been murdered by local guerrillas. He died while attempting to flee his Confederate captors.[17] The whole rationale had been a ruse to pummel innocent civilians. No matter, the valley war was rapidly moving into its "hard" phase.

With a nose for blood, Sheridan's army chased Early's fleeing troops for thirteen miles to New Market, where they were forced to hole up. In letters to his wife, Daniel M. Holt described the military and civilian scene: "Never since I was born, did I have such real *sport* in following up a band of disorganized flying rebels. It pays for all our hard marches and sleepless nights." In confronting the citizens, he noted both their resignation and their hatred: "The women are particularly hostile and wolfish."[18]

With Early bottled up, if not utterly defeated, Sheridan moved to phase two of the plan: destruction of more civilian property. Victory over the rebel army was important, but no more important than the second objective, in Grant's oft-cited command, to turn "the Shenandoah Valley [into] a barren waste . . . so that crows flying over it for the balance of this season will have to carry their provender with them."

Grant's motives in making such draconian orders were twofold. First, by destroying all food and material products that would be useful to Confederate *armies*—principally Lee's Army of Northern Virginia—the enemy might quite literally be starved into defeat. Second, as Sherman discovered in Atlanta and soon rediscovered in the Carolinas, the destruction of food and property could break the will of the Southern white population to continue the war. Bereft of food and shelter, with their own armies unable to protect them from the enemy, the civilians would supposedly crumple.

The plan was sound and, in fact, eventually triumphed. Few asked if it was right. Ultimately, the moral justification for this action, stated or unstated, was relentlessly simple: the Federals recognized no "civilians" or noncombatants in the South. Since some Confederates harbored guerrillas, citizens were rendered de facto "irregulars"—in effect, fair targets. It was no longer simply the Confederate army that brought war to the Union on West Point terms, but "the South," and that meant women, children, and the elderly, as well as soldiers and guerrillas. Many Union soldiers did not have the stomach for such tactics, but those who did justified them on the basis of "military necessity" in fighting a just "defensive" war that was unwillingly brought upon them.

Here again, we come to a moral touchstone of the war. Grant and Lincoln's moral justification for orders to Sheridan and Sherman presumed not only a nation of Confederates but a nation of guerrillas as well. Yet the evidence for widespread terrorism is scant. Just as army atrocity stories were exaggerated, so also were Northern fears about an armed and violent civilian population. Life in Charleston, Richmond, or New Orleans went on. Women were too busy supporting their families to be saboteurs. Men were either impressed or on the run or old. By 1864, moreover, following the savagery in Missouri, Confederate leaders were disbanding irregular forces and would eventually repeal the Partisan Ranger Act.

Still, Lincoln and the North needed a moral rationale if the destruction was to continue. Most Northern civilians—especially Republicans—were more than prepared to endorse virtually any rationalization as long as it came from the state and the army. Emancipation worked as a moral lever for escalating the military destruction of armies in the field but not for inflicting civilian suffering, especially suffering by the nonslaveholding majority of white Southerners in the Shenandoah Valley. There needed to be a terrorist threat to justify the destruction of nonmilitary targets. And that is precisely what the Union generals, and Lincoln, and, to be sure, pesky rebel bushwhackers, provided.

Sheridan understood his commanders' intentions exactly and set out immediately, "carrying out . . . my original instructions for desolating the Shenandoah country, so as to make it untenable for permanent occupation by the Confederates." Valley farmers, of course, had no knowledge of the orders. When with little warning, Sheridan's infantry ominously appeared on the landscape, followed by the dreaded cavalry, no Confederate army was in sight to defend the civilians. Soon, the wrath of God had descended into their midst. The results were immediate and devastating. Wherever the families looked, "the many columns of smoke from burning stacks, and mills filled with grain, indicated that the adjacent country was fast losing the features which hitherto had made it a great magazine of stores for the Confederate armies."[19]

Thus began "Red October" in the valley, when "the work of destruction" began and civilians howled. In all, Sheridan calculated that in a matter of weeks, "I have destroyed over 2,000 barns filled with wheat, hay and farming implements; over 70 mills, filled with flour and wheat; have driven in front of the army over 4,000 head of stock, and have killed and issued to the troops not less than 3,000 sheep." He then added ominously, "The people here are getting sick of the war."

While right about the destruction he wrought in the valley, Sheridan was wrong to assume that "the people" were broken. The people were tired of war but their will had not been broken—especially not that of the women left to view the devastation. The refrain, "we are all loyal," rang throughout the zones of desolation. In Harrisonburg, twenty-eight women petitioned Secretary of War James A. Seddon to raise and arm a regiment of ladies "to leave our hearthstones—to endure any sacrifice—any privation for the ultimate success of our Holy Cause."[20]

If the distant Northern civilian population turned deaf and blind to the civilian suffering unleashed by Sherman and Sheridan, witnesses were not so easily sanguine. Union surgeon Daniel M. Holt considered the destruction appalling. Local "hostility" could not justify the virtually indiscriminate ruin: "A prettier or more fruitful Valley never lay stretched out upon the face of the Earth than this. It goes to destruction by order of General Grant." The next day he wrote, "It might in truth be said that we are *foraging* to an awful extent. Nothing that lives and is used as food or in anywise conduces to the comfort of men, is left behind. We take *all* we can and *burn* what we cannot get away."

One act struck him as especially damnable: "At Mount Jackson, our boys did an act which must be condemned by every lover of humanity. They burned a hospital in which there were a few sick men. Of course the sick were removed, but the act of destruction of their hospital building ought to

be punished by death. None but heathen will thus mar the beauty of civilization. Stonewall Jackson had endeared himself to his people, and won our respect by erecting five comfortable structures like the one destroyed, and in
burying the dead in well laid out ground." Significantly, no Federal soldiers,
let alone officers, were ever called to account.

As the devastation peaked throughout the valley, Holt entered the final
entries in his journal before his medical discharge for diphtheria: "You can
form no idea of the gloom, which overspreads the whole region. One heavy,
black cloud of smoke hangs over the Valley like the pall of death. Lurid
streaks of flame dart up through the pitchy blackness relieving for a second
or two the stately building which is being devoured by hungry flames." Later
he wrote:

> The inhabitants look on like doomed culprits while their property is de-
> stroyed before their eyes. A stoical indifference appears to have taken pos-
> session of them as regards their fate. No resistance is made to any act, which
> we see fit to commit. They appear to think that their day has come, and
> nothing but death or starvation is in store for them.

Yet even in the midst of dissolution, saving acts of kindness appeared:
"The hardest feature in this universal conflagration is, that many real innocent and Union-loving people suffer. These, as everywhere, are poor—less
able to stand the pressure than the more opulent. Hundreds of such are leaving their homes in groups of a dozen or twenty. Some in better circumstances
than others, pick up their little all, and placing it in an old rickety wagon,
drawn by an animal pitiful to behold, while the greater part come straggling
on Gipsey like, fed by our boys from provisions in their haversacks."

For most of the families, Holt remembered old and young alike "sleeping
out as none others can, with scanty covering, either of bedding or clothing."
Some of the "poor white trash" were "trading with and consorting with slaves
who look upon them as inferiors, such as they *really* are." On October 7 he
recorded: "The whole Valley in a blaze. Heavy dark clouds of smoke hang
over it like a funeral pall. Cannot [help] but [feel] compassionate [for] the
case of the poor deluded people."[21]

Although by Sheridan's own self-serving calculations, Early had been destroyed in one of the greatest military displays of the war, he was not yet
gone. There were yet more battles to be fought in October. While visiting
President Lincoln in Washington on October 17, Sheridan learned that
Longstreet was detached from Petersburg to join up with Early in the valley.

Sheridan rushed back to Mill Creek and Winchester the following day, and there witnessed the horrifying reality of his army in pell-mell retreat from their camp behind Cedar Creek. It was an "appalling spectacle of a panic-stricken army—hundreds of slightly wounded men, throngs of others unhurt but utterly demoralized . . . telling only too plainly that a disaster had occurred at the front." Sheridan stormed ahead, enraged, knowing he had the confidence of his soldiers and cursing at them to regroup, shoulder their weapons, and turn on the attacker.

With alacrity the troops rallied and marched toward the enemy, "changing in a moment from the depths of depression to the extreme of enthusiasm." Like a secular revivalist dependent on "enthusiasm" to win a battle, Sheridan took a valuable lesson on leadership: "I already knew that even in the ordinary condition of mind enthusiasm is a potent element with soldiers, but what I saw that day convinced me that if it can be excited from a state of despondency its power is almost irresistible."[22] This was the same lesson that Lee had learned in the Wilderness, again confirming the sheer power of the right generals to snatch victories from the jaws of defeat. It was also a reality to which Republicans thrilled as news of Sheridan's heroic charge spread, adding as much luster to the political campaign as to the military.

In the North, few evidenced regrets at the destruction; even as it escalated, the moral rhetoric remained rote and unchanged. In a September 11, 1864, thanksgiving sermon, preached in recognition of Sheridan's work in the valley, Joseph P. Thompson discoursed on "The Bible Doctrine Concerning War": "We are upon Biblical ground, therefore, when we invoke God in doing battle for a just cause, and we are following Biblical precedent when we ascribe to him the victory." As for the South: "The war which they are waging upon the Government of the United States is an unholy war, a monstrous conspiracy of crime."[23]

The martyred dead remained committed to their altars. In a column titled "How a Soldier Died," the writer described a deathbed scene and then added, "May their memory never be dishonored . . . they are martyrs whose lives have been a free-will offering on our country's altar."[24]

For New Haven's Congregational pastor Elisha Cleaveland, Union victories mandated a partisan Republican endorsement from the pulpit. The Union's duty was clear: "We must crush their armies," and to do that, no equivocating or suing for armistice as the Democrats advocated could be considered. Destruction was the order of the day, and that meant a Republican administration pursuing total war:

Is this the selected moment to talk of an armistice, when Sherman is marching on from conquering to conquer, and our glorious flag is waving triumphantly in the very heart of Georgia,—when Grant is drawing a tourniquet around the neck of the rebel capital that is already producing incipient strangulation? Is it at this supreme hour of hope that we are to withdraw our forces and raise the blockade? When a little more persistence a few more vigorous blows would annihilate the Confederacy is it *then* we would strike our flag and sue for peace? O where is our manhood, where is our patriotism, where is our common sense, where is our faith pledged to the noble men who have fought our battles, the living and the dead?[25]

By 1864 the pulpit had become, in effect, a political platform for Republican rule. Clearly, nothing short of devastation would do. The enabling words "God" and "Providence" no longer needed to be invoked. "Manhood," "patriotism," and "common sense" could do it all, and they required "strangulation."

CHAPTER 39

"A VOTE FOR PRINCIPLE, FOR CONSCIENCE, FOR CHRIST"

Grant, Sherman, and Sheridan did what no Republican editor, orator, or even president could do. With their crushing military campaigns and remorseless destruction of civilian property, they brought the end in sight. With victory the gods would be propitiated, and the nation would be sanctified and made whole. Whatever moral lines were crossed, the political consequences were inevitable. Lincoln would be reelected and Republicans would govern the Republic as they saw fit.

At a thanksgiving service "for recent military successes," conducted at New Haven's Third Congregational Church on September 11, 1864, the Reverend Elisha Cleaveland celebrated the recent victories of Admiral David Farragut at Mobile Bay and Grant at Weldon Railroad, but was especially effusive about Sherman's capture of Atlanta: "It is reasonable to expect that a general so sagacious, energetic and untiring, so patriotic and determined, with so splendid an army at his command, will not be slow to follow up this brilliant success with movements which will soon reduce the rebellion to its last extremity."

In a nation that mythologized its "Puritan" origins, it was no sacrilege to transform the election of Christian leaders into dutiful priests for America's God. By 1864 the pulpit and religious press were so caught up in the holy cause that they supported not only the war but also the Republican Party in explicitly partisan ways. The "spirituality of the church" had long since disappeared, but a new chapter emerged as pulpits and presses endorsed candidates. On the eve of the election, the *American Presbyterian* told its readers in no uncertain terms of their "simple and solemn duty" to vote, and for whom to vote: "Every vote cast for Mr. Lincoln is a declaration for liberty, for law, for humanity."[1] For their part, readers and congregations demanded such endorsements from the church, and any minister who dared quibble suffered the consequences of rebuke and/or termination.

Northern sermons were shamelessly partisan, implying to their listeners that it would be sinful to vote Democratic. Joseph P. Thompson proclaimed it base "to pervert this holy aspiration for peace, into a partisan cry, that means not peace but place; not peace for the nation but place for a candidate." Democrats, he continued, were "partisan" while Republicans were "just." Recognition of the Confederacy meant sectional war for generations, "but if we secure a just peace then will the nation hold the place given to its continent in Mercator's projection of the globe—the central figure of the civilized world; the seas kissing its feet upon either side; the isles and continents bowing their obeisance from afar. That is the recognition that we shall win for the Union itself by a decisive victory."[2]

Denominational reactions to the Democratic convention were swift and, in the main, partisan Republican. Seven Methodist Episcopal annual conferences condemned all talk of "armistice" or "compromise" as "unchristian and sinful." Eleven Baptist associations were outspoken in their opposition to the Democratic platform on religious grounds. Similarly Old and New School Presbyterians instructed their members to support the Lincoln government. At the local level, clergymen participated actively at ward meetings and Republican rallies. At the same time that they urged all to vote for Lincoln, they did not hesitate to brand their Democratic opponents with the ominous label of "disloyalty."[3]

Some clerical voices, few and far between, dared to question the orthodoxy of their denomination and its political preaching. If Republican clergy accused Democrats of tolerating and even promoting sin in their refusal to condemn slavery, Democrats pointed to the hypocrisy of their moralistic critics. If the war was so just, they asked, why were ministers only too eager to allow their congregations to pay the $300 commutation fee to get them out of the draft? And whatever happened to love as "the greatest" Christian virtue, when they preached not only a just war for a just cause, but just "revenge" and "vengeance"? As for national fast and thanksgiving days proclaimed by the state, these were a perversion of the original Puritan holy days and occasions to promote the war and the Republican Party that fomented it.

A writer for the *Chicago Times* complained that Lincoln's thanksgiving proclamations were blasphemous for implying that "the Almighty has indorsed the political policies of the [Lincoln] administration."[4] And when Republicans continued their campaign to put God and Jesus Christ as the "Lord and Savior of all" into the Constitution, Democrats roundly denounced the intrusion of religion into government.

The most sensational cases occurred in Missouri, where partisan loyalties verged on violence and Democratic clergy hounded from their pulpits. One especially famous—or infamous—incident surrounded the Presbyterian minister Samuel B. McPheeters, who refused to speak out against slavery or for the Republican Party. For his silence, he was branded "disloyal," arrested by Major General F. A. Dick, and ordered to leave the state in ten days.

Dick's orders were remanded by Lincoln, but McPheeters's congregation would not leave him alone. At a church trial in St. Louis, congregants ordered that the minister "shall cease all connection with that Church." Charles Hodge, who by this point had come around to see slavery as a sin, and who personally disagreed with the extreme position McPheeters took, nevertheless regarded the punishment as "an injustice which has few, if any, parallels in the history of our church." As later summarized by the denominational historian Lewis G. Vander Velde:

> The first consideration with the majority in this General Assembly of 1864 . . . was not whether justice should prevail, but rather whether the Assembly should avoid any possible suspicion of disloyalty. Thus it was found necessary to sustain the action of a Presbytery which had decided to punish for disloyalty a man in whom the highest Federal authorities could find no fault.[5]

Long a thorn in clerical Republicans' sides, Henry J. Van Dyke, a Democratic Presbyterian of New York, was even more adamant in attacking his denomination. In a sermon preached to the synod of New York on October 18, and with the McPheeters case in mind, Van Dyke launched into a broad-range attack on the wholesale political sellout of the Northern Protestant Church—and Presbyterians in particular. From the lowest to the highest levels, he complained, denominational officials compromised the doctrine of the spirituality and independence of the church from politics—perhaps fatally.

For Van Dyke, it was an open question of whether the church could ever recover a prophetic, spiritual voice. Asking whether the apostles "entered into the political and military contests of the countries through which the saints were scattered abroad," he vented his spleen. Emancipation became the badge of lost innocence, a tool that was shamelessly employed to gain political advantage under the cloak of righteousness: "What I assert and propose to prove, is, that in connection with this subject of slavery, and under the cover of it, the Assembly has handled and determined a question which is purely political, and entirely beyond its appropriate province . . . and invaded the liberty wherewith, according to our standards, Christ has made his people free." The general assembly, he continued,

> had no [ecclesial] constitutional right to step in between these two political parties and take sides with the Republicans in regard to the great question by which they are divided . . . it throws the whole moral influence of the Assembly in favor of one political party and . . . if its recommendations were faithfully carried out in the true spirit and intent, every minister and every member of the Presbyterian Church would be an adherent of that [Republican] party.[6]

Van Dyke was probably right. Rarely, if ever, has a major denomination officially endorsed one party over another since the Civil War. But in 1864, when passions ran high, "the whole moral influence" of the church had become captive of the state and its Republican orthodoxy. Lincoln's wager paid handsome dividends as participants redefined the "cause" of the war to mean emancipation, thereby justifying not only total war for unconditional surrender but also Republican hegemony.

It is doubtful that the political issue of "the Union" could have sustained campaigns of such unmitigated violence, slaughter, and civilian suffering. But when transformed from just war to a Republican-led religious crusade, limitations disappeared, "conduct" was subordinated to victory, and victory apotheosized into one divine right against wrong. God now depended on a righteous American empire as much as the empire depended on Him. Indeed, as explained from most Northern pulpits, the two were one in the same.

With strong support from the churches and the soldiers, Lincoln easily won reelection. McClellan's strongest support in the 1864 presidential election came from Catholics and immigrants, especially Irish, and from rural areas where foreign elements predominated. Lincoln's bedrock were the evangelical Protestant denominations and clergy, native-born citizens, skilled urban workers, and professional classes.[7] In all, Northern Democrats won 45 percent of the popular vote and were especially strong in the border districts and the immigrant wards of large cities. In the congressional elections, most of the Republican losses of the 1862 midterm election were recovered. In the House, Republicans won 145 of the 185 seats, and in the Senate, increased their majority to 42 of 52 seats. The electoral vote was equally definitive, with General McClellan trailing far behind, 212 to 21.

As Sergeant Ransom lay recovering from his stay at Andersonville, he noted that on November 6 the soldiers in the hospital held a mock election that Lincoln won handily. But then he added: "Had this election occurred while we were at Andersonville, four-fifths would have voted for McClellan."[8]

Following the news of Lincoln's resounding reelection, Northern ministers continued to endorse the vote and the Republican Party. In a sermon preached in Harvard Yard, George E. Ellis touted the choice as simple. One party maintained "the one sole purpose of crushing rebellion," while the other was "a party composed of heterogeneous and discordant elements . . . compound, confusing, not definable, except by many distinctions and qualifications."[9]

Confederate presses were equally outspoken in the opposite direction. With word of Lincoln's reelection, the *Richmond Daily Whig* glumly concluded, "There is no middle ground for us to occupy, even if we were so disposed. It is fight, be enslaved, or die; and we feel no hesitation in deciding what to do."[10]

On Thursday, November 25, 1864, Confederate agents did their best to follow Northern examples of civilian intimidation by setting fires in ten or more New York hotels and in Barnum's American Museum. This action followed an earlier raid on October 19 in which Confederate raiders robbed three Vermont banks, making off with more than $200,000 in cash. None did serious damage, but the actions do illustrate a Confederate retaliatory willingness to destroy civilian property and terrorize civilians, insofar as they had the means.

On that same day, Lincoln's national Thanksgiving Day was widely observed by Republican clergy, marking the start of what would become an unbroken chain. The purpose, Lincoln declared, was to observe "a day of Thanksgiving and Praise to Almighty God." Happily, the first observance took place two weeks after his convincing victory at the polls. Again, Republican politics dominated most Northern pulpit oratory. In seeking out a "cause for thanksgiving," Alexander H. Vinton, rector of St. Mark's Church in the Bowerie, did not have far to look: "The huge vote which decided that the war shall go on at whatever cost, was a vote for principle, for conscience, for Christ, and for the blessing of the race whom Christ died to liberate and to save."[11]

By November 1864 Northern clergymen had virtually forgotten their duty to avoid politicking or to care for the oppressed. Since the oppressed—Southern men, women, and children—were the enemy, their plight could be simply noted without judgment. In his address in Paxton, Massachusetts, the Reverend William Phipps urged thanksgiving while others suffered: "Multitudes of families in the land, have been driven from their homes and from all the privileges of a happy household . . . but we have occasion to be thankful, to-day, that such destructions have not reached us."[12]

New England ministers were especially apt to link America's present to their Puritan past and to interpret the national Thanksgiving Day as their gift to the nation. At a "Union Service" in New Britain, Connecticut, the Reverend Lavalette Perrin blatantly ignored the facts of the past and sounded the new orthodoxy that Puritans were not really about the construction of a biblical theocracy and religious intolerance, but about the creation of a democratic redeemer nation, governed by "we the people." Reading back from the Declaration of Independence to New England's Puritan past, Perrin came to the astounding conclusion that "[a]ll men are created equal [was] the pearl of great price for which these spiritual merchantmen of old England, the Puritans, came hither searching."

This patently false but stirring conclusion contained, in embryo, what would become the founding myth of America's civil religion, linking Republican present to Puritan past in one seamless divine destiny where God is "using us . . . in the world's bloody and prolonged struggle for redemption from the grasp and curse of oppression." Having summarized how the Puritans won the Revolution, Perrin went on to show how the Republican Party loyalists were their heirs and constituted the only true party in America: "This was a victory, not of party as against party—not of candidate as against candidate, merely . . . but a victory of principles over prejudice; a victory of patriotism over partisanship; a victory of right and justice over covetousness and selfish ease." Despite being "underdogs" in the struggle, Northern forces had right on their side, and "while the magnificent armies of liberty around Richmond and Atlanta tighten their hold upon the lungs of this writhing monster, let us lift up our hearts with our voices, and sing in grand chorus this one hundredth Psalm."[13]

While Lincoln was singled out for special praise, the generals were not ignored. In a sermon preached on *The Sacrifice of Continual Praise*, Long Island's Cornelius L. Wells singled out the generals for adoration: Grant, "the indomitable hero of Vicksburg . . . and shall I speak of Sherman, the gallant commander of the Army of the South West? . . . From Missionary Ridge to Dalton, from Dalton to Resaca, and Dallas, and Altoon Pass, and Lost Mountain, and on to Marietta; yet on until our victorious hosts enter Atlanta, with banners flying and shouts of victory bursting forth from every heart." Grant and Sherman did not stand alone: "Need I stop to speak of Sheridan; young, bold, intrepid? The victories of the Shenandoah Valley are not eclipsed by any of the whole war."[14]

America's first national Thanksgiving also became the occasion for widespread charitable appeals, in particular for the Christian Commission which, in distinction to the "Unitarian" Sanitary Commission, kept Christ in its charitable activity. In conjunction with Thanksgiving Day, writers for the

American Presbyterian emphasized the need for one million dollars in donations for the Christian Commission, "the only national organization which proposes as its object the salvation of the bodies and souls of our soldiers and sailors." The paper went on in the following week's issue to urge "the best men in the country" to volunteer to visit the army occasionally as members of the commission.

Most writers did not trust the Sanitary Commission and the Unitarians who supported it. One tract, entitled *False Comfort to the Dying Soldier*, told of a Unitarian pamphlet in which was "not a word of a Saviour, not a word of repentance, nor of a day of judgment, but blank, stark universalism." Despite opposing causes, Northern Presbyterians were one with Southern Presbyterians in judging Unitarianism to be "unmitigated heathenism."[15]

CHAPTER 40

"I CAN MAKE THIS MARCH, AND MAKE GEORGIA HOWL!"

While the North did their "simple and solemn duty" by reelecting their war president, Confederates waited anxiously to discover what Sherman would do next. In an attempt to rally the people, President Davis assured the South that Sherman was vulnerable to an attack in his rear. Conventional logic connected armies to their supplies. If you could get in their rear, destroy their supplies, and harass their troops, there would be nowhere to run, "and retreat, sooner or later, he must."

But Sherman had other plans—audacious plans, as it turned out, that took even Grant and Lincoln by surprise. But first he had to attend to Atlanta and Hood's army. With thirty-four thousand infantry and twelve thousand cavalry, Hood remained a formidable but evasive foe who constantly harassed Sherman's superior army without engaging a fixed battle.

After two months of sparring and maneuvering, the two armies remained unchecked, and Sherman was getting edgy. Unwilling to launch a potentially devastating frontal assault on Hood, and knowing he could not protect his rail supplies all the way from Tennessee to Georgia, Sherman came to a radical conclusion. He could eliminate the supply vulnerability by breaking out from his entire army four corps, one cavalry, one artillery—sixty thousand in all—and live off the people of the South, pursuing a course of destruction yet to be determined. The solution to the supply line was brilliantly simple: get rid of the Union supply line altogether, and in the process absolutely demoralize the citizenry whose armies could do nothing to protect them.

On October 9 Sherman telegraphed Grant at City Point:

I propose that we break up the railroad from Chattanooga forward, and that we strike out with our wagons for Milledgeville, Millen, and Savannah. Until

we can repopulate Georgia, it is useless for us to occupy it; but the utter destruction of its roads, houses, and people, will cripple their military resources. By attempting to hold the [rail]roads, we will lose a thousand men
each month, and will gain no result. I can make this march, and make Georgia howl![1]

Sherman had already made the moral leap to justify destroying everything in his path, by redefining citizens as no different from combatants.
Again, civilians would not be directly murdered (though many would no
doubt starve or die of malnutrition), but they would be considered the
enemy. To protect his rear from Hood, Sherman would send a strong holding
detachment under General George Thomas back to Tennessee, where Hood
was heading. Though disappointed, Thomas had an essential role to play: he
would hold Hood's leg while Sherman skinned Georgia alive. Hood could do
nothing about it. Hood would no longer be feared—or even respected; he
would be rendered irrelevant.

Sherman's plan—to head for the Atlantic, out of communication with his
commanders and live off the land and its people as he went along—was unprecedented in scale. Others had done so on a smaller scale: Grant at Vicksburg and Winfield Scott in the Mexican War. But this far outstripped the
earlier occasions. Grant and Lincoln would have to trust Sherman's judgment
to accomplish the plan without their knowing from day to day where he was
or what was emerging.

In time, they trusted him. But not right away. Shortly after proposing his
audacious scheme, Sherman followed up with another, more urgent letter
noting that the rail and communications lines could never remain functioning as long as he was pinned down in Atlanta and Hood's army was free to destroy his lines. But if the offense was taken he could move "with my effective
army . . . through Georgia, smashing things to the sea. . . . Instead of guess-
ing at what [Hood] means to do, he will have to guess at my plans. . . . I can
make Savannah, Charleston, or the mouth of the Chattahoochee. Answer
quick, as I know we will not have the telegraph long."[2]

As Sherman and Grant contemplated the lethal march through the heartland
of the South, Confederates around Virginia were desperately trying to rally
the people to whatever form of fight the war required. The times were bleak.
A writer for the Richmond's *Central Presbyterian* lamented the fact that even
religion was suffering: "There have been many hindrances to the regular and
efficient use of the means upon which the church depends for success."[3]
Some were even considering enlisting slaves in return for their freedom,

though in 1864 that was premature and generally rejected both officially and privately.[4] Orators rushed to recount the great "historic significance" of "The Southern Revolution," but they saw few signs of success.

Inevitably, Confederates began to question whether their leaders had the ear of God, in particular their president. Although a consummate bureaucrat, courageous warrior, and loyal friend, Davis nevertheless lacked rhetorical charisma. He remained unable to harness a moral vision to his cause with sufficient power and clarity to overcome mounting trials and disappointments. When Northern Republicans turned to Lincoln for moral vision, the Confederacy seemed only to turn to their generals, especially Robert E. Lee.

In a desperate message sent to the Confederate Congress on November 7 and timed to influence the North's presidential election the following day, Jefferson Davis signaled a willingness to fight any kind of war that victory over the hated North required. In words that belied the original presumption of fixed armies protecting citizens and cities, he fell back on a different, grimmer rhetoric:

> There are no vital points on the preservation of which the continued existence of the Confederacy depends. There is no military success of the enemy, which can accomplish its destruction. Not in the fall of Richmond, nor Wilmington, nor Savannah, nor Mobile, nor of all combined, can save the enemy from the constant and exhaustive drain of blood and treasure, which must continue until he shall discover that no peace is attainable unless based on the recognition of our indefeasible rights.[5]

Davis's call to fight on without cities or armies was a call to guerrilla warfare and terrorism. If enacted it would complete Sherman's prophecy, making civilians into soldiers. In a profound—if demonic—sense it represented another side of Sherman's moral logic that, if implemented, would hoist Sherman and his commanders on their own petard—a literal blurring of the line between Southern soldiers and civilians. Moreover, by making Sherman's case literally true—no innocents in the white South—it was a war the South *could* win despite Sherman's legions.[6] Many Southerners, moreover, would have agreed that Sherman deserved it. But was it just? With Missouri in view, most Confederate generals resisted this draconian option. Soon enough, all these cities would indeed fall, leading to the question of who would ultimately control the fate of the Confederacy, the president or the generals?

If Davis's communications were the language of a doomed cause, they were also a rich source of intelligence for Sherman, who read the Southern papers carefully and learned of Hood's movements and intentions. He learned as well that Governor Brown of Georgia, a critic of the Davis admin-istration, withdrew his state troops from Hood's army for the purpose of gath-ering in the season's crops. Besides the open feuding between president and governor that this action signaled, it also told Sherman that rich food supplies intended for the people could be his for the taking.

As the country faced its bloodiest battles throughout 1864, the Union generals came to know each other well. They gained a personal sense not only of their fellow generals—with Grant and Sherman being the epitome—but also of the enemy. In correspondence with one another, generals would routinely refer to the enemy army as "Lee" or "Sherman" or Hood" rather than use the name of the armies themselves. When Lincoln ordered Grant to "Get Lee" instead of "Get the Army of Northern Virginia," he was instinc-tively underlining how critical the generals were to the success or failure of the war effort both on the battlefield and, perhaps even more, on the home front.

Well might Lincoln personalize the war around the generals, for in fact, by 1864, they dictated its conduct. And in this arena, at least, it would be in-accurate to say that silence greeted the subject of just conduct in the war. De facto, the generals determined what was "just" conduct through edict and ex-perience and articulated it in the form of orders that were invariably sup-ported by their administrations. And invariably they found any conduct, short of rapine and genocide, just. The generals proved as adept in covering their moral flanks as they were in covering their infantry flanks in time of battle. The war effort depended on both. For the war to play out in the way that it did, it was imperative to protect both flanks or see the cause turned and rolled up.

Many questioned military tactics, especially in defeat, but no voices questioned the generals' deliberations or rethought criteria for just and unjust conduct. Clergy, intellectuals, artists, and journalists remained silent. The generals made the hard pragmatic decisions of war and then turned to the public moralists—chiefly the clergy—to provide moral justification and en-dorsement or, failing that, to turn a deaf ear. This conspiracy of silence over just conduct goes a long way to explain how military destruction and civilian suffering reached the levels they did.

In 1864 Sherman *needed* his moral flanks covered even as he traveled into unknown areas—geographically and ethically. Though prepared to support Sherman, Grant and Lincoln were skeptical. The gains, of course, were im-mense. So were the risks. In the end, the consequences of doing nothing loomed larger than the risks of approving Sherman's march.

In the Confederacy, Davis and Hood proved a horrible match for one another. In their common repudiation of Johnston's policy of protraction, they played right into Union hands. A protracted war might have won the South its independence. An attack risked suicide. Grant recognized that at last both sides had grown weary of war, but the South could hold out longer if its armies remained intact and on the move.

"In the North," Grant later observed, "the people governed, and could stop hostilities whenever they chose to stop supplies. The South was a military camp, controlled absolutely by the government with the soldiers to back it, and the war could have been protracted, no matter to what extent the discontent reached, up to the point of open mutiny of the soldiers themselves."[7] While correct about the South, Grant was wrong to suppose a different North. There, too, war would continue until the soldiers mutinied.

To prepare for his grueling march, Sherman spent much of October neutralizing Hood and ensuring that his army could not be attacked from the rear should Hood decide to reverse directions. By October 26, when Sherman learned that Hood was moving south into Decatur, Alabama, he knew the way was paved for his "long-contemplated project." General Thomas would check (and soon defeat) Hood in Tennessee, and Sherman faced no further significant military obstacles. The heartland would be his for the taking, if only Grant and Lincoln would say yes.

On November 1 a still-skeptical General Grant instructed Sherman to first destroy Hood's army. Sherman replied that if he tried, Hood would simply keep running to draw Sherman out of Georgia and delay the whole campaign. Nothing would be gained, especially with General Thomas's army more than capable of blocking Hood in Tennessee: "I am convinced the best results will follow from our defeating Jeff. Davis's cherished plan of making me leave Georgia by maneuvering."[8] Finally, on November 2, Grant agreed to sign off on Sherman's scheme of a "march to the sea."

With Grant's and Lincoln's approval, Sherman decided to leave soon after the presidential election of November 8. On the morning of November 12, Sherman sent his last telegraph message to General Thomas and then severed the telegraph wire, and with it, all communication with his rear. With twenty days' rations and no supply line, he was effectively on his own.

His army was a marvel. Hardened veterans all, with sick and wounded sent back, it was arguably the most powerful human machine ever assembled. Grant recognized rightly that Sherman's forces were "as good soldiers as ever trod the earth; better than any European soldiers, because they not only worked like a machine but the machine thought. European armies know very little what they are fighting for, and care less."[9]

Among the enlisted men, John Emerson Anderson shared Grant's sense of Sherman's awesome martial machine: "I will not attempt to describe our feelings of astonishment when it was rumored, or announced, that we were going to sever our communications with the north and march right out into the enemies country."[10] While soldiers flexed, Sherman worried. The idea had been his, and all responsibility rested on him as well. Later, he recalled: "There was a 'devil-may-care' feeling pervading officers and men, that made me feel the full load of responsibility, for success would be accepted as a matter of course, whereas, should we fail, this 'march' would be adjudged the wild adventure of a crazy fool."[11]

In a general order issued on November 9, Sherman had addressed the coming campaign and the subject of just conduct. Foraging, a euphemism for plundering valuables regardless of "military value," would be necessary, but "soldiers must not enter the dwellings of the inhabitants, or commit any trespass." In areas where the army was left unmolested, it was to show restraint. But in areas of guerrilla activity or burned bridges, the army should respond in kind, including the destruction of homes: "Army commanders should order and enforce a devastation more or less relentless, according to the measure of such hostility." As for "horses, mules wagons, etc., belonging to the inhabitants, the cavalry and artillery may appropriate freely and without limit."[12] How these limitations were to be enforced with sixty thousand vengeful soldiers in residential streets and neighborhoods Sherman never addressed.

The first stop on the march was Atlanta, where Sherman's soldiers burned what was left of the city to the ground and began moving south toward Savannah. The mobile army organized into two wings, with the Army of the Tennessee on the right under General Howard and the Army of Georgia on the left under General Slocum, Sheridan's roommate at West Point.

Lacking telegraph connections, Grant relied on Richmond newspapers to shadow Sherman's movements across Georgia. As they marched across the countryside, Union bands played "John Brown's Body," striking dread into the hearts of watching civilians who were unable to protect themselves against the devastation they knew was coming. With a front that ranged between twenty-five and sixty miles wide and a pace that covered twelve miles a day, Sherman's vengeful foragers ("bummers") cut a swath of destruction that seemed almost a frolic to the virtually unchecked Yankees, but was a terror to defenseless civilians. One New York soldier described the devastation in chillingly entertaining terms: "Destroyed all we could not eat, stole their niggers, burned their cotton and gins, spilled their sorghum, burned & twisted their R. Roads and raised Hell generally."[13]

Clearly the soldiers were having a good time—the kind of good time that

Foraging. This sketch by Winslow Homer depicts happy Federal soldiers "liberating" a reluctant cow as wheat fields stand in the background ready for plunder.

comes when you are assured that what you are doing is just and conducive to a swift ending of the war. They encountered relatively little resistance, as the total Confederate defenders included only thirteen thousand troops. In addition, a who's who of Confederate generals—including Joseph Wheeler, P. G. T. Beauregard, Braxton Bragg, Dick Taylor, Lafayette McLaws, G. W. Smith, and William J. Hardee—were all present in Georgia to observe Sherman's progress. With no troops, however, they could do nothing but watch as the people of Georgia groaned.

To disguise his initial destination of Milledgeville, Sherman sent one wing to threaten Augusta and the other to Macon. In seven days they would again link up. After a series of feints and minor skirmishes with hapless Confederates, Sherman's wings converged at Milledgeville on November 23 and began moving toward Augusta and Savannah. Along the way, Sherman's bummers destroyed the railroads completely, twisting molten rail tracks around trees to create "Sherman's pretzels." As they went, the army destroyed or confiscated all resources and property that could remotely be considered "of military value." This included, of course, food for civilians now threatened with starvation in the coming winter months.

Not surprisingly, although private homes and property were theoretically protected by Sherman's orders, commanders could not prevent their troops from exacting revenge on the people. The greatest damages reportedly came with General Hugh ("Kilcavalry") Kilpatrick's cavalry, to whom he gave a virtual green light to do as they pleased. By November 22, the pious General Howard (Kilpatrick's moral opposite) had had enough and issued the following general order:

> It having come to the knowledge of the major-general commanding that the crimes of arson and robbery have become frequent throughout the army, notwithstanding positive orders both from these and superior headquarters have been repeatedly issued, and with a view to the prompt punishment of offenses of this kind, it is hereby ordered: That hereafter any officer or man . . . discovered in pillaging a house or burning a building without proper authority, will, upon sufficient proof thereof, be shot.[14]

Noble as Howard's orders were, no one was shot to death for crimes against civilians, and the devastation ground on. Commanders could complain and issue orders, but what did they expect? The very strategy of inflicting sixty thousand battle-hardened and unsupplied men on defenseless communities could not possibly lead to anything else. And the commanders, being intelligent West Point graduates, knew it. It was a classic case of covering their moral flanks with the rhetoric of "orders," while knowing that the frontal assault would continue the urban destruction. They knew as well that carnage on civilians who had no one to defend them would further the war aims of demoralization and despair. Sherman understood this more clearly than the "Christian General" Howard and embraced "terror" as a war aim. Having emptied the acts of war of their moral content, he reduced the action to "which party can whip" by whatever means it took.

Sherman pushed forward even though he recognized that he could not control "the fate of a vast machine" as it rumbled to the sea. Reflecting later on the foraging, he conceded that "no doubt, many acts of pillage, robbery, and violence, were committed by these parties of foragers. . . . [But] I never heard of any cases of murder or rape."[15] His friend and commander, General Grant, backed him up. In his memoirs, Grant concluded: "I do not believe there was much unwarrantable pillaging considering that we were in the enemy's territory and without any supplies except such as the country afforded."[16]

Grant and Sherman could rest content with their tactics because the rules of war had changed. As Sherman explained in a famous letter to his adjutant R. M. Sawyer, the enemy was subject to the government and its armies such that "any and all rights which [the generals] choose to enforce the war—to take their lives, their homes, their lands, their everything"—was permissible. Whatever the designation, be it "hard" war or "total" war, this conflict had certainly become all-encompassing by nineteenth-century standards. For Sherman it represented nothing less than his "theology of the battlefield."[17] Unlike "Christian" generals like Lee, Jackson, or Howard, Sherman did not even have God at one remove. Indeed, he almost defied God by saying that God was not in the war. Almost alone among Civil War generals, Sherman forsook God as well as the rules of war, and, to all appearances, never entertained the possibility that Providence would make him pay.[18]

On the Northern home front, America's clerical arbiters supported the conduct of the war without any real qualifications. For Boston's George E. Ellis, the hoary prospects of failure justified any means, so that *"all inflictions and calamities short of that were to be regarded as conditions for averting it, and therefore to be submitted to, without halting or even protest."* Nothing but the kindest motives governed war strategy: "A grand and holy inspiration of humanity overrules all other motives and aims of the war."

Earlier in his sermon, Ellis acknowledged that his listeners in Harvard Yard hardly knew there was a war going on in any direct sense of the term, let alone how others suffered. He did not know much either: "It is the greatest of wars, because for the greatest stake that was ever at issue in war. It is, in its conduct on this nation's part, the most humane war that was ever waged on the earth, engaging in us the least of ferocity, of barbarity, of reckless and fiendish cruelty, and the most relieved and chastened by forbearing mercy and thoughtfulness as to every needful measure of severity."[19] One can only imagine how relieved Ellis's listeners must have been to hear that it was "the most humane war that was ever waged on the earth."

On December 15 Thomas attacked Hood's army southeast of Nashville. The blow fell, sudden and ruthless. By hitting both of Hood's flanks with his superior numbers, Thomas turned Hood's army into a panicked herd. Hood tried desperately to re-form his army on a second line, but failed miserably. His soldiers broke and raced to the Tennessee River with Yankees nipping at their heels, picking up stragglers and surrendering soldiers. Only Forrest's brilliant delaying campaign saved the army from an utter rout. A thoroughly dispirited Hood was relieved of his command and replaced by Johnston. In Petersburg Grant congratulated Thomas with a two-hundred-gun salute.

Two of Thomas's attacking brigades were black. Colonel Thomas J. Morgan, commander of the Fourteenth U.S. Colored Infantry, later described his troops' behavior as they charged up Overton Hill side by side with white soldiers:

> It was with breathless interest I watched that noble army climb the hill with a steady resolve, which nothing but death itself could check. When at length the assaulting column sprang upon the earthworks, and the enemy seeing that further resistance was madness, gave way and began a precipitous retreat, our hearts swelled as only the hearts of soldiers can, and scarcely stopping to cheer or to await orders, we pushed forward and joined in the pursuit, until the darkness and the rain forced a halt.

For General James B. Steedman, a Democrat who had long opposed the enlistment of African American troops, the battle was definitive. In his official report, he commented:

> The larger portion of these losses, amounting in the aggregate to fully 25 per cent of the men under my command who were taken into action, it will be observed fell upon the colored troops. The severe loss of this part of my troops was in their brilliant charge on the enemy's works on Overton Hill on Friday afternoon. I was unable to discover that color made any difference in the fighting of my troops. All, white and black, nobly did their duty as soldiers.[20]

By October 1864 there were 140 "Negro" regiments in the army with a total strength of 102,000 men. They would serve in every major Union campaign in the last year of the war except Sherman's march through Georgia and the Carolinas.[21]

Unlike Grant and Thomas, Sherman had no black units, preferring instead that African Americans serve behind the lines as laborers and "pioneers." A reluctant abolitionist, Sherman supported the South's right to slaves until they seceded. Even then he favored emancipation but opposed a perfect equality and "[commingling] their blood with ours." As for political rights: "The negro should, of course, be protected in his industry and encouraged to acquire property, knowledge, trade, and every means possible to better his condition, but I think we should all be rather too slow than too fast in extending political rights."

Whatever Sherman thought of the slaves, they perceived him as their savior: "Whenever they heard my name, they clustered about my horse, shouted and prayed in the peculiar style, which had a natural eloquence that would have moved a stone." In inquiring whether they understood the cause of the war, one told Sherman "though we professed to be fighting for the Union, he supposed that slavery was the cause, and that our success was to be his freedom." On that basis, Sherman pleaded with the man to tell the freed slaves not to follow in his train "with useless mouths, which would eat up the food needed for our fighting-men; that our success was their assured freedom." With these warnings, Sherman had very few African Americans follow his army.[22]

The freed slaves revered Sherman as they did Grant and Lincoln. In a letter to the abolitionist Gerrit Smith, General Absalom Baird described how, after the occupation of Savannah:

> I chanced on two or three consecutive days after our arrival to be in General Sherman's rooms when he was receiving the negroes of the place. Poor creatures! They came to him as their deliverer, and one black preacher told him, like Simeon in the Bible, he had prayed for this day, and all he now wanted was to see Mr. Lincoln. Some of them wanted to kneel before him, but the general would not permit it, and told them they must not kneel to any one but their Maker.[23]

By December 10 Sherman's united wings stood at the gates of Savannah defying Confederates to resist. In a letter to General Hardee in Savannah, Sherman did not mince words: "Should I be forced to assault . . . I shall then feel justified in resorting to the harshest measures, and shall make little effort to restrain my army."[24] Meanwhile, Sherman prepared a siege and reestablished communications with the outside world through Port Royal. On December 21 a hopelessly outgunned Hardee abandoned the city and its inhabitants to the invading host. The next day, President Lincoln received a message from Sherman: "I beg to present you, as a Christmas gift, the city of Savannah."

Following the occupation of Savannah and Thomas's sound thrashing of Hood at Nashville, Abraham Lincoln wrote Sherman an appreciative letter that confirms just how independently Sherman had acted in his Southern campaign:

> When you were about leaving Atlanta for the Atlantic coast, I was anxious, if not fearful; but, feeling that you were the better judge, and remembering, "nothing risked, nothing gained," I did not interfere. Now, the undertaking being a success, the honor is all yours . . . in showing to the world that your army could be divided, putting the stronger part to an important new service, and yet leaving enough to vanquish the old opposing force of the whole, Hood's army, it brings those who sat in darkness to see a great light.[25]

Besides validating Sherman, Lincoln's gratitude also reveals Lincoln himself. The reelected and triumphant president increasingly saw things in terms of "the world" observing America. And in his perception of bringing "those who sat in darkness to see a great light," he evidenced the increasing biblicism that marked his last days with an apocalyptic sensibility.

John Emerson Anderson was also confident in the justice of Sherman's cause, though he conceded that it raised questions in his mind of just conduct. While marching, "we were to burn and destroy, that which if left unharmed would be of use to the enemy in prolonging the war. . . . In fact we were to strip the country of every vestige of provender, or forage, for man or beast." In Savannah he uneasily observed

> the Engineer Corps with their fire brands, as they applied the torch to building after building. When we took our departure in the morning the city, except an occupied dwelling house, here, and there, was a mass of smoking and blackened ruins. This burning was only a foretaste of what was to be the fate of the country through which our advancing columns were then moving. War. Terrible war, such as the enemy had carried into the union loving district of eastern Tennessee, and the peace loving hills of Pennsylvania was about to be brought upon this beautiful country that had so long escaped.[26]

Whatever scruples some soldiers may have felt, secular and religious commentators at home gleefully reported the destruction and progress with no hard questions. *The Banner of the Covenant* had no problem with "General Sherman's Invasion" and applauded "the power to destroy mills, houses, cotton gins etc. [and] enforce a devastation, more or less relentless, according to the measure of such [rebel] hostility." For behavior like this, the journal exulted, "the North is blessed with the Fall of Savannah—Sherman's Christmas gift."[27]

By December, a reelected and confident Lincoln was already thinking about the future, and the ultimate meaning of his war. Both had to be concerned with slavery. Earlier, on October 13, Maryland voters had narrowly adopted a new state constitution abolishing slavery. Lincoln would go further. On December 6 he proposed that Congress enact a constitutional amendment forever outlawing slavery on the American continent. With striking clarity, it became apparent that this was what the war was all about. In retrospect, anyway, this atoned for all the bloodshed on the battlefield and the suffering inflicted on defenseless civilians. Now, more than ever, Lincoln understood his messianic destiny as an instrument in the hands of the Almighty to redeem this "almost chosen people."

In his classic history of the Civil War, Bruce Catton fashioned a summary of what, in 1864, Lincoln eventually took to be the innermost meaning of the war—and, by extension, what later Americans have taken to be the innermost meaning of America:

> [T]he war was about to be won, and Mr. Lincoln was looking to the future, which was still plastic. Americans at that moment had a strange, terrifying power. Not only could they shape the future; they had conquered time, so that what they did now could send the future's meaning backward, putting significance in the insensate killings that ran from Franklin all the way back to Shiloh and Bull Run. Out of pain and horror already endured they could light a beacon fire.[28]

Although right about emancipation's "beacon fire," neither Lincoln nor Catton could discern another innermost meaning to the "insensate killings." They could not see a new religion, baptized and confirmed, imbuing a powerful unified nation-state with the power—and sanctity—of God. Therein lay the hidden innermost meaning, the power of which derived, in part, from its very invisibility. Visibly, most believed America (North and South) to be a "Christian nation." Invisibly, few could see that America was incarnating a millennial nationalism as the primal religious faith.

CHAPTER 41

"UPHOLD THE CAUSE AND STRENGTHEN THE HANDS OF THE FAITHFUL"

On January 31, 1865, President Davis appointed Robert E. Lee general in chief of all Confederate armies, explicitly recognizing the obvious, that the South's hope lay fully invested in this one man. By then, however, it was too late. As Sherman prepared to depart Savannah and as Grant held Lee in Petersburg, General Schofield's Twenty-third Corps (re-created as the Department of North Carolina) marched on Fort Fisher— the original target of Winfield Scott's Anaconda Plan, conceived four years earlier at the start of hostilities. On January 15, after a massive bombardment of the fort, an invading force of sixty-five hundred infantrymen and marines stormed the northern wall, compelling the surrender of the fort and taking nineteen hundred prisoners. With Fort Fisher reduced, Wilmington, North Carolina, soon succumbed as well. With Wilmington's fall, Lee's hungry soldiers—surviving miserably in the trenches at Petersburg—lost an indispensable food source from the Carolinas.[1]

The fall of Fort Fisher, though minimal in terms of lives lost, had an enormous psychological impact on the Confederacy. Informed citizens were stunned by the news and recognized that the end of the Confederacy was quite possibly in view. Without the capacity to feed his army from the Carolinas, Lee would eventually be starved into submission. For Petersburg diarist Martha Wayles Robertson, trapped in her home and unable to travel any roads, the fall of Fort Fisher was ominous, but still not hopeless: "The times seem dark and gloomy, but God will uphold the right cause, and let us trust in His justice and mercy! Shall not the judge of all the earth do right?" Despite hopeless odds, the citizens clung to their righteousness. Robertson complained not only of the Yankee invaders but also of the "servants," who posed an increasing problem she regularly described in terms of "the *ingratitude* of servants!"[2]

In a last-ditch attempt to win a negotiated peace, meanwhile, President Davis agreed to an overture from General Francis Preston Blair to send commissioners to meet with Lincoln and Seward on February 3 over the fate of "the two countries." Lincoln agreed to a meeting to secure peace "to the people of our one common country." Neither Davis nor Lincoln expected anything substantive to come of the meetings, and they were not surprised. But both sensed strategic advantages from putting forth an outward show of seriousness.

Davis hoped that a blanket refusal to accept conditional peace from Lincoln might spur on the badly demoralized Confederate troops and citizens. For his part, Lincoln gave the appearance of wanting the bloodshed to cease without any willingness to sacrifice principle. This was precisely what Henry Ward Beecher perceived when, in a confidential letter to Lincoln, he wrote: "I am more than willing that as you will sacrifice no substantial element, you should wave any mere formality—So that the inside of the hand is solid bone I am willing to have the outside flesh soft as velvet."[3]

Lincoln, together with William H. Seward, met with the three Confederate commissioners on board the *River Queen* in Hampton Roads outside of Fort Monroe, Virginia, and, as predicted, the two sides came to no agreement. Lincoln would settle for nothing less than the return of the Confederacy to a reunited Union without slavery. He assured the commissioners that he would be as lenient in reconstructing the South as possible, but passage of the Thirteenth Amendment by the Congress allowed no further compromise over slavery. With that, the conference broke up and Lincoln instructed Grant to continue the onslaught. Once again, Lincoln was confirmed in his sense that blood sacrifice would be the ultimate means of creating cohesion and national survival.

Reactions in the South to the failed peace talks were predictably defiant. In almost caricatured words of arrogance (and denial), the *Richmond Religious Herald* gloated that the South is "in better condition to-day, and the North weaker than ever before, since the war began." The failure of peace talks, moreover, and the smug Northern demand for unconditional surrender would stiffen resolve and "be worth more to us than a victory." Right was still on the South's side:

Those of our people who have grown despondent under the reverses of the times should not think that, because disasters have befallen us, God is unfriendly to our cause. We must remember the terrible character of this war. Our enemy has all the material advantages. We are shut out from the world . . . notwithstanding these things; we have borne the bloody strife, and remain yet unsubdued. Surely God has been the friend of the South and purposes our ultimate independence.

Of course, the question of why the constant defeats continued grew louder, but there was a standard rejoinder: "The answer is found in the condition of his church. . . . We forgot the source of our strength. God in anger withdrew his support. . . . Our cause will be strengthened and our liberty secured as soon as we deserve it."[4] With that assurance, the sacrifices could continue in good faith.

Southern clergymen not only persisted with the jeremiad as means of deliverance but also with the doctrine that slavery was humane. If there was sin connected to the institution of slavery, it was never slavery per se but the abuse of slaves. To stay right with God, ministers repeated their warnings to treat slaves well, albeit in deference to their owner's "privileges." Confederates were reminded to respect slave marriages "in such a form as shall not interfere with the legal rights of the slaveholder."[5]

Defeats were not cause for guilt. Rather, reverses in such a war were arguments "for more humble prayer, for greater sacrifices and united and determined efforts under the counsels of wise and able leaders, and not for gloomy forebodings of evil." By 1865 many Confederate statesmen and journalists were even willing to enlist slaves in the army and give them their freedom in exchange for the preservation of their republic. The *Richmond Daily Dispatch* reversed its earlier opposition to slave enlistments and argued that the Confederacy "must fight negros with negros."[6]

While scholars later posited a Confederate "guilt" over slavery that dampened their war resolve and generated defeatism, contemporary Confederates evidenced no such sentiment. Other writers sympathetic to the Southern cause pointed out "a moral paradox." Slavery was good for freedom, they claimed, and not in conflict with it. It had to do with the nature of societies; the Southern experiment in freedom was demonstrating "that slavery is essentially a feature in the conservatism of every *free* government."[7] Left unspoken and unquestioned was the qualifier every free *white* government.

Archenemies of this viewpoint were the abolitionists, given the most hated epithet in the Confederate lexicon—Puritans. The mere mention of the word would routinely dispel defeatism or acquiescence. A writer for the *Richmond Daily Dispatch* drew his line in the sand: "The loyal sons of this heroic land would sooner see it upheaved from its foundations by some convulsion of nature, and buried in the Atlantic, than to behold its national characteristics submerged by a tide of Puritan manners, selfishness and fanaticism."[8] The same paper told the tale of a "professor of religion" who became an abolitionist and therefore "must needs insult the Christian world with a blasphemy equally as disgusting as any which ever proceeded from the lips of Tom Paine."[9] In 1865 no less than 1860, they believed that abolitionism was the ultimate sin such that "[a]ll who love the Lord Jesus Christ must and will oppose this monster heresy even unto death."[10]

Revivals continued apace in the Confederate armies, and the early winter months witnessed renewals in the hospitals as well. Religious newspapers were happy to report "an encouraging state of religious feeling among the soldiers in Richmond hospitals."[11] To sustain that interest evangelical denominations redoubled their efforts to publish and distribute tracts and religious newspapers through their vendors. Titles like the *Soldier's Closet* (Baptist) or the *Soldier's Visitor* (Presbyterian) or the *Soldier's Paper* (Methodist) all promoted personal conversion and revival.

The *Army and Navy Messenger*, published by the Evangelical Tract Society in Petersburg, Virginia, used the occasion of the siege of Petersburg to preach conversion: "Oh! For the spirit of earnest, agonizing, believing, trusting prayer to be poured upon us, now as we gird our armor, and enter anew upon the terrible conflict." Here, anyway, the soldiers would not disappoint them. Chaplains routinely reported "many conversions in the army during the past year."[12] Religion would never become more central or affirming than in the final months of the Confederacy's life. In fact, the clergy had no choice. Having already sacrificed a prophetic voice of their own to the sacred cause, their fortunes were linked inextricably with their government's.

On the home front, too, calls for conversion displaced calls for victory. Preaching to his Richmond Baptist audience, Jeremiah Bell Jeter opened a late December sermon with the observation: "We have heard much of late of the condition and sufferings of prisoners—their confinement—hard and scanty fare—bad water—sufferings from cold, diseases, the brutality of their keepers. . . . [But] I propose this morning to show you prisoners in a far more pitiable condition than that of those languishing in Yankee prisons."

Jeter then went on to talk about prisoners of sin. He followed this up with a sermon from 2 Timothy 2:3 on "a good soldier of Jesus Christ," whom he went on to describe as "Captain Jesus Christ. Captain of Salvation." If the sinner turned to Christ, then "in death he will triumph and gain an honorable discharge."[13]

Even as revivals in the army convinced Confederates that God was still truly on their side, they worried about demoralization, greed, and insufficient piety on the home front. This religious reversal grew steadily in 1865 as the army prayed for the churches and the nation rather than vice versa. Northern evangelicals might fret constantly over the missing reference to God in their Constitution, but Southern evangelicals, who had God in their constitution, wanted even more: a specific identification with Jesus Christ. The *Richmond*

Christian Advocate called attention to the fact that while Congress proposed prayer to President Davis "in the name of our Lord and Savior Jesus Christ," President Davis invoked God in his fast proclamation but not Jesus, thus risking divine desertion. It was divine desertion—not slavery or Northern superiority—that would prove truly devastating to the cause: "If Christ does not help the people, it will be trampled under foot by its enemies. Will He be our helper, if we persistently exclude His name from our *national* references to the religious duties of the crisis?"[14]

While Northern clergy promoted Lincoln and the Republican Party, Confederate ministers were quick to promote their president and generals. On Sunday, January 1, 1865, in a sermon preached at St. Paul's in Richmond with Jefferson Davis in attendance, the venerable Charles Minnigerode abandoned all pretext to preaching pure "spirituality." Instead, he spoke as if it were a weekday fast:

> God forbid that I should speak as a mere man and not as the minister of Christ, that I should introduce politics where Religion alone should raise her voice, but the times are perilous and it is necessary to "uphold the cause and strengthen the hands of the faithful. . . ." Oh! if we could stop every croaker and nerve every patriot; if we could allay every impatience and rouse all to bear what others have borne before, and drive away their unmanly fears by trust in God . . . the threatening dangers with which the year opens upon us would in God's mercy be changed into blessings, and this year witness the growth of our national strength and our training for the final victory![15]

The theme of "manliness" and piety recurred in Minnigerode's discourse without a hint of defeatism. If there was a problem, it lay with those who complained or found fault with the administration. Instead of criticism, "the literature given to our people chiefly in the daily newspapers should be of an encouraging and inspiring, not a depressing and often demoralizing tendency."[16]

But outside of the leadership elite and Lee's ever-loyal Army of Northern Virginia, voices of dissent grew steadily louder. Georgia remained a sore spot, and on February 15, Governor Joseph E. Brown excoriated President Davis in a speech to the legislature and recommended a constitutional amendment that would remove Davis as commander in chief. For all intents and purposes, Georgia was out of the war. Indeed, the only states really in it were North Carolina and Virginia. The Confederate Congress fought openly with Davis as he chided them on their inability to lead their people. Among the corps of generals, spats broke out between the "political generals" berating

"West Point fools," and the West Point generals aghast at "broken down politicians and drunkards" assuming high ranks in the military.[17]

While Confederates prayed increasingly to God to deliver them, Northern clergy complained of the North's lack of religiosity and a false faith in superior arms. As victory loomed, revivals waned, causing one leading journal to suggest that "[i]f only a sufficient number of evangelists—say five hundred—could be sent into the various divisions to cooperate with, or supply the destitution of chaplains, we have reason to believe that a wide-spread, wonderful and glorious revival would be the result."[18]

The "evangelists" never appeared. Volunteers for promoting revivals, it appeared, required fear—a sentiment largely missing among the North's well insulated civilians. Apart from periodic notices in the religious press, revival was not invoked in the North in any way comparable to the event it had become in the South. Conversions in the camps and hospitals undoubtedly occurred at rates comparable to those of the Confederacy, where death remained imminent. But they lacked the broader cultural significance represented in the Southern secular press. As victory piled on top of victory Northern moral discourse diverted into celebrations of war and "manliness." In a sermon entitled *Manliness*, preached to the Thirteenth Regiment in South Congregational Church of Brooklyn, the chaplain, Edward Taylor, opened with the declaration: "A robust, valorous soul can no more declare itself in soft and feminine words, than a knight of old could lay aside his two-handed sword and heavy coat of mail for a feathery wand and a robe of silk."[19]

Where Confederate "manliness" was moving toward a fusion of bravery and evangelical piety, Northern manliness was moving away, almost in the direction of the antebellum patrician South. Echoing the same theme of manliness in his 1865 Massachusetts election sermon, A. L. Stone offered the view that bloody war was essential to union: "The length of the war has been absolutely indispensable for the full sense of nationality—the unity and authority of the Federal Government, to enter and possess the hearts of the people." Stone went on to revisit the word "Puritan" in a manner strikingly opposite that of his Confederate adversaries: "Oh! That our New England might be, late and forever, what she was at first—PURITAN! Once a word of reproach, veined with sneering irony, History has written it as our proudest eulogy. To keep it unbolted down the ages is our most sacred trust." Then, with a note of bravado that Confederates (and not a few other Northerners) detested, he baldly asserted: "It runs in our [New England] blood to be pioneers of a spreading Christian civilization."[20]

As religious journals on both sides of the war wallowed in self-righteousness and patriotism, they routinely legitimated their own sentiments as pious and those of the enemy as diabolical. In a letter to Robert Dabney, Richmond's Moses D. Hoge complained bitterly about the Northern press throughout the war:

> As for the Northern, so called, religious papers, it is my deliberate opinion that any decent secular journal is better Sunday reading than they. These pretended religious papers are not only secular for the most part as to matter, but satanic as to spirit, and after an article surcharged with falsehood and all uncharitableness the editors make it worse by following it with something very spiritual by way of giving sanctity to the rest of the page. They make a dead run at what McPheeters used to call the "big pious," knowing that the public expect something of the sort in a religious paper, but their saintly talk is so much out of place in such connection that it shocks you as a mock sermon would in a barroom, or bawdy house.[21]

Hoge was exactly right about the North and equally exactly wrong about himself. In fact, the Southern religious papers were no better. The Civil War, which had in many ways become a barroom brawl, extended to the churches on both sides with all trace of Christian forbearance the victim.

CHAPTER 42

"VENGEANCE UPON SOUTH CAROLINA"

Bad weather delayed Sherman's movements until February, and would continue to hound him throughout the Carolinas. But his tactical planning and determination overcame all. Wherever he went he terrorized. When Chaplain William Waring, an African American attached to a Michigan regiment stationed in Beaufort, South Carolina, observed Sherman's army march through, his response was mixed. For sheer intimidation the western soldiers were without peer.

Waring and his fellow soldiers had heard about Sherman's legendary exploits and expected a clean and sparkling professional army. They had a rude awakening as unkempt and loosely disciplined troops walked in disarray before them. Beneath the outward casualness, however, lay a steely resolve that bespoke death to any who got in their way:

> Here comes one. His pantaloons leg is split half way up to the knee; his face is unshaven and his hair unshorn; the crown of his hat, too, is gone, but he is perfectly oblivious to the eyes that are upon him, or the remarks that are made about him, and with his gun swung carelessly over his shoulder, the whole appearance of the man says, "I can hold all the ground that I cover."

A little time later, Waring spotted some foragers bringing back a wagon loaded with hay and chickens and crowing like a rooster (the signal for chicken tonight). Waring evidenced no problem with the soldiers' "addictions," as long as it was directed at rebels. But then a more disturbing sight caught his attention:

> Up the street a little farther, the negro-hating element shows itself. One of them takes a colored woman's pies and then slaps her over because she

complained. Another one inflicts a wound on an already wounded colored soldier. Two more go up to the quarters of the Post Band, who are colored men, and raise a disturbance there.

Instead of dwelling on the racism, however, Waring returned at the end of his account to where he began: the spectacle of the army itself. Why were they so powerful? His answer: "Armies are disciplined and drilled for the purpose of acquiring the greatest possible amount of destructive power, and whether Sherman's army shows that it has been taken through the usual course of instruction or not, it possesses that power in a preeminent degree. It seems to have become part of their nature, and it is irksome to them to be restrained, as they are here, among loyal people."[1]

While American memory and *Gone With the Wind* preserve the Atlanta campaign as the most dramatic achievement of Sherman's army, the march to the sea was logistically far more complex and a tribute to Sherman's organizational genius. Moral genius was another matter. While in Savannah, Sherman authorized the seizure of private property with deliberate sanction for maximal discomfort: "I have adopted in Savannah rules concerning property—severe but just—founded upon the laws of nations and the practice of civilized governments, and am clearly of opinion that we should claim all the belligerent rights over conquered countries, that the people may realize the truth that war is no child's play."[2]

Opposing him was the restored General J. E. Johnston, who was pulled out of retirement by General Lee to direct operations in South Carolina. Serving under Johnston were General Beauregard and General Wade Hampton, who commanded all the cavalry in the state. Johnston was certainly an improvement over Hood, now a thoroughly beaten and bitter man with nothing more than a missing arm and leg to show for his bravery. Ultimately, who was in command mattered not at all; there simply were not enough horses or men to withstand Sherman's juggernaut.

Sherman retained his two-winged army commanded by his trusted generals, Howard and Slocum. To keep the Confederates off balance, he feinted toward Charleston and Augusta, with Columbia his true target all along. Throughout the complex movements, Sherman absorbed the intoxicating fact that no Confederate force in the Carolinas could challenge him in the field, or even slow him down. Sherman's main military concern was whether Lee would remain in Virginia as his food supplies in the Carolinas were destroyed, or whether he would seek to break out from Grant's investment and move south. Repeatedly, Grant assured Sherman that Lee could execute no such move.

No other general in the Civil War duplicated Sherman's experience in his march to the sea. It truly represented a new chapter in the history of war, at least as far as Americans were concerned. With his commanders ignorant of his whereabouts and the enemy in no position to stop him, he was effectively the reigning deity wherever he went, with no higher accountability to check his martial impulses. Harriet Beecher Stowe's apt characterization of him as the "war prophet" was becoming literally true. Everything depended on Sherman. A sort of madness enveloped him and his soldiers as they marched into the heart of darkness, destroying without resistance.

Sherman's only real adversary was the weather, the worst in a decade.[3] Day upon day of rain and mud became a far more serious logistical obstacle than the Confederate army as his troops slogged 425 miles in fifty days. Nonetheless, Sherman's forces displayed a special animus for the Palmetto State, the "seedbed" of the rebellion. Sherman routinely denounced it as the "hellhole of secession." Restraints that were minimal in Georgia all but disappeared as Sherman's hardened veterans marched relentlessly forward.

Sherman's main military target was the railroads, but, with all but no opposition, he made military targets only part of his strategy. The utter psychological destruction of the citizenry also figured large in the plan, and for that to be won, the primary target would be the capital city. By Monday, February 13 Sherman knew that only a token defense existed in Columbia under the command of Wade Hampton.

The Yankees were savoring a go at South Carolina. Sherman was not blind to this, and in a famous aside uttered while the army was still in Georgia, he remarked, "The truth is, the whole army is burning with an insatiable desire to wreak vengeance upon South Carolina. I almost tremble at her fate, but feel that she deserves all that seems in store for her." In a typically moralistic and personal statement, he explained that "I"—rather than "we" or "my commander in chief"—"look upon Columbia as quite as bad as Charleston and I doubt if we shall spare her public buildings there as we did at Milledgeville."[4] As the virtual dictator of his army, Sherman now operated free from all moral, no less than military, reviews.

By February 13, Sherman's forces could see the city and could not resist firing batteries inside the city's habitations. Though not massive, the bombardment succeeded in terrorizing the population and discouraging snipers from taking potshots at Yankee troops. All day Monday, Tuesday, and Wednesday people flocked to the trains in a "contagious panic" to flee Sherman's uncontested rumbling legions. Among those fleeing was the New Orleans firebrand Benjamin M. Palmer, whose sermons had done so much to promote Confederate independence.[5] On February 17 the scanty Confederate forces ran as well, leaving Sherman to accept the mayor's surrender and enter the city.

Already the wind was blowing hard and cotton bales burning, "fired by the rebel cavalry withdrawing from the city that morning." The city streets teemed with white and black citizens as Sherman assured the mayor that he "had no purpose to injure the private citizens or private property." As Sherman and Howard came up, the Fifteenth Corps (Sherman's favorite) marshaled in formation and marched through the town, battle flags whipping in the wind and spirited bands playing "Hail, Columbia" repeatedly. Slaves rushed to the streets, laughing and shouting to the soldiers, "God bless you; I'se free now!" Truly—and nobly—the slaves were indeed freed. Unfortunately, the soldiers had no interest in this aspect of the victory.

Sherman had little to say years later when he wrote his own account of the occupation of Columbia, mindful of the scandal associated with it. Instead, he concentrated solely on self-congratulatory moral stories. One centered on a female friend from his days with the Third Artillery in 1845. In that year, he gave her a book inscribed and signed. When the Yankees came to pillage, she showed the officer the inscription and, Sherman proudly noted, the officer preserved her property intact. In fact, other events and actions were transpiring in Columbia by then, but Sherman chose not to include them. A second anecdote recounted the story of another woman whose home was burning and how Sherman helped to put the fire out: "I mention these specific facts to show that, personally, I had no malice or desire to destroy that city or its inhabitants, as is generally believed at the South."[6]

This was indeed news to the Confederates. With minimal restraints, soldiers of the less disciplined Seventeenth Corps overran the Fifteenth Corps and got into the liquor stores. Soon after, they invaded civilian houses for foraging.

During the afternoon soldiers did their best to loot and terrorize citizens, but few reports of physical assaults on white civilians exist. As the wind continued, fires spread throughout the city, especially in the northern section, where the wind blew most directly. Some of the fires occurred accidentally, but others were set deliberately by soldiers moving from house to house, tossing turpentine pots or burning balls of cotton. Freed Union officers from the prisoner-of-war camp at Columbia were especially bent on revenge. Slaves also joined in the rampage, a relatively small measure of retribution for centuries of violent abuse.

When one woman pleaded with Provost Marshal Jeremiah Jenkins to protect her house, Jenkins replied coldly, "The women of the South kept the war alive—and it is only by making them suffer that we can subdue the men." Another woman got more of the same for saying she would willingly send her sons to die (in fact two had) if it meant defeat for the enemy. The unsurprised Yankee soldier replied harshly, "Yes, damn you women, you are the ones keeping up the war."[7]

Suffer the women did, and the elderly, and the children, as they fled their burning houses all along Main Street to the unfinished capital building. As the white citizens panicked and the former slaves plundered, the soldiers continued to drink and cheer the destruction of Columbia. Predictably, the scene descended into bedlam. The historian Charles Royster recounts:

> Some men grew more and more frenzied with the destruction; it became their sole purpose. They seized possessions only to throw them into the flames. While one group gave finery and valuables to passing black people, another pillaged slave quarters and destroyed blacks' belongings. While one set of men looted banks systematically and extracted buried silver with an experienced touch, others smashed mirrors, slashed paintings, and broke furniture that women had hauled into the streets. . . . Men who were too drunk and too intent on spreading the fire passed out in burning buildings, and the flames closed over them. A few men murdered.[8]

The violence grew so extreme that Sherman was forced to order a roundup of drunken soldiers. In all, 307 were arrested, and in the process, two were killed and thirty more wounded.[9]

It is true that rapes of white women were rare (they were Americans after all), and military court-martial records reveal several soldiers executed for rape. But black women did not receive the same mercies—in fact, most of the executions were for the rape of black women.[10] For obvious reasons, Union commentators gave little attention to the stories of black women being raped, but the facts were plain. While officers complained, they could do little in practice to prevent the violence. Widespread black illiteracy meant that few black women would record their experiences; others were probably too frightened to witness against their triumphant Yankee assailants. Enough accounts survive, however, to confirm the ways in which some white soldiers viewed slave women as "the legitimate prey of lust."

One white woman privy to the violence described Yankee soldiers who stripped black women and then "spanked them around the room. . . . They violated all the women servants publicly and left them almost dead, unable to move."[11] Other accounts describe similar outrages. On the morning of February 18, black women's naked bodies lay on the streets of Columbia "bearing the marks of detestable sex crimes." One older slave was raped by seven Yankees and, with orders to "finish the bitch," she was drowned in a nearby ditch.[12]

The Confederate writer William Gilmore Simms wrote an account of Columbia's burning. A native of Charleston, Simms fled the approaching armies of the North and traveled with his family to Columbia, only to arrive one week before Sherman's Yankees. Though exaggerating the subsequent level of destruction, he had a sound ear for the citizens, especially the women. Despite the taunts and threats, few buckled. Simms observed, "When forced to answer, they did so in monosyllables only, or in brief, stern language, avowed their confidence in the cause of their country, the principles and rights for which their brothers and sons fought, and their faith in the ultimate favor and protection of God."[13] Simms also recognized the differences between white and black women:

> We should grossly err if, while showing the forbearance of the soldiers in respect to our *white* women, we should convey to any innocent reader the notion that they exhibited a like forbearance in the case of the *black*. The poor negroes were terribly victimized by their assailants, many of them . . . being left in a condition little short of death. Regiments, in successive *relays*, subjected scores of these poor women to the torture of their embraces.[14]

To be sure, Sherman never issued direct orders to destroy and plunder private property, let alone to rape "liberated" slaves. But any efforts at restraint were ineffectual; in any case, it was well known that if Sherman expected excesses anywhere it was in Columbia. That expectation amounted to de facto permission in the minds of many. For that, Sherman must take the moral responsibility.

When faced with the ravages of Sherman's army, Confederate women did not evidence the demoralization that Sherman assumed would ensue. Instead, as with soldiers in the field, after the initial shock their hatreds and determination to fight on were renewed by the violence. Women on farms and refugees in cities may have urged their husbands to desert the war and come home. But women experiencing violence directly urged their soldier husbands to remain in the army and repay the Yankees for their outrages, an eye for an eye.[15]

To their credit, not all Union soldiers were so destructive, and some tried valiantly to put out the fires. But most of the more humane soldiers remained in the camp outside of Columbia, leaving the city to the hounds of prey. Throughout, the bands played on and the soldiers complimented themselves on a "good time" had by all. When, near midnight, Sherman walked out into the yard of his "headquarters" to view the city skyline bright with flames, he commented simply, "They have brought it on themselves."

The next morning, as Sherman explored the full extent of destruction wrought by his soldiers, he blamed the mayor for not destroying the liquor. Liquor, and not Union soldiers or their officers, was responsible for the destruction. Left unsaid was why ungoverned soldiers had to be in the city in the first place, when the Confederate "army" of eight hundred was long gone to the northeast. Months after the destruction, William Simms asked the same questions:

> If it could be shown that the whiskey found its way out of stores and cellars, grappled with the soldiers and poured itself down their throats, then they are relieved of [moral] responsibility. . . . But why did the soldiers prevent the firemen from extinguishing the fire as they strove to do? Why did they cut the hose as soon as it was brought into the streets. . . . Why did they suffer the men to break into the stores and drink the liquor wherever it was found? And what shall we say to the universal plundering, which was a part of the object attained through the means of fire?[16]

In his memoirs, Grant insisted that Confederate soldiers or citizens probably torched Columbia. No doubt there was carelessness on the part of Confederate soldiers bent on destroying the cotton. And alcohol was available for plunder. Add high winds, and all the ingredients for self-exoneration to the smoldering city are there. But the evident satisfaction that Union soldiers took in the destruction and the failure of Union officers to adequately police their own men surely added to the tragedy.

Remarkably, neither Grant nor Sherman made any moral commentary except to say, in effect, "You deserved it," no matter what the level of destruction. In a telling concession, Grant argued that even if Sherman's troops had started the fires or been deliberately delinquent in failing to put them out, they were justified in so doing. In other words, their actions would require no moral defense: "The example set by the Confederates in burning the village of Chambersburg, Pennsylvania, a town which was not garrisoned, would seem to make a defence of the act of firing the seat of government of the State most responsible for the conflict then raging, not imperative."[17] In this war, two moral wrongs apparently made one moral right. Sherman agreed: "Though I never ordered [the destruction] and never wished it, I have never shed any tears over the event, because I believe that it hastened what we all fought for, the end of the war."

Like Atlanta, Columbia was effectively "not garrisoned," but the people got what they deserved anyway. It was guilt by geographical association with South Carolina, the state that started the rolling secession of the South. The moral guilt lay not with the Federal soldiers, no matter what they did, but with the people of the South—in particular those of South Carolina. For Sherman, the Confederacy's Original Sin of secession meant that the entire population deserved wrath and damnation:

> I know that in the beginning, I too, had the old West Point notion that pillage was a capital crime, and punished it by shooting. . . . This was a one sided game of war, and many of us . . . ceased to quarrel with our men about such minor things, and went in to subdue the enemy, leaving minor depredations to be charged up to the account of the rebels who had forced us into the war, and who deserved all they got and more.[18]

Few soldiers expressed reservations over the legitimate "foraging" of South Carolina houses for necessary supplies, and most distanced themselves from pillaging for "trophies," which was widespread but always relegated to a few rotten apples. Despite explicit prohibitions in Lieber's Code, the pillaging was systemic, at least in South Carolina, though few owned up to it. Lieber's Code and Sherman's orders may have countenanced civilian punishment and exploitation, but many sensed something new and unprecedented was taking place in South Carolina—maybe even something immoral. The historian Jacqueline Glass Campbell recognizes how "the struggle of essentially moral men to come to terms with the violence and terror they were bringing into southern homes suggests that although Sherman's strategy may have had historical precedent in military terms, in ideological terms, it was understood differently."[19]

Even as Columbia burned, Charleston surrendered to General Alexander Schimmelfenning after a bracing bombardment. That left Lee effectively isolated. Northern headlines rejoiced in the capture: "Charleston Evacuated! A Bloodless Victory! Charleston is Ours, God and the right are vindicated."[20] Others praised the cause: "Never since this horrible war began, have we felt more like pouring out our hearts in thanksgiving to God, for any tidings, than for those which we are permitted to announce to-day. Charleston—the birth-

"The Ruins of Charleston, South Carolina," as seen from the Circular Church. As the "seedbed of rebellion," no target assumed greater significance for Federal troops than Charleston. After months of bombardment the city was left in ruins and would not be repaired until after the war.

place of treason . . . is at length in our hands, and the flag of the Union, once more floats over the stronghold of rebellion."[21]

In none of these accounts was Columbia or the destruction to the city mentioned. Nor was destruction to Charleston mentioned at the time. After the war, a report in a Northern paper revealed the devastation wrought by constant bombardments in the "bloodless victory":

It would be impossible to give even a faint idea of the dreadful effects of this war upon the religious interests of the South. Churches have been shattered and burned, congregations dispersed, benevolent organizations disbanded, Theological Seminaries closed, while many of the clergy wander around without a flock, without a home—some, I fear, without any support except that which may be afforded by the hand of charity.[22]

Again, Union commanders evidenced no remorse over civilian casualties. General Halleck, like Sherman, was an early believer in the West Point Code, and, like Sherman, he got over it. In a communiqué to Sherman, he wrote: "Should you capture Charleston, I hope that by some accident the place may be destroyed, and if a little salt should be sown upon its site it may prevent the growth of future crops of nullification and secession."[23]

Not all delighted in the devastation. At last the bloodlust seemed to wane as victory loomed imminent. Henry Ward Beecher accepted a Federal invitation to deliver a celebratory sermon to consecrate the redeemed city of Charleston. A writer for the *Philadelphia Inquirer* was surprised to discover Beecher's intended theme. According to the account, Beecher informed his congregation of his intent to "appeal for universal unity among the people of both sections," and "now, when it is near its end, his heart yearns for reconciliation with his brethren." As for Columbia: "Along the seaboard we can give essential relief, but all along the route of Sherman's army the description given by the prophet is eminently applicable: 'Before him was the garden of Eden, and behind him was the desert.'" In terms of his own intentions for Charleston, "I would be no man's servant to be the man to go down among them, and when they are burying their dead to taunt them."[24]

PART VIII
RECONCILIATION

MAKING AN END
TO BUILD A FUTURE

CHAPTER 43

"LET US STRIVE ON TO FINISH THE WORK WE ARE IN"

Inauguration Day, March 4, 1865, did not begin well. For several days, Washington had been deluged with rain, and the expectant crowd was soon drenched. Worse was yet to come, for first on the agenda was the inauguration of Andrew Johnson as vice president. Suffering the aftereffects of a bout with typhoid fever, Johnson asked for some whiskey to calm his nerves and proceeded to get rip-roaring drunk. After a rambling speech that Lincoln and his administration could barely endure, he was shown to his seat. A mortified Lincoln leaned over to the parade marshal and instructed him: "Do not let Johnson speak outside."

Then came Lincoln's turn. The applause was ecstatic—the applause of winners. Flags appeared everywhere. Everyone in attendance knew that the defeat of the Confederacy was assured and the time for celebration at hand. In fact, it was a time to gloat. Beyond gloating, the crowd looked forward to words of revenge to punish the demonic South for all the pain and suffering it had imposed on a righteous Union.

The audience would be surprised. Lincoln would offer no lengthy denunciations of the enemy. He would offer no length at all on any theme. In a mere 703 words Lincoln brought together the mystical and fatalistic themes that would later render his speech America's Sermon on the Mount. The address consisted of a series of propositions in response to the unasked questions that were lodged in the back of every Northern American's mind. More meditation than pep talk, the speech led ultimately to a unique jeremiad, unlike any heard in the pulpits, newspapers, or arts. Throughout, Lincoln assumed no personal glory in the effort, but instead spoke in the third person.

How was the war going? Lincoln began with the most important question. Elections, political campaigns, the prospect of reconstruction were all secondary to the great all-encompassing question of war. Happily the signs were good. "The progress of our arms . . . is as well known to the public as to myself." Did this mean that victory was so certain that no further cause for concern existed? Not really. "With high hope for the future, no prediction in regard to it is ventured." So much for the celebration.

Who caused the war? The North surely had its faults, to which he would return later. But causing the war was not one of them: "Both parties depre- cated war; but one of them would *make* war rather than let the nation sur- vive; and the other would *accept* war rather than let it perish." The resulting collision was inevitable: "And the war came."

Why would the South make war on the Union? To protect and extend slavery: "All knew this interest was, somehow, the cause of the war."

So far so good. Now that good had been separated from evil, it would be time to ask how to punish the miscreants. But again Lincoln headed in an unexpected direction. How could like-minded Christians come to such vio- lently opposed answers to slavery and Union? Both, after all, "read the same Bible, and pray to the same God." Each "invokes His aid against the other." Yes, the audience nodded, but we know whose side God was really on. Wrong. Strange as it seemed to own slaves and call it charity, as Southern moralists did to the bitter end, "let us judge not that we be not judged." What? Judgment, as any Northern minister could have told his congregation, was precisely what God required of his obedient servants.

So what cannot be judged? Not what, but *who*. God cannot be judged or contained in human categories. "The prayers of both could not be answered; that of neither has been answered fully. The Almighty has His own pur- poses." This was not the Puritans' God or the abolitionists' God. Their God answered the prayers of the righteous and granted them victory. They had the jeremiad to prove it. And God was bound by its rhetoric to deliver His chosen people.

Lincoln, however, bowed to a different God. Lincoln's God was more in- scrutable. Quoting Jesus, Lincoln condemned both sides: "Woe unto the world because of offences!" Both sides offended God because both sides were implicated in the sin of slavery—a point Lincoln made repeatedly on other occasions. What if slavery was one of those offenses that required hor- rendous penalties for everyone? And what if God's judgment fell equally on both sides, even though only one human agency actually caused the war? How could anyone in the South *or* the North complain? If God "gives to both North and South, this terrible war, as the woe due to those by whom the of- fence came, shall we discern therein any departure from those divine attrib- utes which the believers in a Living God always ascribe to Him?" Any self-respecting Christian knew that the answer to this was of course not. So in place of self-righteous assurance, the best Americans could do was hope:

> Fondly do we hope—fervently do we pray—that this mighty scourge of war may speedily pass away. Yet, if God wills that it continue, until all the wealth piled by the bond-man's two hundred and fifty years of unrequited toil shall be sunk, and until every drop of blood drawn with the lash, shall be paid by another drawn with the sword, as was said three thousand years ago, so still it must be said "the judgments of the Lord, are true and righteous altogether."

Earlier, Lincoln had had little good to say about the black race, even as he had condemned slavery vociferously. But in this address, *Lincoln's* jeremiad, only the blacks escaped the judgments of the Lord. They, after all, had already been judged by white Americans, North and South.

Implicit in everything Lincoln said was the presumption that, as horrific as the war was, it would eventually cease, because this same inscrutable God had unmistakably destined America to be his last best hope. So, when that ecstatic moment came, how ought the victors to respond? This was the answer everyone was waiting for—the denouement of a short but incredibly powerful peroration. Here, on this most pressing issue, Lincoln offered up his greatest surprise. In place of pride and revenge, he could only say:

> With malice toward none; with charity for all; with firmness in the right, as God gives us to see the right, let us strive on to finish the work we are in; to bind up the nation's wounds; to care for him who shall have borne the battle, and for his widow, and his orphan—to do all which may achieve and cherish a just, and a lasting peace, among ourselves, and with all nations.

Clearly the Second Inaugural stands with the Gettysburg Address as America's greatest sermons.[1] But what grants it its enduring power is the fact that it was also his sermon to the world. Peace—an honorable peace—was not only America's destiny for itself but its burden for the world. Lincoln's Christlike "malice toward none" applied not only to Americans but to human beings everywhere. Everywhere. Lincoln's mandated universality set him apart from other national leaders promoting their nationalism as an end in itself.

"With all nations." The last three words of this great speech were the greatest, for they incarnated an enduring civil religion of America the Redeemer Nation. At the same time, they ordained its prophet, soon to become its martyred messiah. Lincoln's Second Inaugural provided the interpretive and mythic context that not only explained America to itself but also explained America to the world. And because of America's sheer power, stunningly apparent in 1865, that world *had* to pay attention.

Lincoln's Second Inaugural realized muted praise in the Northern press. Republican radicals in Congress, led by Thaddeus Stevens of Pennsylvania, resented the irenic tone of Lincoln's address and, instead, pledged "no mercy" on the "conquered provinces." Lincoln himself was aware that his speech would not make him popular. In a letter to New York's politico Thurlow Weed, he wrote:

> I believe it is not immediately popular. Men are not flattered by being shown that there has been a difference in purpose between the Almighty and them. To deny it, however, in this case, is to deny that there is a God governing the world. It is a trust which I thought needed to be told; and as whatever humiliation there is in it, falls most directly on myself, I thought others might afford for me to tell it.[2]

In the Northern religious press, supposedly conscious of a "God governing the world," Lincoln's inauguration was also ignored. The real center of news at the inauguration was Vice President Johnson's intoxication: "Drunkenness in High Places . . . the grief, surprise and shame we feel at this development, cannot be put in words."[3] In like fashion, the *New York Observer* passed over Lincoln's Second Inaugural, reprinting it with no commentary, and focused instead on Johnson's intoxication: "The facts are sufficiently distressing in themselves, but they are less so than the silence, or gentleness of rebuke, with which the political papers favorable to Johnson's election, treat this great national calamity." Then, in an ironically prophetic afterthought: "When we contemplate the relations in which Mr. Johnson stands to the chief magistracy, and that already in our brief political history two presidents have died in office . . . we are appalled by the contingency that may suddenly transfer to the Presidency a man of such infirmity."[4]

With Columbia and Charleston in smoke and rubble behind him, Sherman turned his troops to the north. As he moved on to North Carolina, it was clear (much to Jefferson Davis's frustration) that General Johnston was in no shape either to block Sherman or to come to Lee's defense. But there would be one last try. Sherman moved his two-winged juggernaut toward Goldsboro, North Carolina. Meanwhile, Johnston learned that the wings were far enough apart possibly to concentrate his seventeen-thousand-man army on Sherman's left wing near Bentonville.

The fighting broke out on March 19 and caught the Yankees by surprise. After some initial gains, however, Johnston could not overrun the exposed wing. Once again he had to break off the attack, as Sherman's army recovered and marched in overwhelming force on the hopelessly outnumbered rebels. Unlike Grant—or perhaps learning from him—Sherman was unwilling to engage a costly frontal assault on Johnston. Besides, his army was tired and undersupplied. Instead of pursuing Johnston, Sherman allowed him to retreat, saving Union energies for a move into Virginia and the destruction of Lee's Army of Northern Virginia. While food was plenteous, shoes and uniforms were not. By March Sherman's Federals resembled Confederates: smoke-black faces, dirty and ragged clothes, and many bootless feet wrapped in cloth.

Moving through North Carolina, Sherman's forces did not replicate the wholesale pillaging that drove them in South Carolina. But looting continued, as did the persecution of slaves. African Americans soon learned that Union soldiers, especially those from the West, were no abolitionists; indeed they were outright racists. As in South Carolina, soldiers routinely plundered slave lodgings for food, clothing, and what few belongings the slaves possessed. Instances of racial assault continued even as Sherman made plain his determination to rid himself of freedmen following in his army's wake.

Sherman's strategy of demoralization through direct civilian suffering backfired in the areas most affected. Hatreds grew that would never dissipate. It was not the killing that bothered so many rebels—that was an accepted part of the vagaries of warfare—it was the pillage of civilian property. In particular, the women would not forget. Even more than soldiers in the field, their memories were seared and would find no absolution. In their defiance, the "Religion of the Lost Cause" would be born.[5]

The writer Cornelia Spencer of North Carolina confirmed that hatred for the Yankees did not emerge from the battlefield, heartbreaking as the killing fields were, but by "acts of indiscriminate and licensed pillage which were more to be deprecated than any consequence of the blood shed in fair and open fight during the war."[6] Triumphant Northern statesmen and generals would rewrite the moral economy of war so that civilian suffering was "just." But they could not rewrite the rules in the minds of the victims. All might be fair in war, but this war had gotten very dirty.

By March 25, the railroad link from Goldsboro to New Bern was complete, allowing Sherman to resurface from the journey into darkness and reunite with the army of General Schofield and General Alfred Howe Terry. Immediately he began thinking of moving north to join Grant at Richmond. To that end, he boarded a train for Grant's headquarters at City Point,

Virginia, to persuade his commander to wait until his army could join Grant at Richmond.

But Grant had other things on his mind, including a strategic meeting with Lincoln aboard the *River Queen* on March 27 and 28. By all accounts, Sherman and Lincoln dominated the conversations, with Grant listening closely. Lincoln needed assurances that Lee could never join up with Johnston, which Sherman provided. Both generals assured Lincoln "that one or the other of us would have to fight one more bloody battle, and that it would be the *last*." With that Lincoln responded "that there had been blood enough shed, and asked us if another battle could not be avoided."

Then Lincoln talked about the looming peace, stressing his desire to reunite the country as peacefully as possible with a minimum of revenge or retribution. He hoped Davis would flee the country, and "all he wanted of us," Sherman would later write, "was to defeat the opposing armies, and to get the men composing the Confederate armies back to their homes, at work on their farms and in their shops."[7] All realized that the greatest threat to peace would be a guerrilla war that could go on indefinitely. With Missouri as a microcosm for the nation, that was a scenario to be avoided at all costs.

When not meeting with Lincoln, Sherman again attempted to persuade Grant to postpone his movement on Lee until Sherman and his army could share in the sweet and long-awaited victory. But Grant was not persuadable. Practical considerations and issues of pride dominated Grant's decision. After years of inconclusive engagements with Lee he wanted the Army of the Potomac to beat Lee on its own. Were Sherman to join him for a shared victory, the "westerners" would take the credit for doing what Grant alone had not been able to accomplish, and the whole affair would become politicized.[8] Besides, he did not need Sherman's help.

Lee's only hope was to break free from his entrenchments in Petersburg and attempt to link up with Johnston's forces in North Carolina. But with Sherman now closing in from the south, it was a long shot indeed. Lee remained in his fortified lines as long as he could, hoping for a miracle. One thing was now certain: Richmond would have to be abandoned. The only question was when. In late February he wrote a note of foreboding and faith to his wife in which he conceded:

> I think General Grant will move against us soon . . . & no man can tell what may be the result . . . but trusting in a Merciful God, who does not always give the battle to the strong, I pray we may not be overwhelmed. I shall however endeavour to do my duty & fight to the last. Should it be necessary to

abandon our position to prevent being surrounded, what will you do? Will you remain or leave the city? . . . It is a fearful condition & we must rely for guidance & protection upon a kind Providence. May it guard & comfort you.[9]

Lee understood perfectly that Grant's intent "is now to starve us out," but as long as farmers remained patriotic, that was not likely. Throughout, Lee's faith in the people had remained strong, and they had reciprocated with a blind faith of their own. All were willing to do their duty in a losing cause if only to ensure that those who went before had not been sacrificed in vain.

Others were equally dutiful, especially the clergy. In Campbell County, Virginia, John Blair Dabney, a lawyer-turned-Episcopal-priest to four churches, preached regularly on the need to endure a righteous cause. The signs, he conceded, were ominous, and, in a telling moment, he embraced a scenario of apocalyptic deliverance. In a sermon on Matthew 24:44 ("Be ye also ready, for in such an hour as ye think not the Son of Man cometh"), Dabney underscored the fact that it would be quite foolish to place the Second Coming of Christ "at some remote period."

In a follow-up sermon preached on March 5, Dabney noted that the North needed to learn the lesson Napoleon had learned. In the same sermon, he conceded for the first time that the North might win. But then, in anticipation of postwar rhetoric, he stressed that their victory would never make the North right for waging such a vicious war on innocents:

They may succeed in extirpating or subduing us by their superiour power in giving peace to the South by reducing it to a desert. They may be permitted by a righteous providence to inflict on us unspeakable calamities, [but] when the victims of their savage warfare shall have vanished from the earth, they may be made to suffer untold evils for their cruelty, intolerance, and pride in the destruction of their government, the dissipation of their vaunted wealth.[10]

Winter of 1865 brought decreasing rations, delayed pay, and increased desertions in Johnston's army. Recognizing the impossibility of maintaining defensive lines stretching thirty miles or longer in the face of Grant's superior numbers, Lee concluded, "We shall have to abandon our position on the James River, as lamentable as it is on every account." Lee went on to note that a withdrawal, should it become necessary, "should be concentrated at some point on the railroad line between Richmond and Danville."[11]

On March 2 Lee wrote Grant proposing an "interview" to discuss peace "by means of a military convention." In other words, he suggested that the warrior priests should settle the fates of their countries by themselves. On the same day, he confessed to Davis his belief "that [Grant] will consent to no terms, unless coupled with the condition of our return to the Union."[12]

Clearly generals continued to matter greatly at this stage of the conflict—in particular Lee and Grant—but Grant was not yet ready to act as a statesman. He refused on the grounds that only the president had the authority to make such negotiations. One month later, Grant would change his mind and represent his nation in arranging a peace with Lee. Until a clear prospect of defeat and unconditional surrender appeared, conversations would go nowhere. In prior discussions among Secretary of War Seldon, Senator Robert M. T. Hunter, who had earlier participated in the ill-fated Hampton Roads Conference, and General Lee, the Confederate leaders came to the consensus that defeat was inevitable. Yet no one was willing to tell President Davis.

On March 10, 1865, the Confederacy observed what would be its last national fast. In Richmond, the observance was sincere beyond all precedent. Newspaper accounts marveled at how all stores and shops closed, and religious services were "more marked in Richmond than any previous occasion of its kind."[13]

In an unpublished sermon preached at Castle Craig Episcopal Church in Virginia, John Blair Dabney turned to Job 13:15: "Though he slay me, yet will I trust in him." Until then, millennial rhetoric had been tied to nationalism in both the North and the South. But if God had elected defeat as the fate of his chosen nation, it might be a sign that history itself was about to end. By observing the fast, Confederates might indeed be playing their strongest hand for, to Dabney's increasingly apocalyptic sensibilities, "[i]t is an awful reflexion, that the final issue of this war may probably depend on the manner and the spirit, in which our people discharge the duties of this day."

Then, anticipating the question on everyone's mind, Dabney asked why, when "our cause is a just one," does God not reward us with success? The answer, plain to all listeners familiar with the jeremiad, was that God required repentance and reformation of his chosen Southern people. The fight must go on because the war was just. For those who were waffling, Dabney invited them to think of a Southern defeat and reconstruction that would bring with it "a deluge of black, foreign, and Yankee emigrants who will lord it over us, take us from our homes, and revel in the enjoyment of all that we possess."[14]

If the Confederacy's future hinged on a proper observance of the fast, it was clear by late March that their sincerity must have been insufficient. The bad news continued. Again, at Castle Craig Episcopal Church, Dabney returned to apocalyptic themes with a sermon on Hebrews 6:4–6, preached on March 26, and once more on April 2 at Hopewell Church. The times, he noted, were portentous, "when every hour is big with important events." For all in attendance, life was uncertain in the face of a foe who did not discriminate between soldiers and civilians. No one knew "what unspeakable wretchedness, what a sudden . . . and horrible death may be in store for them." To those who thought they would be spared as civilians, he asked: "Do they dream that the public enemy, so unsparing to others, will spare them? Let them then prepare for the terrible catastrophe, with which we are threatened, by making their peace with God."

In one profound sense, 1865 was different than 1860. Increasingly downbeat Southern moralists evidenced apocalyptic sensibilities. Being in the moral right no longer guaranteed deliverance. Defeat might come, and if it did, it could only mean the end of history. References to the "man of sin"—a mysterious figure who prefigures the end times in the apostle Paul's letters— appeared more frequently as battles were lost. Until then, the South, like the North, incarnated its millennial speculations into nationalism and global salvation in this world. Apocalyptic thoughts about the end of history were thoughts of defeat and worlds to come.

Because no guilt fell on the head of the South, and because things seemed to be going so badly, Dabney wondered if the end of history was dawning in a premillennial reign of terror by the "man of sin" who would, in turn, spark Christ's Second Coming:

We are evidently on the eve of great political revolutions. The signs of the times clearly indicate important changes in the constitution of human society, and the face of the world. The elements of discord are at work, and the explosion cannot be much longer delayed. . . . It behooves us to be prepared for this awful event: for we know not at what moment it may come. Then we shall see our blessed Lord "coming in the clouds of heaven with power and great glory" to judge the world. . . . Then will the second coming of our Christ carry no terrour to your hearts, but will be welcomed by you with songs of rejoicing.[15]

CHAPTER 44

"RICHMOND! BABYLON IS FALLEN!!"

In the field, the continued inability of the Confederate War Department to feed and supply Lee's army was growing acute. In a letter to Secretary of War John C. Breckinridge, Lee outlined the sorry state of military affairs everywhere, but highlighted the imperative to feed his starving army. If his men were fed and supplied, the war would continue, because ultimately it was neither Davis's war nor Lee's war: "Everything in my opinion has depended and still depends upon the disposition and feelings of the people."[1]

Lee was half right. President Davis meant relatively little to the future of the armies, but Lee meant everything to the armies *and* to the people. If Lee was not the sacred totem of the Confederacy, he was the closest of any human to being one, and as long as he survived and joined the fight, the South would not surrender.

Now wholly caught up in last ditch schemes of desperation, Lee ordered General John B. Gordon to lead an assault on Federal forces at Hare's Hill (Fort Stedman) in the early morning of March 25. If Gordon's sharpshooters and following infantry could exploit the vulnerable point and break through, they might have a chance to move south and allow Lee to link up with Johnston's pitifully reduced "army" of 13,500. With great spirit but little hope, Gordon penetrated the Federal lines and succeeded in overrunning Fort Stedman, moving on toward Grant's headquarters at City Point. Then Grant's superior numbers took over. The captured works were recaptured and Gordon was forced to retreat. In the process, Lee lost four thousand men he could ill afford to lose. Worse, the failed assault shortened the intervening distance for a counterattack, for which Grant planned immediately.[2]

Sensing blood, Grant pushed on all fronts. On April 1, he ordered the combined forces of Sheridan's cavalry and Gouverneur Warren's Fifth Corps to smash through Pickett's right wing near Five Forks. On April 2, Longstreet joined up with Lee from north of the James River, bringing the bulk of Lee's army to support the endangered right wing. By then, Lee's exhausted war-crazed troops were literally starving, but still they soldiered on under Lee's charismatic command. Again, the day belonged to Grant, as his early morning assault carried the enemy's lines in the center and on Lee's left. Grant was so pleased, he drove out to observe the progress.[3] This was what he had waited for all those months, and what his commander had been waiting four years to witness. For his part, Lee knew his situation was desperate and in a memo to Breckinridge conceded, "Our only chance, then, of concentrating our forces, is to do so near Danville railroad, which I shall endeavor to do at once. I advise that all preparation be made for leaving Richmond tonight."[4]

That evening, Lee sent out urgent orders to all his generals, commanding them to "abandon our position" immediately and break out to rendezvous at Amelia Courthouse on the Danville railroad line. At 11:30 p.m. Lee left Petersburg for Amelia Courthouse, muttering to his aide, "This is just what I told them at Richmond. The line has been extended until it snapped."

By the afternoon of April 2, a triumphant General Grant informed Lincoln that Petersburg was his and invited the president to visit him in the city the next morning. Instead of pursuing Lee's fleeing army, Grant surmised Lee's destination and determined to get there ahead of him and block his retreat with minimal bloodshed. The Danville Road was virtually the only escape route Lee had, and Sheridan's cavalry beat him to the punch.

Sunday morning, April 12, found churches in Richmond packed with worshippers. Most of those in attendance were women in mourning; a few men entered on crutches, pale and worn with fever. Of St. Paul's, where President Davis sat in attendance at his customary pew, no. 63, the memoirist Cooper DeLeon later observed:

> It was no holiday gathering of perfumed and bedizened godliness, that Sunday in Richmond. Earnest men and women had come to the house of God, to ask His protection and His blessing, yet a little longer, for the dear ones that very moment battling so hotly for the worshippers.[5]

The morning service had been concluded, and the Reverend Minnigerode was preparing for communion when the sexton walked down the aisle, stopped at the president's pew, gently tapped him on the shoulder, and handed him a piece of paper. One communicant, sitting behind Davis, was "so near that I plainly saw the sort of gray pallor that came upon his face as he read." Without a word, Davis rose and walked out. An "uneasy whimper ran through the congregation," and soon word was out that the administration must evacuate Richmond. Immediately, "the vast congregation rose en masse and rushed towards the door."

The Davis administration quickly packed their offices and entered trains that evening. Panic broke out in Richmond. As he prepared to rejoin his unit, an ailing Colonel George Alexander Martin witnessed men, women, and children ransacking commissary stores even as others clogged the streets rushing to leave town. Despite orders to destroy the whiskey, the liquors had been "liberated" and flowed freely into the throats of "skulking men and coarse, half-drunken women gathered before the stores."[6]

That evening (April 2–3) the drinking and plundering continued unabated. Fires broke out all over the city. As the Shockoe warehouse erupted in flames, fires spread to the houses. LaSalle Pickett observed how the flames "stretched out burning arms on all sides and embraced in deadly clasp the stately mansions which had stood in lofty grandeur from the olden days of colonial pride. Soon they became towering masses of fire."

On Monday morning Federal troops under General Godfrey Weitzel announced the occupation of the city and proclaimed, "The people of Richmond are assured that we come to restore to them the blessings of peace, prosperity, and freedom, under the flag of Union." Soon thereafter Union troops from Vermont and New Hampshire led the first brigade up Franklin Street. They were soon followed in orderly fashion by an endless stream of company after company, marching to bands and singing the "Battle Cry of Freedom." The proudest moment for the Union came as Colonel Charles Francis Adams Jr., a descendant of two United States presidents—both opposed to slavery—led the Fifth Massachusetts Cavalry, an all-black regiment, into the city. Adams later remarked that it was "the one event which I should most have desired as the culmination of my life in the army."

The sides of Richmond's streets were crowded with people, mostly black. Federal Major N. D. Stoodley observed, "They shouted, they danced, cried, prayed, sang, and cut up all manner of wild capers." A black band played the "Year of Jubilee" to great applause from soldiers and bystanders alike. Richmond's white inhabitants stayed indoors, still not quite believing what they were viewing and fearing a repeat of the sack of Columbia. Among the litter in the aftermath lay that morning's edition of the *Richmond Whig*, which was defiant to the end. Even as Lee marched out, faith in his army remained, because God was on their side. The editorial announced: "One has only to read the records of battle and campaigns in which the bible abounds to see how frequently, how generally indeed the weaker party in numbers and materiel of war came out victorious."[7]

On April 3 a triumphant Grant notified Lincoln from Richmond that the capital city was now in Federal hands and invited him down from City Point for a visit. Like Columbia, Richmond lay in flames, but not as a result of invading Federal armies. Richmond diarist Sallie A. Putnam described the destruction unleashed by an "exploding arsenal" of several hundred railroad cars carrying loaded shell that had been left behind. "At every moment the most terrific explosions were sending forth their awful reverberations, and gave us the idea of a general bombardment. All the horrors of the final conflagration, when the earth shall be wrapped in flames and melt with fervent heat, were, it seemed to us, prefigured in our capital." Then, when things couldn't possibly get any worse, a cry went out: "The Yankees! The Yankees are coming!" Union soldiers immediately raised the Stars and Stripes over the city capital and "now only the most bitter and crushing recollections awoke within us, as upon our quickened hearing fell the strains of 'The Star Spangled Banner.' For us it was a requiem for buried hopes."

But all was not dark. This Union army would show mercy instead of vengeance, and Richmond would be spared the drunken destruction of Columbia. To save as much of the city as possible, Weitzel sent all unneeded Union troops back to camp, retaining a corps of forty-five hundred officers and soldiers. These stacked their arms and formed fire squads, speeding to all points of the city where help could be rendered. Terrified residents marveled that "no attempt at plunder [was] reported!" Cooper DeLeon reported: "Military training never had better vindication than on that fearful day; for its bonds must have been strong indeed, to hold that army, suddenly in possession of a city so coveted—so defiant—so deadly, for four long years." In West Point terms, *this* was the way a defenseless city in flames should have been treated.

Sallie Putnam also paid grudging thanks to Federal troops who tried to put out the flames. "And the grateful thanks of the people of Richmond are due to General Weitzel and other officers for their energetic measures to save the city from entire destruction." In the end, the West Point Code returned, and for this act of unexpected help, grateful Richmond inhabitants offered "sincere gratitude, for the respect, the kindness, the lenity with which the citizens were treated. For a conquered people, the lines had fallen to us in pleasant places. . . . They softened greatly the first bitter experiences of our subjugation."[8] Left unsaid by Putnam was the fact that many of Weitzel's soldiers who were struggling to put out the flames were African American.

"View in the 'Burnt District,' Richmond, Virginia." Swathed in black mourning clothes, two Richmond ladies pick their way through the streets of their devastated city. Only the timely assistance of triumphant Federal troops prevented total destruction of the city.

Following close behind the Federal armies on April 4 was a triumphant President Lincoln accompanied by his son Tad. The scenes were a jumble of confusion, rage, and worship as he walked down the burned-out streets. One bystander looked closely at her new president and noticed how the war had taken its toll: "He seemed tired and old."

Soon Lincoln was surrounded by a circle of adoring black people shouting, "Bless the Lord! The great Messiah!" Little did they know how literally they spoke. Lincoln, however, fully understood the depth of identification and instructed one black man who fell at his feet: "Don't kneel to me. That is not right. You must kneel to God only, and thank Him for the liberty you will enjoy hereafter."[9]

Lincoln entered a carriage surrounded by an escort of black cavalry to take him to the capital. He was particularly struck by the Confederate White House. As he sat at the executive desk, he had nothing to say except, "This must have been President Davis's chair." No doubt the emotions at occupying the chair of an adversary who had run away only days earlier were intense. Lincoln's use of the term "president" was an unbidden recognition of a "nation" that was not merely "rebels."

In Philadelphia, the *Inquirer* noted Grant's victory with the triumphant headline "Richmond! Babylon Is Fallen!!" It then added: "General Weitzel Enters the City . . . Philadelphia Colored Troops the First to Enter! Weitzel's

Negroes Extinguish the Flames." . . . "The 'Indomitable Ulysses' Marching on. Lee's Army in Full Retreat!"[10] Alongside its tribute to Grant, the paper fawned over Sheridan: "The praises of Phil Sheridan are on every tongue today . . . with the bagging of Ewell and other Rebel Generals . . . victories by Sheridan were now come to be looked upon as matters of course."[11]

But Lee was not done yet. On April 6 he urged General John B. Gordon to march on and then asked the impossible of his dying soldiers and horses: "I know that men and animals are much exhausted, but it is necessary to tax their strength." Amazingly, the wasted soldiers complied and marched in a stupor toward their destination at Farmville on a railroad line to Lynchburg. Lee assumed he would get supplies from Danville, not realizing that Yankees controlled the road in between. The rations would never arrive.

Unaware of the bitter disappointment ahead, Lee pushed out from Amelia Courthouse and almost made it to his supposed provision trains. The middle of his column of escape then became separated from the others and was annihilated at Sayler's Creek, with General Richard S. Ewell and Lee's eldest son, Custis Lee, forced to surrender.

Sheridan, not one to minimize his own importance, summarized the heroics of his troops but later regretted that the subsequent surrender of Lee's army would rob him of the personal praise to which he was accustomed: "The capture of Ewell, with six of his generals and most of his troops, crowned our success, but the fight was so overshadowed by the stirring events of the surrender three days later, that the battle has never been accorded the prominence it deserves." Sheridan, at least, was mindful of the significance of his victory and that night reported to Grant, "If the thing is pressed I think Lee will surrender." When informed of Sheridan's observation, Lincoln wired Grant: "Let the *thing* be pressed."[12]

The next day Lee's skeletal divisions lurched toward Appomattox Station, hoping for supplies from Lynchburg. They camped two miles north of the railroad station at Appomattox Courthouse. Again Grant delivered a message to Lee urging surrender and graciously offering "to meet you . . . at any point agreeable to you, for the purpose of arranging definitely the terms upon which the surrender of the Army of Northern Virginia will be received."[13]

Again Lee declined, still hoping his starving army would be fed. When he learned that Grant's army had beaten him to Appomattox Station with thousands more well-fed and well-equipped Yankees fast closing in on his rear, he determined to attempt one final breakthrough. One last time, Gordon and Longstreet urged their starving troops toward the enemy. The assault was hopeless and the troops were hemmed in on three sides. It failed miserably, but significantly Lee's last military maneuver ended where it all began, on the attack.

On the evening of April 7, Grant met with his generals. All agreed that the end was near and urged a meeting with Lee to avoid unnecessary bloodshed. Once again the generals sought to intercede for their nations, and this time Grant invoked no higher authority in inviting Lee to surrender his army before "any further effusion of blood" be shed. Earlier, when Grant and Sherman had met with Lincoln aboard the *River Queen,* it had been clear that Lincoln thought of his generals as "associates." He would leave it to them to negotiate a "lenient" surrender.[14] When Lee showed Grant's letter to Longstreet, Longstreet replied "not yet," and Lee agreed. Still hoping to extract an honorable peace rather than surrender, Lee proposed instead a personal meeting between the two generals.

As of April 9, Palm Sunday, Lee had not heard back from Grant, who was nursing a massive migraine headache. Assuming that Grant had received his message and planned to meet with him, Lee crossed his picket lines under a flag of truce, only to find that Grant would not see him unless he intended to surrender. At the same time, Sheridan checked the Confederate advance near Appomattox Courthouse and captured Lee's vital supply train. With all gambits played out, Lee wrote to Grant on April 9: "I ask a suspension of hostilities, pending the adjustment of the terms of the surrender of this army."[15] Once Grant read the message, his headache disappeared.

Lee had no idea what to expect. For all he knew, he would soon be in shackles facing a summary court-martial and immediate execution for treason. Nor did he know how his suffering soldiers and officers would be treated by their triumphant foes. For their part, hesitant Yankee soldiers, inured by four years of surprises and disappointments, feared that Lee's communication might be a ruse to allow for escape. Sheridan, impetuous as always, massed his army to attack Lee in the low valley where they were bivouacked. But Grant knew better. Honor counted everywhere with the generals and nowhere more than with General Lee. Just as Custer was about to attack, word reached Sheridan: "Lee has surrendered; do not charge; the white flag is up."[16]

After several hours of anxious waiting, Lee received word from Grant that they would meet in the parlor of the house of the Wilmer McLean family north of the courthouse. Again Lee rode toward his picket line behind a flag of truce, and this time Grant did not disappoint him. Grant was conducted to the McLean house, where Lee waited in full dress uniform, with dress sword glittering at his side.

In a uniform he would never wear in the field, Lee looked like the victor rather than the vanquished. Grant, on the other hand, had just come in from the field and was swordless and mud-splattered. He wore his customary private's blouse, distinguished only by the shoulder straps of a lieutenant general. The two men shook hands, then proceeded to discuss terms of surrender. Though Grant knew Lee from his service in the Mexican War, he could not read Lee's impassive face or discern his reactions:

> Whatever his feelings, they were entirely concealed from my observation; but my own feelings, which had been quite jubilant on the receipt of his letter, were sad and depressed. I felt like anything rather than rejoicing at the downfall of a foe who had fought so long and valiantly, and had suffered so much for a cause, though that cause was, I believe, one of the worst for which a people ever fought, and one for which there was the least excuse.

Southern civilians might still want blood, but the soldiers had had enough. The two generals fell into an animated conversation "about old army times," until finally Lee reminded Grant of the purpose of their meeting. In asking for terms, Grant replied simply, "I meant merely that your army should lay down their arms, not to take them up again during the continuance of the war unless duly and properly exchanged." With that, Grant again rambled until Lee requested the terms be set in writing, which Grant proceeded to do. When Lee learned how generous Grant's terms were—including permission for soldiers to keep their sidearms, horses, and private property—he noted that it would have a "happy effect" on his army.

Only after the two men had parted did Grant telegraph Secretary of War Stanton, almost as an afterthought, with news of the surrender *he* had authorized: "General Lee surrendered the Army of Northern Virginia this afternoon on terms proposed by myself."[17] Grant did not exaggerate. On the occasion of Lee's surrender, Grant spoke for the nation, telling the enemy soldiers that with surrender, "each officer and man will be allowed to return to their homes, not to be disturbed by United States authority so long as they observe their paroles and the laws in force where they may reside." There would be no reprisals, no trials, no humiliating imprisonments and seizures. Following Lincoln's inclinations, Grant determined to cap a convincing victory with a peace worth the purchase.

Lee returned to his anxious and starving army. As the troops gathered before him, many in tears, Lee spoke affectionately to those who had suffered so much and now must go home. But go home they should. In a direct attempt to discourage all notion of guerrilla warfare, he spoke quietly and to great effect: "I have done for you all that it was in my power to do. You have done all your duty. Leave the result to God. Go to your homes and resume your occupations. Obey the laws and become as good citizens as you were soldiers." With that Lee rode off, bareheaded and eyes straight ahead.

When news of the surrender reached the Yankee soldiers, they began firing salutes to their victory. Grant immediately ordered them to cease fire and show respect for an army that was no longer "the enemy" but one of them. One last time the two generals met, each mounted on his favorite horse, respective armies on either side. Lee expressed his hope that no more lives would be lost. Grant, hoping that again Lee (rather than Davis) would speak for his people, replied, "There [is] not a man in the Confederacy whose influence with the soldiery and the whole people was as great as [yours], and . . . if [you] would now advise the surrender of all the armies I had no doubt [your] advice would be followed with alacrity."[18] Lee hedged, noting that he would have to consult President Davis. But the seed was clearly planted.

Grant returned to the McLean house, where "the officers of both armies came in great numbers, and seemed to enjoy the meeting as much as though they had been friends separated for a long time while fighting battles under the same flag." In a profound sense that would only become apparent in time, this was indeed the case.

On April 10 Lee issued his final General Orders No. 9 to the army, subsequently known as "Lee's Farewell Address." Without any thought of ongoing resistance or guerrilla war options, he urged officers and soldiers to "return to [your] homes." Further organized war would be a "useless sacrifice" and guerrilla warfare was unthinkable. Faithful to the end, Lee closed: "You will take with you the satisfaction that proceeds from the consciousness of duty faithfully performed, and I earnestly pray that a Merciful God will extend to you His blessing and protection."[19]

Two days later, a ceremony of surrender took place at Appomattox Courthouse. Federal soldiers lined the principal street to await the formal surrender of Confederate battle flags and arms. General Joshua Chamberlain, with three war wounds and a Congressional Medal of Honor, was selected to be the first general to receive the defeated foe. Confederate Corps Commander John B. Gordon, also wounded five times at Antietam and decorated, rode at the head of the Confederate army. Both generals had suffered and bled for their cause and now would face each other in peace. General Chamberlain later described the ritual:

On they came, with the old swinging route step and swaying battle flags. In the van, the proud Confederate ensign. . . . Before us in proud humiliation stood the embodiment of manhood; men whom neither toils and sufferings, nor the fact of death, nor disaster, nor hopelessness could bend from their resolve; standing before us now, thin, worn and famished, but erect, and with eyes looking level into ours, waking memories.

While the rebels knew the lenient terms of their surrender, they did not know how they would be received by the triumphant Yankees. Would they be jeered? Assaulted? The answer came soon enough as they reached the Federal column where Chamberlain and his officers waited. A bugle sounded. Immediately the Union line snapped to attention and went through the traditional manual of arms, beginning with the position of "salute," and then back to "order arms," and "parade rest." Chamberlain did not command his officers to "present arms," because that was reserved for the highest honor.

But still the command was respectful and this was not lost on Gordon. Hearing the salute, he immediately wheeled his horse and dropped the point of his sword to the boot toe, ordering his men to dip the Confederate banner and answer with the same "carry honors" as they marched, rank upon rank, past the respectful Yankees—"honor answering honor." Chamberlain described the scene: "On our part not a sound of trumpet more, nor roll of drum; not a cheer, nor word nor whisper of vain-glorying, nor motion of man standing again at the order, but an awed stillness rather, and breath-holding, as if it were the passing of the dead!"[20]

Over the next few days, 28,231 soldiers were fed and paroled at Appomattox under the compassionate terms dictated by Grant. In retrospect, he had clearly exceeded his powers as general and negotiated the future of his nation.[21] From the start, the political and military leaders had been closely intertwined within their respective countries, and over time, the generals had gained more and more authority. To be sure, Grant's terms were in accord with Lincoln's wishes, but the fact remains that it was Grant who set the terms for Lee's unconditional surrender and not his commander in chief.

With Lee's surrender, the North had a military icon of its own. Grant was not only the army's greatest general but, more important, the people's greatest general. Only their religious-like faith in his leadership could have permitted the rivers of bloodshed to wash through their homes and towns. But they believed. Grant had a plan and now the fruits of that plan were evident.

In his memoirs, written years later, Sheridan took a brief respite from his own glorification to praise Grant. In highlighting the campaign to "get Lee," Sheridan fastened on his commander's "imperturbable tenacity": "When his military history is analyzed after the lapse of years, it will show, even more clearly than now, that during these as well as in his previous campaigns he was the steadfast centre about and on which everything else turned."[22]

On April 15, Lee returned to his house in Richmond to monitor events and wait out the remainder of the war. Jefferson Davis had escaped south, vowing to continue the fighting "indefinitely" and refusing to rule out guerrilla warfare. On April 20 a concerned Lee, no doubt mindful of Grant's earlier prompt, wrote what was perhaps the most important letter in the course of the entire war. In it, he urged Davis to forgo guerrilla strategies: "A partisan war may be continued, and hostilities protracted, causing individual suffering and the devastation of the country, but I see no prospect by that means of achieving a separate independence . . . to save useless effusion of blood, I would recommend measures be taken for suspension of hostilities and the restoration of peace."[23] Lee's wise counsel was soon circulated throughout the general corps of the Confederate army and weighed far more heavily on their decisions than any words from President Davis in flight.[24]

In Georgia, a spirit of "brotherhood" encompassed war-weary veterans who, days earlier, were prepared to kill. A spirit of mutual forgiveness and admiration (at least among white soldiers) set in almost immediately. They, after all, fought a just war.

The women would not be so forgiving. They had experienced Sherman's hard war most personally and directly, with no postwar fellowship of warriors to heal the wounds or salve the hatreds. In North Carolina, where soldiers from both armies "grouped together around the fires," the women raged. The war against them was not just, and their forgiveness would not be forthcoming. A furious Emma Holmes responded to Appomattox by saying: "Peace on such terms, is war for the rising generations."[25]

Had Davis had his way with guerrilla warfare, Holmes's words might well have been prescient. Thanks in large part to General Lee, he would not prevail, but this generation of Southern women would remember. Even as they deified Lee, they would demonize Northern generals and soldiers. Satan himself would be incarnated in Confederate female memory not in the "butcher" Grant (he, after all, concentrated the killing on fields of battle where it belonged), but in Sherman. The one most sympathetic to the white South and least sympathetic to abolition emerged in Southern memory as the epitome of dark malice and barbarism.[26]

On April 12, the last major city of the Confederacy capitulated as Federal troops under General E. R. S. Canby drove the last Confederate defenders out of Mobile, Alabama. That same day President Davis met with Generals Johnston and Beauregard and his cabinet. Over the objections of Davis and the ever-loyal Judah Benjamin, the generals insisted that Sherman could not be defeated and that further hostilities would be virtually suicidal. For the first time, the generals broke ranks with their commander in chief. And their view prevailed. As news of Lee's surrender reached the generals that afternoon, they agreed that "the Southern Confederacy was overthrown."

That night Johnston summarized the impossible task the army faced, but even more, the loss of a home front. Lee's surrender broke the back of civilian resolve just as surely as a defeat for Sherman at Atlanta would have clinched McClellan's election. At last, three and a half years and hundreds of thousands of sacrificed lives later, Johnston could say to Davis that the *people* "are tired of the war, feel themselves whipped, and will not fight." Therefore, Johnston continued, the South had no choice but to surrender, and it must begin with Sherman. With these words, as the historian Mark Grimsley recognizes, "Johnston thus did what no American commander has ever done, before or since: he exercised the full weight of his military position to tell his government how to conclude a war."[27]

Lincoln and his cabinet, meanwhile, were already past the war and thinking about reconstruction. Secretary of War Stanton ordered the draft halted and discontinued the purchase of war matériel. On the morning of Good Friday, April 14, General Robert Anderson raised the Federal banner over Fort Sumter—almost exactly four years after lowering the same flag to the victorious rebels. Henry Ward Beecher preached the conciliatory sermon he promised. That evening, Lincoln intended to relax by attending the theater.

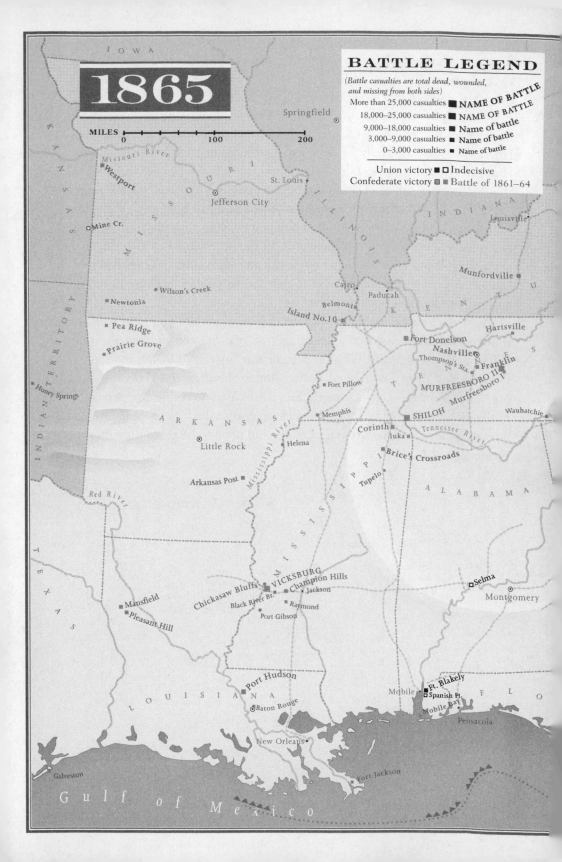

1865

BATTLE LEGEND

*(Battle casualties are total dead, wounded,
and missing from both sides)*

More than 25,000 casualties	■ **NAME OF BATTLE**
18,000–25,000 casualties	■ **NAME OF BATTLE**
9,000–18,000 casualties	■ Name of battle
3,000–9,000 casualties	■ Name of battle
0–3,000 casualties	■ Name of battle

Union victory ■ □ Indecisive
Confederate victory ▦ ■ Battle of 1861–64

IOWA

KANSAS

Springfield

Missouri River

Westport

MISSOURI

St. Louis

Jefferson City

ILLINOIS

INDIANA

Louisville

Mine Cr.

Munfordville

Wilson's Creek

Cairo

Paducah

KENTUCKY

Newtonia

Belmont

Hartsville

INDIAN TERRITORY

Pea Ridge

Island No.10

Fort Donelson

Prairie Grove

Nashville

Thompson's Sta. Franklin

MURFREESBORO II

Murfreesboro I

Honey Springs

ARKANSAS

Fort Pillow

TENNESSEE

Wauhatchie

Mississippi River

Memphis

SHILOH

Little Rock

Helena

Corinth

Iuka

Tennessee River

Arkansas Post

Brice's Crossroads

Tupelo

Red River

MISSISSIPPI

ALABAMA

TEXAS

Mansfield

Chickasaw Bluffs VICKSBURG Champion Hills

Selma

Pleasant Hill

Black River Br.

Jackson

Montgomery

Raymond

Port Gibson

LOUISIANA

Port Hudson

Ft. Blakely

Mobile

Spanish Ft.

FLO

Baton Rouge

Mobile Bay

Pensacola

New Orleans

Galveston

Fort Jackson

Gulf of Mexico

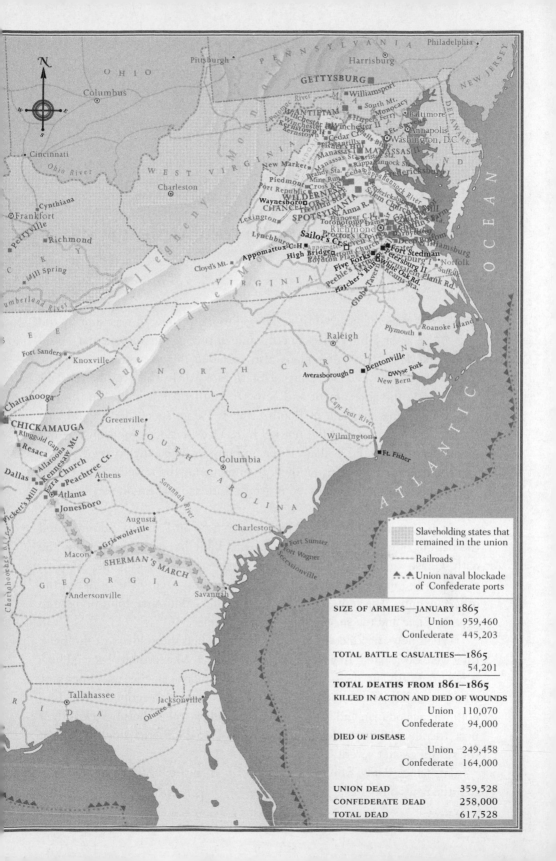

N

OHIO
Columbus
Cincinnati
Ohio River
Frankfort
Perryville
Richmond
K E N T U C K Y
Mill Spring
Cumberland River
Knoxville
Fort Sanders
Chattanooga
CHICKAMAUGA
Ringgold Gap
Resaca
Allatoona Mt.
Dallas
Pickett's Mill
Ezra Church
Kennesaw Mt.
Peachtree Cr.
Athens
Atlanta
Jonesboro
Griswoldville
Macon
SHERMAN'S MARCH
Andersonville
G E O R G I A
Chattahoochee River
Tallahassee
Jacksonville
Olustee
F L O R I D A

Pittsburgh
PENNSYLVANIA
Harrisburg
Philadelphia
GETTYSBURG
Williamsport
South Mt.
Monocacy
ANTIETAM
Harper's Ferry
Baltimore
Winchester I Winchester II
Ft. Stevens
Annapolis
Kernstown Kernstown II
Washington, D.C.
WEST VIRGINIA
Charleston
Fisher's Hill
Cedar Cr. Falls Church
Chantilly
New Market
Manassas I MANASSAS II
Manassas Sta. Bristoe Sta.
Fredericksburg
Piedmont
Brandy Sta.
Rappahannock Sta.
Mine Run
Rappahannock River
Port Republic Cross Keys
Cross Keys
WILDERNESS
Fredericksburg
Salem Church
Waynesboro
Mill
CHANCELLORSVILLE
SPOTSYLVANIA
Lexington
N. Anna R.
Hanover C.H.
Cold Harbor
Gaines' Farm
Totopotomoy
Mechanicsville
Savage's Station
Richmond
Malvern Hill
Lynchburg
Sailor's Cr.
Seven Pines
Proctor's Creek
Drewry's Bluff
Appomattox C.H.
High Bridge
Deep Bottom
Williamsburg
Five Forks
Fort Stedman
Cloyd's Mt.
Boydton Plank Rd.
Petersburg I
Petersburg II
Norfolk
Peeble's Farm
Jerusalem Plank Rd.
Suffolk
Hatcher's Run
White Oak Rd.
V I R G I N I A
Globe Tavern
Reams' Sta.
Allegheny Mountains
Blue Ridge Mountains

Raleigh
Plymouth
Roanoke Island
Bentonville
Averasborough
Wyse Fork
New Bern
N O R T H   C A R O L I N A
Greenville
Cape Fear River
Columbia
Wilmington
Ft. Fisher
S O U T H   C A R O L I N A
Savannah River
Augusta
Charleston
Fort Sumter
Fort Wagner
Secessionville
Savannah

OHIO
NEW JERSEY
DELAWARE
MARYLAND
A T L A N T I C   O C E A N

Slaveholding states that
remained in the union

- - - - Railroads

▲▲▲ Union naval blockade
of Confederate ports

SIZE OF ARMIES—JANUARY 1865
Union   959,460
Confederate   445,203

TOTAL BATTLE CASUALTIES—1865
54,201

TOTAL DEATHS FROM 1861–1865
KILLED IN ACTION AND DIED OF WOUNDS
Union   110,070
Confederate   94,000

DIED OF DISEASE
Union   249,458
Confederate   164,000

UNION DEAD   359,528
CONFEDERATE DEAD   258,000
TOTAL DEAD   617,528

CHAPTER 45

"THE MAN DIES, BUT THE CAUSE LIVES"

On the night of April 14, 1865, President Lincoln was shot by the actor John Wilkes Booth while sitting in the audience at Ford's Theater. Booth's plans also included the assassination of Vice President Johnson and Secretary of State Seward. In this way he thought to dismantle the government and achieve Southern independence through terror. A hulking associate of Booth's, Lewis Paine, succeeded in stabbing Seward several times, but did not kill him. Vice President Johnson was immediately called to the William Peterson house, where Lincoln lay dying. At 7:22 the next morning, Lincoln died. In announcing the tragedy, Secretary of War Stanton purportedly intoned in words both sad and prophetic: "Now he belongs to the ages."

At 11:00 a.m. on April 15, Chief Justice Salmon P. Chase administered the oath of office to Andrew Johnson, with Bible in hand. After issuing the oath, Chase announced, "You are the President. May God guide, support, and bless you in your arduous labors." Johnson answered, "The duties of the office are mine. The consequences are with God." With that, Johnson bent to kiss the Bible and the succession was complete.[1]

When news of Lincoln's assassination reached the soldiers in the field, they were devastated. In a letter to his brother, D. M. Corthell observed how Lincoln's death "no doubt produced a deeper horror in the army then any where else. The indignation of the soldiers is beyond description. Mr. Lincoln was a good man and a great man and I believe the Rebels have lost their best friend." He then added prophetically, "Mr. Johnson I think will treat them with greater severity."[2]

For James Bates, who marched with Sherman from Atlanta to Wilmington, the news hit hard:

For the first ten days of this month the news which came to us was received with intense enthusiasm. But when the news of the assassination of our President reached us, it threw a mantle of sadness over every heart. Never was the death of a public man so deeply lamented as that of Abraham Lincoln. By his wise and judicious management of affairs since he took the presidential chair he has won the esteem and affections of every loyal heart.[3]

Northern papers and preachers saw, in Lincoln's assassination, "the last victim of the Slave Power." Predictably, some secular papers focused on the gory details. By midnight, the *Philadelphia Inquirer* wrote, "[t]he President was in a state of stupor, totally insensible, and breathing slowly, the blood oozing from the wound at the back of his head. The surgeons were exhausting every possible effort of medical skill, but all hope was gone. The parting of his family with the dying President is too sad for description."[4]

On Easter Sunday, following Lincoln's assassination, William F. Morgan of Manhattan employed Christ's last words to form a eulogy: "His precious life was wasted, and the last expiring breath only sufficed for the exclamation, 'It is finished!' " For the South, Morgan held no sentiments but revenge: "Let the south be held answerable, and drink from the chalice which she had prepared for the lips of those she had been so long wont to despise and count of no reputation." Then in words that belied the sentiment, he concluded that Northerners "still do claim for the North, in the sight of Heaven, that [the war] has not been carried on in a spirit of bitterness or revenge."[5]

In fact, themes of revenge permeated the secular and religious press and, even more immediately, the pulpit in the weeks and months following Lincoln's assassination. Robert Russell Booth, pastor of Mercer Street Presbyterian Church in New York City, typified the clerical response when he urged, "Let them [the South] perish! In the grave of our martyred President, let the last vestige of them be buried, and let their memory rot, never to be spoken of with approval hereafter by a true patriot or Christian man."[6]

Besides seeking vengeance Northern preachers, writers, and statesmen immediately set out to complete Lincoln's incarnation as the messiah of the reunited Republic. On the same Easter Sunday that Morgan preached in Manhattan, George Boardman explained to his Presbyterian congregation in Binghamton, New York, that the only parallel to Lincoln was Christ: "His murderer has effected his apotheosis. Our beloved chief magistrate was removed at the height of his fame, his reputation unsullied, the equal of Washington, and beyond Washington, a martyr to the cause of Constitutional liberty. The name of ABRAHAM LINCOLN has entered into history, almost the only one without a spot. . . . The man dies, but the cause lives. Even Jesus

Apotheosis by D. T. Wiest, modeled after John James Barralet's *Apotheosis of George Washington*. Ascending to immortality, Abraham Lincoln is pictured surrounded by angels. At his feet are Columbia—the reunited nation—and a Native American, with heads bowed.

died, but his cause survives and prevails; and ours, so far as it is coincident with his, can never be overthrown."[7]

The Universalist pastor Adoniram J. Patterson, who held the opposite opinion of evangelicals on almost all issues save the nation, agreed with Boardman:

> The haters of liberty crucified the son of Mary. But he rose to life again, and his resurrection is celebrated by the Christian church throughout the world. By his death he acquired a power and influence which he could never have attained in life. So shall it be with our lamented dead [President]. Power shall be born of his ashes, even as a corn of wheat dying brings forth an hundred fold,—and the wrath of man be made to praise thee, O God.[8]

Abraham Lincoln, the single most photographed subject during the Civil War, could not escape the photographers' selective display of images. With his assassination and apotheosis into America's messiah, photographers, statesmen, and family refused to reproduce the most recent photographs of the living Lincoln, taken in 1865 by Alexander Gardner and Henry Warren. The reason? He looked too thin and emaciated:

> Most portraitists resolutely refused to record the physical consequences of the Lincoln presidency on its chief executive, for as a martyr, they probably reasoned, he should not appear wasted or even haggard. Part of the dying-god legend required that its heroes be struck down in their prime. So print-makers romanticized Lincoln's features in their post-assassination portrayals, making his now-gaunt physique heroic rather than taking the commercial risk required to reveal the truth.[9]

As word spread throughout the South of the assassination, no celebrations ensued. Real enemies celebrate enemy deaths at the hands of insurgents as a call for guerrilla warfare. But in this war, they remained Americans all. Richmond's Sallie Putnam, writing from her occupied city, conceded, "In the wonderful charity which buries all quarrels in the grave, Mr. Lincoln, dead, was no longer regarded in the character of an enemy."[10]

On April 17 General Sherman met with a shocked General Johnston at the James Bennett house near Durham Station, North Carolina. Johnston feared the assassination would ruin negotiations for a generous peace and informed Sherman that it was a great "calamity" for the South no less than the North. The two then began negotiating not only the surrender of Johnston's army but the surrender of all armies in the field. Neither president was consulted on these conversations, and even Grant remained in the dark. From these negotiations emerged a remarkably merciful "Memorandum on basis of agreements," drawn up by Sherman, that called for an armistice by all armies in the field. Beyond that, the memorandum dictated terms of reconstruction, agreeing to obey Federal authority, and reestablish the Federal courts. The existing state governments would be recognized when their officials took oaths of allegiance to the United States. In return, the United States would guarantee rights of person and property and issue a general amnesty for Confederates.[11] In that memorandum, General William Tecumseh Sherman, the "scourge of the South," stood incongruously as the Confederacy's last best hope. No one would be more hated in Southern memory than Sherman, but no American showed more generosity of spirit at that moment than Sherman.

Sherman clearly went well beyond anything Grant had negotiated at Appomattox, though he always maintained that everything he did was in the spirit of Lincoln's wishes as they were expressed on the *River Queen*. But clearly he had overstepped his bounds and usurped powers that were not his to exercise. An outraged Congress and cabinet immediately assailed the memorandum, and Grant was promptly dispatched to meet with Sherman and rein him in. On April 24, the two generals and friends met, and Grant gently reminded Sherman that he did not have the authority to impose terms of surrender and reconstruction. President Johnson, Sherman was informed, had rejected the memorandum. Sherman was to apprise General Johnston of the rejection and allow two days for unconditional surrender without terms, after which hostilities would resume.

Throughout the North, an outraged and still mourning nation learned of Sherman's agreement, and Northern newspapers assailed the terms, crying instead for revenge. For his part, Sherman was equally outraged. He fumed against Secretary of War Stanton and the New York papers for printing a communiqué of March 3 from Lincoln to Grant stating that the generals should accept nothing but surrender and should not negotiate peace. Sherman claimed he had never received such a message and reiterated what Lincoln twice told him aboard the *River Queen* on March 27 and 28:

> [I]n his mind he was all ready for the civil reorganization of affairs at the South as soon as the war was over; and he distinctly authorized me to assure Governor Vance and the people of North Carolina that, as soon as the rebel armies laid down their arms, and resumed their civil pursuits, they would at once be guaranteed all their rights as citizens of a common country; and that to avoid anarchy the State governments then in existence, with their civil functionaries, would be recognized by him as the government de facto until Congress could provide others.[12]

Some people looked for plots and conspiracies. Certain that the South was behind the assassination, Northern papers railed against Sherman, complaining that "the favorable terms given to the rebel generalissimo in surrendering" encouraged bold moves. In the view of such critics, however, Southern conspirators had only managed to remove the South's best hope. Ultimately, one religious writer declared, God allowed this to happen "in a way utterly unexpected and afflictive [so that] he has opened the eyes of the blind to the malignant and implacable character of the rebellion. He has removed the one most disposed to a policy of leniency."[13] Now was the time for revenge!

In like fashion, the *New York Observer* spread the rumor of Confederate machinations: "As yet there is no reason to believe that the leaders of the Rebellion had any part or lot in the crime; but the crime itself is nothing more and nothing less than the personification of the whole insurrection. . . . This department has information that the President's murder was organized in Canada, and approved in Richmond."[14]

On April 19 funeral services were held for President Lincoln. In thinking ahead to the ceremonies, Grant instructed his officers to send a black regiment to march in the procession with the Army of the Potomac. After a brief service, the funeral carriage carried the slain president past throngs of mourners to the rotunda of the Capitol.

Throughout the North and in "Union" pulpits in the South, the messianic praises of Lincoln rang like the peals of the mourning bells. Many lauded his Christlike character, averring that "malice seems to have had no place in his nature." To complete the identification, Lincoln's faith was also transformed into that of a converted evangelical. In a sermon preached in the Union Church of Memphis, Tennessee, T. E. Bliss began the mythmaking with the description of Lincoln as "[h]e who but a few months ago told the story of his love for Jesus, in tears, and with all the simplicity of a child."[15]

For Frederick Douglass, Lincoln's assassination spurred apocalyptic sensibilities tied to the American nation and its new birth of freedom. As the news set in, Douglass sensed, "a hush fell upon the land as though each man in it heard a voice from heaven and paused to learn its meaning." The meaning Douglass divined lodged in what his biographer, David Blight, terms a "millennial nationalism" in which

[t]he United States was seen as God's redemptive instrument in history, and with providential appointments went burdens of world significance. The notion of an elected nation included both promise and threat. How could the model republic, called to nationality by the Founding Fathers, endure its own tragic flaws? The Civil War became the crucible in which the nature and existence of that nationalism would be either preserved and redefined, or lost forever.[16]

Alongside his purported lack of malice, Lincoln's morality received significant attention. Lincoln had, one eulogist claimed, given the nation a "moral genius." Another amplified on the theme, noting, "It was mainly his adherence to ethical principles in political discussions that gave such point and force to his reasonings; for no politician of this generation has applied Christian ethics to questions of public policy with more of honesty, of consistency, or of downright earnestness."[17]

If Lincoln had a problem, most eulogists agreed, it was that very likeness to Christ, especially as it appeared in his lack of malice or revenge toward the South. Some went so far as to suggest that in God's Providence, Lincoln had been taken up prematurely because he would not "have been equal" to the harsh penalties that divine justice required of the beaten South, but instead would "have been too lenient."[18]

In an unpublished sermon on Lincoln's death, Abijah Marvin likened Lincoln to Jonathan Edwards and Stephen Douglas. Death spared all three greats from later failures. For Edwards, his magisterial History of Redemption project, if completed, "would never satisfy the majesty of the vision." Douglas "was taken from the evil he might do if his life were prolonged." And "clouds seemed to be gathering over [Lincoln's] head" in regard to reconstruction. But from all of that, he had been saved: "Fortunate in his death he has entered the pantheon of history as the great and good president—Lincoln."[19]

Hard justice required a different president in peace than Lincoln would have been. Many Christian moralists in the North agreed that justice required revenge:

> If now we strip all who have knowingly, freely, and persistently upheld this rebellion, of their property and their citizenship, they will become beggared and infamous outcasts . . . like Cain, with the brand upon their foreheads, and with a punishment greater than they can bear. . . . The Union people of the South . . . would plant farms and villages upon the old slave plantations; and with our help in schools and churches, a new social order would arise upon the basis of freedom and loyalty. [20]

One of the more astute sermons to be preached about Lincoln's assassination came from N. H. Chamberlain, who delivered it to his St. James parish in Birmingham, Connecticut. Chamberlain recognized that blood was needed for America's religion to bloom. The Civil War, together with Lincoln's assassination, provided what mere rhetoric could never achieve—a sacred compact. He began, as he must, with blood: "A nationality is a sublime, a solemn, a sacred thing. It has its history, its prophecy, its destiny. It is always built upon solemn sacrifices; it is a compact always sealed with blood."

From blood he turned to the national totem for which the blood was shed: "Our flag . . . is the symbol of our nationality, and is sacred with its history. As a nation changes or advances, so does its flag, which wraps in its folds its story. . . . The last four years have encircled it with a new halo of glory. It hath endured a new baptism, wherein the smoke of battle stained not and the fire consumed not." From the flag in general, Chamberlain turned to its sacred component parts:

> Henceforth that flag is the legend which we bequeath to future generations, of that severe and solemn struggle for the nation's life. . . . Henceforth the red on it is deeper, for the crimson with which the blood of countless mar-

tyrs has colored it; the white on it is purer, for the pure sacrifice and self-surrender of those who went to their graves upbearing it; the blue on it is heavenlier, for the great constancy of those dead heroes, whose memory becomes henceforth as the immutable upper skies that canopy our land, gleaming with stars wherein we read their glory and our duty.

Only after setting the sacramental context did he come to the martyred messiah:

> Yea, now behold a deeper crimson, a purer white, a heavenlier blue. A President's blood is on it, who died because he dared to hold it in the forefront of the nation. The life of the President, who died in the nation's Capitol, becomes, henceforth, an integral part of the life of the Republic. In Him the accidents of the visible flesh are changed to the permanence of an invisible and heroic spirit.[21]

Consciously or not, when Chamberlain capitalized "Him," he spoke of divinity. Through his death, an innocent Lincoln became transformed from the prophet of America's civil religion to its messiah.

Grant had no love for Stanton, or for his betrayal of Sherman in the press ("he was a man who never questioned his own authority"). But on the issue of Sherman's unauthorized negotiations, Grant had to support the secretary of war and the new president. Although personally aghast at the prospect of a hard peace following on a hard war, Grant was a soldier and he followed his orders. Later, Grant would protect Sherman by insisting that the memorandum was "conditional" on political approval. Since approval was not forthcoming, Grant had instructed Sherman to rescind the agreement and negotiate another surrender with Johnston on the more limited terms that Grant had extended to Lee at Appomattox.[22] At the same time, Grant refused to bow to radicals whose cries for vengeance threatened to upend his armistice with Lee. When some vowed to reverse those concessions, Grant countered that he would resign his command. With that, the movement to punish Lee and the Army of Northern Virginia passed. Even the most determined radical knew better than to take on America's warrior high priest.

On April 26 Johnston surrendered his command to Sherman according to the same conditions specified by Grant at Appomattox. Grant quickly approved the terms, fearing that the vengeful mood in Washington might otherwise prevail. As he returned from Raleigh, Grant reflected on the Southern people and their desire for peace. In a letter to his wife, he commented, "The suffering that must exist in the South the next year, even with the war ending now, will be beyond conception. People who talk now of further retaliation and punishment, except of the political leaders, either do not conceive of the suffering endured already or they are heartless and unfeeling."[23]

Grant was right to worry. The secular and, even more, the religious press led the assault on Sherman's peace plan. A writer for the *Christian Herald* in Cincinnati was incredulous: "The news from General Sherman is startling. If he is not deranged, his course is traitorous. He pledges himself to obtain from his 'principal' terms of peace, giving up all that we have been contending for."[24]

The *American Presbyterian* lashed out against Unitarian-inspired softness and condemned "any namby-pamby, anti-capital punishment, semi-universalist, semi-Pantheistic clique in New York or Boston. . . . Posterity will hold us accountable for a strict, a firm, and a righteous policy towards these engineers of the darkest plot against human happiness that the age has produced."[25] Evangelical presses did not stop with their excoriations of Sherman and singled out Henry Ward Beecher as a turncoat—"In a word, Mr. Beecher, now that the enemy is conquered, may be said to have gone over to the enemy"—for recommending clemency toward Jefferson Davis.[26]

With Johnston surrendered, that left only General E. Kirby Smith's Army of the Trans-Mississippi and General Richard Taylor in Alabama and Mississippi. Both were easily vanquished, and with their fall, the war ended. The last fight occurred on May 12 at Palmito Ranch, Texas. Ironically, it ended with a Confederate victory. On May 26 the Army of the Trans-Mississippi surrendered, and on May 29 President Johnson granted amnesty and pardon to most Confederates.

Victory parades of Federal troops followed in Washington, first by Grant, then by Sherman (who refused to shake Stanton's outstretched hand). In a dark omen of what was to become of race relations in the reunited nation, no black military units were included in the parades as they had been at Lincoln's funeral.

With news of the last armies' surrender, the war disappeared from discourse as suddenly as it had appeared in the aftermath of the surrender of Sumter. After four horrendous years of bloodshed, God or the gods were propitiated and all that remained was the reconstruction of the Union. Never did a war end with more anticlimax. The costly conflict that had obsessed a nation for four years passed into silence. Religious and secular papers spent little time on peace, except to run brief headlines celebrating "End of war!"[27] With that, they moved on to mundane events, as if the war had never taken place.

AFTERWORD

The Civil War may have ended with a whimper, but ongoing debates over its meaning and morality contain a good bit of bang. Throughout this book the focus has been on *how* the war was fought and *how* the home fronts responded. I set aside the question of *why* the war was fought (*jus ad bellum*) because, as I argued at the outset, secession is a moral issue with no moral criterion for a sure answer.

But secession was the catalyst of 1861. The war came. Now it's 1865. All the battles have been fought. The issue of secession has been settled once and, to all appearances, for all. We have witnessed the wanton destruction and inhuman suffering Americans inflicted on one another. We have watched the death toll mount into the hundreds of thousands. We have seen the raw and cynical persecution of innocents enacted by many, from the lowliest soldiers to the greatest commanders, statesmen, and moralists. We have also observed great embodiments of courage, compassion, and nobility.

None of these, taken singly or together, however, resolves the question: was the Civil War just? Having lived vicariously within the spaces of the war, its battlefronts and its home fronts, it is appropriate in closing to reopen the *why* question. To paraphrase Lincoln at Gettysburg: did 620,000 men, and thousands more Confederate women, die in vain?

I have deliberately saved this question for last, because I don't believe any single answer is possible. At the outset I found it more compelling to lay out the evidence. But an honest analysis perhaps requires one personal response. Despite many immoralities that went largely unchecked and were even applauded by both sides at the lowest and highest levels, I cannot bring myself to say that 620,000 men died in vain. Why? In part because, for the most part, *they* did not say it. By the close of the Vietnam War, soldiers aplenty condemned the war as unjust. But this did not happen after the Civil War. Winners and losers alike would concede almost anything, it seemed, except the idea that their internecine war was ultimately meaningless or unjust.

Why did they hold on to its justness? I can only conclude that they supported the rightness of the war because at some profound level they believed in Lincoln's characterization of America as the world's last best hope. And, further, I can only conclude that for reasons Americans don't deserve or understand, we are.

The greatest guarantor of America's claim to global hope as it emerged in the Civil War was surely abolition. Throughout this book I have counterweighted abolition with the tragic perpetuation of racism in American society. But that in no measure diminishes the enormity of the achievement. Indeed, abolition represented the indispensable prelude to equal civil rights, however long that might take to achieve.

In claiming America as the world's last best hope, I certainly do not have in mind particular battles or wars fought in the name of patriotism. There is no lack of such conflicts that were (and are) demonstrably unjust and immoral. Many American wars of conquest and imperialism merely confirm the impalpable truth that because we are the world's last best hope, we are for the same reason the world's greatest threat.[1] Nor do I have in mind some sort of divine Providence that made America the world's last best hope by divine fiat—and, by extension, made America a "Christian nation." Finally, I do not claim that America is the world's last best hope because of emancipation, noble as that end was. While the end of sanctioned slavery was undoubtedly the greatest good to come from the war, it did not mean that the North was all right and the South was all wrong, as Lincoln so eloquently proclaimed in his Second Inaugural Address. There was plenty of guilt to go around on both sides, reflected both in the North's slave-trade profiteering in the past and in the ongoing tragedy of racism and the politics of white supremacy in the present.

People make nations. And the American people, for reasons of culture and environment, created a unique experiment. In the end, they just could not stay apart. Bernard Bailyn correctly argued for the ideological origins of the Revolution.[2] Underlying the Civil War, no less than the American Revolution, was a people's idea: the idea of popular sovereignty. This idea found its resolution, for the most part, in the Civil War, as the North and the South contested to see whose interpretation would prevail. We are and were and forever will be a people of ideas and a nation where people's ideas count. The outcome of the Civil War ensured that America would remain an idea, first and foremost, and lying at the heart of that idea would be "We the people."

From the start, the meaning of "We the people" was contested. The Constitution itself was a compromise reflecting that contest, and slavery was public exhibit number one. In the Civil War, soldiers on both sides self-consciously fought for freedom, even as they differed morally on the definitions and applications of that "freedom." Ideas. Ideas to die for. Ideas to kill for. This was the innermost meaning of the Civil War, no less than of the American Revolution.

As an idea, America was uniquely situated to assume a sacred identity as a chosen nation. An American civil religion incarnated in the war has continued to sacralize for its citizens the idea of American freedom. In fact, for many it enjoys more powerful sway over their lives than the sometimes competing, sometimes conflicting ideas of supernatural religion contained in our nation's many denominations.

For the Civil War to achieve its messianic destiny and inculcate an ongoing civil religion, it required a blood sacrifice that appeared total. While the term "baptism in blood" did not originate in the Civil War, it enjoyed a prominence in the war rhetoric of both the Union and the Confederacy that had no precedent. Speakers and readers came to accept the term literally as the lists of war dead continued to lengthen and civilians watched their lives and properties being destroyed by invading armies. The Civil War was indeed the crimson baptism of our nationalism, and so it continues to enjoy a mythic transcendence not unlike the significance of the Eucharist for Christian believers. For the unbeliever, both blood sacrifices seem irrational. But for the true believer, blood saved. Just as Christians believe that "without the shedding of blood there can be no remission for sins," so Americans in the North and the South came to believe that their bloodletting contained a profound religious meaning for their collective life as nations.

The incarnation of a national American civil religion may have been the final great legacy of the Civil War. How could a people of such diversity, who had more than adequately demonstrated their capacity to live at war, possibly come together in peace without some functioning civil religion? And how does any real religion come into being without the shedding of blood?

Having said all this, I must add that in the process of writing this book it has become irrefutably clear to me that some moral judgments need to be made, judgments that most Americans have been reluctant to make. We have preferred a violent but glamorized and romantic Civil War.[3] Military histories have focused on strategies and tactics and the sheer drama of battles in action. Political histories have focused—especially in the present—on slavery and emancipation, accounting the evil so complete and pervasive as to justify even murder. In this sense, Lincoln's war strategy was and remains genius. That does not make it right.

All too often the moral calculus perfected in the Civil War has been applied to other wars, often in cases involving nothing as noble as abolition. By condoning the logic of total war in the name of abolition—and victory— Americans effectively guaranteed that other atrocities in other wars could likewise be excused in the name of "military necessity." While Lincoln passed tragically from the American scene, Grant, Sherman, and Sheridan remained to carry the new moral logic forward. When Grant became president and commander in chief, his general of the army was William Tecumseh Sherman, and the commander of the Department of the Missouri was Philip Sheridan, supported by George Custer. Together they would pursue wars of extermination in the Indian campaigns of 1868 to 1883, employing the same calculus their commander in chief, Lincoln, had approved in the Civil War.[4] Just as Sheridan wreaked vengeance in the Shenandoah Valley, so he would wreak vengeance on American Indians—and with the same moral justification.

Knowing that the western Indians could roam and attack freely over the warm-weather months, when separated from their wives and children, Sheridan began attacking the Indians in their winter camps. The braves would have to remain to protect the women and children or see them killed before their eyes. Another tactic Sheridan used, one already tried and proved in the Shenandoah Valley campaign of the Civil War, was starvation. By destroying winter foodstuffs (and later exterminating buffalo), Sheridan forced the Indians to flee through the brutal winter cold and snow, where most died of starvation or froze to death.

The system of total war employed in the West aimed at subjugating entire races of people. Incredibly, as he did with Confederate women and children during the Civil War, Sheridan defined the Indians as the "aggressors" deserving destruction. In a letter to Sherman in 1873, Sheridan drew on their Civil War experiences as justification for the Indian wars:

> In taking the offensive, I have to select that season when I can catch the fiends; and, if a village is attacked and women and children killed, the responsibility is not with the soldiers but with the people whose crimes necessitated the attack. During the [Civil] war did any one hesitate to attack a village or town occupied by the enemy because women or children were within its limits? Did we cease to throw shells into Vicksburg or Atlanta because women and children were there?

General Sherman agreed. In response to the Fetterman massacre of December 21, 1866, Sherman had dictated: "We must act with vindictive earnestness against the Sioux, even to their extermination, men, women, and children."[5]

If Sherman did not literally intend extermination, the rhetoric certainly succeeded in bringing terror to the life of every Indian—man, woman, and child.

Americans don't want to concede the unforgivable wrongs committed by the likes of Lincoln, Grant, Sherman, Sheridan, Lee, Forrest, Early, and Davis. Individual acts of immorality occur in all wars. But armies are hierarchies, and responsibility ultimately resides at the top. The web of lies, suppression, and evasion that developed in the Civil War not only shock but also bear witness to the power of war to corrupt—especially at the top. Predictably, as the war continued, the abuses grew ever greater. These were not a rational "measured response" to essentially political challenges, as justifiers of the carnage would like to believe. Rather, the abuses reflected a feeding frenzy of blood for blood's sake. Nobody significant on either side was ever held to account. Privates may have been executed for rape, but no commanding officer was ever executed for creating the orders and culture in which rape could easily take place. No commanding officer that we know of ordered the death of prisoners of war. But by creating a war with no thought for prisons and prisoners and by refusing all attempts at exchange and amelioration, they again created the environment in which unimaginable suffering and death took place.

Why is it important to finally write the moral history of the Civil War? It's important because we are its legates, and if we question nothing from that costly conflict, then we need question nothing in conflicts of the present and future. Issues of discrimination and proportionality recur in every war. The Civil War does not provide an especially encouraging model in this regard, especially if the crimes go largely unnoticed beneath the natural urge to forget and move on. But as with the Holocaust, if we forget, we do so at great peril to our own humanity.

Judging the Civil War is not a brief for pacifism. Rather, it is an endorsement of the idea of a just war. There are no ideal wars. Peace is the only ideal, and every war is at some level a perversion of it. In a less than ideal world, however, in which we sometimes labor under a moral imperative to war, we cannot afford to do less than demand a just war and a merciful outcome.

ACKNOWLEDGMENTS

The idea for this book first took shape during a conversation with my friend and colleague John Demos in the early 1990s. We talked about new research projects and I mentioned long-standing interests in American religious history, and newly emerging interests in the Civil War as the "fulcrum" of American history. I told him that I did not want to write a "religious history" of the war that focused exclusively on chaplains and ministers, though their words would certainly be important. Nor did I want to write an exclusively military history of the war, though battles too would be central. After listening for a little longer he replied, "Well, it sounds to me like you're interested in writing a moral history of the Civil War."

"A moral history of the Civil War." I now possessed a title in search of a book. Twelve years and many turns in the road later, I completed the book and "rewarded" John with the first look. Despite the rigorous demands on his own writing schedule, he read the manuscript carefully and offered critical advice and encouragement. Obviously I remain solely responsible for the arguments (and mistakes) in this book, but without that guiding title, I doubt I would have ever undertaken the project.

Two other early readers slogged through rough drafts of chapters and, in the process, gave friendship and collegiality new meaning. They are Grant Wacker of Duke University Divinity School and Robert Bonner of Michigan State.

While I would not—could not—write a technically sophisticated military history of the Civil War, it increasingly became clear to me that the battles had to represent the spine of the narrative. In writing my way through the war, I have depended heavily on the multivolume classics by Allan Nevins, Bruce Catton, and Shelby Foote. James M. McPherson's *Battle Cry of Freedom* combined all of those chroniclers' verve and style with a social historian's eye for political and economic context that renders his history one for the ages. My footnotes only begin to express how much I have relied on that book, and his other writings on slavery and the Civil War.

Research libraries are every scholar's home away from home. Three have been especially essential to this book. First and foremost, I owe a debt of gratitude to Yale University, whose unrivaled libraries and generous sabbaticals supplied the time needed to engage in the systematic research and writing required to complete this project. A special thanks to Nancy Godleski for introducing me to electronic resources on the Civil War that I never knew existed.

Two research archives deserve special thanks for their long-term support. First, on this project, as with every other book I have written, the American Antiquarian Society has stood in a league of its own. For resources and collegial support I cannot imagine a better environment. In particular, I wish to thank Nancy Burkett, Joanne Chaison, Maria Lamoreux, Thomas Knoles, Georgia B. Barnhill, John Hench, and the Director, Ellen Dunlap. Second, I wish to acknowledge the Presbyterian Historical Society and its staff in Philadelphia for providing access to their superb newspaper collections. A special word of thanks goes to Frederick Heuser, Kenneth J. Ross, and Boyd Reese.

For fellowship awards that funded research assistants and travel monies I am indebted to the Pew Charitable Trusts' senior scholar's awards, administered by Joel Carpenter; to Yale University, especially Susan Hockfield and Barbara Shailor; and to the Association of Theological Schools' Lilly Faculty Fellowship program.

To cover a subject as broad as this it is necessary to visit archival collections throughout the country. Invariably I found the staffs of these libraries and historical societies eager to render assistance on everything from bibliography to local restaurants. In no particular order I wish to thank: the Huntington Library and Art Gallery; the Louisiana State University Archives; the Baptist Historical Society at the University of Richmond; Emory University; the John Hay Library at Brown University; the Robert E. Speer Library at Princeton Theological Seminary; the Newberry Library; Tulane University Archives; the University of Notre Dame; the New York Public Library; the Chicago Historical Society; the Georgia Historical Society; the University of Texas Barker Center for American History; the University of North Carolina Southern Collection; Duke University's Perkin Library; the Southern Baptist Historical Library and Archives, Nashville, Tennessee; the Disciples of Christ Archives, Nashville; Vanderbilt Divinity School; the Confederate Museum in Richmond; the Virginia Historical Society; the South Carolina Historical Society, Charleston; the South Caroliniana Library, Columbia; the William Smith Morton Library at Union Theological Seminary of Virginia; the Alabama Department of Archives and History; and the Library of Congress.

Friends and family helped with penetrating questions and warm accommodations on frequent and far-flung research trips. I especially thank Laura Mitchel Lauretan in Washington, D.C.; Debbie and Scott Robinson in Richmond, Virginia; Douglas Sweeney, then a graduate assistant at Vanderbilt Divinity School; and James Early in Charleston, South Carolina. Closer to home, Susan Stout offered unstinting encouragement—and friendly prodding—to "get back to the book," and I will be forever in her debt. My children, Deborah and James, have always encouraged my work, but in this case they also worked multiple summers Xeroxing sermons and newspapers, cataloguing books, and compiling bibliographies. In every sense of the term they were research assistants and I thank them.

From my first arrival at Yale twenty years ago, my colleagues in history and religious studies have been a scholar's dream come true. They are also wonderful friends who took time from their own busy schedules to read my manuscript in its entirety. I especially thank David Blight, Jon Butler, Johnny Mack Faragher, Glenda Gilmore, Kenneth Minkema, Gene Outka, and the aforementioned John Demos. Towards the end of the project, Sarah Hammond took time away from graduate work to offer insightful assistance with text editing and fact checking.

Outside of Yale, another group of old and new friends also read the completed manuscript, saving me from many errors. I am pleased to acknowledge James F. Cooper Jr., Allen Guelzo, James Block, Bertram Wyatt-Brown, John Boles, Bernard Lytton, and Christopher Grasso.

For expert editorial assistance and guidance on the organization and layout of the manuscript I owe a special debt to Deborah H. DeFord. Deborah also offered expert guidance on the book's illustrations and maps. The maps were prepared ably by Adrian Kitzinger. My agent, Andrew Wylie, has proved to be a vigorous promoter of my book and a careful reader. The staff at Viking Penguin, in particular my unfailingly wise editor, Wendy Wolf, and her assistant, Clifford Corcoran, have offered superb assistance every step of the way.

Several institutions offered me opportunities to present my work in progress, and the exchanges that took place on those occasions invariably clarified my thinking. I want to thank the departments of history and religion at the following universities: Duke University, the Yale Center for the Study of Religion in American Life, the University of Pennsylvania, the University of Notre Dame, Calvin College, Union College in Tennessee, the University of Connecticut, Baylor University, Messiah College, St. Joseph's College in Philadelphia, the University of Florida, Princeton University, and Arizona State University.

Some of the last reading of my father, Harry Stober Stout, consisted of the final chapters of my book, just coming to life as his was ebbing. I am profoundly grateful that he lived to read the first draft and offer his wise observations on war and the meaning of America from his experiences in the Pacific in World War II. Even as I looked back on the life and influence of my father in the writing of this book, I have looked forward to my grandchildren and the moral decisions their generation will be called upon to make. It is to both past and future that I dedicate this book.

NOTES

INTRODUCTION

1. Axtell, "Moral History of Indian-White Relations Revisited," in his *After Columbus*, 20.
2. Of Christian just-war theorists, the most important were Francisco de Vitoria (1486–1546), Francisco Suárez (1548–1617), Hugo Grotius (1583–1645), Samuel Pufendorf (1632–1704), Christian Wolff (1679–1754), and Emmerich de Vattel (1714–1767).
3. Walzer, *Just and Unjust Wars*; Ramsey, *Just War*; Elshtain, *Just War Theory*; Best, *Humanity in Warfare*; Johnson, *Just War Tradition*; O'Brien, *Conduct of Just and Limited War*.
4. Unlike Realpolitik, just-war theory refuses to separate politics from ethics. See Elshtain, "Just War as Politics," in Decosse, *But Was It Just?* 43–60.
5. On civil wars, see Walzer, *Just and Unjust Wars*, 96.
6. See the argument in Parish, "War for the Union as a Just War," in Adams and van Minnen, *Aspects of War in American History*, 82.
7. Allen, *Constitution and the Union*, 12–13. On the moral ambiguities of secession see Buchanan, *Secession*. Less persuasive—because it is more polemical—is Charles Adams, *When in the Course of Human Events*. For an incisive critique of Adams's "neo-Confederate" reading of secession, see Feller, "Libertarians in the Attic," 184–94.
8. Fred Anderson, *Crucible of War*.
9. In terms of total-war language, definitions are crucial. Two important works that challenge my sense of "total" war are Neely, "Was the Civil War a Total War?" 27, and Grimsley, *Hard Hand of War*. Both of these historians aptly employ technical definitions of total war originating in World War II to refer to the deliberate murder of civilians with unprecedented weapons of mass destruction. But, in my opinion, the *mentality* of total war existed in the Civil War and prepared Americans for greater destructions once the technology emerged. "Savage" wars (of which white Americans were superb practi-

tioners) routinely blurred the distinctions between soldiers and civilians, but I would not necessarily term wars against Indians "total." My definition, as will become clear through the text, is more historically relative and traces the seeds of twentieth-century "modern" wars of universal mobilization to the Civil War. For works that take up a total-war terminology see, for example, Johnson, *Just War Tradition*, 281–326; Janda, "Shutting the Gates of Mercy," 7–26; and Winik, *April 1865*.

10. This point is powerfully argued in William Lee Miller, *Lincoln's Virtues*, 436–40.

11. The figure of civilian casualties is taken from McPherson, *Battle Cry of Freedom*, 619. The subject of civilian casualties is astoundingly understudied. Professor McPherson's estimate is the only estimate I have been able to locate.

12. Bellah, "Civil Religion in America," 1–21, reprinted in Ritchey and Jones, *American Civil Religion*. For a sampling of recent scholarship on the subject of civil religion, see Cherry, *God's New Israel*; Bellah and Hammond, *Varieties of Civil Religion*; John Wilson, *Public Religion in American Culture*; Linder, "Civil Religion in Historical Perspective," 399–421; and Henry, *Intoxication of Power*.

13. See, for example, Alley, *So Help Me God*; Hutcheson, *God in the White House*; or Pierarad and Linder, *Civil Religion and the Presidency*.

14. See Marvin and Ingle, *Blood Sacrifice and the Nation*.

15. See, for example, Herberg's classic *Protestant-Catholic-Jew*, or Jewett, *Captain America Complex*.

16. See, for example, Bellah, "Civil Religion in America," 33–35, or Mead, "Nation with the Soul of a Church," 275–83.

17. See Hutchison and Lehmann, *Many Are Chosen*, and Hatch, *Sacred Cause of Liberty*.

18. Ronald Reagan employed this metaphor as the defining image of his presidency.

19. The classic summary of the jeremiad appeared in Perry Miller's *New England Mind*. See also Bercovitch, *American Jeremiad*, and Stout, *New England Soul*.

20. I describe not one but two civil religions during the war, each identical in theological terminology and morally opposed. With Confederate surrender, vestiges of a Confederate civil religion would endure in the "Religion of the Lost Cause." But this would fade and, in time, the white North and South would reunite under one comprehensive and compelling American civil religion.

21. Blight, *Race and Reunion*, 3.

PROLOGUE

1. For a particularly trenchant examination of Lincoln's moral vision, see Guelzo, *Abraham Lincoln: Redeemer President*, especially 185–227.

2. This theme is treated brilliantly in Eric Foner's now classic *Free Soil, Free Labor, Free Men*. See also Sewall, *Ballots for Freedom*.

3. Forman, *West Point*, 117.

4. Schaff, *Spirit of Old West Point*, 146.

5. Basler, *Abraham Lincoln: His Speeches and Writings*, 529, 531. For text and analysis, see Holzer, *Lincoln at Cooper Union*.

6. Basler, *Abraham Lincoln: His Speeches and Writings*, 372.

1. "THE SPIRIT OF THE SOUTH IS RISING"

1. The number of fast-day sermons published is remarkable and itself an evidence of how strongly sentiments had moved in one short month. A brief sampling for the North would include Bellows, *Crisis of Our National Disease*; Beecher, *Peace Be Still*; Breckinridge, *Union to Be Preserved*; Francis Vinton, *Irreligion and Corruption and Fanaticism Rebuked*; Humphrey, *Our Nation*; Fisher, *Sermon Preached in the Chapel of Yale College*; Allen, *Constitution and the Union*; Abbott, *Address upon Our National Affairs*; and Roset, *Sermon on the Preservation of the Union*. For the South, see especially Cuthbert, *Scriptural Grounds for Secession from the Union*, and Dreher, *Sermon*. There were a handful of fast-day sermons calling for calm and moderation; see, for example, Guion, *Sermon Preached*, and William Adams, *Prayers for Rulers*.

2. Quoted in Phillips, "Literary Movement for Secession," in his *Studies in Southern History and Politics*, 33.

3. Despite the efforts of Confederates and present-day neo-Confederates to decouple states' rights from slavery, the connection between the two was symbiotic and reflected in the efforts of South Carolina–dominated secession commissioners sent throughout the slaveholding states to trumpet their gospel of disunion. See Dew, *Apostles of Disunion*.

4. On the interconnections of states' rights and race-based slavery, as well as the movement to reopen the African slave trade, see Sinha, *Counterrevolution of Slavery*, especially 125–52. See also Freehling, *Prelude to Civil War*; Channing, *Crisis of Fear*; and Barnwell, *Love of Order*.

5. McCurry, *Masters of Small Worlds*; see also Fox-Genovese and Genovese, *Mind of the Master Class*.

6. The Confederate constitution was formally ratified on March 11, 1861. It is reprinted in DeRosa, *Confederate Constitution of 1861*, 135–51. On the election and inauguration of Jefferson Davis, see William C. Davis, *Jefferson Davis*, 303–10.

7. Eddy, *Secession—Shall It Be Peace or War?* 17. In New York the Reverend Henry Bellows expressed similar sentiments in *Crisis of Our National Disease*: "Why not consent, then, to pacific and amicable and just terms of separation . . . they ought to be permitted to go out of [the union] in peace." Reprinted in *Fast Day Sermons*, 303.

8. Fiske, *Sermon on the Present National Troubles*, 18–19.

9. Basler, *Abraham Lincoln: His Speeches and Writings*, 579–88.

10. See John L. Thomas, *The Liberator*, 304–37.

11. Martha LeBaron Goddard to Mary W. Johnson, February 11 and March 24, 1861, Civil War Papers, American Antiquarian Society (hereafter AAS). I am indebted to Joanne Chaison for calling these recently assembled letters to my attention.

12. The literature on abolitionism is vast and, since the 1960s, almost exclusively

sympathetic. For representative studies, see Nye, *William Lloyd Garrison and the Humanitarian Reformers*; McPherson, *Struggle for Equality*; Sewart, *Holy Warriors*; Thomas, *The Liberator*; Wyatt-Brown, *Lewis Tappan*; Kraditor, *Means and Ends in American Abolitionism*; Perry, *Radical Abolitionism*; McInerney, *Fortunate Heirs of Freedom*; and Lerner, *The Grimke Sisters from South Carolina*. On black abolitionists, see Quarles, *Black Abolitionists*; Pease and Pease, *They Who Would be Free*; and Blight, *Frederick Douglass' Civil War*.

13. This willingness would not account for the views of the vast majority of Northern blacks, who wished to fight a war for freedom. See Blight, *Frederick Douglass' Civil War*, 1–130.
14. Charles Regan Wilson, "Robert Lewis Dabney," 79–89.
15. Robert Dabney to William Hoge, December 5, 1860, Manuscript Archives, Union Theological Seminary, Richmond.
16. Moses Hoge to T. V. Moore, December 22, 1860, in ibid.
17. Robert Dabney to Charles Hodge, January 23, 1861, in ibid.
18. See Donald, *Lincoln*, 257–94.
19. See Winger, *Lincoln, Religion, and Romantic Cultural Politics*.
20. The best description of Republican ideology remains Foner, *Free Soil, Free Labor, Free Men*.
21. Basler, *Abraham Lincoln: His Speeches and Writings*, 531, 536.
22. Ibid. In his provocative work *On Hallowed Ground*, 10, Diggins argues that with the advent of civil war, Lincoln "returned to the Declaration as the redeeming ethical ideal." On Lincoln's embrace of the Declaration of Independence as the foundational document for American identity and common meaning, and his intellectual affinity with Jefferson, see Wills, *Lincoln at Gettysburg*, 84–89; Maier, *American Scripture*, 196–208; and Farber, *Lincoln's Constitution*, 102–3.
23. Lincoln to Henry L. Pierce, in Basler, *Collected Works of Abraham Lincoln* 3:376; hereafter cited as *CW*.
24. See William C. Davis, *Jefferson Davis*, 316–18.

2. "LET THE STRIFE BEGIN"

1. See Donald, *Lincoln*, 288–92. For a good account of how the Union retained the use of Fort Pickens even as Sumter fell, see Pearce, *Pensacola during the Civil War*, 48–69.
2. The best account of the fall of Fort Sumter, on which these paragraphs depend significantly, is Current's *Lincoln and the First Shot*. Also useful is Potter's *Lincoln and His Party*.
3. The issue of Lincoln's motives in moving to supply Sumter has been hotly debated. From a Northern perspective, it was an innocent attempt to save a Federal property. From a Southern perspective, it was a ruse to force the South to act and, in so doing, cement Northern support for the looming war. A middle path that I find especially persuasive is discussed in Stampp, *And the War Came*, 280–86.
4. For an analysis of the factors influencing Lincoln's decision, see Donald, *Lincoln*, 288–92.
5. *Richmond Enquirer*, March 9, 1861.

6. For a thorough description of the Confederate government in the days immediately prior to the attack on Sumter, see Current, *Lincoln and the First Shot*,
   126–53.
7. Frederick Douglass, *Life and Times*, 324.
8. *Charleston Mercury*, April 13, 1861.
9. Quoted in William C. Davis, *Jefferson Davis*, 325.
10. Alexander H. Stephens, *A Constitutional View of the Late War Between the
    States*, 2 vols. (Chicago, 1868–70), II, 35.
11. Donald, *Lincoln*, 296.
12. Richardson, *Messages and Papers of Jefferson Davis*, I, 60.
13. Too often in the past accusations about who "started" the war merely rein-
    forced sectional prejudices, with Lincoln or Davis entirely innocent and the
    other entirely guilty. Current offers a more balanced perspective *Lincoln and
    the First Shot*, 206–8: "In those early April days both Lincoln and Davis took
    chances which, in retrospect, seem awesome. The chances they took eventu-
    ated in the most terrible of all wars for the American people. Lincoln and
    Davis, as each made his irrevocable decision, could see clearly enough the
    cost of holding back. Neither could see so clearly the cost of going ahead. Both
    expected, or at least hoped, that the hostilities would be limited in space
    and time. . . . Viewed impartially, both sides were guilty of aggression, and nei-
    ther was."
14. Quoted in Ambrose, *Duty, Honor, Country*, 148.
15. Given the engineering focus of antebellum West Point, formal instruction in
    tactics was minimal.
16. Janda, "Shutting the Gates of Mercy," 9–10.
17. Eliot, *West Point in the Confederacy*, 8.
18. J. G. Barnard to Editors, *National Intelligencer*, date February 6, 1859.
19. Howard, *Autobiography*, I, 99.
20. Crary, *Dear Belle*, 87.
21. Forman, *West Point*, 120–21.
22. Kirshner, *Class of 1861*, 9.
23. Crary, *Dear Belle*, 92.
24. Quoted in Kirshner, *Class of 1861*, 11.
25. Burlingame, *With Lincoln in the White House*, 35. See also Guelzo, *Abraham
    Lincoln: Redeemer President*, 279–81.
26. J. Stewart Brown to Alonzo Hill, May 1, 1861, Civil War Papers, AAS.
27. Quoted in Current, *Lincoln and the First Shot*, 193.

3. "OUR FLAG CARRIES . . .
AMERICAN HISTORY"

1. J. B. Jones, *Rebel War Clerk's Diary*, 19, 22–23. See also Emory Thomas, *Confederate State of Richmond*, 6.
2. Andrews, "The Confederate Press and Public Morale," 447.
3. Other notable newspapers and periodicals include the *Southern Literary Messenger*, the *Magnolia Weekly*, the *Record of News, History and Literature* (first
   published June 18, 1863), and a humorous magazine, the *Southern Punch* (first

published August 29, 1863). The *Southern Illustrated News* (fall 1862) became the most popular periodical in the wartime South.

4. Quoted in Current, *Lincoln and the First Shot*, 159–60.

5. Burlingame, *At Lincoln's Side*, 120.

6. See O'Leary, *To Die For*, 20–25.

7. Beecher, *National Flag*, in his *Patriotic Addresses*, 291. Beecher's address was originally delivered in May 1861. The flag over Fort Sumter was the Palmetto state flag of South Carolina. The Confederate flag, sometimes called the "Stars and Bars," went through two iterations and was not formally settled until the Confederate Congress passed an act in 1863. Even in the border state of Kentucky, strong Unionist sentiment was expressed by flag-waving. In Louisville: "The city was ablaze with Union sentiment. Public meetings were held and the most emphatic expressions in favor of the Union were applauded. 'Flag raisings' became popular. Every day's issue of the papers contained notices of these 'flag raisings.' So common did they become that the *Louisville Democrat* said that the city had become known as 'the city of flags.'" Quoted in McDowell, *City of Conflict*, 2–3. On flag culture in the South and in the nation, see Bonner, "Flag Culture and the Consolidation of Confederate Nationalism," 293–332, and Bonner, *Colors and Blood*.

8. On the American flag as a "totem" of American civil religion, see Marvin and Ingle, *Blood Sacrifice and the Nation*.

9. See Andrews's two classics: *The North Reports the Civil War* and *The South Reports the Civil War*.

10. On the rise of the penny press, see Mott's classic *American Journalism*. See also Henkin, *City Reading*, and Leonard, *News for All*.

11. *New York Herald*, March 27 and March 21, 1861.

12. Ibid., April 14, 1861.

13. *New York Tribune*, April 15, 1861.

14. Ibid., April 13, 1861. On the cultural phenomenon of "making" the news, see Schudson, *Discovering the News*.

15. *New York Tribune*, April 15 and 19, 1861.

16. Samuel S. Cox, *Eight Years in Congress*, 193.

17. Northern confidence in their superiority was a commonplace. One typical sentiment, expressed by the Reverend John S. C. Abbott, was unabashedly confident: "Should the Cotton states secede, they will make but a feeble nation. . . . Should the South *provoke war*, it is ruined beyond redemption. . . . Dreadful, beyond imagining, to the South, will be that hour when civil war shall be seriously introduced. May God, in mercy, save them from the awful doom." In *An Address upon Our National Affairs*, 13.

18. *The Age*, May 4, 1861. The only known surviving copy of *The Age* is housed at the American Antiquarian Society. I am indebted to Professor Patricia Cohen for calling this source to my attention.

19. *Charleston Mercury*, April 18, 1861.

20. Ibid., April 20, 1861.

21. On Confederate ideology, see DeRosa, *Confederate Constitution of 1861*, 12–13.

22. *Richmond Examiner*, July 16, 1861. From newspaper circulation rates it is clear that most newspaper-reading inhabitants subscribed to both a religious and a

secular paper. It is, therefore, as important to examine the secular press as well as denominational papers in reconstructing religious meanings in Richmond. The secular papers contained some but not much religious material in their columns, and taken by themselves would give a very different picture of the power and pervasiveness of religion in Richmond public discourse and Confederate ideology than that which appears in the religious press. Interestingly, Beringer et al., *Why the South Lost the Civil War*, derive much of their evidence for religion's supposed abandonment of the Confederacy from the secular press.

23. Emory Thomas, *Confederate State of Richmond*, 30.
24. Andrews, "The Confederate Press," 464, n78.
25. Ibid., 463, n77.
26. For one account of this borrowing see Jones, *Rebel War Clerk's Diary*, 161.
27. *Richmond Enquirer*, December 18, 1860.
28. Wise is quoted in W.M.E.R., "The Thanksgiving Day Contention," 9–11.

4. "THE DAY OF THE POPULACE"

1. On the lack of (fictional) literary classics emerging from the Civil War, see Wilson, *Patriotic Gore*, and Aaron, *Unwritten War*. On writers and intellectuals in the Civil War, see Masur, *"The Real War Will Never Get in the Books,"* and Fredrickson's classic *Inner Civil War*.
2. Quoted in Fredrickson, *Inner Civil War*, 66.
3. See Morris, *Better Angel*.
4. Masur, *"The Real War Will Never Get in the Books,"* 21.
5. Ibid., 163.
6. Quoted in Fredrickson, *Inner Civil War*, 72–73.
7. Masur, *"The Real War Will Never Get in the Books,"* 7.
8. Higginson, "Ordeal by Battle," 8, reprinted in Masur, *"The Real War Will Never Get in the Books,"* 184, 186.
9. Beecher, *Battle Set in Array* in his *Patriotic Addresses*, 276, 287.
10. Bartholomew, *Hour of Peril*, 3–4, 14.
11. Countryman, *Spirit and Purpose of the Conflict*, 14.
12. Goodrich, *Sermon on the Christian Necessity of War*, 5.
13. See Paluden, *"A People's Contest,"* 339–74.
14. See Perry Miller, *Errand into the Wilderness*; Miller, *The New England Mind*; and Bercovitch, *American Jeremiad*.
15. Elsewhere I have traced the rhetorical transformation of the jeremiad from theocracy to democracy in *New England Soul*.
16. See, for example, Hovey, *Freedom's Banner*.
17. *Banner of the Covenant*, May 4, 1861.
18. *Independent*, January 1, 1861. On the development of the nineteenth-century religious press, see Nord, "Systematic Benevolence," in Sweet, *Communication and Change in American Religious History*, 239–69.
19. I have counted column space given over to religious and general news in a sampling of religious newspapers from 1860 to 1865 (cited throughout this book), and find that with the onset of war the ratio of general to religious news

almost reverses, so that for every column of religious news there are three or four columns of general news.

20. *Christian Herald*, April 18, 1861.

21. *Independent*, April 25, 1861.

22. *Christian Herald*, April 25, 1861.

23. Ibid.

24. *American Presbyterian*, April 18, 1861. See also the *Christian Intelligencer*, April 18, 1861.

25. Hodge, *State of the Country* (reprinted from the *Princeton Review*, January 1861). For a summary of the issues raised by this pamphlet, see VanderVelde, *Presbyterian Churches and the Federal Union*, 33–36.

26. *United Presbyterian of the West*, March 21 and April 21, 1861.

27. Now published in Tennessee, the *Christian Recorder* is the oldest continually published black newspaper in the United States. See Williams, *Christian Recorder*, 12.

28. *Christian Recorder*, April 27, 1861.

29. *Christian Instructor and Western United Presbyterian*, July 10, 1861.

30. Ibid.

31. *United Presbyterian of the West*, May 2 and 16, 1861.

32. *Banner of the Covenant*, April 20 and May 4, 1861.

33. *Presbyter*, May 19, 1861.

34. On the "Christianization" of the South, see Loveland, *Southern Evangelicals and the Social Order*, and Schweiger, *The Gospel Working Up*. In claiming Christianity as the most powerful cultural system in the antebellum South, I do not mean to imply it was the only one. Powerful competing systems emerged defined by the slaveholding elite, a cultural heritage of violence, and the culture of honor. For especially good summaries of these, see Wyatt-Brown, *Shaping of Southern Culture*; Stowe, *Intimacy and Power in the Old South*; and Genovese, *Slaveholders' Dilemma*.

35. Smyth, *The Sin and the Curse*, 11–12. The Reverend Benjamin Palmer issued an almost identical argument in New Orleans; see *Slavery, a Divine Trust* published in *Fast Day Sermons*. For an admirable summation of South Carolina clerical reflection on slavery, labor, religion, and morality, see Sinha, *Counterrevolution of Slavery*, and Snay, *Gospel of Disunion*.

36. Joseph Ruggles Wilson, *Mutual Relations of Masters and Slaves*, 11.

37. Thomas Smyth Papers, 1830–1861, Third Notebook, July 31, 1861, William R. Perkins Library, Duke University.

38. Ibid. For similar sentiments, see Rees, *Sermon on Divine Providence*.

39. James H. Elliott, *Bloodless Victory*, 11.

40. See Carwardine, *Evangelicals and Politics in Antebellum America*, 38.

41. A reading room on Eleventh Street in Richmond kept on file all the city papers and all available papers from every state, city, and town in the South. See Kimball, *Starve or Fall*, 74.

42. *Southern Churchman*, April 25, 1862. Religious presses such as the Episcopal *Southern Churchman* and the *Southern Presbyterian* printed "a Religious Family Newspaper" on their mastheads. Virtually all religious weeklies regis-

tered a family focus with sections particularly directed at women and young readers. They also assumed that they were the only source of news. A writer for the *Central Presbyterian* responded on November 24, 1860, to criticisms that the paper included too much secular news with the observation that "many of our subscribers read no other paper. [Our] chief purpose, in this day, is to furnish instructive and useful reading, to discuss religious and ecclesiastical topics, to arouse and develop the Christian zeal and efforts of the church, and to help forward the cause of truth and righteousness." A female writer to the same paper on December 18, 1862, however, informed the editors that her family had other sources of news: "We read the latest news through the week, the Bible and our own 'Southern Presbyterian' on the Sabbath."

43. *Central Presbyterian*, June 2 and 30, 1864.

44. Ibid., December 15, 1860; *Richmond Christian Advocate*, November 14, 1861, and February 20, 1862.

45. *Richmond Christian Advocate*, March 26, 1861. On the doctrinal underpinnings of secession, see Farmer, *Metaphysical Confederacy*.

5. "TO RECOGNIZE OUR DEPENDENCE UPON GOD"

1. The national motto was formally introduced on the Confederacy's seal in 1863. See Bonner, *Colors and Blood*, 115–16.

2. Nineteenth-century churchmen were acutely aware of the absence of God in the federal Constitution and the implications of this for Christian nationhood. See Stout, "Rhetoric and Reality in the American Revolution," in Noll, *Religion and Politics*, 62–76. Southern interpretations of the significance and meaning of the Constitution in the context of new nation-forming are described in Coulter, *Confederate States of America*, and Emory M. Thomas, *Confederate Nation*.

3. See Stout and Grasso, "Civil War, Religion, and Communications," in Randall M. Miller et al., *Religion and the American Civil War*, 313–59.

4. In Love's calendar of printed fast and thanksgiving sermons, only 7 of 622 titles originated in the South. See Love, *Fast and Thanksgiving Days of New England*.

5. In *Confederate Morale and Church Propaganda*, 64–65, James W. Silver lists the following Confederate fasts: June 13, 1861; November 15, 1861; May 16, 1862; September 18, 1862; March 27, 1863; August 21, 1863; April 8, 1864; November 16, 1864; March 10, 1865. In addition, Basil Manly lists February 28, 1862, "Day of Pub. humiliation, fasting and prayer, appointed by the President of the Confederate States." See Hoole, "The Diary of Dr. Basil Manly," 227. Abraham Lincoln proclaimed fasts for September 26, 1861, April 30, 1863, and August 4, 1864. In addition, Lincoln proclaimed four thanksgiving days and Davis two. I have recovered the texts of Davis's proclamations from the Confederate newspapers. Lincoln's proclamations are reprinted in Sickel, *Thanksgiving*.

6. In *Confederate Morale and Church Propaganda*, 64–65, James W. Silver points

to the ubiquity of fast sermons in the South, but by limiting his concept of religion to a form of "propaganda," Silver misses the ritual power of the fast day to shape a people's view of itself in war. More recently, Faust has summarized the fast-day jeremiad in *Creation of Confederate Nationalism*, 26–27, in terms that recognize its inclusive significance as "a recurrent occasion for clerical solemnization of this marriage of sacred and secular." Also useful is Daniel, *Southern Protestantism in the Confederacy*.

7. Davis's proclamation was reprinted in virtually every Confederate religious and secular newspaper.
8. Barten, *Sermon Preached in St. James Church*, 11.
9. Before the Civil War, virtually all Southern Protestants agreed that the doctrine of the spirituality of the church precluded the sort of "federal covenant" on which public fasts rested and through which "political sermons" were preached. See Leith, "Spirituality of the Church," in Hill, *Encyclopedia of Religion in the South*, 731, and Farmer, *Metaphysical Confederacy*, 256–60.
10. See Farmer, *Metaphysical Confederacy*, 235–90.
11. See Faust, *Mothers of Invention*, 179–95.
12. Barten, *Sermon Preached in St. James Church*, 8–9.
13. On the development of the nineteenth-century religious press, see Nord, *Faith in Reading*.
14. Data calculated from Crandall, *Confederate Imprints*, and Harwell, *More Confederate Imprints*. Crandall and Harwell list 1,146 religious titles in 2,828 unofficial publications (these figures exclude periodicals, newspapers, and sheet music).
15. *Richmond Daily Dispatch*, June 14, 1861.
16. See Stowell, *Rebuilding Zion*, 1–48.

6. "THE CHURCH WILL SOUND THE TRUMPETS"

1. Lincoln, "Address to the Young Men's Lyceum of Springfield, Illinois," January 27, 1838, in Basler, *Abraham Lincoln: Speeches and Writings*, 81.
2. Quoted in ibid., 50, 225.
3. Elliott, *God's Presence with the Confederate States*, reprinted in Chesebrough, *God Ordained This War*, 314. See also Sledd, *Sermon*.
4. On the transformation of antislavery from "gradualism" to "immediatism" once the category of "sin" was invoked, see David Brion Davis's classic essay: "The Emergence of Immediatism in British and American Antislavery Thought," 209–30.
5. *New York Tribune*, June 3, 1861.
6. *Christian Instructor and Western United Presbyterian*, July 10, 1861.
7. *Independent*, May 2, 1861.
8. Thomas Smyth Papers, 1830–1861, Third Notebook, July 31, 1861, William R. Perkins Library, Duke University.
9. Hoge, *Discourse Delivered*, 18, 22–23.
10. *Charleston Daily Courier*, July 4, 1861.
11. D. F. Parker to the Reverend Alonzo Hill, May 4, 1861, Civil War Papers, Box 1, Folder 7a, AAS.

12. Elliott, *Silver Trumpets of the Sanctuary*, reprinted in Chesebrough, *God Ordained This War*, 314. For similar sentiments see Gregg, *Duties Growing Out of It*.

13. Longstreet, *Fast-Day Sermon*, 6. See also Mitchel, *Fast Day Sermon*, and Henry Niles Pierce, *God Our Only Trust*.

14. See Sprague, *Freedom under Lincoln* (Boston, 1965); Davis M. Silver, *Lincoln's Supreme Court*; and Hyman, *A More Perfect Union*.

15. On Claiborne Jackson and the creation of a Confederate identity in the Border West, see Christopher Phillips, *Missouri's Confederate*.

16. See Fellman, *Inside War*; Schultz, *Quantrill's War*; and McPherson, *Battle Cry of Freedom*, 292.

17. On "conciliatory" strategies, see Grimsley, *Hard Hand of War*, 23–66.

7. THE BATTLE OF BULL RUN: "A TOTAL AND DISGRACEFUL ROUT"

1. On mobilization for war, see Bensel, *Yankee Leviathan*.

2. "Forward to Richmond," which soon became the motto of the North, was coined in Greeley's *New York Tribune*, June 26, 1861: "The Nation's War Cry: Forward to Richmond!" See Stoddard, *Horace Greeley*, 213.

3. Quoted in McWhiney and Jamieson, *Attack and Die*, 44.

4. On the limitations of technology and the incompetence of untrained civilian amateurs, see Griffith, *Battle Tactics of the Civil War*, and Nosworthy, *Bloody Crucible of Courage*.

5. There is a vast literature on the military strategies of the war and the devastating consequences they would produce. The classic text on war was Clausewitz, *On War*. Clausewitz was probably not read by any generals and Jomini by only a few. In their book *Why the South Lost the Civil War*, the authors use Clausewitz's and Jomini's categories to analyze Civil War battles, even while conceding they were not read by the participants; see Beringer et al., *Why the South Lost the Civil War*, 39–52. Major secondary studies include McPherson, *Battle Cry of Freedom*; McWhiney and Jamieson, *Attack and Die*; and Hagerman, *American Civil War and the Origins of Modern Warfare*. Two multivolume histories of the Civil War that deal fully with the military aspects are Foote, *Civil War: A Narrative*, 3 vols., and Catton, *Centennial History of the Civil War*: vol. 1, *Coming Fury*; vol. 2, *Terrible Swift Sword*; vol. 3, *Never Call Retreat*.

6. In the end, as we shall see, frontal assaults largely ceased. Only then would the offensive tactics of siege and overland marches succeed in defeating the Confederacy.

7. Quoted in Long with Long, *Civil War Day by Day*, 98.

8. Quoted in Andrews, *The North Reports the Civil War*, 86.

9. *Christian Instructor and Western United Presbyterian*, July 3, 1861.

10. See McPherson, *Battle Cry of Freedom*, 340–47.

11. See William C. Davis, *Battle at Bull Run*, 193–98, 248–49.

12. See Eaton, *Jefferson Davis*, 138.

13. Burlingame, *With Lincoln in the White House*, 52, 209.

14. *Charleston Mercury*, July 24, 1861.

15. Presbyterian Synod of Virginia, *Annual Report 1862*.
16. *New York Herald*, July 27, 1861.
17. Martha LeBaron Goddard to Mrs. [Mary] Johnson, October 24, 1861, Manuscipts Collections, AAS.
18. *New York Evangelist*, July 25, 1861.
19. Ibid.
20. *Charleston Mercury*, September 26, 1861. The "contraband" designation applied to slaves was invented in May 1861.
21. For an excellent description of Britain's response to the war, see Blackett, *Divided Hearts*.
22. Russell's report is reprinted in Commager, *Civil War Archive*, 108–11.
23. Adams's letter is reprinted in Masur, *"The Real War Will Never Get in the Books,"* 5.
24. William C. Davis, *Battle of Bull Run*, 257. Because of McClellan's reluctance to embrace total war (to say nothing of Lincoln and his policies), historians have been unkind to him and tend to see him the way Lincoln wanted him to be seen: as a timid, frightened commander who exaggerated enemy strengths to avoid open battle. See, for example, T. Harry Williams, *Lincoln and His Generals*; Kenneth Williams, *Lincoln Finds a General*; or Sears, *George B. McClellan*.
25. *Christian Intelligencer*, July 25, 1861. See also the *American Presbyterian*, August 1, 1861, and the *Christian Instructor and Western United Presbyterian*, August 7, 1861.
26. *New York Evangelist*, August 22, 1861.
27. For a classic description of Bushnell's "Christian interpretation," see Clebsch, "Christian Interpretations of the Civil War," 212–22, and Mullin, *Puritan as Yankee*.
28. Bushnell, *Reverses Needed*, 10–11, 20.
29. Ibid., 14. For a similar arguments see, for example, *Christian Instructor and Western United Presbyterian*, November 6, 1861, or Fisher, *Sermon Preached in the Chapel of Yale College*, 8.
30. On Puritan conceptions of the "meaning of America," see Perry Miller, *Errand into the Wilderness*. By 1861 the term "Puritan" had lost much of its Calvinistic and theocratic content, but the notion of a "city upon a hill" governed by God remained deeply in place.
31. In *On Hallowed Ground*, 19, Diggins lumps Lincoln, Bushnell, and de Tocqueville together as Lockean liberals and misses the substantial differences between Lincoln and Bushnell.

8. TRIUMPHALISM: "ADORNED BY THE NAME OF GOD"

1. Quoted in Fredrickson, *Inner Civil War*, 74.
2. Jackson's letter is reprinted in Commager, *Civil War Archive*, 112.
3. Butler, *Sermon*, 16.
4. See, for example, Jacobs, *Sermon for the Times*.
5. Reed, *A People Saved by the Lord*, 9.

6. Ibid., 10. For similar sentiments, see also Armstrong, *Good Hand of Our God upon Us*, 14.

7. Cooke, "The Sorrows of Fairfax," *Southern Illustrated News*, March 7, 1863.

8. William Gilmore Simms to James Lawson, August 20, 1861, reprinted in Masur, *"The Real War Will Never Get in the Books,"* 219.

9. All of Lincoln's fast-day proclamations are reprinted in Sickel, *Thanksgiving*, 145. This proclamation was most likely written by Secretary of State William Seward.

10. *Banner of the Covenant*, September 21, 1861.

11. *Boston Telegraph*, September 23, 1861.

12. *New York Tribune*, September 23, 1861.

13. On the disappearance of Bull Run from the secular press coverage, see Andrews, *The North Reports the Civil War*, 100.

14. E. A. Adams, *Temple and the Throne*, 9.

15. *New York Evangelist*, October 17, 1861.

16. Scandlin, Diaries 1849–1864, entry for September 26, 1861, AAS.

17. Weller, *Two Firebrands*, 5, 8, 11.

18. Cheever, *God's Way of Crushing the Rebellion*, 6, 11–12. For a contemporary affirmation of this perspective, see Reynolds, *John Brown, Abolitionist*.

19. Dewey, *A Sermon Preached*, 8–9, 12–13.

20. See Fellman, *Inside War*.

21. Gray, *The Warriors*, 31. See also Ehrenreich, *Blood Rites*.

9. "WILL NOT THE MARTYRS BE BLESSED . . . ?"

1. Martha LeBaron Goddard to Mrs. [Mary] Johnson, October 24, 1861, Manuscripts Collection, AAS. In a later letter dated January 12, LeBaron still feared the future of emancipation: "Whether Freedom is to come thro' our present government—or over its ruins I cannot tell—and I dread the failure of this experiment."

2. *Banner of the Covenant*, November 23, 1861.

3. Ibid., January 2, 1862. Bullard's sentiments were frequently echoed in soldiers' letters. See McPherson, *For Cause and Comrades*.

4. Woodward, *Mary Chesnut's Civil War*, 222–23.

5. *Richmond Daily Whig*, November 9, 1861.

6. Charles C. Jones Jr. to Rev. C. C. Jones, October 11, 1861, reprinted in Myers, *Children of Pride*, 128.

7. Mary Jones to Charles C. Jones Jr. in ibid., 138–40. On the role of women in promoting Confederate nationalism, see Faust, *Mothers of Invention*, 16–20.

8. Woodward, *Mary Chesnut's Civil War*, 198. On women's fear of slave insurrections, see Faust, *Mothers of Invention*, 56–62.

9. Woodward, *Mary Chesnut's Civil War*, 228–30.

10. Ibid., 233.

11. *Charleston Daily Courier*, November 15, 1861.

12. *Richmond Daily Dispatch*, November 15, 1861. This same theme was repeated. On January 2, 1862, the *Dispatch* cautioned its readers that "we are inclined to

believe that it is not the intention of Providence that we should owe our inde-pendency to any agency but our own exertions."

13. Ibid., October 7 and November 30, 1861.

14. For a discussion of the paradoxical denigration of Confederate chaplains, see Daniel, *Southern Protestantism in the Confederacy*, 54–81; see also Romero, "Confederate Chaplain," 130. On Union chaplains, see Shattuck, *Shield and Hiding Place*.

15. On the Confederate tendency to feminize chaplains, see Schweiger, *The Gospel Working Up*, 99.

16. On manliness in the Civil War, see Berry, *All That Makes a Man*, 171–74; and McPherson, *For Cause and Comrades*, 78. On the tensions between Christian-ity and manliness in the antebellum South, see Wyatt-Brown, *Shaping of Southern Culture*, 102–5.

17. *Southern Christian Advocate*, November 9, 1861.

18. Thomas V. Moore, *God Our Refuge and Strength*, 11. See also Lamar, *A Dis-course*; DeBeaux, *Fast-Day Sermon*; George Foster Pierce, *Word of God*; and Henry Holcome Tucker, *God in the War*.

19. Elliott, *How to Renew Our National Strength*, quoted in Chesebrough, *God Ordained This War*, 314–15. See also Palmer, *National Responsibility before God*; Henry Niles Pierce, *God Our Only Trust*; and Randolf, *Address on the Day of Fasting and Prayer*.

20. Henry H. Tucker, *God in the War*, quoted in Chesebrough, *God Ordained This War*, 343–44.

21. Woodward, *Mary Chesnut's Civil War*, 237.

22. On the Christian Commission see Shattuck, *Shield and Hiding Place*, 24–33. On educating slaves, see David Brion Davis, *Emancipation Moment*.

23. Beecher, *Modes and Duties of Emancipation*, reprinted in his *Patriotic Ad-dresses*, 328, 333.

24. Spring, *State Thanksgiving*, 17, 34–35.

25. *Richmond Daily Dispatch*, January 10, 1862.

26. *San Antonio Herald*, January 18, 1862.

27. On millennialism in the colonial wars, see Hatch, *Sacred Cause of Liberty*.

28. Hughes's letter was widely reprinted in the press; see, for example, the *New York Herald*, September 4, 1861.

29. *Banner of the Covenant*, December 7, 1861.

10. "TO HUMBLE OURSELVES BEFORE GOD"

1. Richardson, *Messages and Papers of Jefferson Davis*, 1:188. On Davis's drift toward Providence, see Eaton, *Jefferson Davis*, 147–49.

2. J. B. Jones, *Rebel War Clerk's Diary*, 112.

3. *Religious Herald*, February 20 and 27, 1862.

4. Lt. Charles C. Jones Jr. to Rev. and Mrs. C. C. Jones, February 27 and March 3, 1862, reprinted in Myers, *Children of Pride*, 206, 207.

5. *American Presbyterian*, December 19, 1861.

6. Basil Manly, "Sermon on Judges 6:13," February 28, 1862, Manly Family Pa-

pers, William Stanley Hoole Special Collections Library, University of Alabama. For a discussion of Manly's activities as a chaplain during the Civil War, see Fuller, *Chaplain to the Confederacy*; 287–308.

7. Democratic opposition would get its full wind in the fall of 1862, when Lincoln committed himself publicly to emancipation; see Neely, *Union Divided*. On Democratic politics and culture, see chapter 29 of *Upon the Altar of the Nation*.

8. Reverend C. C. Jones to Lt. Charles C. Jones Jr., February 18, 1862, reprinted in Myers, *Children of Pride*, 203–5.

11. "IS IT NOT GRAND . . . ?"

1. *Christian Herald and Presbyterian Recorder*, June 26, 1862.
2. *Presbyter*, October 2 and 9, 1862.
3. Nancie Jourdan to George Frederick Jourdan, December 9, 1861, Civil War Papers, Box 1, Folder 9, AAS.
4. Sarah Baker, *Charlie the Drummer-Boy*, 14–15. On sentimentalized children's literature, see Fahs, *The Imagined Civil War*, 256–86.
5. Ibid., 150–54.
6. Uncataloged panoramas, AAS. I am indebted to Professor Sallie Promey for calling this broadside to my attention.
7. Marten, *Children's Civil War*, 16.
8. *New York Evangelist*, June 26 and April 3, 1862.
9. *Christian Herald*, June 25, 1863. McPherson's *For Cause and Comrades*, 58–60, 77–82, explores the motives of soldiers and shows how the lessons on cowardice were well learned by soldiers and officers alike. See also Linderman, *Embattled Courage*.
10. Marten, *Children's Civil War*, 116.
11. Boykin, *Boys and Girls Stories of the War*, 12.
12. Ezell, "Southern Education for Southrons," 303–27.
13. Rable, *Confederate Republic*, 179–84.
14. For a bibliography of Confederate texts, see Stilllman, "Education in the Confederate States of America," 462–67.
15. Sewart, *Geography for Beginners*, 42–43.
16. Stillman, "Education in the Confederate States of America," 243.
17. See, for example, Lander, *Our Own Primary Arithmetic*, 49, or Moore, *First Dixie Reader*, 56. Northern textbooks developed many of these same themes minus the proslavery apologias. But since they were often reprinted from earlier editions in verbatim fashion, there was no direct commentary on the war. See Marten, *Children's Civil War*, 59.
18. Marinda B. Moore, *Primary Geography*, 14.
19. On slave reform in education, see Stillman, "Education in the Confederate States of America," 396–410.
20. Nancie Jourdan to Fred, December 9, 1861, Civil War Papers, Box 1, Folder 9, AAS.
21. See Faust, *Mothers of Invention*, 40–45, and Rable, *Civil Wars*, 154–201.
22. I am indebted to Joanne Chaison of the American Antiquarian Society for

calling this recently acquired archive to my attention. Of all government jobs available to women, the largest proportion, and best paying, were with the Treasury Department. See Faust, *Mothers of Invention*, 88–92.

23. L. E. Hughes to Memminger, October 21, 1862, Civil War Papers, Box 4, Folder 3, AAS.
24. Eugenia Hyde to Memminger, October 3, 1862, Civil War Papers, Box 4, Folder 3, AAS.
25. Mary Gifford to Memminger, November 28, 1862, Civil War Papers, Box 4, Folder 2, AAS.
26. This estimate is taken from Holmes, " 'Such is the Price We Pay,' " in Vinovskis, *Toward a Social History of the American Civil War*, 174. On widowhood in the Confederacy see Gross, " 'Good Angels,' " in Clinton, *Southern Families at War*, 133–54.
27. Beecher, *National Justice and Penalty* in his *Patriotic Addresses*, 374.
28. *New York Times*, August 5, 1862.

12. "THE POPULAR HEART"

1. Masur, *"The Real War Will Never Get in the Books,"* 45.
2. Bernard, *Lincoln and the Music of the Civil War*, foreword. See also Heaps, *The Singing Sixties*, and Olson, *Music and Musket*.
3. See, for example, Massachusetts Volunteers 25th Regiment Band Books, Manuscript Collection, AAS.
4. *New York Times*, November 23, 1861, quoted in Bernard, *Lincoln and the Music of the Civil War*, 48.
5. Bernard, *Lincoln and the Music of the Civil War*, 58. General McClellan went so far as to forbid Hutchinson from performing before the Army of the Potomac.
6. "The Bonnie Blue Flag" (Baltimore, 1862), Union Imprint Song Sheets, John Hay Library, Brown University.
7. "The Bonnie Blue Flag" (Augusta, 1861). For similar themes see, for example, "Up with the Flag" (Richmond, 1863), Confederate Sheet Music Collection, John Hay Library, Brown University.
8. "All Quiet Along the Potomac To-night" (Richmond, 1862), Confederate Sheet Music Collection, John Hay Library, Brown University.
9. See McPherson, *For Cause and Comrades*, 77–82.
10. *Let Me Die Face to the Foe* (New York, 1862), Union Imprint Song Sheets, John Hay Library, Brown University. The *War Song of Dixie* (Augusta, 1862). Confederate Sheet Music Collection, John Hay Library, Brown University.
11. Howe's account is quoted in Commager, *Civil War Archive*, 378.
12. Masur, *"The Real War Will Never Get in the Books,"* 45.
13. Edmund Wilson, *Patriotic Gore*, 95–97. Howe's poem is reprinted in Commager, *Civil War Archive*, 378–79.
14. Cullen, *Civil War in American Drama*, 17. On Stowe, see Birdoff, *World's Greatest Hit*.
15. See Donald, *Lincoln*, 568–70.

13. "RELIGION HAS GROWN WARLIKE"

1. Livermore, *Numbers and Losses in the Civil War*, 47.
2. Technology was one thing, military practice in the heat of battle another. Many battle lines closed to one hundred yards or less, effectively neutralizing rifles that could hit targets at one thousand yards or more. Nor did accuracy on a practice range extend to the battlefield. One recent analysis of accuracy in Civil War battles concludes that soldiers averaged only one "hit" per one hundred shots—a figure not that different from hit rates in the Mexican War. See Nosworthy, *Bloody Crucible of Courage*, 574–93.
3. William Augustus Willoughby to Wife, April 14, 1862, Papers, 1861–64, Manuscripts Collection, AAS.
4. Following Bull Run, Sherman's fortunes ran temporarily downhill in Kentucky, where he backed away from engagements with the enemy because, out of fear, he exaggerated their strength.
5. On the Battle of Shiloh, see Sword, *Shiloh: Bloody April*; McDonough, *Shiloh—In Hell before Night*; and T. Harry Williams, *P.T.G. Beauregard*, 121–30.
6. Sherman, *Memoirs*, 260.
7. *Christian Instructor and Western United Presbyterian*, September 1, 1862.
8. Edwin Wheelock to Dr. ————, April 17, 1862, Civil War Papers, Box 3, Folder 5, AAS.
9. Halleck's strategy was grounded in the maneuver and siege tactics of Jomini, in contrast to Clausewitz (and Grant), whose strategy centered on the destruction of armies on a massive scale. See Johnson, *Just War Tradition*, 288.
10. John E. Anderson, *Reminiscence*, Civil War Papers, Box 1, Folder 1, 34, AAS.
11. In practice, Lincoln was probably a better military strategist than Jefferson Davis, who refused to appoint a general in chief until forced to by Congress. But in fact, neither was the distinguished military mind he thought he was. On Davis, see Eaton, *Jefferson Davis*, 249.
12. *The Liberator*, March 21, 1862.
13. Ibid., May 2, 1862.
14. Martha LeBaron Goddard to Mrs. [Mary] Johnson, August 3, 1862, Manuscript Collection, AAS.
15. Horace James to Sabbath Society, June 21, 1862, Horace James Correspondence, 1852–1870, Manscript Archives, AAS.
16. *Banner of the Covenant*, May 31, 1862.
17. *Richmond Daily Dispatch,* March 29, 1862.

14. "WHAT SCENES OF BLOODSHED"

1. The literature on McClellan and the Army of the Potomac is enormous. Among the more important works are T. Harry Williams, *Lincoln and His Generals*; Sears, *George B. McClellan*; and McPherson, *Battle Cry of Freedom*, 428–545.
2. The journalistic mythmaking began with the account of Manassas printed in the *Richmond Daily Dispatch*, July 29, 1861. See Royster, *Destructive War*, 68–69.

3. Woodward, *Mary Chesnut's Civil War*, 499–500.

4. T. J. Jackson to R. L. Dabney, July 24, 1862, Manuscript Archives, Union Theological Seminary, Richmond.

5. *Richmond Daily Dispatch*, May 21, 1862.

6. Quoted in Eliot, *West Point in the Confederacy*, 53.

7. See Webb's classic account *The Peninsula* (vol. 3 in Scribner's series *Campaigns of the Civil War*). For more recent accounts see Dowdey, *Seven Days*; and Sears, *To the Gates of Richmond*.

8. Quoted in McPherson, *Battle Cry of Freedom*, 470. In all, McClellan lost 3,214 to Lee's 5,355.

9. In *Just War Tradition*, 290, ethicist James Turner Johnson argues "it is not enough to write off enormous battlefield casualties because they have been inflicted only on combatants."

10. *Richmond Daily Dispatch*, June 26, 1862.

11. *American Presbyterian*, July 10, 1862.

12. Daniel, "The Diary of Mary W. Taylor, 1860–1864," 927.

13. See McPherson, *Battle Cry of Freedom*, 471–72, for casualty figures, and 464–71 on Jackson's failure to arrive on the scene.

14. *Philadelphia Inquirer*, July 1, 1862.

15. Ibid., July 5, 1862.

16. In 1862 Lee was still perceived as a coequal with Davis, Johnston, and Jackson. But by year's end, he would be in a class by himself. See Connelly, *The Marble Man*, 11–26.

17. Richardson, *Messages and Papers of Jefferson Davis*, 1:229–30.

18. Jeremiah Bell Jeter's sermon notes are preserved at the Virginia Baptist Historical Society in Richmond. Special thanks to the society and its director, Fred Anderson, for access to these notebooks. All quotations are taken from the microfilm collection at the Baptist Historical Society.

19. Ibid.

20. *Richmond Daily Whig*, February 26, 1862.

21. Jones, *Rebel War Clerk's Diary*, 124.

22. Richardson, *Messages and Papers of Jefferson Davis*, 1:227–28.

23. *Richmond Examiner*, May 19, 1862.

24. Here I follow the argument set forth in Gallagher, *Confederate War*.

25. *Richmond Examiner*, February 17, 1862.

26. Ibid., February 18, 1862.

27. Ibid., September 5, 1862.

28. Robert L. Dabney to the Board of Directors of Union Theological Seminary, April 21, 1862, Manuscript Archives, Union Theological Seminary, Richmond.

29. Sears, *Civil War Papers of George B. McClellan*, 306–7.

30. Ibid., 344–45.

31. See chapter 29.

32. O. R. (*War of the Rebellion . . . Official Records of the Union and Confederate Armies*), series I, vol. 12, pt. 3, 473–74.

33. Quoted in Grimsley, *Hard Hand of War*, 88–89. Italics mine.

15. "GOD WILLS THIS CONTEST"

1. On Lincoln's resolve to mount a total-war strategy, see Sutherland, "Abraham Lincoln, John Pope, and the Origins of Total War," 567–86.
2. Basler, *Abraham Lincoln: His Speeches and Writings*, 650.
3. See Fellman, *Inside War*.
4. In *Hard Hand of War*, 142–71, Grimsley marks the onset of "hard war" on civilians at 1864.
5. Coulter, *Confederate States of America*, 393–95.
6. Davis, *Jefferson Davis*, 409–10.
7. Among the more important analyses of Confederate nationalism are Gallagher, *Confederate War*, 63–111; Faust, *Creation of Confederate Nationalism*; Emory M. Thomas, *Confederate Nation*; Rable, *Confederate Republic*; McPherson, *For Cause and Comrades*, 94–102, 170–76; and Mitchell, "Creation of Confederate Loyalties," in Abzug and Maizlish, *New Perspectives on Race and Slavery in America*. Still useful is Potter's "The Historian's Use of Nationalism and Vice Versa," in Potter, *The South and the Sectional Conflict*, 34–83.
8. Quoted in Neely, *Last Best Hope of Earth*, 26.
9. Quoted in Grimsley, *Hard Hand of War*, 86.
10. A. W. Bill to "Dear Friend," August 8, 1862, Civil War Papers, Box 2, Folder 8, AAS.
11. Richardson, *Messages and Papers of Jefferson Davis and the Confederacy*, 1:268–74.
12. Quoted in ibid., introduction by Allan Nevins, 1:29.
13. Scandlin, Diaries, 1849–64, AAS.
14. *Christian Instructor and Western United Presbyterian*, July 26, 1862.
15. A. W. Bill to a Friend, August 8, 1862, Civil War Papers, Box 2, Folder 8, AAS. For further descriptions of the effects of General Orders No. 5, see two articles by Sutherland: "Abraham Lincoln, John Pope, and the Origins of Total War," 582, and "Introduction to War," 120–37.
16. See chapter 19.
17. Frederick A. Dickinson to George Dickinson, August 27, 1862, Civil War Papers, Box 1, Folder 7, AAS.
18. The best examination of Second Manassas is Hennessy, *Return to Bull Run*.
19. Jeter, "Notes and Sermons," Virginia Baptist Historical Society, Richmond.
20. MacDonell, "Sermon on Revelation 21:3–4," June 8 and July 16, 1862. Manuscripts Collection, Georgia Historical Society.
21. *New York Evangelist*, September 11, 1862.
22. *Philadelphia Inquirer*, August 18, 1862.
23. Basler, *Collected Works of Abraham Lincoln*, 5:419–25, 433–36. For a discussion of Lincoln's "meditation" and its relationship to his "fatalism," see Donald, *Lincoln*, 370–71.
24. Hodge, "The War," 143.
25. Liggett, "Our National Reverses," printed in Holland, ed., *Sermons in American History*, 250, 253.
26. Henry A. Boardman, *Sovereignty of God*, 21–22.

27. Richardson, *Messages and Papers of Jefferson Davis and the Confederacy*, 1:268–69.
28. *Richmond Daily Whig*, September 18, 1862. On Richmond's suffering, see Kimball, *Starve or Fall*, 119.
29. Jeter, "Sermon on Psalm 126:3," September 18, 1862, Virginia Baptist Historical Society, Richmond.
30. Tupper's sermon is reprinted in Holland, ed., *Sermons in American History*, 240–46. On parallel rhetorical themes in the American Revolution, see Stout, *New England Soul*, 282–311.
31. For an example of comparable sentiments in the secular press, see *Richmond Daily Dispatch*, September 27, 1862.
32. Livermore, *Numbers and Losses in the Civil War*, 47.

16. ANTIETAM: "THE HORRORS OF A BATTLEFIELD"

1. "Give Us Back Our Old Commander," Union Imprint Song Sheet Collection, John Hay Library, Brown University.
2. To be sure, General in Chief Halleck supported McClellan in this theory as both ran scared of Lee's and Jackson's cunning. On the lost orders and Mc-Clellan's tardy response, see McPherson, *Crossroads of Freedom*, 106–9.
3. For outstanding analyses of the battle and significance of Antietam, see, in addition to McPherson's *Crossroads of Freedom*, Sears, *Landscape Turned Red*, and Gallagher, *Antietam*.
4. McPherson, *Crossroads of Freedom*, 122.
5. Charles Ward to Brother Sammy, September 17, 1862, Civil War Papers, Box 2, Folder 6, AAS.
6. On McClellan's timidity and inability to impose his will on demoralized officers, see Sears, *George B. McClellan*, 318–23.
7. Livermore, *Numbers and Losses in the Civil War*, 92–93.
8. *Philadelphia Inquirer*, September 23, 1862.
9. Franklin Bullard to Aunt, October 4, 1862, Civil War Papers, Box 2, Folder 8, AAS.
10. Greiner et al., *Surgeon's Civil War*, 27–28.
11. Bower, "Theology of the Battlefield," 1019.

17. "BROKEN HEARTS CANNOT BE PHOTOGRAPHED"

1. Photography was a relatively new and nonportable medium in the Civil War. The technology had evolved from the original daguerreotype photograph— remarkably detailed but quite expensive and image-reversed—to the more inexpensive and portable collodion technique that bonded photosensitive chemicals to glass and paper. Though cumbersome to employ, photography had reached the point where shots could be taken outdoors.
2. See Meredith, *Mr. Lincoln's Camera Man*, 54.

3. Brady quoted in Andrews, *The North Reports the Civil War*, 88.
4. Frassanito, *Antietam*, 53.
5. Quoted in Keith F. Davis, "A Terrible Distinctness," in Sandweiss, *Photography in Nineteenth Century America*, 170.
6. *New York Times*, October 20, 1862, reprinted in Frassanito, *Antietam*, 15–16.
7. *New York Times*, October 20, 1862.
8. Gardner's view of photography was more modern than Brady's, seeing the image as a form of journalism and current news. Brady, on the other hand, retained a more traditional sense of photography as historical record. As such, Brady was content to arrive at battle scenes days or weeks later, while Gardner rushed to be immediately on the scene.
9. No equivalent to Brady or Gardner existed in the South. There simply were not the extra engravers and paper to allow for such a luxury. See William F. Thompson, *Image of War*, 23, 91–93.
10. Frassanito, *Gettysburg*, 190.
11. William F. Thompson, *Image of War*, 89.
12. On the slow evolution of fine arts in the Civil War, see Holzer and Neely, *Mine Eyes Have Seen the Glory*, introduction.
13. For a comprehensive overview of Homer and the Civil War, see Marc Simpson, *Winslow Homer*. On the avoidance of tragedy in his paintings, see Lloyd Goodrich, *Winslow Homer*, 20.
14. Christopher Kent Wilson, "Marks of Honor and Death," in Marc Simpson, *Winslow Homer*, 28.
15. Henry Joslin to Mother, July 20, 1862, Civil War Papers, Box 1, Folder 8, AAS. Joslin would later die of disease in a Union hospital.
16. Stevens, *Berdan's United States Sharpshooters*, 368.
17. Christopher Kent Wilson, "Marks of Honor and Death," 37, 38.
18. Peters, *Currier & Ives*.
19. LeBeau, *Currier & Ives: America Imagined*, 72.
20. Ibid., 73. The firm of Kurz and Allison rivaled Currier & Ives as Civil War lithographers and chromolithographers and pursued exactly the same heroic themes.
21. For other examples of bayonet charges in Currier & Ives lithographs (all at the American Antiquarian Society) see *The Battle of Gettysburg* (1863), *The Battle of Baton Rouge* (1862), and *The Battle of Malvern Hill* (1862). Of about 245,000 wounds treated by surgeons in Federal hospitals, fewer than 1,000 were from bayonets or sabers. But this statistic does not address the psychological impact that drawn bayonets continued to impose in the Civil War. See Nosworthy, *Bloody Crucible of Courage*, 598.

18. "ALL WHO DIE FOR COUNTRY NOW, DIE ALSO FOR HUMANITY"

1. Quoted in Donald, *Lincoln*, 364. Donald goes on to demonstrate how Lincoln's Emancipation Proclamation was motivated at least in part to "undercut the congressional initiative for emancipation by acting first," 365.

2. The literature on slavery and emancipation during the Civil War is immense. For primary sources, the best compilation is *Freedom: A Documentary History of Emancipation*, the ongoing series of edited documents from the National Archives, edited by Berlin, Fields, Miller, Reidy, and Rowland. Major secondary works include Franklin, *Emancipation Proclamation*; Litwack, *Been in the Storm So Long*; McPherson, *Struggle for Equality*; Klingaman, *Abraham Lincoln and the Road to Emancipation*; and, most recently, Guelzo, *Lincoln's Emancipation Proclamation*.

3. Berlin et al., *Freedom*, series 1, vol. 1, *Destruction of Slavery*, 275.

4. Lincoln's technical objection to the Second Confiscation Act was over the issue of whether Congress had the right to legislate over states. In his view, only the commander in chief could exercise such powers under the war powers of the chief executive. But to see his prior interests in limited emancipation through, he held his tongue and signed the act.

5. Guelzo, *Lincoln's Emancipation Proclamation*, 153.

6. Lincoln's Emancipation Proclamation is reprinted in Delbanco, *Portable Abraham Lincoln*, 271–73.

7. See Berlin, "Destruction of Slavery," in Berlin et al., *Slaves No More*, 40.

8. Randall, *Civil War and Reconstruction*, 495.

9. Basler, *Abraham Lincoln: His Speeches and Writings*, 666–88; quotation at 685.

10. Moses Smith, *Our Nation Not Forsaken*, 11.

11. *Richmond Daily Dispatch*, September 30, 1862.

12. William C. Davis, *Jefferson Davis*, 495.

13. *Southern Illustrated News*, January 12, 1863; *Augusta Weekly Constitutionalist*, October 8, 1862.

14. Coulter, *Confederate States of America*, 266.

15. *Christian Recorder*, June 28, 1862.

16. *Southern Illustrated News*, October 18, 1862.

17. William Williams, *Of the Birth and Death of Nations*, 19, 21, 31. The unnamed source may have been Lincoln's war ethicist Francis Lieber.

18. Dwinell, *Hope for Our Country*, 16, 12–13. See also Joseph P. Thompson, *Christianity and Emancipation*, 67: "Emancipation is not abolition. . . . There are those whose opposition to slavery did not originate in a military necessity. For one, I am opposed to slavery because I am a Christian—a member of that anti-slavery society of which He who came to preach liberty to the captive is the founder and head." The same point was made in Hodgman, *Nation's Sin and Punishment* (New York, 1864), 206: "We have, as a nation, done what was right, but not because it was right. . . . But nevertheless, since the act of Justice, and right and humanity has been passed, and there is an end of slavery, we will say that we are satisfied—that we are thankful!"

19. Sumner, *Emancipation!* 6–7, 23.

20. Hodge, "The War," 152.

21. Shedd, *Union and the War*, 32, 39. See also Spear, *Duty of the Hour*, 9.

22. Philip Foner, *Frederick Douglass Selected Speeches and Writings*, 549.

23. Page, *Speech of Moses B. Page*, 10.

24. Samuel Cox, *Emancipation and Its Results*, 7.

25. Tyson, *Institution of Slavery*, 191–92.
26. Henry Joslin to Mother, July 20, 1862, Civil War Papers, Box 1, Folder 8, AAS.
27. The Illinois State Legislature resolution is reprinted in Commager, *Civil War Archive*, 579.
28. Berlin, "Destruction of Slavery," 68.
29. Quoted in Campbell, *When Sherman Marched North from the Sea*, 65.
30. Masur, *"The Real War Will Never Get in the Books,"* 12.
31. *Spectator* (London), October 11, 1862. Among American historians, a similar argument may be found in Hofstadter's classic *American Political Tradition*, 132–33.
32. See Wiggins, *O Freedom!*
33. Library of Freedom, *Life and Times of Frederick Douglass*, 345, 344.
34. *Christian Recorder*, January 3, 1863.
35. Marshall's letter is reprinted in Berlin et al., *Free at Last*, 85.
36. Banks, *Emancipated Labor in Louisiana*, 8, 23. For similar sentiments, see Seebohm, *The Crisis of Emancipation in America*, 30: "The middle passage out of slavery, here as elsewhere, is one of trial and suffering; but it is short in duration, and the negro emerges out of it with a fair capacity for freedom, and a fair chance of success as a free citizen."
37. Quoted in McKaye, *Emancipated Slave*, 17.
38. *New York Evangelist*, April 3, 1862.

19. LINCOLN, EMANCIPATION, AND TOTAL WAR

1. Randall, *Constitutional Problems under Lincoln*, 343–76.
2. Guelzo, *Lincoln's Emancipation Proclamation*, 71.
3. William R. Williams, *National Renovation*, 18.
4. Neely, *Last Best Hope of Earth*, 105.
5. In *Emancipation Moment*, 19, David Brion Davis argues that "military reverses strengthened the pressure to enlist black troops and to invoke the ultimate weapon of slave emancipation."
6. See chapter 32.
7. Donald, *Lincoln*, 374.
8. Basler, *Abraham Lincoln: His Speeches and Writings*, 652.
9. Douglass, *Day of Jubilee Comes*, reprinted in Commager, *Civil War Archive*, 578. For a fuller discussion of Douglass's response to emancipation, see Blight, *Frederick Douglass's Civil War*, 106–15.
10. Moses Smith, *Our Nation Not Forsaken*, 10–13.
11. This theme is developed brilliantly in Blight, *Race and Reunion*.
12. Quoted in Klingaman, *Abraham Lincoln and the Road to Emancipation*, 169.
13. Quoted in William Wells Brown, *Black Man*, 209.
14. *The Liberator*, August 22, 1862. See also Liggett, "Our National Reverses," 253–54: "What means the recently enacted black code of the great, patriotic and Liberty professing State of Illinois? Do the sons of that would-be-glorious State die by the thousands for the liberty of the black man, as of the white man, and then by a vote almost unanimous, deny him a resting place for the

sole of his weary foot on their own boasted free soil? What means the most extraordinary spectacle of the President of our great nation, inviting to his own council chamber a large number of as intelligent and respectable colored men as he could find . . . to say to you that your expenses shall be paid, if you will be gone from our sight and the land of your unfortunate birth forever?" On the failure of Lincoln's colonization scheme, see McPherson, *Battle Cry of Freedom*, 508–9.

15. This point is made in Belz, *Emancipation and Equal Rights* (New York, 1978), 30–31: "A closer look at Republican Unionism will show . . . that it contained a moral dimension identical to that which historians have more readily discerned in the emancipation policy. Instead of a two-stage progression of war aims from nationalistic reason-of-state to antislavery moral principle, there was in Republican war policy a continuous concern for both expediency and moral idealism in the defense of the Union and in the adoption of an emancipation policy."

16. Quoted in McPherson, *Battle Cry of Freedom*, 769.

17. Hodge, "The War," 157–59.

18. On the prudential Lincoln, see, especially, Guelzo, *Abraham Lincoln: Redeemer President*.

19. On the advances of Lincoln's proclamation over congressional acts, see Oates, *Man Behind the Myths*, 106–7.

20. For an insightful essay tracing the co-optation of Northern clergy by lawyers and politicians during the Civil War, see Fredrickson, "The Coming of the Lord," in Randall M. Miller et al., *Religion and the American Civil War*, 110–30.

21. See chapter 20.

22. Moses Smith, *Our Nation Not Forsaken*, 14.

23. Barnes, *Conditions of Peace*, 7.

24. Skinner, *Light in Darkness*, 4, 8, 11.

25. Moorhead, *American Apocalypse*, 81.

26. On Lincoln's Indian policy, see Weeks, *Farewell, My Nation*, 75.

27. Basler, *Abraham Lincoln: His Speeches and Writings*, 688.

28. Sutherland, "Abraham Lincoln, John Pope, and the Origins of Total War," 580.

20. FREDERICKSBURG: "SO FOOLHARDY AN ADVENTURE"

1. Lieber's Code is printed in Friedman, *Law of War*, 1:158–86, and Hartigan, *Lieber's Code and the Law of War*. These provisions for protection of civilians are reiterated in the Geneva Convention, whose signators pledge: "Persons taking no active part in the hostilities, including members of armed forces who have laid down their arms and those placed hors de combat by sickness, wounds, detention, or any other cause, shall in all circumstances be treated humanely without any adverse distinction founded on race, color, religion, or faith. . . . Outrages upon personal dignity in particular humiliating and degrading treatment . . . shall remain prohibited at any time and in any place whatsoever."

2. Johnson, *Just War Tradition*, 300.
3. The same applied in subsequent American wars. When American officers were accused of torturing Filipino prisoners in the Spanish-American War, they defended themselves (successfully) with General Orders No. 100 and the doctrine of military necessity. In remonstrating against the excesses of American troops in the Philippines, Charles Francis Adams protested the token punishments imposed on American officers as "almost farcical" and continued: "If we are, or appear to be, satisfied with them [the sentences], it would indicate that as a Nation we regard the killing of people and the devastation of a country, and the practice of torture as mere peccadilloes." Quoted in Friedman, *Law of War*, foreword, xix.
4. For an insightful collection of essays on the battle of Fredericksburg, see Gallagher, *Fredericksburg Campaign*.
5. To be sure, Burnside's plan was not wholly without merit if he could launch an immediate attack on Lee's undermanned army. But like McClellan before him, a wary Burnside blinked when he should have attacked, by which time Jackson had rejoined Lee and Longstreet.
6. Quoted in Catton, *Never Call Retreat*, 24.
7. Ibid., 24.
8. John E. Anderson, *Reminiscence*, Civil War Papers, Box 1, Folder 2, 71, AAS.
9. Frank Moore, *Rebellion Record*, 6:107.
10. Quoted in Andrews, *The North Reports the Civil War*, 331.
11. Ibid., 335, 339.
12. *Central Presbyterian*, December 18, 1862.
13. The cartoon is reproduced in Kristen M. Smith, *Lines Are Drawn*, 81.
14. James Gassner to His Mother, December 22, 1862, Civil War Papers, Box 2, Folder 8, AAS.
15. Henry Joslin to Mother, March 10 and April 15, 1863, Civil War Papers, Box 1, Folder 8, AAS.

21. "GOD HAS GRANTED US A HAPPY NEW YEAR"

1. Brooks D. Simpson, *Ulysses S. Grant: Triumph over Adversity*, 163–64.
2. *Richmond Daily Dispatch*, February 23, 1863. Puritan fathers like Thomas Shepard and Cotton Mather, the paper argued, not only inherited the intolerance of their age but were intolerant on principle, with Roger Williams as the lone exception.
3. Ibid., December 31, 1860; January and March 7, 1861.
4. Ibid., May 19, 1861.
5. Ibid., May 2, 1861; January 18, 1862.
6. Ibid., September 27, 1862.
7. Livermore, *Numbers and Losses in the Civil War in America*, 96.
8. Julia Williams to President Davis, Civil War Papers, Box 4, Folder 1, AAS.
9. *Central Presbyterian*, March 12, 1863.
10. For accounts of this battle I have relied chiefly on McPherson, *Battle Cry of*

Freedom, 580–83; Cozzens, *No Better Places to Die*; and Catton, *Never Call Retreat*, 35–47.

11. Catton, *Never Call Retreat*, 42.
12. Basler, *Abraham Lincoln: His Speeches and Writings*, 693–94.
13. John Emerson Anderson to Parents, March 3, 1863, Civil War Papers, Box 1, Folder 2, AAS.
14. Willoughby's letter of January 1, 1863, is preserved in the "William Augustus Willoughby Papers, 1861–64," Manuscript Collections, AAS.
15. *New York Evangelist*, January 8 and January 15, 1863.
16. *American Presbyterian*, December 18, 1862. Presbyterian Historical Society.
17. Rees, *Sermon on Divine Providence*, 11–13.
18. Hovey, *Loyalty*, 7.
19. Spear, *Duty of the Hour*, 14.
20. On internal divisions in the Democratic party see Hettle, *Peculiar Democracy*.
21. Kimball, *Starve or Fall*, 131.
22. For a sampling of the literature suggesting an erosion of nationalism, see Escott, "Failure of Confederate Nationalism," in Owens and Cooke, *Old South in the Crucible of War*, 15–28; Powell and Wayne, "Self-Interest and the Decline of Confederate Nationalism," in ibid., 29–45; Lebergott, "Why the South Lost," 58-74; or Faust, *Creation of Confederate Nationalism*, 36–39. While these works document increasing conflicts they do not, in my view, document an erosion of nationalism any more than increasing controversies in the North indicate a loss of nationalism there. I am indebted to the argument put forward in Carp, "Nations of American Rebels," 5–33.
23. This does not, however, mean that political news sheets critical of Davis were also critical of the rich. The *Richmond Examiner*, for example, ridiculed the "rioters" in the bread riots and suggested they be shot on the spot. In this sense, the poor had no vehicle to express their grievances other than oral demonstration and desertion.
24. J. B. Jones, *Rebel War Clerk's Diary*, 128, 120. On widespread anti-Semitism see Chesson, *Richmond After the War*, 52.
25. J. B. Jones, *Rebel War Clerk's Diary*, 104.

22. "AS SAVAGE AS SAVAGES"

1. *Richmond Daily Dispatch*, March 9, 1863.
2. *Richmond Examiner*, March 21, 1863.
3. Birdwhistell, "Extracts from the Diary of B. F. Hungerford," 28.
4. John Randolph Tucker, *Southern Church Justified in Its Support of the South*, 23.
5. J. B. Jones, *Rebel War Clerk's Diary*, 280.
6. *Richmond Daily Whig*, March 27, 1863.
7. *Central Presbyterian*, March 19, 1863.
8. MacDonell, "Sermon on Matthew 22:21," in Sermons, 1861–67, Manuscript collection, Georgia Historical Society.
9. Elliott, *Sampson's Riddle*.
10. Pierce, *Sermons of Bishop Pierce*.

11. See, for example, Lacy, *Address Delivered at the General Military Hospital*, or Milies, *God in History*.
12. Norwood, *God and Our Country*.
13. *Southern Illustrated News*, April 4, 1863.
14. *Charleston Daily Courier*, March 27 and April 3, 1863.
15. *Central Presbyterian*, April 2, 1863.
16. Dowdey, *Wartime Papers of R. E. Lee*, 419.
17. Bunting's sermon books and diaries are preserved in the Robert Franklin Bunting Papers, Barker Center for Texas History, University of Texas. For a brief sketch of his career see Marks, "Bunting Trusted in God and His Comrades."
18. Kimball, *Starve or Fall*, 131–44.
19. *Central Presbyterian*, January 8, 1863.
20. Jones, *Rebel War Clerk's Diary*, 285.
21. Quoted in Furgurson, *Ashes of Glory*, 196.
22. Putnam, *Richmond during the War*, 208–9.
23. Ann Grymes to Jefferson Davis, April 2, 1863, Civil War Papers, Box 4, Folder 1, AAS.
24. Philo B. Buckingham to Mrs. Buckingham, April 8, 1863, Manuscripts Collection, AAS.
25. *New York Evangelist*, April 23, 1863.
26. *The Liberator*, May 15, 1863.
27. *New York Evangelist*, April 23, 1863.
28. Ibid.
29. Seth Sweetser Papers, 1834–78, AAS.
30. Abijah Marvin, "Fast Sermon on Psalm 80:4–7," April 30, 1863, Manuscript Collection, AAS.

23. CHANCELLORSVILLE: "THE CHAMBER OF DEATH"

1. For this account of Chancellorsville, I have relied heavily on Furgurson, *Chancellorsville, 1863* and Catton, *Never Call Retreat*, 144–67. For technical detail, maps, and complete coverage, the best work on Chancellorsville remains Bigelow, *Campaign of Chancellorsville*.
2. John E. Anderson, *Reminiscence*, Civil War Papers, Box 1, Folder 1, AAS.
3. Robert E. Lee to "My Dear Mrs. Jackson," January 25, 1866, Manuscript Archives, Union Theological Seminary, Richmond.
4. Hooker's version made its way back to the press. A writer for the *New York Evangelist* on May 7, 1863, noted: "Jackson's whole corps, reinforced by D. H. Hill's men, had precipitated themselves on Howard's corps . . . without waiting for a single volley from the rebels, this corps disgracefully abandoned their position . . . and commenced coming, panic stricken, down the road toward head-quarters." In fairness to Hooker, though he was wrong to question Howard's "manliness," he didn't do any worse in the Wilderness than Grant would do a year later. See Neely, "Wilderness and the Cult of Manliness, in Boritt, *Lincoln's Generals*, 79–120.

5. Dowdey, *Wartime Papers of R. E. Lee,* 452–53.

6. Andrews, *North Reports the Civil War,* 370.

7. Philo B. Buckingham to Mrs. Buckingham, May 16, 1863, Manuscript Collection, AAS.

8. Thomas Sherman to William Carthell, May 25, 1863, Civil War Papers, Box 1, Folder 6, AAS. For a discussion of religious themes in soldiers' letters, see McPherson, *For Cause and Comrades,* 62–76.

9. Quoted in McPherson, *Battle Cry of Freedom,* 645.

10. Quoted in Andrews, *The North Reports the Civil War,* 369.

11. *Religious Herald,* May 14, 1863.

12. Quoted in William C. Davis, *Jefferson Davis,* 501.

13. *Richmond Daily Dispatch,* May 11, 1863.

14. See Stowell, "Stonewall Jackson and the Providence of God," in Randall M. Miller et al., *Religion and the American Civil War,* 187–207.

15. Putnam, *Richmond during the War,* 223–24.

16. John Randolph Tucker, *Southern Church Justified in Its Support of the South,* 33.

17. Ibid., 34.

18. *Christian Instructor and Western United Presbyterian,* May 23, 1863.

19. *New York Evangelist,* May 21, 1863.

20. In *Jefferson Davis,* 175, Eaton argues that had Davis been a more forceful commander and not yielded to Lee's local focus, the Army of the Potomac would have been shifted to reinforce Vicksburg. Instead the Confederacy lost both Gettysburg and Vicksburg.

21. Howard Prince to My Dear George, June 6, 1863, Civil War Papers, Box 1, Folder 10, AAS.

24. GETTYSBURG: "FIELD OF BLOOD, AND DEATH"

1. In later reports on Gettysburg, the *Southern Illustrated News* used the "conduct of the Confederate troops" to civilian property as a "victory" of sorts in contrast with "the scandalous outrages committed by Northern troops in Southern territory" August 29, 1863. This report ignored the fact that Confederate troops burned Thad Stevens's factory and attempted to enslave free blacks. See Mitchell, *Civil War Soldiers,* 155–56.

2. William S. Christian to Wife, June 28, 1863, reprinted in Moore, *Rebellion Record,* vol. 7, 325.

3. See McPherson, *Battle Cry of Freedom,* 659, and Catton, *Never Call Retreat,* 185.

4. Quoted in Trulock, *In the Hands of Providence,* 144–45.

5. Catton, *Never Call Retreat,* 190.

6. Dunn quoted in Hess, *Pickett's Charge,* 246.

7. John E. Anderson, *Reminiscence,* Civil War Papers, Box 1, Folder 2, 112, AAS.

8. Charles Ward to Mother, 1863, Civil War Papers, Box 2, Folder 6, AAS.

25. "FOR THE SAKE OF THE CAUSE"

1. *New York Evangelist,* July 9, 1863.
2. On the cultural significance of flags and ritualized violence, see Bonner, *Colors and Blood,* and, more generally, Marvin and Ingle, *Blood Sacrifice and the Nation.*
3. *Christian Intelligencer,* July 16, 1863. Presbyterian Historical Society.
4. Ibid., July 23, 1863.
5. *Independent,* July 9, 1863.
6. Ibid., August 27, 1863.
7. William Thompson Lusk to "Dear Cousin Lou," reprinted in Commager, *Civil War Archive,* 437.
8. *Philadelphia Inquirer,* July 6, 1863.
9. *New York Times,* July 6, 1863.
10. Preface to *"Angel Mother I'm Coming Home,"* Union Imprint Song Sheets, John Hay Library, Brown University.
11. Basler, *Abraham Lincoln: His Speeches and Writings,* 709–10.
12. Ibid., 712.
13. Meade quoted in *Christian Herald,* July 16, 1863.
14. John E. Anderson, *Reminiscence,* Civil War Papers, Box 1, Folder 2, AAS.
15. John Francis Gleason to Father, July 29, 1863, Civil War Papers, Box 1, Folder 1, AAS.
16. The experiences recounted in the unknown Union woman's diary were reprinted in Cable, "A Woman's Diary of the Siege of Vicksburg," 767–75.
17. *Christian Intelligencer,* July 9, 1863.
18. *Philadelphia Inquirer,* July 8, 1863.
19. President Davis agreed. He had Lee in the East, but no one in the West. He too recognized the crucial importance of great generals in a letter to his brother Joseph: "A *General* in the full acceptation of the word is a rare product, scarcely more than one can be expected in a generation, but in this mighty war in which we are engaged there is need for half a dozen." Quoted in William C. Davis, *Jefferson Davis,* 504.
20. *New York Evangelist,* July 9, 1863.
21. DuBois, *Gift of Black Folk,* 82. I am indebted to Professor Edward J. Blum for calling this to my attention.
22. For an outstanding account of the riots see Cook, *Armies of the Streets.*
23. *Christian Intelligencer,* July 16, 1863. Presbyterian Historical Society.
24. Philo Buckingham to Wife, July 17, 1863, Civil War Papers, AAS.
25. John E. Anderson, *Reminiscence,* Civil War Papers, 118, Box 1, Folder 2, AAS.
26. Strong and Daly quoted in Linden and Pressly, *Voices from the House Divided,* 117, 119–20.
27. See, for example, *New York Evangelist,* July 16, 1863.
28. Ibid., July 23, 1863.
29. *Philadelphia Inquirer,* August 5, 1863.

26. "A POLITICAL WORSHIP"

1. *American Presbyterian,* August 6, 1863.
2. *Philadelphia Inquirer,* August 7, 1863.
3. This theme is discussed in Clebsch, "Christian Interpretations of the Civil War," 212–30.
4. Bushnell, "Doctrine of Loyalty," 573.
5. Schaff quoted in Clebsch, "Christian Interpretations of the Civil War," 220. In addition to Clebsch, see Noll, *America's God,* 418–19.
6. *North Carolina Standard,* July 7, 1863; *Central Presbyterian,* July 9, 1863. For similar optimistic assessments, see, for example, *Daily Sun* (Columbus, GA), July 11, 1863; *Richmond Religious Herald,* July 9, 1863.
7. *Christian Observer,* July 16, 1863.
8. *Southern Illustrated News,* August 1, 1863.
9. *Christian Observer,* July 9, 1863.
10. *North Carolina Standard,* July 10, 1863.
11. Myers, *Children of Pride,* 383.
12. *Southern Churchman,* May 15 and July 17, 1863.
13. *Central Presbyterian,* September 17, 1863. For a similar account, see *Richmond Christian Advocate,* September 3, 1863.
14. Bunting's letter of July 30, 1863, was written for the *Houston Tri-Weekly Telegraph,* August 31, 1863, and is preserved in the Robert Franklin Bunting Papers, Barker Center for Texas History, University of Texas.
15. J. B. Jones, *Rebel War Clerk's Diary,* 388–89.
16. Ibid., 390.
17. *Richmond Christian Advocate,* August 20, 1863; *Southern Churchman,* September 11, 1863. Leroy Lee's sermon was extracted in the October 8, 1863, issue of the *Richmond Christian Advocate.* See also *Christian Observer,* August 20, 1863; *Richmond Religious Herald,* August 20, 1863; and *Central Presbyterian,* July 30, 1863.
18. *Richmond Daily Whig,* August 21, 1863.
19. Robert Franklin Bunting, "Letter to Editor," August 23, 1863, Robert Franklin Bunting Papers, Barker Center for Texas History, University of Texas.
20. Ibid.
21. See, for example, the widely circulated soldier's tract by Lee, *Our Country— Our Dangers—Our Duty,* 13, 21.
22. Slaughter, *Coercion and Conciliation,* 7.
23. *Richmond Daily Dispatch,* July 16 and July 28, 1863.
24. *Richmond Daily Whig,* July 10, 1863.
25. *Examiner,* August 2, 1863.
26. Ibid. This theme is amplified in McPherson, "Antebellum Southern Exceptionalism," 230–44.
27. *Richmond Examiner,* July 17, 1863.
28. Ibid., August 6, 1863.
29. Ibid., August 24, 1863.
30. Ibid.
31. Ibid.

27. "THE ROCK OF CHICKAMAUGA"

1. Richardson, *Messages and Papers of Jefferson Davis*, 343–44.
2. Shaw quoted in Commager, *Civil War Archive*, 335–36.
3. Richardson, *Messages and Papers of Jefferson Davis*, 343–44.
4. See Thomas Goodrich, *Bloody Dawn*.
5. *Christian Intelligencer*, August 27, 1863.
6. Sutherland, "Guerrilla Warfare, Democracy, and the Fate of the Confederacy," 290–91.
7. Basler, *Abraham Lincoln: His Speeches and Writings*, 722.
8. Ibid., 701–2.
9. *Richmond Daily Dispatch*, September 4, 1863.
10. For accounts of the battle of Chickamauga, see Glen Tucker, *Chickamauga*.
11. Quoted in McPherson, *The Negro's Civil War*, 215.
12. Quoted in McPherson, *Battle Cry of Freedom*, 675.
13. William C. Davis, *Jefferson Davis*, 518–21.
14. Two recent military histories recount the battles around Chattanooga: Cozzens, *Shipwreck of Their Hopes*, and Sword, *Mountains Touched with Fire*.

28. "IN THAT IMMORTAL FIELD"

1. See Reardon, *Pickett's Charge in History and Memory*, and Desjardin, *Those Honored Dead*.
2. *Banner of the Covenant*, December 3, 1863.
3. *Presbyter*, November 25, 1863.
4. *Times* (London), December 4, 1863.
5. *Banner of the Covenant*, March 23, 1861.
6. Basler, *Abraham Lincoln: His Speeches and Writings*, 737.
7. Edmund Wilson, "The Union as Religious Mysticism," 126. In *Fate of Liberty*, Neely takes issue with Wilson, arguing that Lincoln remained a steely-eyed constitutionalist. While there is much accuracy to this in terms of Lincoln's restraints on issues of habeas corpus and civilian arrests, it ignores the primacy Lincoln granted to the Declaration of Independence, and his increasingly mystical faith in a redeemer nation dedicated to the proposition that "all men are created equal."
8. See especially Wills, *Lincoln at Gettysburg*.
9. *Christian Recorder*, November 28 and November 7, 1863.
10. Basler, *Abraham Lincoln: His Speeches and Writings*, 730.
11. *New York Evangelist*, October 8, 1863.
12. Fish, *Valley of Achor*, 18–19.
13. M'Leod, *Our Country Worth Saving*, 1.
14. Ibid., 3, 11, 16. For similar sentiments, see Rufas W. Clark's Thanksgiving sermon, *Unity of the American Nationality*, 11.
15. *Banner of the Covenant*, December 3, 1863.
16. Wharton, *Willing Reunion Not Impossible*, 21–22.
17. Coxe, *Unjust Reproaches*, 5–7.

18. Carey, *God Doing Wonderful Things*, 13. For similar sentiments, see Lillie, *Discourse Delivered in the Second Reformed Dutch Church*, 14.
19. Schenck, *Songs in the Night*, 9, 12–13.
20. *Richmond Daily Whig*, August 21, 1863.
21. Benjamin M. Palmer, *Discourse before the General Assembly of South Carolina*, 3, 6, 15, 23.
22. *Richmond Daily Dispatch*, January 28, 1864.
23. Ibid., January 13, 1864. On the text in the American Revolution see Stout, *New England Soul*, 282–311.
24. Andrews, *The South Reports the Civil War*, 383.
25. On the divisive issue of states' rights within the Confederacy, see Rable, *Confederate Republic*, 256–63.
26. *Richmond Examiner*, September 18, 1862; April 4, 1864.
27. *Charleston Daily Courier*, April 6, 1864.

29. "THE PRESENT UNHOLY WAR"

1. See Klement, *Limits of Dissent*, 243–45.
2. Silbey, *Respectable Minority*, 72.
3. Cox, *Eight Years in Congress*, 241–42.
4. Ibid., 276.
5. On foreign-born underrepresentation in the Union armies, see McPherson, *Battle Cry of Freedom*, 606.
6. Curran, *Soldiers of Peace*, 89. On the refusal of the American Peace Society to join with the far smaller Universal Peace Union in opposition to the war, see Curran, 111–14.
7. Page, *Speech of Moses B. Page*, 13–14.
8. Cox, *Eight Years in Congress*, 243.
9. Ibid., 244.
10. See especially Litwack, *North of Slavery*; Voegeli, *Free but Not Equal*; and Wood, *Black Scare*.
11. Hancock, *Reminiscences of Winfield Scott Hancock*, 94.
12. Jean H. Baker, *Affairs of Party*, 213. In terms of rioting, Baker recognizes that rioters included white Republicans as well as Democrats, "but Democrats, as the most vehement public opponents of racial change, were found more often than Republicans in the anti-Black mobs that physically and verbally abused Negroes. They were also more likely to organize such affairs and to lead campaigns to exclude blacks from politics" (248).
13. See, for example, Toll, *Blacking Up*; Wittke, *Tambo and Bones*; and Nathan, *Dan Emmett and the Rise of Negro Minstrelsy*.
14. Jean H. Baker, *Affairs of Party*, 221.
15. Samuel S. Cox, *Eight Years in Congress*, 357–58. On the miscegenation controversy, see Wood, *Black Scare*, 53–79. For a description of the "science" that denied mulattos could procreate, see Louis Menand, *Metaphysical Club*.
16. LeBeau, *Currier & Ives: America Imagined*, 96. For a more extended treatment of Currier & Ives's denigrating treatment of African Americans in general, see

LeBeau 215–56. The "Irrepressible Conflict" is reproduced in Peters, Currier & Ives, plate 157. See also Holzer, Baritt, and Neely, The Lincoln Image, 34–43.

17. On Jacksonian religion, see Carwardine's Evangelicals and Politics in Antebellum America.

18. The best treatment of the Bible in political debates is Noll, America's God. See also Noll's "The Bible and Slavery," in Randall M. Miller et al., Religion and the American Civil War, 43–73.

19. Hopkins, Scriptural, Ecclesiastical and Historical View of Slavery, 19, 343.

20. On federal arrests, see especially Neely, Fate of Liberty. In defending Lincoln's critics, Klement failed to explore the role of churches and denominations in suppressing dissent; see Copperheads in the Middle West. See also Andreasen, "As Good a Right to Pray."

21. Carwardine, "Methodists, Politics, and the Coming of the American Civil War," 578–609.

22. Quoted in Victor B. Howard, Religion and the Radical Republican Movement, 42–43.

23. Ibid., 81–82.

30. "FROM HEAD TO HEART"

1. In Southern Cross, 5, Heyrman estimates that by the 1830s the three largest Southern denominations, Baptists, Methodists, and Presbyterians, amounted to at most 50 percent of white and black households.

2. Reprinted in Lexington Presbytery, A Century's History of Presbyterianism, 15.

3. North Carolina Standard, June 4, 1864.

4. Davis's address was reprinted in North Carolina Standard, February 12, 1864.

5. See Watson, "Religion and Combat Motivation," 29–55.

6. Doggett, Discourse Delivered in the Broad Street Methodist Church and The War and Its Close.

7. On the desolation of the churches and spiritual malaise on the homefront, see Shattuck, Shield and Hiding Place, 43.

8. Christian Observer, October 15, 1863. On the collapse of "institutional religion" in the Confederacy, see Faust, Mothers of Invention, 184–85.

9. Central Presbyterian, June 11, 1863.

10. Myers, Children of Pride, 392.

11. Richmond Religious Herald, July 30 and September 10, 1863;

12. Southern Churchman, August 14, 1863. See also Richmond Christian Advocate, September 17, 1863.

13. Richmond Religious Herald, October 1, 1863.

14. Bunting described the army revivals in a "Letter from the Rangers on Silver Creek, near Rome, Georgia," July 30, 1863, Robert Franklin Bunting Papers, Barker Center for Texas History, University of Texas. On Bunting's regiment see Marks, "Bunting Trusted in God and His Comrades," 45.

15. This is not to say that revivals did not flourish in Northern camps bracing for the spring campaigns. Indeed, reports of army revivals appeared in most Northern religious papers. But Northern army revivals did not come to assume

the cultural and political significance that they enjoyed in the Confederacy. On Northern revivals in the army, see Shattuck, *Shield and a Hiding Place*, 73–93.

16. *Central Presbyterian,* February 18 and April 14, 1864.
17. Baker's sermon is reprinted in Lexington Presbytery, *A Century's History of Presbyterianism,* 213–36.
18. Anonymous, *The Soldier's Aim by a Charleston Pastor.* This tract was published by the South Carolina Colportage Board and is in the possession of the South Carolina Historical Society.
19. *Richmond Religious Herald,* February 25, 1864.
20. Ibid., April 21, 1864.
21. The "New South" orthodoxy was captured early on in the books dealing with Confederate army revivals. See especially Bennett, *Narrative of the Great Revival* and William J. Jones, *Christ in the Camp.* On the connections between Civil War revivals and the Religion of the Lost Cause, see Stout and Grasso, "Civil War, Religion, and Communications," in Randall M. Miller et al., *Religion and the American Civil War,* 313–59.

31. "I CAN ONLY THINK OF HELL UPON EARTH"

1. McPherson, *Battle Cry of Freedom,* 802.
2. *The Liberator,* January 29, 1864.
3. Blight, *Race and Reunion,* 242–43.
4. Hesseltine, *Civil War Prisons,* 197.
5. Ibid. Hesseltine's analysis of prison life in the North and South has stood the test of time and remains the only comprehensive survey, although his notions of "war psychology" have been questioned and revised.
6. Wyatt-Brown has exhaustively traced the history and cultural significance of honor in white Southern culture; see especially *Shaping of Southern Culture.* Though not as frequently commented on, similar mores dominated Northern culture, particularly military culture at West Point, whose motto "Duty, Honor, Country" summarized the ethic perfectly.
7. Reprinted in Denney, *Civil War Prisons and Escapes,* appendix 5, 380.
8. Ludlow's letter of June 14, 1863, is reprinted in ibid., 101.
9. Butler's letter is reprinted in *O.R,* series 2 vol. 7, 687–91. (*War of the Rebellion . . . Official Records of the Union and Confederate Armies.*)
10. Ibid., 105.
11. Ibid., 691.
12. James's statement is reprinted in ibid., 117–19.
13. Hesseltine, *Civil War Prisons,* 2. One of the harshest Northern prisons was at Fort Delaware on Pea Patch Island. See Keen, "Confederate Prisoners of War at Fort Delaware," 1–27.
14. Statistics may be found in Denney, *Civil War Prisons and Escapes,* 381.
15. McPherson, *Battle Cry of Freedom,* 802. McPherson goes on to argue that, if anything, northern figures are understated because some paroled Union prisoners died after their release.
16. Cornish, *Sable Arm,* 178.

17. Bryan and Lankford, *Eye of the Storm*, 213.
18. Denney, *Civil War Prisons and Escapes*, 106.
19. McPherson, *Battle Cry of Freedom*, 795.
20. Hesseltine, *Civil War Prisons*, 203.
21. Letter of R. B. Winder to Quartermaster, August 19, 1864, *O.R.*, series 2, vol. 7, 624.
22. Chauncey's Andersonville diary was transcribed by General William Sever Lincoln and is preserved in Civil War Papers, Box 2, Folder 1, AAS.
23. Ransom, *Diary*. Ransom's diary was originally published serially in the *Jackson* (MI) *Citizen* and then bound as a volume in 1881 under the title *Andersonville*. It was reprinted in 1963 with an introduction by Bruce Catton. All of the quotations in this account are from the 1963 edition.
24. Ransom, *Diary*, May 27 and March 30, 1864.
25. *O. R.*, series 2, vol. 7, 616–17. (*War of the Rebellion*)
26. Ibid.
27. Some prisoners did, indeed, seek solace in religion. In contrast to Ransom, Private Sneden attended prayer meetings at Andersonville regularly. Bryan and Lankford, *Eye of the Storm*, 249.
28. Ransom, *Diary*, June 18, 1864.

32. "NO PLEDGE TO MAKE BUT ACTION"

1. *Banner of the Covenant*, October 13, 1862.
2. *American Presbyterian*, September 11, 1862.
3. Kirkwood's letter is reprinted in Berlin et al., *Free at Last*, 67–68.
4. On blacks in the Union military see Joseph T. Wilson's classic account in *Black Phalanx*. See also Quarles, *The Negro in the Civil War*, and Cornish, *Sable Arm*. More recently, see Glatthaar, *Forged in Battle*, and McPherson's edited documentary volume, *The Negro's Civil War*. On the use of slaves for the Confederate army, see Brewer, *Confederate Negro*, and Ervin L. Jordan, *Black Confederates and Afro-Yankees*.
5. Berlin, "The Destruction of Slavery," 65.
6. Taylor, *Sable Arm*, 288-89.
7. McPherson, *The Negro's Civil War*, 176.
8. Thomas Wentworth Higginson to James, November 24, 1862, Thomas Wentworth Higginson Papers, 1853–1911, AAS. Higginson provides a wonderfully written account of his unit in *Army Life in a Black Regiment*.
9. Thomas Higginson to William Brown, December 26, 1862, Brown Family Papers, 1762–1965, AAS.
10. *First Anniversary of the Proclamation of Freedom in South Carolina*, 7.
11. McPherson, *The Negro's Civil War*, 184–85.
12. Ibid., 186. For an account of the battle, see Quarles, *The Negro in the Civil War*, 220–24.
13. *New York Evangelist*, July 2, 1863. Presbyterian Historical Society. Positive responses to African American soldiers was a staple in the religious press. For similar assessments, see the *American Presbyterian*, February 19, 1863, or the *Christian Instructor and Western United Presbyterian*, October 17, 1863.

14. Quarles, *The Negro in the Civil War*, 12–21.

15. Gooding's letter is reprinted in Adams, *On the Altar of Freedom*, 38–39.

16. Gooding quoted in Linden and Pressly, *Voices from the House Divided*, 123.

17. Ibid., 127. On June 15, 1864, Congress passed legislation granting equal pay to black soldiers, retroactive only to January 1, 1864.

18. See Quarles, *The Negro in the Civil War*, 15–16.

19. *Christian Recorder*, August 22, 1863.

20. Harmon's letter of November 7, 1863, is reprinted in Redkey, *Grand Army of Black Men*.

21. McPherson, *Battle Cry of Freedom*, 634.

22. McPherson, *The Negro's Civil War*, 190.

23. *New York Tribune*, September 8, 1865.

24. Ray Palmer, *Opening Future*, 20–21. The issue of "the Bible and slavery" continued to bear commentary in 1863. See, for example, Joseph P. Thompson, *Christianity and Emancipation*, and Harwood, *Canaan, Shem and Japheth*.

25. Gooding's account is reprinted in Virginia M. Adams, *On the Altar of Freedom*, 85.

26. Jones's letter is reprinted in Redkey, *Grand Army of Black Men*, 42.

27. Romero and Rose, *Reminiscences of My Life*, 87–88.

28. McPherson, *The Negro's Civil War*, 209.

29. An early account of the massacre appeared in Joseph T. Wilson, *Black Phalanx*, 348–58. For a balanced assessment of the evidence on all sides, see Castel, "The Fort Pillow Massacre," 37–50.

30. Ransom, *Diary*, July 6, 1864.

31. Cornish, *Sable Arm*, 176.

32. Joseph T. Wilson, *Black Phalanx*, 358.

33. White's letter of March 14, 1864, is reprinted in Redkey, *Grand Army of Black Men*, 38–39.

34. Luis Endicott to Mr. Bradlee, April 27, 1864, Civil War Papers, Box 2, Folder 9, AAS.

33. "THE MOST INTERESTING MEN IN THE COUNTRY"

1. "All Hail to Ulysses!" (Chicago, 1864), Union Imprint Song Sheets, John Hay Library, Brown University.

2. *Southern Illustrated News*, May 30, 1863.

3. Livermore, *Numbers and Losses in the Civil War*, 47.

4. Lyman, *With Grant and Meade*, 121.

5. Grant, *Memoirs*, 473–74.

6. Ibid., 478.

7. On these lesser generals, see Simon, "Grant, Lincoln, and Unconditional Surrender," in Boritt, *Lincoln's Generals*, 181–89.

8. Fort quoted in Faust, *Mothers of Invention*, 138.

9. William T. Sherman to H. W. Hill, September 7, 1863, O.R., series 1, vol. 30, pt. 3, 403. (*War of the Rebellion*)

10. Grant, *Memoirs*, 512.
11. James Longstreet, *From Manassas to Appomattox*, 554.
12. Samuel S. Cox, *Eight Years in Congress*, 395.
13. In the end, Frémont withdrew his candidacy in return for Lincoln's promise to restructure his cabinet.
14. Martha LeBaron Goddard to Mary W. Johnson, May 2, 1864, Manuscripts Collection, AAS.
15. Ibid.
16. Marvin, "Sermon on Daniel 4:27," April 7, 1864, Sermons Collection, AAS.
17. See, for example, Davis's angry reply to North Carolina's governor, Zebulon B. Vance, February 29, 1864 in Crist, ed., *Papers of Jefferson Davis*, 12 vols., vol. 10: 265–70.
18. *Richmond Daily Whig*, April 8, 1864. See also *Richmond Daily Dispatch*, March 17, March 28, and March 30, 1864.

34. "IF IT TAKES ALL SUMMER"

1. For an excellent account of the battle, see Cushman, *Bloody Promenade*.
2. For the description of Lee's rendezvous with Longstreet's Texans, I am indebted to Freeman, *Lee's Lieutenants*, 3:356–57.
3. Gordon is quoted in Freeman, *Lee's Lieutenants*, 3:368.
4. James Longstreet, *From Manassas to Appomattox*, 565.
5. Grant, *Memoirs*, 531.
6. Ibid., 527.
7. Ibid., 540.
8. Lyman, *With Grant and Meade*, 99–100.
9. Freeman and McWhiney, *Lee's Dispatches*, May 18, 1864, 214.
10. Lyman, *With Grant and Meade*, 102.
11. "Grant to Halleck," O.R., series I, vol. 36, pt. 2, p. 672 (*War of the Rebellion*).
12. For the account of this battle, I have relied heavily on Freeman, *Lee's Lieutenants*, 3:402–10; Catton, *Never Call Retreat*, 358–61; and Matter, *If It Takes All Summer*.
13. See Gordon's account in *Reminiscences of the Civil War*, 278–81.
14. Quoted in Freeman, *Lee's Lieutenants*, 3:408.
15. Lyman, *With Grant and Meade*, 114.

35. "JUNE 3. COLD HARBOR. I WAS KILLED"

1. *Mobile Daily Advertiser and Register*, May 27, 1864.
2. *American Presbyterian*, May 19, 1864.
3. Putnam, *Richmond During the War*, 296–97.
4. Helmreich, "A Prayer for the Spirit of Acceptance," 405.
5. Lyman, *With Grant and Meade*, 106. Italics mine.
6. Willoughby's correspondence is preserved in William Augustus Willoughby Papers, Manuscript Collection, AAS.
7. John E. Anderson, *Reminiscence*, 158 in Civil War Papers, Box 1, Folder 1, AAS.

References to "holy war" were becoming commonplace. See also Eustis, *Discourse Delivered at the Funeral of Rev. Samuel Fisk*, 45.

8. Perkins K. Clark, *Sacrifices for Our Country*, 11.
9. Rufus W. Clark, *Discourse Commemorative of the Heroes of Albany*, 8, and Griggs, *No Fear of Death*, 11.
10. See Griffith, *Battle Tactics of the Civil War*, 137–92.
11. Lyman, *With Grant and Meade*, 117.
12. Grant, *Memoirs*, 493–94.
13. Robertson, *Civil War Virginia*, 153.
14. See Brooks D. Simpson's introduction to Lyman, *With Grant and Meade*, xi.
15. Quoted in Furgurson, *Not War but Murder*, 151–52. The fighting continued at Cold Harbor into the evening, but the greatest percentage of casualties came in the opening hour.
16. Charles Watson Washburn Papers, 1862–1865, Manuscript collection, vol. 1, AAS.
17. The correspondence between Lee and Grant is reprinted in Grant's *Memoirs*, 586–87. For an insightful analysis of the exchange in the context of honor and morality, I am indebted to an unpublished paper by Wyatt-Brown, "Robert E. Lee and the Concept of Honor."
18. Quoted in Furgurson, *Not War but Murder*, 212–13.
19. Grant, *Memoirs*, 588.
20. *Philadelphia Inquirer*, July 23, 1864.
21. See McPherson, *Battle Cry of Freedom*, 737.

36. "THE PIOUS MEN WILL BE HELD UP AS THE GREATEST OF PATRIOTS"

1. *Richmond Examiner*, June 4, 1864.
2. *American Presbyterian*, September 8, 1864. For additional accounts see *New York Evangelist*, May 26, 1864.
3. Benjamin Gratz Brown, *Immediate Abolition of Slavery*, 13.
4. Dowdey, *Wartime Papers of R. E. Lee*, 807.
5. George Elsworth to Enron Thomas, November 11, 1864, Civil War Papers, Box 2, Folder 3, AAS.
6. Martin Blynum to Thomas Prince, August 1, 1864, Civil War Papers, Box 2, Folder 3, AAS.
7. Quoted in McPherson, *The Negro's Civil War*, 224–25.
8. *Philadelphia Inquirer*, June 18, 1864.
9. *Richmond Daily Dispatch*, July 16 and 29, 1864.
10. Grant, *Memoirs*, 612.
11. Ibid., 613.
12. Payne's letter is reprinted in Redkey, *Grand Army of Black Men*, 114.
13. Emory M. Thomas, *Robert E. Lee*, 342.

37. "IF THEY WANT PEACE THEY . . . MUST STOP THE WAR"

1. John E. Anderson, *Reminiscence*, 136, Civil War Papers, Box 1, Folder 1, AAS.
2. Sherman, *Memoirs*, 489.
3. Ibid., 492.
4. Quoted in Royster, *Destructive War*, 299.
5. Ibid., 518.
6. Royster, *Destructive War*, 315.
7. Sherman, *Memoirs*, 536.
8. I am indebted to Fellows for first calling this to my attention in " 'The Poor Women Will Make a Howl.' " Many of the primary sources surrounding the deportation are reprinted in Hitt, *Charged with Treason*.
9. *O.R*, series. 1, vol. 36, pt. 5, 76–77 (*War of the Rebellion*).
10. By war's end, many of the women had become sufficiently habituated to their new home that they remained rather than return to their devastated home sites.
11. *Milledgeville Confederate Union*, August 23, 1864.
12. Quoted in Hitt, 70.
13. *New York Tribune*, July 21, 1864.
14. Dowdey, *Wartime Papers of R. E. Lee*, 821.
15. *Richmond Daily Whig*, July 20, 1864.
16. Preston, *Lee: West Point and Lexington*, 32–36, and Sherman, *Memoirs*, 543–44.
17. Sherman, *Memoirs*, 1010.
18. Ibid., 559–60.
19. See McDonough and Jones, *War So Terrible*, 269–90.
20. John E. Anderson, *Reminiscence*, 155, Civil War Papers, Box 1, Folder 1, AAS.
21. Grant, *Memoirs*, 508–11.
22. For descriptions of the destruction see Russell, *Atlanta, 1847–1890*, 114–15.
23. Sherman, *Memoirs*, 598–99.
24. The correspondence between Sherman and Hood is reprinted in Sherman, *Memoirs*, 591–98.
25. Quoted in Bower, "Theology of the Battlefield," 1024.
26. Sherman, *Memoirs*, 596.
27. John M. Howe Letters, 1864, Civil War Papers, Box 2, Folder 5, AAS.
28. *American Presbyterian*, August 4, 1864.
29. Lewin, *National Judgments*, 5.
30. *American Presbyterian*, August 4, 1864.
31. Cruickshanks, *Sermon Preached*, 11–13.

38. "RED OCTOBER": "THE WORK OF DESTRUCTION"

1. Conrad, *Thanksgiving Discourse*, 14.
2. Vandiver, *Jubal Early War Memoirs*, 478.

3. *New York Times*, August 8, 1864.
4. Grant, *Memoirs*, 615.
5. Sheridan, *Memoirs*, 1: 462, 488.
6. All quotes from Anderson are taken from John Emerson Anderson, Letters, Civil War Papers, Box 1, Folder 2, AAS.
7. Dowdey, *Wartime Papers of Robert. E. Lee*, 704.
8. *Valley Spirit*, August 31, 1864. I am indebted to Mochan, "Rebel Vengeance," for bringing this source to my attention.
9. McPherson, *Battle Cry of Freedom*, 619.
10. Grimsley, *Hard Hand of War*, 171–204.
11. Bernard, *Lincoln and the Music of the Civil War*, 245.
12. Quoted in Catton, *Never Call Retreat*, 387.
13. Greiner et al., *Surgeon's Civil War*, 252.
14. Sheridan, *Memoirs*, 2:39–40.
15. Ibid., 2:52.
16. Duncan, *Lee's Endangered Left*, 145. On guerrilla warfare, see Virgil Carrington Jones, *Gray Ghosts and Rebel Raiders*.
17. Greiner et al., *Surgeon's Civil War*, 261.
18. Ibid., 256, 259.
19. Ibid., 56.
20. Quoted in Gallagher, *Confederate War*, 77.
21. Greiner et al., *Surgeon's Civil War*, 245–66.
22. Sheridan, *Memoirs*, II 75–82.
23. Thompson, *Peace through Victory*, p. 13.
24. *New York Observer*, November 17, 1864.
25. Cleveland, *Thanksgiving Discourse*, 11, 13–14.

39. "A VOTE FOR PRINCIPLE, FOR CONSCIENCE, FOR CHRIST"

1. *American Presbyterian*, November 3, 1864.
2. Joseph P. Thompson, *Peace through Victory*, 11, 13.
3. Victor B. Howard, *Religion and the Radical Republican Movement*, 81–87.
4. *Chicago Times*, November 24, 1864.
5. VanderVelde, *Presbyterian Churches and the Federal Union*, 322–23.
6. Van Dyke, *Spirituality and Independence of the Church*, 13, 15, 18.
7. For a voting analysis of the two parties, see Silbey, *Respectable Minority*, 140–57.
8. Ransom, *Diary*, November 6, 1864.
9. Ellis, *Nation's Ballot*, 9.
10. *Richmond Daily Whig*, November 12, 1864.
11. Alexander H. Vinton, *Cause for Thanksgiving*, 22–23.
12. Phipps, *Discourse Delivered in Paxton, Massachusetts*, 8.
13. Perrin, *Our Part in the World's Struggle*, 7–8, 20–22.
14. Wells, *Sacrifice of Continual Praise*, 14–15.
15. *American Presbyterian*, November 24 and December 12, 1864.

40. "I CAN MAKE THIS MARCH, AND MAKE GEORGIA HOWL!"

1. Sherman, *Memoirs*, 627.
2. Ibid., 628–29.
3. *Central Presbyterian*, November 10, 1864.
4. For editorials hostile to enlisting black soldiers, see, for example, *Richmond Daily Dispatch*, November 9, 1864; *Marion Ensign*, November 16, 1864; or *Richmond Examiner*, November 2, 1864.
5. Quoted in Catton, *Never Call Retreat*, 401.
6. If nothing else, America's disastrous experience in Vietnam's civil war confirms that guerrilla warfare can be successful against mighty armies.
7. Grant, *Memoirs*, 633.
8. Sherman, *Memoirs*, 640.
9. Grant, *Memoirs*, 638.
10. John Emerson Anderson, Letters, Civil War Papers, Box 1, Folder 2, AAS.
11. Sherman, *Memoirs*, 656.
12. Ibid., 652.
13. Quoted in Catton, *Never Call Retreat*, 415.
14. O.R., series 1, vol. 64, 21 (*War of the Rebellion*).
15. Sherman, *Memoirs*, 659.
16. Grant, *Memoirs*, 646.
17. The term is Bower's; see "The Theology of the Battlefield."
18. When adopted as a child into the Ewing family, Sherman was baptized Roman Catholic, but he never joined the church. See Marszalek, *Soldier's Passion for Order*, 41.
19. Ellis, *Nation's Ballot*, 14–16.
20. Thompson and Steedman quoted in McPherson, *The Negro's Civil War*, 233.
21. Ibid., 223.
22. Sherman, *Memoirs*, 657.
23. Ibid., 1050–52.
24. O.R., series 1, vol. 102, 737 (*War of the Rebellion*).
25. Basler, *Abraham Lincoln: Speeches and Writings*, 789–90.
26. John Emerson Anderson, Letters, Civil War Papers, Box 1, Folder 2, AAS.
27. *Banner of the Covenant*, January 6, 1865.
28. Catton, *Never Call Retreat*, 376.

41. "UPHOLD THE CAUSE AND STRENGTHEN THE HANDS OF THE FAITHFUL"

1. See McPherson, *Battle Cry of Freedom*, 819.
2. Robertson's diary is edited and reprinted in Helmreich, "A Prayer for the Spirit of Acceptance," 406–7.
3. Henry Ward Beecher to Abraham Lincoln, February 4, 1865, Civil War Papers, Box 2, Folder 8, AAS.
4. *Richmond Religious Herald*, March 9, 1865.

5. *Richmond Daily Dispatch*, January 30, 1865.

6. Ibid., February 20, 1865. For similar sentiments, see *Richmond Examiner*, January 28, 1865.

7. *Richmond Religious Herald*, March 9, 1865.

8. *Richmond Daily Dispatch*, January 19, 1865.

9. Ibid.

10. *Christian Observer*, February 2, 1865.

11. *Central Presbyterian*, February 16, 1865.

12. *Army and Navy Messenger*, February 23, 1865.

13. Jeter, Notes and Sermons, Virginia Baptist Historical Society.

14. The *Richmond Christian Advocate* editorial is summarized with approbation in the *Richmond Religious Herald*, February 9, 1865.

15. Minnigerode, *Sermon Preached*, 9.

16. Ibid., 14.

17. See Coulter, *Confederate States of America*, 555–59.

18. *American Presbyterian*, January 12, 1865.

19. Taylor, *Manliness*, 5.

20. Stone, *The Work of New England*, 22, 16, 19.

21. Moses D. Hoge to Robert Dabney, July 18, 1865, Manuscript Archives, Union Theological Seminary, Richmond.

42. "VENGEANCE UPON SOUTH CAROLINA"

1. Waring's letter is reprinted in Redkey, *Grand Army of Black Men*, 73–76.

2. Sherman, *Memoirs*, 747.

3. Barrett, *Sherman's March*, 45–62.

4. Quoted in Royster, *Destructive War*, 5.

5. Ibid., 9–10.

6. Sherman, *Memoirs*, 766.

7. Quoted in Royster, *Destructive War*, 20, 22.

8. Ibid., 23.

9. *O.R.*, series 1, vol. 47, pt. 1 309 (*War of the Rebellion*).

10. See Lowry, *Story the Soldiers Wouldn't Tell*.

11. Quoted in Campbell, *When Sherman Marched North from the Sea*, 46.

12. Quoted in ibid., 66.

13. Simms, *Sack and Destruction*, 49.

14. Ibid., 55.

15. In *Mothers of Invention*, 238–44, Faust describes demoralization among elite Confederate women that set in during the war's final year. See also Edwards, *Scarlett Doesn't Live Here Anymore*, 83–85. But in *When Sherman Marched North from the Sea*, 69, Campbell discovers a different pattern among South Carolina women, especially the women of Columbia.

16. Simms, *Sack and Destruction*, 84–85.

17. Grant, *Memoirs*, 681.

18. Quoted in Janda, "Shutting the Gates of Mercy," 15.

19. Campbell, *When Sherman Marched North from the Sea*, 56.

20. *American Presbyterian*, February 23, 1865.
21. *New York Evangelist*, February 3, 1865.
22. *New York Observer*, June 18, 1865.
23. Halleck to Sherman, December 18, 1864, O.R., series 1, 44, 741 (*War of the Rebellion*).
24. *Philadelphia Inquirer*, April 8, 1865.

43. "LET US STRIVE ON TO FINISH THE WORK WE ARE IN"

1. See White, *Lincoln's Greatest Speech*.
2. Basler, ed., *Collected Works of Abraham Lincoln*, 7:282.
3. *American Presbyterian*, March 9 and March 16, 1865.
4. *New York Observer*, March 9, 1865.
5. The United Daughters of the Confederacy arguably played the single most important role in remembering Northern injustices to civilians and promoting the Religion of the Lost Cause. See Cox, *Dixie's Daughters*.
6. Quoted in Campbell, *When Sherman Marched North from the Sea*, 91.
7. Sherman, *Memoirs*, 811–12.
8. Grant, *Memoirs*, 434.
9. Robert E. Lee to His Wife, February 21, 1865, in Dowdey, *Wartime Papers of Robert E. Lee*, 907.
10. Dabney, "Sermon on Matthew 24:44," March 5, 1865, John Blair Dabney Manuscripts, 1795–1868," Virginia Historical Society.
11. Dowdey, *Wartime Papers of Robert E. Lee*, 908.
12. Ibid., 911.
13. *Richmond Examiner*, March 13, 1865.
14. Dabney, "Sermon on Job 13:15," March 10, 1865, John Blair Dabney Manuscripts 1795–1868, Virginia Historical Society.
15. Dabney, "Sermon on Hebrews 6:4–6," March 26, 1865, in ibid.

44. "RICHMOND! BABYLON IS FALLEN!!"

1. Dowdey, *Wartime Papers of Robert E. Lee*, 913.
2. See Brooks D. Simpson, *Ulysses S. Grant*, 415.
3. Ibid., 425.
4. Dowdey, *Wartime Papers of Robert E. Lee*, 925.
5. For this account, I have relied on Hoehling and Hoehling, *The Day Richmond Died*, 108–55.
6. Furgurson, *Ashes of Glory*, 326–40.
7. *Richmond Daily Whig*, April 2, 1865.
8. Putnam, *Richmond during the War*, 367.
9. Quoted in McPherson, *Battle Cry of Freedom*, 847.
10. *Philadelphia Inquirer*, April 4, 1865.
11. Ibid., April 8, 1865.
12. Sheridan, *Memoirs*, 2:180–81, 187.

13. Grant, *Memoirs*, 727–28.
14. Brooks D. Simpson, *Ulysses S. Grant*, 419.
15. Dowdey, *Wartime Papers of Robert E. Lee*, 933.
16. Sheridan, *Memoirs*, 2:194.
17. Grant, *Memoirs*, 736–41.
18. Ibid., 744.
19. Ibid., 934–35.
20. Trulock, *In the Hands of Providence*, 304–5.
21. Brooks D. Simpson, "Facilitating Defeat" in Grimsley and Simpson, *Collapse of the Confederacy*, 96.
22. Sheridan, *Memoirs*, 2:203–4.
23. Ibid., 939.
24. See Winik, *April 1865*, 323.
25. Quoted in Campbell, *When Sherman Marched North from the Sea*, 95.
26. Ibid., 108.
27. Grimsley, "Learning to Say 'Enough,'" in Grimsley and Simpson, *Collapse of the Confederacy*, 64.

45. "THE MAN DIES, BUT THE CAUSE LIVES"

1. Winik, *April 1865*, 272.
2. D. M. Corthell to W. P. Corthell, May 8, 1865, Civil War Papers, Box 1, Folder 6, AAS.
3. James Bates to William Carhell, April 24, 1865, Civil War Papers, Box 1, Folder 6, AAS.
4. *Philadelphia Inquirer*, April 15, 1865.
5. Morgan, *Joy Darkened*, 8, 16.
6. In his content analysis of 372 sermons preached on Lincoln between April 16 and June 1, Charles J. Sewart finds "no difference" between the vengeful sentiments of preachers and those of the general public. Virtually to a man they played to themes of hatred, revenge, and a radical reconstruction of the South; see "The Pulpit and the Assassination of Lincoln," 299–307. See also Chesebrough, *"No Sorrow Like Our Sorrow,"* 53–65.
7. Boardman, *Death of President Lincoln*, 13, 16.
8. Patterson, *Eulogy on Abraham Lincoln*, 21.
9. Holzer, Boritt, and Neely, *The Lincoln Image*, 205, 208.
10. Putnam, *Richmond during the War*, 381.
11. Fellman, "Lincoln and Sherman," in Boritt, *Lincoln's Generals*, 157–59.
12. Sherman, *Memoirs*, 813.
13. *American Presbyterian*, April 13, 1865. For similar sentiments, see, for example, the *New York Evangelist*, April 20, 1865.
14. *New York Observer*, April 27, 1865.
15. Bliss, *Discourse Commemorative of the Life and Character of Abraham Lincoln*, 8, 15.
16. Blight, *Frederick Douglass' Civil War*, 111.
17. Storrs, *An Oration Commemorative of President Abraham Lincoln*, 35; and Joseph Thompson, *Abraham Lincoln*, 13.

18. Beard, *Fast Day Sermon*, 12, and Hall, *President Lincoln's Death*, 10–11.
19. Marvin, "Sermon on Ecclesiastes 3:2," April 16, 1865, in Manuscript Collections, AAS.
20. Thompson, *Abraham Lincoln*, 34.
21. Chamberlain, *Assassination of President Lincoln*, 20.
22. Grant, *Memoirs*, 755–56.
23. Simon et al., *Papers of Ulysses S. Grant*, 15:30.
24. *Christian Herald*, April 27, 1865.
25. *American Presbyterian*, April 13, 1865.
26. Ibid., November 1, 1865.
27. See, for example, the *Christian Herald*, June 1, 1865.

AFTERWORD

1. See Anderson and Cayton, *Dominion of War*.
2. Bailyn, *Ideological Origins of the American Revolution*.
3. See Ayers, "Worrying about the Civil War," in Halttunen and Perry, *Moral Problems in American Life*, 144–65.
4. See Janda's "Shutting the Gates of Mercy," 7–26, and Weeks, *Farewell, My Nation*.
5. Quoted in Weeks, *Farewell, My Nation*, 144–45.

BIBLIOGRAPHY

PRIMARY SOURCES

Archives

AMERICAN ANTIQUARIAN SOCIETY (AAS), WORCESTER, MA
  Brown Family Papers, 1762–1965
  Charles Watson Washburn Papers, 1862–1865
  Civil War Papers
  Horace James Correspondence, 1852–1870
  John Emerson Anderson Letters. Civil War Papers.
  John Emerson Anderson, *Reminiscence*. Civil War Papers.
  Manuscript Collection
  Martha LeBaron Goddard Letters
  Massachusetts Volunteers 25th Regiment Band Books
  Sermons Collection
  Seth Sweetser Papers, 1834–1878
  Thomas Wentworth Higginson Papers, 1853–1911
  Uncatalogued Panoramas
  William Augustus Willoughby Papers, 1861–1864
  William Scandlin Diaries, 1849–1864. 2 octavo vols.
BARKER CENTER FOR TEXAS HISTORY, UNIVERSITY OF TEXAS
  Robert Franklin Bunting Papers
GEORGIA HISTORICAL SOCIETY
  Manuscript Collection
JOHN HAY LIBRARY, BROWN UNIVERSITY
  Confederate Sheet Music Collection
  Union Imprint Song Sheets
SPECIAL COLLECTIONS LIBRARY, WILLIAM R. PERKINS LIBRARY,
DUKE UNIVERSITY
  Thomas Smyth Papers, 1830–1861
UNION THEOLOGICAL SEMINARY, RICHMOND, VA
  Manuscript Archives

VIRGINIA BAPTIST HISTORICAL SOCIETY
  Jeter, Jeremiah Bell. Notes and Sermons.
VIRGINIA HISTORICAL SOCIETY
  John Blair Dabney Manuscripts, 1795–1868
WILLIAM STANLEY HOOLE SPECIAL COLLECTIONS LIBRARY,
UNIVERSITY OF ALABAMA
  Manly Family Papers

Newspapers

The Age (New York), American Antiquarian Society
American Presbyterian (Philadelphia), Presbyterian Historical Society
Army and Navy Messenger (Washington, D.C.)
Banner of the Covenant (Philadelphia), Presbyterian Historical Society
Boston Telegraph
Central Presbyterian (Richmond, VA)
Charleston Daily Courier
Charleston Mercury
Chicago Times
Christian Herald and Presbyterian Recorder, Presbyterian Historical
   Society
Christian Instructor and Western United Presbyterian
Christian Intelligencer, Presbyterian Historical Society
Christian Recorder (Philadelphia)
Confederate Union (Milledgeville, GA)
Daily Sun (Columbus, GA)
Houston Tri-Weekly Telegraph
Independent (New York)
The Liberator
London Spectator
Magnolia Weekly (Richmond, VA)
Marion Ensign
Mobile Daily Advertiser and Register
New York Evangelist, Presbyterian Historical Society
New York Herald
New York Observer
New York Times
New York Tribune
North Carolina Standard
Philadelphia Inquirer
Presbyter, Presbyterian Historical Society
Record of News, History and Literature (Richmond, VA)
Richmond Religious Herald
Richmond Christian Advocate
Richmond Daily Dispatch
Richmond Daily Whig

Richmond Enquirer
Richmond Examiner
San Antonio Herald
Southern Christian Advocate (Columbia, SC)
Southern Churchman (Richmond, VA)
Southern Illustrated News (Richmond, VA)
Southern Literary Messenger (Richmond, VA)
Southern Presbyterian (Columbia, SC)
Southern Punch (Richmond, VA)
The Times (London)
United Presbyterian of the West, Presbyterian Historical Society
Valley Spirit (Staunton, VA)
Weekly Constitutionalist (Augusta)
Weekly Constitutionalist (New York)

Books and Articles

"A. Countryman." *Spirit and Purpose of the Conflict*. Boston, 1861.

Abbott, John S. C. *An Address upon our National Affairs*. New York, 1861.

Adams, Ezra Eastman. *The Temple and the Throne*. Philadelphia, 1861.

Adams, Virginia M., ed. *On the Altar of Freedom: A Black Soldier's Civil War Letters from the Front*. Amherst, 1991.

Adams, William. *Prayers for Rulers*. New York, 1861.

Allen, Benjamin Russell. *The Constitution and the Union*. Boston, 1861.

Armstrong, George D. *The Good Hand of Our God upon Us*. Norfolk, VA, 1861.

Baker, Sarah. *Charlie the Drummer-Boy*. New York, 1861.

Banks, Nathaniel. *Emancipated Labor in Louisiana*. Boston, 1864.

Barnard, J. G. *Letter to the Editors of the National Intelligencer*. New York, 1862.

Barnes, Albert. *The Conditions of Peace*. Philadelphia, 1863.

Barten, O. S. *A Sermon Preached in St. James Church, Warrenton, Virginia, on Fast Day, June 13, 1861*. Richmond, 1861.

Bartholomew, J. G. *The Hour of Peril*. Boston, 1861.

Basler, Roy P., ed. *Abraham Lincoln: His Speeches and Writings*. New York, 1946.

———, ed. *The Collected Works of Abraham Lincoln*. 9 vols. New Brunswick, NJ, 1953.

Beard, Edwin S. *Fast Day Sermon*. Rockland, ME, 1866.

Beecher, Henry Ward. *The Battle Set in Array*. In *Patriotic Addresses*. Boston, 1887.

———. *Modes and Duties of Emancipation*. In *Patriotic Addresses*. Boston, 1887.

———. *The National Flag*. In *Patriotic Addresses*. Boston, 1887.

———. *National Justice and Penalty*. In *Patriotic Addresses*. Boston, 1887.

———. *Patriotic Addresses*. Boston, 1887.

———. *Peace Be Still*. New York, 1861.

Bellows, Henry. *The Crisis of Our National Disease*. In *Fast Day Sermons*. New York, 1861.

———. *Fast Day Sermons*. New York, 1861.

Bennett, William W. *A Narrative of the Great Revival Which Prevailed in the Southern Armies during the Late Civil War*. Philadelphia, 1877.

Birdwhistell, Jack, ed. "Extracts from the Diary of B. F. Hungerford, a Kentucky Baptist Pastor during the Civil War." *Baptist History and Heritage* 14 (1979).

Bliss, T. E. *A Discourse Commemorative of the Life and Character of Abraham Lincoln*. Memphis, 1865.

Boardman, George N. *The Death of President Lincoln*. Binghamton, NY, 1865.

Boardman, Henry A. *The Sovereignty of God*. Philadelphia, 1862.

Boykin, Edward. *Boys and Girls Stories of the War*. Richmond, 1861.

Breckinridge, Robert J. *The Union to Be Preserved*. New York, 1861.

Brown, Benjamin Gratz. *Immediate Abolition of Slavery by Act of Congress*. Washington, D.C., 1864.

Brown, William Wells. *The Black Man*. New York, 1863.

Bryan, Charles F., and Nelson D. Lankford, eds. *Eye of the Storm: A Civil War Odyssey*. New York, 2000.

Burlingame, Michael, ed. *At Lincoln's Side: John Hay's Civil War Correspondence and Selected Writings*. Carbondale, IL, 2000.

———, ed. *With Lincoln in the White House: Letters, Memoranda, and Other Writings of John G. Nicolay, 1860–1865*. Carbondale, IL, 2000.

Bushnell, Horace. "The Doctrine of Loyalty." *New Englander* 22 (July 1863).

———. *Reverses Needed*. Hartford, 1861.

Butler, William C. *Sermon*. Richmond, 1861.

Cable, George W., ed. "A Woman's Diary of the Siege of Vicksburg." *Century Illustrated Magazine* 7 (1885): 767–75.

Carey, Isaac E. *God Doing Wonderful Things in Behalf of the Nation*. Freeport, IL, 1863.

Chamberlain, N. H. *The Assassination of President Lincoln*. New York, 1865.

Cheever, George B. *God's Way of Crushing the Rebellion*. New York, 1861.

Chesebrough, David B., ed. *God Ordained This War: Sermons of the Sectional Crisis 1830–1865*. Columbia, SC, 1991.

Clark, Perkins K. *Sacrifices for Our Country*. Greenfield, IN 1864.

Clark, Rufus W. *A Discourse Commemorative of the Heroes of Albany*. Albany, 1864.

———. *The Unity of the American Nationality*. Albany, 1863.

Cleaveland, Elisha Lord. *A Thanksgiving Discourse*. New Haven, 1864.

Commager, Henry Steele, ed. *The Civil War Archive: The History of the Civil War in Documents*. Rev. ed. New York, 2000.

Conrad, F. W. *Thanksgiving Discourse*. Chambersburg, PA, 1864.

Cooke, John Esten. "The Sorrows of Fairfax." *Southern Illustrated News*, March 7, 1863.

Cox, Samuel S. *Eight Years in Congress, from 1857–1865*. New York, 1865.

———. *Emancipation and Its Results—Is Ohio to Be Africanized?* Washington, D.C., 1862.

Coxe, A. Cleveland. *Unjust Reproaches, in Public Calamity, Viewed as Part of the Divine Discipline*. New York, 1863.

Crary, Catherine S., ed. *Dear Belle: Letters from a Cadet and Officer to His Sweetheart, 1858–1865*. Middleton, CT, 1965.

Crist, Lynda Lasswell, ed. *The Papers of Jefferson Davis*. 12 vols. Baton Rouge, 1999.

Cruickshanks, James. *A Sermon Preached*. Worcester, 1864.

Cuthbert, Lucius. *The Scriptural Grounds for Secession from the Union*. Charleston, 1861.

Daniel, W. Harrison, ed. "The Diary of Mary W. Taylor, 1860–1864." *Virginia Baptist Register* 19 (1980).

DeBeaux, T. L. *Fast-Day Sermon*. Wytheville, AL, 1861.

Delbanco, Andrew, ed. *The Portable Abraham Lincoln*. New York, 1992.

Doggett, D. S. *A Discourse Delivered in the Broad Street Methodist Church, Richmond, Virginia, Thursday, September 18, 1862*. Richmond, 1862.

———, *The War and Its Close. A Discourse Delivered in Centenary Church, Richmond, Virginia, Friday, April 8th, 1864*. Richmond, 1864.

Douglass, Frederick. *The Day of Jubilee Comes*. In *The Civil War Archive: The History of the Civil War in Documents*, edited by Henry Steele Commager. Rev. ed. New York, 2000.

———. *Life and Times of Frederick Douglass*. New York, 1993.

Dowdey, Clifford, ed. *The Wartime Papers of Robert E. Lee*. Boston, 1961.

Dreher, Daniel I. *A Sermon*. Raleigh, NC, 1861.

Dwinell, Israel E. *Hope for Our Country*. Salem, 1862.

Eddy, Zachary. *Secession—Shall It Be Peace or War?* Northampton, 1861.

Eliott, James H. *The Bloodless Victory*. Charleston, 1861.

Elliott, Stephen. *God's Presence with the Confederate States*. Savannah, 1861. In *God Ordained This War: Sermons of the Sectional Crisis 1830–1865*, edited by David B. Chesebrough. Columbia, SC, 1991.

———. *How to Renew Our National Strength*. Savannah, 1861. In *God Ordained This War: Sermons of the Sectional Crisis 1830–1865*, edited by David Chesebrough, 314–15. Columbia, SC, 1991.

———. *Sampson's Riddle*. Macon, GA, 1863.

———. *The Silver Trumpets of the Sanctuary*. Savannah, 1861. In *God Ordained This War: Sermons of the Sectional Crisis 1830–1865*, edited by David B. Chesebrough. Columbia, SC, 1991.

Ellis, George E. *The Nation's Ballot and Its Decision*. Boston, 1864.

Eustis, W. T. *A Discourse Delivered at the Funeral of Rev. Samuel Fisk*. New Haven, 1864.

Fast Day Sermons, or The Pulpit on the State of the Country. New York, 1861.

First Anniversary of the Proclamation of Freedom in South Carolina. Beaufort, 1864.

Fish, Henry Clay. *The Valley of Achor, A Door of Hope*. New York, 1863.

Fisher, George P. *A Sermon Preached in the Chapel of Yale College*. New Haven, 1861.

Fiske, John. *A Sermon on the Present National Troubles*. Bath, ME, 1861.

Foner, Philip, ed. *Frederick Douglass: Selected Speeches and Writings*. New York, 1950.

Freeman, Douglas S., and Grady McWhiney, eds. *Lee's Dispatches: Unpublished Letters of General Robert E. Lee, C.S.A., to Jefferson Davis and the War Department of the Confederate States of America, 1862–65*. New York, 1957.

Friedman, Leon. *The Law of War: A Documentary History*. 2 vols. New York, 1972.

Goodrich, William H. *A Sermon on the Christian Necessity of War*. Cleveland, 1861.

Gordon, John B. *Reminiscences of the Civil War*. 1903. Reprint, Baton Rouge, 1993.

Grant, Ulysses S. *Memoirs and Selected Letters*. New York, 1990.

———. *Personal Memoirs of Ulysses S. Grant*. 2 vols. New York, 1885–86.

Gregg, Alexander. *The Duties Growing Out of It, and the Benefits to Be Expected from the Present War*. Austin, 1861.

Greiner, James M., et. al. *A Surgeon's Civil War: The Letters and Diary of Daniel M. Hold, M.D.* Kent, OH, 1994.

Griggs, Leverett. *No Fear of Death*. Hartford, 1864.

Guion, Thomas T. *A Sermon Preached*. Brooklyn, 1861.

Hall, Gordon. *President Lincoln's Death*. Northampton, 1865.

Hancock, A. R. *Reminiscences of Winfield Scott Hancock by His Wife*. New York, 1887.

Harwood, Edwin. *Canaan, Shem and Japheth*. New Haven, 1863.

Helmreich, Jonathan E., ed. "A Prayer for the Spirit of Acceptance: The Journal of Martha Wayles Robertson, 1860–66." *Historical Magazine of the Protestant Episcopal Church* 46 (1977).

Higginson, Thomas Wentworth. *Army Life in a Black Regiment*. Boston, 1870.

———. "The Ordeal by Battle." *Atlantic Monthly* 8 (July 1861). In *The Real War Will Never Get in the Books*, edited by Louis P. Masur. New York, 1993.

Hodge, Charles. *The State of the Country*. Reprinted from the *Princeton Review* (January 1861). New York, 1861.

———. "The War." *Biblical Repertory and Princeton Review* (January 1863).

Hodgman, Stephen. *The Nation's Sin and Punishment*. New York, 1864.

Hoge, William J. *A Discourse Delivered*. New York, 1861.

Holland, Dewitte, ed. *Sermons in American History: Selected Issues in the American Pulpit, 1630–1967*. Nashville, 1971.

Hoole, W. Stanley, ed. "The Diary of Dr. Basil Manly, 1858–1867." *Alabama Review* 4 (1951).

Hopkins, John Henry. *Scriptural, Ecclesiastical and Historical View of Slavery*. New York, 1864.

Hovey, Horace. *Freedom's Banner*. Coldwater, MI, 1861.

———. *Loyalty*. Northampton, 1863.

Howard, Oliver Otis. *Autobiography of Oliver Otis Howard*. 2 vols. New York, 1908.

Humphrey, Heman. *Our Nation*. Pittsfield, MA, 1861.

Jacobs, Ferdinand. *A Sermon for the Times*. Marion, AL, 1861.

Jones, J. B. *A Rebel War Clerk's Diary*. Philadelphia, 1866.

Jones, William J. *Christ in the Camp, or Religion in Lee's Army*. Richmond, 1887.

Lacy, Drury. *Address Delivered at the General Military Hospital, Wilson, N.C.* Fayetteville, 1863.

Lamar, J. S. A. *A Discourse*. Augusta, GA, 1861.

Lander, Samuel. *Our Own Primary Arithmetic*. Greensboro, 1863.

Lee, Leroy M. *Our Country—Our Dangers—Our Duty. A Discourse Preached in Centenary Church, Lynchburg, Virginia, on the National Fast Day, August 21, 1863*. Richmond, 1863.

Lewin, Frederick D. *National Judgments*. New Haven, 1864.

Lexington Presbytery. *A Century's History of Presbyterianism in Tygart's Valley*. Richmond, 1885.

Library of Freedom. *Life and Times of Frederick Douglass*. New York, 1993.

Liggett, James D. *Our National Reverses*. Yale University. In *Sermons in American History: Selected Issues in the American Pulpit, 1630–1967*, edited by Dewitte Holland. Nashville, 1971.

Lillie, John. *A Discourse Delivered in the Second Reformed Dutch Church*. New York, 1863.

Longstreet, Augustus Baldwin. *Fast-Day Sermon*. Columbia, SC, 1861.

Love, W. D. *The Fast and Thanksgiving Days of New England*. Boston, 1895.

McKaye, James. *The Emancipated Slave Face to Face with His Old Master*. New York, 1864.

Masur, Louis P., ed. *"The Real War Will Never Get in the Books": Selections from Writers during the Civil War*. New York, 1993.

Milies, James Warley. *God in History. A Discourse Delivered Before the Graduating Class of the College of Charleston*. Charleston, 1863.

Minnigerode, Charles. *A Sermon Preached*. Richmond, 1865.

Mitchel, J. C. *Fast Day Sermon*. Mobile, 1861.

M'Leod, John. *Our Country Worth Saving*. Philadelphia, 1864.

Moore, Marinda B. *The First Dixie Reader to Succeed the Dixie Primer*. Raleigh, 1864.

———. *Primary Geography*. Raleigh, 1864.

Moore, Thomas V. *God Our Refuge and Strength in This War*. Richmond, 1861.

Morgan, William F. *Joy Darkened*. New York, 1865.

Norwood, William. *God and Our Country*. Richmond, 1863.

Page, Moses. *Speech of Moses B. Page of Berwick*. Augusta, ME, 1863.

Palmer, Benjamin M. *A Discourse before the General Assembly of South Carolina*. Columbia, SC, 1864.

———. *National Responsibility before God*. New Orleans, 1861.

———. *Slavery a Divine Trust: Duty of the South to Preserve and Perpetuate It*. In *Fast Day Sermons, Or the Pulpit on the State of the Country*. New York, 1861.

Palmer, Ray. *The Opening Future*. Albany, 1863.

Patterson, Adoniram J. *Eulogy on Abraham Lincoln*. Portsmouth, NH, 1865.

Perrin, Lavalette. *Our Part in the World's Struggle*. Hartford, 1864.

Phipps, William. *A Discourse Delivered in Paxton, Massachusetts*. Worcester, 1864.

Pierce, George Foster. *Sermons of Bishop Pierce and Rev. B. M. Palmer.* Milledgeville, GA, 1863.

———. *The Word of God a Nation's Life.* Augusta, GA, 1861.

Pierce, Henry Niles. *God Our Only Trust.* Mobile, 1861.

Presbyterian Synod of Virginia. *Annual Report 1862.* Richmond, 1862.

Putnam, Sallie A. *Richmond during the War: Four Years of Personal Observation.* New York, 1867.

Randolf, Alfred M. *Address on the Day of Fasting and Prayer.* Fredericksburg, 1861.

Ransom, John L. *John Ransom's Diary.* Cincinnati, 1881. Reprint, New York, 1963.

Redkey, Edwin S., ed. *A Grand Army of Black Men: Letters from African-American Soldiers in the Union Army, 1861–1865.* Cambridge, MA, 1992.

Reed, Edward. *A People Saved by the Lord.* Charleston, 1861.

Rees, W. A. *A Sermon on Divine Providence.* Charleston, 1861.

———. *A Sermon on Divine Providence.* Austin, 1863.

Richardson, James D., ed. *Messages and Papers of Jefferson Davis.* 2 vols. New York, 1966.

Roset, Joseph. *A Sermon on the Preservation of the Union.* New York, 1861.

Schenck, N. H. *Songs in the Night.* Baltimore, 1863.

Sears, Stephen W., ed. *The Civil War Papers of George B. McClellan: Selected Correspondence, 1860–1865.* New York, 1989.

Seebohm, F. *The Crisis of Emancipation in America.* London, 1865.

Sewart, K. J. *A Geography for Beginners.* Richmond, 1864.

Shedd, William G. T. *The Union and the War.* New York, 1863.

Sheridan, Philip. *Personal Memoirs of P. H. Sheridan.* 2 vols. New York, 1888.

Sherman, William Tecumseh. *Memoirs of General W. T. Sherman.* 1875; rev. ed., 1886. Reprint, New York, 1990.

Simms, William Gilmore. *Sack and Destruction of the City of Columbia, South Carolina.* 1865. Reprint, Milledgeville, GA, 1937.

Simon, John Y., et al., eds. *Papers of Ulysses S. Grant.* Vols. 1–22. Carbondale, IL, 1967–2000.

Skinner, Thomas H. *Light in Darkness.* Stapleton, NY, 1862.

Slaughter, P. *Coercion and Conciliation. A Sermon Preached in Camp, at Centerville, Virginia, by the Rev. P. Slaughter, Chaplain of the 19th Regiment Virginia Volunteers, Condensed, by Request, into a Tract for the Times.* Richmond, 1863.

Sledd, Robert Newton. *A Sermon.* Petersburg, VA, 1861.

Smith, Moses. *Our Nation Not Forsaken.* Hartford, 1863.

Smyth, Thomas. *The Sin and the Curse; or, The Union, the True Source of Disunion, and Our Duty in the Present Crisis.* Charleston, 1860.

The Soldier's Aim by a Charleston Pastor. Published by the South Carolina Colportage Board. South Carolina Historical Society, 1863.

Spear, Samuel T. *Duty of the Hour.* New York, 1863.

Spring, Gardiner. *State Thanksgiving during the Rebellion.* New York, 1862.

Stephens, Alexander H. *A Constitutional View of the Late War between the States.* 2 vols. Chicago, 1868–70.

Stone, A. L. *The Work of New England in the Future of Our Country*. Boston, 1865.

Storrs, Richard. *An Oration Commemorative of President Abraham Lincoln*. Brooklyn, 1865.

Sumner, Charles. *Emancipation! Its Policy and Necessity as a War Measure for the Suppression of the Rebellion*. Boston, 1862.

Taylor, Edward. *Manliness*. New York, 1866.

Thompson, Joseph P. *Abraham Lincoln: His Life and Its Lessons*. New York, 1865.

———. *Christianity and Emancipation*. New York, 1863.

———. *Peace through Victory*. New York, 1864.

Tucker, Henry Holcome. *God in the War*. Milledgeville, GA, 1861.

Tucker, John Randolph. *The Southern Church Justified in Its Support of the South in the Present War*. Richmond, 1863.

Tyson, Bryan. *The Institution of Slavery in the Southern States, Religiously and Morally Considered with Our Sectional Troubles*. Washington, D.C., 1863.

Vandiver, Frank E., ed. *Jubal Early War Memoirs*. Bloomington, 1960.

Van Dyke, Henry J. *The Spirituality and Independence of the Church*. New York, 1864.

Vinton, Alexander H. *Cause for Thanksgiving*. New York, 1864.

Vinton, Francis. *Irreligion and Corruption and Fanaticism Rebuked*. New York, 1861.

War of the Rebellion . . . Official Records of the Union and Confederate Armies. 128 vols. Washington, D.C., 1880–1901.

Weller, R. H. *The Two Firebrands*. St. Joseph, MO, 1861.

Wells, Cornelius L. *The Sacrifice of Continual Praise*. New York, 1864.

Wharton, Francis. *A Willing Reunion Not Impossible*. Boston, 1863.

Williams, William R. *National Renovation*. New York, 1863.

———. *Of the Birth and Death of Nations: A Thought for the Crisis*. New York, 1862.

Wilson, Joseph Ruggles. *Mutual Relations of Masters and Slaves as Taught in the Bible*. Augusta, GA, 1861.

Woodward, C. Vann, ed. *Mary Chesnut's Civil War*. New Haven, 1981.

SECONDARY SOURCES

Aaron, Daniel. *The Unwritten War: American Writers and the Civil War*. Cambridge, MA, 1973.

Abzug, Robert H., and Stephen E. Maizlish, eds. *New Perspectives on Race and Slavery in America: Essays in Honor of Kenneth M. Stampp*. Lexington, KY, 1986.

Adams, Charles. *When in the Course of Human Events: Arguing the Case for Southern Secession*. Lanham, MD, 2000.

Adams, David K., and Cornelis A. van Minnen, eds. *Aspects of War in American History*. Keele, Straffordshire, England, 1997.

Alley, Robert. *So Help Me God: Religion and the Presidency, Wilson to Nixon*. Richmond, 1972.

Ambrose, Stephen E. *Duty, Honor, Country: A History of West Point*. Baltimore, 1966.

Anderson, Fred. *The Crucible of War: The Seven Years' War and the Fate of Empire in British North America, 1754–1766*. New York, 2000.

Anderson, Fred, and Andrew Cayton. *The Dominion of War: Empire and Liberty in North America, 1500–2000*. New York, 2005.

Andreasen, Bryon C. " 'As Good a Right to Pray': Copperhead Christians on the Northern Civil War Home Front." Ph.D. diss., University of Illinois, 1998.

Andrews, J. Cutler. "The Confederate Press and Public Morale." *Journal of Southern History* 32 (1966).

————. *The North Reports the Civil War*. Pittsburgh, 1955.

————. *The South Reports the Civil War*. Princeton, 1970.

Axtell, James. *After Columbus: Essays on the Ethnohistory of Colonial North America*. New York, 1988.

————. "A Moral History of Indian-White Relations Revisited." In *After Columbus: Essays on the Ethnohistory of Colonial North America*. New York, 1988.

Ayers, Edward L. *In the Presence of Mine Enemies: War in the Heart of America, 1859–1863*. New York, 2003.

————. "Worrying about the Civil War." In *Moral Problems in American Life: New Perspectives on Cultural History*, edited by Karen Halttunen and Lewis Perry. New York, 1998.

Bailyn, Bernard. *The Ideological Origins of the American Revolution*. Cambridge, MA, 1967.

Baker, Jean H. *Affairs of Party: The Political Culture of Northern Democrats in the Mid-Nineteenth Century*. New York, 1983.

Barnwell, John. *Love of Order: South Carolina's First Secession Crisis*. Chapel Hill, 1982.

Barrett, John G. *Sherman's March through the Carolinas*. Chapel Hill, 1956.

Bellah, Robert. "Civil Religion in America." *Daedalus* 96 (1967). In *American Civil Religion*, edited by Russell Ritchey and Donald Jones, 1–21, New York, 1974.

Bellah, Robert, and Phillip E. Hammond, *Varieties of Civil Religion*. San Francisco, 1980.

Bells, Herman. *Emancipation and Equal Rights: Politics and Constitutionalism in the Civil War Era*. New York, 1978.

Bensel, Richard. *Yankee Leviathan: The Origins of Central State Authority in America, 1850–1877*. Cambridge, MA, 1990.

Bercovitch, Sacvan. *The American Jeremiad*. Madison, 1978.

Beringer, Richard E., et al. *Why the South Lost the Civil War*. Athens, GA, 1986.

Berlin, Ira. "The Destruction of Slavery." In *Slaves No More: Three Essays on Emancipation and the Civil War*, edited by Ira Berlin et al. Cambridge, MA, 1992.

Berlin, Ira, et al., eds. *Free at Last: A Documentary History of Slavery, Freedom, and the Civil War*. New York, 1992.

————, eds. *Freedom: A Documentary History of Emancipation*. 4 vols. Cambridge, MA, 1982–1993.

————, eds. *Slaves No More: Three Essays on Emancipation and the Civil War*. Cambridge, MA, 1992.

Bernard, Kenneth A. *Lincoln and the Music of the Civil War*. Caldwell, ID, 1966.

Berry, Stephen W., II. *All That Makes a Man: Love and Ambition in the Civil War South*. New York, 2003.

Best, Geoffrey. *Humanity in Warfare*. New York, 1980.

Bigelow, John, Jr. *The Campaign of Chancellorsville: A Strategic and Tactical Study*. New Haven, 1910.

Birdoff, Harry. *The World's Greatest Hit: Uncle Tom's Cabin*. New York, 1947.

Blackett, Richard. *Divided Hearts: Britain and the American Civil War*. Baton Rouge, 2001.

Blight, David W. *Frederick Douglass's Civil War: Keeping Faith in Jubilee*. Baton Rouge, 1989.

————. *Race and Reunion: The Civil War in American Memory*. Cambridge, MA, 2001.

Boatner, Mark Mayo. *The Civil War Dictionary*. New York, 1959.

Bonner, Robert E. *Colors and Blood: Flag Passions of the Confederate South*. Princeton, 2002.

————. "Flag Culture and the Consolidation of Confederate Nationalism." *Journal of Southern History* 68 (2002): 293–332.

Boritt, Gabor S., ed. *Lincoln's Generals*. New York, 1994.

Bower, Stephen E. "The Theology of the Battlefield: William Tecumseh Sherman and the U.S. Civil War." *Journal of Military History* 6 (2000).

Brewer, James H. *The Confederate Negro: Virginia's Craftsmen and Military Laborers, 1861–1865*. Durham, 1969.

Buchanan, Allen. *Secession: The Morality of Political Divorce from Fort Sumter to Lithuania and Quebec*. Boulder, CO, 1991.

Campbell, Jacqueline Glass. *When Sherman Marched North from the Sea: Resistance on the Confederate Home Front*. Chapel Hill, 2003.

Carp, Benjamin L. "Nations of American Rebels: Understanding Nationalism in Revolutionary North America and the Civil War South." *Civil War History* 48 (2002): 5–33.

Castel, Albert. "The Fort Pillow Massacre: A Fresh Examination of the Evidence." *Civil War History* 4 (March 1958): 37–50.

Catton, Bruce. *The Centennial History of the Civil War*. Vol. 1, *The Coming Fury*; vol. 2: *Terrible Swift Sword*; vol. 3: *Never Call Retreat*. Garden City, NY, 1961–65.

Carwardine, Richard J. *Evangelicals and Politics in Antebellum America*. Knoxville, 1997.

————. "Methodists, Politics, and the Coming of the American Civil War." *Church History* 69 (2000): 578–60.

Channing, Steven A. *Crisis of Fear: Secession in South Carolina*. New York, 1970.

Cherry, Conrad, ed. *God's New Israel: Religious Interpretations of America's Destiny*. Englewood Cliffs, NJ, 1972.

Chesebrough, David B., *"No Sorrow Like Our Sorrow": Northern Protestant Ministers and the Assassination of Lincoln*. Kent, OH, 1994.

Chesson, Michael B., *Richmond and after the War, 1865–1890*. Virginia State Library, 1981.

Clausewitz, Carl von. *On War*. 1832. Reprint, Princeton, 1984.

Clebsch, William. "Christian Interpretations of the Civil War." *Church History* 30 (1961): 212–22.

Clinton, Catherine, ed. *Southern Families at War: Loyalty and Conflict in the Civil War South*. New York, 2000.

Connelly, Thomas L. *The Marble Man: Robert E. Lee and His Image in American Society*. Baton Rouge, 1977.

Cook, Adrian. *The Armies of the Streets: The New York City Draft Riots of 1863*. Lexington, KY, 1974.

Cornish, Dudley Taylor. *The Sable Arm: Negro Troops in the Union Army, 1861–1865*. New York, 1956.

Coulter, E. Merton. *The Confederate States of America, 1861–1865*. Baton Rouge, 1950.

Cox, Karen L. *Dixie's Daughters: The United Daughters of the Confederacy and the Preservation of Confederate Culture*. Gainesville, 2003.

Cozzens, Peter. *No Better Places to Die: The Battle of Stones River*. Urbana, 1990.

———. *The Shipwreck of Their Hopes: The Battles for Chattanooga*. Urbana, 1994.

Crandall, Marjorie Lyle. *Confederate Imprints: A Check List Based Principally on the Collection of the Boston Athenaeum*. Boston, 1955.

Cullen, Rosemary L. *The Civil War in American Drama before 1900*. Providence, 1982.

Curan, Thomas F. *Soldiers of Peace: Civil War Pacifism and the Postwar Radical Peace Movement*. New York, 2003.

Current, Richard N. *Lincoln and the First Shot*. Philadelphia, 1963.

Cushman, Stephen. *Bloody Promenade: Reflections on a Civil War Battle*. Charlottesville, 1999.

Daniel, W. Harrison. *Southern Protestantism in the Confederacy*. Bedford, VA, 1989.

Davis, David Brion. *The Emancipation Moment*. Gettysburg, 1983.

———. "The Emergence of Immediatism in British and American Antislavery Thought." *Mississippi Valley Historical Review* 49 (1962): 209–30.

Davis, Keith F. "A Terrible Distinctness." In *Photography in Nineteenth Century America*, edited by Martha Sandweiss. New York, 1991.

Davis, William C. *Battle at Bull Run: A History of the First Major Campaign of the Civil War*. Baton Rouge, 1977.

———. *Jefferson Davis: The Man and His Hour*. New York, 1991.

Decosse, David E., ed. *But Was It Just? Reflections on the Morality of the Persian Gulf War*. New York, 1992.

Denney, Robert E. *Civil War Prisons and Escapes: A Day-by-Day Chronicle*. New York, 1993.

DeRosa, Marshall L. *The Confederate Constitution of 1861: An Inquiry into American Constitutionalism.* Columbia, MO, 1991.

Desjardin, Thomas A. *Those Honored Dead: How the Story of Gettysburg Shaped American Memory.* New York, 2003.

Dew, Charles B. *Apostles of Disunion: Southern Secession Commissioners and the Causes of the Civil War.* Charlottesville, 2001.

Diggins, John Patrick. *On Hallowed Ground: Abraham Lincoln and the Foundations of American History.* New Haven, 2000.

Donald, David H. *Lincoln.* New York, 1995.

Dowdey, Clifford. *The Seven Days: The Emergence of Lee.* Boston, 1964.

DuBois, W. E. B. *The Gift of Black Folk: The Negroes in the Making of America.* Boston, 1924.

Duncan, Richard R. *Lee's Endangered Left: The Civil War in Western Virginia, Spring of 1864.* Baton Rouge, 1998.

Eaton, Clement. *Jefferson Davis.* New York, 1977.

Edwards, Laura F. *Scarlett Doesn't Live Here Anymore: Southern Women in the Civil War Era.* Urbana, 2000.

Ehrenreich, Barbara. *Blood Rites: Origins and History of the Passions of War.* New York, 1997.

Eliot, Ellsworth. *West Point in the Confederacy.* New York, 1941.

Elshtain, Jean Bethke. "Just War as Politics: What the Gulf War Told Us about Contemporary American Life." In *But Was It Just? Reflections on the Morality of the Persian Gulf War*, edited by David E. Decosse, 43–60. New York, 1992.

———. *Just War Theory.* New York, 1992.

Escott, Paul D. "The Failure of Confederate Nationalism: The Old South's Class System in the Crucible of War." In *The Old South in the Crucible of War*, edited by Harry P. Owens and James J. Cooke, 15–28. Jackson, 1983.

Ezell, John S. "A Southern Education for Southrons." *Journal of Southern History* 17 (1951): 303–27.

Fahs, Alice. *The Imagined Civil War: Popular Literature of the North and South 1861–1865.* Chapel Hill, 2001.

Farber, Daniel. *Lincoln's Constitution.* Chicago, 2003.

Farmer, James Oscar. *The Metaphysical Confederacy: James Henley Thornwell and the Synthesis of Southern Values.* Macon, 1986.

Faust, Drew Gilpin. *The Creation of Confederate Nationalism: Ideology and Identity in the Civil War South.* Baton Rouge, 1988.

———. *Mothers of Invention: Women of the Slaveholding South in the American Civil War.* Chapel Hill, 1996.

Feller, Daniel. "Libertarians in the Attic, or A Tale of Two Narratives." *Reviews in American History* 32 (2004): 184–94.

Fellman, Michael. *Inside War: The Guerrilla Conflict in Missouri during the American Civil War.* New York, 1989.

———. "Lincoln and Sherman." In *Lincoln's Generals*, edited by Gabor S. Boritt. New York, 1994.

Fellows, David. " 'The Poor Women Will Make a Howl': General Sherman and the Deportation of the Sweetwater and Rosewell Mill Workers during the Atlanta Campaign of 1864." Senior thesis, Yale University, 2003.

Foner, Eric. *Free Soil, Free Labor, Free Men: The Ideology of the Republican Party before the Civil War*. New York, 1970.

Foote, Shelby. *The Civil War: A Narrative*. 3 vols. New York, 1958–74.

Forman, Sidney. *West Point: A History of the United States Military Academy*. New York, 1952 [1950].

Fox-Genovese, Elizabeth, and Eugene D. Genovese. *The Mind of the Master Class: History and Faith in the Southern Slaveholders' Worldview*. New York, 2005.

Franklin, John Hope. *The Emancipation Proclamation*. New York, 1963.

Frassanito, William A. *Antietam: The Photographic Legacy of America's Bloodiest Day*. New York, 1978.

Fredrickson, George M. "The Coming of the Lord: The Northern Protestant Clergy and the Civil War Crisis." In *Religion and the American Civil War*, edited by Randall M. Miller et al. New York, 1998.

———. *The Inner Civil War: Northern Intellectuals and the Crisis of the Union*. Chicago, 1965.

Freehling, William W. *Prelude to Civil War: The Nullification Controversy in South Carolina, 1816–1836*. New York, 1965.

Freeman, Douglas S. *Lee's Lieutenants: A Study in Command*. 3 vols. New York, 1944.

Fuller, A. James. *Chaplain to the Confederacy: Basil Manly and Baptist Life in the Old South*. Baton Rouge, 2000.

Furgurson, Ernest B. *Ashes of Glory: Richmond at War*. New York, 1996.

———. *Chancellorsville, 1863: The Souls of the Brave*. New York, 1992.

———. *Not War but Murder: Cold Harbor, 1864*. New York, 2000.

Gallagher, Gary W., ed. *Antietam: Essays on the 1862 Maryland Campaign*. Kent, OH, 1989.

———. *The Confederate War*. Cambridge, MA, 1997.

———, ed. *The Fredericksburg Campaign: Decision on the Rappahannock*. Chapel Hill, 1995.

Genovese, Eugene D. *The Slaveholders' Dilemma: Freedom and Progress in Southern Conservative Thought, 1820–1860*. Charleston, 1992.

Glatthaar, Joseph T. *Forged in Battle: The Civil War Alliance of Black Soldiers and White Officers*. New York, 1990.

Goodrich, Lloyd. *Winslow Homer*. New York, 1944.

Goodrich, Thomas. *Bloody Dawn: The Story of the Lawrence Massacre*. Kent, OH, 1991.

Gray, J. Glenn. *The Warriors: Reflections on Men in Battle*. New York, 1959.

Griffith, Paddy. *Battle Tactics of the Civil War*. New Haven, 1989.

Grimsley, Mark. *The Hard Hand of War: Union Military Policy toward Southern Civilians 1861–1865*. Cambridge, MA, 1995.

———. "Learning to Say 'Enough.'" In *The Collapse of the Confederacy*, edited by Mark Grimsley and Brooks D. Simpson. Lincoln, NE, 2001.

Grimsley, Mark, and Brooks D. Simpson, eds. *The Collapse of the Confederacy*. Lincoln, NE, 2001.

Gross, Jennifer Lynn. " 'Good Angels': Confederate Widowhood in Virginia." In *Southern Families at War: Loyalty and Conflict in the Civil War South*, edited by Catherine Clinton, 133–54. New York, 2000.

Guelzo, Allen C. *Abraham Lincoln: Redeemer President*. Grand Rapids, 1999.

———. *Lincoln's Emancipation Proclamation: The End of Slavery in America*. New York, 2004.

Hagerman, Edward. *The American Civil War and the Origins of Modern Warfare: Ideas, Organizations, and Field Command*. Bloomington, IN, 1988.

Halttunen, Karen, and Lewis Perry. *Moral Problems in American Life: New Perspectives on Cultural History*. New York, 1998.

Hartigan, Richard Shelly. *Lieber's Code and the Law of War*. Chicago, 1983.

Harwell, Richard. *More Confederate Imprints*. Richmond, 1957.

Hatch, Nathan O. *The Sacred Cause of Liberty: Republican Thought and the Millennium in Revolutionary New England*. New Haven, 1977.

Heaps, Porter W. *The Singing Sixties: The Spirit of the Civil War Days Drawn from the Music of the Times*. New York, 1960.

Henkin, David M. *City Reading: Written Words and Public Spaces in Antebellum New York*. New York, 1998.

Hennessy, John J. *Return to Bull Run: The Campaign and Battle of Second Manassas*. New York, 1993.

Henry, Maureen. *The Intoxication of Power: An Analysis of Civil Religion in Relation to Ideology*. Dordrecht, Holland, 1979.

Herberg, Will. *Protestant-Catholic-Jew*. New York, 1960.

Hess, Earl J. *Pickett's Charge: The Last Attack at Gettysburg*. Chapel Hill, 2001.

Hesseltine, William B. *Civil War Prisons: A Study in War Psychology*. Columbus, OH, 1998 [1930].

Hettle, Wallace. *The Peculiar Democracy: Southern Democrats in Peace and Civil War*. Athens, GA, 2001.

Heyrman, Christine Leigh. *Southern Cross: The Beginnings of the Bible Belt*. New York, 1997.

Hill, Samuel S., ed. *Encyclopedia of Religion in the South*. Macon, 1984.

Hitt, Michael D. *Charged with Treason: Ordeal of 400 Mill Workers during Operations in Roswell, Georgia, 1864–65*. New York, 1992.

Hoehling, A. A., and Mary Hoehling. *The Day Richmond Died*. Lanham, MD, 1981.

Hofstadter, Richard. *The American Political Tradition and the Men Who Made It*. New York, 1951.

Holmes, Amy E. " 'Such Is the Price We Pay': American Widows and the Civil War Pension System." In *Toward a Social History of the American Civil War*, edited by Maris Vinovskis. Cambridge, 1990.

Holzer, Harold, and Mark E. Neely Jr. *Mine Eyes Have Seen the Glory: The Civil War in Art*. New York, 1993.

Holzer, Harold, Gabor S. Boritt, and Mark E. Neely Jr. *The Lincoln Image: Abraham Lincoln and the Popular Print*. New York, 1984.

Howard, Victor B. *Religion and the Radical Republican Movement 1860–1870*. Lexington, KY, 1990.

Hutcheson, Richard G., Jr. *God in the White House: How Religion Has Changed the Modern Presidency*. New York, 1988.

Hutchison, William R., and Hartmut Lehmann, eds. *Many Are Chosen: Divine Election and Western Nationalism*. Cambridge, MA, 1994.

Hyman, Harold M. *A More Perfect Union: The Impact of the Civil War and Reconstruction on the Constitution*. New York, 1973.

Janda, Lance. "Shutting the Gates of Mercy: The American Origins of Total War." *Journal of Military History* 59 (1995): 7–26.

Jewett, Robert. *The Captain America Complex: The Dilemma of Zealous Nationalism*. Philadelphia, 1973.

Johnson, James Turner. *Just War Tradition and the Restraint of War: A Moral and Historical Enquiry*. Princeton, 1981.

Jones, Virgil Carrington. *Gray Ghosts and Rebel Raiders*. 2 vols. Atlanta, 1973.

Jordan, Ervin L. *Black Confederates and Afro-Yankees in Civil War Virginia*. Charlottesville, 1995.

Keen, Nancy Travis. "Confederate Prisoners of War at Fort Delaware." *Delaware History* 13 (1968): 1–27.

Kimball, William J. *Starve or Fall: Richmond and Its People, 1861–1865*. Ann Arbor, 1976.

Kirshner, Ralph. *The Class of 1861: Custer, Ames, and Their Classmates after West Point*. Carbondale, IL, 1999.

Klement, Frank L. *The Copperheads in the Middle West*. Chicago, 1960.

——.*The Limits of Dissent: Clement L. Vallandigham and the Civil War*. Lexington, KY, 1970.

Klingaman, William K. *Abraham Lincoln and the Road to Emancipation, 1861–1865*. New York, 2001.

Kraditor, Aileen S. *Means and Ends in American Abolitionism: Garrison and His Critics on Strategy and Tactics, 1834–1850*. New York, 1967.

LeBeau, Bryan F. *Currier & Ives: America Imagined*. Washington, D.C., 2001.

Lebergott, Stanley. "Why the South Lost: Commercial Purpose in the Confederacy, 1861–1865." *Journal of American History* 70 (1983–84): 58–74.

Leith, John H. "Spirituality of the Church." In *Encyclopedia of Religion in the South*, edited by Samuel S. Hill. Macon, 1984.

Leonard, Thomas. *News for All: America's Coming of Age with the Press*. New York, 1995.

Lerner, Gerda. *The Grimke Sisters from South Carolina: Rebels against Slavery*. Boston, 1967.

Linden, Glenn M., and Thomas J. Pressly, eds. *Voices from the House Divided: The United States Civil War as Personal Experience*. New York, 1995.

Linder, Robert D. "Civil Religion in Historical Perspective: The Reality That Underlies the Concept." *Journal of Church and State* 17 (1975): 399–421.

Linderman, Gerald. *Embattled Courage: The Experience of Combat in the American Civil War*. New York, 1987.

Litwack, Leon. *Been in the Storm So Long: The Aftermath of Slavery*. New York, 1979.

——. *North of Slavery: The Negro in the Free States, 1790–1860*. Chicago, 1961.

Livermore, Thomas L. *Numbers and Losses in the Civil War in America: 1861–65.* Bloomington, 1957.

Long, E. B., with Barbara Long. *The Civil War Day by Day: An Almanac 1861–1865.* New York, 1971.

Longstreet, James. *From Manassas to Appomattox: Memoirs of the Civil War in America.* Reprint, Bloomington, 1960.

Loveland, Anne C. *Southern Evangelicals and the Social Order 1800–1860.* Baton Rouge, 1980.

Lowry, Thomas P. *The Story the Soldiers Wouldn't Tell: Sex in the Civil War.* New York, 1994.

Lyman, Theodore. *With Grant and Meade from the Wilderness to Appomattox.* Lincoln, NE, 1994 [1922].

McCurry, Stephanie. *Masters of Small Worlds: Yeoman Households, Gender Relations, and the Political Culture of the Antebellum South Carolina Low Country.* New York, 1995.

McDonough, James Lee. *Shiloh—In Hell before Night.* Knoxville, 1977.

McDonough, James Lee, and James Pickett Jones. *War So Terrible: Sherman and Atlanta.* New York, 1987.

McDowell, Robert Emmett. *City of Conflict, Louisville in the Civil War 1861–1865.* Louisville, 1962.

McInerney, Daniel J. *The Fortunate Heirs of Freedom: Abolition and Republican Thought.* Lincoln, NE, 1994.

McPherson, James M. "Antebellum Southern Exceptionalism: A New Look at an Old Question." *Civil War History* 29 (1983): 230–44.

———. *Battle Cry of Freedom: The Civil War Era.* New York, 1988.

———. *Crossroads of Freedom: Antietam.* New York, 2002.

———. *For Cause and Comrades: Why Men Fought in the Civil War.* New York, 1997.

———, ed. *The Negro's Civil War: How American Negroes Felt and Acted during the War for the Union.* New York, 1965.

———. *The Struggle for Equality: The Abolitionists and the Negro in the Civil War and Reconstruction.* Princeton, 1964.

McWhiney, Grady, and Perry D. Jamieson. *Attack and Die: Civil War Military Tactics and the Southern Heritage.* Tuscaloosa, AL, 1982.

Maier, Pauline. *American Scripture: Making the Declaration of Independence.* New York, 1997.

Marks, Paula Mitchell. "Bunting Trusted in God and His Comrades: The Ranger Reverend." *Civil War Times Illustrated* 24 (1985): 40–45.

Marten, James. *The Children's Civil War.* Chapel Hill, 1998.

Marvin, Carolyn, and David W. Ingle. *Blood Sacrifice and the Nation: Totem Rituals and the American Flag.* Cambridge, MA, 1999.

Marszalek, John F. *Sherman: A Soldier's Passion for Order.* New York, 1993.

Matter, William D. *If It Takes All Summer: The Battle of Spotsylvania.* Chapel Hill, 1988.

Mead, Sidney. "The Nation with the Soul of a Church." *Church History* 36 (1967): 275–83.

Menand, Louis. *The Metaphysical Club*. New York, 2001.

Meredith, Roy. *Mr. Lincoln's Camera Man: Mathew B. Brady*. New York, 1946.

Miller, Perry. *Errand into the Wilderness*. Cambridge, MA, 1975.

———. *The New England Mind: From Colony to Province*. Cambridge, MA, 1953.

Miller, Randall M., et al., eds. *Religion and the American Civil War*. New York, 1998.

Miller, William Lee. *Lincoln's Virtues: An Ethical Biography*. New York, 2002.

Mitchell, Reid. *Civil War Soldiers*. New York, 1988.

———. "The Creation of Confederate Loyalties." In *New Perspectives on Race and Slavery in America: Essays in Honor of Kenneth M. Stampp*, edited by Robert H. Abzug and Stephen E. Maizlish. Lexington, KY, 1986.

Mochan, John. "Rebel Vengeance: The Burning of Chambersburg, Pennsylvania." Senior thesis, Yale University, 2003.

Moore, Frank. *The Rebellion Record*. New York, 1861–1873.

Moorhead, James H. *American Apocalypse: Yankee Protestants and the Civil War 1860–1869*. New Haven, 1978.

Morris, Roy. *The Better Angel: Walt Whitman in the Civil War*. New York, 2000.

Mott, Frank Luther. *American Journalism: A History of Newspapers in the United States*. New York, 1947.

Mullin, Robert Bruce. *Puritan as Yankee: A Life of Horace Bushnell*. Grand Rapids, 2002.

Myers, Robert Manson, ed. *The Children of Pride: A True Story of Georgia and the Civil War*. New Haven, 1984 [1972].

Nathan, Hans. *Dan Emmett and the Rise of Negro Minstrelsy*. Norman, OK, 1962.

Neely, Mark E., Jr. *The Fate of Liberty: Abraham Lincoln and Civil Liberties*. New York, 1991.

———. *The Last Best Hope of Earth: Abraham Lincoln and the Promise of America*. Cambridge, MA, 1993.

———. *Union Divided: Party Conflict in the Civil War North*. Cambridge, MA, 2002.

———. "Was the Civil War a Total War?" *Civil War History* 37 (1991).

———. "Wilderness and the Cult of Manliness: Hooker, Lincoln, and Defeat." In *Lincoln's Generals*, edited by Gabor S. Boritt, 79–120. New York, 1994.

Nevins, Allan. *The War for the Union*. 4 vols. New York, 1959, 1960, 1971.

Noll, Mark A. *America's God: From Jonathan Edwards to Abraham Lincoln*. New York, 2002.

———. "The Bible and Slavery." In *Religion and the American Civil War*, edited by Randall M. Miller et al., 43–73. New York, 1998.

———, ed. *Religion and Politics: From the Colonial Period to the 1980s*. New York, 1990.

Nord, David Paul. *Faith in Reading: Religious Publishing and the Birth of Mass Media in America*. New York, 2004.

———. "Systematic Benevolence: Religious Publishing and the Marketplace in Early Nineteenth-Century America." In *Communication and Change in American Religious History*, edited by Leonard I. Sweet, 239–69. Grand Rapids, 1993.

Nosworthy, Brent. *Bloody Crucible of Courage: Fighting Methods and Combat Experience of the Civil War*. New York, 2003.

Nye, Russell B. *William Lloyd Garrison and the Humanitarian Reformers*. Boston, 1955.

Oates, Stephen B. *Abraham Lincoln: The Man Behind the Myths*. New York, 1984.

O'Brien, William V. *The Conduct of Just and Limited War*. New York, 1981.

O'Leary, Cecilia. *To Die For: The Paradox of American Patriotism*. Princeton, 1999.

Olson, Kenneth E. *Music and Musket: Bands and Bandsmen of the American Civil War*. New York, 1981.

Owens, Harry P., and James J. Cooke, eds. *The Old South in the Crucible of War*. Jackson, 1983.

Paluden, Philip Shaw. *"A People's Contest": The Union and the Civil War 1861–1865*. New York, 1988.

Parish, Peter J. "The War for the Union as a Just War." In *Aspects of War in American History*, edited by David K. Adams and Cornelis A. van Minnen. Keele, Straffordshire, England, 1997.

Pearce, George F. *Pensacola during the Civil War*. Gainesville, 2000.

Pease, Jane H., and William H. Pease. *They Who Would Be Free: Blacks Search for Freedom, 1830–1861*. New York, 1974.

Perry, Lewis. *Radical Abolitionism: Anarchy and the Government of God in Antislavery Thought*. Ithaca, NY, 1973.

Peters, Harry T. *Currier & Ives: Printmakers to the American People*. New York, 1942.

Phillips, Christopher. *Missouri's Confederate: Claiborne Fox Jackson*. Columbia, MO, 2000.

Phillips, Ulrich B. "The Literary Movement for Secession." In *Studies in Southern History and Politics: Inscribed to William Archibald Dunning, Ph.D., LL.D., Lieber Professor of History and Political Philosophy in Columbia University, by His Former Pupils, the Authors*. New York, 1914.

Pierarad, Richard V., and Robert D. Linder. *Civil Religion and the Presidency*. Grand Rapids, 1988.

Potter, David M. "The Historian's Use of Nationalism and Vice Versa." In *The South and the Sectional Conflict*. Baton Rouge, 1968.

———. *Lincoln and His Party in the Secession Crisis*. New York, 1942.

———. *The South and the Sectional Conflict*. Baton Rougue, 1968.

Powell, Lawrence N., and Michael S. Wayne. "Self-Interest and the Decline of Confederate Nationalism." In *The Old South in the Crucible of War*, edited by Harry P. Owens and James J. Cooke, 29–45. Jackson, 1983.

Preston, Walter Creigh. *Lee: West Point and Lexington*. Antioch, 1934.

Quarles, Benjamin. *Black Abolitionists*. New York, 1969.

———. *The Negro in the Civil War*. Boston, 1953.

Rable, George C. *Civil Wars: Women and the Crisis of Southern Nationalism*. Urbana, 1989.

———. *The Confederate Republic: A Revolution against Politics*. Chapel Hill, 1994.

Ramsey, Paul. *The Just War: Force and Political Responsibility*. New York, 1968.

Randall, James G. *The Civil War and Reconstruction*. Boston, 1937.

———. *Constitutional Problems under Lincoln*. Urbana, 1951.

Reardon, Carol. *Pickett's Charge in History and Memory*. Chapel Hill, 1997.

Reynolds, David S. *John Brown, Abolitionist: The Man Who Killed Slavery, Sparked the Civil War, and Seeded Civil Rights*. New York, 2005.

Ritchey, Russell, and Donald Jones, eds. *American Civil Religion*. New York, 1974.

Robertson, James I. *Civil War Virginia: Battlefield for a Nation*. Charlottesville, 1991.

Romero, Patricia W., and Willie Lee Rose, eds. *Reminiscences of My Life: A Black Woman's Civil War Memoirs*. New York, 1988.

Romero, Sidney J. "The Confederate Chaplain." *Civil War History* 1 (1955).

Royster, Charles. *The Destructive War: William Tecumseh Sherman, Stonewall Jackson, and the Americans*. New York, 1991.

Russell, James Michael. *Atlanta, 1847–1890: City Building in the Old South and the New*. Baton Rouge, 1988.

Sandweiss, Martha, ed. *Photography in Nineteenth Century America*. New York, 1991.

Schaff, Morris. *The Spirit of Old West Point, 1858–1862*. Boston, 1907.

Schudson, Michael. *Discovering the News: A Social History of American Newspapers*. New York, 1978.

Schultz, Duane. *Quantrill's War: The Life and Times of William Clarke Quantrill, 1837-1865*. New York, 1996.

Schweiger, Beth Barton. *The Gospel Working Up: Progress and the Pulpit in Nineteenth-Century Virginia*. New York, 2000.

Sears, Stephen W. *George B. McClellan: The Young Napoleon*. New York, 1988.

———. *Landscape Turned Red: The Battle of Antietam*. New Haven, 1983.

Sewall, Richard H. *Ballots for Freedom: Antislavery Politics in the United States, 1837–1860*. New York, 1976.

Shattuck, Gardner H. *A Shield and Hiding Place: The Religious Life of the Civil War Armies*. Macon, 1987.

Sickel, H. S. J. *Thanksgiving: Its Source, Philosophy and History with All National Proclamations and Analytical Study Thereof*. Philadelphia, 1940.

Silbey, Joel H. *A Respectable Minority: The Democratic Party in the Civil War Era, 1860–1868*. New York, 1977.

Silver, Davis M. *Lincoln's Supreme Court*. Urbana, 1957.

Silver, James W. *Confederate Morale and Church Propaganda*. Tuscaloosa, AL, 1957.

Simon, John Y. "Grant, Lincoln, and Unconditional Surrender." In *Lincoln's Generals*, edited by Gabor S. Boritt, 181–89. New York, 1994.

Simpson, Brooks D. "Facilitating Defeat: The Union High Command and the

Collapse of the Confederacy." In *The Collapse of the Confederacy*, edited by Mark Grimsley and Brooks D. Simpson. Lincoln, NE, 2001.

———. *Ulysses S. Grant: Triumph over Adversity, 1822–1865*. New York, 2000.

Simpson, Marc, ed. *Winslow Homer: Paintings of the Civil War*. San Francisco, 1989.

Sinha, Manisha. *The Counterrevolution of Slavery: Politics and Ideology in Antebellum South Carolina*. Chapel Hill, 2000.

Smith, Kristen M., ed. *The Lines Are Drawn*. Athens, GA, 1999.

Snay, Mitchell. *Gospel of Disunion: Religion and Separatism in the Antebellum South*. New York, 1993.

Sprague, Dean. *Freedom under Lincoln*. Boston, 1965.

Stampp, Kenneth M. *And the War Came: The North and the Secession Crisis, 1860–1861*. New York, 1950.

Stevens, C. A. *Berdan's United States Sharpshooters in the Army of the Potomac, 1861–1865*. Dayton, OH, 1972 [1892].

Stewart, Charles J. "The Pulpit and the Assassination of Lincoln." *Quarterly Journal of Speech* 50 (1964): 299–307.

Stewart, James B. *Holy Warriors: The Abolitionists and American Slavery*. New York, 1976.

Stillman, Rachel B. "Education in the Confederate States of America, 1861–1865." Ph.D. diss., University of Illinois, 1972.

Stoddard, Henry Luther. *Horace Greeley: Printer, Editor, Crusader*. New York, 1946.

Stout, Harry S. *The New England Soul: Preaching and Religious Culture in Colonial New England*. New York, 1986.

———. "Rhetoric and Reality in the American Revolution: The Case of the Federalist Clergy." In *Religion and Politics: From the Colonial Period to the 1980s*, edited by Mark A. Noll, 62–76. New York, 1990.

Stout, Harry S., and Christopher Grasso, "Civil War, Religion, and Communications: The Case of Richmond." In *Religion and the American Civil War*, edited by Randall M. Miller, et al., 313–59. New York, 1998.

Stowe, Steven M. *Intimacy and Power in the Old South: Ritual in the Lives of the Planters*. Baltimore, 1987.

Stowell, Daniel W. *Rebuilding Zion: The Religious Reconstruction of the South, 1863–1877*. New York, 1998.

———. "Stonewall Jackson and the Providence of God." In *Religion and the American Civil War*, edited by Randall M. Miller et al., 187–207. New York, 1998.

Sutherland, Daniel E. "Abraham Lincoln, John Pope, and the Origins of Total War." *Journal of Military History* 56 (1992): 567–86.

———. "Guerrilla Warfare, Democracy, and the Fate of the Confederacy." *Journal of Southern History* 68 (2002).

———. "Introduction to War: The Civilians of Culpepper Country, Virginia." *Civil War History* 37 (1991): 120–37.

Sweet, Leonard I., ed. *Communication and Change in American Religious History*. Grand Rapids, 1993.

Sword, Wiley. *Mountains Touched with Fire: Chattanooga Besieged, 1863*. New York, 1995.

———. *Shiloh: Bloody April*. New York, 1974.

Thomas, Emory M. *The Confederate Nation, 1861–1865*. New York, 1979.

———. *The Confederate State of Richmond: A Biography of the Capital*. Austin, 1971.

———. *Robert E. Lee: A Biography*. New York, 1995.

Thomas, John L. *The Liberator: A Biography of William Lloyd Garrison*. Boston, 1963.

Thompson, William F. *The Image of War: The Pictorial Reporting of the American Civil War*. Baton Rouge, 1960.

Toll, Robert C. *Blacking Up: The Minstrel Show in Nineteenth Century America*. New York, 1976.

Trulock, Alice Rains. *In the Hands of Providence: Joshua L. Chamberlain and the American Civil War*. Chapel Hill, 1992.

Tucker, Glen. *Chickamauga: Bloody Battle in the West*. Indianapolis, 1961.

VanderVelde, Lewis G. *The Presbyterian Churches and the Federal Union, 1861–1869*. Cambridge, MA, 1932.

Vinovskis, Maris, ed. *Toward a Social History of the American Civil War*. Cambridge, MA, 1990.

Voegeli, V. Jacque. *Free but Not Equal: The Midwest and the Negro during the Civil War*. Chicago, 1967.

Walzer, Michael. *Just and Unjust Wars: A Moral Argument with Historical Illustrations*. New York, 1977.

Watson, Samuel J. "Religion and Combat Motivation in the Confederate Armies." *Journal of Military History* 58 (1994): 29–55.

Webb, Alexander S. *The Peninsula: McClellan's Campaign of 1862*. Vol. 3 in Scribner's series *Campaigns of the Civil War*. New York, 1881.

Weeks, Philip. *Farewell, My Nation: The American Indian and the United States, 1820–1890*. Arlington Heights, IL, 1990.

White, Ronald C., Jr. *Lincoln's Greatest Speech: The Second Inaugural*. New York, 2002.

Wiggins, William H., Jr. *O Freedom! Afro-American Emancipation Celebrations*. Knoxville, 1987.

Williams, Gilbert Anthony. *The Christian Recorder, Newspaper of the African Methodist Episcopal Church: History of a Forum for Ideas, 1854–1902*. Jefferson, NC, 1996.

Williams, Kenneth P. *Lincoln Finds a General: A Military Study of the Civil War*. 5 vols. New York, 1949–59.

Williams, T. Harry. *Lincoln and His Generals*. New York, 1952.

———. *P.T.G. Beauregard: Napoleon in Gray*. Baton Rouge, 1955.

Wills, Garry. *Lincoln at Gettysburg: The Words That Remade America*. New York, 1992.

Wilson, Charles Regan. "Robert Lewis Dabney: Religion and the Southern Holocaust." *Virginia Magazine of History and Biography* 89 (1981): 79–89.

Wilson, Christopher Kent. "Marks of Honor and Death: Sharpshooter and the Peninsular Campaign of 1862." In *Winslow Homer: Paintings of the Civil War*, edited by Marc Simpson. San Francisco, 1989.

Wilson, Edmund. "Abraham Lincoln: The Union as Religious Mysticism." *The New Yorker* 29 (March 14, 1953).

———. *Patriotic Gore: Studies in the Literature of the American Civil War*. New York, 1962.

Wilson, John. *Public Religion in American Culture*. Philadelphia, 1979.

Wilson, Joseph T. *The Black Phalanx*. 1890. Reprint, New York, 1968 .

Winger, Stewart. *Lincoln, Religion, and Romantic Cultural Politics*. De Kalb, IL, 2003.

Winik, Jay. *April 1865: The Month That Saved America*. New York, 2001.

Wittke, Carl. *Tambo and Bones: A History of American Minstrel Stage*. Durham, 1930.

W.M.E.R., "The Thanksgiving Day Contention." *Virginia Cavalcade* 1 (1951): 9–11.

Wood, Forrest G. *Black Scare: The Racist Response to Emancipation and Reconstruction*. Berkeley, 1970.

Wyatt-Brown, Bertram. *Lewis Tappan and the Evangelical War against Slavery*. Cleveland, 1969.

———. "Robert E. Lee and the Concept of Honor." Unpublished paper, 2004.

———. *The Shaping of Southern Culture: Honor, Grace, and War, 1760s–1880s*. Chapel Hill, 2001.

INDEX

Page numbers in *italics* refer to illustrations.